Indigenous Peoples, Title to Territory, Rights and Resources: The Transformative Role of Free Prior and Informed Consent

The right of indigenous peoples under international human rights law to give or withhold their Free Prior and Informed Consent (FPIC) to natural resource extraction in their territories is increasingly recognised by intergovernmental organisations, international bodies, and industry actors, as well as in the domestic law of some States. This book offers a comprehensive overview of the historical basis and status of the requirement for indigenous peoples' consent under international law, examining its relationship with debates and practice pertaining to the acquisition of title to territory throughout the colonial era.

Cathal Doyle examines the development of the contemporary concept of FPIC and the main challenges and debates associated with its recognition and implementation. Drawing on existing jurisprudence and evolving international standards, policies and practices, Doyle argues that FPIC constitutes an emerging norm of international law, which is derived from indigenous peoples' self-determination, territorial and cultural rights, and is fundamental to their realisation. This rights-consistent version of FPIC guarantees that the responses to questions and challenges posed by the extractive industry's increasingly pervasive reach will be provided by indigenous peoples themselves.

The book will be of great interest and value to students and researchers of public international law, and indigenous peoples and human rights.

Cathal M. Doyle is a Research Fellow at Middlesex University Business School. He was previously associated with Middlesex University School of Law, where he completed his PhD. He has extensive experience working with indigenous communities and national and regional indigenous organizations, in particular, in their engagements with the OECO and UN human rights mechanisms. Prior to pursuing his PhD he worked as a management consultant for over 10 years in Accenture with global financial, retail and manufacturing sector clients.

Routledge Research in Human Rights Law

The UN Committee on Economic, Social and Cultural Rights
The Law, Process and Practice
Marco Odello and Francesco Seatzu

State Security Regimes and the Right to Freedom of Religion and Belief
Changes in Europe Since 2001
Karen Murphy

The European Court of Human Rights in the Post-Cold War Era
Universality in Transition
James A. Sweeney

The United Nations Human Rights Council
A Critique and Early Assessment
Rosa Freedman

Children and International Human Rights Law
The Right of the Child to be Heard
Aisling Parkes

Litigating Transnational Human Rights Obligations
Alternative Judgements
Mark Gibney and Wouter Vandenhole

Reproductive Freedom, Torture and International Human Rights
Challenging the Masculinisation of Torture
Ronli Noa Sifris

Forthcoming titles in this series include:

Jurisdiction, Immunity and Transnational Human Rights Litigation
Xiaodong Yang

Applying an International Human Rights Framework to State Budget Allocations
Rights and Resources
Rory O'Connell, Aoife Nolan, Colin Harvey, Mira Dutschke and Eoin Rooney

Human Rights Law in Europe
The Influence, Overlaps and Contradictions of the EU and the ECHR
Kanstantsin Dzehtsiarou, Tobias Lock, Theodore Konstadinides and Noreen O'Meara

Nomadic Peoples and Human Rights
Jérémie Gilbert

Children's Lives in an Era of Children's Rights
The Progress of the Convention on the Rights of the Child in Africa
Afua Twum-Danso Imoh & Nicola Ansell

China's Human Rights Lawyers
Advocacy and Resistance
Eva Pils

The Right to Equality in European Human Rights Law
The Quest for Substance in the Jurisprudence of the European Courts
Charilaos Nikolaidis

Business and Human Rights in South East Asia
Risk and Regulatory Turn
Mahdev Mohan & Cynthia Morel

Indigenous Peoples, Title to Territory, Rights and Resources

The transformative role of free prior and informed consent

Cathal M. Doyle

Routledge
Taylor & Francis Group

LONDON AND NEW YORK

First published 2015
by Routledge
2 Park Square, Milton Park, Abingdon, Oxon, OX14 4RN

and by Routledge
711 Third Avenue, New York, NY 10017

First issued in paperback 2017

Routledge is an imprint of the Taylor & Francis Group, an informa business

British Library Cataloguing in Publication Data
A catalogue record for this book is available from the British Library

Library of Congress Cataloging-in-Publication Data
Doyle, Cathal M. author.
  Indigenous peoples, title to territory and resources : the transformative role of free prior & informed consent / Cathal M. Doyle.
    pages cm — (Routledge research in human rights law)
  Includes bibliographical references and index.
  ISBN 978-0-415-74776-9 (hardback) — ISBN 978-1-315-78066-5 (ebk)
  1. Indigenous peoples—Land tenure.   2. Indigenous peoples—Civil rights.
  3. Indigenous peoples—Legal status, laws, etc.   4. Consent (Law) I. Title.
  K738.D69 2014
  342.08'72—dc23   2014022474

ISBN 13: 978-1-138-28046-5 (pbk)
ISBN 13: 978-0-415-74776-9 (hbk)

Typeset in Baskerville
by RefineCatch Limited, Bungay, Suffolk

To my family, E, J & V

Contents

Preface

Public international law has been a handmaiden in the dismantling of indigenous peoples' rights. If the doctrines governing the occupation of territory had been adhered to in the past, settlers and colonial powers would have been forced to respect indigenous sovereignty, necessitating consensual agreements with those in possession of land since time immemorial. However, the inequality in power, manifested through the use of force, coercion and legal subterfuge, meant that this encounter resulted in the takeover and exploitation of indigenous lands and resources. Where 'consensual' agreements were achieved, these were usually reneged upon, thus denying the rights that they ostensibly sought to recognise and protect. The development of the contemporary human rights regime has promised equal rights to all individuals, communities and peoples. However, in the context of indigenous peoples, realising such rights requires challenging extant relationships of domination.

This book posits that the contemporary requirement for indigenous peoples' consent has its genesis in the initial discussions pertaining to the justification of claims to title to territory and in the associated indigenous response to the colonial encounter. It seeks to examine the implications of the rights which flow from indigenous peoples' territorial dominium for their relationships with external actors, adopting as its focus the particular context of resource exploitation in indigenous territories, a rapidly expanding phenomenon which exemplifies the rights-denying effect of indigenous peoples' treatment as objects rather than subjects of international law.

The book puts forth the hypothesis that the nuances of 'free prior and informed consent' (FPIC) ought to form the basis of the renegotiation of the relationship between indigenous peoples and all the actors impinging on their territorial dominion in different parts of the world. This, it is argued, will ensure that the response to questions and challenges posed by modernity's increasingly pervasive reach are provided by indigenous peoples themselves. In doing so, free prior and informed consent reconstructs the foundations of self-determination which were brutally ruptured in the initial colonial encounters.

Abbreviations

ATCA	Alien Tort Claims Act
AIP	Andean Indian Programme
AIPP	Asian Indigenous Peoples Pact
ATS	Alien Tort Statute
C107	ILO Convention 107
C169	ILO Convention 169
CAO	Compliance Advisor/Ombudsman
CBD	Convention on Biological Diversity
CERD	Committee on the Elimination of Racial Discrimination
CESCR	Committee on Economic Social and Cultural Rights
CRC	Committee on the Rights of the Child
CSR	corporate social responsibility
EBRD	European Bank for Reconstruction and Development
EMRIP	Experts Mechanism on the Rights of Indigenous Peoples
ETOs	Extraterritorial Obligations
FAO	Food and Agricultural Organization
FPIC	free prior and informed consent
FPICon	Free Prior Informed Consultation
FTCC	Federation of Country and City Workers
HRC	Human Rights Committee
IASG	Inter-Agency Support Group
IBAs	Impact Benefit Agreements
IBRD	International Bank for Reconstruction and Development
ICJ	International Court of Justice
ICMM	International Council for Minerals and Metals
IFAD	International Fund for Agricultural Development
IFC	International Finance Corporation
ILO	International Labour Organization
KI	Kitchenuhmaykoosib Inninuwug
MMSD	Mining, Minerals, and Sustainable Development
NCP	National Contact Point
OECD	Organisation for Economic Cooperation and Development
PIC	prior informed consent
REDD	Reducing Emissions from Deforestation and forest Degradation

TSCA	Toxic Substances Control Act
UNDP	United Nations Development Programme
UNDRIP	UN Declaration on the Rights of Indigenous Peoples
UN REDD	UN initiative on Reducing Emissions from Deforestation and Forest Degradation in Developing Countries
UPR	Universal Periodic Review
WIPO	World Intellectual Property Organization

Introduction

The requirement for indigenous peoples' free prior and informed consent is set to become one of the defining issues facing resource-rich States and the global extractive industry.[1] This contentious nexus of native peoples' consent and resource exploitation can be traced back to the initial colonial encounter and founding days of the law of nations. Despite the colonial enterprise's invocation of a Christianising justification, the quest for gold, silver and other natural resources was at the core of the colonising zeal.[2] Guaranteeing access to these highly sought after resources was a major driver in compelling competing colonial powers to devise a system under which they could regulate claims to title over the territories in which these resources were located.[3] Under this nascent law of nations, native consent was recognised as a means of validating territorial claims in the absence of a just war.[4] Implicit in this title-legitimising doctrine was an acknowledgement of native peoples' inherent dominion over their territories, including their lands and resources, and of their capacity to voluntarily incorporate themselves into, or associate themselves with, a more powerful sovereign.[5] The *de jure* requirement for consent was substantially weakened under the nineteenth-century discourse of legal positivism,[6] and duress continued to be used to obtain it in practice.[7] Nevertheless, variants of this consent requirement, some reflecting indigenous perspectives and conceptions of justice, were manifested throughout the colonial era in a spectrum of sovereign-to-sovereign agreements between native peoples and colonising States.[8]

A constant flaw in the colonial conception of native peoples' consent was its formulation based on purely European perspectives of what constituted the

---

1 Buxton 2012; Moody 2007; Sabatini 2014: 3.
2 Wallerstein 2011: 41.
3 For a discussion of the drivers behind the colonial enterprise, see Williams 1990.
4 Vitoria *et al.* 1917 (original published in 1557).
5 Vitoria *et al.* 1917; Vattel 2008 (original published in 1758).
6 See, in general, Oppenheim and Roxburgh 1920; Westlake 1894; Oppenheim 1914.
7 For an account of the initial colonial practices, see De Las Casas 1974 (original published in 1552); Final report by Miguel Alfonso Martínez, Special Rapporteur, *Study on Treaties, Agreements and Other Constructive Arrangements Between States and Indigenous Populations*, UN Doc E/CN.4/Sub.2/1999/20.
8 Lindley 1926.

reasonable behaviour of native peoples. The absence of any consideration of the peoples' own perspectives and self-defined interests ultimately meant that, while premised on the recognition of their inherent sovereignty and territorial dominion, 'consent' served as a mechanism to subvert that sovereignty and dominion. The exceptions to this general tendency were those cases where treaties and agreements were entered into between native peoples with colonial powers on the basis of relative equality. The decolonisation process saw the consent principle set aside, with the territories of unsubjugated native peoples subsumed within the borders of newly formed States.[9] The same period saw the emergence of the modern legal, social and political category of 'indigenous peoples' to describe those culturally distinct peoples descended from the original populations of post-colonial States.

Relatively early in the development of international law, a rule crystallised, under which a change of sovereign was deemed not to infringe upon rights of dominion or property.[10] The associated restrictions which recognition of native dominion should have posed for resource exploitation were, however, overcome by colonial interpretations of native peoples' customs and conceptions of ownership.[11] These interpretations held that natives lacked title over those resources because they purportedly allowed common access to them or lacked the will to exploit them. The ensuing claims to title over these resources by colonial States led to their widespread exploitation with disastrous consequences for native peoples. This model of non-consensual extraction of resources, which emerged in the colonial era, and the legal rationale which underpinned it, still remain in operation in indigenous territories throughout the world and are perhaps the clearest extant vestige of the colonial enterprise.[12]

Daes has described the associated contemporary problems of non-consensual expropriation of indigenous peoples' lands and resources as 'growing and severe'.[13] This widespread phenomenon, which has come to be termed by indigenous peoples as 'development aggression',[14] is particularly pervasive in the extractive

---

9 Castellino and Allen 2003.

10 Oppenheim and Roxburgh 1920.

11 Vitoria *et al.* 1917 Section III, para 390: 153; Nussbaum 1954:, 82; Lindley 1926: 352; Final Report of the Special Rapporteur, Erica-Irene A. Daes 12 July 2004, *Indigenous Peoples' Permanent Sovereignty over Natural Resources*, UN Doc E/CN.4/Sub.2/2004/30/Add.1, para 43.

12 Final working paper prepared by the Special Rapporteur, Erica-Irene A. Daes, *Indigenous Peoples and their Relationship to Land*, 11 June 2001 UN Doc E/CN.4/Sub.2/2001/21, para 66; *Report of the Special Rapporteur on the Rights of Indigenous Peoples, James Anaya*, 6 July 2012, UN Doc A/HRC/21/47 para 74.

13 UN Doc. E/CN.4/Sub.2/2001/21, para 132; UN Doc E/CN.4/Sub.2/2004/30/Add.1, Annex III, para 7.

14 Permanent Forum on Indigenous Issues, 4th session, New York, 16–27 May 2005, Special Theme: Millennium Development Goals Information Received from the United Nations System, UN Doc E/C.19/2005/4/Add.13, 28 March 2005, paras 3–6; see also *Report of the Special Rapporteur on the Situation of Human Rights and Fundamental Freedoms of Indigenous People*, R. Stavenhagen, 21 January 2003, UN Doc E/CN.4/2003/90, para 28.

sector.[15] The unprecedented demand of rapidly industrialising countries and expanding consumer markets,[16] together with technological advances in the mining industry, have served to fuel a highly speculative global commodities market resulting in resource exploitation on a scale hitherto unknown.[17] Indigenous peoples represent in the region of 5 per cent of the global population, and estimates indicate that over half of the world's remaining mineral resources may be located in their territories.[18] When considered in light of the particular relationship that indigenous peoples have with their lands and the small scale of their societies, these factors explain the enormity of the impact the industry has on indigenous peoples.[19] Its extent is such that it constitutes a grave threat to the physical and cultural survival of many indigenous peoples, and poses major challenges to the exercise of the right to self-determination of all indigenous peoples whose territories contain mineral resources.[20] Given this context, it is not surprising that the extant extractive model is leading to escalating tensions and conflict between indigenous peoples, States and transnational corporations.

The beginning of this contemporary era of unprecedented growth in the extractive sector coincided with the end of an era aimed at assimilating indigenous peoples into mainstream society. The recognition of their right to a permanent and enduring way of life replaced the parental and discriminatory objectives of assimilation and integration.[21] Further developments in international law saw the dawn of a new era of self-determination being promised, implicit in which is greater control over land, territories and resources. In large part, this new era of rights recognition emerged in response to indigenous resistance, in regions throughout the world, to the increasingly pervasive encroachment of

---

15 Interim Report of the Special Representative of the Secretary-General on the Issue of Human Rights and Transnational Corporations and Other Business Enterprises, John Ruggie, UN Doc E/CN.4/2006/97, paras 25, 29.

16 Kharas 2010; Doyle and Whitmore 2014.

17 World Investment Report 2010; see also *BHP Billiton Sustainability Report*, 2009, 2010, 2011; and Sibaud 2012; Doyle and Whitmore 2014.

18 Moody 2007: 10; see also Tujan and Bella Guzman 2002: 153; Moody 1992; see also Report of the International Expert Group Meeting on Extractive Industries, *Indigenous Peoples' Rights and Corporate Social Responsibility*, Manila 4 May 2009 UN Doc, E/C.19/2009/CRP, Annex II: Manila Declaration of the International Conference on Extractive Industries and Indigenous Peoples, 2–25 March 2009, Legend Villas, Metro Manila, the Philippines UN Doc, E/C.19/2009/CRP Annex II. For a discussion on the pervasiveness of this impact, see Doyle and Gilbert 2009; Doyle 2010a: 85–94.

19 *Interim Report of the Special Representative of the Secretary-General on the Issue of Human Rights and Transnational Corporations and Other Business Enterprises*, John Ruggie, 22 February 2006 UN Doc E/CN.4/2006/97, paras 25, 29.

20 Report of the Special Rapporteur on the Situation of Human Rights and Fundamental Freedoms of Indigenous People, Rodolfo Stavenhagen, Mission to Philippines, 5 March 2003, UN Doc E/CN.4/2003/90/Add.3, para 63. See also Stavenhagen, 21 January 2003, UN Doc E/CN.4/2003/90, para 20; and Report of the Special Rapporteur on the Rights of Indigenous Peoples, James Anaya, *Extractive Industries Operating Within or Near Indigenous Territories*, 11 July 2011, UN Doc A/HRC/18/35, para 80; see also UN Doc. E/C.19/2013/16.

21 ILO 1988c:31/4–31/5; ILO 1989b:31/2; see Thornberry 2002; Xanthaki 2007; Anaya 2004, for a commentary on this development in human rights law.

non-consensual extractive activities into their territories.[22] In the context of preventing unwanted encroachment and its destructive impact, a core element of this evolving rights framework has been the emergence of a right of indigenous peoples to give or withhold free prior and informed consent (FPIC) to activities in or near their territories. This requirement for consent is derived from self-determination, cultural and territorial rights.[23] It seeks to guarantee indigenous peoples' right to subsistence, facilitate their right to development and protect their right to lands, territories and resources, while allowing them to plan their futures by removing the uncertainty associated with unrestricted outside interference. To a certain extent, FPIC represents a compromise on behalf of indigenous peoples in so far as it falls short of fully challenging the predominant claims asserted by States, under doctrines such as *jura regalia*, to exclusive ownership over resources located in indigenous territories.[24] It does, however, afford some protection to indigenous peoples' resource claims and provides the foundations for the emergence of new resource governance models, premised on notions of shared sovereignty over those resources and partnership in their management and control.[25]

While genuine consent should result in indigenous peoples' rights being safeguarded, consent alone is not a sufficient protection to guarantee this. The absence of consent is, however, one of the most effective barometers of rights' violations. Aspects of the contemporary requirement for indigenous consent resonate with earlier articulations of native consent during the colonial encounter, in particular, those which emerge from prior indigenous conceptions of treaty-making and agreement-making. Its modern-day qualifiers of 'free', 'prior' and 'informed' aim to safeguard consent against rights-denying limitations which had plagued earlier versions. Most significant, when viewed from its potential to deliver on its rights-protecting promise, is the fact that at the core of FPIC is a conception of consent which is based on indigenous determination of its contents and control over its operationalisation.[26] This self-determining dimension of the contemporary consent requirement constitutes its most radical and rights-affirming departure from prior formulations.

There exists an abundance of public international law literature examining the issue of State territorial sovereignty and land rights.[27] This literature addresses the evolution of the legal rules governing territorial acquisition, from their origins in the Roman theory of dominium to the emergence of contemporary doctrines

22 Imai 2009: 290; for an overview of the associated struggles, see Blaser *et al.* 2004; see also Mander and Tauli-Corpuz 2006.
23 UN Doc A/HCR//18/42 Advice no 2, para 20.
24 ILO 1987: Appendix I, Extracts from the Report of the Meeting of Experts on the Revision of the Indigenous and Tribal Populations Convention 1957 (no 107) Geneva 1–10 September 1986, para 82(g).
25 Report of the [Canadian] Royal Commission on Aboriginal Peoples (1996), Chapter 3, Governance Section at 9.
26 Doyle and Cariño 2013.
27 Jennings 1963; Castellino and Allen 2003; Crawford [1979] 2007; Koskenniemi 1989; Wallace-Bruce, 1994; Sharma 1997; Coret 1960; Oppenheim and Roxburgh 1920; Alexandrowicz 1973; Anghie 2007.

legitimising and regulating acquisition of title to territorial sovereignty. A significant body of literature has emerged addressing the issue of territoriality in the context of decolonisation, and the implications of the right to self-determination for democracy in contemporary postcolonial States.[28]

The body of literature addressing indigenous peoples' sovereignty and territorial rights is considerably smaller.[29] It nevertheless makes an important contribution by framing the issue of indigenous peoples' claim to ancestral territories within a rights-based perspective. This rights-based framework grounds indigenous peoples' self-government and land rights in a non-discriminatory approach to their customary tenure systems, cultural integrity and right to self-determination, including its participatory and autonomy dimensions. Within this body of work there has, however, been minimal engagement with the issue of indigenous peoples' ownership and control rights over subsurface resources.[30] The related right to give or withhold free prior and informed consent is attracting increasing attention, but the literature on it remains relatively sparse.[31] That which exists tends to take the contemporary human rights or environmental rights frameworks as its point of departure.[32] In some cases, it presents the idea of seeking indigenous peoples' consent as a novel concept,[33] derived from individual rights in the medical field, or from the rights of States in the context of environmental law. This has led to misunderstandings as to the genesis of the consent requirement and a tendency to decouple it from indigenous peoples' self-determination, sovereignty and dominion over their territories.[34] Such an approach to FPIC could place major constraints on its operationalisation and limit its potential as a facilitator for the realisation of the developmental and resource aspects of the right to self-determination.

This book seeks to delve further into the doctrinal underpinnings of the acquisition of sovereignty in respect of territory occupied by indigenous peoples. In doing so, it aims to shed light on the genesis of the consent requirement at the commencement of the colonial encounter, and examine the role which the theoretical and practical dimensions of this consent requirement played in the legitimisation of title to territory and sovereignty under the then nascent international law. It posits that the contemporary consent requirement has its

28 Castellino 2008; Cassese 1998; Tomuschat 1993; Knop 2002; Espiell Un Doc E/Cn.4/Sub.2/405/ Rev.1 (1980); Hannum 1996.
29 Anaya 2004; Thornberry 2002; Anaya and Williams 2001: 33; Aikio and Scheinin 2000; Richardson, Imai and McNeil 2009a; Gilbert 2006; Xanthaki 2007; Keal 2003; Clinebell and Thomson 1977–1978.
30 UN Doc E/CN.4/Sub.2/2004/30/Add.1; Errico 2011.
31 See, for example, MacKay 2004a; McGee 2009; Rosenthal 2006; Wynberg, Schroeder, and Chennells 2009; Perrault 2004; Nakagawa 2004; Buxton 2010; Lüdert 2008; Goodland 2004; Gilbert and Doyle 2011; Doyle and Cariño 2013; A growing body of non-governmental, UN and industry publications are also addressing FPIC.
32 A notable exception is Colchester and MacKay 2004.
33 Even the UN Experts Mechanism on the Rights of Indigenous Peoples has referred to FPIC as 'relatively new concept internationally', see UN Doc A/HCR/18/42 (17 August 2011), para 63.
34 Rosenthal 2006; Schroeder 2009; Dutfield 2009; Perrault 2004; Nakagawa 2004; Buxton 2010.

genesis in the initial discussions pertaining to the justification of claims to title to territory. As a consequence of this, it suggests that the long-established principle of obtaining indigenous peoples' consent has potentially profound implications for the status of its contemporary manifestation under human rights law.

In examining the genesis and subsequent evolution of this historical consent requirement, the book points to its inherent defect – the unilateral determination of its content and the perversion of its purpose under rights constraining colonial legal doctrines. The book therefore starts from the premise that while the historical consent requirement has important implications for the status of its contemporary FPIC requirement, an understanding of the bases for and content of this long-established legal principle cannot be derived from an exclusive focus on the colonial sources of international law. Fundamental aspects of this consent principle emerge from the position adopted by indigenous peoples themselves during and subsequent to the colonial encounter and, as with its present-day manifestation, these perspectives serve to give it meaning and guarantee its integrity.

In light of this understanding the book examines the bases for, and status and content of, the contemporary consent requirement. It posits that FPIC, rather than being at odds with the realisation of goals such as fulfilment of the genuine public interest or pursuit of egalitarian models of democracy, is instead complementary to them and necessary for their inclusive and non-discriminatory realisation. Based on an analysis of developments in and beyond international human rights law, it suggests that the consent requirement has reached a tipping point in terms of its recognition, and that debate in relation to it is shifting from challenges to its validity to questions around how it should be operationalised. The book concludes by positing that recent decades have seen a major transformation of the content of the consent requirement under international law, so that its contemporary form is increasingly reminiscent of the version articulated by Las Casas as an inherent right of sovereign peoples,[35] its major distinction being that this modern self-determined version draws on indigenous perspectives on law and justice and is premised on indigenous control over its realisation. An insistence on the consent requirement's grounding in inherent indigenous sovereignty and the contemporary right to self-determination will be essential if control over its future operationalisation is to remain with indigenous peoples.

Overview of the book

The book is divided into three parts, and follows a largely chronological order. Part I addresses the period from the initial colonial encounter up to the UN decolonisation era and examines the relationship between consent and title to territory. It comprises two chapters. Chapter 1 focuses on the initial colonial encounter and the formation of the law of nations. It argues that the emergence

---

35 Tierney, 1997: 284–286; Tierney 2004: 11, citing Las Casas, Losada, and Lassègue 1990: 210.

of the requirement of title to territory-legitimising consent of non-European indigenous peoples under international law can be traced back to the early sixteenth century. By tracing the emergence under the law of nations of this natural law based consent requirement, and its subsequent evolution up to the beginning of the nineteenth century, the chapter illustrates that native peoples' consent constituted a core principle underpinning the acquisition of title to territory. It also points to the significance of indigenous perspectives which informed consensual agreements with States, and suggests that it was in these few instances where indigenous perspectives had an equal weight that something akin to a genuine rights-based conception of consent emerges. The *de facto* resistance of many indigenous peoples to colonial encroachment, though not addressed in the book, was also in and of itself an assertion of the consent requirement.

Chapter 2 examines the nature of this colonial conception of indigenous peoples' consent and the role it came to play under the positivist legal discourse in the context of the expansion of the colonial project in the nineteenth century. It posits that, despite being forced into a positivist straitjacket in the latter era of the colonial enterprise, the consent requirement nevertheless remained at the core of the colonial enterprise's expansion until its dying days. It contrasts the theoretical rejection of the relevance of native consent by the late nineteenth- and early twentieth-century positivists, with the *de facto* State practice in the context of territorial acquisition in Africa, in particular, under the protectorate system. The chapter closes with a brief consideration of the role of the consent requirement in the context of the doctrine of guardianship, the trusteeship system, and the emergence of post-colonial States.

Having considered the centrality of indigenous peoples' consent to the debates over acquisition of title to territory and the attempts by legal theorists to dismiss it as bearing no relevance to international relations and native sovereignty, despite State practice to the contrary, Part II of the book, which is composed of four chapters, proceeds to examine the re-emergence of the consent requirement and its current status under international human rights law.

Chapter 3 examines the consent requirement in the work and standards of the International Labour Organization from the end of the 1920s to the beginning of the 1990s. It traces the evolution of the consent requirement from the initial feeble affirmation in ILO Convention 107, to a procedurally strong requirement under ILO Convention 169. Drawing on the text of Convention 169, together with its intent and drafting history, this chapter offers an interpretation of the Convention which holds that it embodies a substantive requirement that is aligned with the extant body of human rights law.

Chapter 4 explores developments in the normative framework of indigenous peoples' rights during and following the drafting of the UN Declaration on the Rights of Indigenous Peoples (UNDRIP), with a particular focus on the implications of the affirmation that indigenous peoples are vested with the right to self-determination. The chapter also examines the sources of law and philosophy which underpin the extant normative framework of indigenous peoples' rights, including the requirement for FPIC. It concludes with a discussion on indigenous peoples' right to self-determination in the post-Declaration era and suggests that the principle of FPIC is a central tenet of this new conception of self-determination.

Chapter 5 aims to provide an overview of some of the sources under human rights law and other emerging international standards, of the requirement for FPIC. Drawing on these sources, it examines the bases for the requirement in terms of the rights which underpin it; the nature of the requirement as a duty, a right, a principle and a safeguard under international human rights law; who the subjects are to whom the duty to obtain FPIC is owed; and the scope of its content and its trigger mechanisms, with a particular focus on the elaboration of this content under the UNDRIP. Its examination of the spectrum of opinion within the human rights regime pertaining to the trigger mechanism indicates that a consensus has emerged that the right to give or withhold FPIC always exists in situations where large-scale extractive operations are located in indigenous peoples' territories or impact on their well-being and the exercise of their right to self-determination.

This evolutionary process of the recognition of FPIC has been accompanied by a range of debates and discussions with regard to the procedural and substantive aspects of the consent requirement. Chapter 6 seeks to engage with these on-going debates. It challenges the veto/no veto dichotomy and critiques the grounds upon which State and industry resistance to the requirement are premised. These include particular conceptions of the public interest, modern democracy, the notion of State sovereignty, and the States' power of eminent domain. The chapter draws on these debates in order to deconstruct the arguments presented. It suggests that ultimately many of these arguments are found wanting, and that the real reason underpinning opposition to FPIC is a simple unwillingness to transfer decision-making power from the organs of the State, and by extension from industry, to indigenous peoples, because of fears of its implications for access to and control over coveted resources located in their territories and a resistance to recognise indigenous peoples as actors who contribute to the common good and development of all peoples within the State.

Part III of the book focuses on the implementation of the FPIC requirement, addressing the evolving positions key actors play in relation to it and the challenges and limitations which an operationalisation of the concept faces as well as the opportunities it affords.

Chapter 7 provides an overview of current State practice in relation to FPIC recognition and describes contexts where there has been some progress in its implementation. It then examines the approaches of the public and private sector arms of the World Bank Group to FPIC, analysing the former's resistance to incorporate the standard into its policies and critiquing the 2012 performance standard of the latter which adopted FPIC as the standard with which its clients must comply. It suggests that while the significance of this development should not be underestimated, in particular, given its implications for the policy of the Equator Banks, caution is also necessary to ensure that the concept of FPIC is not distorted in the process. The chapter also includes a brief foray into the issue of extraterritorial obligations of home States of extractive companies and the relationship of these with FPIC. Finally, it addresses the role of the International Court of Justice (ICJ) in relation to indigenous peoples' issues and considers the potential for the Court to address the consent requirement in the context of a contentious case or an advisory opinion.

The momentum behind the developments in the financial sector, among international organisations and key industry players, indicates that greater industry engagement with FPIC is inevitable, and that the future arena of contestation in the sector will revolve around the manner in which it is operationalised. Chapter 8 outlines the current landscape with regard to the mining industry's engagement with FPIC. It provides an overview of the developments within the broader business and indigenous peoples' rights arena as they pertain to FPIC followed by an examination of the position of the International Council of Mining and Metals (ICMM) in relation to it. It then contextualises the requirement for FPIC in the light of the risk of community hostility and the potential for corporate complicity in infringements on the rights of indigenous peoples. It concludes by addressing some of the progressive policy approaches to FPIC which are emerging from the extractive sector.

Chapter 9 includes some reflections on the challenges which will be faced in the operationalisation of FPIC and the limitations of the concept in light of the broader social, political and economic environments within which indigenous peoples are attempting to assert their rights. The transformative role which FPIC has the potential to play in relation to the extant extractive industry model is considered and possible high-level components of national programmes aimed at operationalising the concept in a culturally appropriate manner are discussed. Finally, the chapter closes with the issue which is at the heart of the indigenous rights' project, namely the empowerment of indigenous peoples to pursue their own self-determined development paths and take control of their own futures. It suggests that indigenous control over the responses to the questions that will inevitably arise in the context of operationalisation of FPIC are central to the realisation of this objective.

The book concludes by suggesting that indigenous peoples have been successful in their engagement with the human rights regime as a platform for reasserting their unsurrendered status as sovereign peoples possessing the right to give or withhold consent to activities affecting their territorial dominion. The obligation now rests with States and the extractive industry to re-negotiate their relationships with indigenous peoples in order to reflect this reality. Indigenous peoples, for their part, will have to continue to proactively assert their own conceptions of FPIC and pursue its implementation across all governance levels, from the local to the international, and spanning all spheres, be they economic, developmental, or environmental, spanning which decisions are taken which have a bearing on industry operations in their territories.

Part I

The role of indigenous peoples' consent in legitimising title to territory

1 The genesis of indigenous consent under international law and its role in legitimising title to territory

1.1 Introduction

In the field of public international law there is a great deal of literature examining the issue of State territorial sovereignty and land rights, both in the context of the Roman law origins of the doctrinal tools that have influenced the direction of the law, as well as in issues concerning decolonisation and title to territory.[1] The body of literature addressing indigenous peoples' sovereignty and land rights is considerably smaller.[2] It nevertheless makes an important contribution by framing the issue of indigenous peoples' claim to ancestral territories within a rights-based perspective.

This chapter seeks to delve further into the doctrinal underpinnings of the acquisition of sovereignty in respect of territory occupied by indigenous peoples. In doing so, it aims to shed light on the genesis of the consent requirement at the commencement of the colonial encounter, and examine the role that this theoretical and practical consent requirement played in the legitimisation of title to territory and sovereignty under the then nascent international law.[3] It suggests that this long-established principle under international law of obtaining indigenous peoples' consent forms a basis for the contemporary requirement for free prior and informed consent (FPIC) and has potentially profound implications for its status under contemporary international law.

The chapter is divided into three sections. Section 1.2 provides the context which led to the birth of the law of nations and the role that the consent requirement played, or did not play, within the medieval doctrines of conquest and their extension to the 'new world'. Section 1.3 examines the emergence of the law of nations under the Spanish School and the centrality accorded to consent in the absence of a just war as a basis for asserting title to territory. Section 1.4 considers the influence of the Spanish School's consent-based discourse on other colonising

---

1 Castellino and Allen 2003; Castellino 2008; Sharma 1997; Coret 1960; Oppenheim 1920; Alexandrowicz 1973; Meisels 2009.
2 Anaya 2004: 20; Thornberry 2002; Anaya and Williams 2001: 33; Aikio and Scheinin 2000; Gilbert 2006; Xanthaki 2007; Keal 2003; Richardson, Imai and McNeil 2009a.
3 See Brierly 1963, for a discussion on the evolution of the concept of international law.

powers in the period up to the early nineteenth century. In doing so it addresses the role which indigenous perspectives on consent played in the context of treaty-making in the initial colonial era.

1.2 Historical context

1.2.1 Consent-based pre-colonial indigenous arrangements

The colonial encounter with indigenous peoples was central to the formation of international law.[4] The bases upon which colonial powers acquired title to territory, and the role of indigenous consent in legitimising it, have, however, long been a contested issue. Jennings suggested that, 'even though force, even considerable force, might be used for the establishment of the settlement [in lands where native peoples lived under tribal organisation], the result in law was not conquest but occupation'.[5] Lindley, on the other hand, presented an alternative view, documenting actual colonial encounters to illustrate that, in the vast majority of cases where the sovereign rights of non-Christians were denied, claims over their territories were either legitimised through conquest, or consent to cession, as opposed to treating their lands as *terra nullius* which could be acquired by occupation.[6] This latter view, at odds with the position of many of the late nineteenth- and early twentieth-century positivists, tends to be supported by contemporary commentators such as Anaya, Thornberry and Crawford.[7] The issue of how title was acquired, and the recognition accorded to the requirement to obtain indigenous peoples' consent as part of that process, is of direct relevance to contemporary assertions under international human rights law of the requirement for indigenous consent in relation to activities impacting on their territories and well-being.

Thornberry observes that '[t]he engagement of international law with indigenous, non-European "others" throws into relief contemporary indigenous claims, both against and on the basis of that system'.[8] In order to fully appreciate the significance of the contemporary requirement for indigenous peoples' free prior and informed consent (FPIC), and to locate its rightful place within the international legal framework, it is necessary to examine the central role which the requirement for native peoples' consent played in the colonial encounter. The approach under colonial practice and theory as to whether or not consent was required for non-conquest-based title to territory is arguably one of the best barometers of the extent to which international law has recognised indigenous sovereignty. The issue is a defining one, not only for indigenous peoples' sovereign and self-determination rights, but also for the legitimacy of the foundations upon

---

4 Anghie 1999: 79.
5 Jennings 1963: 20.
6 Lindley 1926: 11.
7 Anaya 2004: 20; Thornberry 2002: 75; Crawford 2007: 265.
8 Thornberry 2002: 85.

which title to territory rests, and for the integrity of the evolving international legal project itself.

By examining this colonial encounter through the lens of the consent requirement, this chapter seeks to demonstrate that the requirement for indigenous peoples' FPIC has a historically distinct, international law-grounded genesis which differs from, and precedes, the more recent individual or State-centred consent requirements under contemporary human rights and environmental law. These latter requirements are often presented, by both FPIC's proponents and opponents, as the basis for indigenous peoples' right to give or withhold their free prior and informed consent – the most common assertion being that the requirement emerged from, and is a derivate of, the individual consent requirement affirmed in the Nuremberg trials.[9]

Recent developments, within and beyond the human rights arena, suggest that we are nearing a 'tipping point' in terms of international recognition of the FPIC requirement.[10] Most notable among these was the adoption by the International Finance Corporation (IFC), the private sector arm of the World Bank, of the requirement for indigenous peoples' FPIC in its performance standards in 2011 (effective from January 2012). These standards have a far-reaching effect across a range of business sectors, and effectively establish FPIC as the standard for social licence to operate in indigenous territories. This development has been the result of the emergence of an affirmation of a right to give or withhold, or a duty to obtain, FPIC as a central component of the normative framework of indigenous peoples' rights. The arena of contestation consequently looks set to shift from debates over whether the requirement for FPIC exists or not, to the question of who will have control over its operationalisation.

The fact that the requirement for FPIC is grounded in the time immemorial right of indigenous peoples to sovereignty and dominion over their territories, and

---

9 Rosenthal 2006: 120 holds that the 'concept of informed consent was developed mainly for clinical research'. Turner 2006: 136 argues that, 'Historically, discussions of informed consent have focused upon seeking the consent of particular individuals' and that community consent is a recent idea. Wynberg, Schroeder and Chennells, 2009: 4 note that 'obtaining informed consent has become an essential part of modern medical practice' and that '[s]ince the early 1990s, the concept has also been employed systematically in connection with indigenous peoples' rights of self-determination'. Schroeder 2009: 28 suggests that 'the concept of informed consent developed from the relationship between doctors and patients' and subsequently gained significance outside of the medical field when it started to be used in the context of trans-boundary movement of hazardous material in the 1980s and subsequently in relation to indigenous peoples in the context of development projects in their lands and access to genetic resources and traditional knowledge in the 1990s when it became more systematically employed in the context of their right to self-determination. Similar arguments are made by Perrault 2004. Dutfield 2009: 58–59 argues that it is 'well known that informed consent . . . has its origins in medical practice' and that in its 'original context', it 'concerns information exchange between individuals' subsequently finding its way into environmental law where it was applied to States under the Basel and Rotterdam Conventions. Nakagawa 2004: 4 claims that the notion of prior informed consent is 'rooted in U.S. domestic law', in particular, the Toxic Substances Control Act (TSCA) of 1976, suggesting that the requirement under international environmental law for informed consent has its origins in the domestic legislation of the States in the context of transporting hazardous waste and chemicals.

10 See Chapter 8.5 and Chapter 9.2.

is integral to the historical assertion of title to territory under international law, testifies to its indispensable role in the pursuit of indigenous self-determination. It also suggests that, while solid and mutually reinforcing arguments for FPIC can be framed in terms of modern conceptions of social justice and ecological sustainability,[11] the requirement has its roots in the very core of international law. These roots are found in conceptions of inherent rights premised on natural law, in the law of nations premised on consent of nations, and in indigenous responses to colonial enterprise.[12] As a result, the contemporary manifestation of the consent requirement extends beyond the human rights framework from which it has emerged or, perhaps better put, re-emerged. Its operationalisation represents a reassertion of indigenous sovereignty, and consequently, by definition, the locus of its implementation has to be indigenous peoples' own governance institutions, operating in accordance with their self-chosen and autonomously managed decision-making processes and customary laws and practices. The notion of indigenous peoples' FPIC which arises from their distinct historical circumstances is therefore *sui generis* in nature.[13]

Recognition of this fact is essential to counter the emerging trend by which external actors – be they States, international financial institutions, mining companies or even environmental and other non-governmental organisations – seek to play an instrumental role in defining how FPIC should be defined and implemented in practice. To a certain extent this can be interpreted as a contemporary manifestation, cloaked in the human rights, developmental, or corporate social responsibility discourses, of previous parental Christianising and civilising missions. The meaningful operationalisation of FPIC implies addressing a much broader strategic issue, namely, the realignment of the relationship between States and indigenous peoples in a manner that breaks with international law's evolution. This entails an acknowledgement that recognition of indigenous sovereignty, and the requirement for indigenous consent, were at the core of the debates leading to the foundation of international law and its subsequent evolution.

A failure to acknowledge this, and to guarantee that control over FPIC processes is vested in indigenous peoples, would deny their right to self-determination and undermine how they wish to exercise and reassert their sovereignty. Rather than giving effect to FPIC, any attempt to operationalise it, which does not start from this premise, would constitute yet another scripting of indigenous peoples out of their appropriate place in international law. Over the course of the colonial encounter, indigenous consent was gradually divorced from its natural law grounding and divorced from indigenous perspectives, allowing its transformation into a colonial construct which served to facilitate the acquisition of title to territory. Its emergence within the human rights framework, premised on recognition of the right of indigenous peoples' self-determination, constituted a reversal of that trend. The emerging risk for indigenous peoples today is that

11 Buxton 2010; Ludert 2008; Schroeder 2009: 21; Vermeylen 2009: 206.
12 De Grotius 1625: para 40; see also Wheaton 1866: 3–4, 10–11; Williams 1999; White 1991.
13 See Chapter 4.3; see also Kingsbury 2001–2002: 214.

FPIC becomes a corporate or State construct, once again divorced from self-determination and sovereignty rights, thereby facilitating unfettered access to resources in indigenous territories.

Prior to examining the origin and role of indigenous consent in the colonial encounter, it is important to contextualise the consent requirement within pre-colonial indigenous practices, many of which are maintained in varying forms. A cogent argument can be made asserting that the requirement for consent had long been operationalised among and between indigenous cultures prior to their engagement with European colonial powers. This argument is not developed in-depth in this book and constitutes an important subject for further exploration.[14] It is of particular relevance for contemporary assertions of indigenous peoples of their right to give or withhold FPIC through the formulation of their own self-determined processes, policies and protocols governing how their consent should be sought. These articulations constitute a manifestation of indigenous sovereign decision-making and the precedent for them is found both within and prior to the colonial encounter. Oral traditions and documented evidence provide accounts of purely indigenous formal consent-based agreements aimed at furthering the interests of broader collectives encompassing neighbouring communities or multiple peoples. In Asia, pre-colonial alliance-forming traditions premised on mutual consent, such as inter-community peace pacts, continue to be practised by indigenous peoples and constitute contemporary manifestations of FPIC.[15] The British colonist, Lugard, described the traditional practices of the peoples of Africa involving 'blood brotherhood' as 'the nearest equivalent possible to our idea of a contract (treaty)'.[16] Lugard considered this practice to embody the principle of *pacta sunt servanda*, and noted that diverse forms of '[t]reaty making occupie[d] a large place in most works of African travel'.[17] The peoples of what is now Latin America also had their own models of sophisticated inter- and intra-people diplomatic protocols and consent-based agreements. The inscriptions at Tikal, a centre of the pre-colonial Maya civilisation, for example, 'outline significant political relationships both among the Maya themselves and "internationally" between the Maya and other contemporaneous civilizations'.[18] Such consensual alliances, in the form of localised multi-nation groupings, or broader geographic confederacies, and the associated diplomacy necessary for their maintenance, would have been essential to the effective functioning of the extensive pre-colonial trade and the maintenance of peace and military alliances between diverse peoples across pre-colonial North America.[19]

14 Such an exploration faces significant challenges in terms of methodology and sources, however, the works of Williams 1999 and Clavero 2002, 2005a provide useful starting points and methodological guidance.
15 See, for example, Masferré 1999; Cariño and Nettleton 1983: 177.
16 Alexandrowicz 1973: 50–54; Lugard 1893.
17 Alexandrowicz 1973; Lugard 1893; Falkowski 1992: 32, 34. Bull 1984: 106 also notes that *pacta sunt servanda* was deeply respected among African peoples.
18 Montgomery 2001.
19 Williams 1999: 32–36.

The most renowned, and possibly best documented, of these consent-based pre-colonial indigenous arrangements through which native diplomacy was exercised is that of the Iroquois Federation.[20] Described as the 'Romans of the Western World',[21] and 'a remarkable union of tribes that for a century held two European powers at bay',[22] the structure of the Grand Council of the League of the Iroquois consisted of 50 tribal chiefs, or *sachems*, from five tribes, each selecting representatives according to their own customs.[23] Decision-making followed discussion and debate and was based on unanimity, with each tribe having one vote, and the chiefs required to repeat the process at clan and tribe levels where consensus was sought through the communities' own diverse processes.[24] This indigenous diplomatic and consent-based structure existed prior to the colonial encounter and played a significant role in regulating it.[25] Treaty-making between the European powers and the Iroquois adhered to Iroquois protocol and ritual,[26] with *wampum* belts serving to track council proceedings, seal the words of the Iroquois, and in addition to constituting 'sacred symbols of agreement', also served as 'instruments for establishing and maintaining contact'.[27] This *wampum* belt tradition, which was a widespread and long-standing one among North American Indian peoples, was reflective of 'the legal ideas that [these] peoples sought to apply in their relations with the West during the North American Encounter era'.[28] Such legal ideas and principles informed indigenous resistance, decision-making and diplomacy throughout the colonial encounter. An understanding of indigenous conceptions of consent during this encounter era can thus be gleamed from their perspectives on those treaties that were entered into with them, a subject to which the book will return later. Prior to doing so, it will first examine the role that the theoretical colonial conception of the consent requirement played in the legitimisation of title to territory under the then nascent international law.

1.2.2 Medieval historical context

The conquest of the Americas has been described as 'a legal enterprise'.[29] The law both legitimised and moderated the use of power. Legal justification was fundamental to the assertion of sovereignty, to claims to title over territory vis-à-vis other States, and to the manner in which colonising power was exercised over the newly claimed territories and their peoples.[30] In his insightful analysis appropriately

---

20 Jennings 1985a; Jennings 1984; Fenton 1985: 16. Williams 1999: 52–61, 114–123.
21 Williams 1999: 114, 174–175.
22 Sturtevant 1974: 118.
23 Fenton 1985: 7–9.
24 Sturtevant 1974: 118; Fenton 1985.
25 Fenton 1985: 16.
26 Jennings 1985b: xv.
27 Foster 1985: 104; see also Sturtevant 1974: 127.
28 Williams 1999.
29 Williams 1990: 6.
30 Ibid.: 7–8.

entitled 'The American Indian in Western Legal Thought', Williams traces the influence of medieval doctrine and discourse on the justification for the Renaissance era colonial enterprise.[31] Together with similar historical inquiries, this analysis serve to contextualise the evolution of the colonial powers' legal justification for their claims to the territories of native peoples, and to shed light on the fundamental role which the consent requirement came to adopt as the legitimising concept underpinning title to territory.[32]

During the era of the Crusades, a practice emerged of issuing papal bulls to justify title to foreign lands in the interest of spreading Christianity to infidels.[33] Commencing with the first issuance in 1055, these initial bulls were premised on the 'supreme arbitral powers' of the Popes over temporal matters.[34] Some even extended to justifying title on the basis of remedying deviant forms of Christianity practised by 'barbarous' peoples, with Henry II being granted authority to invade Ireland on the basis of a papal bull (*Laudabiliter*) issued in 1155 – this by the only English Pope, Adrian IV – under the pretext of bringing the Church there into order.[35]

From the time of Pope Urban II to the Peace of Westphalia, religious reasons were used to justify European expansion. At the same time, debates within the Church sought to clarify the bases upon which claims to territories and properties therein could be justified.[36] In 1199, in *Quod super his*, Pope Innocent III raised questions as to the legitimacy of Christian power over non-Christians.[37] The view that dominion was grounded in a reason-based natural or human law, as opposed to divine law, was asserted by St Thomas Aquinas (1227–1274).[38] According to Aquinas's logic, this reason-based natural law was the source of sovereignty and, while not on a par with divine law, was nevertheless not annulled by it.[39] Instead, Christianity was regarded as being consistent with natural reason.[40] Aquinas also framed the arguments for a just war. Such a war had to be based on a 'just cause', be authorised by a sovereign, and have the intent of advancing good or avoiding evil.[41] Some have argued that his writing supports a theory of government based on consent of the governed.[42] Tierney points out that this principle of consent to

31 Ibid.: 13.
32 Castellino and Allen 2003; Castellino 2008: 503–568; Koskenniemi 1989; Sharma 1997; Coret 1960; Muldoon 1977; Falkowski 1992; Oppenheim 1920; Williams 1991: 51.
33 Muldoon 1977: 4; see also Weckman 1949; Clavero 2005a.
34 Falkowski 1992: 5.
35 Hull 1926–1931, 'Appendix I – Pope Adrian's Bull "Laudabiliter" And note upon it'. The original text of the Bull is included in Cambrensis and Dimock 1867: 317–319; see also Muldoon 1977: 26, 127–129; Williams 1990: 136–137. The bull *Laudabiliter* is reproduced in English in Ehler and Morrall 1967: 53–55.
36 Muldoon 1977: 5.
37 Green and Dickason 1989: 149.
38 Lindley 1926: 11.
39 Green and Dickason 1989: 163; Lindley 1926: 11; De Grotius 1633: 12. See also Greig 1988: 148.
40 Muldoon 1977: 186.
41 Brownlie 1963: 6.
42 Tierney 1987: 647.

political governance was elaborated on by numerous medieval theologians, such as Herveus Natalis (1315) who held that political jurisdiction could only come from 'consent of the peoples'.[43] In light of this fact, he holds that:

> the distinctive feature of medieval thought was not that it preserved the old notion of hierarchy but that it introduced a radical innovation by using the egalitarian concept as a foundation for new legal and philosophical theories of government by consent.[44]

This 'medieval consent theory', which would inform Vitoria's and Las Casas' thinking,[45] eventually made its way into the consciousness of the American Founding Fathers and contemporary democratic systems.[46] Aquinas' contemporary, Sinabaldo Fiesco, who became Pope Innocent IV (1243–1254), shared a somewhat similar perspective to Aquinas.[47] His commentary on Pope Innocent III's *Quod super his* was central to the emergence of the Spanish colonising doctrine.[48] In it, Pope Innocent IV established the conditions under which invasions of territories possessed by 'Moslem infidels' were justified.[49] By virtue of natural law, infidels could hold dominium over their territories and choose their leaders.[50] However, these rights were qualified by the Church's universal mandate to provide spiritual care for all, thereby justifying its jurisdiction over infidels.[51] According to Pope Innocent IV, the Pope was the only one who could authorise the 're-taking' of the Holy Land and of Spain from the Muslims.[52] At the core of his argument, which provided the necessary pretext for war, was that Europe's conversion to Christianity had been voluntary, unlike the infidels' conversion to Islam.[53] Hostiensis, a student of Innocent IV, presented an alternative view which held that infidels, who lacked divine grace, could not hold dominium or possess governmental authority, and consequently on these grounds alone a just war could be pursued to acquire the lands they possessed.[54] In merging the Church's 'hierocratic' discourse with natural law and combining it with the notion of 'divine reason' – in other words, a monopoly on rationality – Pope Innocent IV provided a more sophisticated rational and theological basis for dismissing those who resisted conversion.[55] They could be classified as irrational and deluded and therefore in need

43 Ibid.: 649.
44 Ibid.: 650.
45 Tierney 2004: 11.
46 Tierney 1987: 650–651; See also Tierney 1997: 70.
47 Tierney 1988: 150.
48 Green and Dickason 1989: 161.
49 Ibid.: 150, 151.
50 Pope Innocent IV, Commentary on *Quod Super His* (ca. 1245) X 3.34.8, quoted in Green and Dickason 1989. 151.
51 Zion and Yazzie 1997; Stogre 1992; Zavala 1963: 17.
52 Green and Dickason 1989: 150, 151; Donelan 1984: 79.
53 Ibid.: 150, 151; see also Brownlie 1963: 5.
54 Muldoon 1977: 186.
55 Williams 1990: 47.

of redemption. In doing so, he succeeded in establishing a doctrine which 'authorized conquest and conversion'.[56]

This justification for the invasion of infidels' lands was expanded on in the 1414 Council of Constance, which addressed the rights of Poland to defend Lithuania from the invasions of the Teutonic Knights.[57] The Council saw the hierocratic belief, corresponding to Hostiensis' theory that dominium depended on grace, as put forward by Wycliffe, rejected in favour of a natural law right to dominium, as had been framed by Innocent IV.[58] It accepted the arguments made by Poland's lawyer that exclusive power rested with the Pope to authorise conquest of the lands of infidels, with the qualification that this was only permissible in cases where natural law rights were being violated, or where necessary for the spread of the faith.[59] This view recognised infidel dominium, while simultaneously affirming that it could be legitimately terminated under certain conditions, including where the spread of the faith was prevented.[60] As Williams succinctly captures it, Innocent VI provided the logic under which 'power facilitated truth' and 'truth facilitated power':

> [with knowledge and power] placed in the service of each other so that the medieval crusading idea might not only be legitimised but, more important, be preserved in a form more palatable for Renaissance Europe's will to empire directed at the New World.[61]

1.2.3 Papal justification for title to non-European territories

Innocent VI's logic was reaffirmed in the mid-fifteenth century through a series of papal bulls (including *Romanus Pontifex*) issued at the behest of Portugal, purportedly to fulfil its desire to save pagan souls, while gaining nothing from conquering their territories in the process.[62] The bulls emerged in the context of contestation between Portugal and Spain over areas of Northern Africa, in particular, the Canary Island, hitherto not possessed by Christian powers.[63] Having initially banned Christian entry into the Island, the Pope proceeded to issue further papal bulls authorising Portugal's conquest of Africa on the basis of the parental responsibility of Rome to ensure the salvation of the region's inhabitants.[64] In effect, it represented the assertion of a 'doctrine of discovery' over such territories, treating them in a manner akin to *terra nullius*, and

---

56 Ibid.
57 Muldoon 1979: 107–119.
58 Williams 1990: 66; Muldoon 1979: 119; see also Lindley 1926: 11.
59 Vladimiri 1414; see also Muldoon 1979: 113.
60 Green and Dickason 1989: 159; see also Williams 1983; Muldoon 1977: 3.
61 Williams 1990: 47, 50.
62 Falkowski 1992: 7; Williams 1990: 74; Sharma 1997: 38; Lindley 1926: 24.
63 Muldoon 1979: 120.
64 Williams 1990: 72; Greig 1988: 140 holds that the removal of the ban reflected the impotence of the Church vis-à-vis States; Muldoon 1979: 120.

the subordination of the dominium of the native peoples to the papal power to 'save their souls'.[65]

The rights of these natives to dominium were addressed in two separate legal opinions sought by Pope Eugenius IV, and prepared by the canonical lawyers Minucci and Roselli. The arguments of Minucci reflected the views of Pope Innocent IV. However, Minucci framed dominium of the natives as flowing from the law of nations, or *jus gentium*, as opposed to natural law, thereby rendering it more vulnerable to removal. According to Minucci, Popes held *de jure* power to revoke this dominium on the basis of refusal of access to Christian missionaries.[66] Roselli asserted a dominium based on natural and civil law, but held that in the higher interests of saving the souls of all men this dominium could be removed by the Pope.[67] Consequently, under both theories, native dominium was not absolute and Portugal could justify conquest, not as an end in itself, but as a means to bring civilisation and Christianity. Portugal thus became the executioner of Rome's fiduciary duty of universal guardianship, and in return could impose tributes 'as they would with regard to their own properties and their other lordships'.[68] As Muldoon observes, the justification was imbued with a hint of the 'White man's burden' argument which would later be employed in the scramble for Africa.[69]

On 'discovery' of the Bahamian islands in 1492, Columbus proceeded to claim them as Spanish territories on the basis of the barbarian nature of their inhabitants.[70] Given the absence of any papal authorisation, the claim, which sought to assert Spanish sovereignty and deny the infidels' dominium over their lands, had no basis under the existing Church doctrine.[71] A number of bulls (*Eximiae devotionis* and two entitled *Inter castera*) were subsequently issued in haste in 1493,[72] this time by a Spanish Pope in accordance with Spain's wishes, and based on text it had drafted. Described as the 'zenith of the popes' assertion of temporal authority over Christian princes',[73] they provided legal ownership of any discovered lands in which the peoples were 'well-disposed to embrace the Christian faith'.[74] Subsequently, the 1494 Treaty of Tordesillas between Spain and Portugal established that Spain could claim any territories 370 leagues west of the Cape Verde

---

65 While similar in effect, from a legal doctrinal perspective, the practice was distinct from the notion of *terra nullius* which deemed inhabited lands open to occupation on the basis of the nature of the political society that existed, or on the basis that no social or political organisation existed at all.
66 Muldoon 1979: 126.
67 Ibid.: 127.
68 Papal Bull of Pope Nicolas V of 1453, quoted in Williams 1990: 73–74; Ehler and Morrall 1967: 144–153.
69 Muldoon 1977: 48; see also Davidson 1992.
70 Williams 1990: 78; Ehler and Morrall 1967: 153.
71 Muldoon 1979: 136.
72 The three bulls were issued on 3 May and 4 May 1493 by Pope Alexander VI, see Falkowski 1992: 8.
73 The bull is reproduced in Falkowski 1992: 8–11.
74 Ibid.

Islands which it discovered.[75] Following the 'discovery' of South-East Asia, another papal bull, *Praecelsae devotionis*, was issued in 1514 which divided the globe from north to south, providing Portugal with claims over the Pacific. However, the 'discovery' of the Philippines signalled the unacceptability of this division to the Spanish, and led to its replacement by another basis for partition of claimable territories under the 1529 Treaty of Saragossa.[76]

The issuance of the bulls to Portugal and Spain, and the treaties entered into by them, consequently represented little more than a shift from an era of papal-sanctioned, internal European colonisation, premised on the purported reacquisition of once Christian territories, to a papal-sanctioned taking of non-European lands which had never been under the dominium of Christian rulers or peoples.[77] Non-Christian native dominium was not denied, but respect for it was conditional and could be removed by the Pope. This fiction, that conquest was based on Church-sanctioned spiritual grounds, served to facilitate an era of relatively unfettered Spanish and Portuguese colonial expansion in significant parts of the Americas and Asia.[78]

The system of forced labour put into effect in the colonies and the continued shipment to Spain of slaves by Columbus contributed towards his falling out of favour with the Spanish Queen Isabella, who ended his governorship by 1500,[79] apparently fearing that such practices were not compliant with the papal bulls and could potentially lead to a revocation of Spain's privileges.[80] However, opposition by the Spanish colonialists to attempts to end the system of forced labour, or '*encomienderos*', on the grounds that it limited the supply of mine labour, was successful. The result was a rapid reversion to the *encomienda* system, the legal system which effectively constituted a form of enslavement.[81] As a result, within less than two decades, during which time the Church's presence in the region was minimal, native populations were brought to the point of extinction on many of the islands.[82]

The system remained unquestioned until 1511, when Montesinoss, a Dominican missionary, challenged its legality.[83] Concerned with the implications of Montesinoss's arguments, King Ferdinand convened the Council of Burgos in 1512, to address the issue of whether the Indians were 'slaves by nature' in need of tutelage or inhumanly abused under the *encomienda* system leading to their

75 'Treaty between Spain and Portugal concluded at Tordesillas', 7 June 1494, ratification by Spain, 2 July 1494; ratification by Portugal, 5 September 1494 (original manuscript in National Archives in Lisbon, Gav. 17, Maco 2, no. 24), reproduced in Davenport and Paullin 1917: 84. See also Greig 1988: 141; Ehler and Morrall 1967: 153–159; Tuck 1999: 72.
76 Treaty of Saragossa, 22 April 1529; Muldoon 1979: 139.
77 Muldoon 1977: 3.
78 Grote 1999: 497–528.
79 Thomas 2004: 164.
80 Williams 1990: 82–83. Thomas 2004: 261.
81 For an account of the effects of the *encomienda* system, see Macnutt 1909: 311–425.
82 Williams 1990: 85.
83 Zavala 1963: 33.

extermination.[84] At the time, the unquestioned basis for Spanish title was discovery in accordance with the papal concession, a position reaffirmed by Charles V in 1519.[85]

The laws emerging from the Council recognised Indian freedom, but could be interpreted to imply that the use of force was permissible in order to inculcate them with 'the virtues of Christianity and civilization'.[86] The natives were to be informed of the intent of establishing Spanish settlements – to bring Christianity and civilisation and to 'reserve friendship with them' – however, the laws explicitly held that if they withheld their consent, settlements would proceed regardless, on the condition that they did not do the natives 'any greater damage than shall be necessary'.[87] The *encomienda* system was consequently not challenged in practice.[88] 'Indian consent to be ruled was logically irrelevant to the drafters of the code', as the divine basis upon which Spain exercised its guardianship over them, by definition 'excluded the possibility of their capacity to consent or dissent in rational fashion'.[89]

The debates at Burgos promoted King Ferdinand to seek opinions as to the basis of Spain's legal rights in the Indies and led to the drafting of the *Requerimiento*. This served a dual purpose. It attempted to control the conquistadores and ensured they did not pose a challenge to the royal power, while also appeasing the Church and avoiding criticism of the colonial policy or allegations of heresy on the grounds that it was not consistent with the recognition of the rights of the infidels.[90] The *Requerimiento*, which was to be read to the natives, required them to acknowledge the Pope, and by extension the King and Queen as his representatives. If their consent to permit missionaries to preach was not forthcoming, or if it was 'maliciously' delayed, the Spanish were justified in declaring war on them and enslaving them.[91] Some debate exists as to whether the *Requerimiento* implicitly recognised native dominium, and provided for its removal if any obstacles to the spread of the faith were encountered, or rather, if it denied the existence of dominium, and merely provided the natives with a choice between acquiescence and conquest.[92] Given that the *Requerimiento* effectively functioned to legitimise conquest, the debate as to its underlying philosophy is somewhat academic.[93] Attempts to achieve comprehension of its contents, or its intent, were completely disregarded in practice.[94] Instead, driven by the 'love of gold',

---

84 Francis 2006: 648; Williams 1990: 87.
85 Hanke 1949: 147.
86 Williams 1990: 87.
87 Laws of Burgos (Leyes de Burgos) promulgated on 27 December 1512; see also Simpson 1960.
88 Sanderlin 1971; see also Himmerick and Valernisa 1996.
89 Williams 1990: 88.
90 Fernández 2001: 130–131.
91 Williams 1990: 92.
92 Muldoon 1980: 301–316; see also Muldoon 1979: 141–142; Orique 2011: 220.
93 Thornberry describes it as offering the choice between accepting its terms or being 'attacked and subjugated'; Thornberry 2002: 65.
94 Hanke 1949: 47. Muldoon 1979: 140.

attacks of a genocidal nature[95] were perpetuated on the native peoples.[96] In one reported case, an Inca leader, aware of the *Requerimiento's* contents, rejected as absurd the notion that the Pope had the power to give away territories which did not belong to him.[97]

Opposition from Church groups, in particular the Dominicans, to Spain's treatment of the natives continued following the Council of Burgos, and was premised on the grounds that there existed a universal human power for reason, which the natives also held. This position was forcefully rejected by the colonialists as it challenged what was effectively native slavery, though not termed as such. The approach of the Dominicans to attempt to resolve the dispute was to use *reducciones* – settlements of Indians far from 'Spaniards interested in gold' – which sought to educate the natives and provide them with an environment in which to exercise individual rational thought, but which were fundamentally flawed from the perspective of ensuring native peoples' cultural survival as they provided little outlet for their cultures and world-views.[98]

1.3 Theological and legal challenges to papal grants as basis for title to territory

Theological and legal critiques of the Spanish colonial practice also emerged in the first half of the sixteenth century. The notion of the universal power of humans for rational thought underpinned Vitoria's highly influential thesis, 'On the Indians Lately Discovered' – which he delivered as a series of lectures in 1532, and which is regarded as having constituted a significant step towards the articulation of a law of nations.[99] The Dominican, and former *encomiendero*, Bartolomé de Las Casas was another prolific and influential writer on the subject.[100] Following the philosophy espoused by Vitoria and Las Casas, the papal bull of 1537, *Sublimus Deus*, forbade the enslavement of the natives and asserted

95 Thornberry 2002: 86; see also Schabas 2005.
96 Dobyns 1966: 415; see also Stavenhagen 1997: 28; Macnutt 1909: 315–316; Diffie 1967: 200.
97 Prescott 1847: 218.
98 Williams 1990: 95; Cariño and Nettleton 1983: 30.
99 Mainly Vitoria's seminal work: F de Vitoria, *Relecciones: De Potestate Civili* (1528), F. de Vitoria, *De Indis Recenter Inventis* (1530) and *De Jure Belli* (1539) Vitoria *et al* 1917; Barcia 1927; Nussbaum 1954: 80–81; Scott 1934.
100 Las Casas' extensive work includes: *Memorial de Remedios para las Indias* (1516); *Del Único Modo de Atraer a Todos los Pueblos a la Verdadera Religión* (1537); *Brevísima Relación de la Destrucción de las Indias* (1552); *Historia de la Destrucción de las Indias* (1561); *Apologética Historia Summaria de las Gentes Destas Indias* (1559). The following is a selection of some compilations of his writing: *The Devastation of the Indies: A Brief Account* (trans. H Briffault) (Baltimore, MD: Johns Hopkins University Press, 1974); *Obras Completas* 14 volumes (Madrid: Alianza Editorial, 1992); *The Only Way* (ed. H.R. Parish and J. Parish, trans. F. P. Sullivan) (New York: Paulist Press, 1992); *Brevissima Relación de la Destrucción de las Indias*: Primera Edición Crítica (ed. I. Pérez Fernández) (Madrid: Punto Print, 1999); *Relación de la Destrucción de Africa: Preludio de la Destrucción de Indias. Primera Defensa de Los Guanches Negros Contra su Esclavización* (ed. I. Pérez Fernández) (Salamanca: Editorial San Esteban, 1999). Readers are: *Witness: Writings of Bartolomé de Las Casas* (G Sanderlin, trans. and ed.) (Maryknoll, NY: Orbis Books, 1992, first edition 1971); *Indian Freedom: The Cause of Bartolomé de Las Casas, 1484–1566, A Reader* (P F. Sullivan, trans and annotated) (Kansas City: Sheed and Ward, 1995).

that they were rational beings not to be deprived of their liberty or their possessions.[101] Unlike the 1492 Bull, it did not assert a right to Spanish title over the territories of the infidels. However, it did reaffirm a right to preach Christianity. Las Casas interpreted *Sublimus Deus* as superseding the early bull, and that consequently subjugation of the natives, and claims to possession of their territories, could no longer be justified, absent their consent.[102] The royal proclamation issued by Philippe II in 1573 also embodied much of Vitoria's and Las Casas' doctrines by establishing a new Spanish policy premised on subjugation through 'pacifications' as opposed to 'conquest'.[103] As a result, at least in theory, voluntary consent was officially recognised as the primary basis upon which title to territory could be claimed under peaceful circumstances.[104]

Despite its humanist basis, its affirmation of the natural law rights of natives, and its dismissal of the papal grant of title as grounds for denying these rights, Williams regards Vitoria's discourse as being 'thoroughly medieval in its totalising trajectory, desire for the plenitude of a rationalised world order, and critical focus on Indians' normative difference'.[105] Those espousing this perspective hold that in practice, apart from its introduction of the notion of the equality of Indians with Europeans, subject to the potential for guardianship of those less intelligent natives, Vitoria's discourse merely served to change the basis upon which conquest was justified.[106]

Anaya describes Vitoria as having introduced a 'normative duality' into the discourse on Indian peoples – on the one hand, they were possessors of rights by virtue of their humanity, on the other, they could be deprived of these rights if they deviated from Eurocentric standards dictating the rules pertaining to contact between them and Europeans.[107] Thornberry and Bennet also address this double-edged nature of Vitoria's discourse, which, while recognising indigenous dominium nevertheless established a legal framework for 'just wars', and acknowledged, however reluctantly, the potential emergence of a guardian–ward style relationship.[108] Cohen regards the Spanish laws premised on Vitoria's doctrine as humane and premised on equality of the Indians with the Spaniards, and views the oppressive colonial practices as being 'in defiance of, rather than pursuant to, the laws of Spain'.[109]

---

101 Papal Bull, *Sublimus Deus*, English translation in Macnutt 1909: 198 and Appendix II, 427–431.
102 Falkowski 1992: 29.
103 *Ordenanzas de Descubrimientos de Nueva Población y Pacificación de las Indias* 1573, included in Titles V, VI, VII, VIII and XII of Book IV of the '*Recopilación de Leyes de los Reinos de las Indias*', see Delcaza Dufour (ed.) 1987; Hanke 1949: 142–143; Williams 1990: 106.
104 Translated version reproduced in Hanke 1967: 151–152. For the Spanish version, see Morales, 1979: 489–518.
105 Williams 1990: 97–98; Muldoon 1979.
106 Anaya 2004: 18; Anghie 2007: 30.
107 Anaya 2004: 18–19.
108 Thornberry 2002: 64, 67.
109 Cohen 1942: 13.

Others have argued that Vitoria articulated 'the seminal doctrine of human rights' with regard to native peoples, under which Spain could only claim dominium on obtaining 'the voluntary consent of the majority of the American nations'.[110] The work of Las Casas also attracts a divergence of opinion.[111] Some have compared his writings on the rights of native peoples with the emergence of the human rights doctrine.[112] Others, such as Clavero, argue that Las Casas' role in relation to indigenous peoples' rights has been vastly exaggerated and romanticised. One of the central concerns is that Las Casas, instead of amplifying the voice of native peoples, appropriated their voices, according a limited role to their agency and political will. As a result, whether intentionally or not, Las Casas effectively contributed to their colonisation and subjugation.[113] Marks notes that there have been a range of interpretations of the 'Spanish School' of international law, with Vitoria and Las Casas representing its major theorists on native peoples rights,[114] but that 'preponderantly the assessment is that [this School] was favourable to the recognition of indigenous rights in law'.[115] While these discourses critiqued the colonising enterprise, they were articulated in, and from a contemporary perspective unacceptably constrained by, a language and constructs which drew on theological, philosophical, and legal argumentation of their day.[116] Critically, from the perspectives of the peoples whose sovereignty had been violated, these discourses were articulated after the event and did not propose a return to the *status quo ante*.

Nevertheless, a consideration of Vitoria's influential doctrine,[117] and Las Casas' perspective on it, as well as Las Casas' own alternative views of indigenous peoples' inherent rights, help to shed light on the principles underpinning the emergence of international law of title to territory and its relationship with aspects of the contemporary normative framework of indigenous peoples' rights. While demonstrating that international law's origins are grounded in relations between colonisers and native peoples, they also provide an important insight into, and explanation for, aspects of subsequent Spanish, and other colonial powers', engagement with those peoples in their colonies who resisted acculturation and domination throughout the colonial period.

1.3.1 Vitoria and legitimate basis for title to territory

In his analysis of the lawful basis upon which 'the Indians and their lands have come, or might come, into the possession and lordship of Spain', Vitoria, regarded

---

110 Youngblood Henderson 1985: 188.
111 Authors such as Marcel Bataillon, David Brading, Sabine MacCormack, Anthony Pagden and Vidal Abril Castelló are among those who have provided a historiography of Las Casas.
112 Tierney 2004: 11; Hanke 1959: 116; Yanez 2014.
113 Clavero 2002; see also Castro 2007.
114 Marks 1990–1991: 7; see also Scott 1934.
115 Marks 1990–1991: 1; for an alternative view, see Allen 2011: 241.
116 Thornberry 2002: 64; Nussbaum 1954: 83–84.
117 Hanke 1949: 151, citing Friar L. Getino of Madrid, Friar V. Beltran de Heredia of Salamanca, Friar H. Muñoz of Manila and J. Brown Scott as supporting this view.

by many as the father of international law,[118] dismissed papal grants and discovery as a basis for legitimate claim to title, thereby challenging Spanish claims to territories in the Americas. According to his theory, the refusal of the natives to consent to the dominion of the Pope or Christian princes, or to accept the faith, was also dismissed as a legitimate basis for war,[119] with just wars framed as defensive rather than punitive in nature.[120] However, he proceeded to outline seven possible legitimate exceptions – effectively limitations on the rights of natives – by which this title to territory could be obtained.[121]

According to Vitoria, six out of seven of these legitimate titles could flow from situations where a just war was necessary, with one other title (number six in his list) based on free choice. The six lawful titles, numbered one to five and seven, which could be based on a 'just war' were:

First title, the denial of 'natural society and fellowship' which implied the right to travel among, and trade with, the Indians on the condition of doing no harm to them.[122]

Second title, the prevention of the propagation of Christianity.[123]

Third title, attempts to force converted Christians to revert to their former 'idolatry' ('a title based on human friendship and alliance').[124]

Fourth title, the Pope's power 'for a reasonable cause' to provide peoples converted to Christianity, but whose leaders were not, with 'a Christian sovereign and dispose of their other non-believing rulers'.[125]

Fifth title, the existence of tyrannical aboriginal rulers or laws, or the refusal of natives to abandon certain rituals which were against natural law, even if the 'natives assent to rules and sacrifices of this kind'.[126]

Seventh title, victory in the cause of allies and friends, in cases where the Indians wage war upon each other and summoned the Spanish to assist them.[127]

Under this framework, no legal basis for unilaterally declaring war against the natives existed if preaching of the faith, travel, and trade were permitted, and there were no attempts to reconvert Christians or maintain 'tyrannical' leaders or laws. However, it appeared that a Spanish sovereign would be excused if, in good faith, they pursued what they believed to be a just war.[128] This applied even if the

---

118 Vitoria *et al.* 1917; see also Kingsbury and Straumann 2010: 12–13.
119 Vitoria *et al.* 1917: Section II, paras 370, 374, 376, 377 at 143, 145–147; see also Hanke 1949: 151.
120 Kingsbury and Straumann 2010: 13.
121 Vitoria *et al.* 1917: Section III, paras 383–405 at 151–160.
122 Ibid., Section III, paras 386–396 at 151–156 (paras 392–393).
123 Ibid., Section III, paras 396–401, 156–158.
124 Ibid., Section III, para 401 at 158.
125 Ibid., Section III, para 401–402 at 158.
126 Ibid., Section III, para 403–404 at 159.
127 The titles are listed here in order to group those related to a 'just war' (titles 1–5 and 7) separately from the consent-based title (title 6).
128 Brownlie 1963: 9–10.

war was objectively unjust.[129] The sixth title in Vitoria's list was one based on voluntary choice of the majority of the natives, and is addressed in the section below in detail.[130]

To these seven grounds for title, Vitoria added an eighth, possibly legitimate, basis under which the Spanish could potentially claim title – namely a title based on guardianship or tutelage, where the natives were deemed to be 'unfit to found or administer a lawful State', in which case, Spain could act in their interests to administer them.[131] Vitoria would neither condone nor condemn this basis for title, but he insisted that for it to be legitimate, it would have to be in the interests of the natives, and not merely for Spanish profit. While refusing to condone it outright, Vitoria nevertheless held that, if all the natives were 'wanting in intelligence', such a course of action could be necessary.[132] It has been suggested that this, albeit partially condoned basis for title, facilitated the introduction of a system of guardianship justified on secular, as opposed to religious grounds, and represented the precursor of the guardian–ward relationship adopted by States vis-à-vis indigenous peoples.[133] As will be discussed in Chapter 2, this guardianship role was eventually formalised in the *Berlin Act of 1885*,[134] and continued under the Mandate system of the League of Nations and subsequently under the Trusteeship system of the UN. The guardianship model envisaged by Vitoria effectively negated the consent requirement on the basis of a lack of capacity. As with its subsequent manifestations, this guardianship relationship was theoretically to be of a temporary nature, with its purported purpose being to facilitate self-government once native capacity for this had been realised.[135]

Vitoria's theory essentially held that where territories were already occupied by a native people who had the capacity to govern themselves, and where there was no basis for a just war, voluntary consent obtained in good faith was the only premise upon which the Spanish could lay claim to their territories and sovereignty over them.[136] In other words, in the absence of consent of the natives, where there were no grounds for a just war (or by extension where such a war, if waged, was not victorious), claims to sovereignty over indigenous peoples or to their lands could not be legally justified. In accordance with this belief, Vitoria argued that if none of the conditions legitimising title were met, Spain could continue to trade with the peoples without subjugating them, and to substantiate his argument provided the example of how the Portuguese had profited greatly from such arrangements.[137]

129 Ibid.
130 Vitoria *et al.* 1917: Section III, paras 404–405 at 159–160.
131 Ibid., Section III, paras 406–407at 160–161.
132 Ibid., Section III, para 409 at 162.
133 Bennett 1978a: 4–11; Williams 1990: 104; Thornberry 2002: 77.
134 *General Act of the Berlin Conference on West Africa*, 26 February 1885.
135 Vitoria *et al.* 1917: 160–161; Falkowski 1992: 24.
136 Vitoria *et al.* 1917: Section II at 143, para 370 held that refusal to accept the faith which was declared to them could not be a basis for a just war.
137 Ibid.: 162.

Finally, Vitoria introduced another level of ambiguity into his doctrine by suggesting that, due to the numbers of 'native converts' in the Americas at the time of his writing, the Spanish sovereign had a responsibility for some role in 'the administration of the lands in question'.[138] However, he did not clarify how this administrative role could legitimately be executed in the absence of meeting the requirements which he had laid out for legitimising title to territory – i.e. grounds for a just war, consent or his final questionable reference to a trustee system. Arguably, this on-going administrative role could be considered akin to the nineteenth-century protectorates that were formalised under the Berlin Act of 1885, or to obtaining a title by acquisitive prescription under contemporary international law.[139]

While representing a major advance from the rights denying presumption of native people as natural slaves lacking rationality, native sovereignty under Vitoria's doctrine nonetheless affirmed a lesser form of sovereignty than that of the European nations,[140] with a clear lack of reciprocity existing in relation to Spain's sovereign rights and obligations vis-à-vis the 'natives', and the native sovereign rights and obligations vis-à-vis Spain.[141] In doing so, it afforded colonial regimes the manoeuvring space necessary to justify suppression of native sovereignty in practice. The doctrine, while purporting to elaborate on the neutral basis of a universal law of nature and human law, nevertheless, was premised on purely European perspectives as to which practices were 'natural' and by extension permissible. The terms of engagement were therefore culturally biased euro-centric ones, ostensibly upholding the principle of equality of peoples but in practice facilitating further penetration into indigenous peoples' territories.

1.3.2 Vitoria's consent-based title

As noted above, one of Vitoria's enumerated legitimate titles was based on the 'true and voluntary choice' of the Indians, both rulers and ruled, who could by 'their own motion . . . accept the King of Spain as their sovereign'.[142] Vitoria qualified the nature of the consent upon which claim to this title could be founded, with 'free and voluntary choice' constituting a necessary pre-condition for it to be granted. Pointing to inadequacies in the claims of the early conquistadors that the natives had consented to the King as their 'lord and king', and to the transfer of property to the Spanish, he argued that:

> [F]ear and ignorance, which vitiate every choice, ought to be absent. But they were markedly operative in the cases of choice and acceptance under

---

138 Ibid.
139 For a discussion on acquisitive prescription, see Jennings 1963: 21–23.
140 Thornberry 2002: 85–86.
141 Nussbaum 1954; for a view that Vitoria did not recognise native sovereignty, see Anghie 2007: 26–27.
142 Vitoria *et al.* 1917: 159–160.

consideration, for the Indians did not know what they were doing; nay, they may not have understood what the Spaniards were seeking. Further, we find the Spaniards seeking it in armed array from an unwarlike and timid crowd. Further, inasmuch as that aborigines, as said above, had real lords and princes, the populace could not procure new lords without other reasonable cause, this being to the hurt of their former lords. Further, on the other hand, these lords themselves could not appoint a new prince without the assent of the populace. Seeing, then, that in such cases of choice and acceptance as these there are not present all the requisite elements of a valid choice, the title under review is utterly inadequate and unlawful for seizing and retaining the provinces in question.[143]

Vitoria therefore affirmed not only the substantive requirement for the consent of both the native population and their leaders, and their legal personality as subjects of the law of nations to give and withhold consent, but also asserted that their consent had to be obtained in a manner which was in accordance with the principles of natural law. As a result, adherence to a number of objective criteria – freedom from fear and ignorance; comprehension of what they were consenting to; absence of any threat of force; respect for indigenous authorities which have the support of the people – was mandatory for consent to be legitimate and to justify title and acquisition of territories.[144] Under natural law therefore, consent could not be coerced and required prior understanding and the support of both the leaders and the people. Theoretically, these criteria imposed strict procedural obligations on Spain in order avoid vitiated consent.

Implicit in Vitoria's acknowledgement of the possibility for a legitimate Spanish title based on free and voluntary choice of the native people and their leaders, was the recognition of their sovereignty and capacity for self-government and dominion 'over themselves and other things'.[145] According to Vitoria, 'The aborigines undoubtedly had true dominion in both public and private matters, just like Christians, and neither their princes nor private persons could be despoiled of their property on the grounds of their not being true owners.'[146]

Vitoria's doctrine of consent was, however, fatally compromised, taking with one hand what it gave with the other. While it affirmed that consent must be based on free and voluntary choice to constitute a legitimate basis for title to territory, it simultaneously placed severe limitations on the voluntary and free dimension of this consent requirement by eliminating indigenous peoples' option to withhold consent to trade with, proselytisation by, or travel of, the Spanish in their territories. To attempt to prevent any of these activities was instead grounds for a

143 'On the illegitimate titles for the reduction of the aborigines of the New World into the power of the Spaniards', ibid.: 148, para 380.
144 Marks 1990–1991: 42.
145 Vitoria *et al.* 1917: 128, para 335, Section 1.
146 Ibid.: 128, para 334, Section 1.

'just war' and loss of dominion. Vitoria also rejected the notion that minority opposition among the natives vitiated their consent, holding that it would be impossible to do anything for the 'welfare of the State' if all had to have the 'same way of thinking'.[147] The implications for the treatment of the minority where they refused consent were not clarified by Vitoria, however, he refers to situations where the majority are Christians voting 'in the interest of the faith' to replace a leader. Such a situation suggests that: (a) he recognised that no title existed even in such cases where the majority were Christians until they expressed their consent to subjugation; (b) the argument did not apply in cases where the population were not Christians; and (c) a majority of Christians in a certain province could assert power over a minority of non-Christians. These limitations may, in part, have been a result of a rather naïve assessment of Vitoria of their *de facto* implications for indigenous peoples, whom he assumed would benefit from his theoretical framework. Given the reality of the Spanish engagement with the natives, of which Vitoria had no first-hand experience, and the scope of these exceptions, consent was in practice obtained under threat of a 'just war', and consequently, in many contexts, represented little more than a legiti-mising tool for Spanish title. If consent was not forthcoming, the capacity of a native people to maintain their dominium over lands in which the colonial power could settle, travel, trade, and preach, or usurp rulers and practices they deemed to violate natural law, was in most cases severely limited. Indeed, the absence of consent could imply resistance, which under the defensive just war doctrine was akin to aggression. Furthermore, at a more fundamental level, native peoples were not asked to consent to this 'universal' framework which established the conditions under which they could 'voluntarily consent' to Spanish title. Instead, this new 'law of nations' assumed their consent to its operation, and it was imposed on them, regardless of their perspectives on the universal nature and terms of the principles it espoused.

1.3.3 Las Casas' position on the rights of the Indios

Las Casas supported Vitoria's grounds for rejecting earlier Spanish claims to title based on papal authority to bestow power on Christian princes over native peoples. However, his view differed significantly from those of Vitoria in relation to legitimate titles in many other regards. His perspective with regard to native peoples' capacity to make choices is captured in his oft-quoted statement that:

> All the races of the world are men, and of all men and of each individual there is but one definition, and this is that they are rational. All have understanding and will and free choice, as all are made in the image and likeness of God . . . Thus the entire human race is one.[148]

---

147 Ibid.: paras 404–405, 160.
148 Sanderlin 1971: 174–175, quoting from Las Casas (1559) *Apologética Historia*.

For Las Casas, there appeared to be only one basis for a legitimate and perfected title to territory – namely, the voluntary uncoerced choice of the native.[149] His theory of consent was intentionally formulated as a legally, rather than theologically, based one.[150] It was premised on two mutually reinforcing legal pillars, combining the medieval doctrine of *Quod omnes tangit* ('What touches all is to be approved by all') with the natural law-based recognition of the natives' dominium and right to select their own rulers by consent.[151] In *De thesauris*, Las Casas clarified that the Pope could only grant an inchoate right to title under *jus ad rem*, valid as against other Christian princes, but that native consent was necessary for that title to be perfected under *jus in re*.[152] In other words, free consent was the essential ingredient, or as Las Casas framed it the 'natural foundation and efficient cause' to transform a right 'to' a thing (preference vis-à-vis others), into a right 'in' a thing (a right to exercise sovereignty).[153] Tierney suggests that by engaging such legal arguments Las Casas maximised the appeal and force of his defence of Indian rights by invoking the 'juridical tradition that undergirded the earlier development of natural rights theories'.[154]

Las Casas dismissed the limitations on the rights of native peoples, which Vitoria regarded as justifiable grounds for obtaining title, as illustrative of Vitoria's carelessness and as based on false assumptions with regard to the actual circumstances of the native peoples. According to Las Casas, Vitoria had introduced these limitations in an attempt to 'moderate' the harshness of his revocation of the extant basis upon which Spain claimed title to territories in the New World.[155] In light of their effects – the perpetuation of the exploitation and elimination of native peoples – which Las Casas, unlike Vitoria, had himself witnessed, he rejected each of Vitoria's premises for the declaration of a 'just war'.[156]

Las Casas also dismissed Vitoria's assumption that, where the consent of the majority was obtained, the dissent of the minority could be ignored,[157] by extrapolating from the theories of Pope Innocent III that there were particular contexts where rights were held at the corporate and individual level. Under Las Casas' theory of consent, in cases where the natural right to liberty was concerned, minority dissent prevailed as the rights of all to liberty were at stake and could not be subordinated to the preferences of a majority or a particular ruler.[158] Liberty under Las Casas' theory effectively constituted a non-derogable right, which

---

149 Lupher 2006: 128–133; see also Lindley 1926: 126.
150 Muldoon 1979: 150, citing Pennington 1970: 157–158; see also Clavero 2002: 67, arguing that Las Casas was a poor jurist.
151 Tierney 2004: 11; Muldoon 1979: 152.
152 Tierney 1997: 283.
153 Ibid.
154 Tierney 2004: 11.
155 De Las Casas, Poole (ed.) 1992: 17–18.
156 Ibid.; 341; see also Marks 1990–1991: 34.
157 Tierney 1997: 284–286, also Tierney 2004: 11.
158 Ibid.

required the consent of all to legitimise any limitation. This broad-based inclusive conception of consent was captured in his requirement that 'all, both great and small, the whole people and individual persons, are to be summoned and their consent sought and obtained'.[159]

Las Casas consequently did not rely on Vitoria's theories in order to assert his position. Instead he held that Spanish jurisdiction in the Americas could not be justified based on war, as the inherent right of peoples to jurisdiction over their territories was, according to Las Casas, 'in the bones of the persons of each community or state' and inseparable from them.[160] As a consequence, any attempts to justify title through the use of force would, within a short time, lead to 'the empire of the Indies [being] entirely overthrown and destroyed'.[161]

Las Casas' opposition to the use of force was most clearly articulated in his vociferous rejection of Sepúlveda's radical thesis that war against the Indians was justifiable on the basis that they lacked rationality, did not have dominion and were natural slaves.[162] Sepúlveda and Las Casas had been called upon by Charles V in 1550 to address the issue of whether war was justified against the natives. At the debates in Valladolid, Sepúlveda, an Aristotelian and believer in the notion of natural slaves, held that war should precede preaching of the faith, so that the natives could be placed under 'civilized government and tutelage, with or without their consent' in order to facilitate their adoption of the faith.[163] Las Casas, on the other hand, started from a premise of equality of all men and peoples. He advocated the seeking of voluntary consent to conversion to Christianity and to the dominion of the Spanish Crown, arguing that this consent would be forthcoming without the use of force, and citing specific examples in Mexico where this had been achieved.[164] Peaceful conversion of the natives, together with voluntary consent to Spanish dominion, while maintaining existing native authorities, was the only legitimate basis for title according to Las Casas.[165] Las Casas' position with regard to the role and entitlements of the Spanish Crown evolved over time. In his initial writings he regarded it as a protective shield for the natives against the wrongs of the *encomienderos*. In his later writing, particularly *De Thesauris*, he denied any legitimacy of the Crown's powers over the natives, on the basis that it had been acquired by force in the absence of consent.[166]

For Las Casas, this unique basis for title in seeking voluntary subjection was even to be found in the instructions of the Papal Bull of 1492, which stated 'the

---

159 De Las Casas *et al.* 1992 *De Thesauris*, in *Obras Completas*, 1992, vol.11.1 210; Tierney 1997: 285.
160 De Las Casa and Poole (ed.) 1992: 84.
161 Ibid.: 18.
162 Sepúlveda, Losada (ed.) 1951; Las Casas' opposing view was articulated in De Las Casas, Poole (ed.) 1992. For an account of the background to, and debates at, the 1550–1551 Valladolid dispute between Las Casas and Sepúlveda, see Macnutt 1909: 277–293; see also Hanke 1949: 109–132; Marks 1990–1991 and Clavero 2002.
163 Parry 1940: 37.
164 Macnutt 1909: 365–367.
165 De Las Casas, Poole (ed.) 1992.
166 Tierney 1997: 281.

aforementioned continents and islands, as well as their natives and inhabitants, subject to yourselves and to lead them to the Catholic faith'. Las Casas' interpretation of 'subject to yourselves' as requiring voluntary subjection of the natives was radically different from that of Sepúlveda, who considered the same wording a justification for war in order to subjugate the natives.[167] In light of the inherent rights of the natives, Las Casas reasoned that the 1492 Papal Bull could only provide spiritual as opposed to temporal dominium over them.[168] His view has consequently been interpreted as holding that the bull provided a basis for the assertion of *de jure* sovereignty, but for this sovereignty to be exercised, *de facto* consent was necessary.[169] Las Casas' argument therefore implied that, prior to the Spanish arrival, the natives were sovereign peoples exercising self-government.[170] In his later years he went so far as to argue that they exercised this in a manner more effective than the Spanish and would be better off if all the Spanish were cast out 'except for a few chosen few ones, so that the Indians could receive the faith'.[171] This preaching of the faith had to be through persuasion, through reason. According to Las Casas, an approach which first demanded that native peoples be subjected against their will could only lead to war, which he condemned as nothing more than 'general murder and robbery among many'.[172]

Certain views put forward by Las Casas, in particular those relating to the slave trade and evangelisation based on a failure to respect others' religious beliefs, are indisputably inconsistent with contemporary human rights standards.[173] Even his views on native sovereignty were to some extent inherently contradictory. The rational nature of all men, including natives, and their associated capacity for making choices, are premised on a notion of equality. However, this is framed within, and underpinned by, the notion of a universally applicable religious framework, which through its propagation had *de facto* constraining implications for the exercise of native sovereignty. Nevertheless, while advocating evangelism, and holding that the King could maintain some form of overarching authority where consent was given for this,[174] Las Casas, in recognising native jurisdiction and territoriality and the requirement for native consent, went significantly further than Vitoria in his doctrine of natural law-based native rights.[175] Not only was consent a requirement to justify an overarching Spanish claim to sovereignty, but where consent had not been forthcoming prior to taking of lands and mines, Las Casas held that restitution 'to the penny' for the taking of 'boatloads of gold and

---

167 De Las Casas, Poole (ed.) 1992: 351, 354; Marks 1990–1991: 36.
168 See Muldoon 1979: 152–153 and Clavero 2002, for a critique of Las Casas' logic.
169 Orique 2011: 241; De Las Casas *et al.* 1992c: 455–456; De Las Casas *et al.* 1992e: 315–318; see also Carro 1971: 274–275.
170 Sanderlin 1971: 195–196; see also Hanke 1959: 47–48.
171 Sanderlin 1971: 21.
172 Ibid.: 28.
173 For a critical commentary, see Clavero 2002; see also Castro 2007; Keen 1971: 39; see also Comas 1971: 505–506 ; Zavala 1944: 149–154.
174 Carro 1971: 269.
175 Carozza, 2003: 286, 295.

silver' was appropriate.[176] While advocating for full restitution, he acknowledged that this was highly unlikely and the natives may have to accept much less.[177] Las Casas' influence in the 1542 New Laws which restricted the powers of the *encomienderos* was evident. However, it was not surprising that the reforms he advocated, which many viewed as challenging the integrity of the entire colonial enterprise, were eventually rejected under pressure from the colonialists.[178]

Diverging opinions exist with regard to how Las Casas should be judged and his legacy interpreted.[179] One view holds that he advocated for native peoples to be treated as 'independent kingdoms', similar to the autonomous Naples or Sicily, governed 'according to their own customs and civilization' and invited to become 'equal subjects of a paternalist crown'.[180] In contemporary terms, one could perhaps equate this reasoning to the promotion of a sort of internal right to self-determination, recognising native peoples' rights over their territories but affording them little opportunity to extradite themselves from their subordinate position under the colonial empire. The extent to which Las Casas could be regarded as having advocated for an unrestrained external right to self-determination, namely the rejection of any form of sovereign authority of the Spanish Crown or the Roman Catholic Church on the basis that consent had not been obtained, seems to have fluctuated over time. In his initial writing, Las Casas appeared to accept, rather than challenge, the *de facto* situation of the non-consensual Spanish presence. That presence was taken as given, and the focus was on how it could be legitimised in a peaceful manner through voluntary religious conversion.[181] Interpretations of his later writing, however, suggest a more radical stance affording greater support to an unencumbered right of native peoples to reject the imposition of colonial power and to be compensated for non-consensual taking of their lands and resources. Another dimension of Las Casas' writing and legal practice which has also been critiqued is its impersonal accounts of actual people and events, its tendency to ignore the diversity of peoples that existed, and its failure to adequately project the perspectives and legal justification for the actions of indigenous leaders such as Tenamaztle of Xalisco, whose case he argued at the Council of the Indies.[182] Instead of arguing Tenamaztle's defence on the grounds of indigenous law and sovereignty, arguments were instead framed in terms of pleas to natural law and the laws of Castilla.[183] Las Casas, from this perspective, could be seen as erroneously attempting to 'empower the dominated with the voice of the dominant' rather than 'open[ing] up the dominant discourse to the transformative voice of the dominated'.[184]

---

176 Friede 1971: 177; see also Hanke 1949: 154; Yanez 2014: 18, 21.
177 Orique 2011: 821.
178 Hanke 1949: 104.
179 Clavero 2002; Castro 2007.
180 Rubies 2007.
181 Clavero 2002.
182 Ibid.: 33.
183 Ibid.: 40.
184 Hutchinson 1989: 565–566.

In many regards, Las Casas' doctrine, which posed more than an academic challenge to colonial powers and eliminated much of the wriggle room introduced by Vitoria, would eventually be largely relegated to the side-lines of international law in favour of doctrine which continued to justify the use of force.[185] Nevertheless, his doctrine did have an influence in the Spanish colonies with many friars across the Spanish colonies adopting a similar stance.[186] As an articulation of indigenous peoples' rights, it served to limit the effect of the rights-denying theories of Sepúlveda, and to highlight the logical inconsistencies of Vitoria's discourse and the rights-restricting effects of the limitations which it imposed on the consent requirement and indigenous sovereignty. Interpreted in light of the extant international order, and freed of its religious baggage and sixteenth-century political discourse, it has an on-going relevance for the contemporary and still evolving normative framework of indigenous peoples' rights.[187] The fundamental caveat to this is that indigenous voices have to be heard and their perspectives respected.

The requirement for native consent was at the core of Las Casas' theory of legitimate title to territory. Without the consent of the native authorities, temporal power over them appeared unjustifiable and any imposed government structures were illegitimate.[188] Even where that consent was forthcoming, they maintained their dominium over their lands and resources. As this consent had generally not been obtained, overarching claims to title to territory and sovereignty by the colonial government and the associated exploitation of native peoples' lands and mines could not be justified. However, as noted, Las Casas' articulation of the rights of native peoples, while progressive for its time, was nevertheless deficient in terms of the extent to which it was infused with the perspectives of the peoples themselves. If sovereignty 'permits the expression of collective difference',[189] then recognition of sovereignty must be facilitative of the expression of that difference. It is with regard to this self-determining dimension of consent and sovereignty that Las Casas' discourse is arguably most deficient.

1.4 The influence of the Spanish School in legal discourse beyond Spain

A thinly cloaked version of Vitoria's discourse was subsequently adopted by the English in their colonising discourse in relation to the Americas.[190] As noted earlier,

---

185 Brownlie 1963; see also Tierney 1997: 275–276; Tierney 2004: 11; Carozza 2003; Beuchot 1994: 37–39.
186 *Archivo de Indias*, Lima 29, Lib. 5. *Report of Toledo to the King, from Potosí*, 20 March 1573, quoted in Hanke 1949: 163, 157; see also Comas 1971: 487–539. For a contrary view, see Castro 2007; for a critique of Castro's analysis, see Boruchoff 2008: 497–504.
187 See Clavero 2002, for a critical critique on the interpretations of Las Casas' writing.
188 Hanke 1949: 156.
189 Macklem 1993: 1348.
190 For a colonialist's account of British policy from 1457 onwards, see Egerton 1897; see also Egerton 1903. For an overview of the colonisation of North America, see Robertson 2005; see also Miller 2006; Williams 1990; Abbot 1975.

the English Crown had made use of papal bulls in its colonising enterprise as far back as 1155. England's mechanism of choice for the spreading of Christianity and civilisation was the 'planting' of Christians, or the Christian seed, in the fertile lands of the infields – a practice which it pioneered in the colonisation of Ireland.[191] If the natives gave their consent, planting could proceed and possession of property was permitted. If, upon explanation by the English of their intent to settle peacefully in native peoples' territories, and to trade and traffic with them, native consent was not forthcoming, then the use of force or a just war was permissible.[192] Subsequent justifications would be in line with Vattel's theories of productive land usage.[193]

Under this doctrine, the natives would benefit from true (non-papal) Christianity and civilisation (leading to more productive of use of lands in accordance with the Puritan ethos), and would be liberated from Spanish cruelty and the abuses documented by Las Casas.[194] The natives were consequently expected to be grateful for the plantations in their lands. England, on the other hand, would fulfil the dual goal of spreading the true form of Christianity, while profiting from the gold and silver of the Americas.[195] In 1498, in a manner similar to the expansive Spanish and Portuguese claims to rights over non-European territories, Henry VII asserted that England had a right to conquer, occupy and possess the lands of the infidels and thereby acquire title to territory over them. He commissioned John Cabot to realise this and claimed the Gulf of Mexico based on his voyage of discovery.[196] Cabot's voyages would also act as a basis for subsequent British justification for discovery-based titles. Following Henry VIII's abandonment of the Catholic Church, the English continued to challenge the *de facto* authority of the Pope while at the same time justifying their claims to discovery vis-à-vis the papal bulls up to the time of James I in the 1620s.[197]

1.4.1 Early state practice: perfecting discovery through conquest or consent

Together with the French, the English added the notion of actual possession (while at the same time not necessarily complying with it) to the requirement for discovery.[198] The Dutch, for their part, adopted a similar approach premised on the theories of Grotius, which rejected title on the basis of discovery alone, but upheld the notion of a just war where commerce was not permitted. In accordance with this, the treaties they entered into with Asian rulers had more commercial

---

191 Hakluyt 1877: xlv.
192 Ibid.: xlv; see also Williams 1990: 169.
193 Smith 1877: 7–8; see also Miller *et al.* 2010: 27.
194 Williams 1990: 172–174; Macnutt 1909.
195 Bannister 1838: 58.
196 Falkowski 1992: 15; Lindley 1926: 130. For an account of conflicting colonial powers' claims, see Weddle 1985: 372–387; and Trelease 1997.
197 Hakluyt 1877: 134–135.
198 Miller *et al.* 2010: 18–21; see also Richardson 2009a: 57; Eccles 1972.

than political effect.[199] The notion of settlement and the productive agricultural use of land also served to justify the English claims over territories which had earlier been claimed by the Spanish on the basis of prior discovery. The Spanish claims were challenged by the English on the Vattellian grounds that they were not in effective possession of those territories, as they did not occupy substantial portions of their lands, and consequently had no right to maintain claim over them.[200] Competing claims to the territories of the 'heathens and infidels' were also made by the Dutch and French.[201] This gradually led to the declining relevance of the papal bulls, and the emergence of other doctrines upon which disputes vis-à-vis other European powers and claims to title to territory were addressed, culminating in the agreements reached in the 1648 Peace of Westphalia and the emergence of the consent of territorial sovereign nation-states as the cornerstone of international law.[202]

One approach which emerged was that 'discovery' of territories not held under claim of a European power provided an inchoate title which had to be perfected through actual possession.[203] According to Jennings: 'Not since the 16th century, for example, has it been possible to argue that a mere discovery, coupled with an intention to eventually occupy, is sufficient to create a title.'

This position was asserted by the British against the Spanish in 1790, in the context of their discovery-based claims to portions of the United States where Britain affirmed that the consent of the natives supported its right to possession.[204] In 1765, Blackstone asserted that possession over inhabited lands was realised either through conquest (presumably in accordance with natural justice) or consent manifested by treaties.[205] Where native populations existed, perfecting this title consequently implied the need for: (a) their consent to cede (and purchase of their land necessary for settlement), or (b) conquest, by forcing them to acquiesce following the successful conduct of a just war.[206] This 'doctrine of discovery' largely served to avoid disputes between European powers. However, the fact that the rules of conquest which applied to indigenous peoples differed from those applied to European States,[207] and the manner in which native consent was obtained was not subject to any form of oversight, implied that indigenous peoples were frequently dispossessed of their territories and sovereignty by whatever method the coloniser had the power to realise.[208]

---

199 In general, see Alexandrowicz 1967.
200 Hakluyt 1877: 234; see also Williams 1990: 180.
201 Jennings 1975: 5.
202 Brownlie 1963: 14; see also Falkowski 1992: 13–14; and Jennings 1963.
203 Jennings 1963: 4.
204 Lindley 1926: 26; TWISS 1846: 80–81.
205 Blackstone 1765, Book I, 106–107 qualified the right of conquest, stating 'with what natural justice I shall not at present enquire'.
206 US Supreme Court, *Johnson v. M'Intosh*, 21 U.S. 543, 5 L. Ed. 681, 8 Wheat. 543 (1823) 545, 587–578; see also Lindley 1926: 31.
207 Falkowski 1992: 15, citing Sereni 1943: 85–117.
208 Castellino and Allen 2003.

The practice of purchasing lands from the tribes in North America adopted by the Swedish and the Dutch, in part to challenge British 'discovery'-based claims to sovereignty, reflected the reality that, where sizable indigenous populations existed, their consent to colonial settlement 'was a practical necessity'.[209] This was also illustrated by the treaty-making, often driven out of military necessity, between the French and the English with the native peoples,[210] and the orders provided to Cook as part of his expedition to the North-west of America 'to take possession of [any inhabited lands] with the consent of the natives'.[211] This practice of treaty-making and consent-premised purchases of lands was continued and expanded upon by the United States following independence. The United States held that it had acquired the British right to claim native territories by cession or conquest, and entering into these treaties was necessary for it to protect its territorial rights vis-à-vis the British.[212]

Cornell describes the initial encounter between European societies and North American Indian tribes in the context of the fur trade as the 'market period', throughout which both parties were *de facto* equals from an economic, political and military perspective.[213] During this period of relative equality, consensual and mutually beneficial arrangements were reached between these societies based on a composite of European and American Indian conceptions of law and justice. Williams focuses on the frequently overlooked, yet fundamental, question of American Indian perspectives on these and other colonial era treaties signed between 1600 and 1800 and the constitutional principles that they embodied for the signatory native peoples.[214] Core among these principles were: the sacred and intergenerational nature of the trust-based relationships they established between treaty parties; the constitutional duties attributable to the stronger party in the treaty relationship, together with the increased importance of compliance with these duties as power imbalances amplified over time; and the indispensable requirement to respect indigenous protocol, customs and perspectives in treaty-based relationships.[215] As noted earlier, native peoples entered into consent-based agreements among themselves prior to the colonial era, the Iroquois League of the Haudenosaunee being exemplary. Williams suggests that a reason the Iroquois had such an influence on treaty-making in North America was because for them proactively seeking to enter into consent-based treaties with other peoples was 'a constitutional tradition of law and peace'.[216] The fundamental principle of indigenous consent as the foundation for a constitutional order underpinning covenants, which started among indigenous groups, was extended to include settler

---

209 Sanders 1983: 7, fn 11; see also Colchester and MacKay 2004: 3–6.
210 Williams 1999; Orange 2011; see also Ruru 2009: 114. Miguel Alfonso Martínez, Special Rapporteur, *Study on Treaties, Agreements and Other Constructive Arrangements Between States and Indigenous Populations*, UN Doc E/CN.4/Sub.2/1999/20, para 117–122.
211 Twiss 1846: 58–59; see also Bennett and Castles 1979: 253–254.
212 Mellor 1951: 374.
213 Cornell 1988: 17.
214 Williams 1999; see also Clavero 2005a. For a study on treaties in Latin America, see Levaggi 2002.
215 Williams 1999.
216 Ibid.: 116.

peoples in the form of treaty-making and the continuous intergenerational renewal and interpretation of their commitments.[217] As Clavero suggests, these treaties should be recognised as constitutive elements of the State which precede and have primacy over their Constitutions.[218] This indigenous legal tradition was premised on principles of good faith, justice, friendship, solidarity, equality and unity, mandating respect for indigenous territories, while guaranteeing mutual support and cooperation in times of need among treaty parties bonded together as brothers in perpetuity.[219] Through the operation of such treaties, the peace and security necessary for trade and mutually respectful co-existence based on the 'sacredly revealed truth of their shared humanity' were assured. [220] Unlike colonial conceptions of consent, entering into consensual agreements in accordance with principles insisted on by indigenous peoples, and accepted by their treaty parties, was not a one-off activity which served only the interests of the colonial power. Instead indigenous conceptions of consent served to affirm and protect the rights of both parties and clarify their duties towards one another.

Indigenous peoples have consistently affirmed that the consent-based treaties entered into with them constitute formal acknowledgements of their self-determination and sovereignty rights. They do so irrespective of State interpretations.[221] UN expert seminars have called on States to continue 'to explore ways of redressing historical and contemporary injustices related to treaties, agreements and other constructive arrangements through negotiation and underline the principle of free, prior and informed consent'.[222] This position is reflective of the need to understand the perspectives of both parties to agreements which were purportedly entered into on a consensual basis. From the commencement of the colonial encounter, indigenous peoples have offered alternative conceptions of law and justice. They have responded in a variety of ways to this encounter – resisting, negotiating agreements, forming new alliances, and at times merging into other groups. This history has, by and large, been ignored in State-centric versions of international law. However, as contemporary historians have observed '[t]he wretched of the earth are talking, and we are all trying to listen, we now aim for a bifocal vision, a bilateral history, a mirror-image ethnography'.[223] Extended to international law, this bilateral understanding necessitates a re-engagement

---

217 Ibid.: 110–111.
218 Clavero 2005a.
219 Williams 1999: 118.
220 Ibid.: 123.
221 Final report by Special Rapporteur, Miguel Alfonso Martínez, *Study on Treaties, Agreements and Other Constructive Arrangements between States and Indigenous Populations*, UN Doc E/CN.4/Sub.2/1999/20 paras. 55, 57, 104, 105, 110; see also UN, *Study on Treaties, Agreements and Other Constructive Arrangements Between States and Indigenous Populations - First Progress Report*, E/CN.4/Sub.2/1992/32, paras 138–139; and UN, *Study on Treaties, Agreements and Other Constructive Arrangements between States and Indigenous Populations: Second Progress Report* E/CN.4/Sub.2/1995/27, para. 130; and UN Doc E/CN.4/Sub.2/AC.4/2004/7; see also Littlechild 2011: 118–119.
222 *Conclusions and Recommendations of the Seminar on Treaties, Agreements and Other Constructive Arrangements between States and Indigenous Peoples*, UN Doc E/CN.4/2004/111, 3.
223 Morgan 1999: 43.

with indigenous principles of consent and sovereignty which were increasingly supressed during the colonial encounter as power imbalances grew between indigenous peoples and colonialists.

1.4.2 Post-Spanish School legal theorists

Vitoria and Las Casas and other members of the Spanish School were not alone among the founding fathers of the law of nations in their affirmation of consent-based titles to territory, and their rejection of discovery alone as legitimising claims over indigenous lands. Over the subsequent centuries a number of eminent jurists have regarded consent or cession as the only bases for justifying title to territory over native lands in the absence of a just war.[224] Gentili (1550–1608), an Italian Protestant, proposed a more nuanced approach to the concept of a just war, which was authorised only where all types of trade were refused, but not on religious grounds.[225] He was the first to perform an in-depth analysis of the law of treaties, affirming that treaties were binding beyond the life of the signatories, provided conditions remained unchanged, and holding that entering into them under duress following military defeat did not constitute grounds for their subsequent annulment.[226]

Hugo de Grotius, alongside Vitoria, is recognised as one of the founding fathers of international law and was the first publicist to consolidate existing theory into comprehensive doctrine.[227] Grotius adopted a modified secularised version of Vitoria's thesis which dismissed discovery as a legitimate basis for title (as it did not constitute grounds for a just war) and recognised the inherent natural law-based capacity for consent of all peoples.[228] Like Gentili, Grotius recognised the capacity of all men to enter into treaties.[229] In his seminal work, *De Jure Belli ac Pacis* (1625), Grotius articulated the restrictions that should be placed on the use of force in order to limit conflicts between States, as well as private actors, such as joint stock companies.[230] The conditions he imposed on native sovereignty, including the requirement to permit free commerce in their territories (which was rejected by the Portuguese jurist, De Freitas), nevertheless continued to place limitations on native peoples' territoriality through the justification of a just war where they were not complied with.[231]

---

224 Lindley includes in this list Brumus (Germany 1548), Gentilis (Oxford 1588) Selden (1618), Grotius (1609), Pufendorf (1672), Gunther (1778), Kluber (1819), Blackstone (1765), Heffter (1844), Praider-Fodere; Salomon; Bonfils and Jeze; see Lindley 1926: 11–17.
225 Lindley 1926: 13; Brownlie 1963: 11.; Kingsbury and Straumann 2010.
226 Nussbaum 1954: 96.
227 Brownlie 1963: 13; see also Nussbaum 1954: 111, 114.
228 Grotius 1625: 10.
229 Ibid.: 128; see also Nussbaum 1954: 110.
230 Ibid.
231 Alexandrowicz 1967: 51; Brito Vieira 2003.

Pufendorf (1672), who also rejected mere discovery as a basis for title, interpreted Grotius as affirming that inhabited lands could not be acquired by occupation on the grounds that:

> every man is, by nature, equal to every man, and consequently not subject to the dominion of others, therefore this bare seizing by force is not enough to found a lawful sovereignty over men, but must be attended with some other title.[232]

The Swiss publicist Vattel (1714–1767) was influential in the shift from a natural law to a positivist-based approach to questions pertaining to title to territory and the status of native peoples. His conception of the Law of Nations was informed by a combination of Hobbes's (1588–1679) post-Westphalian conception of nation-states, as premised on a social contract and possessing an absolute sovereign, and Lockean conceptions of property rights, as derived from labour and the associated necessity for productive land use.[233] Locke echoed the views of Grotius, Pufendorf and Suarez that claims over property in a political society had to be based on consent, however, he held that consent was not required to claim property in the absence of a political society.[234] This Enlightenment-consistent model afforded the potential to undermine the natural law rights of native peoples, as it could be argued that those peoples who did not meet the characteristics of nation-states were no longer deemed to be vested with such rights.[235] Consistent with the post-Westphalian conception of natural law rights as vested exclusively in sovereign nation-states and individuals, those native peoples not recognised as meeting the nation-state criteria found themselves no longer classified as subjects of the law.[236] The notion of a single 'nation' was therefore becoming synonymous with the 'State', despite the fact that multiple nations co-existed within many of these so-called nation-states. This ultimately facilitated a new reality in which, instead of the nation defining the State, the State would define the nation. The question therefore arose as to which native nations met the status of nation-states. For Vattel, a nation's *de facto* self-government, by 'its own authority and laws', implied it should be recognised as a sovereign nation-state.[237] However, the extent to which Vattel regarded this as exclusively applicable to those native nations possessing centralised power structures, such as the Aztecs, is unclear. He explicitly mentioned these powerful nations as illustrative of territories which should not have

---

232 Pufendorf 1672, quoted in Lindley 1926: 14, 131; for a commentary on Pufendorf's theory of property rights under international law, see Tully 1993.
233 Thornberry 2002: 71; Anaya 2004: 20; for a comment on Hobbes, see Nussbaum 1954: 135; for a comment on Vattel, see Brownlie 1963: 17.
234 Tully 1980: 98–99; see also Tully 1993: 145.
235 Vattel 1758; see also Anaya 2004: 19–24; see Lindley 1926: 17.
236 Crawford 2007: 7–9; Thornberry 2002: 71; see also Anaya 2004: 20; Oppenheim 1920: 126 §63 and 305 §168.
237 Vattel 1758, in Haakonssen 2008: Book I, Chapter i, §4, 83.

been colonised,[238] as opposed to the territories of wandering tribes in the United States, portions of which he regarded as open to acquisition by European powers.[239] If the restrictive interpretation of Vattel's theory is adopted, then, under a Vattel-compliant model of international law, many indigenous peoples would be effectively defined out of existence as nations and sovereign entities.[240] At best, those which could not claim to meet the nation-state criteria could become 'domestic dependent nations' within sovereign nation-states,[241] and, at worst, they would be totally subsumed within those States with no rights as communities.

A certain degree of ambiguity therefore existed in Vattel's approach to native peoples. On the one hand, he conceded that those peoples possessing and cultivating lands held rights to property over them which they could not be denied against their will.[242] However, in the absence of a 'civilised' political organisation, these property rights did not appear to pose an obstacle to the assertion of title to territory over them, absent their consent.[243] In this regard, Vattel's view was consistent with that of British and French theorists who based territorial claims on usufructuary arguments, giving precedence to agricultural land use over any native title deemed to be premised on hunting and gathering activities.[244] On the other hand, Vattel's assertion that uncultivated lands could be taken by Europeans can be interpreted as only constituting a limitation on native peoples' property rights without necessarily representing a complete denial of their sovereign right to self-government and independence.[245] This latter interpretation has some degree of resonance with the experience of Native Americans in the United States where the Supreme Court, while relying on Vattel's conception of the law of nations, affirmed that native sovereignty was affected by conquest and cession but not by discovery – in other words, occupation was not the mode of acquisition to be applied to them.[246] Vattel's theory was also ambiguous in relation to the status of the sovereignty of nations which consented to place themselves under the authority of another nation-state.[247] Addressing this issue the United States Supreme Court held that native sovereignty continued, albeit in a modified form, following their incorporation into the United States in a manner equivalent to dependent States.[248]

The sovereignty-constraining dimension of Vattel's eighteenth-century theory constituted a precursor for the even more radical sovereignty-denying discourses which would emerge under the purely positivist conceptions of international law

238 Ibid.: Book IV, Chapter iv, §37, 672–673.
239 Ibid.: Book I, Chapter xviii at 100 §209.
240 Anaya 2004: 20–23.
241 *Cherokee Nation v. Georgia*, 30 U.S. (5 Pet.) 1, 16 (1831).
242 Lindley 1926: 23; Alexandrowicz 1973: 46, citing Vattel, Book II, Chapter XII, §163.
243 *Fletcher v Peck* (1810)10 US 87; see also Thornberry 2002: 79–80.
244 Pagden 1995.
245 Clinebell and Thomson 1977–1978: 686–687; see also Anaya 2004: 23.
246 *Worchester v Georgia* 31 U.S. (6 Pet.) 515 (1832) 559–560.
247 Anaya 2004: 23.
248 Clinebell and Thomson 1977–1978: 671; Crawford 2007: 266, fn 54.

in the nineteenth century. Despite continued engagement with indigenous peoples in order to obtain their colonial enterprise-legitimising 'consent', the principles underpinning indigenous conceptions of consent reflected in their treaty-making and agreement-making practices were increasingly ignored by colonial legal theorists as power imbalances with indigenous peoples grew more pronounced and Britain emerged as the dominant colonial empire. The nature of this colonial conception of consent and the role it came to play during the nineteenth and into the beginning of the twentieth centuries are the subject of Chapter 2.

2 Nineteenth-century positivists and divergence between the role of consent in theory and practice

2.1 Introduction

A common thread running through the conceptions of the law of nations of Vitoria, Las Casas, Grotius and Vattel was that it derived 'its authority from the consent of all, or at least of many nations'.[1] The emerging consensus in the eighteenth century among nation-states was that they only recognised each other as subjects of international law. This premise would be solidified and further refined over the subsequent century by the Positivist School which regarded international law as exclusively grounded on the consent of sovereign nation-states.[2] Indigenous peoples were not alone in losing legal personality as a result of this emergence of an exclusively sovereign State conception of international law. The Church, which previously had held the role of arbitrator, lost its power by the time of the Peace of Westphalia in 1648,[3] while feudal entities were also squeezed out of the subjects whose legal personality was recognised.[4]

The global reach of this European colonial project reached its peak in the nineteenth century. From the mid-nineteenth century until the commencement of the First World War, despite the contrary views of some notable publicists,[5] this positivist approach sought to completely deny indigenous sovereignty.[6] The version of international law which accompanied this globalised colonial project was in many regards a simplified one from that of previous centuries, in so far as it abandoned the naturalist precepts in favour of exclusively positivistic ones.[7] It was also totalising and exclusionary. Instead of emerging from an equal meeting of legal traditions, international law re-emerged as a monolithic project

---

1 Wheaton 1866: 3–4, 10–11; see also Vattel 1758: Book 3, Chapter 12, §188–192 at 381–383 §192; Vitoria *et al.* 1917: Section III, 153 §391.
2 Damerow 1978: 76–81.
3 Brownlie 1963: 14. From Grotius onwards the leading publicists were Protestant, see Nussbaum 1954: 146.
4 Nussbaum 1954: 90.
5 Among these were Heffter (Germany, 1844), Pasquale Fiore (Italy, 1868), Woolsey (United States, 1874), see Lindley 1926: 15–17; see also Phillimore 1871: 23.
6 Alexandrowicz 1973: 6; see also Wheaton 1866; Oppenheim 1920: 317 §214.
7 Anghie 1999: 1–81; see also Anghie 2007.

subordinating all non-European traditions which had yet to accommodate themselves to its principles. The consent of the family of nations, essentially, European States,[8] determined its content and the extension of the club to which it applied. Positivism conferred power on European States to 'grant' sovereignty and to determine its implications. It eliminated the problem associated with natural law under which sovereignty was understood as inherent to political societies whose recognition was mandated under principles of equality and justice. With native sovereignty constrained within this positivist straitjacket, the principle of native consent could be deployed as and when desired by the colonial power, with no implications for the rights of the consent giver of its exercise under international law beyond those which it was convenient for that power to recognise.

This chapter seeks to examine the nature of this colonial conception of indigenous peoples' consent and the role it came to play under the positivist legal discourse in the context of the expansion of the colonial project in the nineteenth century. It is divided into eight sections. Section 2.2 provides a brief overview of the context within which the positivist discourse emerged. Section 2.3 explores the role of consent in the colonial practice leading to the acquisition of territory, contrasting the legal theories in relation to acquisition of title to territory which the positivists espoused with the *de facto* colonial practice. Section 2.4 addresses the discussion around the consent requirement under the Berlin Act. Section 2.5 examines the views of the positivists in relation to membership of the family of nations. Section 2.6 considers the implications of this for 'colonial' protectorates. Section 2.7 looks at the nature of the consent requirement during the positivist era. Section 2.8 addresses the role of the consent requirement in the context of the doctrine of guardianship, the trusteeship system, and the emergence of post-colonial States. Section 2.9 considers self-determination and the decolonisation project.

2.2 Socially sanctioned racist theories and the positivist discourse

The nineteenth century has been coined 'Britain's Imperial Century'.[9] The emergence of the rights-denying positivist legal discourse was symptomatic of broader changes in British society's perspectives of indigenous peoples. The discourse both drew from, and endorsed, evolving socially sanctioned racist theories. Three distinct historical developments fuelled these racist theories, bolstering the notion of native peoples as backward children and savages, unworthy of treatment as sovereign peoples and incapable of functioning as independent nations. The first consisted of a series of rebellions. Commencing in the 1840s, they led to what has been referred to as a 'crisis of liberalism' in the British Empire.[10] These rebellions

---

8 Gong 1984.
9 Porter 1999b: ix.
10 Bank 1999: 364-6.

played a formative role in the emergence of the new racist discourse underpinning the final wave of British Colonial expansion in Africa. The exposure of the fragility of the Victorian belief in the inevitable universalisation of British civilisation commenced during the 1835 Xhosa War in the Cape.[11] The subsequent Indian Mutiny of 1857, the Jamaican Morant Bay Rebellion of 1865, the Māori Wars in the 1860s, among other rebellions involving 'ungrateful natives', shattered that illusion and exposed a new dominant ideology based on the superiority of 'the conquering race'.[12] This perspective was captured in an 1883 statement on behalf of the British Raj in the media that it had been 'founded on conquest and not consent'.[13]

The racist discourse found further support in the emergence of a new scientific anthropology. The creed of this new 'science' was social evolutionism, according to which, races, like individuals, were held to conform to the Darwinist notions of survival of the fittest.[14] The judgemental and racist character of the evolutionary theorising implicit in the notion of social evolutionism which emerged in the 1860s remained unchallenged until the 1920s, and to a certain degree, as discussed in Chapter 3, continued to influence international law as it pertained to indigenous peoples into the 1960s, with remnants of it arguably still remaining in some present-day legal thinking.[15] The international legal project was also influenced by its reconceptualisation as a scientific discipline. This served to justify a transition from a discipline concerned with deciphering pre-existing universally applicable principles of justice and morality to one based on studying and ordering of rules agreed upon by States.[16] This scientific approach to international law was aligned with the scientific approach to the study of races, as international law was now to be exclusively the domain of civilised races.

A third contributor to the emergence of this racist discourse appears to have been the transmission of the racism in North America to Britain in the 1850s.[17] In North America, early colonial settlers regarded the 'drawing of "tribal" social boundaries as key components of their English "liberty"' and resisted efforts to 'collapse the difference between Indians and ordinary English colonists'.[18] As discussed in Chapter 1, they were, however, frequently obliged to enter into treaties with native peoples, and negotiate under conditions of relative equality, in accordance with principles derived from both European and tribal legal and diplomatic traditions. By the nineteenth century, these treaties had increasingly been reneged on, with a positivist version of international law invoked to justify such practices. Reduced significance was accorded to indigenous perspectives in new treaties that were entered into, which were frequently interpreted as the cession of Indian

---

11 Ibid.: 364.
12 Bellich 1988: Moore 1999: 433.
13 Moore 1999: 433.
14 Bolt 1971; Bank 1999: 364; see also Fukuyama 2011: 50.
15 Anghie 2007.
16 Lawrance 1895: 1; quoted in Anghie 2007: 49.
17 Curtin 1964: vi, 372.
18 Breen 1999: 104.

sovereignty, irrespective of whether this understanding was shared with the indigenous signatories.[19] As reflected in the rulings of Chief Justice Marshall, despite affording some recognition to residual Indian sovereignty and 'measured separatism', the language of the Indian as 'savage' permeated North American legal thought at the end of the eighteenth and outset of the nineteenth centuries.[20]

In Britain, the eighteenth century's racist sentiments had been increasingly masked under the Christianising zeal of Puritan missionaries and overshadowed by the humanitarian liberalism underpinning groups such as the Aborigines' Protection Society.[21] The ensuing mid-nineteenth-century shift towards an overtly racist discourse and consensus was so dramatic that it has been described as a transition from this 'era of humanitarianism' to 'the era of imperialism'.[22] This cocktail of fear and superiority, which native uprisings, distorted Darwinist concepts and imported racism combined to foment within the British Empire, served to establish a context within which the legitimising role of indigenous consent in the acquisition of title to territory could be manipulated and perverted to suit colonial ends, inevitably to the detriment of indigenous sovereignty.

2.3 State practice and the acquisition of indigenous peoples' territories by occupation

2.3.1 Tensions between positivist theory and state practice

The inherent tension between dismissing indigenous sovereignty *de-jure*, while relying on obtaining their consent *de-facto* in order to legitimise title to territory, and the contradictions it introduced in relation to indigenous legal personality under international law, represent an unresolved paradox at the core of the positivist approach to international law. In the interest of minimising conflict between colonial States, the practice of seeking native consent remained one of the predominant means of legitimising title to territory until the end of the colonial era.[23] The practice also continued due to the inability of the colonial powers to suppress native resistance and guarantee 'security of life and property' for their subjects, which was necessary for occupation to be considered 'effective'.[24] Consequently, despite the emergence of this positivist model of international law, and the affirmations by many of its major publicists that the treatment of the uncivilised natives was only conditioned by the 'conscience' of the civilised State claiming sovereignty over them,[25] States nevertheless continued

---

19 UN Doc E/CN.4/Sub.2/1999/20, para 117–122.
20 Williams 1999: 132.
21 Porter 1999a: 345.
22 Curtin 1964: xii; Bolt 1971.
23 *Study on Treaties, Agreements and Other Constructive Arrangements Between States and Indigenous Populations*, UN Doc. E/CN.4/Sub.2/1999/20, para 300.
24 UN Doc E/CN.4/Sub.2/1999/20, paras 117–122; see also Lindley 1926: 141, 159, citing Institut de Droit International X, *Annuaire* 1888: 201.
25 Westlake 1894: 142–143.

to seek the consent of indigenous peoples and sign treaties with them right up to the dying days of the colonial enterprise.[26] Maintaining that colonial system in the face of African resistance, which became formalised as Indirect Rule after 1900 and championed by Lugard, also necessitated some form of local consent based on achieving 'a sufficient balance of interests . . . for the colonial power's presence to be tolerated by those who carried most weight in colonial societies'.[27]

In light of this reality, a number of contemporary commentators have suggested that the notion of *terra nullius* played little practical part in the pursuit of the colonial agenda. Thornberry suggests that in light of colonial State practice, the notion put forward by nineteenth-century publicists that indigenous lands were regarded as *terra nullius*, thereby permitting not only the denial of indigenous sovereignty but also the taking of their lands, constituted 'something of an academic conceit'.[28] Bennett also notes that in many parts of the world obtaining title to territory by occupation based on the principle of *terra nullius* 'bore little relation to the actual practices of colonial powers'.[29] This view appears to be shared by Crawford who argues that *terra nullius* under international law always constituted 'desert and uncultivated' or 'uninhabited lands' and the colonial practice in Africa was consistent with obtaining consent.[30] Shaw likewise points to the existence of treaties in Africa as evidence of the recognition of territorial sovereignty of native authorities.[31] Echoing these perspectives, Castellino and Allen acknowledge the role played by these treaties but suggest that the ideology of attributing the principle of *terra nullius* to the context of the lands of non-European peoples lay behind the colonisation of Africa, as it was premised on a presumed right of European powers to acquire the continent's territory.[32] A number of publicists such as Lindley and Alexandrowicz have conducted extensive analysis of the actual practice of States in relation to *terra nullius*. This analysis provides insightful perspectives on the *de facto* undeniable, if theoretically inconvenient, role of consent in the assertion of title to territory, as well as touching on some of the highly inadequate practices associated with obtaining that 'consent'.

2.3.2 Surveys of actual state practice

Lindley's conclusion, based on his 1926 survey of global State practice and an analysis of the previous four centuries of international legal doctrines and diplomatic relations, was that international law rejected the notion of *terra nullius*

---

26 Lindley 1926: 24–44.
27 Porter 1999b: 18–19; Burroughs 1999: 196.
28 Thornberry 2002: 75.
29 Bennett 1978a: 5.
30 Crawford 2007: 178–179.
31 Shaw 1986: 37.
32 Castellino and Allen 2003: 98; see also Fisch 1988: 360–363.

and occupation as a means of obtaining title to territory over lands inhabited by native peoples, in all but a very few particular cases.[33] Instead, it recognised cession where natives consented to 'place themselves under the sovereignty of the acquiring State', and conquest where lands were taken without their consent 'by superior force'.[34] According to Lindley, the widespread practice of seeking native consent and using it as a basis for asserting title to territory was a reflection of the legal rule *nemo dat quod non habet* ('no one gives what he doesn't have') and an implicit recognition of native sovereignty.[35]

This assessment of State practice, which canvassed the situation of 35 colonised countries, indicated that the only instance where occupation was deemed 'the appropriate method of acquisition' was in Australia, on the grounds that 'there appeared to be no political society to be dealt with'.[36] However, despite the subsequent practice rendering aboriginal dissent irrelevant,[37] early British instructions and Acts illustrate that, even in the case of Australia, the requirement for consent of the natives had initially been affirmed, and the sovereignty and dominium of the aboriginal peoples acknowledged,[38] with Cook required

> with the consent of the natives to take possession of convenient situations in the country in the name of the King, or if you find the country uninhabited to take possession for his majesty by setting up proper marks and inscriptions, as first discoverers.[39]

In the case of New Zealand, on the other hand, notwithstanding some debate in relation to the status of the South Island as potentially constituting *terra nullius*,[40] the express orders of the British Secretary of War issued in 1839, as a precursor to the Treaty of Waitangi, acknowledged the country as '[a] sovereign and independent state' and affirmed that

> the Queen . . . disclaims . . . every pretension to seize on the islands of New Zealand, or to govern them as a part of the dominions of Great Britain, unless the free and intelligent consent of the natives expressed according to their established usages, shall be first obtained.[41]

33 Anghie 1999: 60; see also Thornberry 2002: 75.
34 Lindley 1926: 44.
35 Ibid.
36 Ibid.: 41; see also Castellino and Keane 2009: 35–45; Mcrae *et al.* 2009: 9–29; Clarke 2009: 92–95.
37 Goodall 1999.
38 *The Pacific Islanders Protection Act 1875*, Sections 2 and 7 which applied to the colonies of New South Wales, New Zealand, Queensland, South Australia, Tasmania, Victoria and Western Australia.
39 Bennett and Castles 1979: 253–254; see also Secret Instructions to Lieutenant Cook (1768).
40 Lindley 1926: 41–42. See also Crawford 2007: 265, fn 54, quoting H.V. Evatt that the acquisition was 'uncertain as between occupation and cession'; Kawharu, 1977: 75; *Ngai Tahu Land Report Waitangi Tribunal Claim* 27 (Waitangi Tribunal, 1991), Section 4.2. Ngai Tahu Accession to the Treaty.
41 Mackay 1873: Part 1 at 5 and Public Documents Relating to the Colony of New Zealand, No. 6, The Marquis of Normanby to Captain Hobson, R.N., Downing Street, 14 August 1839, at 14; see also Parlty Papers 1840, Vol. XXIII (238), quoted in Lindley 1926: 41; Castellino and Keane 2009: 102–110; Ruru 2009: 114–115.

Drawing on extensive empirical evidence, Alexandrowicz illustrates that treaty-making peaked in the years prior to and following the 1885 Berlin Conference, during which time the scramble for titles to territory in Africa was at its most ferocious.[42] In practice, therefore, consent as manifested in these treaties, while of a highly dubious standard when viewed from contemporary human rights or natural law criteria, formed the primary basis upon which claims to title to territory and protectorates were justified in the colonisation of Africa, with only a few incidences of actual conquest documented.[43]

These catalogues of State practice suggest that the requirement to enter into such consent-based agreements with native chiefs constituted a widely accepted practice or 'rule of law'.[44] This view stands at odds with the theories of positivists such as Westlake,[45] Oppenheim[46] and Hall,[47] all of whom rejected the notion of 'uncivilized' or even 'organized' natives (who were not considered States) possessing sovereignty over their territories and dismissed the consent requirement by affirming that their territories could be acquired by occupation. While acknowledging native peoples' capacity to enter into treaties with civilised States or private individuals, they nevertheless held that the treaties entered into with them had, or would have, no effect under international law. In doing so, these late nineteenth- and early twentieth-century Positivist School publicists sought to deny any implications of the widespread State practice of seeking native consent for their theoretical position that title to territory over native lands could be obtained by mere occupation.

Just as it had been in the formative years of the law of nations, the issue of native sovereignty and the associated requirement for native consent were at the core of the contentious issues pertaining to nineteenth-century discussions on title to territory. It was therefore not surprising that its relevance to colonial powers' right to claim title and sovereignty over African peoples and their territories emerged in the 1885 Berlin Conference which sought to regulate colonial trade on the continent.[48]

2.4 The consent requirement under the Berlin Act

The Berlin Conference reflected the tension at the core of the Positivist School of thought. One of the stated purposes of the Conference was to address the 'formalities to be observed in order that any new occupation of territory upon the African coast should be deemed to be effective' and to prevent the scramble for Africa from 'degenerating into anarchy'.[49] During the debates,

---

42 Alexandrowicz 1973: 141.
43 Bull and Watson 1984: 111, 113–114; see also Alexandrowicz 1973: 12, 144.
44 Lindley 1926: 176.
45 Westlake 1894: 152–156.
46 Oppenheim 1920.
47 Hall 1890: 106.
48 Ibid.: 94.
49 Alexandrowicz 1973: 8, 46.

the American representative, Kasson, proposed that the consent of the natives should constitute a requirement 'before occupation can be recognized as valid', stating that:

> *modern international law* follows closely a line which leads to the recognition of the right of native tribes to *dispose freely of themselves and of their hereditary territory*. In conformity with this principle my government would gladly adhere to a more extended rule, to be based on a principle which should aim at the *voluntary consent* of the natives whose country is taken possession of, in all cases where they had not provoked the aggression.[50]

Bull suggests that the Kasson proposal 'sought to uphold the idea that African native chiefs had rights in international law'[51]. Sanctioning Kasson's notion of 'voluntary consent' under 'modern international law' would have implied a transition from the positivist conception of the law of nations, back towards natural law-based principles under which free consent was regarded as sacrosanct.[52] The shift to a positivist approach to the law of nations had removed the theoretical constraints on conquest imposed by the notion of a 'just war' and significantly lowered the standards pertaining to obtaining consent, which could now be arbitrarily determined by the colonising State and involve coercion and the threat of force.[53] Sidestepping this issue, the presiding under-secretary of the conference described the proposal as a 'delicate question, upon which the Conference hesitated to express an opinion'.[54] The final text of the Berlin Act therefore omitted any explicit reference to a consent requirement.

Under the Act, colonial States were only required to notify each other of their territorial claims, providing them with an opportunity to raise any objections they had in relation to the claims of other colonial States. The Act therefore provided little clarity as to the grounds upon which title to territory could be obtained.[55]

The silence of the Act in relation to the role of native consent, and its effective transformation of 'colonial' protectorates into mechanisms for asserting control over internal affairs by the colonial power (as opposed to traditional protectorates where only external sovereignty was vested in the powerful State),[56] gave rise to disagreement between the positivists and those advocating for native sovereignty as to whether the Act contained an implicit consent requirement regulating claims to title to territory as well as the establishment and functioning of protectorates. In order to contextualise these contrasting views, it is first necessary to consider the

---

50 Emphasis added. Quoted in Oppenheim 1914: 140.
51 See also Bull 1984: 110.
52 Alexandrowicz 1973: 46.
53 Anghie 1999: 61; see also Brownlie 1963: 35.
54 Crawford 2007: 264.
55 *General Act of the Berlin Conference on West Africa*, 26 February 1885, Articles 34 and 35.
56 Alexandrowicz 1973: 62; Koskenniemi 2001: 124; see also Egerton 1897: 431, who held that the 'British colonial system is based on the consent of the governed'.

status accorded to native peoples under the positivist conception of international law. The writings of two of its founding fathers, Westlake and Oppenheim, will be used as illustrative of this view.

2.5 Positivist theories on membership of the family of nations

Oppenheim's view, that only the consent of 'civilized States' determined 'membership of the Family of Nations', represented the pinnacle of positivist thinking.[57] Membership of the family of nations was not, however, a necessary precondition for a State or nation to prohibit occupation of their territory.[58] The requirement instead was recognition as a State with the potential to be a member of the family. Oppenheim clarified that this right to prevent occupation did not extend to tribal peoples, even if they were organised, unless they were considered a State:[59]

> Only such territory can be the object of occupation *as is no State's land*, whether entirely uninhabited, as e.g. an island, *or inhabited by natives whose community is not to be considered as a State*. Even civilised individuals may live and have private property on a territory without any union by them into a State proper which exercises sovereignty over such territory. And *natives may live on a territory under a tribal organisation which need not be considered a State proper*. But a part or the whole of the territory of any State, even although such State is entirely outside the Family of Nations, is not a possible object of occupation, and it can only be acquired through cession or subjugation.[60]

According to Oppenheim, not only could title to territory over native lands be obtained by occupation,[61] but this right continued even if the natives successfully resisted occupation. In cases where a native tribe managed to resist a foreign power which did not seek to reoccupy the area, other members of the Family of Nations could acquire the territory though occupation.[62] Under this restricted 'scientific' positivist version of international law, natural law principles protecting indigenous sovereignty and the requirement for these peoples' consent were emaciated or abandoned while State sovereignty was aggrandised.[63]

An apparent paradox inherent in Oppenheim's position emerges from his affirmation of occupation as basis for claim to title over native territories, while

---

57 Oppenheim 1920: 134 (§71). See also Hyde 1922: 163–164; Anaya 2004: 28–29.
58 Crawford 2007: 13.
59 Oppenheim 1920: 383–384 (§221). Other publicists in this category included Hall 1894, Westlake 1914 and Field 1876.
60 Emphasis added. Oppenheim 1920: 383 §221.
61 Ibid.
62 Ibid.: 389 §228.
63 Thornberry 2002: 74; Nussbaum 1954: 232; see also Alexandrowicz 1973: 6.

also acknowledging that the acquisition of land 'together with sovereignty over it' by private individuals or corporations was made 'by cession from a native tribe living on the land' but took place 'outside the dominion of the Law of Nations, and the rules of this law, therefore cannot be applied'.[64] He likewise held that cessions of territory made by tribes 'to States which are members of the Family of Nations' also fall outside 'the sphere of International Law',[65] while simultaneously affirming that:

> cession of territory made to a member of the Family of Nations by a State as yet outside that family is real cession and a concern of the Law of Nations, since such State becomes through the treaty of cession in some respects a member of that family.[66]

In addressing this conundrum, Westlake reasoned as follows:

> [N]o document in which such natives are made to cede the sovereignty over any territory can be exhibited as an international title, although an arrangement with them, giving evidence that they have been treated with humanity and consideration may be valuable as obviating possible objections to what would otherwise be a good international title to sovereignty. And this is reasonable. A stream cannot rise higher than its source, and the right to establish the full system of civilized government, which in these cases is the essence of sovereignty, cannot be based on the consent of those who at the utmost know but a few of the needs which such a government is intended to meet.[67]

This specific role of native consent was addressed by Westlake in his response to Kasson's proposal and the possibility that the Berlin Act could be interpreted as imposing a consent requirement on States. According to Westlake, this would have been inconsistent with the General Act as:

> the result [of the Act] is that when an accession of territory on the coast of Africa is notified to the powers they will have the opportunity of objecting. It cannot be doubted that if the aggrandisement was made at the expense of a civilized population without its consent, or was attended with proceedings of great inhumanity to an uncivilized population, this would be a good ground of objection on the part of any power that pleased to take up the cause. But *it would be going much further, and to a length to which the conference declined to go, if we were to say that, except in cases of unprovoked aggression justifying conquest, an uncivilized population has rights which make its free consent necessary to the establishment over it of a*

64 Oppenheim 1920: 373 §209(2).
65 Ibid.: 377 §214.
66 Ibid.
67 Oppenheim 1914: 146.

government possessing international validity. Any such principle, had it been adopted, would have tended to defeat one of the chief objects of the conference, namely to avoid collisions between its members by regulating more clearly their mutual position on the African coast. [68]

Westlake sought to further strengthen this argument by holding that chiefs, elders and bodies of 'fighting men' might not have the authority to cede territory, as doing so may not be permitted 'by the ideas of the tribe'.[69] Ironically, this did not seem to impose any barriers to the acquisition of their territory by occupation. He also argued that even in cases where such cession was permitted, there would be a lack of clarity as to the formalities required.[70] At the core of Westlake's argument was that being 'uncivilized', native peoples were unable to understand the concept of sovereignty and its implications and consequently claiming they had ceded sovereignty could not constitute the basis for title to territory.[71] While Westlake recognised native peoples' capacity to hold property rights, he nevertheless held that 'the inflow of the white race cannot be stopped where there is land to cultivate, ore to be mined, [and] commerce to be developed'.[72] Drawing on the arguments of de Martens Ferrao, and (rather selectively) on the rulings of United States Chief Justice Marshall, [73] Westlake affirmed the view that uncivilised natives did not have sovereignty, and concluded that native consent was not required in order that they pass 'under political subjection'.[74]

What emerges from the positivist perspective is an ambiguous and inconsistent stance on the status of indigenous peoples' legal personality.[75] This is assumed to exist for the purpose of legitimising title to territory by cession, but at the same time the consent-based agreement entered into would have no effect under international law, and the consent provider was assumed to lack the sovereignty necessary to become, even 'in some respects', a member of the family of nations. Native peoples were therefore empowered with a once-off capacity to provide consent for the benefit of the colonial power's acquisition of title to territory but with no positive implications for their own current or future legal status.

2.6 Protectorates as a colonial tool

Ironically, given their central role in the acquisition of control over Africa, even less focus was given in the Berlin Act to the requirements for establishing protectorates, with protectorates excluded from Article 35, which established the

---

68 Emphasis added. Ibid.: 141–142.
69 Ibid.: 142.
70 Ibid.
71 Ibid.: 151.
72 Ibid.: 145.
73 *Worchester v Georgia* 31 U.S. (6 Pet.) 515 (1832) at 554; see also Anaya 2004: 18.
74 Oppenheim 1914: 146–147.
75 Anghie 2007.

requirement for effective occupation, at the behest of the British.[76] The establishment of protectorates generally followed the 'prolific' division of the continent into colonial 'spheres of influence' premised on agreements between European powers.[77] Consistent with their sovereignty-denying view of native peoples, both Oppenheim and Westlake differentiated between protectorates over 'real States' and those over 'African tribes', despite the fact that treaties formed the basis of both. Oppenheim categorised the latter as third-class protectorates which paved the way for future occupation. His outline of the purpose and status of these 'so-called' protectorates is worth quoting in full:

> The growing desire to acquire vast territories as colonies on the part of States unable to occupy effectively such territories at once has, in the second half of the nineteenth century, led to the contracting of agreements with the chiefs of natives inhabiting unoccupied territories, by which these chiefs commit themselves to the 'protectorate' of States that are members of the Family of Nations. These so-called protectorates are certainly not protectorates in the technical sense of the term designating the relation that exists between a strong and a weak State through a treaty by which the weak State surrenders itself into the protection of the strong and transfers to the latter the management of its more important international relations. Neither can they be compared with the protectorate of members of the Family of Nations exercised over such non-Christian States as are outside that family, because the respective chiefs of natives are not the heads of States, but heads of tribal communities only. Such agreements, although they are named 'Protectorates,' are nothing else than steps taken to exclude other Powers from occupying the respective territories. They give, like discovery, an inchoate title, and are preparations and precursors of future occupations.[78]

This echoed Westlake's view that while protected States were 'semi-sovereign', with their sovereignty divided between them and the protecting State in accordance with the protectorate agreement,[79] in cases where 'uncivilized' peoples were under protectorates, territorial sovereignty was in 'suspense' and that sovereignty 'as far as it extended' was acquired by the protecting State.[80]

As noted above, the positivist interpretations of the Berlin Act have been challenged by those who emphasised the role of native consent and sovereignty in legitimising territorial claims. Lindley held that Article 6 of the General Act implied the express or implied consent of native chiefs was a necessary, but not sufficient, condition for the establishment of a protectorate with powers over

---

76 Koskenniemi 2001: 124.
77 Shaw 1986: 48.
78 Oppenheim 1920: 388 §226.
79 Oppenheim 1914: 181–183.
80 Ibid.: 183.

native peoples.[81] Furthermore, the extent of the internal powers transferred was to be determined based on the 'express or tacit' consent given by the native authorities which maintained rights over property unless these were voluntarily transferred.[82] In direct contrast to the position of Westlake, Lindley reasoned that:

> It is not necessary to the possession of powers which are in fact sovereign powers that the nature of sovereignty as a political conception should be understood; and it is difficult to see why, if the natives are to be regarded as capable of possessing and transferring property, they should not also be considered competent to hold and transfer the sovereignty which they actually exercise.[83]

His response to Westlake's concern that the consent requirement could be used to invalidate existing titles of the colonial powers was, however, less affirmative of native sovereignty, as it justified acquisition of territory on the basis of *post facto* tacit consent, as opposed to prior express consent. In this regard, he held that where a colonial power had already established a responsible local authority, other powers could not contest its title as that title would be valid under prescription.[84] According to Jennings, acquisitive prescription can address 'an adverse possession which in its origin is demonstrably unlawful' and 'indicates the acquisition of title by a long-continued and undisturbed possession', implying that title of the former owner is extinguished.[85] Lindley therefore appeared to regard the prior establishment and operation by the protecting State of a competent local authority (which generally took a significant period of time) as a manifestation of the tacit consent of the native authorities to the protectorate arrangement, on the presumption that a responsible local authority could only function in the absence of native resistance and would have to guarantee their rights.[86]

The positivist perspective on the role of native consent in the establishment of protectorates also contrasts with the evidence emerging from Alexandrowicz's survey of African treaty-making in the context of establishing protectorates. The survey provided 'overwhelming evidence for the proposition that the treaty of Protectorate was applied in Africa in accordance with the traditional rules of international law'.[87] These treaties transferred (external) sovereignty and also frequently contained additional clauses 'transferring land in private law', with the distinction between sovereignty and associated title to territory and property rights being clear.[88] In practice, what followed was a gradual non-consensual replacement of

81   Lindley 1926: 322.
82   Ibid.: 322–323.
83   Ibid.: 21.
84   Ibid.: 176, 178.
85   Jennings 1963: 20–21, 30.
86   Lindley 1926: 78–79, 158. See Lindley's reasoning in the context of similar arguments regarding Putumayo in Peru.
87   Alexandrowicz 1973: 123.
88   Ibid.: 126.

international law by European municipal laws, in breach of the protectorate treaties, and the appropriation of internal sovereignty by the European powers.[89] As Koskenniemi notes: '[Colonial] Protectorates had emerged as the main vehicle through which European States extended their colonial empires in Africa, [while these] were generally based on treaties with native chiefs . . . their result were often indistinguishable from annexation.'[90]

Colonial protectorates following the Berlin Act effectively became 'an instrument of colonialism'[91] and 'a mode of acquisition',[92] providing a means for colonial powers to exercise effective internal and external control over the affairs of African peoples, without assuming the burden of administration associated with claims to full sovereignty.[93] Therefore, while the argument that the Berlin Act constituted 'tactic acceptance' of the Kasson position by the Conference[94] had a degree of validity in terms of the continued practice of entering into treaties and agreements with native peoples, ultimately when this 'once-off' consent requirement was exhausted, and the colonial power met the requirement of effective occupation, a guardianship model premised on the European civilising mission effectively applied in both protectorates and ordinary colonies.[95]

2.7 Consent-seeking practices in the positivist era

Engaging with the issue of the identity of African natives became a 'central preoccupation' in the context of efforts to systematise European assertion of colonial territorial sovereignty.[96] The positivists sought to eliminate native peoples completely from the purview of international law by establishing a construct in which their views, resistance or lack of consent to the loss of sovereignty and control over territory had no bearing on the legality of claims to sovereignty over them. In this model, the elimination of the slave trade and the opening up of Africa to commerce were bundled together as humanitarian objectives which would raise the native on the scale of civilisation. The deceit was therefore twofold. Not only was there discordance between the theoretical justification of sovereign power and actual practice in relation to its acquisition, but there was also an unbreachable chasm between the stated objectives of pursuing the colonial agenda and its actual effects.[97] While not all treaties were coerced or without advantage to

---

89 Alexandrowicz 1973: 127.
90 Koskenniemi 2001: 124.
91 Alexandrowicz 1967: 55.
92 Shaw 1986: 46.
93 Alexandrowicz 1973: 124; see also Andrews 1978.
94 Lugard 1922: 11; Alexandrowicz 1967: 47 and Lindley 1926: 34, 176.
95 For a comment on the guardianship doctrine emerging from the Act, see Bennett 1978a: 5; Koskenniemi 2001: 126.
96 Anghie 2007: 94.
97 UN Doc E/CN.4/Sub.2/1999/20, para 173.

the native peoples,[98] and native resistance did play a role in determining the content of some treaties,[99] the stark reality of the failure of the Conference's model to deliver on its humanitarian promise was evidenced by the fact that its only significant achievement was the establishment of the Congo Free State under the personal sovereignty of King Leopold II of Belgium, whose treatment of the natives was notoriously inhumane.[100] This reality suggests that it was largely immaterial if the Berlin Conference accepted Kasson's consent requirement or not, as the positivist conception of international law would have rendered any assertion of native sovereignty, through the mechanism of a consent requirement, relatively benign. Three factors which point to this are: (a) the inadequate conditions under which that consent was obtained; (b) the restricted choices available; and (c) the potential for the invocation of the notions of *terra nullius* or conquest.

The conditions under which native consent was sought raise serious doubts as to the extent of the native peoples' understanding of the consequences of providing consent and their capacity to negotiate its terms and conditions. Many of the treaties entered into consisted of standardised forms prepared by European companies. These were signed by minor leaders, often in the presence of a witness and interpreter, and included a clause stating that the chiefs understood, and had freely consented to, their contents.[101] Direct, non-standard, treaties were also signed between European States and senior African chiefs or kings.[102] In some cases, evidence of negotiation exists from different versions of the signed and unsigned treaties, with, for example, the chiefs and King of Gabon rejecting versions where they forfeited their political rights.[103] The minor local chiefs often had little choice or bargaining power in their treaty negotiations once a treaty was signed with an overarching chief or king.[104] Alexandrowicz notes that 'the Europeans acted on the presumption that in the external sphere the transfer of a complete title constituted a valid transaction in international law' in order to overcome situations where, under customary law, community land may not have been alienable and sovereignty and territory could not be ceded by the ruler as 'public authority was in the community and not in its organs'.[105]

Apart from cases documented by Lugard in East and West Africa, which present the native chiefs as effective negotiators,[106] the actual degree of understanding of what was being consented to by the native chiefs in many of these treaties, and the effectiveness of their negotiating power, are impossible to ascertain.[107] Lugard

98 Touval 1966.
99 Bull 1984: 114.
100 Anghie 1999: 63; Lindley 1926: 112–113; see also O'Sullivan and Ó Síocháin 2003.
101 Alexandrowicz 1973: 46–47, 121.
102 Ibid.: 46, 50.
103 Ibid.: 49.
104 Ibid.: 50.
105 Ibid.: 50–54.
106 Ibid.: 50–54, citing Lugard 1893; see also Falkowski 1992: 32, 34.
107 Alexandrowicz 1973: 121.

himself was involved in signing some treaties on behalf of the East Niger Company which allowed for no more than a few days of negotiation time, casting doubt on the credibility of his assessment of the degree of understanding and negotiation which the chiefs required to make an informed decision.[108] Accounts of the consent-seeking indicate that at times it consisted of little more than a race between competing powers to obtain an agreement from a particular chief, without ensuring their, or their peoples, understanding of the implications.[109] Indeed, the opinion of the people appears to have been of little, if any, consideration to the colonial powers. The Delagoa Bay Arbitration case between Portugal and Britain, which arose out of the Portuguese cancellation of an American citizen's concession for an extension of the railway in Eastern Africa, is illustrative of the contested nature of the process through which native consent was obtained by the colonial powers.[110] In challenging the basis of the British authority over the territory, the Portuguese argued that the native chiefs considered what the British defended as treaties of cession 'to be merely lists of merchandise which had been promised them'.[111] Unsurprisingly in Africa, as happened in North America and New Zealand, differences emerged in texts and interpretation of the versions of treaties documented in the languages of native peoples and the coloniser in relation to the cession of native sovereignty.[112]

In many instances, it was also acknowledged that consent was 'obtained under compulsion'. This practice, regarded as morally repugnant by some, was not uncommon in treaties entered into with native peoples during the positivist era, both in Africa and in other jurisdictions,[113] and was considered acceptable as it was in keeping with the legitimacy of 'forced treaties' in international affairs.[114] The irony, in the context of treaties entered into with indigenous peoples, was that while they were not regarded as international treaties, they were nevertheless subject to a duress threshold which would have vitiated consent under domestic contracts. While sound arguments had been made that this principle was questionable in contexts where power imbalances between the two parties were so extreme; these appear not to have had any traction.[115] In such circumstances, as Anghie notes, rather than an expression of their independent will, native consent constituted a 'construct dictated by the colonial scramble'.[116]

108 Lugard, Lady F. L. 1997: 355–358; see also Alexandrowicz 1973: 36; Lindley 1926: 36.
109 Alexandrowicz 1973: 36; Lugard, Lady F. L. 1997: 355–358; Lindley 1926: 36.
110 *Award on the claims of Great Britain and Portugal to certain territories formerly belonging to the Kings of Tembe and Mapoota, on the eastern coast of Africa, including the islands of Inyack and Elephant (Delagoa Bay or Lorenzo Marques)*, 24 July 1875, XXVIII, pp. 157–162; see also *The Western Australian*, 18 July 1898, available at: http://trove.nla.gov.au/ndp/del/article/3213374
111 Lindley 1926: 173.
112 Alexandrowicz 1973: 53–54, for a commentary on the case of Italy and Ethiopia, see also Baer 1976.
113 *Choctaw Nation v. Oklahoma*, 397 U.S. 620, 630–631 (1970); see also Meredith 2006: 2–3.
114 Lindley 1926: 44.
115 MacDonell 1911: 285–286. Alexandrowicz 1973: 46–47.
116 Anghie 1999: 71.

The situation was further compounded by the attitude among European powers that treaties did not imply that 'sovereignty resided in the native community' and instead 'constituted a flexible means for staking a claim of precedence and maintaining a free hand against such communities without the establishment of formal administration'.[117] Instead of affording indigenous peoples the option to enter into arrangements under which they could associate themselves with other States while maintaining their sovereignty, the assumption of the positivists was that native peoples were consenting to a total surrender of their sovereignty.[118] In such a context, Kasson's, presumably well-intentioned, consent requirement, had it been accepted, may ultimately have constituted little more than a mechanism to bolster the pretence that native peoples had consented to dispossession of their rights and extinguishment.[119]

Finally, if consent was not forthcoming, the possibility existed for the doctrine of *terra nullius* to be invoked as the notion that certain peoples existed without any social or political organisation was fully endorsed by many, though not all, publicists at the time.[120] This logic, which was applied in Australia, considered in New Zealand,[121] and, but for the operation of the *Monroe Doctrine*, had the potential to be invoked in the Amazon,[122] would have afforded a convenient means to circumvent a consent requirement in the African context.[123] In addition, under the positivist conception of international law, rules regulating the conduct of wars of conquest in relation to native peoples were effectively non-existent. Once conducted, these wars were regarded as a *fait accompli* which international law neither justified nor condemned[124] and it merely remained up to the State in question 'to justify its acquisition to public opinion as a conquest'.[125]

The practice of obtaining indigenous consent therefore proceeded within a framework within which those peoples had little choice but to accept the terms offered to them. Empowered with this once-off consent-granting capacity, they legitimised the colonial acquisition of title over their territories and transformed themselves into wards of their imposed colonial guardians. By the end of the nineteenth century, the doctrine of guardianship or trusteeship had crystallised as the preferred colonial model of relationship between States and indigenous peoples, purportedly for the benefit of the latter. This doctrine, premised on the notion of indigenous peoples as uncivilised and lacking in self-governing capacity, was by definition amenable to the negation of any subsequent assertions of a consent requirement.

---

117 Koskenniemi 2001: 12.
118 Oppenheim 1914: 181–183.
119 Anghie 1999: 71.
120 Austin and Austin 1869.
121 *Ngai Tahu Report* (Waitangi Tribunal, 1991); Brownlie 1992: 4–5.
122 Lindley 1926: 78–79.
123 Shaw 1986.
124 Lindley 1926: 47; Anaya 2004: 29–30.
125 Lindley 1926: 47.

2.8 The doctrine of guardianship and trust

As outlined above, under the positivist model, indigenous international legal personality was recognised in order to establish 'consent-based' colonial sovereignty over them and then reclassify them as wards under the protection of the colonial power in accordance with a doctrine of trusteeship.[126] While this doctrine was systematised in the nineteenth century, precedence for it can be found in the religious-based guardianship role affirmed in the fifteenth-century papal bulls, Vitoria's non-comittal reference to a secular guardianship doctrine and the practice of the *encomienda* system which endured into the seventeenth century.[127] Driven by practical considerations Britain actively pursued the guardianship doctrine from the eighteenth century onwards.[128] The doctrine underpinned its Royal Proclamation of 1763 and its post-American War of Independence proposal concerning a buffer area with the newly independent States.[129] Burke advocated for it in the 1780s as a means to ensure respect of natural and native laws and to limit the powers of the East India Company to annex territory.[130] It was also reflected in the appointment of protectorates for Australian Aboriginal peoples following an 1837 report of the Select Committee on Aboriginal Tribes. Over the course of the nineteenth century, the doctrine gained prominence in North America. In Canada, the guardian–ward relationship was embodied in the notion of the Crown's fiduciary relationship with First Nations and dates back to the British Royal Proclamation of 1763 which affirmed that Indian Nations or Tribes 'live under our Protection'.[131] In the United States, the judiciary established a trusteeship system classifying indigenous peoples as 'domestic dependent nations' over which Congress held plenary power, while paradoxically also recognising aspects of their continued sovereignty, albeit subject to Congressional plenary power.[132] In 1898, only three years after it advocated for 'the voluntary consent of the natives whose country is taken possession of', the United States invoked the guardianship doctrine in an effort to legitimise its non-consensual takeover of the Philippines, leading to a three-year unsuccessful war for independence.[133]

Concerning the British colonial Empire, Porter notes that in the nineteenth century:

> a sense of trusteeship reinforced the notion of good government, with its ideals of law and order, economy and efficiency, as well as settled expectations of how society ought to be organized. It might include . . . some measure of

---

126 Snow 1919: 36, 122; see also Sanders 1983: 18–19; Sanders 1985: 299–300; and Lynch 1988: 113; Phelan 1957: 223–224.
127 For an overview of the *encomienda* system, see Keith 1971.
128 Bennett 1978: 8, 10.
129 Mellor 1951: 374.
130 Stanlis 1993: 31.
131 *The Royal Proclamation* - October 7, 1763 by The King. A Proclamation, George R.
132 *Cherokee Nation v. Georgia* 30 U.S. 1 (1831); *Worcester v Georgia* U.S. (6 Pet.) 515 (1832). See also Bennett 1978b; Berman 1978; Clinebell and Thomson 1977–1978.
133 Olcott 1916: Vol. II, 110.

popular consent to government, even if not representative institutions. More expansively, contemporaries associated Imperial rule with Britain's 'civilizing mission', to which the character of government was everywhere both fundamental and definitive.[134]

Under this doctrine, intrinsic value was not necessarily attributed to indigenous peoples' customs and institutions or their perspectives on self-governance. Instead, a pragmatic approach to maintaining the colonial order was adopted which implied a constant dilemma as to whether to promote assimilation though the imposition of British institutions or to allow 'colonial inhabitants to maintain traditional laws and customs and to fashion their own [institutional] arrangements'.[135]

The deliberations around the proposed South African Natives' Land Act 1913, Amendment Bill 1927, are illustrative of such dilemmas and the philosophy of guardianship underpinning them. The Bill was targeted at the Bantu people 'living in Native territories and locations under tribal conditions and, for the most part, with communal tenure'.[136] The Joint Council examining the Bill grounded its own obligations towards the Natives on South Africa's commitment to the Government of England to deal with Natives 'with the most scrupulous justice and with the uttermost toleration' given that '[o]ne of the great tasks imposed upon the white men of South Africa was to civilise and bring the Natives up, and not to trample on them and repress them'.[137] In light of this, the Council considered if the Bill 'aimed at the development of Natives to a higher state of civilization' and was 'just', 'practical', and framed 'with due allowance for the essential factors of Native life'.[138] Citing the 1925 Rhodesian Land Commission's finding that natives are 'hampered by the insecurity of tenure (inseparable from tribal conditions) and by the unprogressive attitude of the chiefs and people', the Council observed that 'the progressive Native requires individual tenure of land for his continued development, and this is not obtainable in tribal areas'.[139] Its guardianship-based reasoning for finding the Bill defective in terms of ensuring the Bantu's well-being was consequently infused with derogative perspectives on native governance and tenure systems.

This tension between the guardianship doctrine and the realisation of native peoples' rights was recognised at the doctrine's conception.[140] The view was nevertheless advocated throughout the intervening centuries that a good faith approach to the doctrine would yield outcomes that were compatible with the recognition of native sovereignty and serve to benefit native people 'who were not

---

134 Burroughs 1999: 173.
135 Ibid.: 174.
136 Johannesburg Joint Council of Europeans and Natives, General Hertzog's Solution of the Native Question, Memorandum No. 1, Native Land Act 1913, Amendment Bill 1927 (R. L. Esson and Co. Ltd., Johannesburg 4979), para 4.
137 Ibid.: para 53.
138 Ibid.
139 Ibid.: para 25.
140 Vitoria *et al.* 1917: §3, para 18.

yet able to stand by themselves under the strenuous conditions of the modern world'.[141] Early twentieth-century commentators such as Snow pointed to the parallels between the guardianship responsibility of 'civilized States' towards peoples in their colonies and the guardian–ward 'relationship between civilized States and aboriginal tribes under its sovereignty'.[142] Commenting on its application in relation to Indian nations, Hannum notes that its actual implementation by governments has been 'woefully inadequate and duplicitous'.[143] As pointed out by Anaya, the doctrine's failure to live up to its potential flowed from the fact that it was 'rooted in negative regard for indigenous cultural attributes' and has meant that it has served, rather than tempered, colonial ends.[144] Attributing the status of wards to indigenous peoples led to responsibilities towards them being domesticated and transferred from the international sphere to the sphere of national public law.[145] Short of denying their existence, this domestication represented the final demotion of indigenous status and constituted a major obstacle to the exercise of their rights.[146] Within this sovereign State-controlled sphere, the notion that indigenous peoples lacked capacity for rational decisions was again widely invoked to deny them autonomy over their own affairs. Described as barbarous communities, equivalent to 'old children', they were regarded as incapable of expressing or realising their will, and consequently could be 'deprived of their internal freedom' until such time as they developed that capacity.[147] Indigenous peoples possessed only a 'right to guardianship' under which they were to be protected to enable them to realise their potential, and eventually potentially form part of the more 'developed races'.[148]

This trust doctrine was given significant impetus at the international level by the Berlin Conference, the outcome of which was held by some to have included native populations within the community of international law by imposing guardianship obligations towards them on dominant nations.[149] The Act stated that '[a]ll the Powers exercising sovereign rights or influence in the aforesaid territories bind themselves to watch over the preservation of the native tribes, and to care for the improvement of the conditions of their moral and material well-being' and to support all institutional activities aimed at 'instructing the natives and bringing home to them the blessings of civilization'.[150]

A corresponding trust doctrine was affirmed in the 1919 Convention of St Germain-en-Laye and enshrined in the Covenant of the League of Nations

---

141 Covenant of the League of Nations, 28 June 1919, Article 22.
142 Snow 1919: 36.
143 Hannum 1996: 102
144 Anaya 2004: 25–26.
145 UN Docs E/CN.4/Sub.2/1999/20; E/CN.4/Sub.2/AC.4/2004/7; and E/CN.4/2004/111; see also Brownlie 1992: 9; Mcnair 1961: 53.
146 Ibid.
147 Lorimer 1883–1884: I, 157.
148 Ibid.; see also Rodríguez-Piñero 2005: 19.
149 Lindley 1926: 327; Alexandrowicz 1973: 115. For a contrary view on the extent of the guardianship obligations, see ICJ, *Case of South-West Africa* 65 AJIL 149 (January 1971).
150 *General Act of the Berlin Conference on West Africa*, 26 February 1885, Article 6.

under Article 22 as a sacred trust of civilisation.[151] This doctrine of guardianship was also embodied in Article 23 of the Covenant of the League of Nations in its native inhabitants clause, which practice confirmed also extended to native peoples in independent countries.[152] This trust or guardianship doctrine was regarded as having coalesced into a standard against which the actions of colonial powers were to be judged in mandated and non-mandated territories and corresponded to 'actual duties of a legal or quasi-legal character'.[153] Such a view had been advocated by Snow, who held that there was an obligation on all three branches of government to train the dominated communities for civilisation to ensure their equality-based participation in government.[154] Under the League's Mandate System, a Permanent Mandates Commission, composed of experts in colonial administration, including representatives of the International Labour Organization,[155] was established with oversight responsibility in relation to the policies in mandate territories,[156] operating an ineffective complaint mechanism, through which natives could theoretically air grievances in relation to the implementation of mandates.[157]

The emerging post-First World War emphasis on the principle of self-determination and self-government of peoples, as affirmed by US President Wilson and the establishment of the League of Nations, marked a shift in international law away from the positivist discourse.

However, while developments in political and legal thinking contributed towards the opening up of the question of the legal status of entire peoples within certain territorially defined units, it did not have the same positive implications for the legal status of those peoples who constituted culturally distinct groups in dependent territories or independent States. The attempt in 1923 by Chief Deskaheh of the Cayuga Nation and representative of the Six Nations of the Grand River Land to obtain a hearing before the League in relation to a dispute with Canada over indigenous self-governance reaffirmed the absence of legal personality of these groups in the eyes of the international community.[158] The request was initially considered by the League's Secretary General and obtained the support of a small number of States. However, following objections by Great Britain, on the grounds that the issue Deskaheh wished to raise was 'an internal affair of the British Empire', it was removed from the agenda.[159]

---

151 The seminal work on the Mandate system is Wright 1930; see also Matz 2005, for an overview of the mandate system's history and its implications for contemporary contexts.
152 Rodríguez-Piñero 2005: 22, citing Walters 1952: 568–571.
153 Lindley 1926: 330, 336. Alexandrowicz 1973: 6, 116; see also *Treaty of Peace between the Allied and Associated Powers and Austria; Protocol, Declaration and Special Declaration* (St Germain-en-Laye, 10 September 1919). Entry into force for Australia and generally (Treaty): 16 July 1920, Australian Treaty Series 1920, No. 3.
154 Snow 1919: 108; see also Oppenheim 1920: §227.
155 Rodríguez-Piñero 2005: 27–30.
156 Wright 1930: 140–141.
157 Duncan Hall 1948: 198.
158 For an overview of Deskaheh's attempt, see Niezen 2003: 31–36.
159 Thornberry 2002: 82, citing Minde 1996: 102–104.

Māori and other Iroquois delegations were similarly refused an audience in 1924 and 1927 respectively.[160]

The view underpinning the guardianship/trusteeship doctrine that indigenous peoples were no longer considered subjects of international law consequently remained well entrenched during the lifetime of the League. Indigenous peoples' consent, or absence thereof, was generally reduced to merely one of many facts to be considered in resolving inter-State disputes with regard to sovereignty and title to territory over the lands which they traditionally occupied. This status, or rather lack of it, was unambiguously reaffirmed in three emblematic cases in the 1920s and 1930s, namely:[161] the 1926 *Cayuga Indians* and the 1928 *Islands of Palmas* international arbitration cases;[162] and the 1933 *Eastern Greenland* Permanent Court of International Justice case.[163] In all three cases, indigenous peoples' international legal personality was denied and their historical consent (as manifested in the form of a treaty between the Cayuga Indians and the state of New York, and 'contracts' between the native princes of Las Palmas and the Dutch) or absence thereof (as evidenced by the successful resistance of the Inuit to Nordic settlers) were deemed immaterial to, or a mere fact to be considered in, the determination of the State claims. This underlying conception of the State 'as a person of international law' with the exclusive right to sovereignty was subsequently reaffirmed under the 1934 Montevideo Convention on the Rights and Duties of States,[164] despite the fact that many indigenous nations could lay claim to meeting its four criteria of: 'a) a permanent population; b) a defined territory; c) government; and d) capacity to enter into relations with the other states'.[165] Upon the establishment of the United Nations, the guardianship doctrine was incorporated into its Charter under Chapters XII and XI addressing International Trusteeship System and Non-Self-Governing Territories respectively.[166] Nevertheless, despite its widespread recognition, 'efforts to derive legally enforceable rights from the doctrine ... [were] far from successful' as courts were unwilling to elaborate on the fiduciary duties it implied.[167]

Given that the doctrine of guardianship or trust was premised on the lack of capacity of indigenous peoples, it was logical that under the Trusteeship System a third party 'competent public authority' would be vested with the power to give or withhold consent on indigenous peoples' behalf in relation to measures impacting

---

160 Thornberry 2002: 82.
161 See ibid.: 83–84; Anaya 2004: 30–31.
162 *Cayuga Indians (Great Britain) v. United States*, 6 UNRIAA 173 (1926); *Island of Palmas (United States v Netherlands)* 2 UNRIAA 831 (1928).
163 *Legal Status of Eastern Greenland (Denmark v. Norway)*, 1933 P.C.I.J. (ser. A/B) No. 53 (Apr. 5) at paras 101 and 363.
164 Montevideo Convention on the Rights and Duties of States (1933), 49 Stat 3097, T.S. 881. For an overview of the evolution of the notion of territory in international law, see Castellino 2008: 503–568; see also Castellino and Allen 2003.
165 Mckay 1999: 32.
166 Thornberry 2002: 77; see also Sanders 1985: 299–300; and Falkowski 1992: 48.
167 Bennett 1978a: 8.

on them.[168] In order to meet the objectives of the Trusteeship System, 'no indigenous land or natural resources [could] be transferred, except between indigenous persons, save with the previous consent' of this competent public authority and '[n]o real rights over indigenous land or natural resources [could] be created in favour of non-indigenous persons except with the same consent'.[169] As the colonial powers had done in certain instances, the UN Trusteeship Council proposed replacing indigenous authorities and customs in order to provide for 'the political and social advancement of the indigenous inhabitants'.[170] The incompatibility of the proposals with the culture of the peoples in question was raised by the Administrating Authorities and the recommendations rejected due to the resistance they would face from indigenous peoples.[171] Such proposals and responses illustrated the on-going perspective of indigenous peoples as backward while also indirectly demonstrating that indigenous assertions of *de facto* sovereignty continued, despite the imposed structural impediments to its exercise. The requirement for consent was, however, formally acknowledged in one particular context under the Trusteeship System. During the first decade of its operation, resolutions of the Trusteeship Council clarified that under Article 76b of the UN Charter addressing 'progressive development towards self-government or independence': '[The] Administering Authority should be guided ... by the principle that African communities settled on the land should not be moved to other areas unless a clear expression of their collective consent had been obtained.'[172] This principle of requiring consent prior to relocation continued to inform engagement with indigenous peoples in independent countries under the first ILO Convention adopted in 1957 to address their particular situation.

2.9 Self-determination and the decolonisation project

The international self-determination project took on a new momentum following the establishment of the UN in light of the affirmation in its Charter of the applicability of the principle of self-determination to 'all peoples'. Chapter XI addressing Non-Self-Governing Territories, which included a reporting requirement for administering States, eventually constituted the basis for the promotion of self-determination and decolonisation by the General Assembly.[173] A proposal of the Belgian government in 1953, referred to as the Belgian Thesis, in the context of the decolonisation process would, had it been

---

168 See Repertory of Practice of United Nations Organs (1945–1954), Volume 4, Article 76, para 32, available at: http://untreaty.un.org/cod/repertory/art76/english/rep_orig_vol4-art76_e.pdf
169 Ibid.: para 33.
170 Lauterpacht 1988: 685.
171 Ibid.
172 Repertory of Practice of United Nations Organs (1945–1954), Volume 4, Article 76, paras 50–51, citing TC Resolution 468 (XI) and General Assembly third session, Suppl. No. 4 (A/603) 31.
173 Thornberry 2002: 92.

adopted, have opened the possibility of extending the scope of that process to all non-self-governing indigenous peoples.[174] The Belgian Thesis proposed that the right to self-determination be applicable to all 'non-self-governing territories' as stated in the UN Charter, and addressed all 'homogeneous peoples differing from the rest of the population in race, language and culture'[175] residing in both colonial and non-colonial States.[176] It interpreted peoples in 'non-self-governing territories' under Chapter IX of the UN Charter as including all native peoples with 'backward cultures', regardless of their geographical location or territorial contiguity and explicitly listed groups such as the scheduled tribes in India, the Indians in Brazil, while classifying Latin American States among those with colonial policies.[177] The rejection of the thesis at the behest of the Latin American States on the basis that non-self-governing territories only applied to territories that were distinct from independent States implied that the protections afforded under the UN Charter's Chapter IX were not extended to indigenous populations in independent countries.[178]

The self-determination right instead remained confined to 74 'geographically separate' territories with the 'self' interpreted as the entire people contained within these inviolable territories. The principle applied was that of *uti possidetis juris*, whereby colonial borders were effectively rendered sacrosanct and served to demarcate the people, rather than the peoples demarcating the territory. As a result, self-determination in the context of the decolonisation of Africa was transformed from its political people-based definition, to a 'strict territorial concept of international practice'.[179]

As it had done during the formation of Latin American States, the process of recognition of new African States combined with the principle of *uti possidetis juris*, which established State borders along colonial administrative lines based on the notion of *colonial effectivités*, dismissed any need, or even possibility, to assess the legitimacy of the claims over indigenous peoples' territories of these new, and in all but name, colonial entities.[180] Any potential under international law for culturally distinct indigenous peoples to challenge their inclusion within these borders was frustrated by the fact that the creation of new States, and their acquisition of title to territory, did not fit into any of the standard five modes of territorial acquisition associated with already existing States, namely: occupation,

174 Kunz 1954: 98, 108–110; Van Langenhove 1956: 409–412; and Van Langenhove 1954, citing UN General Assembly, A/AC. 67/2, May 8, 1953, pp. 3–31 'speech of the Belgian representative, Joseph Nisot, in the Ad Hoc Committee on Factors (Nations Unies, Communiqué de Presse PM/2550, 21 juillet 1953)'.
175 Ibid.; see also Thornberry 1989.
176 Ibid.: 873–874; see also Van Langenhove 1954; Bennett 1978a: 12–13. Anaya 2004: 54, 76; Cassese 1998.
177 Text of Replies to the Ad Hoc Committee on Factors (May 8, 1952), UN Doc A./AC.67/2 at 3–31.
178 Sanders 1983: 18; see also Bennett 1979: 42.
179 Shaw 1986: 140.
180 Castellino and Allen 2003: 153–155.

prescription, cession, accession/accretion or subjugation/conquest.[181] Border disputes between these newly formed States in relation to areas, where there had been minimal, if any, prior colonial presence, were resolved on the basis of determining the *uti possidetis juris* line with the claims of indigenous groups ignored.[182] Subsumed within the larger population, the culturally distinct groups which fall under the contemporary social and political category of 'indigenous peoples' were effectively excluded from self-determination's potential subjects [183]

The judgemental and racist character of the evolutionary theorising implicit in the social evolutionist theories which underpinned the emergence of the positivist discourse was challenged by anthropologists such as Franz Boas by the 1920s, who argued that human behaviour was socially constructed and consequently dismissed comparative approaches to social organisation.[184] Notions of race were challenged and the problem of backwardness and inferiority came to be perceived as an issue of culture.[185] The nascent international rights regime pertaining to these indigenous peoples emerged during the decolonisation era in the context of the ILO standard setting and technical assistance activities in Latin America took a trusteeship style approach as their point of departure. In doing so, this new regime carried with it the new anthropological perspectives which saw the solution to the 'Indian problem' as their integration into mainstream society to be achieved through their modernisation. As a result, the first international recognition of this category and their inherent rights was framed in a context that envisaged, and aimed to facilitate, their eventual disappearance. Within this context, indigenous peoples' capacity to give or withhold consent was recognised and recourse to force or coercion excluded from methods to promote their integration. As in the trusteeship system, consent was also recognised in the context of relocation but subject to the overarching caveat that where it was sought, it could always be overridden in the economic interests of the State. The emergence of this ILO regime of indigenous rights and its subsequent evolution are the subject of Chapter 3.

181 Jennings 1963: 6–7.
182 Castellino and Allen 2003: 83–84.
183 Falkowski 1992: 52; Thornberry 2002: 93.
184 Boas 1921; see also Fukuyama 2011: 50.
185 Caso 1948: 239, 247, cited in Rodríguez-Piñero 2005: 56; Tennant 1994: 14.

Part II

The requirement for free prior and informed consent in the normative framework of indigenous peoples' rights

3 The evolving consent requirement under the ILO system

3.1 Introduction

This chapter traces the emergence of the consent requirement within the contemporary normative framework of indigenous peoples' rights. In particular, it focuses on developments in the ILO system, from initial references to consent under the Andean Indigenous Peoples (AIP) programme, through to its rights-constraining articulation in ILO Convention 107, and eventually to a more procedurally sound, if substantively limited, consent requirement under Convention 169. The chapter suggests that the rights-denying framing of the consent requirement under ILO Convention 107's overtly pro-integration and assimilation agenda reflected a similar consent consert requirement under the trusteeship doctrine in dependent territories. However, it also posits that Convention 107 embodied the emaciated remnants of the prior natural law-based consent requirement. In doing so, it offered the seed from which the contemporary self-determination-based requirement for free prior and informed consent would eventually be fleshed out, first, through the revision of Convention 107 and subsequently through indigenous participation in the elaboration of its content under the human rights regime.

Drawing on the text of ILO Convention 169 (C169) together with its objective and intent, the chapter suggests that, in addition to its well-elaborated procedural dimension, a context-specific substantive consent requirement can also be derived from C169. This represents a novel interpretation of the Convention and consequently necessitates a thorough engagement with its drafting history and subsequent interpretations of its content by the UN and ILO supervisory bodies. Having examined the basis under the Convention for a requirement to obtain indigenous consent, the chapter concludes by contextualising this requirement in light of subsequent developments in human rights law.

3.2 The International Labour Organization and indigenous peoples

Following the emergence of Latin America's newly independent States, the United States articulated the Monroe Doctrine, protecting them from any European claims over areas within their borders. The presumption was that the entire territory of the continent pertained to the American States, regardless of whether or not indigenous peoples had consented to their inclusion under the new sovereign States. While analogous to the operation of the principle of *terra nullius* at an internal level,[1] the process of incorporation of indigenous peoples was arguably even more totalising in its colonial effect, as it applied to all indigenous peoples, irrespective of their social or political organisation. When combined with the principle of *uti possidetis juris*, the application of the Monroe Doctrine guaranteed that disputes in relation to claims over 'frontier' territories would be resolved exclusively between the newly formed Latin American States, while the territorial claims of the indigenous peoples located within them remained outside the purview of international law. As noted by Alverez:

> Not only do no territories 'nullius' exist on the American continent, but further, and in consequence thereof, no international value is given to the possession of certain regions held since time immemorial by native tribes not recognizing the sovereignty of the country within whose limits they find themselves. Two important consequences follow therefrom: that the occupation of those regions by the natives is a matter of internal public law of each country and not of International Law; and second, that the governments have, in certain cases, an international responsibility for the acts of the natives within their boundaries; even though those natives do not recognize the sovereignty of the state.[2]

In many of these post-colonial Latin American States, the very concept of the *Indios*, or indigenous peoples, would come to be regarded as inconsistent with the State's founding principles.[3] The concept, however, gained popularity again in the 1920s with legislation enacted in post-revolutionary Mexico providing for land restitution and establishing *ejidos*, while in Peru and Bolivia indigenous communities were recognised in the 1920 and 1938 Constitutions respectively.[4] In parallel, agrarian reform legislation addressed, with varying effects, the land issues of these indigenous populations.[5] These revised political perspectives at the national level were complemented by the International Labour Organization's (ILO) foray into issues of indigenous peoples.[6]

Shortly after its foundation in 1919, the ILO commenced a series of studies on indigenous workers in dependent territories. This focus on native populations was

---

1 Gilbert 2006: 31; Castellino and Allen 2003: 82.
2 Alvarez 1909: 342–343 fn 95; see also Castellino 2008: 533–538.
3 Lipschutz 1952: 75. However, the 1824 Constitution of Mexico did recognise the Indian tribes, see Clavero 2005a.
4 Ibid. ILO 1987: 48.
5 Ibid. Lipschutz 1952: 75 fn 2.
6 *ILO Convention No. 50 on the Recruiting of Indigenous Workers* was drafted in 1936; *ILO Convention No. 64 on Contracts of Employment* in 1939; Sanders 1983: 19. The Andean Indian Programme was established in 1953, see ILO 1953; see also Rodríguez-Piñero 2005: 18.

reflected in its 1930 Convention on Forced Labour (No. 29). The ILO's engagement with the issue of indigenous peoples, or 'descendants of aborigines', in independent countries (essentially Latin American States) in the labour context can be traced back to 1936. Its 1949 report on the 'conditions of Life and Work of Indigenous Populations in Latin American Countries' was a precursor to its landmark 1953 report entitled 'Indigenous Peoples'. The latter emerged from the Andean Indian Programme (AIP) which addressed the situation of indigenous peoples in the Andean region. The 'democratically-phrased integration' of the region's indigenous peoples into mainstream society was the explicit objective of the AIP. In theory, this implied replacing the 'prevailing master–subordinate integration' with a model of integration based 'upon consent rather than upon coercion, and to be achieved without destroying for the Indian his present satisfying community organisation and valued way of life'.[7] The logic behind this was a pragmatic one, as 'without the consent [and full and continuing co-operative participation] of Indian groups no programme of social and economic betterment, . . . could have the faintest chance of developing organic roots in Indian community life.'[8] In practice, however, the programme failed to deliver on this promise of consent-based integration, and instead was ultimately seen as little more than a vehicle for the pursuit of a de-politicised development agenda in indigenous territories.[9] The most tangible outcome of the programme was to set the stage for the standard-setting activity around Convention 107 – thereby positioning the ILO as the leading international organisation with a role in the formalisation of universal law and policy as it pertained to indigenous peoples' rights.[10]

3.3 The constrained consent requirement under ILO Convention 107

The drafting of Convention 107 followed the standard ILO two-year process involving the production of a series of reports in 1955 and 1956 on the 'Living and Working Conditions of Aboriginal Peoples in Independent Countries'. The reports relied to a large extent on the 1953 'Indigenous Peoples' report, buttressed by input from a number of other countries.[11] The concept of 'indigenous' proposed by the ILO Office in its reports was largely accepted. This represented a shift in the use of the term indigenous from the entire native populations of non-self-governing territories to a narrower, more culturally defined subset of those populations in independent countries. The term 'indigenous peoples' had been included in the initial draft, but was removed at the behest of India.[12]

---

7 Beaglehole 1953: 523; see also Rens 1961: 423.
8 Ibid.: 532.
9 Rodríguez-Piñero 2005; see also Ferguson 1990: 255.
10 ILO 1953; Swepston 2005: 53.
11 Rodríguez-Piñero 2005: 121–122.
12 Ibid.: 163.

The requirement for historical descent from pre-colonial populations differentiated indigenous populations from tribal populations, while the notion of 'semi-tribal' reflected the extent to which certain tribal populations were integrated into the national community.[13] The final terminology thus was indigenous, tribal and sub-tribal populations.

Convention 107, the first international law treaty on indigenous peoples' rights, was novel in that it represented the first time a legal instrument had been directed specifically towards those groups now recognised as indigenous peoples.[14] It was premised on extending the protectionist measures under the doctrine of trusteeship to backward indigenous populations in independent countries,[15] with the solution to their backwardness being their integration and assimilation into 'the national community'.[16] The Convention reflected dominant anthropological conceptions on achieving this integration objective while avoiding the use of force.[17] Consistent with this logic, the rights-protecting aspects of the Convention are facilitative of, and subordinate to, the fulfilment of its integration objective,[18] which essentially involved promoting changes in the indigenous way of life to render it more compatible with 'Western standards of culture' and development.[19] In effect, 'progressive integration' under the Convention corresponded to a development agenda conditioned by the prevailing scientific methods of applied anthropology within a framework that recognised indigenous peoples as distinct but transient societies.[20]

Articles 11 and 13, which recognise indigenous peoples' land ownership rights and oblige States to respect the role of custom in their transmission, are its most empowering. Read together with Article 7(1), they embody the recognition of ownership flowing from possession since time immemorial.[21] This important recognition aside, the Convention's provisions on land rights and those addressing recognition of, and engagement with, indigenous customs and institutions are, on the whole, reflective of the subordination of its rights-protecting aspects to its overriding integration agenda.

This subordination is evident in the Convention's subjection of its requirement for indigenous peoples' 'free consent' prior to their removal from their lands to the extremely broad exception of national economic development.[22] The provision consequently represents an assertion of State power to infringe on, and terminate, the inherent land rights recognised under Articles 11 and 13. The provision has its

---

13 *Indigenous and Tribal Populations Convention, 1957* (No. 107), Article 1.
14 See Van Langenhove 1956 and Rodríguez-Piñero 2005, for the background to the Convention.
15 Hannum 1996: 76.
16 ILO 1953; ILO 1955; ILO 1956a; ILO 1956b; ILO 1956c: 530–546; ILO 1957a; ILO 1957b: 400–417.
17 Bennett 1978a: 18–21; Rodríguez-Piñero 2005: 98.
18 Bennett 1978a: 18.
19 ILO 1956a: 24; see also Thornberry, 1992: 344, 346; Bennett 1978a: 19; Xanthaki, 2007: 55–56.
20 Rodríguez-Piñero 2005: 112, 116; see also Sanders 1983: 64.
21 Thornberry 1992: 357; see also Bennett 1978a: 20 and 33; ILO 1956a: 33.
22 Other exceptions to the free consent requirement in Article 12 include national security and health.

origin in the 1955 ILO report which noted the growing recognition of the 'principle that indigenous peoples should not be removed from their habitual territories without their freely given consent'.[23] Despite the Convention's requirement that removals constitute 'exceptional measures', its all-encompassing notion of 'national economic development' effectively reduces Article 12 to a mere requirement for compensation.[24] Commentators have pointed to the requirement that removals must be in accordance with 'national laws and regulations' as the provision's most significant restriction, implying that removals cannot be conducted in an arbitrary manner such as through the use of 'unbridled administrative fiat[s]'.[25] This requirement for compensation in the form of land was intentionally affirmed in an absolute manner,[26] requiring that indigenous peoples shall: 'be provided with lands of quality at least equal to that of the lands previously occupied by them, suitable to provide for their present needs and future development'.[27]

However, this requirement was *de facto* unrealisable as comparable lands were unavailable in contexts of rapid industrialisation and high population densities.[28] It also ignored indigenous peoples' unique perspectives on their environment and the potentially devastating effect on their physical and cultural survival when the bonds with their traditional lands were severed. Furthermore, it has been suggested that the finality of the wording 'removing' as opposed to 'relocating' indigenous peoples suggests the lack of a restitution requirement.[29] Article 12 was consequently palatable to States, generating little debate during the drafting process, as it enabled recognition of indigenous rights over traditional lands without hindering State capacity to dispose of those lands.[30]

The Convention does not affirm a requirement for consultation. However, Article 5(a) includes a requirement for the State to 'seek the collaboration' of indigenous populations and of their representatives. The operative verb 'seek' and the dual nature of the requirement to collaborate with the population in addition to their representatives, together with impositions on customary decision-making processes in Articles 5(c) and 7(1), serve to weaken the collaboration requirement and potentially legitimise the circumventing of the indigenous authorities.[31] Apart from this loosely framed requirement for collaboration, indigenous peoples' role in determining the nature of their own development is minimal under the Convention.[32] Many of its provisions, in particular its limited

---

23 The same report recommended the use of 'psychological and anthropological techniques' to adapt customs which inhibited natural resource development, see ILO 1955: 68–69.
24 Barsh 1987: 756; Bennett 1978a: 40.
25 Bennett 1978a: 39; Thornberry 1992: 360–361.
26 ILO 1956b: 22.
27 ILO Convention 107, Article 12(2).
28 Ferch 1992: 322; see also Barsh 1987: 757.
29 Barsh 1987, and Ferch 1992: 323.
30 ILO 1956a: 34, 37–38; see also Thornberry 1992: 357.
31 Thornberry 1992: 349–350.
32 See ILO Convention 107, Articles 6, 12(2) and 17(2).

consent requirement, can be regarded as reflective of a palliative approach to the question of indigenous existence, facilitating indigenous peoples' inevitable disappearance in a manner that States regarded as morally acceptable and pragmatic.

The Convention's affirmation of the obligation to obtain the free consent of indigenous peoples was nevertheless an important affirmation for a number of reasons. First, it appears to represent the first such affirmation of a free consent requirement in relation to non-State entities in a treaty under contemporary international law.[33] It consequently indicated a tentative step towards a return to the initial recognition under the law of nations of indigenous peoples' capacity to give or withhold consent in their relationship with States. Second, it reflected an, albeit highly qualified, acknowledgement of the fact that externally proposed activities which have profound impacts on indigenous peoples should trigger the consent requirement in order to legitimise State actions. Furthermore, this consent had to be 'freely' given, in the absence of force and coercion, which the Convention forbids as a means of promoting integration.[34] Third, the Convention also represented a tentative step towards the recognition of the role of traditional decision-making authorities in internal affairs of indigenous peoples, while simultaneously introducing the notion of the need for participation of their representatives in decision-making involving external actors.[35] Finally, perhaps most importantly, despite its rights-denying character, the consent provision, to a certain extent, provided the opening for the evolution of a more procedurally sound and substantively meaningful requirement for indigenous peoples' free prior and informed consent, in particular, in relation to resource extraction activities in their territories.[36] The similarity between the arrangements under the Trusteeship System and the Convention are also worthy of mention. In both cases, the consent is only considered relevant in the case of relocation, with non-indigenous authorities making decisions for indigenous peoples on the basis of a guardianship relationship in all other contexts. Under both regimes, a degree of recognition is accorded to customary decision-making institutions, however, these institutions and traditional forms of decision-making are vulnerable to external assessments of their appropriateness. Both regimes, as such, imposed considerable constraints on the potential for the exercise of self-government, as decisions were inevitably subject to external oversight, approval or rejection.

3.4 Discontent with Convention 107

By the 1970s, technological developments were leading to increasingly pervasive resource exploitation in indigenous territories. The nascent international indigenous

---

33 Article 3 of the Vienna Convention on the Law of Treaties, 1155 U.N.T.S. 331, 8 I.L.M. 679, entered into force 27 Jan. 1980. ICCPR (1966) Articles 7 and 23.
34 ILO Convention 107, Article 2(4).
35 ILO Convention 107, Article 5(a) and Article 12(1).
36 Swepston 1990: 683.

movement drew the attention of the UN Sub-Commission on Prevention of Discrimination and Protection of Minorities to their plight, leading to an Economic and Social Council-mandated, decade-long, *Study of the Problem of Discrimination against Indigenous Populations* (the Martínez Cobo study) – the first major UN initiative addressing indigenous peoples' rights.[37] The voluminous report constituted a benchmark for subsequent standard-setting activities of the ILO and the *UN Working Group on Indigenous Populations*.[38] The study is best known for its 'working definition' of indigenous peoples, which continues to be invoked as reflective of the characteristics of indigenous peoples.[39] The study also addressed the issue of FPIC, holding that land and resource ownership and control rights should not be extinguished or resources taken without consent. It further held that indigenous peoples were entitled to determine the manner and scale of natural resource development,[40] to take decisions in accordance with their 'own values, social structures and rules and at their own pace',[41] and to enter into prior negotiated agreements.[42]

By 1977, a total of 28 countries had ratified C107,[43] however, during this period of almost two decades, the ILO supervisory machinery accorded little attention to the legal and political arenas which fell under its protectionist provisions.[44] From 1979 onwards, starting with the Yanomami case in Brazil, a number of egregious cases involving mining and hydroelectric projects were brought before the supervisory bodies invoking Article 11.[45] In response, the ILO supervisory bodies interpreted the land rights protections as extending protection to subsoil resources and embodying a right to consultation, in relation to their exploitation.[46] The ILO had started questioning the integration-based model by 1973, in light of the alternative model premised on maintaining indigenous peoples' separate identity

---

37 Final report submitted by the Special Rapporteur, Mr. José Martínez Cobo, *Study of the Problem of Discrimination Against Indigenous Populations*, UN Doc. E/CN.4/Sub.2/476 and Add. 1–6 (1981); UN Doc. E/CN.4/Sub.2/1982/2 and Add. 1–7 (1982); UN Doc. E/CN.4/Sub.2/1983/21 and Add. 1–7 (1983).

38 UN Doc. E/CN.4/Sub.2/1987/22, para 64; See also Economic and Social Council resolution 1982/34: 7 May 1982; UN Doc. E/CN.4/Sub.2/1982/33, (1982), para 13.

39 Castellino and Doyle forthcoming, 2015.

40 UN Doc. E/CN.4/Sub.2/1987/22, para 542.

41 Ibid.: paras 234, 541, 542.

42 Ibid.: para 544.

43 The only country to ratify the Convention after 1977 was Iraq in 1986. The Convention was closed for ratification in 1989 and remains in force for those States which ratified it but did not subsequently ratify ILO Convention 169.

44 Rodríguez-Piñero 2005: 246; Bennett 1978b: 47.

45 *Individual Observation on Brazil, International Labour Conference, 71st Session Report of the Committee of Experts on Application of Conventions and Recommendations Concerning Convention No. 107, Indigenous and Tribal Populations*, 1957 Brazil (ratification: 1965) Published: 1990, Document No. (ilolex): 061990BRA107; see also *Individual Observation on India, International Labour Conference, 72nd Session Report of the Committee of Experts on Application of Conventions and Recommendations* concerning Convention No. 107, Indigenous and Tribal Populations, 1957 India (ratification: 1958) Published: 1990, Document No. (ilolex): 061990IND107); and Rodríguez-Piñero 2005: 249–256; Xanthaki 2007: 52.

46 *Report of the Working Group on Indigenous Populations on its Third Session* E/CN.4/Sub.2/1984/20, para 28.

and their traditional way of life.[47] In 1975, reflective of the organisation's emerging constructive interpretation of C107, the then Director-General expressed concerns that a revision of C107 could potentially result in a lowering of standards around natural resource exploitation.[48]

The revision of C107 into what was to become Convention 169 (C169) consequently followed a period of increased international focus on the issues of indigenous peoples and a rejection of its outdated approach by indigenous peoples, academics, the ILO and States.[49] The decade-long Martinez Cobo study (1971–1983) had raised the issue of discrimination against indigenous peoples to centre stage. The formation of the UN Working Group on Indigenous Populations in 1982, which from the outset adopted a rights-based agenda in the drafting of the *UN Declaration on the Rights of Indigenous Peoples* (UNDRIP), signalled a clear end to the pursuit of integration.[50] These and other developments at the international level, coupled with the emergence of a new form of anthropology advocating indigenous self-determination, and increased demands of indigenous peoples for recognition of their right to determine their own development processes, resulted in a 'steady crescendo of criticism' of C107.[51]

3.5 The revision of C107

The revision of C107 was considered necessary to strengthen provisions protecting land rights, remove those directed at integration, and emphasise the necessity of respecting indigenous peoples' identity and their wishes.[52] The revision process followed the standard ILO formula. A decision to revise the Convention was taken by the ILO Office, a Committee composed of experts prepared a report on the relevant standards, questionnaires were sent to States, and over the course of two sessions the final text was agreed under the guidance of the ILO Office, with the entire process completed within a three-year window.[53] Contentious

---

47 Sanders 1983: 20.
48 Rodríguez-Piñero 2005: 267, citing letter from Director-General F. Blanchard to J. Rens, 29 April 1975.
49 ILO 1988c, 36/3, *Statement of the Chairman of the Committee on Convention 107*; see also Berman 1988: 49; see also Sanders 1983: 20; Thornberry 1992: 333; Xanthaki 2007: 67; Barsh 1987; and Barsh 1983.
50 Sub-Commission on Prevention of Discrimination and Protection of Minorities Resolution 2 (XXXIV), 8 September 1981; Commission on Human Rights Resolution 1982/19, 10 March 1982; Economic and Social Council Resolution 1982/34, 7 May 1982; *Report of the Working Group on Indigenous Populations on its Fourth Session*, UN Doc. E/CN.4/Sub.2/1985/22 (27 August 1985), Annex III at 14, para 61; Daes 2011: 17.
51 Another example of a significant UN agency action in the area was the 1981 *Declaration of San José, Adopted by the UNESCO Meeting of Experts on Ethno-Development and Ethnocide in Latin America*, UNESCO Doc. FS 82/WF.32 (1982). Non UN international initiatives addressing the question included the International NGO Conference on Discrimination Against Indigenous Populations in the Americas, 20–23 Sept. 1977 Palais des Nations, Geneva, which resulted in the *Draft Declaration of Principles for Defence of the Indigenous Nations and Peoples of the Western Hemisphere*, see Treaty Council News 1977; see also Sanders 1983; Swepston 1987.
52 Samson 1989: 44.
53 Xanthaki 2007: 67–68.

provisions are decided by vote, with States, employers and employee representatives all having equal voting power.[54] Throughout the process the ILO Office maintained an influential role in negotiating agreement on its controversial provisions. A degree of indigenous participation in the drafting process was facilitated, primarily through the employers group.[55] This was unprecedented from an ILO perspective, however, it was considered inadequate by indigenous representatives, the obvious irony being fact that a Convention, premised on effective consultation and participation, lacked adequate consultation in its drafting.[56] The limited extent of this consultation, and in particular the absence of any participation in the decision on whether to initiate the revision or not, have been described as C169's 'original sin' and significantly influenced its initial credibility among indigenous peoples.[57] The decision to revise C107 was particularly controversial in light of the parallel, and more ambitious, drafting of the UNDRIP under the UN Working Group which had established working methods facilitative of effective indigenous participation almost on par with that of State representatives. A commonly held perception is that the ILO regarded this process as a threat to its prominent reputation in the arena of indigenous peoples' issues.[58]

The C169 drafting process has also been criticised for failing to adequately address issues which were central to indigenous peoples' demands in the decade leading up to the revision,[59] and in their engagement with the UN Working Group.[60] The four most contentious issues centred around: (a) the right to self-determination and the implications of the term 'peoples'; (b) the political dimension implicit in the term 'territory'; (c) ownership rights over natural resources; and (d) the requirement for informed consent in relation to measures and activities impacting on indigenous peoples.[61]

Each of the issues was dealt with in a distinct manner. The introduction of the terminology 'peoples' was justified on the grounds that it was reflective of indigenous peoples' 'distinctive identity' which C169 aimed to recognise.[62] In line

---

54 Despite proposals by the employees group, the scope of the Convention was not extended to include indigenous peoples outside of independent countries who continued to be governed under the trusteeship doctrine, see Berman 1988: 52–53.

55 Swepston 1987: 451.

56 Clavero 2002: 141 (Annex II, Tratados entre Pueblos o Constituciones por Estados: Un Dilema para América).

57 Rodríguez-Piñero 2005: 281–282, 318–319 and 342, citing Swepston, *Report of Participation in Working Group on Indigenous Populations: 29 July to 2 August 1985* (ILO Archives ACD 4/107, 4, undated) and internal memo from L. Swepston, ILO Archives, ESC 1005/21/1/0/1, *Resolution of the Indigenous Peoples Preparatory Meeting Relating to International Labour Organization's Convention Concerning Indigenous and Tribal Peoples in Independent Countries* (Geneva, 28 July 1989), Appendix at 66–67.

58 Berman 1988: 48, 49; see also Rodríguez-Piñero 2005: 273, 275, suggesting that the drafting of the UNDRIP was the primary impetus behind the decision to revise Convention 107.

59 Treaty Council News 1977: 23; and Ligue internationale des femmes pour la paix et la liberté 1981: 16.

60 Eide, UN Doc. E/CN.4/Sub.2/1982/33, (1982) paras 72 and 98; Berman 1988: 49.

61 Rodríguez-Piñero 2005: 306.

62 ILO 1988a: 12–14.

with its identity-affirming philosophy, the fundamental criterion of self-identification was introduced, the Social Darwinist notion of 'semi-tribal' peoples removed, and the timeline for historical continuity linked to the formation of the State as opposed to pre-colonial times. To allay the concerns of those States objecting to the political connotations of 'peoples', a caveat was introduced that the term peoples should 'not be construed as having any implications as regards the rights which may attach to the term under international law'.[63] The use of 'peoples' under the Convention was thereby divorced from the burning issue of the right to self-determination which was the crux of parallel debates in the context of the UN Declaration.[64] The intent of the Convention was neither to affirm nor inhibit its recognition.[65] Instead, it was clarified that, as political considerations lay outside of the ILO's mandate, other UN fora would address the right to self-determination[66] – the other fora being the UN Working Group, with the final decision on the right ultimately resting with one of the 'highest political organs' of the UN, its General Assembly.[67]

Another contentious issue was the political dimension of the term 'territories'. Together with the requirement for consent, the notion of territory was objected to on the grounds that it was perceived as infringing on 'national sovereignty'. The ILO Office clarified that 'territory' in the Convention 'does not appear to carry the implications of legal title, but only a geographical area subject to a particular jurisdiction'.[68] However, the term 'territories' was replaced by 'lands' in Articles 7 and 14. As a result, while the Convention provides important elements for a framework upon which a right to territorial jurisdiction can be asserted, it is nevertheless weighted heavily towards recognition of land rights as opposed to territorial rights.[69] This issue of indigenous peoples' rights to ownership and control over resources located in their territories was the subject of extensive discussion. The experts noted that the Martínez Cobo Study had urged 'unrestricted ownership and control of land, including all natural resources' and had provided detailed guidelines in relation to activities involving resource extraction.[70] In keeping with the report's recommendations, the experts acknowledged that indigenous peoples maintain claims over subsoil resources under their traditional or customary systems.[71] However, the general view of the ILO experts was that States would be unwilling to recognise indigenous resource ownership rights, and that affirming such a right in the Convention would give rise to 'practical problems'.[72]

63 Ibid.: 12–14.
64 ILO 1987: 30; see Swepston 1990: 695.
65 ILO 1988c: 36/19. Statement of Mr Watchorn, employers' adviser, Australia.
66 Ibid. 32/6, see also ILO 1988a: 14.
67 Alexander *et al.* 2009: 13.
68 ILO 1989a: 33.
69 Myntti 2000: 121.
70 ILO 1987: Appendix 1, para 57.
71 Ibid.: 112, para 73.
72 Ibid.: 112, para 74.

3.5.1 Debates pertaining to the requirement for consent in the drafting of Convention 169

The notion that indigenous peoples should participate in decisions affecting them was central to a shift from an integration objective to one which sought to maintain indigenous peoples' identities in accordance with their own aspirations.[73] The consent requirement associated with decisions impacting on those aspirations and identities was consequently one of the more controversial issues that emerged during the revision process.

The views expressed at the ILO experts meeting in relation to indigenous consent can be grouped into three categories: (a) those advocated by the employee expects and by international non-governmental organisation experts,[74] which held that obtaining consent constituted an essential principle and a required outcome (a substantive consent requirement); (b) those proposed by the employer experts, which rejected consent outright (no consent position); and (c) views expressed by a government expert suggesting that where consent was sought, but not forthcoming, procedural protections requiring public inquiry were necessary before a decision could be overridden (a strong procedural consent requirement).[75]

The substantive consent requirement was framed as a derivative of indigenous peoples' claims to natural resources, their way of life and land rights. It was also argued that the requirement for consent would not stop development, but would constitute a shift to a more equitable power balance,[76] and was necessary in light of the dispossession, environmental damage and disruption of indigenous peoples' way of life resulting from the increased frequency of resource exploitation.

Yllanes Ramos, the Mexican representative of the employers group who had previously described indigenous peoples as suffering from 'social retardation',[77] was the primary dissenting voice to a consent provision.[78] His objections were on the grounds that no State would ratify the Convention were indigenous peoples provided with a right to prevent development and 'that its application could even lead to dissolution of States'.[79]

The intermediary position (a strong procedural consent requirement) arose from a discussion on the requirement for consent in *Aboriginal Land Rights (Northern Territory) Act* 1967, which was presented as a means of accommodating the different views and needs of governments and indigenous peoples in a context where subsoil ownership rights were maintained by the State.[80] It was noted that while referring to a 'veto', the Act includes a provision allowing for a government

---

73 Barsh 1987: 756; Bennett 1978a: 47; ILO Convention 169, preamble para 5.
74 ILO 1987: Appendix 1, para 2, noting that two international NGO experts participated.
75 ILO 1987: paras 70–83.
76 Ibid.: para 77.
77 Statement of Mr Yllanes Ramos, Mexican employers' delegate, ILC, 29th Session, Geneva, 1946. Quoted in Rodríguez-Piñero 2005: 2.
78 Barsh 1987: 761.
79 ILO 1987: Appendix 1, para 58.
80 The Act is not specified in the report, see ILO 1987: Appendix 1, para 74.

override in exceptional circumstances, subject to certain rigorous procedural requirements.[81] What was described corresponded to the procedural steps involved in seeking and obtaining consent, together with the requirement for 'appropriate' and effective checks to ensure that the substantive outcome could only be overridden under exceptional and exhaustively justified circumstances.

A general, though not unanimous, consensus emerging from the experts meeting was that the requirement for consent represented a form of compromise which accommodated both indigenous peoples' and States' claims over resources.[82] While this view was regarded as reflecting the concerns and essential principles discussed,[83] suggestions were also made by some experts that 'exceptions or limitations' would be necessary. The recommendation was encapsulated in two of the conclusions upon which the experts placed particular emphasis, namely, that:

> Indigenous and tribal peoples should enjoy *as much control as possible* over their own economic, social and cultural development[84] [and that] [t]he authority of States to appropriate indigenous or tribal land, or to remove these peoples from their lands, should be limited to exceptional circumstances, and should take place only with their informed consent.[85]

In those exceptional circumstances, where governments sought to override indigenous peoples' decisions, appropriate procedures which guaranteed the opportunity for their effective representation were proposed.[86] Commentators have suggested that it was reasonably clear from these initial debates that many experts regarded self-determination and consent 'to be the only acceptable organizing principles for a Convention on indigenous rights'.[87]

In preparing the draft text, the ILO Office noted the lack of unanimity among the experts on the position that 'indigenous peoples should have *absolute control* and the right of ultimate decision'.[88] Its view was that there existed 'a wide measure of agreement' that consent should 'always be sought' prior to mineral development and that the process for seeking consent had to be context-specific.[89] The 'fears', which had been expressed by Ramos, were repeated by the Office as grounds for 'leaving the degree of control to be exercised by these peoples and by governments to decisions at the national level'.[90] The pragmatism inherent in the text proposed by the Office resonated with the positions of a significant number

81 Ibid.: 1, para 74; see also Sub-section 40(b) of the *Aboriginal Land Rights (Northern Territory) Act.*
82 ILO 1987: Appendix 1: para 82(g).
83 Ibid.: para 83.
84 Emphasis added. Ibid.: para 159(2).
85 Ibid.: para 159(6).
86 Ibid.: para 159(6).
87 Berman 1988: 50. For a response to Berman, see Swepston 1989.
88 ILO 1987: 29–30 and Appendix 1, paras 58 and 159(2).
89 Ibid.: 53–54.
90 Ibid.: 32.

of States on the basis that it 'accorded closely with existing national legislation'[91] and avoided constitutional and other legal impediments to ratification.[92]

A series of proposals and counter-proposals were made by governments, employees and employers at the 1988 Conference in relation to the wording of the consent requirement. A proposal of the employee group to change the wording to 'obtain the informed consent' was objected to by the employers group and Canada on the grounds that it implied a right of veto.[93] Representatives of the employer group stated that their objections were not based on the pursuit of their own 'self-interest', but on the national interest, which they held was, in the long term, also in the interest of indigenous peoples.[94] Canada also repeatedly objected to any form of consent requirement on the grounds that it would be 'unrealistic', would 'threaten the supremacy of legislative bodies' and would 'jeopardise ratification of the revised Convention'.[95] At the 1989 Conference the wording proposed by the Office requiring consultation 'in good faith with the objective of achieving agreement or consent' was accepted by a narrow majority.[96] The provision was included in Article 6 and is applicable to all consultations mandated under the Convention. The consultation requirement under Article 6 was complemented by the requirement under Article 15(2) to consult and conduct impact assessments and ensure benefit sharing in relation to natural resource exploitation.

In the final discussion on the proposed provisions, a number of government delegations supported Bolivia's objections to Article 15(2) on the grounds that it would vest ownership of sub-surface resources with indigenous peoples living on the land.[97] This view was supported by Argentina and Venezuela. New Zealand suggested that the requirement for benefits under Article 15(2) was problematic where States maintained ownership of subsoil resources,[98] while Argentina held that the inclusion of the word 'consult' would make it difficult to ratify the Convention.[99] In response, a number of other governments argued that the consent requirement was consistent with State claims of ownership over sub-soil resources. Australia again pointed to the legalisation in its Northern Territories, as illustrative of the fact that the consent requirement in no way violated the principle of State ownership.[100] This position was supported by Colombia.[101]

During the drafting of the Convention, Colombia had raised concerns that protections under Article 15(2) needed to address the 'the rights of the indigenous peoples, the protection of their habitat and crops or their community as regards

91 ILO 1988c: 32/16, 130.
92 ILO 1989b: 25/17.
93 Ibid.: 32/10.
94 ILO 1988c: 36/19. Statement of Mr Watchorn, employers' adviser, Australia.
95 ILO 1988c: 32/3, 17, 48; ILO 1989b: 25/11, 68 and 32/10, 73.
96 ILO 1989b: 25/13, para 74.
97 Ibid.: 25/19, para 127.
98 Ibid.
99 Ibid.
100 Ibid.: para 128.
101 Ibid.: 25/20, para 140.

the consequences of the exploitation of these resources'.[102] The implication being that the provision should not be interpreted as providing a *carte blanche* to States to proceed with extractive activities, regardless of their impact on indigenous peoples' rights, their way of life, cultural integrity and existence. The addition of 'informed' to 'free consent' came as a result of Colombia's emphasis on the need for the provision of 'all necessary information' leading to a 'clear understanding' of the peoples concerned.[103] Denmark likewise insisted that the wording of Article 15(2) could not be weakened and noted the resource-sharing arrangement with indigenous peoples of Greenland and their right of veto in relation to exploitation.[104] The Government member of the USSR interpreted Article 15 as recognising States' 'exclusive' right of ownership of natural resources, but as also requiring the consent of indigenous peoples prior to exploitation.[105] Ecuador's inter-pretation was that the article required governments to promote agreements with indigenous peoples in relation to resource usage.[106] The ILO Secretary General clarified that the Office envisaged consent as an objective rather than a requirement of consultations.[107] The Workers Group expressed their disappointment with the compromise wording and the fact that some parties still considered it to be 'too onerous'.[108] In their view, consent over matters affecting a people was implied in the 'removal of the assimilationist sentiments' from the Convention.[109]

3.6 Positive and constraining dimensions of C169: a procedural requirement for consent

Compromise language with regard to a consent requirement was inevitable, given the aggressive two-year timeframe for the revision process coupled with the ILO's objective of maximising ratification and its tripartite structure, which severely constrained indigenous influence over the outcome while providing industry representatives with some power in determining the content of their rights. This outcome was signalled in the Office's draft text's emphasis on the palatable, but potentially nebulous, procedural requirements of consultation and participation, as opposed to the controversial but concrete substantive self-determination-based consent and control rights.[110] By 1984, the Human Rights Committee had clarified that constitutional and legislative frameworks should be consistent with the exercise of the right to self-determination.[111] The non-recognition of that right under the

---

102   Ibid.: 31/16.
103   ILO 1988a: 56.
104   Ibid.: 25/20, para 137.
105   Ibid.: 25/19, para 132.
106   Ibid.: 25/20, para 139.
107   Ibid.: 25/12, para 74.
108   Ibid.: 31/4.
109   Ibid.
110   Berman 1988: 55; see also Simpson 1987: 282.
111   Human Rights Committee, General Comment 12, Article 1 (1984), Compilation of General Comments and General Recommendations Adopted by Human Rights Treaty Bodies, UN Doc. HRI/GEN/1/Rev.1 at 12 (1994).

Convention effectively implied that realignment of these frameworks was not considered mandatory in the context of indigenous peoples' rights, thereby legitimising objections to the recognition of a consent requirement on the basis of extant legislation.

Unsurprisingly, given the existing consent requirement in C107 and the extent of impacts on indigenous peoples' way of life as a result of relocation, C169's strongest express requirement for consent emerges from Article 16, which Thornberry notes reformed C107's 'draconian Article 12' 'to establish the basic principle that indigenous peoples shall not be removed from territories occupied without their free consent, and only as an exceptional measure'.[112] While the revised provision removed the economic development justification for non-consensual relocation, it did not eliminate the possibility of other 'exceptional' justifications for non-consensual relocation. A procedural safeguard was introduced to address any exceptions and requires appropriate legal procedures including public inquiries ensuring the effective representation of the people whose consent is being sought.[113] According to the ILO Office, the decision not to specify the permissible exceptions was premised on eliminating the 'unduly permissive' nature of the exceptions under C107, while avoiding undue limitations in contexts where such relocation was deemed essential to meet certain unforeseeable imperatives.[114] However, during the drafting process, several experts had suggested that exceptions should be limited to emergency situations and should not be of a permanent nature.[115] Venne, who acted as the spokesperson on behalf of indigenous groups observing the ILO drafting process, disparagingly referred to the provision as 'a work of art', noting that its 'very nice language' in the first paragraph is dismissed in the following one in the case of 'exceptional circumstances'.[116] In her eyes, this consent requirement was a thinly disguised justification for a continued agenda of assimilation, shrouded under the cloak of politically correct language.[117] The Convention's potential to support a situation where compliance with procedural requirements could justify relocation or other potentially severe non-consensual impacts on indigenous rights, failed to address one of the primary critiques levied against C107, namely that it afforded the potential to resolve disputes over the usage of indigenous lands and resources simply by compensating disposed peoples, even if the proposed usage was driven by individual or corporate interests.[118] Indeed, the absence of a requirement to respect the outcome of consent-seeking processes was described as reflective of the Convention's

---

112 Thornberry 1992: 382.
113 ILO Convention 169, Article 16(2).
114 Partial Revision of the Indigenous and Tribal Populations Convention 1957 (No. 107), ILO Conference Report IV (2A), 76th Session 1989: 44.
115 Report VI(1) 1988: Appendix 1, para 78.
116 Venne 1990: 63.
117 Ibid.: 58–60.
118 Barsh 1983: 82; Venne 1990: 63; Berman 1988: 55–56; Mackay 1999: 157; UN Doc E/Cn.4/Sub.2/1990/42, para 47.

'paternal statist approach' and implying 'no power [for indigenous peoples] to resist pressures of assimilation and cultural domination'.[119]

The Convention nevertheless outlines extremely important procedural obligations in relation to consent-seeking consultations regarding natural resource access and related requirements around impact assessments, benefits, and compensation. This procedural requirement emerges from Article 6 which requires that:

> consultations carried out in application of this Convention shall be undertaken, in good faith and in a form appropriate to the circumstances, [through appropriate procedures and in particular through their representative institutions] with the objective of achieving agreement or consent to the proposed measures.[120]

The obligation to consult and seek consent is framed within the context of the requirements under Articles 2 and 33 for 'co-ordinated and systematic action', developed with indigenous peoples' participation, to achieve the substantive right of 'guarantee[ing] respect for their integrity'.[121] This is to be read together with Article 15(2) requiring consultations with the affected peoples in the context of sub-surface resources exploitation:

> with a view to ascertaining whether and to what degree their interests would be prejudiced, before undertaking or permitting any programmes for the exploration or exploitation of such resources pertaining to their lands. The peoples concerned shall wherever possible participate in the benefits of such activities, and shall receive fair compensation for any damages which they may sustain as a result of such activities.[122]

The central importance of the consultation provisions is reflected in the ILO's Committee of Experts on the Application of Conventions and Recommendations' observation that the 'obligation to consult' had been among the issues that it has most often examined in the last two decades.[123] The interpretation

---

119 Strelein 1996: 77.
120 ILO Convention 169, Article 6.
121 GB.282/14/3, ibid.; see also Committee of Experts, 76th Session, 2005, Individual Direct Request, Bolivia, submitted 2006; Committee of Experts, 75th Session, 2004, Observation, Mexico, published 2005; and Governing Body, 289th Session, March 2004, Representation under Article 24 of the ILO Constitution, Mexico, GB.289/17/3; Committee of Experts, 77th Session, 2006, Observation, Guatemala, published 2007; General observation, Indigenous and Tribal Peoples Convention, 1989 (No. 169), reproduced in CEACR Report III (Part 1A) ILC.100/III/1A, Ibid. at 783–788; for an overview of these cases, see *Indigenous and Tribal Peoples' Rights in Practice: A Guide to ILO Convention No. 169* (Geneva: ILO, 2009).
122 ILO Convention 169, Article 15(2).
123 General observation, Indigenous and Tribal Peoples Convention, 1989 (No. 169), reproduced in International Labour Conference, 100th Session, 2011, *Report of the Committee of Experts on the Application of Conventions and Recommendations* (CEACR) Report III (Part 1A) ILC.100/III/1A: 783.

accorded to Convention 169 by the Committee of Experts has, in the main, sought to constructively build on the procedural dimensions of this obligation. In addition to focusing on the requirement to treat consent as the objective of all consultations, and to contextualise this requirement in light of the right to determine development priorities under Article 7, the supervisory body has repeatedly emphasised the requirement that consultations be conducted through 'appropriate procedures and in particular through [indigenous peoples' own] representative institutions', 'in good faith and in a form appropriate to the circumstances',[124] and has provided important insights into the procedural aspects of the components parts of free, prior and informed consent.

The ILO Office has suggested that the difference in the outcomes between legal frameworks requiring good faith consultations and those requiring consent is primarily a function of the political will of the State to engage with indigenous peoples in good faith and the availability of adequate oversight mechanisms, rather than the legislative requirement *per se*.[125] This perspective finds a certain degree of support in the fact that Constitutional Courts in Colombia and Guatemala, and courts in Argentina, as well as the ILO Supervisory mechanisms and the Inter-American Commission on Human Rights, have all cited the Convention's provisions when holding that inadequate consultations are grounds for suspending projects and freezing concession issuance. While they do not go as far as requiring indigenous peoples' permission for projects, these decisions and recommendations indicate that consent-seeking consultations, and associated measures required to address potential impacts and assess alternatives, nevertheless have an important binding dimension.[126]

Much of the ILO's impressive corpus of guidance has been invoked by national courts, with its influence also extending beyond State parties.[127] UN treaty and charter bodies regularly refer to it when addressing indigenous peoples' rights, while the Inter-American Commission on Human Rights regards certain provisions of C169 as providing 'evidence of modern international opinion on questions related to indigenous peoples and, therefore . . . [can be] appropriately

---

124 Governing Body, 282nd Session, November 2001, Representation under Article 24 of the ILO Constitution, Colombia, GB.282/14/3. General observation, Indigenous and Tribal Peoples Convention, 1989 (No. 169), reproduced in CEACR Report III (Part 1A) ILC.100/III/1A, ibid.: 783–788.
125 L. Swepston on behalf of the ILO, oral statement to the UN Permanent Forum on Indigenous Issues, Sixth Session (2007) (notes on file with author).
126 For a summary of a selection of these national cases, see *Application of Convention No. 169 by Domestic and International Courts in Latin America: A Casebook* (Geneva: ILO, 2009); see also Inter-American Commission on Human Rights, Precautionary Measure PM 382/10 – Indigenous Communities of the Xingu River Basin, Pará, Brazil, 1 April 2011; see also Chapter 2.
127 See, for example, ILO 2010; for example, the Philippines, *Indigenous Peoples Rights Act* (1997) was in part modelled on ILO Convention 169. See also IFC 2007a as illustrative of financial institutions tending to follow the Convention's provisions. See ILO 2009 for examples of where requirements have been echoed by national courts.

considered for the interpretation and application of the Articles of the American Declaration'.[128]

A similar logic is applied by the Inter-American Court of Human Rights. The African Commission on Peoples and Human Rights also uses the Convention as an interpretative guide for the African Charter in relation to non-State parties. In this regard, C169 has lived up to the expectations of those who greeted its adoption with optimism.

Writing immediately after its adoption, Barsh acknowledged C169's short-comings but argued for its potential to be substantially strengthened if a 'progressive' interpretation were accorded to it.[129] Likewise, Anaya suggests that those who employ 'formalism to interpret the Convention' and thereby dismiss its relevance, act in a manner counterproductive to their interests.[130] Instead, he proposes constructing legal arguments around 'the Convention's central affirmation of indigenous cultural and group integrity'.[131] Given the developments in the normative framework of indigenous peoples' rights in the quarter of a century since the adoption of C169, it is essential that it be constantly reinterpreted in light of the 'entire legal system prevailing at the time of its interpretation'. In light of the increasing influence of C169 on indigenous peoples' participatory rights both in, and beyond, ratifying States, the necessity for legal clarity with regard to the consent requirement emerging from the Convention is of growing importance. This urgency is further evidenced by four tendencies in interpreting C169. The first is the misinterpretation by some States of the compatibility of its provisions with legislative or judicial recognition of a substantive consent requirement.[132] The second is the emerging gulf between, on the one hand, the ILO supervisory body's hesitancy to acknowledge that a substantive consent requirement can be derived from the rights affirmed under the Convention and, on the other, the progressive jurisprudence of international and regional human rights bodies deriving such a requirement from essentially the same corpus of substantive rights. A third factor, which, in light of the *pro-homine* principle,[133] should influence the interpretation of the Convention, is the reality that violations of indigenous peoples' rights in the context of natural resource extraction in their territories are far more extensive today than when the Convention was adopted.[134] Finally, the

128   Inter-American Commission on Human Rights *Maya indigenous community of the Toledo District v. Belize*, Case 12.053, Report No. 40/04, Inter-Am. C.H.R., OEA/Ser.L/V/II.122 Doc. 5 rev. 1 at 727 (2004).
129   Barsh 1990: 211.
130   Anaya 2005: 237.
131   Ibid.
132   Bolivia Constitutional Judgment 0045/2006, File 2005–12440–25-RDL, Judgment of 2 June 2006 see also *Application of Convention No. 169 by Domestic and International Courts in Latin America: A Casebook* (Geneva: ILO, 2009), 57–59.
133   Requiring that laws be interpreted in the manner which is most advantageous to the human being, see *Mayagna (Sumo) Awas Tingni Community v. Nicaragua*, judgment of 31 August 2001, Inter-Am. Ct. H.R., (Ser. C) No. 79 (2001), Concurring opinion of Judge Sergio García Ramírez, para 2.
134   Moody 2007; Doyle and Gilbert 2009; Whitmore *et al.* 2012; Doyle and Whitmore 2014.

acknowledgement by the UN General Assembly that indigenous peoples are vested with the right to self-determination establishes a new interpretative frame within which protections for their substantive and procedural rights have to be considered by all organs of the UN, including the ILO.

3.7 Bases for a substantive consent requirement under the Convention

The perception that the Convention affirmed a veto right and created a 'state within a state' was initially regarded as constituting an impediment to its ratification in Latin America.[135] Indeed, the limited ratification of the Convention suggests that some States may continue to regard the Convention from this perspective. To counter this perception, the ILO Office and supervisory mechanisms have clarified that such an interpretation exaggerates the Convention's requirement for full participation, and that a 'right to veto' is not provided under Article 6, which instead represents a right to participate in, and to influence, decision-making.[136] This interpretation that the Convention does not provide an absolute veto power is an accurate reflection of its drafting intent and textual expression, a fact that has been reiterated by numerous commentators.[137] However, it is suggested here that this tendency to view the Convention's provisions around resource exploitation, through the veto/no veto lens, misconstrues the consent requirement emerging from the rights the Convention affirms. The framing of consent in terms of a veto power was introduced during the drafting process by those opposed to any form of consent requirement.[138] In essence, it was, and remains, a reductionist and polarising approach to the issue of rights-based decision-making, serving to detract from discussion of the substantive bases for a consent requirement.[139]

The remainder of this chapter seeks to examine the bases of a context-specific substantive consent requirement under the Convention. Its premise is as follows: the Convention's overarching objective of guaranteeing indigenous peoples' permanent and enduring way of life has profound implications for activities threatening this way of life and the rights necessary for its enjoyment, as it logically prohibits rights' infringements which pose a threat to indigenous peoples' way of life. Articles 6 and 7 of the Convention recognise indigenous peoples as autonomous actors with the right to make decisions in relation to their current and future way of life, thereby acknowledging that they may choose to alter that way of life. Consequently, an interpretation of the Convention, which is consistent with its

---

135 Swepston 1998: 33.
136 M. Tomei and L. Swepston, *Indigenous and Tribal Peoples: A Guide to ILO Convention No. 169* (Geneva: ILO, 1996) at 24, see also ILO 2003: 16; ILO 2001: Representation (Article 24) Colombia (GB.277/18/1): (GB.282/14/4), para 59.
137 Myntti 2000: 120; see also Mackay 1999: 75; see also Gilbert 2006: 82.
138 Swepston 1990: 690.
139 See Chapter 6.2.

objective of protecting diverse ways of life and its recognition of indigenous decision-making autonomy, would be that activities which could pose a threat to indigenous peoples' way of life may not proceed unless their consent is obtained to any associated infringements on the rights protected under the Convention. In accordance with the general rule of interpretation under the *Vienna Convention on the Law of Treaties*, this argument will be supported by reference to C169's object and purpose, its text, including its preamble, its drafting history and subsequent developments in international law.[140]

The Convention's rejection of the failed integration agenda has profound implications for the conception of indigenous peoples' rights which it articulates. It represented an abandonment of the palliative philosophy of C107 and the underlying presumption of the inevitable disappearance of indigenous cultures under its assimilationist orientation. This transformation of indigenous peoples' right to exist, from a transitional and temporary right, to a permanent and enduring one, premised on respect for the 'unique identity' of indigenous peoples, was the fundamental change introduced in C169.[141]

In his speech submitting C169 to the plenary for adoption at the 76th session of the International Labour Conference, the Rapporteur of the Committee held that the text had achieved the objective of removing C107's assumption that indigenous peoples should disappear, and replacing it by one which assumed respect for their cultures and way of life.[142] In light of this, the Rapporteur suggested that the importance of the requirement to consult indigenous peoples 'in good faith and in a form appropriate to the circumstances, with the objective of achieving agreement or consent', would be appreciated by both States and indigenous peoples.[143] This echoed a similar intervention at the 75th session by the Chairman of the Committee noting that the Convention consecrated:

> respect for the integrity of the values, practices and institutions of these peoples in the general framework of guarantees enabling them to maintain their own different identities and ensuring self-identification, totally exempt from pressures which might lead to forced assimilation, but without ruling out the possibility of their integration with other societies and life-styles as long as this is freely and voluntarily chosen.[144]

This objective has subsequently been affirmed in ILO publications which clarify that '[i]n contrast with the previous Convention which had an integrationist character, this new instrument presumes the permanent and enduring existence of these people if they so decide it'[145] and 'Convention no 107 was revised in order

---

140 General principle of interpretation as reflected in the Vienna Convention on the Law of Treaties (1969), Article 31(1), (2), (3).
141 International Labour Conference Proceedings, 75th Session (1988) at 32/2, para 11.
142 International Labour Conference Proceedings, 76th Session (1989) at 31/2.
143 Ibid. at 31/1.
144 Ibid. at 31/4–31/5.
145 Author's translation. See ILO 2002: 6.

to include the fundamental principle that the way of life of indigenous and tribal peoples was permanent and enduring.'[146]

This intent to protect their 'permanent and enduring' way of life and existence finds expression in Articles 2 and 5(b), which require indigenous peoples' physical and cultural integrity to be guaranteed. Logically, this intent gives rise to a requirement for the prohibition of measures which threaten indigenous peoples' existence and way of life, as a failure to do so would defeat the objective of the Convention.[147] Adherence to this objective constitutes the doctrinal basis for the implicit substantive consent requirement which emerges from the Convention. The logic of the Convention implies that measures which threaten indigenous peoples' permanent and enduring way of life and their integrity are only permissible with their free and informed consent. In other words, rather than constituting a veto power of indigenous peoples over State decisions, consent provides the mechanism through which the State can seek to legitimise what would otherwise be prohibited measures under the Convention. This distinction, while subtle, is fundamentally important to safeguard the rights the Convention affirms. The implicit substantive consent requirement is consequently complementary to the procedural consent requirement in Article 6(2). The latter always applies, while the former is triggered by circumstances which pose a threat to indigenous peoples' enduring way of life, with respect for the outcome of the consultations mandatory in contexts where the Convention's objective would otherwise be compromised. While the ILO supervisory bodies have not yet addressed this consent requirement, support for such an interpretation can be found in the jurisprudence of the Inter-American Court and some national courts, such as the Colombian Constitutional Court. A 2003 decision of the latter placed a particular emphasis on C169's objective to guarantee indigenous peoples' permanent and enduring way of life. It interpreted this as a right not to be assimilated, and as a basis for the requirement to consult with the objective of consent.[148] This ruling was identified by the ILO Office as 'one of the constitutional judgements to develop the application of Convention 169 in greatest detail'.[149] In 2009 and 2011, the Colombian Court invoked this decision when affirming that contemporary international law imposes a duty on States to obtain indigenous peoples' FPIC in the context of projects which threaten their way of life.[150] In doing so, it explicitly rejected the veto argument as a basis for denying the requirement to obtain FPIC and held that C169 was consistent with this logic.[151]

---

146 Author's translation. See ILO 2007a: 7.
147 International treaties must be interpreted in the light of their objective and intent, see Vienna Convention on the Law of Treaties, 1155 U.N.T.S. 331, 8 I.L.M. 679, entered into force 27 Jan. 1980.
148 Constitutional Court of Colombia SU-383/03, 13 May 2003.
149 Ibid.; see also ILO 2009: 89, 97.
150 Constitutional Court of Colombia, Sentencia T-769/09 (2009) (Referencia: expediente T-2315944); see also Colombia Constitutional Court Sentencia T-129/11, (2011) (3 March 2011) Referencia: expediente T-2451120.
151 See Chapter 6.1.

The question therefore arises as to how determination is to be reached as to when indigenous peoples' integrity, existence and enduring way of life are threatened. The subjective nature of this determination in the context of resource extraction projects and activities is reflected in the need for participatory assessments of the 'social, spiritual, cultural and environmental' impacts to ascertain 'whether and to what degree [indigenous peoples'] interests would be prejudiced'.[152] This suggests that indigenous peoples must have an influential role in assessments of when their way of life or existence is at risk, and if they deem this to be the case, the burden of proof rests with the State to demonstrate that such impacts can be avoided. If the State is unable to do so, and consent to the project or activities is not forthcoming, then they are prohibited under the Convention. In less extreme cases where cultural integrity and way of life are not threatened, but enjoyment of substantive rights protected under the Convention is nevertheless infringed upon, the principles of non-discrimination, compliance with the law, necessity and proportionality would imply that the State has to demonstrate that it has balanced any infringement of indigenous rights against a legitimate need. Again, if the State is unable to demonstrate this, consent provides the only means to legitimise such rights infringements.

The view that a substantive consent requirement emerges from C169 is also supported by the drafting history of Article 7, which is inspired by internal self-determination.[153] The provision, which embodies 'one of the fundamental principles of the Convention',[154] recognises

> [indigenous peoples'] right to decide their own priorities for the process of development as it affects their lives, beliefs, institutions and spiritual well-being and the lands they occupy or otherwise use, and to exercise control, *to the extent possible*, over their own economic, social and cultural development.[155]

During the drafting, the ILO Office clarified that the qualification 'to the extent possible' was not to be regarded as a limitation on the right under Article 7, but as providing flexibility where 'involvement at all stages' of decision-making was not logistically possible.[156] This suggests that the flexibility afforded to States under it was not intended to constitute grounds for imposing limitations on, or denying, those developmental choices which indigenous peoples perceive as necessary to guarantee their integrity and way of life.

The Convention's implicit substantive consent requirement is further reinforced by the constraints on the range of legitimate options available to the State in its pursuit of non-consensual measures under Article 3(2), which states that

---

152 ILO Convention 169, Articles 7(3) and 15(2).
153 ILO 1988a: 8, 17, 19, 30.
154 ILO 2001: Representation (Article 24) Colombia (GB.277/18/1): (GB.282/14/4), para 59.
155 Emphasis added. ILO 1987, para 55.
156 ILO 1988a: 17–19 and 34–35.

'[n]o form of force or coercion shall be used in violation of the human rights'.[157] While the ILO Secretary General has clarified that 'the legitimate use of force, for instance in connection with law enforcement, would not be excluded by the text',[158] its Committee of Experts has noted that laws must avoid the criminalisation of indigenous peoples who are attempting to exercise their land rights.[159] The burden of proof therefore also rests upon the State to illustrate that any related restrictions on indigenous peoples' rights, such as their right to peaceful assembly, are legitimate, necessary and proportionate. Such restrictions are only permissible when they are 'imposed in conformity with the law', and are 'necessary in a democratic society'.[160] The associated emerging trend towards limiting State power to infringe on indigenous rights is evident in the progressive rulings of international and regional bodies, such as the assertion by the African Commission that: '[f]orced evictions, [of indigenous communities] by their very definition, cannot be deemed to satisfy . . . the . . . test of being done "in accordance with the law".'[161]

In summary, an implicit substantive requirement for consent can be derived from a good faith interpretation of the Convention's terms in light of its objective and intent. The requirement is reflected in Article 2 (right to physical integrity) and Article 5(b) (right to cultural integrity) and reinforced by Article 3.2 (prohibition on the use of force), together with the Convention's affirmation of land, resource and development rights and the principle of non-discrimination.[162] The procedural dimensions of the consent requirement under Article 6(2) are in addition to and not in place of its substantive dimensions.

If the above argument is accepted, then, under C169 any measures which threaten indigenous peoples' permanent and enduring way of life or integrity always give rise to a substantive consent requirement. Those measures with lower levels of impact may trigger this substantive consent requirement if the conditions of legality, necessity and proportionality are not met. Measures which do not trigger the substantive dimension of the consent requirement nevertheless always give rise to the procedural requirement for good faith consultations with the objective of consent or agreement.

As a result, a textual interpretation of the Convention in light of its purpose suggests that the determination of whether or not to maintain their way of life rests with indigenous peoples, while the conditions under which they exercise

157 Goodland 2008: 342.
158 ILO 1989b: 25/9, para 50.
159 Argentina Indigenous and Tribal Peoples Convention, 1989 (No. 169) Observation, CEACR 2009/80th Session reproduced in ILO 2010: 16, quoting Magistrate's Court of the Fourth District of the Province of Neuquén in the case of Antiman, Víctor Antonio y Linares, José Cristóbal Linares s/usurpación, of 30 October 2007.
160 ICCPR Article 21.
161 Communication No. 155/96 (2001) *The Social and Economic Rights Action Center for Economic and Social Rights v Nigeria* and Communication No. 276 (2003); African Commission on Human and Peoples Rights Case 276/2003 – *Centre for Minority Rights Development (Kenya) and Minority Rights Group International on behalf of Endorois Welfare Council v Kenya* (2009), para 218.
162 Aidesep *et al.* 2011.

their right to exist remain, to a certain extent, subject to State discretion, provided the fundamental rights affirmed in the Convention are not violated. This limitation on indigenous control over the conditions of their existence is reflective of the unequal relationship between States and indigenous peoples implied in the absence of recognition of the right to self-determination under the Convention.

During the revision of C107 it was repeatedly held that the new Convention should not promote positions which were contrary to a consensus emerging in the UN, or fail to take account of developments in international law.[163] This philosophy has been subsequently restated by the ILO Office[164] and is embodied in the Convention itself under Article 35, which affirms that its application 'shall not adversely affect rights and benefits of the peoples concerned pursuant to other Conventions and Recommendations, international instruments, treaties, or national laws, awards, custom or agreements'.[165]

The intent of C169 was consequently not to be a hindrance to the development of indigenous rights. However, a frozen interpretation of the substantive rights emerging from the Convention has precisely that effect. It gives rise to a situation whereby C169 plays a restraining role on the emergence of a core component of the right to self-determination and safeguard for indigenous peoples' collective rights.[166]

Constructive approaches to C169 recognise that its emphasis on indigenous institutions and their participation in decision-making establish certain conditions which are necessary for the realisation of the right to autonomy.[167] The ILO Office affirmed in 1996 that an aim of the Convention is to 'set up the conditions for self-management' and that it is compatible with 'any future international instrument which may establish or define [a right to self-determination]'.[168] Reflective of this is the fact that it presumes a good faith engagement between States and indigenous peoples who possess autonomous decision-making capacity and are capable of providing or withholding consent. When interpreted in light of the right to self-determination, C169's affirmation of the requirement for cooperation and good faith consultations takes on an additional dimension. It requires that the articulation between State and indigenous governance systems, each with its own 'precise autonomy', must occur within a framework of informed consent, in which both the State party and the indigenous peoples commit to be bound by the outcome of consent-seeking processes and any agreements into which they enter.[169] Such agreements can be governed and regulated under international law, national

---

163 ILO 1988a: 32; see also ILO 1987: Appendix I, paras 40, 51–52.
164 Tomei and Swepston 1996: 9.
165 ILO Convention 169, Article 35.
166 Urteaga Crovetto 2009.
167 Myntti 2000: 120–122; see also Alfredsson 1998: 125–128; Gilbert 2006: 231; Gilbert 2002: 353.
168 *ILO Convention on Indigenous and Tribal Peoples, 1989 (No. 169): A Manual* (Geneva: ILO, 2003) at 10.
169 Jimeno Santoyo 2002: 25.

law, indigenous customary law, or a combination of all three depending on the arrangement reached between the parties.[170]

As will be discussed in Chapters 4 and 5, the recognition by the human right regime of indigenous peoples' unqualified right to self-determination has gone hand in hand with the affirmation that a requirement to obtain their FPIC is derived from their cultural, development and territorial rights. Human rights bodies have held that C169 is compatible with this FPIC requirement, and have requested States to take C169 into account when assuring respect for the 'right to' free prior and informed consent.[171] Indeed, the Independent Expert on minority issues has suggested, as proposed in this chapter, that a right to withhold consent is implied in C169,[172] while the Committee on the Elimination of Racial Discrimination (CERD) has interpreted C107's requirement for collaboration under its Article 5 as supporting the requirement to obtain indigenous peoples' FPIC.[173] The ILO supervisory bodies have, since the 1970s, rejected the integration objective of C107 and interpreted its provisions in light of 'generally accepted human rights principles . . . such as the principle of consultation'.[174] As an international treaty, C169 also has to be constantly reinterpreted and 'applied within the framework of the entire legal system prevailing at the time of its interpretation'.[175] This is essential to ensure that account is taken of relevant rules of international law and that interpretations of its provisions do not lead to results which are manifestly unreasonable.[176] In light of the body of human rights law affirmation of a self-determination-based requirement for FPIC, an interpretation of C169 which negates this requirement would be unreasonable and inconsistent with the legal framework of which it forms a part. Finally, given the central role of indigenous peoples' traditional occupations to the preservation of their way of life, this consent requirement may also flow from a constructive interpretation of the non-discrimination provisions under ILO Convention 111 (C111) addressing discrimination in employment and occupation.[177] This Convention, which the ILO has interpreted as covering indigenous peoples' traditional and non-wage occupations,[178] is one of

---

170 A parallel exists with agreements entered into between States and international organisations which may be governed by international law, national law or internal rules of the organisation, see *Draft Articles on the Law of Treaties between States and International Organizations or Between International Organizations with Commentaries 1982* (New York: United Nations, 2005), *Yearbook of the International Law Commission*, Vol. II, Part II, 1982 A/CN.4/SER.A/1982/Add.l (Part 2), Chapter 2.

171 CERD Early Warning Urgent Action, letter to Peru, dated 2 September 2011; see also UN Doc. E/C.12/COL/CO/5 (7 June 2010), para 9.

172 Statement by the United Nations Independent Expert on Minority Issues, Ms Gay McDougall, on the conclusion of her official visit to Colombia, 1–12 February 2010 (12 February 2010).

173 CERD/C/PAN/CO/15–20 (19 May 2010), para 14.

174 ILO Supervisory Body Comments (2010), ibid.: 4.

175 Ibid.: 332.

176 Vienna Convention on the Law of Treaties (1969), Articles 31 and 32.

177 ILO Convention No. 111, Discrimination (Employment and Occupation) Convention, 25 June 1958: 362 UNTS 31; see also ILO 2007b.

178 See El Salvador Observation, Discrimination (Employment and Occupation) Convention, 1958, No. 111, CEACR 2008/79th Session reproduced in ILO 2010: 68; and Direct Request

the ILO's eight fundamental instruments and has been ratified by 170 countries, including most countries with significant populations of indigenous peoples. Such an interpretation would hold that non-consensual activities which threaten a people's capacity to continue their traditional occupations constitute *de facto* or indirect discrimination and are prohibited under the Convention in light of its objective of eliminating any discrimination in respect of occupation.[179] The case would appear to be particularly strong for indigenous communities with a tradition of small-scale mining or other traditional activities which are displaced by large-scale mining or other major development projects. Given the degree of resistance which States have demonstrated towards the ILO supervisory bodies' insistence on compliance with the procedural aspects of the consultation requirement, these bodies may continue to feel constrained in affording recognition to the substantive consent requirement emerging from C169 and other ILO Conventions. Nevertheless, the potential for such an obligation to arise from C169, C107 and C111 exists and is of significance when viewed in the light of the implications it could have in the context of the obligations of the host and home States of transnational mining companies, an issue which is touched on in Chapter 7.

3.8 Conclusion

The adoption of ILO Convention 107 in 1957 introduced some minimal degree of international oversight and protection in relation to indigenous peoples' rights. However, its rights-denying consent requirement was reflective of the Convention's overtly pro-integration agenda and assimilationist orientation. That flawed requirement, which can be traced to the ILO's Andean Indian Programme and the trusteeship system, nevertheless provided the seeds for the inclusion of an explicit procedural consent-seeking requirement under Convention 169 and represented the first step in the process towards the affirmation of a rights-based requirement for FPIC.

This chapter has argued that to date there has been an unduly narrow interpretation of the consent requirement under the Convention, arising from a narrow focus on the issue of a veto power.[180] It attempts to reorient this perspective by examining the Convention's overarching objective of guaranteeing indigenous peoples' permanent and enduring way of life and suggesting that this prohibits any rights' infringements that pose a threat to that way of life. However, the parallel recognition of indigenous peoples as autonomous actors with the right to decide how their way of life should evolve implies that indigenous peoples can consent to potential changes in that way of life, thereby legitimising activities that would otherwise be prohibited under the Convention. Consequently, a substantive

---

(CEACR) - adopted 2010, published in 100th ILC session 2011, Discrimination (Employment and Occupation) Convention, 1958 (No. 111) - Philippines (Ratification: 1960); see also ILO 2007b: 14.

179 ILO Convention 111, Article 2.
180 ILO 1988b: 4; ILO 1989a: 5–6.

consent requirement emerges from the Convention. This requirement is further strengthened by the need for any measures impacting on indigenous peoples' rights to meet the requirements of legality, necessity and proportionality.

Such an interpretation of Convention 169 has not, as of yet, been adopted by the ILO Supervisory bodies, which, while affirming the procedural aspects of the consent requirement, appear trapped in the veto/no veto dichotomy in relation to its substantive dimension. This procedural requirement should not be interpreted as limiting the substantive consent requirement emerging from Convention 169 or any other international instrument. Recognising an impact-based substantive consent requirement as a derivation of the rights recognised in C169 would be consistent with the jurisprudence of a range of human rights bodies. The emergence from within the broader human right regime of a self-determination and consent-orientated framework of indigenous rights augurs for an even more radical interpretation of Convention 169. It implies that not only does a substantive consent requirement exist but that the threshold for justification of non-consensual activities now has to meet the test of legitimate limitations on the right to self-determination.

The ILO's Committee of Experts has engaged extensively with the issue of consent-seeking consultations. Where it has found that consent has not been the objective of such consultations, it has, in the case of extractive industries, issued recommendations to suspend activities.[181] The grounds now exist for it to recommend adherence to the more exacting and rights-affirming requirement of respecting the outcome of these consultations and actually obtaining consent.

Indeed, doing so could be a way to resolve the issue of the legal nature of the consent requirement which emerges from C169 when interpreted in light of developments in the normative framework of indigenous peoples' rights. If, following a complaint to the ILO under Article 26 of its Constitution, an ILO Commission of Inquiry were to hold that a State party was in breach of C169 for failing to obtain the consent of an indigenous peoples, prior to adopting measures which threaten their existence, cultural integrity or way of life, and the implicated government refused to accept the finding, that government could, following publication of the recommendation, appeal it to the ICJ for a final decision.[182] This would bring the issue before the ICJ for consideration and, as discussed in Chapter 7, would provide it with the opportunity to engage with a range of issues pertaining to indigenous peoples' status and rights under international law.

Recognition by the ILO supervisory bodies that a substantive consent requirement emerges as a derivation of the Convention's intent and the rights it affirms would represent an important step in the evolution of the normative

181 See, for example. recommendations to Colombia and Guatemala in International Labour Conference, 98th Session, 2009 Report of the Committee of Experts on the Application of Conventions and Recommendations Report III (Part 1A), International Labour Conference, 98th Session, 2009: 677 and 680; See also Indigenous and Tribal Peoples Convention, 1989 (No. 169) Observation, CEACR 2009/80th Session (Colombia), reproduced in ILO 2010: 55.
182 Constitution of the International Labour Organization (1946) 15 U.N.T.S. 40, Articles 29 and 31.

framework of indigenous peoples' rights towards one premised on the equality of peoples. Interpreting the Convention in light of indigenous peoples' right to self-determination would also finally absolve C169 of its original sin of denying the indigenous voice at its conception. Doing so would be consistent with the rules of treaty interpretation under the Vienna Convention on the Law of Treaties as this contemporary requirement for FPIC is recognised as premised on and necessary for the realisation of the right to self-determination and permeates the entire normative framework of indigenous peoples' rights.

4 The self-determination-based normative framework of indigenous rights

4.1 Introduction

One of the core controversies surrounding the drafting of ILO Convention 169 (C169) revolved around the recognition of the right of indigenous peoples to self-determination. The decision of the ILO Office to exclude this 'political consideration' from the scope of the discussion facilitated the rapid revision of ILO Convention 107 (C107) and the adoption of the new Convention significantly strengthened indigenous peoples' procedural and substantive rights. Convention 169, which remains the only international treaty specifically dedicated to indigenous peoples currently open to ratification, also introduced the contemporary notion of 'indigenous peoples' into international legal parlance. It did so, however, without any implications for indigenous peoples concerning the rights which are inherent in the concept of 'peoples' as understood under contemporary international law. The concept of 'indigenous peoples', devoid of its self-determination implications, became palatable to States as it appeared to implicitly sanction certain limitations on indigenous peoples' rights, in particular their decision-making rights, which would not have to meet the self-determination threshold. This power of the State to limit self-determination rights under C169 was manifested in the absence of an explicit requirement to obtain indigenous consent prior to authorising activities infringing on their rights. As outlined in Chapter 3, despite this shortcoming, the Convention can be interpreted as providing a framework for the articulation of a contextualised substantive, as well as procedural, consent requirement emerging from the right of these peoples to exist and maintain their way of life and integrity in perpetuity. However, even under this constructive interpretation, C169 stops short of fully empowering indigenous peoples to determine their own social, cultural and economic development, as any decisions taken by them can effectively be overwritten by the State, provided those decisions follow certain procedural steps and do not put indigenous peoples' way of life and existence at risk.[1]

---

1 See Chapter 3 for a discussion. For a general commentary on Convention 169, see Rodríguez-Piñero 2005: 290–331 and Thornberry 2002: 339–367.

During the drafting of C169, reference was made to the fact that the question of indigenous self-determination was being considered in other UN fora and would be decided on by the 'highest political organs' of the UN system.[2] This process, which commenced in 1982, culminated in the adoption of the *UN Declaration on the Rights of Indigenous Peoples* (UNDRIP). The provisions of the UNDRIP, in particular, those pertaining to the right to self-determination, development, resources, and free prior and informed consent (FPIC), reflect the evolution in the normative framework of indigenous peoples' rights in the years which followed the adoption of C169.[3] Indeed, the foundational right of indigenous peoples to self-determination and the repeated references to the State duty to obtain FPIC can be regarded as forming the UNDRIP's skeletal frame.

This chapter explores some of these developments in that normative framework, with a particular focus on the implications of the affirmation of a right to self-determination. Doing so allows the consent requirement, discussed in subsequent chapters, to be contextualised within the rights framework from which it emerges. The chapter commences with an examination of the UNDRIP's status and its drafting history. It addresses the debates during the two-phase drafting process which spanned over two decades, with a particular focus on discussions pertaining to self-determination rights over resources and consent. Having outlined the positions adopted by indigenous peoples and States during these negotiations, the chapter proceeds to examine the sources of law and philosophy which underpin the extant normative framework of indigenous peoples' rights, including the requirement for FPIC. It concludes with a discussion on indigenous peoples' right to self-determination in the post-Declaration era and suggests that the principle of FPIC is a central tenet of this new conception of self-determination.

4.2 The UN Declaration on the Rights of Indigenous Peoples (UNDRIP)

As a General Assembly Resolution, the UNDRIP is not a legally binding document *per se*.[4] Some authors and indigenous rights advocates have, however, highlighted that this Declaration distinguishes itself from other UN declarations as a result of the legalistic and mandatory manner in which each of its provisions, couched in the language of rights, is drafted.[5] Ahren, one of the Sami negotiators, describes its contents as 'clones of provisions found in legally binding international treaties and/or binding customary international law'.[6] Another, complementary interpretation, supported by the Special Rapporteur on the rights of indigenous

---

2 ILO 1987: 30. Eventually the issue was addressed by the UN Human Rights Council and the General Assembly.
3 Ahren 2007: 127.
4 For a commentary, see Brownlie 1990; Cassese 1995; Schwebel 1979.
5 Ibid.: 128; Lenzerini 2008: 624.
6 Ahren 2007: 128.

peoples, is that many of the rights articulated in it are reflective of, or strengthen, existing contemporary international legal interpretations of positive law as they pertain to indigenous peoples.[7]

The assertion that the UNDRIP constitutes customary international law has been questioned on the grounds of potentially insufficient 'consistent state practice and *opinio juris* globally' to meet the threshold.[8] However, these challenges have been directed towards the UNDRIP as a whole as opposed to its recognition of specific rights, such as indigenous peoples' land rights, for which the case could potentially be made.[9]

By consolidating this human rights jurisprudence in a single instrument, the provisions of which are mutually reinforcing, the UNDRIP has created something larger than the sum of its parts. Particular significance has to be accorded to its affirmation that the right of self-determination under common Article 1(1) of the 1966 Human Rights Covenants is applicable to all indigenous peoples.[10] The provisions of the UNDRIP are framed in light of this overarching *erga omnes* and *ius cogens* norm.[11] This acts as a counterweight to the view that the non-binding nature of the document in which they are articulated diminishes the legal significance of the rights and obligations affirmed therein. In certain contexts, it exposes the disingenuous intent behind repeated references to this non-binding status, such as those which arise in the context of the mining industry's challenge to the requirement for FPIC.[12]

It is beyond the scope of these pages to engage with the debate over the legal nature of normative declarations of the General Assembly in general, and whether or not this specific declaration reflects pre-existing or emerging customary law.[13] Instead the chapter adopts as a point of departure the perspective advocated by Daes, that the UNDRIP's normative nature provides indigenous peoples with an opportunity to invoke its provisions, regardless of their legal nature.[14]

Prior to moving to a discussion on the UNDRIP's drafting history, this section seeks to highlight a number of factors which contribute to the unique nature and evolving importance of this Declaration, in relation to other UN normative declarations, and by extension the normative framework which it affirms. These

---

7 UN Doc. A/HRC/9/9 (2008); Wiessner 2008: 1141; Anaya and Wiessner 2007; Wiessner 1999: 57. For a contrary view, see Allen 2011: 227–234.

8 Castellino 2011: 371.

9 See Castellino 2011: 371 fn 17; Allen 2011: 233–235.

10 Prior to the adoption of the UNDRIP, there was debate as to whether indigenous peoples met the criteria for peoples identified by Cristescu and Espiel, see Scheinin 2005: 12; Xanthaki 2007: 136; see also H. G. Espiel, *Implementation of United Nations Resolutions: Relating the Right of People Under Colonial and Alien Domination to Self-Determination*, UN Doc. E/CN.4/Sub.405 (20 June 1978); and A. Cristescu, *The Right to Self-Determination: Historical and Current Development on the Basis of United Nations Instruments* E/CN.4/sub.2/404/Rev.1 (1981).

11 *East Timor (Portugal v. Australia)*, Judgment, I.C.J. Reports 1995, p. 90, para 29; see also Cassese 1995: 130–132.

12 See ICMM (2008a).

13 For a general commentary on the issue of customary law and the UNDRIP, see Voyiakis 2011: 222–223.

14 Daes 2011: 38.

factors include: (a) its use by UN treaty and charter bodies, in particular, the Committe on the Elimination of Racial Discrimination (CERD) and the Special Rapporteur on the rights of indigenous peoples, as well as the UN Permanent Forum on Indigenous Issues (the Permanent Forum) and the Experts Mechanism on the Rights of Indigenous Peoples (the Experts Mechanism); (b) the engagement of UN Agencies, funds and bodies with its implementation; (c) its impact at national level; and (d) its use by indigenous people. Also of relevance is the process of its adoption, including its voting patterns.

The distinctive nature of the UNDRIP is evidenced by the manner in which UN mechanisms, established in order to provide UN agencies and States with guidance in relation to the realisation of indigenous peoples' rights and issues, have engaged with its interpretation and implementation. Both the Permanent Forum and the Experts Mechanism have adopted practices, accepted by the Economic and Social Council and the Human Rights Council respectively, of issuing 'General Comments' or thematic guidance in the form of legal and policy 'advice'. These mechanisms, together with the Special Rapporteur on the rights of indigenous peoples, have effectively assumed an interpretative role in relation to the UNDRIP's provisions. Their advice has been heeded by UN Specialized Agencies, leading to the incorporation of the UNDRIP's provisions into their policies and operational guidance notes.[15] In doing so, they are consolidating its status as a key interpretative guide for other sources of international law.

In its first General Comment on the implementation of the UNDRIP, the Permanent Forum argued that because it is not a treaty does not imply that the UNDRIP does not have any legal effect or influence.[16] This legal effect comes from the contextualisation of the UNDRIP within 'the wider normative context of the innovations that have taken place in international human rights law in recent years'.[17] In this regard, the General Comment argues that the 'Declaration is part of a practice that has advanced a growing "rapprochement" between declarations and treaties'.[18] These views resonate with the opinions of some independent experts and academics who contextualise the UNDRIP within the overall normative human rights framework and emphasise its import as an interpretative guide for existing human rights instruments.[19] This interpretative role was already reflected in the decisions of regional and international human rights bodies and in the UNDRIP's influence on national legislation even prior to

---

15 *Guidelines on Indigenous Peoples' Issues* (Geneva: UNDG, 2008); see also the policies of UNDP, the IFAD and the FAO addressed in the context of FPIC in Doyle forthcoming 2015.
16 *General Comment on Article 42 of the UN Permanent Forum on Indigenous Issues on the UN Declaration*, UN Doc. E/C/19/2009/14, Annex to UN PFII Report of the 8th session, paras 6–13.
17 Ibid.: para 6.
18 Ibid.: para 9.
19 *Briefing on the United Nations Declaration on the Rights of Indigenous Peoples*, UN Doc. CERD/C/SR.1848/ Add.1, para 10 (22 February 2008); see also Schabas 2011; Gilbert and Doyle 2011: 326–327.

its adoption.[20] Following its adoption, this role has increased significantly.[21] One example of this was CERD's recommendation to the United States that, despite the fact that it had voted against the UNDRIP, it should 'be used as a guide to interpret the State party's obligations under the Convention relating to indigenous peoples'.[22] Use of the UNDRIP by UN treaty and charter bodies as a benchmark against which to assess State treatment of indigenous peoples exemplifies a broader trend towards the use of non-treaty documents as the basis for calibrating States' human rights performance. One of the most tangible illustrations of this emerges from the Human Rights Council's Universal Periodic Review (UPR) process, where the UNDRIP is frequently addressed, which includes as part of the basis of the review the Universal Declaration of Human Rights and '[v]oluntary pledges and commitments made by States'.[23] The UNDRIP has also had a significant impact on the decisions of the Inter-American Court of Human Rights,[24] the Inter-American Commission[25] and the African Commission on Human and Peoples Rights.[26]

At the national level, consideration has been given to the content of the UNDRIP in the drafting of the Constitutions of Bolivia and Ecuador.[27] It has been incorporated into legislation in Bolivia and has informed the drafting of legislation and regulations in Peru.[28] It has also informed judicial decisions in States such as Colombia and Belize.[29] Citing the UNDRIP, the Supreme Court of Belize stated: 'General Assembly resolutions are not ordinarily binding on member states. But where these resolutions or Declarations contain principles of general international law, states are not expected to disregard them.'[30]

---

20 See, for example, Inter-American Commission of Human Rights, *Mary and Carrie Dann v United States*, Case No. 11.140, Report 75/02 (2001); *The Philippines Indigenous Peoples Rights Act* (1997) includes an express reference to the UNDRIP. See also UN Doc. CERD/C/USA/CO/6 (2008), para 29.
21 Doyle forthcoming 2015.
22 Concluding observations of CERD United States of America, 7 March 2008, CERD/C/USA/CO/6, para 29.
23 Human Rights Council Resolution 5/1. Institution-Building of the United Nations Human Rights Council, 18 June 2007.
24 Rodríguez-Piñero 2011: 468.
25 See, for example, *Mary and Carrie Dann v United States*, p. 19.
26 See, for example, Communication No. 155/96 (2001) *The Social and Economic Rights Action Center for Economic and Social Rights v Nigeria* and Communication No. 276 (2003); African Commission on Human and Peoples Rights Case 276/2003 – *Centre for Minority Rights Development (Kenya) and Minority Rights Group International on behalf of Endorois Welfare Council v Kenya* (2009).
27 UN Doc A/HRC/9/9/Add.1 15 August 2008, Annex 1.
28 Bolivia: *Ley No. 3760* de 7 de noviembre de 2007, modified by *Ley No. 3897* de 26 de junio de 2008; Peru: Reglamento de la Ley No 29785, Ley del Derecho a la Consulta Previa a los Pueblos Indígenas u Originarios Reconocido en el Convenio No. 169 de la Organización International del Trabajo Decreto Supremo No 001–2012 MC, 3 abril 2012.
29 See Chapters 3 and 5 for references to the Colombian Supreme Court's engagement with the UNDRIP.
30 *Mayan Village of Santa Cruz v. The Attorney General of Belize and the Minister of Natural Resources and Environment*, Belize Supreme Court, Consolidated Claims Claim Nos 171, 172, 2007, para 131.

It also noted that Articles of the UNDRIP reflect 'the growing consensus and the general principles of international law on indigenous peoples and their lands and resources'.[31]

Indigenous peoples, as custodians of the UNDRIP, are actively engaged in all major developmental, environmental and human rights fora that have a potential role in furthering its implementation.[32] As Castellino has suggested, the effectiveness of indigenous peoples in this custodial role will be a determining factor in any assessment of the potential creation of 'momentum towards [the UNDRIP's] implementation and/or articulation as a set of legally binding obligations on States'.[33]

The UNDRIP was adopted by the General Assembly by a vote of 143 States in favour to four against. In addition, there were 11 abstentions. The subsequent attention directed towards the implementation of the UNDRIP by UN organs, and by indigenous peoples themselves through their direct engagement with States, was an important component in impelling the four opposing States, Australia, Canada, New Zealand and the United States,[34] and those which abstained in the General Assembly, to issue statements expressing support for it.[35] At one level, the UNDRIP can be regarded as a consolidated and synthesised codification of the broad spectrum of human rights jurisprudence addressing indigenous peoples' issues in a range of contexts. As with the jurisprudence it mirrors, the UNDRIP provides 'a contextualized elaboration of general human rights principles and rights as they relate to the specific historical, cultural and social circumstances of indigenous peoples'.[36] On another level, the UNDRIP can be understood as reflective of the broadening of the human rights framework in order to cater to new philosophical and legal perspectives. As Thornberry observes, the 'message of the Declaration is that ways of seeing human rights may be subject to change and expansion away from political vision and dominant epistemologies of those who have hitherto "controlled" both the concept and its implementation'.[37] The resolution adopting the UNDRIP can consequently be regarded as an express

31 Ibid.
32 Doyle 2009: 44; see also Nijar 2011; Tobin *et al.* 2008; UN Doc. A/HRC/WG.12/2/1 at 7; Rio+20:Indigenous Peoples International Declaration on Self-Determination and Sustainable Development, 21 June 2012, available at: www.iwgia.com.
33 Castellino 2011: 383–385.
34 For a comment on the role of these States in drafting, see Merlan 2009: 303.
35 *United States Department of State Announcement of U.S. Support for the United Nations Declaration on the Rights of Indigenous Peoples* (16 Dec. 2010), 1, available at: www.state.gov/documents/organization/153223. pdf; *Canada's Statement of Support on the United Nations Declaration on the Rights of Indigenous Peoples* (12 November 2010) available at www.aadnc-aandc.gc.ca/eng/1309374239861; *New Zealand Parliament Ministerial Statements—UN Declaration on the Rights of Indigenous Peoples—Government Support* [Volume:662;Page:10229] (20 April 2010) available at www.parliament.nz/en-NZ/PB/Debates/ Debates/6/5/a/49HansD_20100420_00000071-Ministerial-Statements-UN-Declaration-on. htm; *Statement on the United Nations Declaration on the Rights of Indigenous Peoples Parliament House Canberra*, 3 April 2009, available at: www.un.org/esa/socdev/unpfii/documents/Australia_official_ statement_endorsement_UNDRIP.pdf
36 UN Doc. A/HRC/9/9, 15 August 2008, para 86.
37 Thornberry 2011: 90.

acknowledgement by States of the universal applicability of this extant body of human rights law addressing indigenous peoples and of the relevance of a multiplicity of sources of law in the determination of indigenous rights. In this regard, the significance of the voting record appears to go beyond the usual legal implications derived from voting patterns associated with normative resolutions.[38]

The drafting of the UNDRIP, discussed in detail below, was a unique process in the history of international law-making. In marked contrast to the drafting of other UN Declarations, it was a multi-decade process premised on the full and effective participation of its subjects.[39] Xanthaki hints at the fact that this is one of the reasons why, during its drafting, the UNDRIP was of greater significance than the draft American Declaration on the Rights of Indigenous Peoples, which had not resulted from an equally participatory mechanism.[40] To an extraordinary extent, the text of the draft UN Declaration, submitted to the Sub-Commission in 1994, reflected the proposals of indigenous peoples.[41] These, and subsequent, proposals of indigenous peoples drew extensively on, and contributed to, the body of human rights law which developed in parallel with the drafting process. The subsequent discussions under the Commission on Human Rights' Working Group on the Draft Declaration on Indigenous Peoples Rights[42] were regarded by States as 'a negotiation' with indigenous peoples.[43] They aimed at ensuring indigenous support for any modifications to the 1994 text, on the grounds that adopting a declaration without it would be of no significance.[44] In this regard, the process represented an unprecedented manifestation of the operation of the principle of consent of indigenous peoples at the international level in the formulation of principles and rights under international law which pertain directly to them.[45]

The culmination of this two-decade-long drafting and negotiation process was the agreement between States and indigenous peoples on the unqualified right to self-determination of indigenous peoples as framed in common Article 1(1) of the Human Rights Covenants. While, certain disagreements remained in relation to provisions on lands, territories and natural resources, the final text adopted by the Human Rights Council reflected indigenous peoples' key demands in relation to ownership and control rights over lands, territories and natural resources and the requirement for their FPIC. Some subsequent modifications, necessary to receive

---

38 Domínguez-Redondo 2011; Tammes 1958.
39 Knop 2002: 249.
40 Xanthaki 2007: 121, note 1.
41 Burger 1996: 210; see also the 1984 and 1985 *Declaration of Principles*, UN Doc. E/CN.4/ Sub.2/1985/22 (27 August 1985), Annex III at 1–2. See also Daes 2011: 13–16.
42 Commission on Human Rights Resolution 1995/32 (3 March 1995) (endorsed by Economic and Social Council resolution 1995/32, 25 July 1995).
43 General Comment on Article 42 of the UNPFII on the UN Declaration, UN Doc. E/2009/43-E/C.19/2009/14, Annex to UNPFII Report of the 8th session, para 9.
44 See, in particular, statements of Australia and Russia, UN Doc. E/CN.4/1996/WG.15/CRP.2, paras 7, 9, 16, 19.
45 UN Doc. E/CN.4/2001/85, para 61. see also Ahren 2007: 84–129; Charters and Stavenhagen 2009.

the support of the African States, were also accepted by indigenous peoples prior to the General Assembly vote on its adoption.[46] In light of this unique drafting history and its invocation of indigenous sources of law, the interpretation accorded to the UNDRIP's provisions by both States and indigenous peoples have to be examined for a full appreciation of its spirit and intent.[47]

4.2.1 Phase 1 Drafting under the Working Group on Indigenous Populations

The drafting of the UNDRIP was split into two clear phases.[48] The first from 1982 to 1994 was under the auspices of the Sub-Commission on Human Rights' Working Group on Indigenous Populations which was composed of five experts.[49] The Working Group was chaired, from 1983 onwards, by Erica-Irene Daes who initiated the drafting exercise in 1985.[50] Its working methods provided equal participation of indigenous peoples and States.[51] Indigenous organisations submitted their own proposals for the UNDRIP text, with particular emphasis on control over sub-surface resources.[52] Their claims to rights over natural resources were premised on their inherent, based on natural and indigenous law, right to self-determination,[53] which they argued under international law 'necessarily encompass[es] the right of indigenous peoples to use and control their own lands and natural resources'.[54] An unqualified right to self-determination was also considered to flow from a non-discriminatory application of the rules of positive law to all peoples. The argument was also made that control over sub-soil resources was necessary for their subsistence as peoples.[55] Indigenous representatives repeatedly emphasised the need to obtain their FPIC which 'constituted an essential element of any and all self-determination exercises'.[56] The weaknesses in ILO Convention 169 in this regard were also noted.[57]

During the drafting a number of governments raised concerns with regard to the proposed recognition of rights over sub-surface resources on the grounds that

---

46 *Decision on the United Declaration on the Rights of Indigenous Peoples*, Assembly/AU/Dec. 141 (VIII), 30 January 2007.
47 For an account of the UNDRIP drafting, see Eide 2007.
48 Barsh 1998; see also Davis 2008: 439.
49 Economic and Social Council Resolution 1982/34.
50 Daes 2011: 12–13.
51 Commission on Human Rights Resolution 1995/32, para 4; see also Knop 2002: 249.
52 UN Doc. E/CN.4/Sub.2/1985/22 (27 August 1985), Annexes III and IV, principle 10 and principle 4.
53 Ibid. See also UN Docs. E/CN.4/Sub.2/1987/22 Declaration of 22 Principles; E/CN.4/Sub.2/1987/22, para 36, 52; E/CN.4/Sub.2/1988/24, para 82; E/CR.4/Sub.2/1992/33, para 123.
54 UN Doc. E/CR.4/Sub.2/1992/33, para 69.
55 UN Doc. E/CN.4/Sub.2/1988/24, para 82.
56 UN Docs E/CN.4/Sub.2/1987/22, para 22; E/CN.4/Sub.2/1988/24, paras 75, 83; E/CN.4/Sub.2/1989/36, para, 62–63; E/Cn.4/Sub.2/1990/42, para 118.
57 UN Doc. E/Cn.4/Sub.2/1990/42, para 47.

it was inconsistent with constitutional and legislative frameworks.[58] This position was generally premised on the rejection of indigenous peoples' unqualified right to self-determination, based on a particular interpretation of positive law. This interpretation either regarded the right as vested exclusively in States or the entire people of a State, or recognised indigenous peoples as subjects of a qualified right to self-determination with a limited scope.[59]

The final 1994 draft text included an unqualified right to self-determination justified on the basis that indigenous peoples were not seeking to have or to exercise a right to secession.[60] The approach to indigenous peoples' natural resources rights during this initial decade of drafting can be traced from the initial proposed text in 1988 which only included recognition of rights over 'surface resources',[61] to an interim text in 1989–1990 which included reference to both surface and sub-surface resources,[62] and ultimately to the more ambiguous final draft in 1994 which recognised rights to those natural resources 'traditionally owned or otherwise occupied or used', without specifying if this was inclusive of all resources or limited only to surface resources.[63] This was complemented by the affirmation of a right:

> to determine and develop priorities and strategies for the development or use of their lands, territories and other resources, *including the right to require that States obtain their free and informed consent prior to the approval of any project* affecting their lands, territories and other resources, particularly in connection with the development, utilization or exploitation of mineral, water or other resources.[64]

4.2.2 Phase 2 Negotiations under the Working Group on the Draft Declaration

The second phase of the UNDRIP's drafting process, which commenced in 1995, under the auspices of the Commission's Working Group on the Draft Declaration,[65] culminated in 2006 when the newly formed Human Rights Council voted to adopt the draft Declaration.[66] During the intervening years many of the same arguments that had been raised in the Working Group on Indigenous Populations were revisited, but this time with a greater degree of State engagement

58 UN Doc. E/Cn.4/Sub.2/1990/42, para 115; see also UN Doc. E/CN.4/Sub.2/AC.4/1990/1/ Add.1.
59 See Iorns 1992.
60 Daes 2011: 27.
61 UN Doc. E/CN.4/Sub.2/1988/24, Annex II; UN Doc. E/CB.4/Sub.2/1908/25, paras 12 and 14.
62 UN Doc. E/CN.4/Sub.2/1989/36, paras 12 and 14.
63 UN Doc. E/CN.4/Sub.2/1993/29/Annex I, Article 26.
64 UN Doc. E/CN.4/Sub.2/1993/29/Annex I (23 Aug. 1993), Article 30.
65 Resolution of the Commission on Human Rights 1995/32, 3 March 1995.
66 Human Rights Council Resolution 2006/2.

in the process. At the outset indigenous peoples stated that the final report 'must be produced [and transmitted to the Commission on Human Rights] with the full involvement and consent of Indigenous Peoples', a requirement which they regarded as inherent in their request for their equal and full participation in the Working Group deliberations.[67] They likewise insisted that they would 'not consent to any language which limit[ed] or curtail[ed] the right of self-determination'.[68]

Throughout the ensuing decade of negotiations indigenous peoples insisted on this maintenance of an unqualified right to self-determination and repeatedly argued that 'ownership and control of their lands, territories and resources' were essential for its exercise.[69] They also argued that the right to self-determination was accepted under international law as embodying a resource dimension; that human rights law recognised this as applicable to indigenous peoples; and that as peoples they maintained an inherent right to permanent sovereignty over natural resources.[70]

A number of governments continued to object to affording recognition to the right to self-determination on the grounds that it was inconsistent with national sovereignty and territorial integrity.[71] The recognition which it would imply for indigenous peoples' sovereignty over natural resources also contributed to State resistance to its recognition.[72] Canada proposed the elaboration of principles premised on the conception of self-determination as a right to negotiate political status and socio-economic and cultural development.[73] This proposal was rejected by indigenous peoples who regarded it as an unacceptable restriction on the right. They also held it would be ineffective in practice, as had been demonstrated by the slow progress of such negotiations over land and natural resource rights in Canada.[74] The use of the term territories was also considered objectionable by certain governments,[75] with some suggesting that the notion of 'traditional ownership' was too broad a basis for claiming rights to lands, territories and resources.[76]

Other governments supported indigenous peoples' right to self-determination and conceptions of territories.[77] Denmark emphasised the need to ensure that rights to natural resources were addressed in a manner satisfactory to indigenous

---

67   *Joint Statement by the Indigenous Caucus to the Working Group on the Draft Declaration on the Rights of Indigenous Peoples*, 53rd Session, 22 October 1996; see also *Statement by Ambassador Dr. Ted Moses on behalf of the Grand Council of the Crees, to the Working Group on the Draft Declaration on the Rights of Indigenous Peoples*, 21 October–1 November 1996.
68   Pritchard 1998: 46.
69   UN Docs. E/CN.4/1996/84, para 84; E/CN.4/2000/84, para 72; and E/CN.4/2001/85, para 100.
70   UN Docs. E/CN.4/2001/85, para 104; E/CN.4/1999/82, para 20; E/CN.4/2002/98, para 38; and UN Doc. E/CN.4/2003/92, para 49.
71   For a discussion, see Knop 2002: 212–275; see also Xanthaki 2007: 109–112.
72   UN Doc. E/CN.4/1996/84, para 37.
73   UN Docs. E/CN.4/2000/84, para 50; and E/CN.4/2001/85, para 85.
74   UN Doc. E/CN.4/2000/84, para 89.
75   UN Docs. E/CN.4/2001/85, para 108; and E/CN.4/2005/89, para 31.
76   UN Doc. E/CN.4/1996/84, para 83.
77   UN Doc. E/CN.4/2000/84, para 104.

peoples.[78] Canada endorsed the principles relating to ownership and control rights over resources, but held that these needed to cater to the various arrangements indigenous peoples had with States.[79] Australia adopted a more radical stance, stating that it would be guided by national legislation affirming State ownership of resources – a position that indigenous peoples rejected as fundamentally inconsistent with an international human rights standard-setting process.[80] They also rejected the notion that the UNDRIP's provisions afforded exclusive rights to indigenous peoples over natural resources, at the expense of third parties, on the basis that competing claims would be addressed on a case-by-case basis.[81]

In the process of negotiations around the FPIC requirement, deletion of the concept from the UNDRIP was rejected, while a range of wording proposals in relation to its mandatory nature, deviating from the aforementioned 1994 draft provision, were considered.[82] Government positions included the views that 'prior informed consent might not be required in all cases'[83] and that indigenous people should have 'the right to require that States take account of their free and informed opinion in the approval of any project affecting their lands and their resources'.[84] Indigenous representatives continued to insist on the inclusion of a requirement to obtain FPIC,[85] insisting that 'a Government could not be negotiator and judge at the same time', and invoking the language of CERD's 1997 General Recommendation's FPIC requirement.[86] Those States opposed to FPIC's interpretation as a veto[87] insisted on the language to 'seek' consent, while those States supportive of indigenous peoples' position maintained that the operative verb had to be 'obtain' consent. The final wording, proposed by the Chair, of 'consult . . . in order to obtain their free and informed consent', while it maintained the verb 'obtain' represented a form of compromise between these positions, the nature of which is discussed in Chapter 5. Of fundamental importance for indigenous peoples was that FPIC remained framed as a derivation of an unqualified self-determination right to determine their own social, cultural and economic development.

78 UN Doc. E/CN.4/2000/84, para 95.
79 UN Doc. E/CN.4/2000/84, para 96.
80 UN Doc. E/CN.4/2000/84, para 92; For indigenous peoples' objections, see UN Docs. E/
    CN.4/2000/84, para 106 and E/CN.4/2001/85, para 115. See also *Wik Peoples v Queensland*
    [1996] HCA 40; (1996) 187 CLR 1; (1996) 141 ALR 129; (1996) 71 ALJR 173 (23 December
    1996); Brennan 1998.
81 UN Docs. E/CN.4/2002/98, para 42 and E/CN.4/2003/92, para 35.
82 UN Doc 1995/32 E/CN.4/1997/102, paras 251, 208.
83 UN Doc. E/CN.4/2003/92, para 46.
84 UN Doc 1995/32 E/CN.4/1997/102, para 280.
85 UN Docs. E/CN.4/1997/102, para 275; E/CN.4/2001/85, para 61; and E/CN.4/2002/98,
    para 40.
86 UN Docs E/CN.4/1997/102, para 282; and E/CN.4/1998/106, para 25.
87 France, Canada, Japan and Norway raised concerns in relation to consent as a veto. UN Doc. E/
    CN.4/1997/102, paras 209; 217.

4.3 The theory and sources of indigenous rights

Consideration of the bases for the requirement for FPIC under, and indeed beyond, international human rights law necessitates a brief engagement with who is recognised as indigenous and the related theory and sources of indigenous peoples' rights. Anaya explains that indigenous peoples are 'generally understood as groups that are descended from the original or long-time inhabitants of lands now dominated by others'.[88] Despite this succinct explanation which captures many possible aspects of indigenousness, such as historical and on-going connection with particular territories, collective identity and cultural distinctiveness, and non-dominance,[89] the question of who are indigenous peoples was one of the recurring and intractable issues addressed throughout the drafting of the UNDRIP.[90] Given the diversity of groups included under the concept and political opposition to an 'overly inclusive' classification, efforts to reach a sufficiently comprehensive definition, which would not exclude legitimate aspirants to the indigenous status, proved fraught with complications.[91] The pragmatic approach adopted by Daes during her chairmanship, and subsequently maintained as the neutral position when agreement on a definition proved impossible, was to dismiss the necessity of a definition and use Martínez Cobo's 'working definition' as a guide.[92] While the UNDRIP does not explicitly stipulate the characteristics of those groups to whom it applies, these characteristics nevertheless emerge from both the sources of rights it recognises and the rights which it affirms.[93] This broad and flexible definition of indigenous peoples which emerges tends to subsume the category of tribal peoples and suggests overlapping and fuzzy boundaries with other loosely defined categories such as peoples, minorities, and ethnic groups.[94] It could be argued that the emphasis on self-identification and the very absence of a fixed definition, despite the opposition of many States to such an open-ended approach to the determination of the rights holders, constitutes an important element of the indigenous rights framework, as it shifts the locus of control over legitimisation of membership of the 'community of indigenous peoples' to that community itself.[95] At the very least it implies that indigenous peoples are equal to all other peoples, vested with the rights to self-determination and self-identification,[96] and that indigenous consent is necessary to legitimise State classifications which should in no way infringe on the rights pertaining to these groups.

---

88 Anaya 2004: Preface.
89 Kingsbury 2001: 246.
90 Willemsen Díaz 2009: 30; Daes 2009: 54–55, 68; Henriksen 2009: 80; Chávez 2009: 99 and 103; Regino Montes and Torres Cisneros 2009: 150, 152–154; Barume 2009: 171, 174–175; Anaya 2009: 190–191; and Åhrén 2009: 202.
91 Castellino and Doyle forthcoming 2015.
92 Daes 2009: 48–77, 54.
93 Castellino and Doyle forthcoming 2014.
94 Ibid.
95 Ibid.
96 Corntassel 2003: 75.

The normative framework of indigenous peoples' rights which has emerged both from within and beyond the human rights regime is unique and *sui-generis* in nature.[97] Its uniqueness is evidenced by the fact that it is the first articulation of a framework of rights on the basis of the right of peoples to self-determination beyond the traditional decolonisation context.[98] In doing so, it broke the mould of the western individual rights philosophy which had underpinned the human rights regime since its inception, and expanded its content in at least two regards.[99] By drawing on indigenous philosophical conceptions and Cosmo visions it infused the heretofore normatively constrained human rights regime with a new collective rights discourse. This extended the rights regime beyond traditional conceptions based on individual human dignity, generally understood from western theories and conceptions of justice.[100] Individual rights nevertheless remain a core component of indigenous rights, sitting alongside collective conceptions of rights as derived from indigenous sources of law and philosophy, within a framework premised on justice, equality and non-discrimination.[101] As with individual human rights, the collective rights of indigenous peoples are recognised by the international community as 'inherent' in nature.[102] At the core of this framework is a revitalised concept of self-determination which demands the construction of a new relationship between States and indigenous peoples premised on mutual trust and equality, thereby drawing on long-established indigenous traditions and conceptions of justice.[103] While also drawing on the decolonisation and apartheid-inspired notions of self-determination, it offers new perspectives as to the meaning of self-determination and extends the scope of its subjects beyond those populations of classically defined territorial units with actual or potential claims to statehood.[104] In effect, this unqualified right to self-determination is, like the indigenous rights framework itself, *sui-generis* in nature, and has to be given content through a multiplicity of legal systems and perspectives. This *sui generis* nature of the contemporary indigenous rights framework is evidenced in the UNDRIP, which constitutes its most accomplished affirmation. The international community, through the UNDRIP, acknowledged a convergence of thinking around four distinct, yet interrelated, sources of indigenous rights, each of which is articulated in the UNDRIP's preamble and reflected throughout the document. These sources are: indigenous law and philosophies; treaties, agreements and other constructive arrangements between States and indigenous peoples; historical claims and the

---

97 For commentary on this rights framework, see Thornberry 2002; Anaya 2004; Xanthaki 2007; Kingsbury 2001; Castellino and Walsh (eds) 2005; Kymlicka 1999; for commentary on historical indigenous perspectives underpinning contemporary rights framework, see the works of Williams 1999 and Clavero 2002.
98 MacKay 2013: 1; Castellino 2008: 552–553.
99 Quane 2012: 77 also argues that it has served to expand on the content of human rights leading to a greater interdependency and indivisibility between rights.
100 Follesdal and Maliks 2014.
101 MacKlem 2007.
102 UNDRIP preamble.
103 Williams 1999: 136.
104 Quane 2012: 53.

related issue of remedial measures; and the principle of equality of all peoples. While some of these sources of rights will find greater traction than others in particular contexts, a predominant conceptual feature common to all four is their implication that indigenous peoples must have a central role in the articulation and operationalisation of their rights.

This first recognised source of rights is indigenous peoples' 'cultures, spiritual traditions, histories and philosophies' including their traditions, customs and laws.[105] The *sui generis* nature of the indigenous rights framework flows from the fact that it is premised on this recognition of indigenous law and philosophies as the source of rights. In doing so it embodies their distinctive custom-based relationships and connection with their lands, territories and resources and their legal systems governing this.[106] The use of the term *sui generis* as a descriptor of indigenous rights and associated body of law appears to have been first coined by academics in the 1970s.[107] The Canadian Supreme Court invoked the classification in 1984, and it has subsequently gained traction in judicial rulings and a range of academic commentary.[108] Indeed, the very category of 'indigenous peoples' has been characterised as a 'distinctive *sui generis* concept' 'important to the development of international legal norms and institutional practice'.[109] By extension, the *sui generis* classification applies to the legal claims associated with this distinct conceptual structure which underpins them.[110] This *sui generis* dimension of the indigenous rights framework seeks to capture 'the complex, overlapping, and exclusive identities and relationships' of indigenous and non-indigenous parties, extending to the interests indigenous peoples share with other parties as well as their own particular interests.[111] The recognition of the distinctive nature of these rights as flowing from indigenous law and philosophy can be traced back to the colonial encounter era, and is found in the very origins of colonial indigenous rights jurisprudence as well as in early treaty-making and agreement-making practices with indigenous peoples.[112] Even during the height of the positivist discourse, the inherent *sui generis* character and source of indigenous rights were implicitly recognised, as evidenced by the Privy Council's affirmation that 'indigenous peoples whose legal conceptions, though differently developed, are hardly less precise [or enforceable as rights] than our own'.[113]

This source of rights in indigenous custom, law and philosophy is closely related to the second recognised source of indigenous peoples' rights under the extant normative framework, namely 'treaties, agreements and other constructive

105 UNDRIP Preamble and Articles 9, 11, 12, 26, 27, 33, 34, 40.
106 Dannenmaier 2008.
107 Wilkinson and Volkman 1975: 612.
108 Borrows and Rotman 1997.
109 Kingsbury 1998: 441.
110 Kingsbury 2001.
111 Borrows and Rotman 1997: 11.
112 Ibid., citing *Mohegan Indians v Connecticut* (1705–1773); see also Walters 1995.
113 *Re Southern Rhodesia* 1919 A.C. 211 (P.C.), 234.

arrangements with States'.[114] As discussed in Chapter 1, where such treaties have been entered into under conditions approaching equality, they provide unique sources of law based on indigenous perspectives of law and justice. Their international character is acknowledged under the normative framework of indigenous rights which holds that in some situations they constitute 'matters of international concern, interest, responsibility and character'.[115] The wording 'treaties, agreements and other constructive arrangements' encompasses not only historical treaties with indigenous peoples primarily in settler States, but a range of more recent agreements involving indigenous peoples throughout the world.[116] As a source of rights it also recognises the potential for the expansion of the normative framework to address future constructive arrangements between indigenous peoples and States and acknowledges, if somewhat obliquely, the international legal personality of all indigenous peoples. This is consistent with the findings of the 1999 *UN Study on Treaties and Constructive Agreements between States and Indigenous Peoples*, which emphasised that the fact that many indigenous peoples never entered into treaties with States, or their colonial predecessors, does not undermine their status as 'peoples' or 'nations'.[117] Instead, the 'key question' is whether or not the indigenous peoples in question voluntarily surrendered this status, with the assumption being they did not, unless proven otherwise.[118] The notion of FPIC is inherent in both of these sources of rights, flowing from indigenous custom and law and representing a fundamental principle of agreement and treaty-making.

The third source relates to historical injustices resulting from colonisation and dispossession of lands, territories and resources, denying indigenous peoples the opportunity to exercise their rights, 'in particular, their right to development in accordance with their own needs and aspirations'.[119] Though not explicitly stated, this source of rights, which is invocative of the remedial dimensions of the indigenous rights framework,[120] relates to aspects of claims to historical sovereignty and rights which pre-exist the colonial encounter or the formation of contemporary States. Such historically based claims very rarely constitute claims for statehood, as these are constrained by the principle of territorial integrity as well as practical considerations arising from the small scale of most indigenous societies. They are nevertheless one of the sources for indigenous peoples' claims to rights over lands, territories and resources and to consent-based development. The related issue of indigenous legal personality and sovereignty, which has been buried in the annals of international law, remains equally obscured at the national level, with the United States being one of the few jurisdictions where the notion of indigenous sovereignty, albeit a restricted and legally fragile one, has been recognised by the

---

114 UNDRIP Preamble and Article 37.
115 UNDRIP Preamble.
116 Castellino and Doyle forthcoming 2015.
117 UN Doc E/CN.4/2004/111, 3.
118 UN Doc E/CN.4/Sub.2/1999/20, paras 284–288.
119 UNDRIP Preamble.
120 See Lenzerini (2008) and Anaya 2004, for a discussion on reparations and the remedial aspect of self-determination.

Courts.[121] Anaya acknowledges the important role that historical claims have in demonstrating the systematic nature of indigenous oppression as a result of State-imposed institutional arrangements, but suggests that arguments based on a 'human rights frame' addressing the present-day manifestations of past violations, associated inequality and on-going oppression tend to have greater traction with governments than those framed around notions of historical sovereignty within a 'state-centred frame'.[122] Others, such as McNeil, suggest that national courts will eventually have to address these historical sovereignty claims.[123] Undoubtedly, the historical sovereignty argument alone would not have delivered the unprecedented progress in the recognition of indigenous peoples' rights. However, while operating within the 'prevalent positivist conception' of international law as 'an expression of sovereign wills',[124] the human rights regime, through the indigenous rights framework, is nevertheless establishing the platform for indigenous peoples to reassert their own self-determined conception of sovereignty.[125] Such conceptions of sovereignty do not envisage a return to the *status quo ante*, but are related to a historically continuous, if legally unrecognised, *de facto* exercise of sovereignty. A core component of its realisation, in accordance with the principle of self-determination, is the assertion of decision-making rights, including FPIC, which seek to address the most pressing sovereignty-related issues facing contemporary indigenous peoples, in particular, the increasingly pervasive and profound impact of extractive activities in their ancestral territories.[126]

The fourth source of indigenous rights is the principle of equality of all peoples and the associated 'right of all peoples to be different, to consider themselves different, and to be respected as such'.[127] This, together with the recognition of indigenous peoples' 'political, economic and social structures'[128] as a source of rights, is the basis upon which indigenous peoples' unqualified right to self-determination has been affirmed and constitutes the foundation from which the panoply of indigenous peoples' collective rights flows. As a right to control cultural, social and economic development, it is, by extension, a right to protect against non-consensual interference with such development, or in the extreme case, should a people voluntarily so choose, a right to choose a development path which results in integration into or assimilation with other indigenous or non-indigenous peoples.[129] The recognition of this unqualified right to self-determination, and the associated collective rights which flow from its exercise, is also reflective of another *sui generis* aspect of the indigenous rights framework, namely, its negotiated nature. As a result of this nature, the rights it encapsulates are effectively direct

---

121 *Cherokee Nation v. Georgia* 30 U.S. 1 (1831).
122 Anaya 2005a: 237, 242–243.
123 McNeil 1998: 298.
124 O'Schachter 1998: 7.
125 Wiessner 2008.
126 Doyle and Gilbert 2009: 219.
127 UNDRIP Preamble.
128 UNDRIP Preamble.
129 Wiessner 2011: 122.

derivations of indigenous peoples' claims and consequently reflective of their perspectives.

Arguably the core aspects of all four sources of rights find expression in indigenous peoples' right to self-determination, as essentially the extant normative framework of indigenous peoples' rights can be understood as premised on the notion of equality of peoples, and the corresponding right of indigenous peoples, as peoples, to perpetuate their distinctive existence, while freely determining the conditions of that existence in accordance with their own aspirations. The exercise of this self-determination right is envisaged within a framework where all peoples mutually accommodate and respect each other's self-determination claims. How the right is exercised and operationalised, and by extension its actual content in specific contexts, will, to a certain degree, be a function of the particular needs, aspirations and characteristics of the indigenous peoples in question. The content of these new models of self-determination cannot be determined through traditional State-based structures as they must, along with the entire indigenous rights framework, be infused with indigenous philosophies of law and justice and lead to a rights-based consensual relationships with States and other actors.

4.4 On-going debates in relation to indigenous self-determination

The most significant outcome of the negotiations on the text of the UNDRIP was the affirmation of indigenous peoples' right to self-determination as affirmed in common Article 1(1). This right serves to inform and condition the constellation of indigenous peoples' rights and associated State obligations. During the initial engagement of the human rights regime with the notion of indigenous peoples' right to self-determination, debates tended to focus on whether the external dimension of the right was applicable to indigenous people and what its internal aspects entailed.[130] Considerable effort was expended on demonstrating that an inherent right of indigenous peoples to self-determination existed, and that this was compatible with the notion of State sovereignty.[131] The logic employed was consistent with the opinions of the International Court of Justice (ICJ), the supporting conclusions of eminent jurists, and UN studies on the issue of self-determination.[132]

The largely constructive critiques of the concept of indigenous self-determination which emerged were aimed at examining how indigenous peoples could ensure recognition of the right and maximise the potential for its recon-ceptualisation and meaningful exercise. In this context various conceptions of

130 Thornberry 1993; Daes 1993.
131 Aikio and Scheinin 2000.
132 *Western Sahara, Advisory Opinion, I.C.J. Reports 1975*, p. 12; *Legal Consequences for States of the Continued Presence of South Africa in Namibia (South West Africa) notwithstanding Security Council Resolution 276 (1970), Advisory Opinion, I.C.J. Reports, 1971*, p. 16; Cassese 1995: 128; Espiel 1978; and Cristescu 1981.

self-determination emerged. It was envisaged as embodying the right to make meaningful choices with regard to political status and development alternatives premised on free prior and informed consent.[133] It was also envisaged as an on-going right to resist territorial and structural encroachment.[134] Analysis grounded on constructivist approaches framed self-determination as a consensual relational right.[135] Viewed from a historical and contemporary perspective, emphasis was also placed on its remedial dimensions, as well as on its on-going political or constructive dimension.[136] The extensive debates as to whether the right should be limited to its internal dimension proved to a large degree to be much ado about nothing.[137] The issue was eventually addressed by the inclusion of a requirement that the right be exercised in accordance with the principles of international law pertaining to territorial integrity.[138] The implication is that for indigenous peoples, as for all peoples, where the right to freely determine their political status and development is denied, a right to secession may exist under international law.[139] The exclusion of any reference to an 'internal' only right also implies that some form of international guarantees must exist which ensure that the right can be fully exercised. Indigenous peoples' negotiating power with States is thereby amplified beyond that which they would have if the right were purely an internal one and points to the possibility of the emergence of mutually acceptable independent oversight, conciliation or arbitration mechanisms.

Such a scenario is catered for by the indigenous rights framework as reflected in Articles 19, 38 and 40 of the UNDRIP. When read together, they require States to cooperate and consult with indigenous people in order to obtain their free and informed consent prior to taking 'appropriate measures, including legislative measures, to achieve the ends of this Declaration'.[140] Negotiations on the basis of equality in relation to the operationalisation of the indigenous rights framework, including the right to self-determination, are therefore necessary. What is implied is a reconceptualisation of the rights to self-determination of the indigenous peoples and of the non-indigenous population of the State. Such a process should culminate in a constructive agreement between the State and indigenous peoples,

---

133 Anaya 2004: 290; Imai 2009: 292; Henriksen 1999: 27; Thornberry 2000; Daes 2000: 80; Kingsbury 2000: 26.
134 Imai 2009: 290; Lâm 2000: 60.
135 Kingsbury 2000: 26, 28; see also *International Workshop on the Draft United Nations Declaration on the Rights of Indigenous Peoples*, Patzcuaro, Michoacán, Mexico, 26–30 September 2005. Information provided by the Government of Mexico. UN Doc. E/CN.4/2005/WG.15/CRP.1 (29 November 2005), 5; and Canadian Royal Commission on Aboriginal Peoples 1996, *Looking Forward, Looking Back*, Chapter 2.
136 Anaya 2004.
137 See Castellino and Gilbert 2003: see also Anaya 2004: 97–115; Lâm 2000; Colchester and MacKay 2004: 3; Henriksen 1999: 14; Weissbrodt and Mahling 1994; Berman 1985: 190, 192.
138 See 1970 *Declaration on Principles of International Law concerning Friendly Relations and Cooperation among States in accordance with the Charter of the United Nations*, GA Res 2625, Annex, 25, UN GAOR, Supp. (No. 28), UN Doc. A/5217 at 121 (1970) and common Article 1(3) of the ICCPR and ICESCR; see also Quane 2011: 285.
139 Charters 2009: 164; see also *Reference re Secession of Quebec*, [1998] 2 S.C.R. 217, para 124.
140 UNDRIP Article 38.

premised on the principle that indigenous rights are 'in some situations, matters of international concern, interest, responsibility and character' and that conflicts of rights need to be addressed in accordance with principles of international law while also according due consideration to indigenous peoples' laws and legal systems.[141] Therefore, implicit in the indigenous rights framework is the notion that, where intractable issues arise and agreement cannot be reached with the State in relation to the realisation of their rights, recourse to external arbitration or mediation may be appropriate. A range of other non-secession-based aspects of the external right to self-determination may also apply to indigenous peoples. Practical examples include formal participation of indigenous governance institutions in international fora (such as the Norwegian Sami Parliament before the International Labour Organization),[142] powers to enter into trade agreements with States (such as the Navajo with Cuba's State food purchasing agency),[143] or development cooperation arrangements directly with foreign governments or between indigenous peoples themselves across national borders.[144]

The last 15 years have seen the emergence of some State practice recognising indigenous peoples as subjects of the right to self-determination.[145] However, despite the recognition of the applicability of common Article 1 to indigenous peoples and the termination of secession-related debates, the issue of indigenous self-determination continues to provoke a degree of scepticism among some commentators as to its moral legitimacy, and questions still arise as to scope of the right as it applies to indigenous peoples. Prior to the adoption of the UNDRIP, questions had been raised by Scheinin and Brownlie as to the unit to which the right of self-determination applied, supporting its recognition for some indigenous groups, but potentially challenging its application to others.[146] This issue was largely put to rest by the adoption of the UNDRIP and subsequent jurisprudence of human rights bodies. More recent critiques have suggested that indigenous peoples' right to self-determination is a privileged right vis-à-vis other groups in society.[147] A somewhat similar perspective holds that it is 'at odds with the moral logic of multiculturalism, and is politically unsustainable' on the grounds that the same right will not be extended to national minorities in international law.[148] Others describe it as a 'limited' right to self-determination to be realised through

---

141 UNDRIP Preamble, Article 40.
142 International Workshop on FPIC and Indigenous Peoples, *Contribution of the ILO* (Geneva: ILO, 2005), UN Doc. PFII/2005/WS.2/4, para 4.
143 Miller 2008: 1109; see also Comaroff and Comaroff 2009.
144 Miller 2008: 1109.
145 Article 2 of the Mexican Constitution (Constitución Política de los Estados Unidos Mexicanos, Reformada mediante Decreto Publicado en el Diario Oficial de la Federación el 14 de Agosto del 2001); Article 2 of the Bolivian Constitution (Constitución Política del Estado de Bolivia de 2009); Philippines *Indigenous Peoples Rights Act* 1997, Section 13; *Reference re Secession of Quebec*, [1998] 2 S.C.R. 217. See also HRC Concluding Observations to Canada, UN Doc. CCPR/C/79/Add.105 (7 April 1999); and Aguilar *et al.* 2010: 44.
146 Brownlie 1992: 48; Scheinin 2005: 12.
147 Allen 2011: 243.
148 Kymlicka 2011: 206–207.

a process of negotiation with States in which 'indigenous peoples' will . . . is not paramount'.[149] Another perspective holds that it embodies a limited resource dimension, without a right to control over sub-soil resources and to withhold consent to their exploitation.[150] Some of these commentators imply that the right to self-determination under the UNDRIP may have gone too far, while others suggest it has not gone far enough.[151]

While this summary represents a simplification of the arguments presented, it serves to highlight two basic premises, also asserted by States as potential grounds for limiting indigenous self-determination. One holds that indigenous peoples' right to self-determination lacks moral standing because the same right of self-determination will not be extended to other groups by States.[152] Recognition of the right to self-determination is therefore presented as representing differential treatment and as inconsistent with the equality argument upon which it was asserted.[153] The other more pragmatic argument holds that indigenous peoples will have to accept compromises as they effectively lack the power vis-à-vis the State to enforce those rights which would otherwise flow from the right to self-determination. It is therefore up to the States alone to 'spell out how they are going to reconcile the inevitable conflicts that will occur between competing self-determination rights'.[154]

The moral argument is questionable. It is true that international law currently distinguishes indigenous peoples from groups which do not pursue the status of peoplehood, while leaving unaddressed the question of other groups who do not self-identify as indigenous but who have legitimate claims to peoplehood.[155] However, the fact that the international community is currently unwilling to acknowledge the right to self-determination of other non-dominant peoples or groups is a dubious basis for denying indigenous peoples that right as it appears somewhat analogous to arguing that 'two wrongs make a right'. The moral argument underpinning indigenous peoples' claim to a right to self-determination on the basis of equality of peoples is not weakened by the potential immorality underpinning the position of States vis-à-vis other non-dominant groups or peoples. The equality argument invoked by indigenous peoples is premised on their right of self-determination vis-à-vis the right to self-determination of the dominant group in the State, based on a non-discriminatory interpretation of the principles of international law and distributive justice.[156] It is not an attempt to claim rights to which other peoples should not be entitled nor does it imply that other peoples are not entitled to those rights. This would be contrary to the manner in which the indigenous rights framework itself has evolved. That framework does

---

149 Quane 2011: 270.
150 Errico 2011: 364–366.
151 Contrasting, for example, Kymlicka 2011 with Engle 2011.
152 Kymlicka 2011: 206–207.
153 Allen 2011: 243.
154 Quane 2011: 279.
155 Kymlicka 1999: 284–286; Allen 2011: 243.
156 Macklem 1993: 1311; see also Anaya 2004: 97–115.

not foreclose the possibility of engaging with provisions framed under the minority rights or individual rights regimes, which affirm rights pertaining to indigenous peoples. Indeed, the framework is buttressed by an interpretation of such rights, informed by the right to self-determination, as manifested by the jurisprudence of the Human Rights Committee in the context of Articles 25 and 27 of the International Covenant on Civil and Political Rights (ICCPR) and the Committe on Economic, Social and Cultural Rights (CESCR) interpretation of Article 15 of the International Covenant on Economic, Social and Cultural Rights (ICESCR). The affirmation in this jurisprudence that the right to self-determination is vested in indigenous peoples is reflective of the fact that 'rights are generally tailored to, or triggered by, particular characteristics or needs (and thus in large part factually based)'.[157] Other groups whose needs, circumstances and characteristics merit recognition of similar rights should also be assessed on the basis of their particular claims.[158]

The pessimistic analysis, which holds that the rights affirmed in the UNDRIP are unsustainable because other groups will demand them, leading to their eventual denial as the 'firewall' buffering them collapses, can be countered by the optimistic perspective that indigenous peoples' rights have provided an opening for the assertion of collective rights, grounded in the right to self-determination, within what was essentially an individualistic rights framework that failed to cater to the reality of groups and peoples which exist within States.[159] As Thornberry notes, the 'human rights projects are an unfinished project'.[160] Furthermore, there is no inherent reason to believe that a model of State sovereignty and international order, premised on the recognition of collective rights, including the right to self-determination of peoples who form part of the overall population, is any less stable that one premised on individual rights. Indeed, strong arguments have been made to the contrary.[161]

Another argument that supports indigenous peoples' right to self-determination is the fact that the right to self-determination is increasingly affirmed in contexts in which identity and participation are recognised 'as elements of equality'.[162] Within such a context, international law appears to have moved beyond undifferentiated rights as a basis of realising *de facto* equality.[163]

The second critique, which invokes pragmatism as a reason for accepting certain State-imposed limitations on indigenous self-determination, raises two concerns. The first is that, in the context of resource extraction, the pragmatic argument potentially underestimates the pressure indigenous peoples can and do exert on

---

157 MacKay 2013: 3.
158 Ibid.
159 Stavenhagen 2011: 162; see also Kymlicka 2011: 201–208.
160 Thornberry 2011: 90.
161 Van Dyke 1982: 21–40; see also Van Dyke 1985; Freeman 1995: 25–40, Holder and Corntassel 2002: 126; and Sanders 1991: 368.
162 Knop 2002: 110; see also Goodland 1985: 14.
163 Kymlicka 1995: 45–48.

States through local-level resistance and international campaigns.[164] These strategies of resistance, which vary in nature from legal and political to more direct forms of action, are in themselves an exercise of self-determination and have been particularly effective in the context of resource extraction where they have led to major projects being stalled by decades, at times resulting in their cancellation, or forcing States and corporations to enter into mutually acceptable agreements with indigenous peoples which recognise their decision-making powers.[165] They are frequently responsible for bringing the opposing parties to the table in order to negotiate on a rights basis, in influencing national or international mechanisms when considering the extent to which indigenous rights have been respected, and in driving policy change among actors with power to influence the State.[166]

The second concern with the pragmatic argument is that it may be somewhat of a self-fulfilling prophesy. If the starting premise is that indigenous peoples' right to self-determination is limited by the power of the State, then there is limited possibility for indigenous peoples to invoke that right in order to challenge the inappropriate exercise of State power. A 'limited right to self-determination' suggests that States can legitimately place, what they consider to be, reasonable constraints on its exercise. This fails to alter the power dynamics between indigenous peoples and States and perpetuates a fiduciary-type relationship which negates the transformative potential of the right to self-determination.[167]

The fact that the unqualified right to self-determination, as affirmed in common Article 1 of the Covenants, is recognised as applying to indigenous peoples, suggests that discussions pertaining to any limitations on that right should be considered in light of the drafting history of common Article 1. During the drafting process, proposals that the substance of the right be outlined in 'a concrete form' were rejected on the grounds that 'any enumeration of the components of the right of self-determination was likely to be incomplete. A statement of the right in an abstract form, as in paragraph 1 of the Article, was thought to be preferable.'[168] This same logic should now apply to indigenous peoples' right to self-determination. To hold *a priori* that indigenous peoples have a limited right to self-determination, without first considering the potential limitations this self-determination right may impose on the right of self-determination of other peoples in the State, would appear inconsistent with the principles of equality and

164 Zibechi 2012; Laplante and Spears 2008: 72–78.
165 See Report of the Office of the United Nations High Commissioner for Human Rights, *International Workshop on Natural Resource Companies, Indigenous Peoples and Human Rights: Setting a Framework for Consultation, Benefit-Sharing and Dispute Resolution*, Moscow, 3–4 December 2008 (Geneva: OHCHR, 2009) (notes of meeting on file with author). See also Mander and Tauli-Corpuz 2006: 139–152; see also Caruso and Colchester 2005; see also Evans, Goodman and Lansbury 2002.
166 Doyle and Cariño 2013.
167 Calma 2003.
168 UN Doc. A/2929 (1953), para 15.

non-discrimination. Instead, where the exercise of those self-determination rights comes into conflict, a dialogue premised on equality may require a reconceptualisation of, and limitation on, the right of self-determination of all 'peoples' within the State,[169] including that of indigenous peoples.[170]

It is suggested here that indigenous peoples themselves should be the ones to decide where lines of compromise in relation to their right to self-determination are to be drawn. The compromises which are necessary and acceptable will differ by community, people, national jurisdiction and region, leading to a diversity of self-determined outcomes.[171] Viewed from this perspective, rights to internal autonomy, self-government, participation and consent represent some of the components of the abstract right to self-determination, but fail to capture all its potential modalities and outcomes.[172] A constructive suggestion, which may help shift the locus of power from State organs and ground the resolution of disputes in relation to the exercise of the right to self-determination on a more principled human rights basis, is the establishment of a 'permanent good offices commission' under the auspices of the UN to assist in seeking negotiated solutions where conflicts and seemingly intractable issues arise in relation to the exercise of the right.[173] Finally, the potential for a tension to arise between self-determination and human rights programmes has been noted, particularly in relation to issues such as group membership and identity.[174] Another possibility raised is that self-determination could be facilitative of indigenous nationalism premised on the notions of indigenous nations' superiority over other nations.[175] As with States, indigenous peoples' sovereignty and self-determination are conditioned by respect for minimum human rights standards, including the principle of non-discrimination.[176] The diversity of opinion and perspectives across the international community of 193 UN Member States with regard to their obligations in relation to particular universal human rights is reflected in the UPR process and could potentially offer evidence of *opinio juris* in relation to a degree of cultural sensitivity regarding the process of realisation of these standards, while simultaneously rejecting cultural relativism as a basis for their non-applicability.[177] An equal, or even greater, diversity of perspectives with regard to approaches toward implementing these rights across the global community of thousands of indigenous peoples can be expected. The availability of fora such as the Experts Mechanism, the Permanent

---

169 Quane 2011: 279, 286; see also Quane 2005: 666.
170 Thornberry 2011; see also *Statement of M Ahren on behalf of the Arctic Council under Agenda Item 3, Study on Indigenous People's right to participate in decision-making*, Experts Mechanism on the Rights of Indigenous Peoples, 3rd session, July 2010, available at: www.docip.org
171 Barsh 1994: 78; Erueti 2011: 109–110; see also Knop 2002: 212–275.
172 Imai 2009; Thornberry 2000: 51; see also Barsh 1994: 78.
173 Weyl and Weyl 2008; cited in Özden and Golay 2010: 61.
174 Kingsbury 2001–2002: 237.
175 Niezen 2003: 200–202; Thornberry 2011: 86, noting CERD's engagement with the case of 'Fiji about indigenous rights not overbearing the rights of others'.
176 Wiessner 2008: 1175.
177 Statistics on States' positions and the issues raised during the UPR process can be found in the database developed by the NGO 'UPR Info', available at: www.upr-info.org/database/statistics

Forum and other non-UN regional indigenous gatherings and networks provide a context within which the community of indigenous peoples can converge on commonly shared perspectives with regard to culturally sensitive human rights operationalisation.

Others challenge the normative framework of indigenous rights, in particular, the UNDRIP, as a basis for indigenous assertions of self-determination, suggesting that it has been overly compromised in the negotiation process, which focused too much attention on cultural rights rather than genuine autonomy. The critique flows from a view that the post-Cold War era human rights project is ideologically aligned with neo-liberalism which 'eschews strong forms of indigenous self-determination and privileges individual civil and political rights'.[178] Rather than seek to strengthen this indigenous framework's legal architecture, they question the human rights foundations underpinning it. These concerns reflect the opposition which indigenous peoples faced in the negotiation of the UNDRIP and the compromises to which this gave rise, including the compromise on the wording of the FPIC requirement from the 1994 draft text. They also point to the political obstacles indigenous peoples will face in asserting their rights. As with the suggestion that a limited form of self-determination emerges from the UNDRIP, this ideological critique perhaps also underestimates what indigenous peoples have achieved in terms of the UNDRIP's content (as will be argued in relation to the FPIC requirement in Chapter 5). It may also underestimate their capacity to mobilise and pursue their own self-determination projects in pragmatic ways by drawing on the aspects of the rights regime which further their political ends. The negotiated nature of the UNDRIP inevitably implied compromise. However, as Daes notes, its normative nature has the potential to drive cultural and political transformation while enabling indigenous peoples to critique and challenge any potential right-limiting provisions, such as the affirmation of territorial integrity or the political unity of sovereign States or the justification of militarisation on the basis of a relevant public interest.[179] The UNDRIP as a component of the international normative indigenous rights framework affirms rights which supersede national legislation.[180] That framework draws on a multiplicity of conceptual sources, including indigenous law and philosophies, suggesting that its foundation runs deep, and providing a basis for optimism that the human rights project is capable of reconciliation with indigenous self-determination, leading to the flourishing of indigenous identity and autonomy.

In practice, complex scenarios will inevitably arise where an appropriately contextualised combination of consequentialist and non-consequentialist approaches may be required to resolve tensions between collective indigenous self-determination rights and the individual human rights of members of those groups. However, while affirming the individual rights of members of indigenous peoples

---

178 Engle 2011: 142.
179 Daes 2011: 38; UNDRIP Articles 30 and 46.
180 Ibid.

as well as the collective rights of the group, the normative framework of indigenous rights does not assume that States should make decisions for indigenous peoples as to how to resolve these tensions. Indeed, requiring indigenous consent for any measures impacting on their self-determination projects will be a crucial determinant in ensuring that this is not the case. The constraints of State territorial integrity and potential tensions between collective and individual human rights may pose certain challenges to the pursuit of indigenous self-determination. In some cases, the potential for elites within indigenous communities to take advantage of the rights framework for their own ends will also serve to undermine genuine self-determination. The response to these challenges will be context-specific. However, for most indigenous communities and their members, a greater challenge which is likely to remain is how to assert their decision-making power vis-à-vis external actors with vested interests over resource-rich indigenous territories. It is for this reason that the requirement for indigenous-controlled FPIC associated with the unqualified right to self-determination remains so central to indigenous struggles.

The concept of self-determination which emerges from the normative framework of indigenous peoples' rights, and is most clearly manifested in the UNDRIP, represents a radical transformation and expansion of the classical concept. It no longer constitutes a one-off outcome-orientated right, primarily aimed at establishing the conditions under which consent to independence can be granted within a territorially defined unit. Instead, in the indigenous context, it is widened to represent an on-going right. The exercise of that right enables indigenous people to determine the conditions of their existence on the basis of equality with other peoples, with their consent required in a manner determined by them, whenever others seek to alter those conditions. Subsequent chapters will examine the contours and content of that consent requirement, progress towards, and obstacles to, its implementation, and the conditions which are necessary for this to be realised in a rights-consistent manner.

5 FPIC and the normative framework of indigenous peoples' rights

5.1 Introduction

Commencing in 1997 with the Committee on the Elimination of Racial Discrimination's (CERD) General Recommendation XXIII on the rights of indigenous peoples, affirmations of the requirement for free prior and informed consent (FPIC) under the human rights and environmental regimes, as well as other normative frameworks and voluntary standards, have gradually become the norm in the context of resource exploitation impacting on indigenous peoples.[1] This trend has been particularly notable following the adoption of the UN Declaration on the Rights of Indigenous Peoples (the UNDRIP) in 2007 which contains no fewer than six references to the requirement to obtain FPIC. A substantial body of jurisprudence has emerged at the international, regional and national levels elaborating on the content, scope and trigger mechanisms of FPIC. This chapter aims to provide an overview of some of the sources under human rights law and other emerging international standards, of the requirement. Drawing on these sources, it examines the bases for the requirement in terms of the rights which underpin it; the nature of the requirement as a duty, a right, a principle and a safeguard under international human rights law; who the subjects are to whom the duty to obtain FPIC is owed, and the scope of its content and its trigger mechanisms, with a particular focus on the elaboration of this content under the UNDRIP.[2]

5.2 Bases for the requirement for FPIC

The requirement for indigenous peoples' FPIC is derived from a range of collective rights. The Committee on Economic Social and Cultural Rights (CESCR) has affirmed the requirement in light of the right 'to own, develop, control and use their communal lands, territories and resources',[3] and has increasingly linked it

---

1 Doyle 2008.
2 *Declaration on the Rights of Indigenous Peoples*, G.A. Res. 61/295, UN Doc. A/RES/47/1 (2007) (henceforth UNDRIP in the footnotes).
3 General Comment 21, Right of everyone to take part in cultural life (Article 15, para 1 (a), of the ICESCR) UN Doc. E/C.12/GC/21, 21 December 2009, (GE.09–46922), paras 36–37.

with the right to self-determination and cultural rights.[4] The Human Rights Committee (HRC), under its optional protocol jurisprudence, has effectively held that the requirement for consent emerges from a self-determination-informed right of indigenous peoples to maintain their culture and way of life and to participate in decisions impacting on them. A component of this is a right to continue to 'benefit from their traditional economy' which necessitates non-interference with 'culturally significant economic activities'.[5] In the HRC's concluding observations the requirement is affirmed in light of the right to self-determination, cultural rights, effective remedies, non-discrimination and the derivative rights to lands.[6] In a range of concluding observations, and under its early warning urgent action and follow-up procedures, CERD has addressed the requirement for consent in the general context of non-discriminatory impacts on indigenous peoples' rights and interests,[7] and specifically in relation to the rights to land and resources,[8] culture,[9] ability to pursue their traditional way of life[10] and traditional lifestyles,[11] enjoyment of their economic, social and cultural rights,[12] customary laws and practices,[13] the rights to life and physical safety and freedom of movement.[14] Under CERD's General Recommendation XXIII, the requirement emerges from the non-discriminatory enjoyment of the rights of indigenous peoples to, *inter alia*, culture, economic, social and cultural development, participation, property, including lands and natural resources, and effective remedies.[15]

---

4 Colombia, UN Doc. E/C.12/COL/CO/5 (21 May 2010); Sri Lanka UN Doc. E/C.12/LKA/CO/2–4, 9 December 2010; Argentina, UN Doc. E/C.12/ARG/CO/3; UN Doc. E/C.12/RUS/CO/5, para 7b, 11 May 2011.

5 *HRC Angela Poma Poma v Peru, Communication No. 1457/2006 CCPR/C/95/D/1457/2009, 24 April 2009, paras 7.6, 7.7.*

6 HRC Concluding Observations to Panama, UN Doc. CCPR/C/PAN/CO/3, 17 April 2008, para 21. Nicaragua, UN Doc. CCPR/C/NIC/CO/3, (12 December 2008), para 21, citing Articles 26 and 27 Inter-American Court of Human Rights and *The Mayagna (Sumo) Awas Tingni Community v. Nicaragua*, Inter-Am. Ct. H.R., (ser. C) No. 79, 31 Aug. 2001; Colombia, UN Doc. CCPR/C/COL/CO/6, 4 August 2010, para 25, citing Articles 2, 26 and 27; UN Doc. CCPR/C/TGO/CO/4, para 21, citing Articles 2 and 27. See also CERD Urgent Action Decisions: United States (2006) UN Doc. CERD/C/USA/DEC/1; *Suriname* (2005) UN Doc. CERD/C/DEC/SUR/2.

7 UN Doc. CERD/C/GUY/CO/14, 4 April 2006, para 14.

8 UN Doc. CERD/C/IND/CO/19, 5 MAY 2007, para 19; UN Doc. CERD/C/PHL/CO/20, 28 August 2009, paras 24, 25; CERD Early Warning Urgent Action letter to Canada, 15 August 2008; UN Doc. CERD/C/USA/DEC/1 (b), 11 April 2006; CERD Early Warning Urgent Action letter to Peru, 13 March 2009.

9 UN Doc. CERD/C/ECU/CO/19, 15 August 2008, para 16, Article 5(d)(v).

10 UN Doc. CERD/C/ETH/CO/15, 20 June 2007, para 22, Article 5(c), (d) and (e).

11 UN Doc. CERD/C/IND/CO/19, 5 May 2007, para 19.

12 UN Doc. CERD/C/LAO/CO/15, 18 April 2005, para 18, Article 5.

13 UN Doc. CERD/C/PHL/CO/20, 28 August 2009, paras 24, 25; CERD Early Warning Urgent Action letter to Philippines, 24 August 2007.

14 CERD Guatemala, 15 August 2008, Follow-up (Letter).

15 General Recommendation XIII; Concluding Observations to the Philippines 2009 and Guyana 2006; CERD Early Warning Urgent Action letter to Peru, 13 March 2010; CERD Follow-up Letters to Government of Australia, 18 August 2006; Government of Guatemala, 15 August 2008, Government of Canada, 12 March 2010; Government of Chile, 27 August 2010.

The Special Rapporteur on the rights of indigenous peoples adopted the extractive industry as a thematic focus of his mandate from 2011 to 2014. He has repeatedly addressed the issue of FPIC in his annual reports to the Human Rights Council, in communications and statements to governments, and in his commentaries on particular controversial projects such as the Marlin mine in Guatemala and the El Diquis dam in Costa Rica.[16] In his comments, the Special Rapporteur explained that under contemporary human rights law, indigenous peoples' consent is required for measures which have a potentially substantial impact on indigenous peoples' basic physical or cultural well-being[17] or on their lands, territories or natural resources.[18] The rights implicated include indigenous peoples' rights to property, to cultural integrity, to equality, to participation, to development and to self-determination as well as the 'related principles of democracy and popular sovereignty' conditioned by indigenous peoples' 'distinctive cultural patterns and histories'.[19] The requirement is also closely related to respect for rights flowing from indigenous customary land tenure.[20] According to the Special Rapporteur, the inevitability of extractive projects infringing on one or more of these rights gives rise to a 'general rule that indigenous consent is required for extractive activities within indigenous territories'.[21]

In 2003, the former Special Rapporteur on the situation of human rights and fundamental freedoms of indigenous peoples (subsequently renamed the Special Rapporteur on the rights of indigenous peoples), described FPIC as being of 'crucial concern' in relation to decision-making rights concerning large-scale development projects,[22] and concluded that due to the significant potential impacts, '[f]ree, prior and informed consent is essential for the [protection of the] human rights of indigenous peoples in relation to major development projects'.[23] The Special Rapporteur on the right to food has affirmed that, under international law, indigenous peoples have been afforded 'specific forms' of land rights which, in light of their rights to self-determination and development, includes the requirement to consult them in order to obtain their FPIC.[24]

In its 2007 ruling, in the case of *Saramaka v. Suriname*, which addressed mining concessions issued in the territory of the Saramaka people absent their consent,

16 UN Doc. A/HRC/9/9/Add.1, 15 August 2008, Annex 1; 'Declaración pública del Relator Especial sobre los derechos humanos y libertades fundamentales de los indígenas, James Anaya, sobre la "Ley del derecho a la consulta previa a los pueblos indígenas u originarios reconocido en el Convenio No. 169 de la Organización Internacional de Trabajo" aprobada por el Congreso de la República del Perú', 7 de julio de 2010. See also UN Docs. A/HRC/18/35/Add.3 (2011); and A/HRC/18/35/Add.8 (2011).
17 UN Doc. A/HRC/9/9/Add.1, Annex 1, ibid.: para 39.
18 UN Doc. A/HRC/18/35/Add.3 (2011), para 41; UN Doc. A/HRC/12/34 (2009), paras 47–49.
19 UN Doc. A/HRC/12/34 (2009), paras 41, 42. These rights underpin the duty to consult with the objective of consent.
20 UN Doc A/HRC/24/41 (2013), para 27.
21 UN Doc A/HRC/24/41 (2013), para 28.
22 UN Doc. E/CN.4/2003/90, (2003), para 13.
23 Ibid.: para 66.
24 UN Doc.A/HRC/12/31 (2009), para 21(j).

the Inter-American Court of Human Rights held that the right to give or withhold consent is premised on the nature of the impact to indigenous peoples' self-determination-informed right to property over their lands, territories and natural resources.[25] The Court linked the requirement for FPIC to impacts on the integrity of the lands and to the right of indigenous and tribal peoples to cultural and physical survival.[26] In its 2012 decision, in the case of *Sarayaku v Ecuador*, which addressed oil exploration activities in Sarayaku territory, the Court also affirmed that the duty to consult, with its associated objective of consent, is derived from the right to cultural integrity.[27] The ruling placed a particular emphasis on the 'prior' dimension of consultations holding that, in order for the community to have the potential to influence the decision-making process, this had to occur at the initial stages of planning and not only at the point in time when the community's approval was sought.[28] While the ruling affirmed that consent had to be the objective of consultations, it remained silent on consent as a required outcome and consequently did not expand on the substantive dimension of FPIC.[29]

The Inter-American Commission, for its part, has argued that the requirement for consent is derived not only from the right to property and non-discrimination,[30] but also 'the right to life, cultural identity and other essential human rights, in relation to the execution of development plans or investments that affect those rights'.[31] This extension of the bases for the consent requirement beyond the right to property is of fundamental importance, given that Article 21 of the American Convention allows for the right's subordination and deprivation on grounds of public utility or social interest.[32] This aspect of the right to property under Article 21 was noted by the Court in the 2007 *Saramaka v Suriname* ruling. The limitation on their right to property was, however, made subject to the requirement not to 'deny their survival as a tribal people', with any activities threatening this triggering the FPIC requirement.[33] Establishing the FPIC trigger threshold as threats to a people's cultural or physical survival potentially exposes indigenous peoples to adverse impacts which a lower threshold would avoid. By affirming, as the

---

25 *Saramaka People v. Suriname*, Judgment of November 28, 2007 (Preliminary Objections, Merits, Reparations, and Costs) Inter-Am. Ct. H.R., (Ser. C) No. 172 (2007).

26 *Saramaka People v. Suriname* (Interpretation) Judgment of August 12, 2008. Series C No. 185, paras 17, 37; *Saramaka v. Suriname* (2007), op. cit. 25, paras 129–134.

27 Inter-American Court of Human Rights, Case of *Pueblo Indígena Kichwa de Sarayaku v. Ecuador. Fondo y reparaciones.* Judgment of June 27, 2012. (Only in Spanish) Series C, No. 245, paras 212–220.

28 Ibid.: para 177.

29 Ibid.: paras 185–186.

30 Inter-American Commission of Human Rights Report No. 27/98 (Nicaragua), para 142, quoted in *Awas Tingni v. Nicaragua* (2001), op. cit. 6, para 25; and *Mary and Carrie Dann v. United States*, Case 11.140, Report No. 75/02, Inter-Am. C.H.R., Doc. 5 rev. 1 at 860 (2002), para 165.

31 (Author's translation.) Resolución del Presidente de la Corte Interamericana de Derechos Humanos, 17 de junio de 2011, Caso *Pueblo Indígena Kichwa De Sarayaku v Ecuador* (2012), op. cit. 27, para 29.

32 Article 21(b) and (c) of the convention; see also Shelton 2011: 77.

33 *Saramaka v Suriname* (2007), op. cit. 25 at 127.

Commission has done, that FPIC is derived from other non-property rights, such as the right to cultural identity and right to life, the trigger threshold is lowered significantly, as these rights are subject to a much narrower range of limitations.

In its 2009 *Endorois v Kenya* ruling, which addressed tourism and prospecting for rubies in Endorois traditional lands, the African Commission on Human and Peoples Rights invoked the aforementioned jurisprudence of the Inter-American system and concluded that the requirement for consent was a derivation of the right to property and the peoples' right to development.[34] The broader range of rights, affirmed under the African Convention and the interpretation of the African Commission that the collective rights of peoples, such as the rights to development and natural resources, are vested in indigenous peoples, provides a stronger normative underpinning for the consent requirement than affirmed by the Inter-American Court.

Taken together, this body of jurisprudence indicates that the requirement for consent constitutes the canopy for, and is a derivative of, a myriad of human rights, *inter alia* the right to self-determination and self-determined development, the right to property – including traditionally owned lands, territories and resources and associated customary laws – the right to practise traditional livelihoods, and collective dimensions of rights to health, food, life, housing, participation and cultural rights. The requirement for FPIC is further buttressed by (a) the necessity of guaranteeing indigenous peoples' cultural and physical survival; (b) ensuring they can maintain and transmit their historical identity, and (c) the need to cater to their particular historical contexts.[35] This latter point relates to the extent of violations of their rights associated with imposed extractive projects as well as the historical and non-surrendered sovereignty of indigenous peoples, both those which entered into treaties and agreements with States and those who did not.

As with its predecessor under the law of nations and natural law, at the core of this contemporary human rights law-based consent requirement is the recognition of indigenous peoples as peoples, equal to all other peoples, whose sovereign and self-determined perspectives and decisions with regard to their social, cultural and economic development must be respected. Where it differs from its predecessor is that this self-determination requirement mandates the indigenous definition of the concept and control over its implementation.

5.3 Nature of the requirement for FPIC

The right to self-determination constitutes the primary foundation of the requirement for FPIC in the context of development projects in or near indigenous peoples' territories. The Human Rights Committee (HRC), the Committee on

34 African Commission on Human and Peoples' Rights, Case 276/2003 – *Centre for Minority Rights Development (Kenya) and Minority Rights Group International on behalf of Endorois Welfare Council v Kenya* (2009), paras 226, 291, 293 and 296.
35 EMRIP (2011) A/HRC/18/42, para 22; CERD General Recommendation XXIII.

Economic Social and Cultural Rights (CESCR) and the Committee on the Elimination of Racial Discrimination (CERD) have all clarified that this right applies to indigenous peoples.[36] This was also recognised by the UN General Assembly when it adopted the UNDRIP in 2007. The relationship between FPIC and self-determination is a mutually reinforcing one. The imposition of development projects denies indigenous peoples the possibility of determining their own development priorities. Therefore, to realise the developmental aspect of the right to self-determination, indigenous peoples must be able to withhold consent. Conversely genuine choice, implicit in the notion of granting informed consent, is only possible if a people has been afforded the possibility of considering developmental alternatives and determining priorities in advance of making such a choice. Viewed from this perspective, FPIC is integral to the right to self-determination, being not only necessary to prevent unwanted developments, but also essential in ensuring that indigenous peoples shape developments by and for themselves.[37]

The requirement for good faith consultations, which aim to achieve consent, and the requirement to respect the outcome of those consultations are clearly interdependent. As a result, to be effective, guidance has to address both the procedural and substantive aspects of the requirement. Prior to 2007, human rights treaty bodies frequently limited their recommendations to the requirement to 'seek' consent, without necessarily making reference to the requirement to respect its outcome.[38] Rather than constituting a restriction on the substantive aspect of FPIC, these recommendations instead reflect the need to address the widespread and glaring procedural and institutional deficiencies associated with consultations before the requirement's substantive aspect can be realised.[39] This interpretation is consistent with the fact that, following the adoption of the UNDRIP, all three treaty bodies which are most engaged with indigenous rights have, in general, been consistent in their usage of unambiguous language which affirms not only a requirement to 'seek' consent but also to guarantee that consent is obtained or secured.[40] Taken as a whole, this body of jurisprudence therefore clarifies the mandatory aspects of the FPIC process necessary for respect of indigenous peoples' rights.

To date, CERD has been the most engaged and innovative international human rights body on the subject of FPIC. Its General Recommendation XXIII, issued in 1997, on the Rights of Indigenous Peoples states that 'no decisions directly

---

36 Doyle forthcoming 2015; Gilbert and Doyle 2011.
37 Doyle and Gilbert 2009: 219; Raja Devasish Roy, an indigenous leader from Bangladesh, has suggested that the acronym FPIC might more appropriately be understood as referring to 'Free Prior and Informed Choice', author's discussion with Raja Devasish Roy, Geneva, 2009.
38 CESCR: Mexico UN Doc. E/C.12/MEX/CO/4 9 June 2006, para 28; Canada UN Doc. E/C.12/CAN/CO/5, 19 May 2006, para 38.
39 See Chapter 9.
40 For example, see Ecuador UN Doc. CERD/C/ECU/CO/19 15 (2008); CERD's Early Warning Urgent Action letter to the Philippine Government (7 March 2008) and HRC *Poma-Poma v Peru* UN Doc. CCPR/C/95/D/1457/2006 (24 April 2009).

relating to their rights and interests are [to be] taken without their informed consent'.[41] Its increased emphasis on the requirement to obtain FPIC is evident in its concluding observations to States,[42] its follow-up procedure and its examination of cases in the context of its Early Warning Urgent Action procedure.[43] The CESCR has also significantly increased its focus on the consent requirement, with unambiguous affirmations of it under its General Comment no. 21 and its concluding observations.[44] The HRC has likewise affirmed the requirement under its concluding observations in 2008, 2010, 2011, and 2012 and under its individual complaint jurisprudence in 2009.[45]

All three treaty bodies have affirmed that indigenous peoples have a 'right to free prior and informed consent'.[46] This notion that giving or withholding free prior and informed consent constitutes a right also finds support in the statements of a number of UN Special Rapporteurs.[47] One of the earliest affirmations of such a right is found in the 2003 report of the Special Rapporteur on the situation of human rights and fundamental freedoms of indigenous peoples, which clarified that the 'right to free prior and informed consent by indigenous peoples' includes the 'right to say no' in the context of large-scale development projects.[48] In 2007, the Inter-American Court of Human Rights, in *Saramaka People v Suriname*, also affirmed the existence of a 'right to give or withhold their free prior and informed consent' in cases where there exists a potentially major impact to a community's cultural or physical well-being.[49] Logically, if self-determination is conceived of as a right to choose, then FPIC is the aspect of that right which allows a people to refuse a particular option and select the alternative. As such, the conception of FPIC as a right (or rather a right to give or withhold FPIC) flows from the fact that it is an exercise of the right to self-determination and necessary for its realisation.

The Special Rapporteur on the rights of indigenous peoples has on occasion referred to FPIC as a right, but has also argued that it should not be conceived of

---

41 CERD, General Recommendation XXIII, para 4(d).
42 For example, Ecuador UN Doc. CERD/C/ECU/CO/19 (2008), Russia UN Doc. CERD/C/RUS/CO/19 20 (2008), and Philippines UN Doc. CERD/C/PHL/CO/20 (2009).
43 See Doyle forthcoming 2015.
44 Ibid.
45 Ibid.
46 For example, see CESCR: UN Doc. E/C.12/COL/CO/5 (2010), para 9; HRC: Togo UN Doc. CCPR/C/TGO/CO/4 (2011), para 21; CERD: Early Warning Urgent Action letter to Peru, dated 2nd September 2011.
47 Report of the independent expert on minority issues, Gay McDougall Addendum Mission to Colombia, 25 January 2011; UN Doc. A/HRC/16/45/Add.1 para 78; see also Statement of Special Rapporteur on the right to participation, to the EMRIP, 2010, 12 July 2010, 3; and Statement by Professor James Anaya, Special Rapporteur on the Situation of the Human Rights and Fundamental Freedoms of Indigenous People, Ninth Session of the UN Permanent Forum on Indigenous Issues, 22 April 2010, New York, at 4; and Report of the Special Rapporteur on adequate housing as a component of the right to an adequate standard of living, UN Doc. A/HRC/4/18 (11 June 2007), Annex 1, Basic Principles and Guidelines on Development-based Evictions and Displacement, paras 55(e), 56(b).
48 Stavenhagen, UN Doc. E/CN.4/2003/90 (2003), paras 13 and 66.
49 *Saramaka People v. Suriname*, Judgment of 28 November 2007 (Preliminary Objections, Merits, Reparations, and Costs), Inter-Am. Ct. H.R., (Ser. C) No. 172 (2007), para 194(d).

as a 'stand-alone right' or an end in itself.[50] The notion of FPIC as a non-stand-alone right is consistent with the principle that all human rights are interrelated, interdependent and indivisible.[51] What the Special Rapporteur's suggestion implies is that the requirement for FPIC cannot be abstracted from the rights its purpose is to protect. This suggestion resonates with similar arguments addressing individual consent which hold that consent is not a 'free-standing principle' and must be supported by a right which it aims to protect.[52] By extension it has argued that a failure to obtain an individual's consent where no right is violated does not constitute a wrong.[53] This reasoning could also be applied in contexts where there is no potential infringement of indigenous peoples' rights as a result of a proposed measure. However, proceeding with an extractive project or activity which has a potential impact on indigenous peoples' enjoyment of their rights, including the free pursuit of their economic, social and cultural development, without having obtained consent, would represent an infringement of the right to self-determination, as giving or withholding consent is by definition an exercise of that right. It has also been posited, in the context of the individual consent requirement in the medical sphere, that if consent is divorced from the notion of individual autonomy and ownership over, and integrity of, the body, that 'informed consent will remain a hollow aspiration'.[54] An analogy exists with the collective consent requirement of indigenous peoples, which would also remain a hollow aspiration, if divorced from their collective right to self-determination, cultural and territorial integrity, and ownership of lands, territories and resources. In such a scenario, consent runs the risk of being transformed into something which undermines the realisation of the rights it aims to protect.

An alternative, complementary, position to envisaging FPIC as a right frames the requirement to obtain it as a duty of the State. This position emerges from the 2011 advice of the Experts Mechanism on the Rights of Indigenous Peoples (EMRIP) to States in the context of indigenous peoples' right to participation in decision-making. The mechanism held that 'The State's duty to obtain free, prior and informed consent affirms the prerogative of indigenous peoples to withhold consent and to establish terms and conditions for their consent.'[55] This argument which frames consent as a prerogative, while, on the surface, less empowering for indigenous peoples than a perspective which affirms a right to give or withhold consent, is not without normative force. From a logical perspective, it has a basis in the textual formulations pertaining to the FPIC requirement in international legal instruments and jurisprudence. These frequently use a formulation such as 'States shall obtain consent, consult in order to obtain consent, or consult with the objective of obtaining consent'. From the normative perspective, the argument

50 UN Doc. A/HRC/21/47, (2012) para 47.
51 Donnelly 2003: 27–32; Quane 2012.
52 Beyleveld and Brownsword 2007: 242.
53 Ibid.
54 Katz 1994: 77.
55 EMRIP Advice 2 UN Doc. A/HCR//18/42, Annex 1, para 23.

can be made that the corollary right of this duty to obtain FPIC is the right to self-determination, or more specifically the right to self-determined development. This changes the nature of the right in question from one that is primarily reactive (a right to give or withhold consent) to a proactive right embodying the requirement for FPIC. The qualification that indigenous peoples also have the prerogative to 'establish terms and conditions for their consent' is another reflection of the intimate relationship between the decision-making right to self-determination and the FPIC requirement. It places emphasis on the fundamental importance of ensuring that the indigenous voice has precedence in all aspects of the processes involved in defining, seeking and granting consent.

Finally, FPIC is also frequently framed as a principle[56] and more recently, as a safeguard and a standard.[57] The interchangeable categorisation as a right or a principle is not unique to the concept of FPIC, with a similar practice common in relation to self-determination. While each conception of FPIC has relevance in a particular context, none should be regarded as exhaustive of the concept's content. Indigenous peoples themselves invoke both the notion of FPIC as a right and as a 'principle of negotiating in good faith on the basis of mutual respect and equality'.[58] Framing FPIC as a principle and a safeguard to be complied with has been useful in facilitating the extension of this normative standard beyond the human rights framework within which it has been framed as a duty of States, or a right of indigenous peoples vis-à-vis States. Indeed, the capacity of the human rights framework itself to deal with the nature of indigenous claims against non-State actors remains to be seen. As a principle governing the interaction of all third party actors with indigenous peoples, the concept of FPIC is already demonstrating its potential to transform the relationship of private sector actors with indigenous peoples.[59] An understanding of FPIC as a principle is complementary to its legalistic dimension as a right. The latter is more rigid and rule-based, while the former suggests a framework which provides the flexibility for a diversity of consent-seeking rules which apply to all actors and are to be self-defined as an exercise of each people's right to self-determination. This avoids the potential for co-option of the procedural aspect of FPIC by

56 See, for example, IFC 2012c; *UN Development Group Guidelines on Indigenous Peoples' Issues* (Geneva: Inter-Agency Support Group (IASG) on Indigenous Issues, 2009); *Standard-Setting Legal Commentary on the Concept of Free, Prior and Informed Consent, Expanded Working Paper* submitted by A. I. Motoc, UN Doc. E/CN.4/Sub.2/AC.4/2005/WP.1, 14 July 2005; *Report of the International Workshop on Methodologies regarding Free, Prior and Informed Consent and Indigenous Peoples* (New York, 17–19 January 2005), UN Doc. E/C.19/2005/3; Programme of Action of the Second International Decade of the World Indigenous Peoples Objective (ii), Draft Programme of Action for the Second International Decade of the World's Indigenous People, UN Doc. A/60/270 (18 August 2005), para 9(ii).

57 UN Doc. A/HRC/21/47 (2012), para 80.

58 Doyle and Cariño 2013: 17.

59 IFC 2012a; Statement by Professor James Anaya, Special Rapporteur on the Situation of the Human Rights and Fundamental Freedoms of Indigenous People, Ninth Session of the UN Permanent Forum on Indigenous Issues, 22 April 2011, New York; see Doyle forthcoming 2015, for an overview of policies of other financial institutions.

unscrupulous States or corporate entities, and ensures that it acts as a framework for the exercise of self-determined, autonomously controlled, *sui generis* decision-making processes.

The notion of FPIC as a 'safeguard' emerges from the approach of international financial institutions to indigenous peoples' rights. Having observed the potential practical utility of this approach, the Special Rapporteur suggested in his 2012 report on indigenous peoples and the extractive sector that 'consultation and free, prior and informed consent are best conceptualized as safeguards against measures that may affect indigenous peoples' rights'.[60] A concern has been raised that framing FPIC as a safeguard establishes States and the industry as protectors of indigenous peoples' rights.[61] The potential disempowerment of indigenous peoples implicit in such a conception of FPIC can be avoided if it is clarified that FPIC acts as a safeguard which indigenous peoples themselves define and use to protect their fundamental rights, including their rights to sovereignty and self-determination, when these are impacted on by extractive activities. This should be a self-evident requirement but it is nevertheless of fundamental importance to emphasise, as otherwise the 'safeguard' for the right to self-determination could end up constituting an infringement of the exercise of that right, potentially rendering it a self-defeating oxymoron. This is consistent with the view of the Special Rapporteur that FPIC establishes the extremely high threshold which needs to be met before the rights it safeguards can be infringed upon.[62] As is evident from the growing corpus of recommendations of various human rights bodies engaging with the issue of indigenous peoples' consent, these concepts of consent as a duty (or requirement), a right and a principle or safeguard are used interchangeably, depending on the specific context. Any risk inherent in framing FPIC as a safeguard for the right to self-determination is countered by its simultaneous framing as a 'duty' imposed on the State, a principle to be complied with by all actors, and as a right pertaining to indigenous peoples, which includes the right to say 'no'. Each conception of FPIC has particular and important dimensions associated with it and the use of any one term should not be taken to limit the rights-reinforcing dimensions of the others.[63] Understood as an exercise of the right to self-determination, the requirement for FPIC implies that where indigenous people choose not to enter into consultations, an obligation to do so cannot be imposed on them[64] and where they do agree to engage in such processes, their format must be determined with or by them and cannot be mandatory.[65]

60 UN Doc. A/HRC/21/47 (2012), para 80.
61 B. Clavero, *Relator Especial: Misión Imposible*, 7 September 2012, previously available at http://clavero.derechosindigenas.org/?p=12597
62 J Monet *James Anaya: A Sit-Down with the UN's Man in Indian Country*, 9 May 2012, available at: http://indiancountrytodaymedianetwork.com/2012/05/09/james-anaya-a-sit-down-with-the-un%E2%80%99s-man-in-indian-country-111990
63 UN Docs. A/HRC/EMRIP/2012/2, para 26(d); and A/HCR//18/42, paras 28, 63.
64 E/C.19/2009/CRP. 8, 4 May 2009, para 13.
65 Doyle and Cariño 2013: 12; see also UN Doc A/HRC/24/41, para 25.

5.4 The subjects of FPIC

The question of who are the holders of the right to FPIC, or to whom the principle or safeguard applies, has also been addressed by a range of human rights bodies. In the Americas, the Inter-American Court has clarified that FPIC applies to indigenous peoples and other communities which:

> share similar characteristics with indigenous peoples, such as social, cultural and economic traditions different from other sections of the national community, identifying themselves with their ancestral territories, and regulating themselves, at least partially, by their own norms, customs, and traditions.[66]

This position is reflected in the reports of Special Rapporteurs of the Human Rights Council, the concluding observations of UN treaty bodies and in the jurisprudence of national courts, such as the Constitutional Court of Colombia.[67] It is also reflected in the scope of ILO Convention 169 which applies to both indigenous and tribal peoples. In a number of Latin American countries the consultation and consent-seeking requirements are similar for indigenous and Afro-descendant peoples.[68] In Africa, where the concept of indigenous as first peoples is controversial,[69] the approach of the African Commission has been to provide criteria, not all of which must co-exist, that can be used to identify those groups falling under the rubric of indigenous peoples. One set of criteria it invoked were those suggested by Daes, which correspond largely to those of the Martínez Cobo study, namely:

> i) the occupation and use of a specific territory; ii) the voluntary perpetuation of cultural distinctiveness . . . ; iii) self-identification, as well as recognition by other groups, as a distinct collectivity; iv) an experience of subjugation, marginalisation, dispossession, exclusion or discrimination.[70]

---

66 *Saramaka v Suriname* (2007), op. cit. 25, para 79.
67 Constitutional Court of Colombia, Sentencia T-769/09 (2009); Report of the independent expert on minority issues, Gay McDougall, Addendum Mission to Colombia, 25 January 2011, UN Doc. A/HRC/16/45/Add.1, para 78.
68 The Constitution of Ecuador, Articles 57–59; Federal Constitution of Brazil, Article 231 and the Transnational Constitutional Provisions Act. Constitutional Court of Colombia, Sentencia T-769/09 (2009).
69 Report of the African Commission's Working Group of Experts on Indigenous Populations/ Communities Adopted by The African Commission on Human and Peoples' Rights at its 28th Ordinary Session (2005, Banjul, Copenhagen, IACHPR and IWGIA); see also Kingsbury 1998: 414–457; 'Advisory Opinion of the African Commission on Human and Peoples' Rights on the United Nations Declaration on the Rights of Indigenous Peoples', adopted by the African Commission on Human and Peoples' Rights, at its 41st Ordinary Session (May 2007, Accra, Ghana), available at: www.achpr.org/mechanisms/indigenous-populations/un-advisory-opinion/
70 Report of African Commission on Indigenous Populations, ibid.: 93.

The Commission has also issued a resolution affirming that the FPIC of communities is a requirement in relation to extractive projects, which does not specify that it refers exclusively to indigenous peoples.[71] However, its jurisprudence in the *Endorois v Kenya* case suggests that this is applicable only to those peoples and communities who meet some or all of the aforementioned criteria. The prevalence of community customary land tenure systems in Africa, and associated traditional institutions and collective identities, suggests that the requirement for FPIC can be derived from the collective rights of such communities.[72] Indeed, it has been suggested that this criterion of local living customary law would have been more appropriate than reliance on the category indigenous.[73] This is supported by the fact that the African Charter, which includes peoples' rights, represents a significant departure from the individualistic manner in which rights, with the exception of the right to self-determination, have been framed under other instruments of international human rights law.[74] Similar arguments can be made for forest peoples in other jurisdictions who do not self-identify as indigenous, but who nevertheless maintain collective claims over lands and practise traditional ways of life.[75]

The Human Rights Committee, in affirming the requirement for FPIC in the *Poma Poma v Peru* case, also introduced the potential for the requirement to be extended to non-indigenous ethnic, linguistic or religious minorities.[76] However, as with the Inter-American Court, the logic of the ruling appears to imply that such communities would have to have somewhat similar traditional economic, social or cultural characteristics to indigenous peoples.[77] Similarly, in its General Comment no. 21, the Committee on Economic Social and Cultural Rights has affirmed that FPIC may be required from non-indigenous minorities and communities as well as indigenous peoples in the context of threats to their cultural resources, way of life or cultural expressions.[78] Implicit in its Comment is that these groups maintain distinct social and culture traditions, and that the requirement for their FPIC can consequently be derived from their cultural rights. The groups falling under this category also share characteristics in common with indigenous peoples. Consequently, in addition to indigenous peoples, marginalised collectivities that maintain a distinct way of life, shared sense of identity or customary land tenure regimes associated with a particular territory may have legitimate claims to be eligible to give or withhold their FPIC to extractive industry projects.

71 The African Commission on Human and Peoples' Rights (African Commission) Resolution 224 Human Rights-Based Approach to Natural Resources Governance at its 51st Ordinary Session held from 18 April to 2 May 2012 in Banjul, The Gambia.
72 Wicomb and Smith 2011.
73 Smith *et al.* 2011: 15. For a discussion on customary law as living law see Tobin 2014.
74 Obinna Okere 1984: 141, 148; see also M'baye 1978; Ssenyonjo 2011: 55; and Umozurike 1997.
75 Mackay 2013.
76 HRC, *Poma Poma v Peru* (2009), op. cit. 5, para 7.6.
77 Ibid.
78 Committee on Economic, Social, and Cultural Rights, General Comment No. 21: Right of Everyone to Take Part in Cultural Life, UN Doc E/C.12/GC/21 (2009).

The *Draft UN Declaration on the Rights of Peasants and Other People in Rural Areas* is illustrative of developments beyond the indigenous rights framework. The current version of the draft affirms the right of peasants 'to participate in policy design, decision-making, implementation, and monitoring of any project, programme or policy affecting their land and territories' but only requires FPIC in the context of relocation, on the basis of the right to security of tenure.[79] It does, however, recognise a 'right to reject' 'all forms of exploitation which cause environmental damage' and 'interventions that can destroy local agricultural values' in the context of the rights to 'a clean and healthy environment' and 'recognition and protection of their culture and local agricultural values' respectively.[80] The drafting process, which is in its infancy, nevertheless highlights the reluctance of States to recognise other groups, such as peasants, as holders of collective rights. As noted by Mackay, the claims of such non-indigenous groups remain relatively unexplored under the human rights regime and will have to be assessed on a case-by-case basis with their validity depending on the particular needs and characteristics of the group in question.[81]

Under international environmental law, and within the broader framework of sustainable development, the principle of FPIC is being invoked in the context of local communities as well as indigenous peoples.[82] In order to reconcile this approach with developments in the normative framework of indigenous peoples' rights, one proposal is that FPIC, when conceived of as 'a right' under international law is exclusive to indigenous and tribal peoples, but as 'a principle' can be extended to all communities.[83] A potential risk inherent in such an approach is that the extension of the principle could serve to abstract FPIC from the rights-based grounding from which derives its normative force, thereby rendering it open to restrictions which are inconsistent with respect for indigenous and tribal peoples' rights.[84] It is therefore necessary that any extension of the requirement beyond those groups who self-identify as indigenous peoples, or share similar characteristics

---

79 UN Doc A/HRC/15/1/2 (2013), Articles 2(4) and 4(5).
80 Ibid.: Articles 9(1,3) and 11(1,3).
81 MacKay 2013: 3.
82 Convention on Biological Diversity (1992–06–05) (entry into force 1993–12–29) 1760 UNTS 79; 31 ILM 818 (1992); *Akwé: Kon Voluntary guidelines for the conduct of cultural, environmental and social impact assessments regarding developments proposed to take place on, or which are likely to impact on, sacred sites and on lands and waters traditionally occupied or used by indigenous and local communities* (Geneva: Secretariat of the Convention on Biological Diversity, 2004), Decision VII/16 F COP-7 UN Doc. UNEP/CBD/COP/7/21 (13 April 2004); Nagoya Protocol on Access to Genetic Resources and the Fair and Equitable Sharing of Benefits Arising from their Utilization to The Convention on Biological Diversity, Nagoya, 29 October 2010, C.N.782.2010.Treaties-1 (Depositary Notification); Overview of Recommendations Arising from Comments on the UN-REDD Guidelines on Free, Prior and Informed Consent (FPIC) (Geneva: UNREDD Programme, UNDP, FAO, UNEP, February 2012); The Conference on Sustainable Development noted the importance of the UNDRIP in the realisation of sustainable development, see *The Future We Want*, General Assembly resolution 66/288 (11 September 2012).
83 Voss and Greenspan 2012; see also Rumler 2011.
84 See comments of Indian Law Resource Center in *Overview of Recommendations Arising from Comments on the UN-REDD Guidelines on Free, Prior and Informed Consent (FPIC)* (Geneva: UNREDD Programme, UNDP, FAO, UNEP, February 2012), at 4–5.

with them, be grounded on a clearly articulated rights basis.[85] It is also essential that it in no way serve to limit or constrain the notion of indigenous peoples' FPIC as a peoples' right flowing from their exercise of the right to self-determination and as a manifestation of their inherent sovereignty. As a result, should the concept of FPIC gain traction for local communities in general, clear distinctions need to be made in contexts where the case for FPIC is made as flowing purely from the amalgamation of individual rights of local community members, as opposed to flowing from peoples' collective self-governance, autonomy and territorial rights. This latter point relates back to the discussion on the bases for FPIC and is of particular significance in determining the modalities of its operationalisation. Its status as a derivative of the right to self-determination implies that indigenous peoples must be the ones who define what FPIC means and how it will be operationalised in their own particular contexts and in accordance with their own laws, customs and institutions. As a derivation of individual rights the modalities for its operationalisation would tend to be more generic in nature and lack the distinctive governance features associated with indigenous decision-making processes.

5.5 Scope of FPIC under the contemporary normative framework

The fact that FPIC is derived from a myriad of rights is reflective of the fact that while it is of particular significance to issues pertaining to control over lands, territories and natural resources, it is also essential for the realisation of other self-determination rights.[86] As a result, references to FPIC under international human rights and environmental law tend to be broad in scope and extend to such areas as redress for the taking of cultural, intellectual, religious and spiritual property[87] and the requirement to obtain FPIC 'before adopting and implementing legislative or administrative measures that may affect' indigenous peoples.[88]

Within the context of rights to lands, territories and resources, the requirement for FPIC has been affirmed in at least four contexts. First, consent is required prior to any relocation of indigenous peoples from their lands or territories.[89] Second, FPIC must be obtained for the storage or disposal of hazardous materials in

---

85 For steps in this direction, see Mackay 2013; see also Greenspan 2014.

86 UN Doc. E/CN.4/Sub.2/AC.4/2005/WP.1, para 33. See also *Statement to the Third Session of the UN Expert Mechanism on the Rights of Indigenous Peoples Presentation under Agenda Item 3, Cathal Doyle on behalf of University of Middlesex Department of Law and Philippines Indigenous Peoples Links* (Geneva, 2010). Available at: www.indigenousportal.com/Human-Rights/Cathal-Doyle-Presentation-under-Agenda-Item-3-III-EMRIP.html

87 UNDRIP, Article 11; see also Nagoya Protocol (2010) C.N.782.2010.Treaties-1, op. cit. 82; see also UN Doc. UNEP/CBD/COP/10/5/Add.4, 16; CESCR General Recommendation No 21 E/C.12/GC/21, para 37; see also Halesa *et al.* 2013.

88 UNDRIP, Article 19.

89 UNDRIP, Article 10; ILO Convention 169, Article 16; ILO Convention 107, Article 13.

their lands or territories.[90] Third, indigenous peoples' right to redress is framed in light of the absence of FPIC wherever 'lands, territories and resources, which they have traditionally owned or otherwise occupied or used . . . have been confiscated, taken, occupied, used or damaged without their free, prior and informed consent'.[91] Finally, FPIC has emerged as the standard to be complied with in the context of development projects that impact on indigenous peoples' lands, territories and resources.[92]

In the context of development projects, the requirement for FPIC is triggered by proposed activities in, or affecting, indigenous territories, irrespective of whether formal title is held over them.[93] The FPIC of all communities whose rights are impacted must be sought and obtained.[94] Impact areas, as a result, have to be based on the social, cultural and spiritual links to territories as well as the direct physical impact area, as those communities with spiritual links to the affected territory may extend beyond groups that are resident in the physical impact area. Furthermore, physical impacts in one area may damage the territorial integrity of a far more extensive area. Cultural impacts, in addition to potentially having a more expansive geographical reach than physical impacts, will also frequently precede physical impacts in time. For example, the knowledge that a threat is imminent can have a destabilising effect on peoples' perceptions of their traditional authorities' capacity to uphold their rights and guarantee their well-being if FPIC is not sought in advance of the development of plans or decisions in relation to potential land use.

The procedural dimensions of the consent requirement have been elaborated on by a number of UN human rights treaty and charter bodies as well as the ILO supervisory bodies. All of these mechanisms have clarified that consent-seeking processes should be consistent with the requirements of both ILO Convention 169 and the UNDRIP. This guidance indicates that good faith consultation processes must be held with indigenous peoples and be free from all external manipulation, coercion and intimidation and occur in 'a climate of mutual confidence';[95] that all the affected indigenous peoples be notified that their

---

90 UNDRIP, Article 29; Special Rapporteur on the Rights of Indigenous Peoples Addendum UN Doc. A/HRC/9/9/Add.1, 15 August 2008, Annex 1 Ecuador Report; Declaración pública del Relator Especial sobre Ley del derecho a la consulta en Perú (2010); ICESCR General Comment 14 (Twenty-second session, 2000): Article 12: The Right to the Highest Attainable Standard of Health, UN Doc. E/2001/22 (2000) 128 at para 27.

91 UNDRIP, Article 28; CERD General Recommendation No. 23, para 5; CESCR General Recommendation No. 21, para 36.

92 See Doyle forthcoming 2015.

93 UN Doc. A/HRC/21/47 (2012); A/HRC/12/34 (2009), para 44; see also *Report of the Committee Set Up to Examine the Representation Alleging Non-observance by Guatemala of the Indigenous and Tribal Peoples Convention, 1989 (No. 169), Made under Article 24 of the ILO Constitution by the Federation of Country and City Workers (FTCC)*, para. 48.

94 Constitutional Court of Colombia, Sentencia T-769/09 (Referencia: expediente T-2315944) 29 de Octubre 2009.

95 *Report of the Committee Set up to Examine the Representation Alleging Non-Observance by Guatemala of the Indigenous and Tribal Peoples Convention*, 1989 (No. 169), made under Article 24 of the ILO Constitution by the Federation of Country and City Workers (FTCC) GB.294/17/1; GB.299/6/1

consent will be sought sufficiently in advance of the approval and commencement of any activities;[96] that the procedures for consultation are consistent with their respect for their institutions and customary laws and are developed with them based on a consensus approach;[97] and that there be full disclosure of information regarding all aspects of a potential project in a manner that is accessible and understandable to the impacted indigenous peoples.[98] The substantive aspect arises by virtue of their right to self-determination and their cultural and territorial rights, and implies that indigenous peoples can approve or reject or conditionally approve a project or activity.[99]

One aspect of this decision-making process is the possibility to influence and select alternatives to particular proposals.[100] This decision to approve or reject, or approve on certain conditions, should be based on the consensus of all indigenous peoples and communities affected and be reached through their traditional decision-making processes and representative institutions in accordance with their customary laws and practices.[101] Consent may be required at multiple

(2007), para 53; see also UN Doc. A/HRC/12/34/Add.6, Apéndice A, para 23; see also *Sarayaku vs. Ecuador* (2012), op. cit. 27, paras 186 and 194.

96 *Saramaka v Suriname* (2007), op. cit. 25, paras 129, 134 see also fn 127 and paras 137 and 194 d, e; *Sarayaku vs. Ecuador* (2012), op. cit. 27, paras 180–184, both cases citing UNDRIP Article 32(2); International Labour Conference, 98th Session, 2009 Report of the Committee of Experts on the Application of Conventions and Recommendations Report III (Part 1A) at 677 and 680. See also Indigenous and Tribal Peoples Convention, 1989 (No. 169) Observation, CEACR 2009/80th Session (Colombia), reproduced in ILO 2010: 55; UN Permanent Forum on Indigenous Issues, *Report of the International Expert Group Meeting on Extractive Industries, Indigenous Peoples' Rights and Corporate Social Responsibility*, Manila, 4 May 2009, UN Doc, E/C.19/2009/CRP.8, para 13; CERD, Concluding Observation to Colombia, CERD/C/COL/CO/14, 2009, para 20; see *Sarayaku vs. Ecuador* (2012), op. cit. 27, fn 241, for list of national jurisprudence in Latin America addressing the prior dimension of consultations.

97 CERD Concluding Observations, Philippines 2009, UN Doc. CERD/C/PHL/CO/20, para 24; CERD Early Warning Urgent Action letters to the Philippines 7 March 2007; 28 August 2007, 7 March 2008, 15 August 2008, 27 August 2010; ILO Representation Guatemala GB.294/17/1 (2007), op. cit. 95, para 53; Representation (Article 24) - Brazil - C169 - 2009; *Report of the Committee Set up to Examine the Representation Alleging Non-Observance by Brazil of the Indigenous and Tribal Peoples Convention*, 1989 (No. 169), made under Article 24 of the ILO Constitution by the Union of Engineers of the Federal District (SENGE/DF)). (GB.295/17) (GB.304/14/7), para 42; *Sarayaku v Ecuador* (2012), op. cit. 27, paras 194, 201.

98 See *Sarayaku v Ecuador* (2012), op. cit. 27, paras 204–211; *Saramaka v Suriname* (2007), op. cit. 25, para 194(c); ILO Convention 169, Article 7(3) and 15(2); UNDRIP, Article 32(2); WGIP (2004) UN Doc. E/CN.4/Sub.2/AC.4/2004/4 (2004), paras 21–25; EMRIP (2011) UN Doc. A/HRC/18/42, Annex 1, Advice no. 2 (2011), para 25.

99 UN Doc. E/CN.4/2003/90 (2003), para 13, UNPFII UN Doc, E/C.19/2009/CRP.8 (2009), para 13; EMRIP UN Doc. A/HRC/EMRIP/2012/2 (2012) Annex Advice 4, para 27.

100 UN Doc. A/HRC/21/47 (2012), para 66; Colombia Constitutional Court Sentencia T-129/11, (2011), Section 8, viii.

101 Philippines, *Indigenous Peoples Rights Act* (1997); CERD Concluding Observations, Philippines (2009), UN Doc. CERD/C/PHL/CO/20, para 24; CERD Early Warning Urgent Action letters to the Philippines, 7 March 2007; 28 August 2007, 7 March 2008, 15 August 2008, 27 August 2010; ILO 2001: Representation (Article 24) Colombia (GB.277/18/1):(GB.282/14/4) para 68; see also *Final Statement Complaint from the Future In Our Hands (FIOH) against Intex Resources ASA and the Mindoro Nickel Project: The Norwegian National Contact Point for the OECD Guidelines for Multinational Enterprises* (Oslo: OECD, 2011) at 6, 7, 21.

phases during the consultation and negotiation processes and throughout the project's lifecycle (e.g. at the land use planning stage, prior to concession issuance and prior to commencement of exploration and exploitation activities and for any other rights-impacting activities).[102] If consent is given following good faith negotiations, it should result in a legally binding agreement that ensures equitable benefit-sharing arrangements.[103]

Effective grievance mechanisms spanning the entire project lifecycle, including any post-project impacts, should be guaranteed.[104] The State maintains ultimate responsibility for holding the consultations and ensuring that consent is obtained within a legislative framework which respects indigenous peoples' rights, however, it can delegate operational aspects of this responsibility to corporate entities.[105] Free prior and informed consent therefore establishes the processes for consultation and negotiations that have to be followed by all parties and imposes a requirement that the outcome of these processes be recognised and upheld. Both the process and outcome components of FPIC are necessary to ensure indigenous peoples' effective participation in the decision-making process. While the requirement has been affirmed by numerous human rights bodies, Article 32 of the UN Declaration represents its clearest affirmation under an international legal instrument.

5.6 The most accomplished affirmation of FPIC: scope of the requirement under the UN Declaration on the Rights of Indigenous Peoples

5.6.1 Obligations flowing from the requirement for free prior and informed consent

The UNDRIP contains no fewer than six references to the requirement to obtain FPIC, addressing all of the aspects of FPIC listed in the preceding section.[106] It reflects an acknowledgement by States that FPIC is, in principle (if not yet

---

102 See, for example, consent requirement prior to concession issuance: *Saramaka v Suriname* (2007), op. cit. 25, para 137; prior to exploration: CESCR Cambodia UN Doc. E/C.12/KHM/CO/1, (22 May 2009), para 16; prior to exploration and exploitation, Colombia, CERD/C/COL/ CO/14 (28 August 2009), para 20.

103 UN Doc. A/HRC/15/37 (2010), para 46 and UN Doc. A/HRC/12/34 (2009), para 53; ILO Convention 169, Article 15(2); UN Doc. A/HRC/EMRIP/2012/2, para 40; IFC 2012a: 18–20; see also B. Clavero, *Perú: Convenio necesario y ley innecesaria* 7 November 2008, previously available at: http://clavero.derechosindigenas.org/?p=800.

104 World Commission on Dams 2000: 281; CERD Philippines, UN Doc. CERD/C/PHL/CO/ 20 (2009) para 23–4; Report of the International Expert Group Meeting on Extractive Industries, Indigenous Peoples' Rights and Corporate Social Responsibility (4 May 2009), UN Doc. E/C.19/2009/CRP. 8, para 46.

105 Anaya, *Extractive Industries Operating Within or Near Indigenous Territories*, UN Doc. A/HRC/18/35 (2011), para 63; see also EMRIP UN Doc. A/HRC/EMRIP/2012/2 Advice No. 4 (2012), para 8.

106 UNDRIP does not include an express requirement for benefits. However, the principle of FPIC embodies that requirement in so far as it becomes a component of the consent-based negotiations.

in practice), the minimum standard to be respected 'for the survival, dignity and well-being of the indigenous peoples of the world'.[107] Article 32 of the UNDRIP states that:

1. Indigenous peoples have *the right to determine and develop priorities* and strategies for the development or use of their lands or territories and other resources.
2. States shall *consult* and *cooperate* in *good faith* with the indigenous peoples concerned through their own representative institutions *in order to obtain their free and informed consent* prior to the approval of any project affecting their lands or territories and other resources, *particularly in connection with the development, utilisation or exploitation of mineral, water or other resources.*
3. States shall provide effective mechanisms for just and fair redress *for any such activities*, and appropriate measures shall be taken to mitigate adverse environmental, economic, social, cultural or spiritual impact.[108]

The first paragraph of Article 32 contextualises the requirement for FPIC which is articulated in the second paragraph. It frames FPIC as a prerequisite for the realisation of a self-determined development path premised on control over lands and resources.[109] Consequently, FPIC is required for 'any project affecting their lands or territories and other resources'.[110] This differs from the FPIC protections afforded in Articles 10 (addressing relocations) and 29(2) (addressing disposal of hazardous materials) in two significant ways. On the one hand, the focus of Article 32 is limited to projects, whereas Articles 10 and 29(2) are not subject to this restriction. On the other hand, Article 32 does not link the requirement for FPIC to specific impacts of projects, and in this regard its scope is broader than that of Articles 10 and 29(2). Article 32 places FPIC at the core of indigenous peoples' right to development. It requires FPIC for all projects affecting indigenous peoples, and does not place any express limitations on FPIC in relation to either the type of project or its potential impact. It does, however, place special emphasis on projects that involve the development, utilisation or exploitation of mineral, water or other resources.

Article 32 also requires that States consult with indigenous peoples in good faith through their own representative institutions. Article 33 states that indigenous peoples have the right to 'determine the structures and to select the membership of their institutions in accordance with their own procedures'. Taken together, these articles address one of the most common issues encountered by indigenous peoples in consultations with States and companies: that of portraying individuals amenable to the interests of these external entities, but who are not selected according to the community's procedures, customs or traditions, as being

---

107 UNDRIP, Article 43.
108 UNDRIP, Article 32.
109 UNDRIP, Articles 3 and 23; see also Doyle and Gilbert 2009.
110 UNDRIP, Article 32(2).

representative of the community.[111] The wording of the FPIC requirement in Article 32(2) is, however, less definitive than that of Articles 10 and 29(2) and consequently merits further consideration.

5.6.2 FPIC from an objective to a requirement

Some commentators note that the text of Article 32(2) leads to some ambiguity with regard to the obligations of States where consent has not been obtained.[112] The following section proposes that if a combination of textual analysis, construed in the context of the UNDRIP as a whole, and interpreted in the light of its drafting history is applied to Article 32,[113] then the strong presumption emerges that the UNDRIP supports the principle that a decision to withhold FPIC, particularly in the context of natural resource exploitation, should be respected and only overridden in exceptional circumstances and under very particular conditions outlined in Article 46 of the UNDRIP. This proposition is based on the following logic.

The requirement for FPIC affirmed in Article 32(2) is effectively a derivation of the right to development affirmed in Article 32(1). Article 32(2) outlines the mechanism to guarantee the realisation of the right affirmed in Article 32(1). It identifies obtaining FPIC as the purpose of good faith consultations on the basis of the right affirmed in Article 32(1). The State's obligation in contexts where an indigenous people withhold FPIC is not explicitly addressed in Article 32(2). Consultations which have the purpose of seeking consent only imply a procedural guarantee. Irrespective of their outcome, the purpose is satisfied by the act of seeking consent. By contrast, consultations with a purpose of obtaining consent embody both elements of an obligation of conduct and an obligation of result. Read in light of the right affirmed in Article 32(1), Article 32(2) consequently affirms a right of choice.[114] The requirement for States to cooperate with indigenous peoples, affirmed under Article 32(2), also reinforces the consent requirement, as inherent in the concept of cooperation and working together towards a common end is a willingness to respect and comply with the requests of the other party.

Article 32(2) places extra emphasis on FPIC in the context of 'development, utilisation or exploitation of mineral, water or other resources'. This is indicative of the pervasiveness and extent of the impacts associated with these activities, including their potential irreversibility, on the enjoyment of the right in

---

111 See Philippines Indigenous Peoples ICERD Shadow Report Submission to the Committee on the Elimination of Racial Discrimination, 75 Session, 3–28 August 2009 (Manila, 2009) (henceforth Philippines ICERD Shadow Report 2009) at 56–59 available at:www2.ohchr.org/english/bodies/cerd/cerds75.htm; see also *Saramaka People v Suriname* (2007), op. cit. 25, para 164.

112 Davis 2008: 465 suggests that indigenous peoples see it as a 'quasi-veto' right; see also Engle 2011: 141–163 and Chávez 2009: 104.

113 Article 27, General rule of interpretation of the Vienna Convention on the Law of Treaties. See also Driedger 1983: 1.

114 Roy 2011.

Article 32(1) and the resource aspect of the right to self-determination. Article 32(3) affirms that there is a duty on the State to ensure that appropriate redress is guaranteed, including compensation or restitution, and mitigation measures are provided. The wording 'any such activities' suggests that it should be read in the light of Article 32(2), and not interpreted separately as justifying the pursuit of activities without FPIC.[115] The silence of Article 32(2) in relation to States' obligations where FPIC is not obtained has therefore to be interpreted in the light of limitations that can legitimately be placed on the right affirmed in Article 32(1).

This right, as indicated in the UNDRIP's drafting discussions, is an aspect of the right to self-determination in Article 3.[116] This categorisation of Article 32 as a self-determination right was recognised by States during and after the drafting process.[117] The Permanent Forum on Indigenous Issues[118] and the Expert Mechanism have subsequently highlighted the need for recognition that: 'the right to self-determination of indigenous peoples constitutes a duty for States to obtain indigenous peoples' free, prior and informed consent, not merely to be involved in decision-making processes, but a right to determine their outcomes'.[119]

The only limitation permissible on the self-determination right affirmed under Article 32(1), and by extension on the FPIC requirement in Article 32(2), is found under Article 46(2) of the UNDRIP. Article 46(2) establishes that limitations placed on the rights affirmed in the UNDRIP must be:

> determined by law and in accordance with international human rights obligations [and] . . . non-discriminatory and strictly necessary solely for the purpose of securing due recognition and respect for the rights and freedoms of others and for meeting the just and most compelling requirements of a democratic society.

Article 32 of the UNDRIP is therefore consistent with the evolution of the consent requirement under the normative framework of indigenous peoples' rights following the adoption of C169. Rather than framing consent as a mere objective of consultation, it requires that consent shall be obtained in all but the most exceptional circumstances. These exceptions must be justified in light of their strict necessity for upholding human rights and must be balanced in a proportional manner against indigenous peoples' enjoyment of their right to self-determination. As will be discussed in Chapter 6, neither the common good nor

---

115 Article 28 addresses such situations requiring redress for taking or use of resources without FPIC.
116 Report of the Working Group established in accordance with Commission on Human Rights resolution 1995/32 (6 January 2003), UN Doc. E/CN.4/2003/92, paras 19, 20 and 44.
117 UN Doc. A/61/PV.107 at 25.
118 UNPFII Report on the ninth session (19–30 April 2010), Special theme: 'Indigenous peoples: development with culture and identity: Articles 3 and 32 of the United Nations Declaration on the Rights of Indigenous Peoples', UN Doc. E/2010/43-E/C.19/2010/15, paras 4–35.
119 EMRIP (2011), UN Doc. A/HCR/18/42 Annex Advice No. 2, para 34.

the public interest were envisaged as legitimate limitations to the self-determined development-based requirement for FPIC.

5.7 Relationship between the requirement for FPIC and the degree of impact

Given the relatively rapid uptake of the consent requirement by the various bodies of the human rights regime in the period following the adoption of the UNDRIP, it is not surprising that some divergence of opinion emerged as to the circumstances which trigger a requirement to obtain consent. These opinions can be broadly grouped into two categories. The first is aligned with the view of many indigenous peoples and holds that FPIC is required for any project or activity affecting their lands, territories and resources or their well-being. This is reflected in requirements of Article 32 of the UNDRIP that FPIC be obtained for 'any project' and CERD's General Recommendation XXIII requirement that 'no decisions that impact on the rights and interests of indigenous peoples be taken without informed consent'. It is also reflected in the CESCR General Recommendation 21 which requires FPIC for resource usage. None of these affirmations of the requirement for FPIC place any explicit limitation on when it should be obtained.

The second, which also requires respect for FPIC, holds that consent should always be sought for development projects but is only absolutely essential that it be obtained when there is the potential for a profound or major impact on the property rights of an indigenous people or where their physical or cultural survival may be endangered.[120] This position is reflected in the Inter-American Court ruling in the case of the *Saramaka People v Suriname* and in some of the earlier statements of the Special Rapporteur on the rights of indigenous peoples which indicate that where the basic well-being or physical or cultural survival of the community is not at risk or where a project does not have a 'major impact', consent may not be an absolute condition for pursuing the project. It is also consistent with a constructive interpretation of ILO Convention 169. These two perspectives, and the evolving nature of the latter, are discussed in Section 5.7.1.

5.7.1 Consent requirement triggered by any project impacting on rights or interests

The first position is premised on the fact that giving or withholding consent to activities which impact on a people's developmental, cultural, territorial or subsistence rights is integral to the right to self-determination. This implies that indigenous peoples have a right to determine if any projects that directly impact on them may, or may not, proceed and under what conditions. Indigenous peoples view the right to give or withhold FPIC as 'a requirement, prerequisite and

---

120 *Saramaka v. Suriname* (2008) (Interpretation), op. cit. 25, para 37.

manifestation of the exercise of their right to self-determination'.[121] In putting forward this argument, indigenous peoples have acknowledged that this exercise of their right to self-determination must be consistent with respect for the right to self-determination of others in the State.[122] This perspective on the consent requirement consequently represents a more nuanced rights-based argument than a claim to hold an absolute and unconditional veto power in all circumstances. Instead, the position holds that the consent requirement always exists as a result of a people's right to choose their own forms of economic, social and cultural development. The right to say 'yes' or 'no' or 'yes but' must be exercised through a self-determined process and the outcome is assumed to be binding on all parties. The only exception envisaged is where there is a legitimate limitation to their exercise of the right to self-determination based on the necessity to protect the self-determination rights of others in a manner which guarantees that the restriction to the enjoyment of indigenous peoples' rights are proportionate to the interests of the rights holder being served. This is consistent with the ordinary meaning of the term 'obtain consent' used by human rights bodies and the manner in which consent is framed in the UNDRIP, when considered in the context of its recognition of indigenous peoples' right to self-determination and its acknowledgement of historical injustices, 'preventing them from exercising, in particular, their right to development in line with their needs and interests'.[123]

In addition to being grounded in the developmental, or choice, dimension of the right to self-determination, the requirement for consent in relation to all extractive projects impacting on indigenous peoples' lands or resources is supported by the resource dimension of the right to self-determination. Any threat to the absolute right of peoples not to be deprived of their subsistence triggers the consent requirement. In addition, as will be discussed in Chapter 6, the consent requirement provides the middle ground in which the apparently irreconcilable claims of indigenous peoples to an inherent right to permanent sovereignty over natural resources can be reconciled with States' claims to sovereignty over these same resources.[124] This perspective on FPIC is closely aligned with the position of many indigenous peoples that it must be required for 'any' projects that impact on their control over these sub-soil resources, or any other impact on lands or resources.[125] It is also largely consistent with the position which the Special

---

121 *Progress Report on the Study on Indigenous Peoples and the Right to Participate in Decision-making.* Report of the Expert Mechanism on the Rights of Indigenous Peoples, UN Doc. A/HRC/EMRIP/2010/2 (17 May 2010), para 34.

122 Statement by M. Ahren on behalf of the Arctic Council under Agenda Item 3, Study on Indigenous People's right to participate in decision-making to the EMRIP, 3rd session, July 2010, www.docip.org

123 *UN Declaration on the Rights of Indigenous Peoples*, Preamble, interpreted in light of the general principle of law as reflected in Article 31 of the Vienna Convention on the Law of Treaties (1969).

124 See Chapter 6.7.

125 Pronunciamiento Estado Peruano Consuma Violación de Derechos de los Pueblos Indígenas, Mediante la Reglamentación de una Inconstitucional Ley de Consulta Pacto de Unidad

Rapporteur on the rights of indigenous peoples has developed in his 2012 and 2013 reports on the extractive industry which are discussed below.[126]

In its commentary addressing when consent is a mandatory requirement, the Expert Mechanism on the Rights of Indigenous Peoples referred to the jurisprudence of CERD as being 'highly instructive, as it sets out the factual circumstances in which it has found that indigenous peoples' consent is required'. [127] A review of the CERD's communications and concluding observations to governments suggests that while it insists on the necessity for impact assessments,[128] it does not indicate that only a subset of impacts should trigger the consent requirement. Instead, consistent with the text of its General Recommendation XXIII, this body of jurisprudence suggests that the requirement for consent is always triggered by extractive projects which could affect indigenous peoples' rights or interests. The reason behind this is CERD's awareness of the inevitable gravity of the impacts of such projects due to the vulnerability of relatively small-scale indigenous societies.[129] A similar affirmation of the requirement for consent emerges from the concluding observations and General Comment 21 of the CESCR. A limited basis exists for an assessment of the CESCR's position on the consent requirement as its optional protocol only entered into force in May 2013 and to date only has 14 State parties.[130] The position of the Inter-American Commission on Human Rights resonates with that of CERD's 1997 General Recommendation XXIII, which the Commission has invoked on multiple occasions in relation to FPIC. The Commission held that informed consent is required prior to any changes to indigenous peoples' time-immemorial, possession-based, title over lands and resources.[131] Extending this to extractive projects, it affirmed that:

> [The consent requirement was] equally applicable to decisions by the State that will have an impact upon indigenous lands and their communities, such as the granting of concessions to exploit the natural resources of indigenous territories.[132]

As such, the Commission does not condition the applicability of consent requirement on the degree of impact.[133]

Confederación Nacional Agraria Perú, CONACAMI, AIDESEP, ONAMIAP (Lima, 4 de marzo de 2012).

126 UN Doc. A/HRC/21/47 (2012), para 65.

127 EMRIP, UN Doc. A/HRC/EMRIP/2012/2 (2012) Advice No. 4, para 25.

128 See, for example, CERD Ecuador, UN Doc. CERD/C/ECU/CO/19 (2008), para 16; CERD Follow-up Letter to Guyana (24 August 2007).

129 Thornberry 2011: 79; see also CERD Early Warning Urgent Action procedure guidelines (2007) available at www.ohchr.org.

130 Optional Protocol to the International Covenant on Economic, Social and Cultural Rights, GA resolution A/RES/63/117, 10 December 2008.

131 *Mary and Carrie Dann v. United States*, op. cit. 29, paras 130, 140.

132 *Maya indigenous community of the Toledo District v. Belize*, Case 12.053, Report No. 40/04, Inter-Am. C.H.R., OEA/Ser.L/V/II.122 Doc. 5 rev. 1 at 727 (2004), paras 143 and 153.

133 See also *Awas Tingni v Nicaragua* (2001), op. cit. 6, para 143.

5.7.2 The degree of impact as the threshold

The second position in relation to FPIC, which has gained some traction within the human rights regime, is that it is qualified and subject to limitations based on additional grounds to those acknowledged under its more absolute formulation discussed above. This position holds that the extent of the requirement to obtain consent is a function of the degree of impact of the proposed activity. In effect, under this approach, FPIC is provided to an activity's impact rather than to the activity *per se*. In an attempt to shift the discussion away from the polarised veto/ no veto dichotomy, the Special Rapporteur on the rights of indigenous peoples has explained that the principles of consultation and consent are 'aimed at avoiding the imposition of the will of one party over the other'.[134] Consistent with this position, the Special Rapporteur has stated that FPIC does not imply indigenous peoples have a general veto power, provided impacts are not profound and the requirements of Articles 46 and 32(3) of the UNDRIP are respected.[135] Article 32(3) addresses the right to redress, while Article 46(2) holds that limitations on rights are only acceptable when they are necessary to uphold the human rights obligations of others. According to the Special Rapporteur, the extent of the obligation to obtain consent is a function of the potential impact of a proposed measure on indigenous peoples' lives and territories, with significant and direct impacts leading to a 'strong presumption' of the requirement for consent.[136] Qualifying this position, the Special Rapporteur explains that this requirement could 'in certain contexts . . . harden into a prohibition of the measure or project in the absence of indigenous consent'.[137] The Special Rapporteur has asserted this position in a number of concrete cases, including his report on the El Diquis hydroelectric project in Costa Rica, where he stated that:

> consent to the impacts of the project should be provided in a manner that is free and informed, prior to the decision of the State permitting the commencement of the project activities, and should be explicitly enshrined in an agreement . . . which contains the State's commitment. [138]

Activities with minor impacts consequently may not necessarily trigger the consent requirement. Under this interpretation, the provisions of the UNDRIP and the jurisprudence of the human rights bodies allow for limitations on the exercise of indigenous peoples' rights, including their right to self-determination and the associated right to, or requirement for, FPIC. This position is based on the

---

134 UN Doc. A/HRC/12/34 (2009), para 49.
135 UN Doc. A/HRC/9/9/add.1 Annex 1 (2008), paras 38–39; UN Doc. A/HRC/12/34 (2009), paras 46, 48.
136 UN Doc. A/HRC/12/34 (2009), para 47.
137 Ibid.: para 47.
138 Author's translation from the original Spanish version. Anaya, *Adición La situación de los pueblos indígenas afectados por el proyecto hidroeléctrico El Diquís en Costa Rica*, UN Doc. A/HRC/18/35/Add.8 (2011), para 15.

Inter-American Court of Human Rights' derivation of the consent requirement from the American Convention on Human Rights when interpreted in light of the UN Declaration on the Rights of Indigenous Peoples.[139] The Court's position is articulated in the *Saramaka v Suriname* decision where it held:[140]

> regarding large-scale development or investment projects that would have a major impact within Saramaka territory, the state has a duty, not only to consult with the Saramakas, but also to obtain their free, prior, and informed consent, according to their customs and traditions.[141]

The ruling envisages the consent requirement as varying on a case-by-case basis,[142] ranging from an ILO Convention 169 (C169) Article 6-style 'consultation with the objective of consent' requirement for measures or projects with minor impacts, to a strict 'obligation to obtain consent' for those with potentially major impacts or which threaten the physical or cultural survival of a people. According to the Court, survival as an indigenous or tribal people implies their ability to 'preserve, protect and guarantee the special relationship that [they] have with their territory', so that 'they may continue living their traditional way of life, and that their distinct cultural identity, social structure, economic system, customs, beliefs and traditions are respected, guaranteed and protected'.[143]

Measures that threaten any of these elements, including denying the possibility to exercise customs and traditions which are integral to a people's way of life, consequently trigger the requirement for FPIC.[144] If the notion of spectrum of impacts is used to determine when consent is required, then impacts which threaten peoples' existence sit at one extreme. The substantive consent requirement emerging from C169 addresses such scenarios. Meanwhile, the consent requirement flowing from the recognition of indigenous peoples' right to self-determination covers the entire spectrum of potential impacts which infringe on their capacity to make decisions pertaining to their social, cultural and economic development. The fact that the Inter-American Court invokes the right to self-determination in the context of affirming the consent requirement[145] suggests that the notion of a major impact under this jurisprudence extends beyond threats to cultural or physical survival to include limitations on their developmental choices. In addition, any such restrictions on the enjoyment of rights must also satisfy the criteria of

---

139 UN Doc. A/HRC/18/35/Add.3 (2011), para 41, footnote 42, citing *Saramaka v. Suriname* (2007), op. cit. 25, para 134.
140 *Saramaka v Suriname* (2007), ibid.
141 Ibid.: para 134.
142 *Saramaka People v. Suriname* Interpretation of the Judgment of Preliminary Objections, Merits, Reparations and Costs, Judgment of August 12, 2008. Series C No. 185, para 42.
143 Ibid., para 37 quoting from *Saramaka v. Suriname* (2007), op. cit. 25, paras 91, 121, 129.
144 *Saramaka v. Suriname* Interpretation (2008), op. cit. 26, paras 34 and 35.
145 *Saramaka v Suriname* (2007), op. cit. 25, para 93; *Sarayaku v Ecuador* (2012), op. cit. 27, para 231, fn 301.

(a) prior establishment by law; (b) necessity; (c) proportionality, and must have (d) the 'aim of achieving a legitimate objective in a democratic society'.[146]

Under this interpretation of when FPIC is required, it could be argued that, in the context of projects in their territories, the UNDRIP already identifies those circumstances in which FPIC is always essential on the grounds of the profundity of their impact on indigenous peoples. Those explicitly mentioned are: (a) the development, utilisation or exploitation of mineral, water or other resources (Article 32); (b) relocation (Article 10); (c) disposal of any hazardous materials (Article 29); and (d) the taking of cultural, intellectual, religious and spiritual property (Article 11). This position provides a counter-argument to the objections raised by New Zealand, Australia and the United States to FPIC on the grounds that it 'would apply regardless of circumstances'.[147]

This notion that consent is always required in the context of large-scale extractive projects was the object of analysis in the August 2008 Inter-American Court of Human Rights' interpretation of its judgment in the *Saramaka* case. The interpretation indicates that extensive impacts are synonymous with large-scale development or investment projects, and consequently such activities always trigger the FPIC requirement. This emerges from the Court's statement that:

> The Tribunal has emphasized that when large-scale development or investment projects could affect the integrity of the Saramaka people's lands and natural resources, the State has a duty not only to consult with the Saramaka, but also to obtain their free, prior, and informed consent in accordance with their customs and traditions.[148]

MacKay, the attorney for the Saramaka people, suggests that the absence of an impact-based trigger for the FPIC requirement in such contexts is one of the most notable aspects of the interpretation.[149] The implication being that a high level of impact is assumed. The reference to the integrity of indigenous peoples' lands and resources is also noteworthy as is the Court's clarification that the requirement to obtain FPIC 'depend[s] upon the level of impact of the proposed activity',[150] thereby divorcing it from any notion of the quantum of the territory impacted by a project.[151]

---

146 *Saramaka v. Suriname* Interpretation (2008), op. cit. 26, paras 34 and 35.
147 Statement of Peter Vaughn to the Permanent Forum, on Indigenous Issues, Representative of Australia, on behalf of Australia, New Zealand and the United States of America, on Free, Prior and Informed Consent, 22 May 2006, New Zealand Ministry of Foreign Affairs and Trade. www.australiaun.org/unny/soc_220506.html
148 *Saramaka v Suriname* Interpretation (2008), op. cit. 26, para 17.
149 MacKay 2009.
150 *Saramaka v Suriname* Interpretation (2008), op. cit. 26, para 17.
151 *Saramaka v Suriname* (2007), op. cit. 25, para 137. The original ruling mentioned 'a large part of their territory'.

The position that consent is always required in extractive sector projects is reinforced by the general recognition that it can be assumed that large-scale extractive projects will always have significant impacts on indigenous peoples. As Goodland, a former senior environmental advisor to the World Bank, explains:

> [N]o modern, large-scale, open-pit mine can be operated without significant long-term impacts, partly because 99 per cent of all rock moved and processed at modern open-cast mines ends as waste. To pretend otherwise is to ignore the world's mining track record. [152]

These impacts extend beyond the environmental domain and include major social, cultural and spiritual impacts. The UN Special Representative on the issue of human rights and transnational corporations and other business enterprises has acknowledged this unique and profound nature of the extractive sector's social and environmental footprint on indigenous peoples' rights, stating:

> The extractive sector – oil, gas and mining – utterly dominates this sample of reported abuses with two thirds of the total . . . The extractive industries also account for most allegations of the worst abuses, up to and including complicity in crimes against humanity. These are typically for acts committed by public and private security forces protecting company assets and property; large-scale corruption; violations of labour rights; and a broad array of abuses in relation to local communities, especially indigenous people. [153]

The analysis of Successive Special Rapporteurs on the rights of indigenous peoples also points to these potentially devastating impacts. The first Special Rapporteur held that consent was crucial in the context of large-scale extractive-based development, while the next Special Rapporteur, who adopted a particular focus on extractive industries, has pointed to large-scale mining operations as one of the scenarios where consent is required as a result of the significance of their impacts. [154] As noted by the Special Rapporteur, under the extant extractive model, indigenous peoples 'continue to be vulnerable to human rights abuse, which erodes the basis of their self-determination and, in some cases, endangers their very existence as distinct peoples'. [155]

The Special Rapporteur further refined his position in relation to the consent requirement in the context of extractive projects in his 2012 report, stating that:

> It is generally understood that indigenous peoples' rights over lands and resources in accordance with customary tenure are necessary to their survival.

---

152 Goodland 2012: 7.
153 UN Doc. E/CN.4/2006/97 (2006), para 25.
154 Anaya, (2010), *Declaración pública del Relator Especial sobre Ley del derecho a la consulta en Perú*, available at: www.ohchr.org
155 UN Doc. A/HRC/18/35 (2011), para 80.

Accordingly, indigenous consent is presumptively a requirement for those aspects of any extractive project taking place within the officially recognized or customary land use areas of indigenous peoples, or that otherwise affect resources that are important to their survival.[156]

This framing of the consent requirement, as triggered by project activities affecting lands and resources held under customary tenure, is closely aligned with that which regards consent as being triggered by any project which affects indigenous peoples' rights and interests. This in fact is reflected in the affirmation of the Special Rapporteur's 2013 report – the final one of his six-year mandate and the culmination of his examination of the extractive sector – that the consent requirement constitutes a general rule applicable to extractive activities within indigenous territories.[157] Victoria Tauli-Corpuz, who took over the Rapporteur mandate in June 2014, has in her previous capacity as chair of the Permanent Forum emphasised the relationship between FPIC and self-determined development and the fact that the former is triggered whenever a proposed activity affects the exercise of the latter.[158] It can therefore be assumed that as Special Rapporteur she will further elaborate on this relationship, and its implications for indigenous conceptions of FPIC.

Other Special Rapporteurs have also affirmed that FPIC is necessary for extractive projects.[159] Likewise all four treaty bodies which have focused on indigenous issues in a concerted manner to date, have made recommendations to States in their concluding observations in relation to the need to obtain indigenous peoples' consent in the context of extractive projects.[160]

The 2009 *Poma Poma v Peru* decision of the HRC and the 2010 *Endorois v Kenya* decision of the African Commission address the requirement for FPIC in contexts relevant to the extractive sector. Both suggest an impact-based trigger for the consent requirement. However, the *Endorois* decision suggests that where indigenous

---

156 UN Doc. A/HRC/21/47 (2012), para 65.
157 UN Doc A/HRC/24/41 (2013), para 28.
158 Tauli-Corpuz 2008.
159 Report of the Special Rapporteur on adequate housing as a component of the right to an adequate standard of living, UN Doc. A/HRC/4/18 (2007) Annex 1 Basic Principles and Guidelines on Development-based Evictions and Displacement, paras 35, 55 (e), 56 (b); Bangladesh open-pit coal mine threatens fundamental rights, warn UN experts [28 February 2012], Geneva, Statement issued by the Special Rapporteurs on: the right to food; right to water and sanitation; extreme poverty; right to freedom of opinion and expression; right to freedom of peaceful assembly and of association; the rights of indigenous peoples; and adequate housing as a component of the right to an adequate standard of living. Available at: www.ohchr.org/en/NewsEvents/Pages/DisplayNews.aspx?NewsID=11878andLangID=E; See also Report of the independent expert on minority issues, Gay McDougall, Addendum Mission to Colombia, 25 January 2011 A/HRC/16/45/Add.1 para 78; and Statement by the United Nations Independent Expert on minority issues, Ms Gay McDougall, on the conclusion of her official visit to Colombia, 1–12 February 2010, Section V, available at: www.ohchr.org/en/NewsEvents/Pages/DisplayNews.aspx?NewsID=9821andLangID=E; see Doyle forthcoming 2015.
160 Doyle and Whitmore 2014: 61–3, addressing Recommendations of the HRC, the CESCR, CERD and the Committee on the Rights of the Child.

property rights are affected, the consent should by default be triggered, while *Poma Poma* suggests that a spectrum of impacts, including those which do not necessarily threaten a people's survival, may trigger the requirement.

In *Poma-Poma v Peru*, the HRC stated that for indigenous participation in decision-making to be effective, their FPIC was required and that 'mere consultation' was inadequate to ensure protection of their rights under Article 27 of the ICCPR. For measures which 'substantially compromise *or* interfere with culturally significant economic activities' to be permissible, consent must be obtained.[161] The wording suggests that interference which is deemed to have anything beyond a limited effect on a people's way of life or livelihood will trigger the consent requirement.[162] The ruling also states that:

> [P]articipation in the decision-making process must be effective, which requires not mere consultation but the free, prior and informed consent of the members of the community. *In addition*, the measures must respect the principle of proportionality so as not to endanger the very survival of the community and its members.[163]

The first sentence makes no reference to the extent of impact, and consequently supports an interpretation of the FPIC requirement as extending beyond cases where cultural or physical survival are threatened, to include a broader range of impacts related to interference with the enjoyment of the right to maintain and develop their cultures. The fact that the consent requirement is 'additional' to compliance with the proportionality principle also suggests that the HRC regards it as extending beyond such contexts. The silence of the decision in relation to the implications for the consent requirement of indigenous peoples' right to self-determination under Article 1 of the Covenant leaves open the prospect of a broader interpretation of the trigger threshold in the future.

In its 2009 ruling in *Endorois v Kenya*, the African Commission derived a consent requirement from the right to property and the peoples' right to development. The consent requirement affirmed in the context of the right to development is associated projects which would have a major impact on their territory,[164] while that affirmed in relation to the right to property is independent of the extent of the potential impact.[165] The invocation by the Commission of a strongly worded restitution provision applicable in all cases where consent is not obtained, and its reference to the links between the right to property and rights to self-determination and right to life, are consistent with the latter all-encompassing trigger where

161 Emphasis added. HRC *Poma Poma v Peru* (2009), op. cit. 5, para 7.6.
162 Ibid., paras 7.4 and 7.6, citing Communications Nos. 511/1992 and 1023/2001, *Lansman v. Finland*, Views adopted on 26 October 1994 and 15 April 2005 respectively.
163 Emphasis added, ibid.: para 7.4.
164 *Endorois v Kenya* (2009), op. cit. 22, para 291.
165 Ibid.: para 226.

property rights are at risk.[166] One possible conclusion from the ruling would be that the African Commission is of the view that: (a) where proposed projects overlap with indigenous peoples' territories, irrespective of formal title, FPIC is always required, and (b) where projects are outside those territories but impact on indigenous peoples' rights, in particular, their right to development, the trigger for FPIC would be related to the degree of impact determined in accordance with indigenous perspectives.

5.7.3 Reflections on the trigger mechanisms

In light of the profound impact of extractive projects on indigenous peoples, the Expert Mechanism on Indigenous Peoples Rights conducted a study focused exclusively on the extractive sector as a follow-up to its 2011 report on the right to participation. It concluded that:

> Under their international human rights obligations, States have a duty to establish legal and policy frameworks that effectively monitor and enforce relevant international laws, norms and standards, including the right to free, prior and informed consent.[167]

The study held that the determination of when consent is required for on-going and proposed extractive projects should be based on the existence of a 'major, significant or direct' impact on indigenous peoples' lives or territories, and an assessment:

> from the perspective and priorities of the indigenous peoples concerned [of impacts to their] rights, survival, dignity and well-being . . . taking into account, *inter alia*, the cumulative effects of previous encroachments or activities and historical inequities faced by the indigenous peoples concerned.[168]

This raises two important issues which have to be borne in mind when considering an impact-based trigger. The first is the issue of cumulative impacts. In addition to considering historical encroachments and their on-going effects as suggested by the study, a full consideration of cumulative impacts would require consideration of any foreseeable future events to which the project could give rise. This is consistent with the reasoning of the HRC in the *Lubicon Lake Band* case where it held that cumulative effects of disparate 'step-by-step' developments can constitute

---

166 Ibid.: paras 212 and 232, citing Daes, UN Doc. E/CN.4/Sub.2/2004/30 (2004) and the Draft Declaration on the Rights of Indigenous Peoples E/CN.4/Sub.2/1994/2/Add.1 (1994).
167 EMRIP UN Doc. A/HRC/EMRIP/2012/2 (2012), para 26(d).
168 Ibid.: Annex: Advice No. 4, para 27.

a violation of Article 27.[169] It is also reflective of jurisprudence at the national level affirming the requirement to consider all foreseeable cumulative impacts.[170] This is of particular importance in the context of small-scale mining operations which are frequently a precursor for further mining operations, including large-scale more invasive operations and the creation of extractive industry-dependent local economies.[171] The fact that small-scale mining can trigger the consent requirement is reflected in national jurisdictions where experience has been gained in the operationalisation of the consent requirement. In the Philippines and Australia's Northern Territory, no differentiation is made under legislation between small-scale and large-scale mining, with both triggering the requirement for consent. [172] Viewed from an impact perspective, a perverse situation exists under legislation in Guyana whereby consent is required for small-scale but not large-scale mining.[173] The Supreme Court in Belize affirmed the requirement for consent independent of the scale of activities and based on actions which 'affect the existence, value, use or enjoyment of the property'.[174] In Colombia, the Constitution Court held that the requirement for consent could apply in the context of small-scale mining when considered in light of the peoples' rights to self-determination, to physical and cultural existence and to their way of life and to practise their customs.[175]

The second issue touched on in the Expert Mechanism study is the role of indigenous peoples in the determination of impacts which trigger the consent requirement. From an implementation perspective, basing the requirement to obtain FPIC on the possible impact of a project raises the question of how such potential impacts on indigenous peoples' well-being or property rights are determined, and by whom. Indigenous peoples' complaints in relation to natural resource extraction are generally targeted at States and corporate entities. Leaving control over determining the impact to these actors, and consequently the decision as to whether FPIC is required or not, would therefore appear to change little in practice and is unlikely to be readily accepted by indigenous peoples. This view is reflected in the position of the Experts Mechanism that the 'perspective and priorities of the indigenous peoples concerned' is a relevant factor in the

169 *Lubicon Lake Band v. Canada*, Communication No. 167/1984 (26 March 1990), UN Doc. Supp. No. 40 (UN Doc. A/45/40) at 1 (1990) 32.2 and 3.3; see also Scheinin 2000: 194.
170 *Te-Moak Tribe of Western Nevada v. U.S. Department of the Interior*, 9th Cir., No. 07–16336, 6/18/10 8999–9007; *Taseko Mines Limited v. Phillips*, 2011 BCSC 1675 Date: 20111202 Dockets: S117685, 114556, para 46.
171 Houghton 2011: 89.
172 Philippines NCIP, *Administrative Order No. 3 Series of 2012: The Revised Guidelines on Free and Prior Informed Consent (FPIC) and Related Processes of 2012*, Sections 19 and 24; *The Aboriginal Land Rights (Northern Territory) Act* 1976 (Section 18 c).
173 *Guyana Amerindian Act* (2005), Section 48; Colombia Constitutional Court Sentencia T-129/11, (2011), Section 6.
174 *Aurelio Cal and the Maya Village of Santa Cruz v Attorney General of Belize; and Manuel Coy and Maya Village of Conejo v Attorney General of Belize*, The Supreme Court of Belize, 2007 Consolidated Claims Claim Nos. 171 and 172 of 2007, para 136(d).
175 Author's translation. Colombia Constitutional Court Sentencia T-129/11, (2011), Section 7(i).

determination of when consent is required,[176] and by the fact that indigenous peoples are working at national, regional and international levels, in conjunction with the Permanent Forum on Indigenous Issues, to develop their own framework of indicators for monitoring their well-being.[177] If the principles underlying the development of this framework are to be respected, then the logical conclusion is that indigenous peoples must have a determining say as to the circumstances under which FPIC is required. Indeed, at a more fundamental level, a model of FPIC consistent with the exercise of a right to self-determination would have to be premised on the principle that assessments of potential impacts on rights are conducted by the rights holders themselves. The emerging practice by indigenous peoples of asserting their right to conduct core aspects of these impact assessments is reflective of this. So too is the practice whereby indigenous peoples develop their own FPIC policies, protocols, templates and manifestos outlining when and how their consent is to be sought in accordance with their own customary laws and practices. A consent-seeking model which removes control over such determination from indigenous peoples would be a reversion to now antiquated trusteeship-type relationships and stands at odds with the notion of constructing new and enduring relationships based on legal principles of equality and consent between indigenous peoples and States.

A pragmatic perspective also supports the recognition of indigenous peoples' role in the determination of triggers for a consent requirement. Projects with impacts which indigenous peoples do not regard as posing any significant threat to their rights are likely to be granted consent. On the other hand, consent for projects with major impacts, or those which they perceive as potentially threatening their physical or cultural survival, is far less likely, and will be contingent on adequate benefits and compensation which offset the perceived risks. As a result, the divergence between positions which assert consent for any project, and that which holds that it is only required for major impacts should, from a pragmatic perspective, be relatively insignificant, suggesting that indigenous determination of when consent is required is a logical approach to follow. In practice, however, an externally determined impact-based trigger provides a space within which vested interests can manoeuvre to gain access to indigenous territories by claiming that particular types of projects, such as small-scale mining, or activities such as exploration, have minor impacts and consequently do not trigger a consent requirement. Once they have gained access to the territory, experience proves that successful resistance to further activity becomes immensely more difficult for a range of reasons, including the potential for manipulation and division of communities and the reluctance on the part of companies and States to disengage once substantial investments have been made.[178]

---

176 EMRIP 2011 Report, UN Doc. A/HRC/18/42 Annex Advice no. 2, para 22; EMRIP (2012) UN Doc. A/HRC/EMRIP/2012/2 Annex Advice no. 4, para 27(a).
177 *Indicators of Well-being, Poverty and Sustainability Relevant to Indigenous Peoples*, February 2008, UN Doc. E/C.19/2008/9.
178 Franks *et al.* 2014.

One of the interesting models in the context of the discussion on triggers for the FPIC requirement is the International Finance Corporation's (IFC) 2012 Performance Standard 7 on Indigenous Peoples, which establishes FPIC as a safeguard for indigenous rights. [179] The approach adopted by the IFC is more restrictive than a self-determination-based conception of FPIC but, depending on how it is implemented, is potentially less restrictive than a trigger based on major impacts to territories or well-being. To a certain degree, it avoids delving into the subjective waters of determination of the extent of impact as a basis for triggering the consent requirement by requiring proof of consent in the event of projects with 'adverse impacts'. Adverse economic, social and cultural impacts are defined as including 'impacts from loss of access to assets or resources or restrictions on land use resulting from project activities',[180] 'loss of identity, culture, and natural resource-based livelihoods as well as exposure to impoverishment and diseases' and threats to food security.[181] A further qualification specifies four categories of projects associated with these impacts, namely those: (a) located on lands, or natural resources on lands, subject to traditional ownership or under customary use; (b) requiring relocation of communities; (c) significantly impacting on critical cultural heritage of indigenous peoples; or (d) using cultural heritage, including knowledge, innovations or practices for commercial purposes.[182] A valid, but unadopted, suggestion was made by the Special Rapporteur on the rights of indigenous peoples during the drafting of the performance standard that a caveat be added that this list is not exhaustive.[183] Despite this omission, the four categories of projects triggering the consent requirement nevertheless appear largely consistent with the UNDRIP and those areas addressed by the jurisprudence of the human rights bodies. The extent to which the IFC's interpretation of the content of FPIC is consistent with the normative framework of indigenous peoples' rights and provides for indigenous control over its operationalisation is, however, less clear. This issue will be addressed in Chapter 7 when examining the role of non-State actors in the operationalisation of the consent requirement.

Drawing on decisions and recommendations at the international, regional and national levels, the chapter has sought to emphasise the jurisprudential trend towards affirming a requirement for FPIC in order to constrain State power to infringe on indigenous peoples' enjoyment of their rights in the context of resource extraction projects impacting on their well-being or territories. In addressing the nature, scope, bases, subjects and triggers of the right to FPIC, the chapter concluded that while certain grey areas may remain in relation to some of these aspects, it is nevertheless reasonable to conclude that under international human

---

179 International Finance Corporation (IFC) Performance Standard No. 7 (2012) on Indigenous Peoples 'forms part of the IFC's Sustainability Framework and is an integral part of IFC's approach to risk management'. See IFC 2012a.
180 IFC 2012a,, paras 1, 8, 14 (footnote 8).
181 IFC 2012b,, para 1, GN 9, GN 12.
182 IFC 2012a, paras 13–17.
183 Anaya (2011) *Memorandum Re: Draft Performance Standard 7 on Indigenous Peoples to: Reider Kvam IFC Environment and Social Development Department Policy and Quality Assurance*, 2 March 2011.

rights law the requirement for FPIC always applies in the context of large-scale, and indeed small-scale, extractive projects. Despite this trend at the international level, State resistance to incorporation of the requirement into legislation remains the norm and debates in relation to its validity continue at the national level. Chapter 6 seeks to critically engage with these debates and associated assumptions underpinning arguments invoked by State actors when challenging the legitimacy of the requirement for FPIC.

6 Debates in relation to the consent requirement

6.1 Introduction

The inherent tension between indigenous peoples' assertion that no resource extraction projects in, or impacting on, their territories should proceed without their FPIC, and the growing demand for access to resources located in those territories by third parties, poses a challenge for States.[1] In most, if not all, States, legislative and policy frameworks have traditionally limited indigenous autonomy and their land and resource rights in favour of external actors interested in exploiting their resource-rich territories. Despite the growing constitutional, legislative and judicial recognition of indigenous peoples' rights, the vast majority of States have yet to fully align these rights-regulating frameworks with the standards affirmed under international human rights law and instead continue to subordinate indigenous peoples' rights to the interests of the extractive industry. This gap between the international framework and national legislation is particularly notable when viewed through the lens of FPIC. In order to justify this divergence, the compatibility of the requirement for FPIC with notions such as State sovereignty, democracy and the power of eminent domain continues to be challenged by States, both in the context of international standard-setting and oversight processes and in national contexts through judicial, legislative and administrative processes. In addition, those States and industry actors opposed to according greater recognition to the requirement attempt to abstract the concept from its rights bases. This has two effects. The first is that it enables them to frame the debate pertaining to its acquisition as a question of whether or not indigenous peoples possess a veto power over State decisions, while ignoring the rights implications of those decisions. The second is that it permits them to frame FPIC as a purely procedural requirement, something which has to be sought as opposed to obtained, thereby rendering impotent its core rights-protecting and substantive component, namely 'consent'. The debates during the drafting of ILO Convention 169 (C169) and the discussions around the negotiation of the UN Declaration on the Rights of Indigenous Peoples (the UNDRIP) illustrate the range of positions

---

1 Eide 2009: 44.

in relation to these objections put forward by States and industry to prevent FPIC's configuration as a duty upon States, embodying an obligation of conduct and of result and a self-determination right of indigenous peoples which all actors are obliged to respect. The chapter draws on these debates in order to deconstruct the arguments presented. It suggests that ultimately many of these arguments are found wanting, and that the real reason underpinning opposition to FPIC is a simple unwillingness to transfer decision-making power from the organs of the State, and by extension from industry, to indigenous peoples, because of its potentially profound implications for access to and control over coveted resources located in their territories.

6.2 Objections based on consent as a veto power

6.2.1 State perspectives on the veto in the context of the UN Declaration

As the requirement to obtain consent implies respecting the right to say 'no', one of the key contentious issues raised by certain States, during the drafting of the UNDRIP, revolved around the notion of a 'right to veto'. Objections to the inclusion of a requirement to obtain FPIC came primarily from the four countries that voted against the adoption of the UNDRIP, namely Australia, Canada, New Zealand, and the United States. This same argument had been raised, most forcibly by Canada and the employers group, during the drafting of C169.[2] These four countries, in particular, Australia and Canada, are home to most of the world's transnational mining companies, many of which have operations or interests in indigenous territories at home and abroad. The position of Australia, New Zealand, and the United States with regard to FPIC is laid out in joint statements submitted to the Permanent Forum and the Human Rights Council: '[I]t is our firm position that there can be no absolute right of free, prior, informed consent that is applicable uniquely to indigenous peoples and that would apply regardless of circumstances.'[3]

They further stated that giving a 'veto' to particular sub-groups of the population was not a position that a democratic government could accept.[4] Commenting on Article 32(2) in its vote against the UNDRIP in the General Assembly, New Zealand had stated that '[it had] some of the most extensive consultation mechanisms in the world, where the principles of the Treaty of Waitangi, including

---

2 International Labour Conference Proceedings, 75th Session (1988) at 32/10; see also Chapter 1.2.3 in this volume.
3 Statement of Peter Vaughn to the Permanent Forum on Indigenous Issues, Representative of Australia, on behalf of Australia, New Zealand and the United States of America, on Free, Prior and Informed Consent, 22 May 2006, New Zealand Ministry of Foreign Affairs and Trade. Available at: www.australiaun.org/unny/soc_220506.html
4 *Note verbale dated 2 August 2006 from the Permanent Mission of Australia to the United Nations Office at Geneva addressed to the Office of the United Nations High Commissioner for Human Rights*, see UN Doc. A/HRC/2/G/1, 24 August 2006.

the principle of informed consent, are enshrined in resource management law.'[5] However, it held that the UNDRIP's provisions implied 'different classes of citizenship, where indigenous people have a right of veto that other groups or individuals do not have'.[6] Canada also objected to the use of the concept of FPIC in the UNDRIP, which it argued could be interpreted as 'giving a veto to indigenous peoples over many . . . development proposals . . . which concern the broader population and may affect indigenous peoples'.[7] During the drafting process these States were the primary drivers behind the attempts to weaken the requirement for FPIC by proposing that the operative verb 'obtain' be changed to 'seek', in relation to FPIC.[8]

Somewhat ironically, in their opposition to the notion of a veto right, these States have clarified that the text of the UNDRIP actually affirms a strong substantive requirement for FPIC – a view largely consistent with its interpretation by human rights bodies. All four States acknowledge the potential for Article 32 to be interpreted as affording indigenous peoples a veto over development projects impacting on their lands, territories and natural resources.[9] Similarly one of the grounds provided by Colombia for abstaining in the General Assembly vote was that '[t]he Declaration's approach to prior consent is different [from that of C169]

5 UN Doc. A/61/PV.107 at 14.
6 UN Doc. A/61/PV.107 at 14; see Young 1995: 171–174, for a commentary on the bicultural system which has emerged in New Zealand.
7 Canada's position on the United Nations Draft Declaration on the Rights of Indigenous Peoples, 29 June 2006, available at: www.ainc-inac.gc.ca/ap/ia/pubs/ddr/ddr-eng.asp
8 Carmen 2012: 4; see also Report of the Working Group established in accordance with Commission on Human Rights' resolution 1995/32 of 3 March 1995 on its eleventh session (22 March 2006), UN Doc. E/CN.4/2006/79.
9 General Assembly 61st Session 2007, UN Doc. A/61/PV.107, 11 (Australia), 12, 13 (Canada), 14 (New Zealand), 15 (United States); See also *Observations of the United States with Respect to the Declaration on the Rights of Indigenous Peoples*, USUN Press Release #204(07), 13 September 2007. Explanation of vote by Robert Hagen, U.S. Advisor, on the Declaration on the Rights of Indigenous Peoples, to the UN General Assembly, 13 September 2007, reproduced in Cummins 2007: 372; and UN Doc. GA/10612 Sixty-first General Assembly Plenary 107th and 108th Meetings, *General Assembly Adopts Declaration on Rights of Indigenous Peoples;* see also Joint Australia, New Zealand and the United States Statement, *Statements and Speeches by Ministry Representatives,* 2006, United Nations General Assembly, 61st session, Third Committee: Item 64(a) The Declaration on the Rights of Indigenous Peoples Statement by H.E. Ambassador Rosemary Banks on behalf of Australia, New Zealand and the United States, Monday, 16 October 2006 [internet] 2006 (accessed 20 August 2012), available at: www.mfat.govt.nz/Media-and-publications/Media/MFAT-speeches/2006/0-16-October-2006b.php; Canada's Position: United Nations Draft Declaration on the Rights of Indigenous Peoples [internet] 2006 (accessed 20 August 2012), available at: www.ainc-inac.gc.ca/ap/ia/pubs/ddr/ddr-eng.asp; Declaration on the Rights of Indigenous Peoples General Assembly, 13 September 2007, Explanation of vote by the Hon. Robert Hill, Ambassador and Permanent Representative of Australia to the United Nations (As delivered) [Internet], 2007, (accessed 20 August 2012), available at: www.unny.mission.gov.au/unny/GA_070913.html; and New Zealand Ministry of Foreign Affairs and Trade (MFAT), Explanation of Vote, HE Rosemary Banks, New Zealand Permanent Representative to the United Nations, 13 September 2007, [Internet], 2007, (accessed 20 August 2012), available at: www.mfat.govt.nz/Media-and-publications/Media/MFAT-speeches/2007/0-13-September-2007.php

and could amount to a possible veto on the exploitation of natural resources in indigenous territories in the absence of an agreement'.[10]

On their subsequent adoption of the UNDRIP in 2010, following pressure from indigenous peoples and States through the Universal Review Process,[11] Canada and the United States of America issued statements with somewhat contradictory interpretations of the consent requirement to their original position, with both States emphasising the 'non-binding' nature of the UNDRIP. Addressing its concerns regarding the notion of FPIC 'when used as a veto', Canada stated it was confident that it could 'interpret the principles expressed in the UNDRIP in a manner that is consistent with our Constitution and legal framework'.[12] While acknowledging the moral and political force of the UNDRIP, the United States stated that it understood the Declaration's requirement for FPIC 'to call for a process of meaningful consultation with tribal leaders, but not necessarily the agreement of those leaders, before the actions addressed in those consultations are taken'.[13]

Two other States had made qualifications in relation to the requirement to obtain consent when voting in favour of the UNDRIP. Sweden held that Article 32(2) 'shall be interpreted as a guarantee that indigenous peoples must be consulted, not as giving them a right of veto' and it should only apply to 'such lands or territories that are formally owned by indigenous peoples'. [14]

In a slightly more constructive interpretation of Article 32(2), Suriname suggested that it represented a requirement '[to] seek prior consultations in order to prevent unjustified disregard for human rights. The level, nature and extent of such consultations depend, in every instance, on the specific circumstances.'[15]

Another interesting development has been the acceptance by States such as Russia, which abstained from the vote on the UNDRIP, of recommendations made at the UPR process that they support the UNDRIP and comply with the principles contained in it.[16] Russia also committed to implementing 'the recommendations raised by Committee on the Elimination of Racial Discrimination (CERD) as to how to improve the situation of the indigenous communities'.[17]

---

10 General Assembly, 61st Session 2007, UN Doc. A/61/PV.107, 18.
11 Recommendations made by Austria, Bolivia, Denmark, Norway and Pakistan to Canada at the 4th Session of UPR in February 2009. Recommendations made by Austria, Iran, Mexico and Pakistan to New Zealand at the 5th session in May 2009.
12 Indian and Northern Affairs Canada, 'Canada's Statement of Support on the United Nations Declaration on the Rights of Indigenous Peoples', 12 Nov. 2010, available at: www.ainc-inac.gc.ca/ap/ia/dcl/stmt-eng.asp.
13 US Department of State, 'Announcement of U.S. Support for the United Nations Declaration on the Rights of Indigenous Peoples', 16 Dec. 2010 at 5, available at: www.state.gov/documents/organization/153223.pdf.
14 General Assembly, 61st Session 2007, UN Doc. A/61/PV.107 at 24.
15 Ibid. at 27.
16 Accepted recommendation by Mexico to Russia, UPR, 4th session (February 2009) (29 May 2009) UN Doc. A/HRC/11/19 at 85.56,
17 Accepted recommendation by Denmark to Russia, UPR, 4th session (February 2009). Ibid. at 85.56.

A similar recommendation was made to Kenya which it rejected,[18] however, it accepted a recommendation '[to] [i]mplement the recommendations and decisions of ... the African Commission on Human and Peoples' Rights, particularly those relating to the rights of indigenous peoples'.[19]

In both cases, respect for the principle of FPIC is addressed under the commitments made by these States. Respect for the principle of consent has also been addressed in the UPR process. A recommendation by Denmark to 'undertake effective consultations with indigenous peoples based on free, prior and informed consent' was rejected by Tanzania.[20] New Zealand accepted the recommendation made to it in relation to the role of FPIC in the resolution of disputes between the State and indigenous peoples, that consistent with the observations of CERD and the Special Rapporteur on the rights of indigenous peoples:

> [It should] continue the new dialogue between the State and the Maori regarding the Foreshore and Seabed Act of 2004, in order to find a way of mitigating its discriminatory effects through a mechanism involving prior informed consent of those affected.[21]

Canada has likewise accepted the recommendation that:

> [It] [e]nsure that all consultation and consent duties are respected by all responsible government agencies at federal and provincial level as well as to ensure that the relevant recommendations of United Nations treaty bodies are fully taken into account and that the specific claims processes do not restrict the progressive development of Aboriginal rights in the country.[22]

Commitments made by States during the UPR process have a potentially significant legal dimension under international law, possibly representing sources of legal obligations and ultimately contributing towards evidence of *opinio juris*.[23] In addition, further recommendations and commitments under the process to implement the jurisprudence of human rights bodies and uphold standards requiring consent contribute not only to the legal standing of the principle under international law but also to the propagation of the norm of FPIC beyond the ambit of State actors and institutions.

---

18 Rejected recommendation by Mexico to Kenya, UPR, 8th session (May 2010) (17 June 2010), UN Doc. A/HRC/15/8 at 103.6.
19 Accepted recommendation by Bolivia to Kenya, UPR, 8th session (May 2010) (17 June 2010), UN Doc. A/HRC/15/8 at 101.114.
20 Rejected Recommendation by Denmark to Tanzania, UPR, 12th session, October 2011 (8 December 2011) UN Doc. A/HRC/19/4 at 86.49.
21 Accepted recommendation by Mexico to New Zealand, UPR, 5th session, May 2009 (4 June 2009) UN Doc. A/HRC/12/8 at 81.58.
22 Accepted recommendation by Austria to Canada, UPR, 4th session, February 2009 (3 March 2009), UN Doc. A/HRC/11/17 at 86.55.
23 Domínguez Redondo 2012: 701–705.

6.2.2 Discussion on the veto in the drafting of CERD general recommendation XXIII

In the past three decades debates over the requirement for FPIC have frequently been reduced to a binary question of whether or not indigenous peoples hold veto powers over national development. This approach to the concept of FPIC is ideologically inconsistent with the manner in which the consent requirement has been framed under human rights jurisprudence. Under that jurisprudence the requirement has been addressed from the perspective of its role in guaranteeing indigenous peoples enjoyment of their rights and their empowerment to determine their own future, rather than the extent to which it infringes on State power by conferring a veto power on indigenous peoples.

The issue of a veto power has, however, on occasion, been directly addressed by human rights bodies. The drafting history of CERD's General Recommendation XXIII is one such example. Interestingly, a remark by Van Boven during the drafting process suggests that, in part, the General Recommendation may have been the product of a concern that CERD was being 'side-lined' as, '[s]ome matters which might have been referred to the Committee, such as indigenous issues, were being referred to the Human Rights Committee'.[24] The issuance of its General Recommendation on the Rights of Indigenous Peoples, with its affirmation of a requirement for informed consent, placed CERD at the cutting edge of collective rights in general,[25] and indigenous peoples' issues in particular, and has acted as a catalyst for the emergence of the requirement for FPIC under human rights jurisprudence.[26] The discussions on the Recommendation's drafting indicate that the consent requirement was introduced in light of 'the magnitude of the problem' of land deprivation that had become evident from the Committee's consideration of the situation in various States,[27] with Brazil cited as one such example.[28] In its report to CERD, the year prior to the drafting process, Brazil had held that it was addressing the issue of exploitation of indigenous peoples' lands by ensuring that '[n]othing could be done . . . without [indigenous peoples'] own consent'.[29]

---

24 Summary Record of the 1215th meeting, 4 August 1997, UN Doc. CERD/C/SR.1215 (7 August 1997), para 84.
25 Castellino 2006: 1.
26 For examples of where General Recommendation XXIII has been invoked, see Inter-American Commission, *Mary and Carrie Dann v. United States*, Case 11.140, Report No. 75/02, Inter-Am. C.H.R., Doc. 5, rev. 1 at 860 (2002) and *The Mayagna (Sumo) Awas Tingni Community v. Nicaragua*, Inter-Am. Ct. H.R., (ser. C) No. 79 (Aug. 31, 2001); Inter-American Court of Human Rights in *Saramaka People v. Suriname*, Judgment of November 28, 2007 (Preliminary Objections, Merits, Reparations, and Costs), Inter-Am. Ct. H.R., (Ser. C) No. 172 (2007); and the African Commission Communication No. 155/96 (2001) *The Social and Economic Rights Action Center for Economic and Social Rights v Nigeria*, and Communication No. 276 (2003); African Commission on Human and Peoples' Rights Case 276/2003 – *Centre for Minority Rights Development (Kenya) and Minority Rights Group International on behalf of Endorois Welfare Council v Kenya* (2009).
27 Summary record of the 1183rd meeting, UN Doc. CERD/C/SR.1183 (3 January 1997), para 104.
28 Ibid.
29 Summary record of the 1159th meeting: Brazil, Republic of Korea. UN Doc. CERD/C/SR.1159 (5 November 1996), para 26.

Wolfrum, the primary drafter of the Recommendation, which was originally intended to focus only on compensation and restitution issues,[30] was of the opinion that indigenous peoples' future should be 'determined together with them as partners' so that 'their rights are neither neglected nor are they treated as objects'.[31] He regarded a mere right to participate in decision-making as inadequate to safeguard these rights, and instead held that informed consent was the necessary standard.[32] In effect, his proposal was that respect for the principle of non-discrimination implied a self-determination-based approach to engagement with indigenous peoples. Wolfrum argued that his proposed text was consistent with the then draft *UN Declaration on the Right of Indigenous Peoples*, the proposed *Inter-American Declaration on the Rights of Indigenous Peoples*[33] and legislative developments in some States.[34] Addressing concerns expressed by some committee members regarding a veto power over decisions of central government, Wolfrum pointed to legislation in Australia which 'stipulated that mines could not be sunk in land occupied by the Aborigines without their consent'.[35] The third State he pointed to was Argentina which he held had recently adopted legislation very similar to the proposed general recommendation.[36] Other committee members emphasised the importance of the power to protect their rights in decision-making processes which the consent requirement provided to indigenous peoples but which the notion of participation did not.[37] It was also noted that the General Recommendation did not have to be constrained by the weaker consultation requirement in C169.[38]

Commenting on these discussions and the final text of the Recommendation, which included an unambiguous FPIC requirement, Thornberry, a long-standing CERD committee member, concludes that there was a consensus that the formulation that had been reached distinguished:

> between the general right of effective participation in public life, and the narrower issue of decisions directly affecting those indigenous groups. In the latter case, the sense of the Committee's deliberations appears to be that the peoples do have a right of veto.[39]

The self-determination right to withhold consent clearly embodies the right to reject proposed activities. However, as emerges from the Recommendation's

---

30 Summary record of the 1171st meeting: Democratic Republic of the Congo, Swaziland, UN Doc. CERD/C/SR.1171 (14 November 1996), para 44.
31 Wolfrum 1999: 369–382; see also Wolfrum 1999: 498, 515.
32 Ibid.: 515; see also Summary record of the 1235th meeting: Algeria, Democratic Republic of the Congo, Mexico, Poland, UN Doc. CERD/C/SR.1235 (5 August 1997), para 67.
33 UN Doc. CERD/C/SR.1235. Ibid.: para 93.
34 Ibid.: para 80, 93.
35 UN Doc. CERD/C/SR.1171 (14 November 1996), para 80.
36 Ibid.: para 93.
37 Ibid.: paras 72, 76, 82.
38 Ibid.: paras 71, 72.
39 Thornberry 2002: 217.

drafting history and CERD's subsequent jurisprudence, this right, where it is invoked, is premised on its necessity to protect the realisation of other indigenous rights rather than emerging from a discourse advocating a veto power. Finally, from the perspective of norm adoption and emergence, the drafting of the FPIC requirement in the Recommendation is interesting in that it is illustrative of the connection between local, domestic and international norms. The requirement for consent in national policy and legislation, itself driven by indigenous advocacy and perspectives, served to inform the emergence of the FPIC norm in the international arena, a process in which CERD's Recommendation and indigenous advocacy played a catalytic and mutually reinforcing role.

6.2.3 The Colombian Constitutional Court's engagement with FPIC and the veto question

Another noteworthy engagement with the veto argument from a human rights perspective is found in the jurisprudence of the Colombian Constitutional Court. Since 1991 the court has developed an expansive body of jurisprudence addressing consultation, and more recently consent, rights of indigenous and tribal peoples, with the ILO supervisory bodies describing it as 'exemplary in identifying problems regarding the holding of prior consultations'.[40] The court suggests that one approach to reconciling the two extremes between a veto power and mere information provision is by using a 'degree of impact' criterion, with consultation and consent acting to protect the communities by determining the least harmful measures. This perspective has to be contextualised within the understanding that what is at stake is not only the potential economic benefits which may be derived from a project, but 'also the present and future of a people, and its members, that have the right to self-determination and to defend its physical and cultural existence'.[41] This self-determination right applies 'regardless of how "absurd or exotic" their customs and way of life way appear to some'.[42] Having contextualised the requirement for consent as a self-determination issue integral to a people's physical and cultural survival, the court then proceeded to explain the necessity of avoiding situations in which the discussion is framed in terms of 'who can veto whom'.[43] In rejecting the veto framework as an appropriate lens through which to address the requirement for FPIC, the court held that the 'abstract general interest and the majority vision of development and progress associated with infrastructure works' cannot be given precedence when these projects are to be developed in indigenous peoples' territories.[44] Building on this principle, it reasoned that 'an ethnic community cannot be forced to give up their way of life and culture due to

---

40 Observation, CEACR 2009/80th Session in ILO 2010: 58.
41 Colombia Constitutional Court Sentencia T-129/11, (2011) Section 6.
42 Ibid.
43 Author's translation. Ibid.
44 Author's translation. Ibid.

the mere arrival of an infrastructure or mining project'. [45] Instead, the court held that, when a project had the potential to cause a community's way of life to be transformed or to disappear, consent is necessary to guarantee the least harmful outcome, and should be respected by the courts and organs of the State.[46]

The CERD deliberations and the reasoning of the Colombian Constitutional Court illustrate that rejecting the requirement for indigenous peoples' consent on the basis that it accords them a veto power obscures the reality that what is actually being affirmed is that the State, and in practice the extractive industry, are themselves exercising a veto power over indigenous peoples' exercise of their right to self-determination. Instead of reconciling and balancing potentially competing claims to self-determination, this position holds that an abstract and undefined public interest, which 'happens' to coincide with the private interests of the extractive sector, always overrides the legitimate exercise of indigenous peoples' right to self-determined decision-making. It also fails to address the potential impact of extractive projects on the broad range of rights which the consent requirement aims to protect. In addition to the public interest grounds, a number of other related arguments are presented by States for rejecting the consent requirement. These include the view that the notion of FPIC is not compatible with the principle of democracy, the idea that it represents a limitation on State sovereignty and the argument that the power of eminent domain conditions all property rights. These lines of reasoning opposing the consent requirement are addressed below.

6.3 Public interest, common good and national development objections

The case for limiting or even denying the requirement for FPIC is frequently premised on the argument that indigenous peoples cannot stop projects that are deemed to be in the public interest or justified under the notion of national development. This argument can be traced back to ILO Convention 107 (C107) and is evident in subsequent discussion on its revision in 1986, where it was strongly advocated by industry representatives.[47] Indeed, the case could be made that the very notion of imposing development in the public interest has undertones of long-discredited integration policies and the colonial civilising mission. The counter-argument, that the notion of 'public interest' 'is open to abuse as a lazy justification (or, even worse as a rhetorical defence of the indefensible)',[48] is particularly relevant in the context of extractive sector activities. As evidenced by a range of international empirical studies questioning the macro economic

---

45 Author's translation. Ibid.
46 Ibid.
47 International Labour Conference, Partial Revision of the Indigenous and Tribal Populations Convention, No. 107 (1957), Provisional Record 36, 75th session, 19.
48 Beyleveld and Brownsword 2007: 272, citing Brownswood 1993.

benefits of mining, this public interest argument is strongly contested and rarely substantiated in the context of such activities.[49] The concerns raised in these studies regarding the limited benefits accruing to developing countries from resource extraction are exacerbated in many countries by generous tax incentives to entice foreign investment, by high levels of corruption associated with the sector, and by the potential long-term impact on other economic sectors such as agriculture, fisheries and tourism. On the other hand, the local-level impacts are undeniable, pervasive and severe.[50] Narrowly framed initiatives, such as the Extractive Industries Transparency Initiative, aimed at addressing the pervasive corruption in the sector, remain largely blind to the sector's other rights-denying impacts, and may even have the perverse effect of legitimising them by detracting attention from them.

International legal instruments also challenge the use of the public interest argument. The text and drafting of the UNDRIP indicate that neither the public interest nor the common good were envisaged as legitimate grounds for placing limitations on the right to self-determined development and FPIC in the context of resource extraction under Article 32. No reference is made to either as grounds for limitations on rights in Article 46(2). A proposal to add the 'common good' to Article 46 as a basis for placing such limitations was considered but rejected.[51] In contrast, Article 30 includes an express reference to a 'relevant public interest' as a basis for overwriting the outcome of consultations in relation to military operations in indigenous territories.[52] The absence of such a qualification under Article 32 suggests it should not be assumed to apply. The threshold under Article 46 in terms of the burden of proof for imposing limitation on rights protected by the FPIC requirement therefore remains extremely high. An interpretation of the UNDRIP that justifies derogations from the requirement to obtain FPIC on the basis of general public interest or national development-based arguments could therefore lead to a shift in the burden of proof away from the State and onto indigenous peoples in a manner that is incompatible with the spirit and intent of the UNDRIP. This position is also reflected in the Vienna Declaration and Programme of Action which affirms that 'development may not be invoked to justify the abridgement of internationally recognised human rights'.[53] As a result, development must proceed consistently with indigenous peoples' right to self-determination. Furthermore, international and regional human rights bodies and national courts have cautioned States against infringement of indigenous peoples'

---

49 Sachs and Warner 1997; Sachs and Warner 2001: 827–838; Auty 1998; Power 2002; see also Humphreys *et al.* 2007.
50 Ruggie, UN Doc. E/CN.4/2006/97 (2006), para 25; The World Bank Group and Extractive Industries, The Final Report of World Bank Extractive Industry Review, *Striking a Better Balance*, Volume 1, December 2003; for case studies, see Evans *et al.* (eds) 2002; Caruso *et al.* 2005; see Padel and Das 2010; see also Kirsch 2006.
51 Article 45 at the time, UN Doc. E/CN.4/2006/79 at 76.
52 Daes 2011: 38 notes this weakness in the Article.
53 Vienna Declaration and Programme of Action, adopted by the World Conference on Human Rights on 25 June 1993, Part I, at para. 10. UN Doc. A/CONF.157/23, 12 July 1993.

rights on the basis of national development and public interest.[54] CERD has held that the exploitation of resources for national development 'must be exercised consistently with the rights of indigenous and tribal peoples'.[55] The Human Rights Commission (HRC) has affirmed in its 1994 decision in the case of *Länsman v Finland*, that the scope of a State's freedom with regard to development on indigenous peoples' lands cannot be 'assessed by reference to a margin of appreciation but by reference to the obligations it has undertaken in Article 27', which, it subsequently clarified, includes an obligation to obtain FPIC.[56]

In his explanation of the consent requirement, the Special Rapporteur on the rights of indigenous peoples held that it does 'not bestow on indigenous peoples a right to unilaterally impose their will on States when the latter act legitimately and faithfully in the public interest'.[57] In light of actual State practice, the qualification 'legitimately and faithfully', and the question of how this is to be guaranteed, are of fundamental importance. So too is the manner in which the public interest is determined, as due consideration must be given to the fact that guaranteeing indigenous peoples' rights is fundamental to it.[58] The public interest argument appears strongest in contexts where the requirement for FPIC is exclusively linked to property rights which are made subject to public interest limitations. However, where the right to property is addressed under human rights law, such limitations are generally made subject to 'conditions provided for by the law'.[59] The African Commission ruling in the *Endorois v Kenya* case provides some guidance in this regard. Article 14 of the African Charter states '[t]he right to property shall be guaranteed. It may only be encroached upon in the interest of public need or in the general interest of the community *and* in accordance with the provisions of appropriate laws'.[60] The African Commission interpreted this as establishing a conjunctive test, whereby any limitation on property rights on the basis of the public interest also had to meet the condition of being 'in accordance

54 *Länsman et al. v. Finland*, Communication No. 511/1992, UN Doc. CCPR/C/52/D/511/1992 (1994). See also footnotes 55, 61, 66 and 67.

55 *Suriname*, UN Doc. CERD/C/64/CO/9/Rev.2, (2004), para 15. See also *Handolsdalen Sami village and others v Sweden* application no. 39013/04.

56 Communications No. 511/1992, *Länsman v. Finland*, Views adopted on 26 October 1994, para 9.4.; HRC *Angela Poma Poma v Peru*, Communication No. 1457/2006 CCPR/C/95/D/1457/2009, 24 April 2009.

57 UN Doc. A/HRC/12/34 (2009), para 49.

58 MacKay 2011.

59 American Convention on Human Rights, O.A.S. Treaty Series No. 36, 1144 U.N.T.S. 123, entered into force July 18, 1978, reprinted in *Basic Documents Pertaining to Human Rights in the Inter-American System*, OEA/Ser.L.V/II.82 Doc. 6, rev..1 at 25 (1992), Article 21(2); Protocol to the Convention for the Protection of Human Rights and Fundamental Freedoms, 213 U.N.T.S. 262, entered into force May 18, 1954, Article 1; African [Banjul] Charter on Human and Peoples' Rights, adopted June 27, 1981, OAU Doc. CAB/LEG/67/3 rev. 5, 21 I.L.M. 58 (1982), entered into force Oct. 21, 1986, Article 14 (henceforth African [Banjul] Charter on Human and Peoples' Rights).

60 Emphasis added. African [Banjul] Charter on Human and Peoples' Rights, Article 14.

with the law' and being proportional.[61] Particularly stringent constraints were to be imposed on the invocation of public interest in the context of resource exploitation in indigenous territories, as the rights at stake included 'the right to life, food, the right to self-determination, to shelter, and the right to exist as a people'.[62] According to the Commission, meeting the 'in accordance with the law' component of the test necessitated that consultations be held.[63] However, owing to the exacting threshold established in relation to the protection of indigenous peoples' property rights, these consultations required 'that consent be accorded'.[64] The ruling effectively held that the public interest justification for infringements on indigenous peoples' rights, in addition to having to serve a legitimate aim and be proportional, also had to meet the threshold of consent. This was similar to the conclusion reached by the Inter-American Court of Human Rights, that the requirement for consent formed part of the safeguard against potentially significant limitations on indigenous peoples' right to property. This consent-based constraint on the public interest justification, in the context of resource extraction activities, could in future inform the European Court of Human Rights' interpretation of indigenous peoples' property rights as any limitations on them are subject to general principles of international law.[65]

The public interest argument as a basis for limiting indigenous peoples' rights has also been rejected by courts at the national level. The Canadian Supreme Court has held that it was 'so vague as to provide no meaningful guidance and so broad as to be unworkable as a test for the justification'.[66] A similar argument as to the public interest argument being inadequate to justify limitations on indigenous peoples' rights was made by the Constitutional Court of Colombia in light of the axiological character of the Constitution.[67] The court held that this character was inconsistent with the notion that the function of public authorities was to guarantee the public interest and ensure progress for the majority in accordance with their particular mandates and statutory powers, even if this infringed on the rights of ethnic groups.[68] Instead it held that the axiological character of the Constitution 'imposes the need to balance the relative importance of the values protected by the constitutional norm such as diversity and pluralism and those protected by mandatory legal rules'.[69] In this regard it is important to highlight that, as recognised by provincial Supreme Courts in Canada,[70] respect for indigenous

---

61 *Endorois v Kenya* (2009), op. cit. 26, para 211.
62 Ibid., para 212, citing Daes, UN Doc. E/CN.4/Sub.2/2004/30 (2004), 48.
63 *Endorois v Kenya* (2009), op. cit. 26, para 225.
64 Ibid., para 226.
65 Protocol to the Convention for the Protection of Human Rights and Fundamental Freedoms, 213 U.N.T.S. 262, entered into force, May 18, 1954, Article 1; To date, the court has not ventured into such issues, see Koivurova 2011: 7.
66 Canadian Supreme Court case *R v Sparrow* [1990] 1 S.C.R. 1075.
67 Colombia Constitutional Court, Sentencia T-129/11, (2011) Section 5.
68 Ibid.
69 Author's translation. Ibid.
70 *Wahgoshig First Nation (WFN) v Her Majesty the Queen in Right of Ontario et al.* 2011. ONSC 7708 2012 01, para 72.

peoples' rights is an essential dimension of the public interest. The Canadian Courts have also held that 'the integrity of the consultation process itself' is a consideration in assessing the public interest.[71] This centrality of indigenous peoples' rights, including the right to consultation and FPIC, to the public interest and common good is something which tends to be overlooked in the context of natural resource extraction in their territories, even in contexts where the FPIC requirement has legislative force.[72] The public interest must be understood from a principled, and not 'moral majority' perspective, and consequently has to be consistent with guaranteeing respect for rights and the requirements of proportionality and necessity.[73] The centrality of indigenous peoples' unique relationship with their territories to the realisation of their right to self-determination and to their continued existence as peoples implies that the additional requirement of obtaining their FPIC is necessary to safeguard these rights. This does not necessarily frame FPIC as an absolute principle which will always override the rights of others in society. Rather, it acknowledges the threshold established by the disproportionate negative impact of non-consensual extractive industry projects, not only on indigenous peoples' property rights but also on their physical and cultural existence and their self-determination rights. In general, even if a particular extractive project is proven to be indispensable for meeting a given need, that need will be far from proportionate to the potential negative impacts on the self-determination rights of an indigenous people if it proceeds in the absence of their consent. This gives rise to the strong presumption that the self-determination-based right to withhold FPIC is not subject to a general public interest limitation. In order to provide a context in which extreme cases where the human rights of others, in particular, their self-determination rights, come into conflict with the self-determination rights of indigenous peoples, a mechanism aimed at balancing these competing claims on the basis of respect for human rights principles, together with the standards of necessity and proportionality, is required. Such mechanisms should be participatory in nature, be developed in cooperation with indigenous peoples and agreed to by them, and ensure that equal weight is accorded to their perspectives. The operation of such a mechanism would have to be based on the consent of indigenous peoples and assumes that the State has established the preconditions for obtaining FPIC. It does not, however, imply that indigenous peoples are obliged to enter into consultations in relation to activities proposed in their territories.[74] Finally, when considering the issue of national development as a purported justification for non-recognition of the requirement for FPIC, it is important to remember that this was precisely the justification deployed under the rights-denying assimilation-orientated provisions of C107.

---

71 *Platinex Inc. v. Kitchenuhmaykoosib Inninuwug First Nation*, 2006 CanLII 26171, para 109.
72 See, for example, Philippines Supreme Court cases *Didipio Earth-Savers' Multi-Purpose Association, [DESAMA] Inc. et al. vs. Elisea Gozun, et al.* G.R. No. 157882 (30 March 2006); see also *La Bugal-B'lann Tribal Ass'n v. Ramos*, G.R. No 127882 421 S.C.R.A. 148 (1 Dec. 2004), for a commentary on the La Bugal-B'lann ruling, see Khee-Jin Tan 2005–2006; and Doyle 2010: 85–94.
73 Beyleveld and Brownsword 2007: 272.
74 UN Doc A/HRC/24/41, para 58.

6.4 FPIC and democracy: inclusive versus exclusive democracy

The argument that the FPIC requirement is inconsistent with the notion of democracy, as it allows one group to 'veto' the activities of others has been raised by those States opposed to the concept.[75] This argument against FPIC raises the question as to what is meant by democracy and what relationship it bears to the right to self-determination and principle of consent of the governed, as well as the application of these concepts to indigenous peoples.[76] Cassese has suggested that models of self-determination which recognise the right of territorial concentrated group to make autonomous decisions over lands and natural resources are not a threat to democracy but 'a way of solving the problems of democracy'.[77] Indeed, the notion of an evolving right of democratic governance under international law as a derivation of the right to self-determination was one of the primary arguments used by indigenous peoples in their negotiation of the UNDRIP provisions.[78]

Barsh posits that conceiving contemporary democracy as based on the consent of individuals is not consistent with contemporary political realities.[79] Instead, he holds that modern democracies involve inter-group competition for decision-making power and are pluralistic in nature, affording recognition to a number of 'organizations of interest'.[80] The politically marginalised situation of indigenous peoples has resulted in their *de facto* exclusion from this pluralistic model of governance, perpetuating a situation whereby their interests are not reflected in national policy and legislation. This is consistent with the critique of pluralist theories of democracy as favouring powerful vested interests in determining the political agenda.[81] This reality is epitomised by the elite theory which draws attention to the hermetically sealed social sphere in which the political elite and powerful interest groups co-exist.[82] It consequently acknowledges the extent to which power within ostensibly democratic systems is exercised by the elite, either consciously or subconsciously, in the interests of this substratum of society, in particular, the business sector.[83] This sector has long been recognised as having an inordinate influence on policy agenda-setting, determining both the issues that are considered for decision-making and the outcome of those decisions.[84] Another

---

75 See Chapter 6.2.1 on the State perspective on consent as a veto.
76 For a discussion of the concept of democracy based on consent of the governed under international law, see Franck 1992: 46; for a view which questions the centrality of consent as a foundation for the territorial State, see Brilmayer 1989–1990: 1; for a discussion on the relationship between liberal democracy and the concept of indigenous peoples, see Merlan 2009: 303.
77 Cassese 1995: 355, 359.
78 Davis 2008: 459–460; Franck 1992: 52.
79 Barsh 1992: 120.
80 Ibid.: 121, citing Vanhanen 1990: 11.
81 For a critique of various models of democracy, see Rowbottom 2010.
82 Bachrach and Baratz 1962.
83 Ibid., see also Wright Mills 2000.
84 Ibid.

dimension to the exercise of power in democratic systems is ideological power.[85] This dimension of power disinvests the subject over which it is exercised of awareness that they are complying with normative values determined by the dominant forces.[86] Instead these values or realities are regarded as preordained, unchangeable or natural, and no other realistic alternative to them is envisaged.[87] As a result, disempowerment can become self-perpetuating and serves to 'sustain internal constraints upon self-determination'.[88]

Both elite and ideological domination are manifested in the exercise of power over decision-making in relation to extractive policies and operations. Regulatory capture and dominant developmental discourses function to narrow the democratic space available to question resource usage and developmental strategies. The worldwide, industry-driven, revision of resource regulatory frameworks which commenced in the 1980s is evidence of this.[89] Together with international financial institutions, the extractive sector has been successful in promoting a 'shift in the policy orientation of developing countries in favour of enabling and facilitating private investment in mineral resource development'.[90] At the same time, the industry has played and, despite some potentially positive recent developments, continues to play a significant role in constraining the recognition of indigenous rights in national and international frameworks.[91] In many developing countries such as the Philippines, where the resource sector is traditionally notorious for corruption,[92] regulatory capture is perceived as determining the *modus operandi* of the agencies responsible for mining promotion and licencing.[93] Parallel to this, the ideology of the predominant neo-liberal developmental discourse presents an extractive-based foreign direct investment-driven model as the unique solution to poverty alleviation, identified as the primary driver for growth and sustainable development.[94] The common good or public interest is assumed to be served by rapid and widespread expansion of industries under this development paradigm.[95] Within it, indigenous peoples' rights are marginal considerations, classifiable as parochial interests,[96] which are easily dismissed, ignored, or excluded from the

85 Lukes 1974.
86 Ibid.: 122.
87 Ibid.: 128.
88 Ibid.: 122.
89 Bridge 2004: 406–421; see also Caruso and Colchester 2005: 57–58.
90 Campbell 2005: 816; see also Naito, Remy, and Williams 2001.
91 Mcrae *et al.* 2009: 273, 277–279, 301, 307, 311, 312, 314, 317. See also Report by G. McDougall, Country Rapporteur, to the 1323rd meeting of the Committee on the Elimination of Racial Discrimination, 12 March 1999; Libby 1989; and Altman 2009: 290–293. For an overview of Aboriginal Rights in Australia, see Castellino and Keane 2009: 31–97; Doyle 2010a: 86; Goodland and Wicks 2009; Caruso and Colchester 2005.
92 Doyle *et al.* 2007: 9.
93 Goodland and Wicks 2009; Doyle *et al.* 2007; Philippines ICERD Shadow Report 2009: 46.
94 Whitmore 2006.
95 Valbuena Wouriyu 2005: 158. Mining is declared in the public interest under *Colombian Mining Code Law 685*, 15 August 2001, Article 13.
96 *La Bugal-B'lann Tribal Ass'n v. Ramos*, G.R. No 127882 421 S.C.R.A. 148 (1 Dec. 2004).

elite-dominated political space where policy agendas and decisions affecting them are determined.

The question of whether or not a right of indigenous peoples to give or withhold FPIC is inconsistent with the practice of democracy therefore has to be considered in light of the actual distribution and exercise of power within democratic systems. This in turn requires an examination of the extent to which democracies are successful in ensuring effective indigenous participation in decision-making and protecting their rights and interests, particularly when viewed from the historical perspective of marginalisation and discrimination. Viewed from this perspective, attempts to delegitimise the principle of FPIC on the grounds that it is inconsistent with democracy are perhaps more reflective of the desire to maintain extant power structures, which are inherently exclusionary of indigenous peoples. The reality that the FPIC of indigenous peoples is a legal requirement in a number of democracies lends weight to the perception that the crux of the issue is maintaining the status quo in terms of power distribution as opposed to concerns for the exercise of genuine democratic governance and any inconsistency between it and the principles of FPIC.

Indeed, the requirement for FPIC can be justified on the grounds that democracy is premised on the consent of the governed, and that this consent can be provided by groups possessing the right to self-determination.[97] Self-determined free prior and informed consent is merely the culturally appropriate mechanism through which indigenous peoples, as collectives, accord their consent to measures directly impacting on them on the basis of equality with other peoples.[98] Consequently, for democracy to be inclusive, recognition of the FPIC requirement is necessary.[99] This precise issue was raised by the Australian Aboriginal and Torres Strait Islander Commission when opposing the deletion of the concept of FPIC, from the then draft UNDRIP, on the grounds that 'the historical and contemporary marginalisation and the often small numbers in society of indigenous peoples meant that the normal operation of a democratic system of government did not necessarily allow for adequate expression of indigenous perspectives'[100]. As Goodland notes, on the 'continuum between the poles of democracy and autocracy, [community] consent lies at the democratic pole while involuntary displacement is the autocratic pole'.[101]

It has been argued that consent of the governed implies that a utilitarian approach to agreement on rules is inadequate, and instead a contractarian stance must be adopted in which we should 'take the point of view of those who stand to lose' in order to optimise their position.[102] Such a view supports the notion of

97 Van Dyke 1995: 45–46.
98 The need for a culturally appropriate model of political participation for indigenous peoples has been affirmed by the Inter-American Court of Human Rights in *Yatama v. Nicaragua* (Preliminary Objections, Merits, Reparations and Costs), Judgment of 23 June 2005.
99 Young 2000: 31–32, 100, 106; see also Van Dyke 1985: 201; Calhoun 1947: 24–25.
100 UN DOC. E/CN.4/1997/102 (10 December 1996) para 203.
101 Goodland 2004: 69.
102 Lane Scheppele 1988: 66.

respecting autonomous decisions in relation to the development priorities of indigenous peoples, particularly in the context of resource extraction where they stand to lose more than any other group in society. It can also be argued that if democracy consists of competing groups vying for decision-making power, then FPIC seeks to level the playing field by enabling indigenous peoples to compete on equal terms with more powerful actors and groups in determining the outcome of decisions that impact on them. From this perspective, FPIC provides the mechanism for addressing these structural deficiencies and the associated democratic deficit as it pertains to indigenous peoples.

Emerging notions of democracy such as participatory and deliberative democracy appear largely consistent with the principle of indigenous peoples' FPIC. The premise underpinning participatory democracy is that proposals which are negotiated and agreed through participatory process have greater economic and political viability,[103] as they address deficits in accountability and the erosion of public trust dominating contemporary models of representative democracy.[104] The mobilisation of indigenous peoples in Bolivia which led to reforms in the country's democratic system has been described as an example of participatory democracy in action.[105] Meanwhile, the emergence of deliberative democracy as a means of addressing the weakness of representative democracy has seen an increased emphasis placed on the objective of pursuing consensus-based decision-making.[106] Advocates of this model of democracy regard self-determination as the foundational ideal for inclusive democracy[107] and have noted the particular claims to distinctiveness of indigenous peoples in seeking to preserve their identity.[108] The critiques of the power dynamics at play in pluralist or elite models of democracy, and the arguments underpinning participatory and deliberative democracy, all point to the consistency of indigenous peoples' FPIC with the ideals embodied in democratic principles. They also highlight FPIC's role in the *de facto* realisation of these ideals by ensuring that democratic processes are inclusive of indigenous peoples and lead to just outcomes.[109] Contemporary invocation of democratic principles by States in their attempts to dismiss indigenous conceptions of FPIC are ironic when considered in light of the fact that the American federal system of democracy and those systems inspired by it owe much to the structures underpinning indigenous peoples' historical confederacies. It was with these confederacies that consent-based agreements were entered into by States during the colonial encounter era only to be subsequently ignored by them.[110] Indigenous peoples are once again articulating their own conceptions of the

---

103 Coelho and Favareto 2008: 2949.
104 Crozier Huntington and Watanuki 1975.
105 Albro 2006: 387–410, see also Schilling-Vacaflor 2012; Bascopé 2010.
106 Young 2000; Dryzek 2000: 24, 100, 106.
107 European Court of Human Rights, *Freedom and Democracy Party (OZDEP) v Turkey* No. 23885/94, Judgment of 8 December 1999, para 43, for a commentary, see Thornberry 2002: 293.
108 Young 2000: 31; Young 1995: 171–174.
109 Lüdert 2008; see also Masaki 2009.
110 Grinde and Johansen 1991.

principles underpinning self-determination-based democratic governance on the international stage.[111] However, without respect for FPIC, these indigenous principles will yet again be subordinated to a modern wave of conquest-style colonisation in the form of 'democratically' justified but territorial autonomy denying intrusions of extractive industries into indigenous territories.[112]

6.5 Invocation of the State sovereignty argument

Another argument which is frequently invoked against recognising indigenous peoples' decision-making rights and FPIC is that to do so would infringe on State sovereignty. Alston has observed the striking frequency with which notions of State sovereignty are 'invoked within international settings to prevent developments which seek to adapt the overall system in order to enable it to respond adequately, or even just plausibly, to new challenges'. [113] This sovereignty argument was repeatedly raised in discussions pertaining to the consent provisions, and the impact of extractive projects on indigenous peoples' rights, during the drafting of both C169[114] and the UNDRIP.[115] It continues to constitute the basis upon which some States, international financial institutions, industry bodies and their members reject, or disassociate themselves from, the principle of FPIC.

There are a number of counter-arguments to this notion that State sovereignty is compromised by respect for the requirement for FPIC. The first holds that it is simply a red herring. State sovereignty, as conceived of under international law and relations,[116] is exercised vis-à-vis other States and the issue of indigenous peoples' exercise of FPIC within State borders does not affect this.[117] The analogy of recognising indigenous peoples' autonomous decision-making powers and structures with the decentralisation of power inherent in federal States addresses this sovereignty-based argument. National sovereignty does not equate to centralised power structures, as federal or consociational States are no less sovereign or stable than unitary States, and consequently should not pose an obstacle to indigenous peoples' territorial autonomy.[118] Indeed, indigenous governments exercise a degree of *de facto* sovereign power alongside federal and State structures in a number of jurisdictions.[119] The fact that FPIC is recognised under legislation and

---

111 Thirteenth Session of the United Nations Permanent Forum on Indigenous Issues, 12–23 May 2014, Special Theme: 'Principles of good governance consistent with the United Nations Declaration on the Rights of Indigenous Peoples: Articles 3 to 6 and 46'.
112 García Hierro 2014.
113 Alston 2005: 36.
114 ILO 1988c: 32/12.
115 UN Doc. E/CN.4/1997/102 (10 December 1996) at 209; see also UN Doc. GA 2007 A/61/ PV.107 at 26.
116 Crawford 2007: 27.
117 Macklem 1993: 1315 argues that in cross-border contexts addressing indigenous sovereignty has the potential to convert borders to bridges.
118 Hannum 1996: 463–464; Xanthaki 2007: 137; see also Rufus Davis 1978; see also Van Dyke 1985: 201.
119 Macklem 1993: 1347.

jurisprudence in unitary and federal States also serves as a counterweight to the argument that the external aspect of State sovereignty is jeopardised by recognising the requirement for FPIC. This argument should not, however, detract from the fact that indigenous peoples' right to self-determination can also have external dimensions. Where indigenous peoples whose location spans State borders are potentially affected by the activity of one State, respect for those peoples' FPIC offers a mechanism for ensuring respect for the sovereignty of both States, as well as that of the indigenous peoples in question.[120]

The second counter-argument addresses the internal aspect of State power embodied in the notion of sovereignty. It holds that this aspect of sovereignty has evolved with the development of human rights and that rather than being at odds with each other, State sovereignty and respect for human rights are mutually reinforcing. Respect for human rights, including indigenous peoples' rights, is therefore part and parcel of the modern conception of the legitimate exercise of State power.[121] This view is reflected in the jurisprudence of the HRC which has affirmed that indigenous peoples' enjoyment of their rights under Article 27 'does not prejudice the sovereignty and territorial integrity of a State party', while simultaneously affirming that the requirement for FPIC is derived from Article 27.[122] The argument against FPIC on sovereignty grounds is therefore at odds with the underlying sovereignty conditioning premise of the human rights project.[123]

A third counter-argument embodies elements of these two arguments and is based on the historical reality underpinning the notion of State sovereignty. From this perspective, sovereignty is viewed as embodying a State's power of imperium and dominium over its territories. These powers are exercised vis-à-vis other States but also have implications for groups within the State. Prior indigenous sovereignty and dominium are also a source for indigenous peoples' rights over their territories. This sovereignty, which is granted little *de jure* recognition under national legal systems, continues to be exercised on a *de facto* basis by indigenous peoples through their traditional authorities and is manifested in their customary laws. It is also implied in their right as peoples to self-determination. The requirement for FPIC is a manifestation of this sovereignty and a safeguard for its realisation.[124] Experience illustrates that mining by external entities in the absence of FPIC results in a diminishment of this *de facto* sovereignty which indigenous peoples

120 See Chapter 7.5.
121 Application of the Convention on the Prevention and Punishment of the Crime of Genocide (*Bosnia and Herzegovina v. Yugoslavia (Serbia and Montenegro)*), Separate Opinion of Judge Weeramantry, para 2 (1996).
122 HRC General Comment no. 23 on Article 27, para 3.2; HRC, *Poma Poma v Peru* (2009), op. cit.: 56.
123 Castellino 2000: 75–108.
124 Monet, *James Anaya: A Sit-Down with the UN's Man in Indian Country*, 9 May 2012, available at: http://indiancountrytodaymedianetwork.com/2012/05/09/james-anaya-a-sit-down-with-the-un%E2%80%99s-man-in-indian-country-111990

exercise over their territories.[125] Indigenous consent, therefore, rather than conflicting with State sovereignty provides a mechanism to reconcile the existing legal tension between these two competing claims to dominium.

Finally, peoples' sovereignty can be conceived of as a social good and a means to express collective difference and to protect a people's identity from encroachment by the opinions and perspectives of others.[126] Rather than framing State sovereignty as a constraint on indigenous decision-making power, Macklem advocates applying the principle of distributive justice to the concept, on the basis of formal and substantive equality of peoples. This, he argues, would result in the recognition of indigenous sovereignty and respect for indigenous government[127] necessary to rectify current distributions of sovereignty which 'are tainted by the injustice of the distributional context in which they have occurred'.[128] Viewed from each of these perspectives, indigenous FPIC is consistent with and even reinforces State sovereignty.

Recognising the requirement for FPIC clearly involves a transfer of power from State structures to indigenous peoples. The question to be answered is therefore whether or not the extant distribution power meets the criteria of distributive justice and respect for indigenous rights. The argument that State sovereignty prohibits FPIC, without engaging with its justice and rights dimensions or indeed with what is implied in the notion of State sovereignty, is essentially an argument that State bodies should maintain power simply because they currently hold that power. It offers no principled legal or moral justification as to why current power configurations have greater legitimacy than those based on the pursuit of justice and rights.

6.6 Eminent domain and the right to free prior and informed consent

The two legal principles frequently invoked by States seeking to justify non-consensual taking of resources located in indigenous peoples territories are the Regalian doctrine (or its offspring in the form of State claims to ownership of subsoil resources) and the principle of eminent domain or *jus eminens*. A range of opinions exists as to when this right of eminent domain can be invoked. A 1795 ruling of the United States Supreme Court referred to it as a 'despotic power' with the presumption being that it would not be called 'into exercise except in urgent cases, or cases of the first necessity'.[129] Legal theorists have echoed this view that it applies 'in cases of emergency', when necessary for the public good, with others

---

125 Downing 2002: 3.
126 Macklem 1993.
127 Ibid.
128 Ibid.: 1365.
129 According to the court, this was the case 'in time of war or famine, or other extreme necessity', U.S. Supreme Court, *Vanhorne's Lessee v. Dorrance*, 2 U.S. 304 (1795) 2 U.S. 304 (F.Cas.) 2 Dall. 304 at 311. For a discussion on the subsequent expanded but controversial use of eminent domain in the United States, see Ely Jr 2003: 32–36.

suggesting that it can be invoked as 'necessity for the public good [or interest] requires'.[130] In general, however, there has been a tendency to lower the threshold for its exercise.[131] Increasingly this power of eminent domain is invoked in order to justify compulsory acquisition of lands to facilitate extractive projects on the grounds that they serve the common good where land-owners are unwilling to consent to such projects.[132]

Daes suggests that 'States rarely or never have truly urgent or compelling need to take indigenous lands or resources', and that as a result the power of eminent domain should not be invoked against them.[133] According to her analysis: 'The principal question is whether under any circumstances a State should exercise the State's powers of eminent domain to take natural resources from an indigenous people for public use while providing fair and just compensation.'[134]

The State power of eminent domain is 'a right of the State over the property of individuals' and is not applicable to the property of the State.[135] The manner in which Daes' question is framed therefore appears to presume that indigenous peoples' claims over their resources are recognised by the State. However, the question still has validity in relation to the use of the power of eminent domain over indigenous peoples' lands in the context of accessing resources located beneath them, even in cases where the State refuses to recognise indigenous peoples' legitimate ownership claims over those resources. An analysis of: (a) the circumstances under which the public good triggers the power of eminent domain; (b) how indigenous peoples' rights are factored into the determination of the public good; and (c) how their rights are balanced with the exercise of the power of eminent domain, is likely, as suggested by Daes, to provide sufficient grounds for restricting the exercise of eminent domain over indigenous lands. MacKay argues that this is the case because:

> eminent domain is subject to human rights law in the same way as any other prerogative of state and, therefore, should not be granted any special status or exemption, in this case, to justify denial of the right to FPIC.[136]

130 Halleck, 1878: 129–130, citing Cooper's Justinian, and Bowyer and Chancellor Walworth.
131 Stennett 1985: 213; see also Purely Economic Justifications Sufficient to Permit Exercise of Federal Eminent Domain Power--*United States v. Certain Parcels of Land* 64 *Mich. L. Rev.* (1965–1966), 347
132 Information received from non-governmental organisations with ECOSOC consultative status, International Work Group for Indigenous Affairs (IWGIA) and Tebtebba Foundation, UN Doc. E/C.19/2007/7 (13 March 2007) at 11, 17. For an example of the courts declaring that mining companies could exercise eminent domain, see Philippines Supreme Court case, *Didipio Earth-Savers' Multi-Purpose Association, [DESAMA] Inc. et al. vs. Elisea Gozun, et al.* G.R. No. 157882 (30 March 2006).
133 *Indigenous Peoples' Permanent Sovereignty over Natural Resources*, Final report of the Special Rapporteur, Erica-Irene A. Daes UN Doc. E/CN.4/Sub.2/2004/30, para 48.
134 Ibid.: para 48.
135 Halleck 1878: 129–130.
136 MacKay 2004b: 53.

Leonen has also noted that FPIC is problematic for the exercise of eminent domain and as a result will be subject to numerous legal interpretations.[137] An additional legal rationale exists for rejecting the application of the power of eminent domain over indigenous lands in the absence of FPIC. This is derived from an examination of the source of the power of eminent domain. Addressing the source of eminent domain, Vattel held that:

> Every thing in the political society ought to tend to the good of the community [and] their property cannot be excepted . . . The right which belongs to the society or the sovereign of disposing, in case of necessity and for the public safety, of all the wealth contained in the State is called eminent domain . . . When therefore the people confer the empire on any one, they at the same time invest him with eminent domain, unless it be expressly reserved.[138]

This view was dismissed by Halleck as 'obviously defective and incorrect' in favour of the explanation for eminent domain provided by Walworth.[139] Walworth, Chancellor of New York, considered the right of eminent domain to be held by the State by virtue of the fact that it was retained when grants of property were made to individuals or ownership transferred to them.[140] It consequently represents a 'right of resumption' and:

> remains in the government, or in the aggregate body of the people in their sovereign capacity, and they have a claims to resume the possession of the property in the manner directed by the constitution and laws of the State, whenever the public interest requires it.[141]

As Halleck notes, eminent domain is a right: 'which, from its very nature, is inseparable from the sovereignty, and is necessarily transferred with the sovereignty'.[142] As a result, regardless of which of these two theories represents the source of the right to eminent domain, its applicability to the traditional lands of indigenous peoples is legally questionable. Vattel's conception would imply that there had to be a consensual transfer of the power of eminent domain from native peoples to their new sovereign. The notion that such a transfer took place is at odds with most native peoples' conceptions of agreements they entered into with States.[143] It also fails to account for the fact that many indigenous peoples found

---

137 Leonen 1998: 22 and 40.
138 Vattel 1758: Book I, Chapter XX, 112, para 244.
139 Halleck 1878: 130.
140 Ibid.
141 Ibid.
142 Ibid.
143 For comments on conflicting conceptions of transference of sovereign powers in agreements between indigenous peoples and States, see Brownlie 1992: 48; Walters 2009: 28; Littlechild 2011: 115–116.

themselves incorporated into States in the absence of either consent or conquest. If Walworth's definition is assumed to be correct, eminent domain is premised on the assumption that the State transferred to, or granted, private individuals owner-ship of its property, and in doing so retained a right of resumption of that property. The fact that under contemporary international law, the recognised source of indig-enous peoples' property is immemorial possession, and not State grants,[144] with their rights of ownership governed by custom, is irreconcilable with the notion that these lands were 'transferred' or 'granted' to them by the State. Voluntary surrender and re-granting of lands would be necessary for the State to make a legal argument that it retained a right to eminent domain over indigenous territories. It would also have to demonstrate that indigenous peoples knowingly relinquished this aspect of their sovereignty on the surrender of their lands. There is, as a result, a fundamen-tal obstacle to the operation of the principle of eminent domain in indigenous territories, as it is premised on a right to resume possession over property which was never possessed by the State. As such, inherent in the very notion of eminent domain itself resides a legal argument for obtaining indigenous peoples' free and informed consent prior to the acquisition of their lands or resources.

In light of the recognition of indigenous peoples' right to self-determination, the power of eminent domain over lands and resources in their territories remains vested in the indigenous peoples as sovereign entities. As a result, where a small number of individuals within the community refuse consent, the communities or peoples can themselves invoke the power of eminent domain to give effect to their decision, provided this is done in accordance with their own laws and customs and ensures the appropriate level of respect for the rights of individual community members.

6.7 Rights to sub-soil resources and FPIC

In most national jurisdictions, States assert ownership over sub-soil resources. At the same time most indigenous peoples also maintain ownership claims over the sub-soil resources located in their territories, claims which are embodied in the notion of a right to permanent sovereignty over natural resources.[145] While international human rights law has recognised indigenous peoples' inherent rights to their lands, based on customary tenure regimes and long-time possession, it has been slow to apply the same logic to sub-soil resources,[146] despite the fact that logically many of the same arguments could be made in relation to surface and sub-surface resources. Notable exceptions to this are the engagements with the issue of sub-surface rights based on immemorial possession by the Inter-American Commission on Human Rights and CERD's concluding observations to the

---

144 See, for example, ILO Convention 107, Article 11; ILO Convention 169, Article 14; UN Declaration on the Rights of Indigenous Peoples, Article 26; see also Bennett 1978a: 20, 33.
145 Final working paper prepared by the Special Rapporteur, Addendum, Erica-Irene Daes, *Indigenous Peoples' Permanent Sovereignty over Natural Resources*, E/CN.4/Sub.2/2004/30/Add.1.
146 Errico 2011: 335–341.

Philippines and Guyana.[147] There is also some support for these rights in the jurisprudence of the Inter-American Court and the African Commission on Human Rights. While debates exist as to whether resource rights are vested in peoples or States,[148] under Human Rights law, common Article 1 of the ICCPR and ICESCR, and the UN Declaration on the Right to Development, clearly affirm the former as its subjects.[149] The recognition by the HRC and the CESCR that the self-determination rights under common Article 1 are vested in indigenous peoples strengthens their claim to resource rights, including sub-surface resources. Article 15 of C169 recognises these rights in a context where States do not retain the ownership over sub-surface resources. The UNDRIP goes further, affirming a self-determination-based right 'to own, use, develop and control . . . resources' which indigenous peoples possess 'by reason of traditional ownership or other traditional occupation or use' without differentiating between surface or sub-surface resources.[150]

At the national level, some exceptions exist to the general rule of State claims to ownership of sub-soil resources. In common law jurisdictions, the rights to sub-surface resources remains vested in the surface owner unless evidence exists showing their valid extinguishment,[151] and ownership rights over sub-soil resources have been accepted under common law based on traditional usage of those resources as reflected in *Alexkor Ltd and the Republic of South Africa v. The Richtersveld Community*.[152] In the United States, sub-surface and surface ownership go together. In the Philippines, the 1997 *Indigenous Peoples Rights Act* affirms that Ancestral Domains contain the mineral resources therein, however, a decision of the Supreme Court in 2000 casts some doubt as to the implications of this.[153] In contexts where the right to permanent sovereignty over natural resources is vested in a part of the population of a State, such as an indigenous people, the presumption is that it imposes an obligation on the government of that State to obtain the consent of those peoples as a precondition to freely disposing of the natural resources in the region they inhabit.[154]

The relationship between the peoples' right to give or withhold consent and their rights over resources under common Article 1(2) is a mutually reinforcing

147 *Mary and Carrie Dann v United States*, op. cit.: 26; CERD Concluding Observations to Guyana, UN Doc. CERD/C/GUY/CO/14, 4 April 2006, para 16; CERD Concluding Observation to the Philippines, UN Doc. CERD/C/PHL/CO/20, 23 September 2009, para 22

148 Brownlie 1990: 119; Duruigbo 2006.

149 *Declaration on the Right to Development*, G.A. res. 41/128, annex, 41 U.N. GAOR Supp. (No. 53), 186, UN Doc. A/41/53 (1986).

150 UNDRIP Article 26.

151 MacKay, 2004b: 57–58; see also *Western Australia v Ward* [2002] HCA 28; 213 CLR 1; 191 ALR 1; 76 ALJR 1098, 8 August 2002, para 382.

152 *Alexkor Ltd and Another v Richtersveld Community and Others* (CCT19/03) [2003] ZACC 18; 2004 (5) SA 460 (CC); 2003 (12) BCLR 1301 (CC) 14 October 2003; see also Chan 2004.

153 Doyle 2010; see also *Isagani Cruz et al. v. Secretary of Environment and Natural Resources et al.* G.R. No. 135385, December 6, 2000; *Indigenous Peoples Rights Act* 1997, Republic Act No. 8371 (the Philippines).

154 Crawford 1992b: 64.

one. Free prior and informed consent protects indigenous peoples against being 'deprived of their own means of subsistence'. This is reflected in indigenous peoples' conception of FPIC as 'the right to protect the sovereignty of lands and resources'.[155] It is also captured in its description as a *de facto*, if somewhat weak, property right to minerals.[156] The requirement for FPIC is also necessary to facilitate the free disposal 'of their natural wealth and resources'. This relationship has been addressed by the Expert Mechanism which noted that the requirement for consent in the UNDRIP provides analogous protections to that provided under common Article 1, paragraphs 2 and 3 of the Human Rights Covenants.[157] A similar view has been articulated by the African Commission which noted the similarity between the right of all peoples to freely dispose of their wealth and natural resources under Article 21(1) of the African Charter and common Article 1(2) of the Covenants with the FPIC provisions of the UNDRIP in Articles 10, 11(2), 28(1) and 32.[158] This reasoning illustrates that FPIC is regarded as a manifestation of the exercise of permanent sovereignty over natural resources. Conversely, the right to permanent sovereignty over natural resources is one of the rights from which the requirement for FPIC can be derived.[159]

However, the lack of jurisprudence supporting sub-surface resource ownership rights under the extant international legal framework and the *de facto* practice of most States, which are unwilling to recognise indigenous ownership and control over sub-soil resources, mean that it will be some time before indigenous claims over sub-surface resources gain legal traction. Indeed, one of the arguments which States make when challenging the legitimacy of the FPIC requirement is that, as owner of the resource, the State is not required to obtain consent for its exploitation. It is within this context that human rights regimes have focused on the middle ground of affirming a rights-protecting consent requirement for extractive operations. In light of this reality, the operationalisation of indigenous peoples' right to give or withhold their consent and to ensure reasonable benefits and compensation by negotiation of consent-based agreements takes on greater significance.

Indigenous rights are increasingly afforded constitutional and legislative protection, and it is not beyond the bounds of possibility that their rights over resources will gain increasing traction over time as greater recognition is accorded to customary law as a source of property rights. At the same time, many national legal frameworks will most likely continue to affirm State ownership over natural resources. A principle of constitutional interpretation holds that the systematic or

155 Joint Statement of the Global Caucus of Indigenous Peoples, 10th Session of the UNPFII, New York, 16–27 May 2011 at 2, available at: www.docip.org
156 Altman 2009: 291; see also Hunt 2005: 675.
157 *Report of the Experts Mechanism on the Rights of Indigenous Peoples*, July 2012, A/HRC/EMRIP/2012/2, para 11.
158 African Commission on Human and Peoples Rights, Advisory Opinion on the United Nations Declaration on the Rights of Indigenous Peoples (Banjul, Copenhagen: CHPR and IWGIA, 2010), paras 32–35.
159 UN Doc. A/HRC/EMRIP/2012/2, para 44.

structural interpretation of constitutional provisions should not lead to provisions undermining each other, but should instead be directed towards a harmonisation that negates any basis for conflict.[160] In this regard, the principle of consent may provide a means to reconcile the apparent contradiction between indigenous peoples' inherent, natural and customary law-based rights to resources, protected under an evolving framework of international human rights law which affirms their right to self-determination, with national legal frameworks and certain international resolutions asserting States' rights of ownership of sub-soil resources.

When viewed from the legal perspective of indigenous peoples' right to permanent sovereignty over the natural resources located in their territories, FPIC could be seen as a compromise between two antagonistic sets of international norms. It allows the international community to attempt to reconcile the apparently irreconcilable, namely indigenous peoples' inherent right to natural resources under the principle of permanent sovereignty, with States' claims to sovereignty over these same resources under doctrines, such as the Regalian doctrine, which are upheld by most States where natural resource extraction occurs.[161] It also provides a natural resource governance framework within which local customary law, national law and international law can interact on an equitable basis and inform one another.[162]

A word of caution is necessary when considering the consent requirement through such a reconciliatory lens. When asserting their right to FPIC, it should not be assumed that indigenous peoples are abandoning their claims of ownership over sub-soil resources located in their territories. They may instead be seeking to afford a minimum level of protection to their resource rights in contexts where States insist on maintaining exclusive ownership claims.[163] In such contexts, asserting their right to give or withhold their free prior and informed consent, based on the human rights framework, may be the most pragmatic option available to them when faced with imminent threats to their rights and well-being. This does not, however, imply that indigenous peoples do not have legitimate claims over sub-surface resources. Theoretically sound arguments supporting indigenous peoples' rights over sub-soil resources, or permanent sovereignty over natural resources can be made, drawing on principles of human rights and indigenous sources of law. Such arguments can be supported through an examination of the historical basis for State claims over subsurface resources in indigenous territories when contrasted with recognition of sources for indigenous claims over lands rights.[164] Future attempts to assert such claims by indigenous peoples in national and international arenas based on such arguments may result in the emergence of

---

160 *Etcheverry Ruben A. y Otros C/ Provincia del Neuquen*, Tribunal Superior de Justicia de Argentina S/Acción de Inconstitucionalidad, Nro de Fallo: 1532/08 at XIV.1.
161 Pagayatan and Victoria 2001; see also Leonen 2000.
162 Loarca 2009.
163 Pagayatan and Victoria 2001.
164 The author is currently finalising a paper which further develops these arguments.

a body of jurisprudence which challenges narrow conceptions of resource ownership as being exclusively vested in States.

6.8 Grievance mechanisms and judicial review

The availability of some form of fair and impartial oversight and dispute resolution mechanism and a right to judicial review are essential elements for the operationalisation of FPIC.[165] The World Commission on Dams recommended that indigenous peoples and States agree to third party mediation at the outset of the FPIC process to address any potential conflicts that arise.[166] This should complement, but not replace, access to judicial review procedures.[167] In addition, the role of indigenous peoples' own governance systems and judicial processes in oversight and dispute resolution needs to be agreed upfront. Where the requirement for FPIC is respected, State agencies should accept the self-determined decision of indigenous peoples in relation to activities in their territories. In such contexts, the need for mediation, arbitration or judicial review could arise in cases where members of the indigenous community contest the outcome of the FPIC processes, or where the right to self-determination of another people is alleged to be threatened by a decision to give or withhold consent.

In most national jurisdictions the standard of FPIC remains something which indigenous peoples assert and States refuse to recognise. A range of 'less than FPIC' participatory engagement models have, however, emerged since the 1980s. These include the World Bank's 'free prior informed consultation' leading to 'broad community support', C169-style 'consultation with the objective of consent', a requirement for 'consultation and accommodation' under Canadian jurisprudence, and a 'right to negotiate' under Australia's Native Title Act. This range of engagement models, some of which contain a substantive dimension, but none of which are equivalent to FPIC, is likely to expand as legislators respond in partially or substantively restrictive ways to indigenous peoples' continued and increasingly effective assertions of their right to withhold consent.[168] In such contexts the requirement for judicial review is of particular importance as the State maintains the possibility to override the outcomes of consultation process.

Judicial review in these contexts will inevitably involve value judgments which will have to be guided by core international and constitutional legal principles. Among these core principles are respect of indigenous peoples' cultural and territorial integrity, the exercise of their right to self-determination and the need to address contemporary manifestations of historical discrimination. Determination of how to proceed must be based on a balancing of rights in accordance with the principles of necessity and proportionality. The proposed project should be assessed in light of its necessity for the realisation of the right to self-determination of other

165 Williams 2010, Statement to United States Federal Committee on Natural Resources Hearing.
166 Report of the World Commission on Dams 2000: 282; see also Cariño and Colchester 2010: 430.
167 Report of the World Commission on Dams 2000: 281.
168 Szablowski 2010: 119; see also Doyle and Cariño 2013.

peoples in the State and of the 'just and most compelling requirements of a democratic society'.[169] General public interest or common good arguments would fail to meet this threshold. If this necessity test is met, then the proportionality requirement is triggered. In light of the existential nature of indigenous peoples' self-determination-based claims which arise in the context of imposed resource exploitation, the principle of proportionality must be the foundation upon which competing claims are balanced.[170] The absolute nature of the subsistence dimension of the right to self-determination implies that overriding the outcome of consent-seeking processes should be prohibited where rights necessary for subsistence and cultural or physical survival are at risk of being violated. Arguably a limitation to this right should only be considered in cases where a non-derogable right of another party is at risk of being violated.[171] Addressing the social, cultural and spiritual dimensions of the right to exist will require that judicial bodies develop an appreciation of the potential impacts through the lens of each people's particular Cosmo vision and relationship with their environment. This is crucial to the capacity to engage in the type of legal analysis necessary to ensure a just balancing of rights. While the 2012 Inter-American Court of Human Rights ruling in *Sarayaku People v Ecuador* did not specifically address the consent requirement, it remains exemplary in terms of its engagement with indigenous perspectives on project impacts.[172] However, in the context of indigenous self-determination, ensuring progress towards legal plurality and an appropriate role for indigenous legal systems and principles in the adjudication of the adequacy of consultation processes is a necessity.

In situations where survival does not appear to be threatened and the refusal to grant consent is grounded on the implications for indigenous peoples' developmental options, the threshold to be met for the proportionality test remains onerous, as what is being considered is a limitation on the right of indigenous peoples to self-determination. To justify the override of a decision to withhold consent in such a context, the proportionality test would require conclusive demonstration by the State that the impact on the developmental aspect of the right to self-determination of other peoples was disproportionate to the impact on that same right of indigenous peoples.[173] Such a disproportionate impact on the right to development of the majority of the population of the State is highly unlikely in the context of a single extractive project which impacts directly on an indigenous people's developmental options.[174] The implication is that even where legislative recognition

169 UNDRIP Article 46(2).

170 Sachs 2009: 206–210.

171 For a discussion of the hierarchy of rights noting that a non-derogable right will not always prevail over a derogable right unless it is a peremptory norm, see Meron 1986: 16.

172 Inter-American Court of Human Rights, case of *Pueblo Indígena Kichwa de Sarayaku v. Ecuador*. Fondo y reparaciones, judgment of 27 June 2012, para 212–20.

173 Perrault, Herbertson and Lynch 2007: 501; see also De Sadeleer 2002: 292–301.

174 The Ok Tedi mine which represents 10 per cent of mining in Papua New Guinea GDP is exceptional, see Colley, 'Political Economy of Mining', in Evans, Goodman and Lansbury (eds.), 2002: 29–30. The industry as a whole contributes 30 per cent of Mongolia's GDP, see EITI 2012: 8. The industry contributes 6 per cent of Peru's GDP while representing 70 per cent of its exports, see www.revenuewatch.org/countries/latin-america/peru/overview; see also EITI 2011.

is not accorded to the right to give or withhold FPIC, the presumption should be that consent requirement can only be overridden in extremely exceptional and exhaustively justified circumstances.[175] In cases where a decision to override the consent requirement is taken, the requirement for participatory impact assessments, the mitigation of risks to indigenous peoples' rights and reasonable benefit sharing and adequate compensation and respect for human rights and the law continue to apply.[176]

The above assumes a functioning and impartial judiciary open to engaging with indigenous perspectives. In many jurisdictions where indigenous peoples' rights are violated, this does not exist. In the absence of effective remedies at the national level, and the lack of enforcement of decisions of international human rights mechanisms, the emergence through participatory processes of complementary judicial structures at the international and national levels, such the special jurisdictions proposed by Martínez with the capacity to address self-determination-related disputes,[177] may ultimately be necessary to give effect to the consent requirement.

6.9 Parallels with objections to inter-state prior informed consent requirement

As noted earlier, the consent requirement has also emerged in a number of other spheres of law, including the medical context, in relation to an individual's autonomy rights over their body. Another area where the requirement has emerged is in the context of environmental law regulating inter-state hazardous trade. The requirement for prior informed consent (referred to as PIC) of States is embodied in the 1998 *Rotterdam Convention on the Prior Informed Consent Procedure for Certain Hazardous Chemicals and Pesticides in International Trade.*[178] The legal and economic grounds upon which pesticide manufacturers objected to the consent requirement have interesting parallels with the objections to indigenous peoples' FPIC and consequently merit some attention. On the legal front it was argued that informed consent (a) posed a threat to the sovereignty of developing countries and placed limitations on their development options;[179] (b) would force exporting countries to exercise significant extra-territorial control over businesses, thereby extending the

---

175 Daes, UN Doc. E/CN.4/Sub.2/2004/30 (2004), para 48; McGee 2009: 584.
176 UN Doc. A/HRC/21/47 (2012), para 52; *Saramaka v Suriname* (2007), op. cit.: 26, paras 138–140; ILO Convention 169, Article 15.2, UNDRIP Articles 32(3) and 28.
177 Final report by Special Rapporteur Miguel Alfonso Martínez, *Study on Treaties, Agreements and Other Constructive Arrangements between States and Indigenous Populations*, UN Doc. E/CN.4/Sub.2/1999/20, paras 306–311.
178 *Rotterdam Convention on the Prior Informed Consent Procedure for Certain Hazardous Chemicals and Pesticides in International Trade* (1998), United Nations, Treaty Series, vol. 2244, p. 337; C.N.846. 2002.
179 Walls 1988: 766, senior counsel for the Chemical Manufacturers Association, outlined the legal and economic grounds for opposition to the PIC requirement; see also Colopy 1994/1995; and Uram 1990: 470; and Ross 1999.

traditional notion of State responsibility;[180] (c) opened up the potential for exporting countries to face liability in cases where their companies exported waste without consent;[181] (d) could be illegal under GATT rules;[182] and (e) was unnecessary as domestic and international law already provided sufficient remedies under tort, contract and commercial law.[183] The economic arguments centred on the implications of the delays the PIC process could cause.[184] Arguments were also made that it could lead to an uneven playing field, with responsible companies which complied with PIC disadvantaged, ultimately leading to the unintended effect of increasing unregulated trade with consequent risks for health and the environment.[185] The final framing of the PIC requirement in the Rotterdam Convention was regarded as unsatisfactory by those advocating for greater environmental and health protection,[186] but was described by those arguing for it from an industry perspective as 'a reasonable alternative to a stringent PIC program'.[187] The fact that the objections to informed consent had come from both those seeking to alter the traditional dominance of trade over environment and health concerns, and those seeking to maintain the status quo and avoid impacts on trade provides an important lesson for the operationalisation of indigenous peoples' FPIC. It suggests that it is the context and constraints within which the consent requirement operates, and not necessarily the notion of consent itself, which determine if it is regarded as a 'liberal' industry-friendly concept or a 'protectionist' environmental and health concept. This same issue also arises in the context of indigenous peoples' FPIC, which, depending on the extent to which indigenous peoples control its operationalisation, can be a powerful self-determination-based rights safeguarding mechanism or merely a means to rubber stamp mining operations without changing the underlying self-determination-denying engagement and operational dynamics.

The experience of States and civil society with informed consent requirements in the context of the transport of hazardous waste also points to the significant role which industry has played in the recognition and regulation of the requirement. A similar influential role is played by industry in the context of indigenous peoples' FPIC. However, given the financial considerations, which hostile relations with indigenous communities create for extractive industry companies, an additional incentive exists for them to respond to indigenous demands to recognise the requirement for FPIC in contexts where States are unwilling to do so. Chapter 8 will examine the response of industry and the broader framework of business and human rights to these demands. Before addressing this dynamic area, Chapter 7

---

180 Walls 1988: 766.
181 Ibid.: 767, citing the ICJ *Corfu Channel* Case and the *Trail Smelter* case (*U.S. vs Canada*) 3 Rep International Law Arbitration 1905, 1965–66 (1949) U.N. Sales No. 1949 v.2.
182 Ibid.: 769.
183 Ibid.: 774.
184 Ibid.: 770.
185 Ibid.: 771.
186 Barrios 2004: 679.
187 Walls 1988: 774–775.

will look at the actual practice to date of States in relation to FPIC recognition and also consider the role which financial institutions, home States and the ICJ are playing, or could potentially play, in the establishment of FPIC as the normative standard to which States and corporations must comply.

Implementation of free prior and informed consent: challenges and opportunities

7 The evolving practice of States and international organisations

7.1 Introduction

States maintain the primary responsibly to consult with and obtain indigenous peoples' FPIC. Their role in this process is indispensable in terms of ensuring the coordinated and systematic nature of indigenous participation, guaranteeing that independent oversight structures exist and facilitating adequate capacity-building and resourcing. The extractive industry, international financial institutions and investors, the NGO community and the UN system and home States also have a major role to play in determining the status of FPIC as a normative standard and in its realisation in practice.

When considering the status of FPIC as an emerging international norm, three factors can be examined: (a) *opinio juris*; (b) State practice; and (c) recognition by highly influential non-state actors including international organisations, the extractive industry and the financial sector. The extensive body of human rights jurisprudence at the international and regional levels, some of which is reflected in the decisions of national courts, has been addressed in Chapter 5 and provides strong grounds to support the view that the threshold for this criterion has been met or is close to being met. The second consideration relates to State practice. Chapter 6 engaged with the arguments put forward by some of the States that oppose the requirement. This chapter will provide a brief overview of some of the existing practice in relation to its recognition. It suggests that while a growing number of States have committed to the substantive FPIC requirement, they still constitute a small percentage and the rate of increase remains slow. The third criterion which relates to non-State actors' recognition of the requirement is the most dynamic and potentially the most significant area in terms of its potential for actual tangible impacts on indigenous peoples. The extent of FPIC adoption into the policies and practices of international institutions has increased rapidly following the adoption of the UN Declaration on the Rights of Indigenous Peoples (UNDRIP), which includes a specific provision requiring UN bodies, UN Specialized Agencies and UN funds to promote its realisation. Most UN Specialized Agencies now have policies, or are in the process of developing or updating policies, which are consistent with the UNDRIP and its requirement for FPIC. Beyond the UN, in the arena of international financial institutions, the requirement has also gained significant traction. This has major implications for other corporate actors and has led to scenarios in which private sector initiatives are leapfrogging many States in their engagement with the requirement. These tentative steps currently being taken by the extractive industry towards acknowledgement of FPIC's relevance for their operations, and the broader context of business and human rights within which these developments are occurring, will be considered in Chapter 8. To these three traditional criteria, a fourth criterion has to be added in the context of FPIC, namely the recognition which indigenous peoples have afforded to the requirement and the measures which they are taking to implement it in practice. This criterion will be addressed in the final chapter.

The chapter is divided into four sections. Section 7.2 looks at the actual practice to date of States in relation to FPIC recognition. It provides a non-exhaustive overview of contexts where there has been progress in implementation and other contexts where retrogressive steps have been taken. Section 7.3 addresses the approach of the public and private sector arms of the World Bank Group to FPIC. It examines the rationale behind the refusal to date of the public sector arm, the International Bank for Reconstruction and Development (IBRD), to adopt the principle of FPIC in its operational policy and suggests that, despite the hurdles it will face in incorporating FPIC during its revision process, doing so is necessary to ensure consistency across the organisation and to fulfil its human rights obligations. The section also addresses the significance of the incorporation of the requirement for FPIC into the policy of the Bank's private sector arm, the International Finance Corporation (IFC). It suggests that while the significance of this development should not be underestimated, caution is also necessary to ensure that the concept of FPIC is not distorted in the process. With this in mind the section briefly critiques certain aspects of the IFC's guidance in relation to FPIC operationalisation. Section 7.4 then provides a brief foray into the issue of the extraterritorial obligations of the home States of extractive companies and examines the relevance of the requirement for FPIC in a context where, despite increased focus on the need for remedies of corporate-related human rights violations, access to judicial and non-judicial remedies in home States remains sparse. As a closing comment, Section 7.5 addresses the role of the International Court of Justice (ICJ) in relation to indigenous peoples' issues and draws on the opinions of a number of its justices which point to a potential role for it in addressing indigenous peoples' claims. It concludes with a brief consideration of the potential for the ICJ to address the consent requirement under one of its pending contentious cases.

7.2 Emerging State practice in relation to FPIC

Despite the unprecedented progress in the international arena in establishing the legal underpinning and content of the requirement for FPIC, and the impetus which this has given to developments within the private sector, which will be discussed below, significant changes in attitudes and approaches towards indigenous peoples' rights are still necessary at the national level before FPIC can be operationalised. A relatively small but growing number of States have nevertheless accorded, or are considering according, some recognition, either through legislative, administrative or judicial mechanisms, to the consent requirement. This section provides a cursory overview of some of these contexts.

Two well-established FPIC requirements are found in the Philippines and Australia's Northern Territories which have legislation requiring consent prior to the approval of any extractive activities in indigenous peoples' territories. While these legislative acts represent the 'high water mark' in terms of recognition of the consent requirement in the context of extractive activities, both embody some compromise that weakens certain aspects of that requirement.[1] Both cases need to be viewed not only on the basis of their legislative provisions but also on the associated State practice in relation to them.[2] This is particularly relevant in the Australian context where the provision in the *Aboriginal Land Rights (Northern Territory) Act* (1976), allowing for a possible override of the aboriginal 'veto' power under the Act, has never been invoked by the State.[3] The operation of the consent requirement under the Act provides an example of a functioning model of FPIC which protects the rights of the traditional land-owners, while also providing sufficient certainty to mining companies to enable them to plan for the future.[4] Mining revenues in the territory are in excess of $1 billion per annum, pointing to the fact that FPIC can be consistent with a thriving mining industry.[5] In the Philippines' context, the FPIC requirement is affirmed under the *Indigenous Peoples Rights Act* (1997), which recognises indigenous peoples' inherent rights to self-determination and to their ancestral territories and provides them with prior rights to exploit sub-surface resources.[6] Informed consent is required prior to concession issuance and for subsequent mining activities and is defined as:

> the consensus of all members of the ICCs/IPs to be determined in accordance with their respective customary laws and practices, free from any external manipulation, interference and coercion, and obtained after fully disclosing the intent and scope of the activity, in a language and process understandable to the community.[7]

In Papua New Guinea, the fact that over 90 per cent of land rights flow from customary law implies that a *de facto* consent requirement exists.[8]

---

1 Altman 2009; Rumler 2011; Doyle 2010a; *Philippines Indigenous Peoples, ICERD Shadow Report*, Manila, 2009.
2 For case studies on FPIC implementation in the Philippines and Australia, see Doyle and Cariño 2013: 29–32, 53–55.
3 *Aboriginal Land Rights (Northern Territories) Act* 1976, Sections 40(b) and 43; Mcrae *et al.* 2009.
4 Doyle and Cariño 2013: 60–63.
5 Northern Land Council, available at: www.nlc.org.au/articles/info/the-mining-industry-and-the-nlc/
6 Republic Act No. 8371, *The Indigenous Peoples Rights Act of 1997*.
7 Ibid., Section 3(g).
8 Jorgensen 2007: 57–69.

The *Land Act* (1996) requires the agreement of traditional land-owners prior to leasing of their lands. The National Court of Justice has addressed how these agreements with land-owners are to be effected and evidenced,[9] however, jurisprudence and practice suggest that the standard applied is less stringent than FPIC.[10] In Fiji, approximately 87 per cent of the land is classified as native land. Consent for leases must be obtained from the Native Lands Trust Board as opposed to the land-owner.[11] Prior to Greenland's acquisition of full control over its natural resources in 2009, a mutual consent-based regime governed the relationship between the peoples of Greenland and Denmark with regard to mining projects.[12]

In Guyana, the consent of village councils is required in the context of small-scale and medium-scale mines but only on titled lands.[13] The Mexican *Forestry Law* (1992) and *Agrarian Law* (1992) require consent prior to the issuance of forestry concessions in *ejidos* of indigenous communities.[14] In the state of Chihuahua, Mexico, under the 2013 Law on the Rights of Indigenous Peoples, consultation in order to obtain consent is required and a 'right to FPIC' is recognised in relation to project concessions, as well as legislative and administrative measures, with the State required to respect the outcome of consultations – the only permissible exceptions being in cases of emergencies, fortuitous events and natural disasters.[15] A proposal was also submitted in the Mexican parliament in 2013 requesting an amendment to Article 2 of the Constitution of Mexico to include the requirement to obtain FPIC in cases of relocation, storage of hazardous waste or large-scale projects with potentially significant impacts on indigenous peoples.[16] In Panama, a 2010 decree requires consultations in order to guarantee FPIC to projects within indigenous peoples' collectively held territories.[17] In New Zealand, consent is required for any impact on *waahi tapu* (sacred areas) for non-minimal impacts to other lands.[18] In Canada, the *Yukon Oil and Gas Act* (2002) requires the consent of First

---

9 *Land Act* (1996), Section 10, 11 and 102(2); PNG, National Court of Justice OS (JR) No. 10 of 2009 N3827, *Musa Valley Management Company Ltd et al. v/s the Department of Lands and Physical Planning et al*, 16, 17 June 2009, 22 January 2010. See also Moore 2011.

10 *Musa Valley Management Company Ltd et al v/s the Department of Lands and Physical Planning et al.*, ibid. CERD Early Warning Urgent Action letter to Papua New Guinea (11 March 2011); see also Macintyre 2007.

11 *Native Land Trust Act* [Cap 134] Part II, Section 12.

12 The *Greenland Home Rule Act*, Act No. 577, (1978), Section 8(1) included 'a mutual right of veto' over mining projects. This Act has been superseded by the *Act on Greenland Self-Government*, adopted 19 May 2009, which transfers responsibility for the mineral resource area to Greenland's Self Government authorities.

13 *Amerindian Act* (2005), Section 48.

14 *Ley Forestal Diario Oficial de la Federación*, 22 de diciembre de 1992, Artículo 19 Bis 4; *Ley Agraria Nueva Ley*, publicada en el *Diario Oficial de la Federación*, el 26 de febrero de 1992, *Texto Vigente Última Reforma*, publicada DOF 09–04–2012, Artículo 77.

15 *Ley de Derechos de los Pueblos Indígenas del Estado de Chihuahua*, Nueva Ley P.O.E. 2013.06.29/ No. 52, Articles 9(VII), 13, 15, 19.

16 *Gaceta Parlamentaria*, No. 3892-VI, jueves 24 de octubre de 2013. Available at: http://gaceta.diputa-dos.gob.mx/Black/Gaceta/Anteriores/62/2013/oct/20131024-VI/Iniciativa-16.html

17 *Gaceta Oficial*, No. 26,193 (30 de diciembre de 2008), reglamentada por el Decreto Ejecutivo 223 de 29 de junio de 2010, publicada en la *Gaceta Oficial* de 7 de julio de 2010, Artículo 14.

18 *Crown Minerals Act* 1991, Section 50, 53–54.

Nations prior to the issuance of licences in their traditional territories.[19] Consent is also required under negotiated agreements such as the Nunavut Final Agreement (1993) and the Kaska-Yukon Government Bilateral Agreement (2003).[20] In the United States, consent is required for mining on American Indian tribal lands, however, on federal lands the lesser standard of meaningful consultation applies.[21]

Jurisprudence in countries such as Canada, Belize, India and Colombia is indicative of the increasing acknowledgement of this universal requirement for consent. The Supreme Court of Canada has clarified that where Aboriginal people hold title to land, the government's duty to consult is 'in most cases' 'significantly deeper than mere consultation' and, depending on the nature of the breach, can extend to the more demanding requirement of 'full consent'.[22] The Canadian Supreme Court subsequently clarified that the consent requirement did not apply where title was claimed but not yet proven.[23] In such contexts a lesser duty to consult and accommodate exists. In 2014, the Special Rapporteur on the rights of indigenous peoples recommended that Canada apply the FPIC standard to land subject to aboriginal claims.[24] This Recommendation was subsequently supported by the Supreme Court in its 2014 Tsilhqot'in Nation v. British Columbia decision, which noted, that if consent was not obtained projects might be cancelled once title was established.

A similar position exists under the *Native Title Act* in Australia.[25] The Act, which is applicable nationally, affirms a right to negotiate as opposed to a requirement for consent.[26] It has nevertheless been interpreted by the Native Title Tribunal in 2009 as including the entitlement of Aboriginal Peoples to say 'no' to development projects and to expect that 'considerable weight' would be given to their 'view about the use of the land in the context of all the circumstances' projects'.[27]

Landmark cases in South Africa such as the 2003 *Richtersveld Community* ruling, recognising indigenous peoples' ownership of sub-soil resources based on traditional usage, mean that FPIC is automatically required should the State wish to pursue extractive activities in those peoples' territories.[28]

In its October 2007 landmark ruling, and subsequently in its 2010 and 2014 rulings, the Supreme Court of Belize referenced, *inter alia*, the FPIC requirements in the UNDRIP and CERD's General Recommendation XXIII on Indigenous

---

19 *Revised Statutes of the Yukon (RSY) Oil and Gas Act*, 2002, Section 13(1) b.
20 Gibson 2012: 5.
21 Harvard Project on American Indian Economic Development 2014: 27.
22 *Delgamuukw v. British Columbia* [1997] 3 SCR 1010, para 186.
23 *Haida Nation v. British Columbia (Minister of Forests)* 2004 SCC 73; see also *Blueberry River Indian Band v. Canada* (Department of Indian Affairs and Northern Development), [1995] 4 S.C.R. 344, para 73.
24 UN Doc A/HRC/27/52/Add.2 (2014).
25 Hunt 2005: 661–680. For a critique of the right to negotiate under the Act, see Ritter 2009.
26 *Native Title Act* 1993, Section 29.
27 *NNTTA Western Desert Lands Aboriginal Corporation (Jamukurnu - Yapalikunu) / Western Australia / Holocene Pty Ltd* [2009] NNTTA 49, 27 May 2009, para 215.
28 See, for example, *Alexkor Ltd and Another v Richtersveld Community and Others* (CCT19/03) [2003] ZACC 18; 2004 (5) SA 460 (CC); 2003 (12) BCLR 1301 (CC), 14 October 2003.

Peoples.[29] The Court ordered the State to cease and abstain from any acts, including granting of mining permits or issuing any regulations concerning resource use, impacting on the Mayan indigenous communities 'unless such acts are pursuant to their informed consent'.[30]

In Colombia, the 2001 *Mining Act* recognises the power of indigenous authorities to declare certain areas off limits to mining activities.[31] In addition, in 2009, the Constitutional Court of Colombia affirmed the applicability of the consent requirement, emerging from the Inter-American Court of Human Rights *Saramaka v Suriname* decision, to Colombian indigenous and afro-descendant communities in the context of large-scale mining operations in their territories.[32] In 2011, the court expanded on this jurisprudence, addressing the implications of these peoples' right of self-determination for the requirement for FPIC, affirming its mandatory nature in relation to small-scale as well as large-scale activities.[33] Despite this affirmation of the consent requirement, the government and industry have taken up legal challenges in attempts to overturn the decisions, based on arguments that it is inconsistent with ILO Convention 169 and State ownership of sub-soil resources.[34] In 2011, the court also held that a 2010 amendment to the Mining Code was unconstitutional due to the absence of consultations with indigenous and tribal peoples prior to its enactment.[35]

The relevance of the requirement for 'full consent' was also touched on by the Malaysia Court of Appeals in 2005 when it noted that the Department of Aboriginal Affairs:

> made a significant policy statement in 1961 ... which it considers still applicable and forming the policy of the department ... In respect of the land rights of the aborigines, the statement states ... Aborigines will not be moved from their traditional areas without their full consent.[36]

India's *Scheduled Tribes and Other Traditional Forest Dwellers (Recognition of Forest Rights) Act*, 2006 requires 'the free informed consent of the Gram Sabhas [village council]' in the context of resettlement.[37] In a 2013 decision, the Indian Supreme Court

---

29 *Aurelio Cal and the Maya Village of Santa Cruz v Attorney General of Belize; and Manuel Coy and Maya Village of Conejo v Attorney General of Belize*, The Supreme Court of Belize, 2007, Consolidated Claims Claim Nos. 171 and 172 of 2007.

30 Ibid., para 136(d).

31 Colombia, *Codigo de Minas* del año 2001, Artículo 127. See Moncloa 2007, for a commentary on the provision.

32 Colombian Constitutional Court, Sentencia *T-769* (2009).

33 Colombian Constitutional Court, Sentencia *T-129/11* (2011).

34 Referencia: Nullidad Sentencia T-769–09 Expediente T-2315944, Ministerio del Interior y de Justicia Republica de Colombia, Bogotá, 14 de Abril de 2010 (government petition seeking the annulation of the ruling).

35 Colombian Constitutional Court, Sentencia 366 (2011).

36 *Kerajaan Negeri Selangor and 3 Ors v Sagong Bin Tasi and 6 Ors* 2005 [CA], para 18.

37 Scheduled Tribes and Other Traditional Forest Dwellers (Recognition of Forest Rights) Act, 2006 Chapter 2 4(2)(e).

extended the protection under the *Forest Rights Act* (2006) beyond property rights or inhabited areas and held that if Vedanta's proposed Bauxite Mine in the Dongria Kondh's sacred Niyamgiri hills in Odisha 'in any way, affects their religious rights, especially their right to worship their deity . . . in the hill's top . . . that right has to be preserved and protected'.[38]

The court required that the Gram Sabhas' decision be obtained in relation to community cultural or religious claims over the impacted areas prior to a final decision of the Ministry of the Environment and Forest in relation to the necessary forest clearance.[39] In community referenda, the Gram Sabhas of all 12 villages unanimously rejected the project and in January 2014 the Ministry confirmed it would deny the forest clearance certificate in accordance with these referenda.[40] In May 2014, Vedanta announced that it would not mine the Niyamgiri hills in Odisha until it had community consent.[41]

However, given the non-linear nature of indigenous peoples' struggles for rights recognition, it is not surprising that there have been attempts to roll back this progress in a number of jurisdictions. These efforts, often at the behest of the industry, have taken various forms. In 1987, in Australia, restrictions were placed on the consent requirement under the *Aboriginal Land Rights (Northern Territory) Act* (1976). The amendment changed the original provision in the Act requiring consent at both exploration and exploitation, limiting it to a single requirement at the commencement of exploration.[42] In the Philippines, a series of increasingly restrictive implementing regulations issued in 2002 and 2006 served to effectively amend the consent requirement under the 1997 *Indigenous Peoples Rights Act*.[43] A number of these infirmities have been remedied in the 2012 FPIC guidelines as a result of greater participation of indigenous peoples in their drafting and a more assertive position by the National Commission on Indigenous Peoples vis-à-vis the extractive sector following recommendations to this end by CERD, the CESCR and the ILO.[44] However, the industry, with the support of the Mines and Geosciences Bureau, continues to challenge these guidelines, claiming that they are detrimental to foreign direct investment in the mining sector. In practice, the requirement for FPIC in the Philippines is regularly circumvented due to inadequate oversight mechanisms, corruption and a lack of accountability of the government agency facilitating the consent-seeking processes.[45]

---

38 Indian Supreme Court judgment dated 18/04/2013, in W.P.(C) No. 180/2011, *Orissa Mining Corporation. Vs. MoEF and Ors*, para 58.

39 Ibid., paras 59–60.

40 www.thehindubusinessline.com/industry-and-economy/govt-rejects-vedantas-niyamgiri-mining-project/article5570028.ece

41 http://zeenews.india.com/business/news/companies/vedanta-to-await-local-consent-for-indian-bauxite-mine_99180.html

42 Libby 1989; see also Altman 2009: 290–293.

43 Bennagen 2007: 179.

44 NCIP Administrative Order No. 3 Series of 2012, the Revised Guidelines on Free and Prior Informed Consent (FPIC) and Related Processes of 2012.

45 *Philippines Indigenous Peoples ICERD Shadow Report*, Manila, 2009; Doyle and Cariño 2013: 30–33, 58–60.

In Belize, the government adopted a narrow interpretation of the 2007 Supreme Court decision requiring FPIC as applicable only to the claimant communities and continued to issue concessions without the consent of other Mayan communities.[46] A second ruling of the Supreme Court in 2010 clarified that the requirement applied to all impacted Mayan communities.[47] The government appealed the case but the ruling was upheld in March 2014.[48] The possibility exists that it may appeal the case to the Caribbean Court of Justice.[49] In Colombia, the government and industry jointly sought the annulment of Constitutional Court 2009 ruling affirming FPIC.[50] In Peru, after extensive debates and objections by the indigenous networks, Article 15 of the 2011 law of consultation reserved the final decision-making power to the government and was reinforced through its 2012 implementing regulations.[51] The 2010 ruling of the Peruvian Constitutional Court affirmed a similar position.[52] However, the government maintains that it will guarantee respect for indigenous peoples' rights in any decision taken. following prior consent-seeking consultations.[53] In Guatemala, a 2007 ruling of the Constitutional Court recognised the requirement for consent-seeking consultations under C169 but held that indigenous peoples' own self-initiated and managed consultations at the municipal level do not have a legally binding effect.[54] In Bolivia, the Supreme Court in 2006 declared the requirement to consult in order to secure consent to be unconstitutional.[55] A consent requirement was included in Bolivia's (2006) *Hydrocarbons Act*,[56] however, a controversial ruling by the Supreme Court held the consent provision to be unconstitutional on the grounds that it was inconsistent

46 University of Arizona Indigenous Peoples Law and Policy (2008).
47 *The Maya Leaders Alliance and the Toledo Alcaldes Association on Behalf of the Maya Villages of Toledo District v. the Attorney General of Belize and the Minister of Natural Resources and Environment*, Claim No. 366 of 2008, Supreme Court of Belize, A.D. 2010.
48 Supreme Court of Belize Claim No. 394 of 2013, April 3 2014.
49 Update to the CERD 81st Session in anticipation of the Committee's review of Belize in the absence of a State report, submitted by the Maya Leaders Alliance (Belize) (1 July 2012), para 15, available at: www2.ohchr.org/english/bodies/cerd/docs/ngos/TheMayaleadersAlliance.pdf
50 Solicitud Nulidad Sentencia T-769–09 14, Ministerio de Interior y de Justica Republica de Colombia, April 2010.
51 (Peruvian law on the right to consultation) *Ley del Derecho a la Consulta Previa a los Pueblos Indígenas u Originarios Reconocido en el Convenio No 169 de la Organización Internatíonal del Trabajo Ley No 29785*, 23 August 2011; (Peruvian implementing regulation on the law on the right to consultation) *Reglamento de la Ley No 29785, Ley del Derecho a la Consulta Previa a los Pueblos Indígenas u Originarios Reconocido en el Convenio No 169 de la Organización International del Trabajo Decreto Supremo No 001–2012 MC*, 3 April 2012; (Position of Peruvian indigenous organisations on the regulations) *Pronunciamiento Estado Peruano Consuma Violación de Derechos de los Pueblos Indígenas, Mediante la Reglamentación de una Inconstitucional Ley de Consulta Pacto de Unidad Confederación Nacional Agraria Perú*, CONACAMI, AIDESEP, ONAMIAP (Lima, 4 March 2012).
52 EXP. No. 05427–2009-PC/TC Lima Asociación Interétnica de Desarrollo de la Selva (AIDESEP), 60.
53 Decreto Supremo No. 001–2012-MC, art 15.
54 Apelación de Sentencia de Amparo Expediente 3878–2007 Corte de Constitucionalidad: Guatemala, 21 de diciembre de 2009, 26.
55 Sentencia Constitucional 0045/2006, Expediente 2005–12440–25-RDL, sentencia de 2 de junio de 2006.
56 *Ley de Hidrocarburos Ley No 3058* del 17 Mayo 2005, Artículos 114, 115.

with ILO Convention 169.[57] Commenting on the ruling, the ILO Office has clarified that while the Convention did not 'establish that the results of the consultation are mandatory or binding on the State, providing for such mandatory nature is not in contradiction with the Convention'.[58]

In 2008, Bolivia incorporated the UN Declaration, including its six provisions requiring FPIC, into its national legislation.[59] However, concerns have been raised that the consultations in relation to the construction of a road through the TIPNIS National Park did not adhere to the requirement of FPIC as framed under human rights law,[60] and Bolivia subsequently passed a specific consultation law to address the TIPNIS case.[61] Those opposing the road claim that consultations were not held in good faith.

States have also been vocal in their resistance to precautionary measures issued by the Inter-American Commission on Human Rights and the ILO supervisory bodies, calling for the suspension of projects on the basis of failing to consult prior to conducting activities.[62] In many instances, this resistance has been driven by the industry. If recent developments discussed below and in Chapter 8 are indicative of the genuine intent of certain highly influential private sector actors to engage with FPIC, it is possible that in the future rather than constituting a restraining factor on State approaches to FPIC, the private sector could potentially act as a catalyst for greater engagement with it.

7.3 The World Bank and the International Finance Corporation's recognition of FPIC

7.3.1 The World Bank review of operational policies affecting indigenous peoples

The World Bank was the first UN Specialized Agency to adopt a policy on 'tribal' peoples, which in 1982 constituted a ground-breaking development.[63] In the intervening years, in particular, following the adoption of the UNDRIP, this practice has been emulated by a range of UN Agencies and bodies, including

57 *Sentencia Constitucional 0045/2006*, Expediente 2005-12440-25-RD L, sentencia de 2 de junio de 2006.
58 ILO 2009: 59.
59 Ley 3897 (26 June 2008).
60 Amnesty International open letter to the authorities of the Plurinational State of Bolivia in the context of the dispute concerning the Isiboro Sécure Indigenous Territory and National Park (Territorio Indígena y Parque Nacional Isiboro Sécure - TIPNIS) AI Index: AMR 18/002/2012 (3 May 2010), 3.
61 *Ley de Consulta a los Pueblos Indígenas del Territorio Indígena y Parque Nacional Isiboro Sécure* – TIPNIS Ley 222 (10 February 2012).
62 See *Report of the Committee on the Application of Standards*, International Labour Conference Record of Proceedings, 99th Session (Geneva: ILO, 2010) Part I, para 54 and Part II, paras 102–107; see also M. Picq, 'Is the Inter-American Commission of Human Rights too progressive?' (9 June 2012), available at: www.aljazeera.com/indepth/opinion/2012/06/2012658344220937.html
63 Griffiths 2005: 2.

the International Fund for Agricultural Development (IFAD), the Food and Agricultural Organization (FAO) and the United Nations Development Programme (UNDP), whose newly drafted policies, standards and safeguards comply with developments in international human rights law, affirming FPIC as the appropriate standard for engagements with indigenous peoples.[64] A similar development has taken place in the context of the environmental and social safeguard policies of international financial institutions. The European Bank for Reconstruction and Development (EBRD) addresses the requirement for FPIC in a number of contexts, including the development of natural resources.[65] Its 2008 Environmental and Social Policy recognises that 'the prior informed consent of affected Indigenous Peoples is required for the project-related activities ... given the specific vulnerability of Indigenous Peoples to the adverse impacts of such projects'.[66] A draft of the revised 2014 version of the policy contains a similar consent requirement. The policy introduces some potential ambiguity in the definition of consent, linking it to 'involvement in', rather than authorisation of, a project.[67] Similarly, the 2009 safeguard policy of the Asian Development Bank affirms the requirement for FPIC. However, the definition of FPIC is also somewhat ambiguous as it is equated with broad community support, and if interpreted narrowly, is potentially inconsistent with the rights underpinning FPIC.[68] The Inter-American Development Bank does not explicitly require FPIC in its 2006 policy, which was issued prior to the adoption of the UNDRIP. However, an interpretation of the policy in a manner consistent with the regional and international framework of indigenous peoples' rights to which it requires adherence, suggests that the consent requirement for a large-scale mining project is implicit in the policy.

These and other developments in the policies and practices of international organisations are significantly strengthening the normative status of FPIC and have possible implications for the formation of international legal rules in the area.[69] They are reflective of the international community's official position in relation to the requirement and are also serving to influence national governments' position in relation to it in specific contexts, in particular, where funding is contingent on compliance with these rights safeguards as, once agreements are entered into with States, they can become legally binding standards.[70] An example of this is the UN initiative on Reducing Emissions from Deforestation and forest

---

64 See Doyle forthcoming 2015, agencies such as UNESCO and the UNEP are drafting similar poli-
    cies, see www.unesco.org/new/en/indigenous-peoples/related-info/unesco-policy-on-indigenous-
    peoples/launch-event-policy-on-indigenous-people/
65 European Bank for Reconstruction and Development (EBRD), Environmental and Social Policy,
    issued May 2008, para 4.
66 Ibid.
67 Asian Development Bank, Safeguard Policy Statement July 2009 at 3.
68 Ibid., para 4.
69 Kingsbury 1999: 323.
70 Ibid.: 338.

Degradation (REDD) in developing countries, with pilot projects in Vietnam implementing FPIC processes.[71]

The policies of the public sector arm of the World Bank Group have, despite revisions in 1991 and 2005, fallen behind those of other UN agencies as well as other international financial institutions. This lag in the Bank's policies pertaining to indigenous peoples' rights is reflected in its failure to include the FPIC requirement, despite strong recommendations that it do so, emerging from two major international reviews it had commissioned, one on dams and the other on the extractive industry.[72] The Bank rejected the recommendation of its own 2004 Extractive Industry Review on the grounds that:

> Where a country is not one of the few that have incorporated FPIC into their domestic legal framework, requiring FPIC would be inconsistent with the Bank Group's role as a global institution whose members are sovereign governments, possessed of their own rights to determine whether to follow the terms of any international convention. Indeed, this would create a conflict with the Articles of Agreement, as the Bank Group would, in effect, be giving the equivalent of a veto right to parties other than those specified in the country's legal framework. This would be inconsistent with the Bank Group's governance structure, which establishes the critical role of member governments in Bank Group financing.[73]

Instead, the Bank has opted to include what it termed Free Prior Informed Consultation (FPICon) resulting in 'broad community support'.[74] In their response, indigenous organisations rejected the concept of FPICon, referring to it as a 'misappropriation and misinterpretation of FPIC' and as 'negat[ing] indigenous peoples' self-determining status and rights by casting indigenous peoples as nothing more than a sub-set of local communities'.[75] The Bank proceeded to include FPICon in its policy which, while highly controversial among indigenous peoples, has been recognised as consistent with certain elements of C169.[76] Its concept of 'broad community support' nevertheless suffers from a fundamental flaw as, under it, the entity seeking community 'support' maintains control over the determination of whether the indigenous people or community has agreed or not to a proposed activity. The Bank's own Compliance Advisor/Ombudsman has expressed concern in relation to the ambiguity of the Bank's determination of broad

71 'Applying Free Prior and Informed Consent in Viet Nam', UN REDD Programme, April 2010.
72 World Commission on Dams 2000; and the World Bank Group and Extractive Industries 2003. The Final Report of World Bank Extractive Industry Review *Striking a Better Balance*, Volume 1.
73 The World Bank 2004.
74 MacKay 2004a.
75 Letter from 60 indigenous peoples' organisations and indigenous NGOs to the World Bank's Board of Directors, 19 July 2004, quoted in Griffiths 2005: 11; see also MacKay 2004a.
76 Shelton 2011: 62.

community support.[77] This insistence on FPICon rather than FPIC has been strongly criticised by non-governmental organisations, indigenous peoples and the Eminent Person responsible for the Extractive Industry Review.[78] In 2003, the Special Rapporteur on the Rights of Indigenous Peoples recommended that the Bank's policy 'on indigenous peoples should strictly adhere to all existing and evolving international indigenous human rights standards'.[79] This recommendation is consistent with the opinion of a number of independent experts. All have argued that in order to realise its obligation under international law, to ensure that peoples affected by its projects and strategies have the opportunity to participate effectively in decisions affecting them, the World Bank should respect the right of indigenous peoples to self-determination and FPIC.[80] Addressing the Bank's position, Goodland, a former senior advisor at the Bank, suggests that it is inconsistent for it to invoke the argument that its Articles of Agreement are limited to the economic arena as a basis for rejecting FPIC.[81] This is the case for economic as well as moral and legal reasons. The requirement for FPIC embodies a fundamental economic principle with which the Bank must comply, namely 'willing seller, willing buyer'. The rejection of FPIC therefore implies economics based on the use of force.[82] The Bank's position that FPIC is in contravention of State sovereignty also rings particularly hollow when viewed in light of its capacity to influence domestic legislation and facilitate 'norm internalisation'.[83] It is also at odds with the Bank's position on environmental agreements which it does not oppose on State sovereignty grounds.[84] Indeed, Kingsbury argues that the Bank may have legal obligations of consultation arising from '[its] constitutive documents and legal relations with its member states, or from the Bank's own commitments to participation, or general principles of international law applicable to international organisations, or otherwise from public international law'.[85]

As a UN Specialized Agency, the Bank is coming under pressure to respect the rights and principles contained in the UNDRIP and to uphold its obligations under Articles 41 and 42 to contribute to its full realisation and to 'promote respect for and full application of [its] provisions'. In 2012, the Bank launched a review of its environmental and social safeguard policies, including its Operational Policy 4.10 on indigenous peoples.[86] During all of its consultations with indigenous

---

77 'IFC's Policy and Performance Standards on Social and Environmental Sustainability and Disclosure Policy, Commentary on IFC's Progress Report on the First 18 Months of Application', Office of the Compliance Advisor/Ombudsman (CAO) IFC and MIGA, World Bank Group, Advisory Note, 17 December 2007; see also Rai *et al.* 2011: 8, 10, 45, 50.
78 MacKay 2005; see also Salim 2005; see also Statement by C. Doyle, EMRIP 2010.
79 Stavenhagen, UN Doc. E/CN.4/2003/90, para 67.
80 Tilburg Guiding Principles on World Bank, IMF and Human Rights, para 33, Tilburg University, The Netherlands, April 2002, reproduced in Van Genugten, Hunt and Mathews 2003: 247–255.
81 Goodland, 2008: 345.
82 Ibid.
83 Sarfaty 2005: 1809.
84 Kingsbury 1999: 327.
85 Ibid.: 325.
86 The World Bank's Safeguard Policies Proposed Review and Update Approach Paper (World Bank, 10 October 2012), para 35.

peoples in 2013–2014, the need to adopt FPIC has been emphasised.[87] The Special Rapporteur on the rights of indigenous peoples has also clarified that 'the revised policy should be consistent with rights of indigenous peoples affirmed in the UN Declaration' which should 'apply to all the Bank's financial and technical assistance, and not just its investment lending'.[88] The Bank's initial response was relatively positive, identifying FPIC as one of the major themes to be addressed in the review process and agreeing to establish an independent Indigenous Peoples Advisory Council which would serve as a mechanism for its on-going engagement with indigenous peoples.[89] However, past experience of indigenous peoples with participation in World Bank policy reviews, along with the Bank's discretionary approach to its policy review process and the US effective veto power over the Bank's policy, suggest that incorporation of FPIC into the Bank's policy is by no means a foregone conclusion.[90] The Bank's 2014 draft standard on indigenous peoples includes the requirement for FPIC but provides borrowees with an unacceptable, from an indigenous rights perspective, "opt-out" option. Nevertheless, in light of developments within the international framework of indigenous peoples' rights following its last policy update, in particular, the adoption of the UNDRIP and the incorporation of FPIC into the policies of other international financial institutions, including the IFC as well as other UN Specialized Agencies, further delay in the Bank's recognition of FPIC will be difficult to justify.

7.3.2 IFC Performance Standards and safeguard policy requiring FPIC

The World Bank's private sector arm, the International Finance Corporation (IFC), initiated a review of its Performance Standards in 2009, identifying FPIC as one of four 'key operation topics'.[91] It initially resisted the adoption of FPIC, maintaining that its standard of free prior informed consultation was 'functionally equivalent'.[92] However, following lobbying from indigenous groups and input from the Special Rapporteur on the rights of indigenous peoples, in 2012, the IFC incorporated FPIC into its Performance Standard 7, which forms part of its overall safeguard policy. The significance of this development for the operationalisation of FPIC, given the IFC's role as the flag bearer of global standard setting for the private sector, including both banks and extractive industry

---

87 World Bank Safeguard Policies Review and Update Dialogue with Indigenous Peoples, October 2013–March 2014, available at: http://consultations.worldbank.org/

88 http://unsr.jamesanaya.org/notes/world-bank-operational-policies-must-be-in-line-with-the-united-nations-declaration-on-the-rights-of-indigenous-peoples

89 Letter from World Bank President Jim Yong to Asian Indigenous Peoples Pact (6 August 2012) (on file with author).

90 Griffiths 2005; see also Bradlow 2012: 57; Woods 2003: 111–112; Sarfaty 2009.

91 *Progress Report on IFC's Policy and Performance Standards on Social and Environmental Sustainability, and Policy on Disclosure of Information Review and Update Process* (Washington, DC: IFC, 2010), paras 34–35 and Annex A, 'Review and Update of IFC's Sustainability Framework: Overview of Key Issues'.

92 Ibid.: 26.

companies, is enormous and has been described as a 'watershed moment in international development history'.[93]

The policy justifies this additional requirement for indigenous peoples on the grounds that they may be 'particularly vulnerable to the loss of, alienation from or exploitation of their land and access to natural and cultural resources'.[94] The FPIC requirement applies to projects: impacting on land or natural resources subject to traditional ownership or under customary use; requiring relocation of communities; or significantly impacting on critical cultural heritage of indigenous peoples. Under the standard, indigenous peoples' FPIC is required for project design, implementation and outcomes,[95] which in terms of extractive projects would logically translate into planning, exploration and project feasibility phase (design); exploitation (implementation/operation) and project closure and decommissioning (outcomes).[96]

One of the most significant features of the Performance Standard is that the requirement for FPIC is framed together with the objectives of avoiding 'adverse impacts' on indigenous peoples and ensuring full respect for their human rights,[97] implying that its implementation must be consistent with those rights. As a result, any ambiguities in the Standard must be interpreted in light of the contemporary framework of indigenous peoples' rights. On the other hand, its most significant ambiguity is the absence of an explicit statement with regard to what should happen where indigenous consent is not forthcoming in contexts other than relocation.[98] The interpretation provided by the IFC, in response to questions during its drafting consultation process, was that it would not fund such projects, or projects associated with on-going violations of indigenous peoples' rights.[99]

The IFC subsequently developed a set of implementation Guidance Notes, the production of which lacked a similar public consultation process but did involve discussions with IFC extractive industry clients. While the Notes are helpful in providing direction to corporations unfamiliar with the concept of FPIC, they do introduce further ambiguities, in particular, in relation to sequencing. This arises from a suggestion that consent may not be required prior to exploration.[100] The suggestion, which is based on the fact that a complete impact assessment may not be feasible until later in the project lifecycle, is at odds with the requirement of the Performance Standard that FPIC processes are triggered by adverse impacts at the project design stage. The implication of an impact-based trigger, as affirmed by a range of authoritative human rights bodies and standards, is that consent-seeking

93 Baker 2013.
94 IFC 2012a, para 11.
95 Ibid.: para 11.
96 There is some inconsistency in the use of the term 'outcomes' which refers to project decommissioning and elsewhere to 'expected outcomes related to impacts affecting the communities of Indigenous Peoples', see IFC 2012a,, GN 11 and 15.
97 IFC 2012a, para 2.
98 Doyle 2011, *Input to IFC Sustainability Policy.*
99 IFC Consultation, Paris, 23 February2011, notes on file with author.
100 IFC Guidance Note 7, *Indigenous Peoples* (Washington, DC: IFC, 2012), para GN 39.

consultations have to start at the earliest stage possible prior to any activities commencing in indigenous territories based on full disclosure of the information available at that time.[101] Further FPIC processes will be required as the project progresses through different stages. Another potential ambiguity introduced in the Guidance Notes relates to the absence of clarity with regard to the role which indigenous peoples themselves are entitled to play in defining and implementing FPIC processes. The Guidance Note does not address contexts where indigenous peoples have defined, or may wish to define, their own FPIC process or conduct and control key aspects of project-related impact assessments themselves. Finally, the Guidance Note makes some assumptions in relation to indigenous self-governance which may not be appropriate in particular contexts, such as a reference to majority decision-making and to conducting joint FPIC processes with non-indigenous groups. While this may be considered appropriate by some indigenous communities, the requirement under the Performance Standard, and human rights law in general, to ensure respect for indigenous cultures and associated decision-making processes, implies that the communities themselves should determine the appropriate approach to such issues.

In addition to these ambiguities in the Performance Standard and associated Guidance Note, a number of structural limitations associated with the *modus operandi* of the IFC and other international financial institutions act as constraints on their potential role in the operationalisation of FPIC. First, these safeguard policies rely on the project operators, the clients of the financial institutions, for their enforcement – something which has been described as a fox guarding the henhouse.[102] The IFC's safeguards apply in relation to the responsibilities of its staff vis-à-vis those to whom it provides loans. As a result, apart from a limited supervisory role, the Bank is largely disconnected from the policy implementation at community level.[103]

Second, the use of intermediary financial entities by the IFC in the provision of loans to project executors has increased dramatically. In the late 1990s, the IFC's portfolio consisted primarily of clients to which it provided direct project financing. By 2010, over 40 per cent of its portfolio had shifted to global financial markets.[104] This method of funding projects further distances the institution and its oversight mechanisms from the impacted indigenous communities and significantly increases the probability that the FPIC requirement will not be triggered.[105]

101　Doyle and Cariño 2013:11; UN Doc A/HRC/24/41 (2014), para 68.
102　Szablowski 2007: 135.
103　Supervision is primarily based on reports received from the project proponent and a visit to the project site prior to project approval, ibid. at 114.
104　IFC Compliance Advisor Ombudsman, *The CAO at 10: Annual Report FY2010 and Review FY2000–10* (Washington, DC: IFC, 2010), 6.
105　For an overview of IFC procedures in relation to the environmental and social review process for financial intermediaries, see IFCDCESI, *Environmental and Social Review Procedures, Manual Financial Intermediary Investments: Early Review and Appraisal, Disclosure and Commitment, and Supervision*, Version 4, 14 August 2009.

Third, the safeguard policies apply as part of the contractual relationship between the Bank and its clients. As a result, the impacted communities do not have a direct recourse to remedies either against the Bank or its clients under those policies. The IFC's 'independent accountability mechanism' in the form of a Compliance Advisor/Ombudsman (CAO) was established in an attempt to respond to this deficiency.[106] Its effectiveness is constrained by the fact that the responsibility of the audit arm of the mechanism is limited to ensuring that Bank staff act in accordance with the guidelines, a responsibility which does not extend to an investigation of the activities of the project proponent itself.[107] A related concern with regard to the implementation of the Performance Standards is that, despite the presence of an active Compliance Advisor/Ombudsman, there is no known case of funding being withdrawn based on a failure to adhere to safeguard policies.[108]

Finally, given that the IFC funds private sector clients, and not governments, the consent requirement does not address the concession issuance by the State, as it only applies to the decision-making phases of IFC clients. A major restraint on the exercise of a genuine choice as a result is the absence of the requirement for a participatory analysis of alternative development options prior to seeking consent to a particular externally driven project proposal. The recommendation that a comprehensive options assessment be conducted prior to consent-seeking processes in relation to a particular project proposal was one of the major findings of the World Bank-commissioned World Commission on Dams and is equally applicable to all projects within the resource extractive sector.[109] It should, as a result, be a core component of the revised World Bank policy.

The incorporation of FPIC into the policies of the IFC, and most other international financial institutions, represents a major milestone on the path towards FPIC's crystallisation as the standard to be complied with by all private sector actors. The acknowledgement of the human rights-based nature of FPIC should serve to guarantee indigenous peoples' central role in its definition and implementation and act as a corrective force on any potential distortion of the concept arising out of ambiguities in safeguard policies or guidance of financial institutions. It is therefore essential that these institutions come to terms with the fact that the primary source for guidance on FPIC operationalisation should be indigenous communities themselves and that their views must have primacy in the concept's operationalisation. If this principle is respected in practice, then despite its shortcomings, the IFC's adoption of FPIC consequently would represent an important step on the path towards the widespread operationalisation of a genuine self-determination-based model of FPIC.

---

106 Szablowski 2007: 42, 240; see also IFC 201a: 4; see also *CAO Ethos International Conference Business and Civil Society in the New Economy, Office of the Compliance Advisor Ombudsman (CAO) for IFC and MIGA* (13 June 2012), available at: www.slideshare.net/institutoethos/meg-taylor
107 IFC 2010a.
108 Coumans 2010: 30 (1–2).
109 Report of the World Commission on Dams 2000: xxxiv, 221.

One of the reasons why the IFC Performance Standards are of particular significance to indigenous peoples is their role as the basis for the Equator Principles. These voluntary principles apply to 79 financial institutions which cover in excess of 70 per cent of international project finance debt in emerging markets.[110] The Equator Principles were revised in 2014 to bring them into line with the IFC's policy. The two core changes introduced were the requirements for indigenous peoples' FPIC and for human rights due diligence. Both respond to the affirmation of the responsibility of financial institutions to respect human rights in the 2011 UN Guiding Principles on Business and Human Rights as well as the revised 2011 OECD Guidelines for Multinational Enterprises. Some of these institutions have commenced research into the implications of the human rights due diligence requirement for their operations,[111] however, similar research in relation to the implications of the FPIC requirement have yet to be initiated.[112] Guaranteeing compliance with the requirement for FPIC necessitates a context-specific understanding of the extent to which the particular governance and decision-making processes of impacted indigenous peoples have been respected. Implementing a rights-consistent concept of FPIC consequently gives rise to a range of operational challenges, in areas such as monitoring and oversight, staff incentives, and client sanctions. Financial institutions and their extractive industry clients have yet to fully comprehend these challenges or what will be required to develop appropriate and effective operational responses. As will be discussed in Chapter 8, in relation to the policy of the International Council for Minerals and Metals (ICMM), developing an understanding of how to respond will necessitate extensive engagement with indigenous peoples.

In addition to banks, investors also play a significant role in funding extractive projects. Increasing demand from customers for ethical investment options has resulted in some investors advocating respect of indigenous peoples' rights and attempting to encourage extractive companies to commit to obtaining FPIC.[113] To date, however, such initiatives are rare.[114] The UN Principles for Responsible Investment are currently examining the issue of the extractive sector and human rights, and research endorsed by them acknowledges that the sector needs to focus greater attention on its impacts on indigenous communities.[115] Outside the arena of sustainable and responsible investor initiatives, most investment policies continue to be driven by the standards produced by and for extractive industry

---

110 www.equator-principles.com/index.php/about-ep/about-ep
111 Thun Group, 'UN Guiding Principles on Business and Human Rights Discussion Paper for Banks on Implications of Principles 16–21', 2013, available at: www.business-humanrights.org/media/documents/thun-group-discussion-paper-final-2-oct-2013.pdf
112 Allen & Overy 2013.
113 Ethical Funds Company (2008); see also EIRIS 2010; Position of Calvert Investment, in Voss and Greenspan 2012: 17, 18; Kropp 2010; De Cordova (NEI Investments) 2012: 66, 67, 99; and First Peoples Worldwide 2012.
114 Nikolakis, Cohen and Nelson 2012.
115 Knoepfel 2011: 20.

bodies themselves. Investors have emerged as a focus group for indigenous peoples' advocacy. The obvious synergy between investment risk management and human rights' realisation suggests that further constructive engagement between indigenous peoples and investors around the operationalisation of FPIC is inevitable.[116]

7.4 The developing issue of home State responsibility

The duty of States to obtain FPIC is a result of indigenous peoples' rights to self-determination and to non-discrimination. The *erga omnes* character of these rights raises questions as to the duties of home States to ensure that their corporations comply with FPIC in order to safeguard these rights.[117] The HRC has clarified that common Article 1, paragraph 3 imposes obligations: 'not only in relation to [a State's] own peoples but vis-à-vis all peoples which have not been able to exercise or have been deprived of the possibility of exercising the right of self-determination'.[118]

While acknowledging the caveat that 'States must refrain from interfering in the internal affairs of other States and thereby adversely affecting the exercise of the right to self-determination', the Committee affirmed that:

> [i]t follows that all States parties to the Covenant should take positive action to facilitate realisation of and respect for the right of peoples to self-determination [irrespective of whether the people depend on a State party to the Covenant or not].[119]

Human rights bodies, in particular, CERD[120] and the CESCR,[121] have delved into the related evolving issue of home State responsibility, or Extraterritorial

116 First Peoples Worldwide 2013; Doyle and Cariño 2013.
117 The Inter-American Court of Human Rights has noted that the *erga omnes* character of the rights to equality and non-discrimination 'give rise to effects with regard to third parties, including individuals', see Inter-American Court of Human Rights Advisory Opinion, Oc-18/03 of 17 September 2003, Requested by The United Mexican States Juridical Condition and Rights of Undocumented Migrants, para 110. The relevance of this in the context of indigenous peoples' rights has been noted by Justice Trindade, see Inter-American Court of Human Rights, *Sarayaku People v Ecuador*, 17 July 2005, Separate Opinion of Judge Cançado Trindade, para 20 (Spanish version only).
118 CCPR General Comment No. 12: Article 1: The Right to Self-determination of Peoples (13 April 1984), para 6.
119 Ibid.
120 CERD, *Concluding Observations to Canada, United States, Norway and UK from 2006 to 2011*, see Doyle forthcoming 2015.
121 CESCR, *Statement on the Obligations of States Parties Regarding the Corporate Sector and Economic, Social and Cultural Rights*, UN Doc. E/C.12/2011/1 (20 May 2011), para 5; CESCR, General Comment 15, The right to water (Twenty-ninth session, 2003), UN Doc. E/C.12/2002/11 (2002), para 33; General Comment 18, Article 6: The equal right of men and women to the enjoyment of all economic, social and cultural rights (Thirty-fifth session, 2006), UN Doc. E/C.12/GC/18 (2006), para 52. The CESCR specifically noted that 'States Parties should extraterritorially protect the right to social security by preventing their own citizens and national entities from violating this right in other countries', General Comment 19, The right to social security (art. 9) (Thirty-ninth session, 2007), UN Doc. E/C.12/GC/19 (2008), para 54.

Obligations (ETOs), for the actions of their corporate actors.[122] In doing so, CERD has emphasised the need for home State regulation to ensure that extractive corporations registered in their jurisdictions respect indigenous peoples' rights. It has also emphasised to home States the important role obtaining FPIC plays in ensuring these rights are guaranteed.[123] In its 2014 Concluding Observations to China, the CESCR recommended that it '[a]dopt appropriate legislative and administrative measures to ensure legal liability of companies and their subsidiaries *operating in or managed from* the State party's territory regarding violations of economic, social and cultural rights in their projects abroad'.[124]

The Committee on the Rights of the Child (CRC) addresses the extraterritorial obligations of States for their corporate actors in its General Comment on Child Rights and the Business Sector stating that 'States should enable access to effective judicial and non-judicial mechanisms to provide remedy for children and their families whose rights have been violated by business enterprises extraterritorially.'[125]

However, evidence of exercise by home States of regulatory responsibility for the overseas operations of their corporations remains sparse, and relatively few offer effective access to judicial remedies to overseas victims of corporate-related rights abuses.[126] The importance of addressing this deficiency in the context of the extractive sector has been noted by the Special Rapporteur on the rights of indigenous peoples.[127] This emerging issue has also been the subject of extensive consideration by the Special Rapporteur on the Right to Food, who holds that a component of the State duty to protect includes: 'a duty on the State to regulate its corporations and non-State actors in order to protect the inhabitants of other countries'.[128]

In their commentary on the *Maastricht Principles on Extraterritorial Obligations of States*,[129] a number of human rights experts, including the Special Rapporteur on the right to food, noted that the UNDRIP 'may also be the source of extraterritorial

122 The extent of the extraterritorial responsibility of States is an on-going debate, see McCorquodale and Simons 2007; see also Clapham 2006; Alston 2005; see also *Legal Consequences of the Construction of a Wall in the Occupied Palestinian Territory, Advisory Opinion*, ICJ Reports 2004: 136, paras 107–113. See Doyle forthcoming 2015.

123 In the letter CERD referred to the draft UN Norms on Transnational Corporations. See CERD Early Warning Urgent Action letter to France, 28 September 2009 and Chapter 3 for a commentary.

124 UN Doc. E/C.12/CHN/CO/2 (2014), para 13.

125 General Comment No. 16 (2013) on State obligations regarding the impact of business on children's rights, UN Doc. CRC/C/GC/16 para 44. Available at: www2.ohchr.org/english/bodies/crc/callsubmissionsCRC_BusinessSector.htm

126 The best known is the US *Alien Tort Claims Act* (ATCA), 28 U.S.C. §1350 (2001). An attempt to pass a bill in Canada providing for extraterritorial jurisdiction in the context of mining was narrowly defeated in March 2011, see Canadian *Bill C-300 (Historical) Corporate Accountability of Mining, Oil and Gas Corporations in Developing Countries Act, An Act Respecting Corporate Accountability for the Activities of Mining, Oil or Gas in Developing Countries*. A follow-up bill was introduced in April 2012. Bill C-418 Extraterritorial Activities of Canadian Businesses and Entities Act.

127 *Mining Must Respect Indigenous Peoples' Rights* (21 August 2012), available at www.galdu.org/web/index.php?odas=5836

128 For a discussion on the issue of extraterritorial responsibility and the right to food, see Report of the Special Rapporteur on the Right to Food, Jean Ziegler, 24 January 2005, UN Doc E/CN.4/2005/47, para 53.

129 *Maastricht Principles on Extraterritorial Obligations of States in the Area of Economic, Social and Cultural Rights* (Maastricht: Maastricht University Press, 28 September 2011).

obligations, to the extent that it reflects customary international law'.[130] They also suggested that the CERD's 2007 recommendation to 'explore ways to hold transnational corporations registered in [home States] accountable' for violations of indigenous peoples rights is consistent with the general obligation on States to provide effective remedies.[131]

The legal foundations for ETOs, their scope and the remedies required under them, are an evolving area of debate under international law.[132] The *UN Guiding Principles on Business and Human Rights* acknowledged the recent recommendations of treaty bodies in the area of home State obligations, but did little to promote them, maintaining instead that treaty body guidance 'suggested that the treaties do not require States to exercise extraterritorial jurisdiction over business abuse'.[133] The issue is cautiously addressed under guiding principle number two, which holds that contemporary international human rights law does not generally require States to regulate the extraterritorial activities of businesses domiciled in their jurisdiction.[134] It also suggests that for States' actions in this arena to be reasonable, certain conditions, including being grounded in multilateral agreements, may be necessary.[135] The conservative nature of the guidelines in relation to ETOs was justified by the Special Representative on the grounds that he sought the consensus of all States in relation to their content.[136] Alternative perspectives, such as those articulated in the Maastricht Principles, argue that tentative foundations exist for asserting the ETOs of States, and advocate building on these, so that 'the accountability gap that economic globalisation has created can be closed'.[137] One of the landmark cases cited in relation to ETOs in the context of international agreements is *Sawhoyamaxa Indigenous Community v Paraguay*.[138] In *Sawhoyamaxa*, the Inter-American Court on Human Rights affirmed that property rights under Article 21 of the American Convention on Human Rights spring from 'culture, uses, customs, and beliefs of each people'.[139] It also addressed the need to ensure that a Bilateral Investment Treaty, which addressed land restitution to indigenous people, be applied in accordance with human rights obligations under the Convention.[140] In its *Saramaka v Suriname* ruling, the court derived a requirement for FPIC from the property right affirmed in *Sawhoyamaxa*. A constructive reading of this jurisprudence, in light of indigenous peoples' right to self-determination,

---

130 De Schutter *et al.* 2102: 1099.
131 Ibid.: 1135, 1150.
132 Langford *et al.* 2013.
133 Ruggie 2013: 45.
134 UN Doc A/HRC/17/31 (2011), Principle 2.
135 Ibid.
136 Ruggie 2013: 117.
137 De Schutter 2012.
138 *Sawhoyamaxa Indigenous Community v. Paraguay*, Inter-Am. Ct. H.R., Merits, Reparations and Costs (ser. C) No. 146 (29 March 2006).
139 *Sawhoyamaxa*, para 120.
140 *Sawhoyamaxa*, para 140; Coomans and Kunnemann 2012:40–52; De Schutter *et al.* 2012: 1122; Suarez-Franco 2013: 297.

would consequently suggest that the court's interpretation of the American Convention supports an ETO in relation to guaranteeing respect for the FPIC of overseas indigenous peoples.

The UN Guiding Principles also refer to 'multilateral soft-law instruments such as the *Organisation for Economic Cooperation and Development [OECD] Guidelines for Multinational Enterprises* and to Performance Standards required by institutions that support overseas investments, as examples of how home States establish expectations for the conduct of their businesses abroad.[141] The *OECD Guidelines for Multinational Enterprises*, which list 42 adhering States, constitute a legal commitment on the part of governments to ensure that multinational enterprises comply with the standards and to establish National Contact Points as the mechanism to facilitate this commitment.[142] They do not, however, impose mandatory obligations on corporations, and have been described by a National Contact Point (NCP) as 'soft law with hard consequences'.[143] The guidelines are of particular relevance in the context of extractive industries as over half of the complaints made under them are in relation to this sector.[144] A chapter on human rights, modelled on the UN guidelines for business and human rights, was included as part of an update in 2011,[145] and includes a commentary on their implementation, stating that enterprises should consider UN instruments on indigenous peoples.[146] In addition, the *OECD Common Approaches for Export Credits and Environmental and Social Due Diligence* may trigger the FPIC requirement as they can require benchmarking of Environmental and Social Impact Assessments (including adverse project-related human rights impacts) against IFC Performance Standards.[147]

In the case of Norway, both its OECD NCP, and its Export Credit Agency have sought to give effect to the recommendation made by CERD to ensure Norwegian extractive and hydroelectric corporations respect indigenous peoples' rights in other jurisdictions.[148] In 2011, the Norwegian NCP issued a Statement in relation to the activities of a Norwegian mining company in indigenous peoples' territories in the Philippines. The Statement held that CERD's recommendation '[had] placed a duty on Norway to ensure that the standards affirmed in ILO Convention no. 169 are applied not just in indigenous territories in Norway, but also by Norwegian companies operating overseas'.[149] This is consistent with the view that under human rights treaties, home States have a duty to ensure that their

---

141 UN Doc A/HRC/17/31 (2011), Principle 2.
142 Workshop of the OECD National Contact Points and the Extractive Sector, The British Academy, 10–11 Carlton House Terrace, London, 23 March 2012 (notes on file with author).
143 Ibid.
144 Institute for Business and Human Rights 2012: 1.
145 *OECD Guidelines for Multinational Enterprises*, 2011 Edition (Paris: OECD, 2011), Chapter IV, Human Rights at 31.
146 Ibid. at 32.
147 OECD Recommendation of the Council on Common Approaches for Officially Supported Export Credits and Environmental and Social Due Diligence TAD/ECG(2012)5 (28 June 2012), para 20.
148 UN Doc. CERD/C/NOR/CO/19–20 (8 April 2011), para 17.
149 Norwegian NCP 2011: 21.

corporations safeguard indigenous peoples' rights by obtaining their FPIC. The Norwegian Export Credit Agency adhered to CERD's recommendation as part of its due diligence by conducting a field visit to the Philippines in order to validate FPIC processes involving a Norwegian hydroelectric company.[150] The NCP Statement also provides extensive guidance regarding the mining company's obligations in relation to consultations and obtaining FPIC,[151] with which the Norwegian NCP has encouraged all ICMM members to comply.[152] This is particularly relevant, given the recommendations of the UK and Norwegian NCP Statements respectively that Vedanta in India and Intex Resources in the Philippines comply with the outcome of good faith consultations.[153] Both Statements referenced the IFC Standards and the Akwé Kon Guidelines, as providing appropriate guidance for corporations in relation to engagements with indigenous peoples.[154]

The potential extraterritorial applicability of C169 within the Spanish legal framework is also being considered by academics and indigenous support organisations.[155] The arguments put forward for extraterritorial responsibility for violations of human rights under C169 build on the recognition of extraterritorial responsibility in the context of criminal law and the principle of universal justice under the Spanish Judiciary Act.[156] A complementary argument holds that failure to address violations by Spanish transnational corporations outside of Spanish territorial jurisdiction could lead to a situation where a ratified Convention had no legal force.[157] Furthermore, as part of its development cooperation strategy, Spain has recognised the requirement for indigenous peoples' FPIC.[158]

If the limitations traditionally associated with territorial jurisdiction can be overcome in the context of C169, then perhaps similar arguments can be made in relation to C111. The fact that the *ILO Tripartite Declaration of Principles Concerning Multinational Enterprises and Social Policy*, which has international coverage,[159] makes specific reference to C111, could help to strengthen this argument.

Another avenue available to indigenous peoples pursuing violations of their rights associated with non-consensual extractive activities is that of tort-based

150 As part of the process, the author provided advice to the Norwegian Export Credit Agency in relation to the Philippines' legal framework and experiences of indigenous peoples with FPIC processes.
151 Norwegian NCP 2011.
152 OECD Norwegian NCP Workshop, op. cit.: 142. Denmark's development cooperation strategy also includes the requirement for FPIC, see *Strategy for Danish Support to Indigenous Peoples* (Danish Ministry of Foreign Affairs, Danida), May 2004.
153 Norwegian NCP 2011: 10; UK NCP 2009, para 73.
154 Norwegian NCP 2011: 6, 8, 23; see also UK NCP 2009, para 70.
155 Martínez de Bringas 2009.
156 Ibid.; *Ley Orgánica 6/1985*, de 1 de julio, del Poder Judicial.
157 Martínez de Bringas 2009: 16.
158 *Estrategia Sectorial Española de Cooperación Española con los Pueblos Indígenas* (2006), 20, see also Chapter 3.
159 *Report of the United Nations High Commissioner on Human Rights on the Responsibilities of Transnational Corporations and Related Business Enterprises with Regard to Human Rights* (15 February 2005), UN Doc. E/CN.4/2005/91, para 29(d).

claims. This avenue is generally limited to post-facto challenges and financial compensation for harm caused and negligence. It consequently does not provide an opportunity to challenge human rights violations and the nature of the extractive activity *per se*. As a result of its limitations, Westra argues that 'the whole concept of "torts" and compensation for environmental injuries [associated with violations of indigenous peoples' rights in the context of extractive operations] is legally insufficient and morally inadequate'.[160] However, in the absence of other remedies, tort provides one of the few avenues available to indigenous peoples to pursue extractive companies, including those with offices in the UK, and may potentially act as a deterrent to future human rights abuses.[161] A 2009 report of the UK's Joint Committee on Human Rights, examining the nexus of business and human rights, indicated a willingness to address extraterritorial effects in the context of parent company-based regulation.[162] However, it expressed reluctance to enact legislation providing for extraterritorial jurisdiction over the human rights impact of its companies overseas.[163]

In its concluding observations, CERD has recommended that the United States hold its corporations to account for activities in indigenous territories overseas.[164] The United States tort legislation, while not specifically aimed at human rights, is capable of catering to claims under international law and has been interpreted as applicable to the actions of US-based corporations operating overseas.[165] The 1789 United States Alien Tort Statute (ATS), also known as the Alien Tort Claims Act (ATCA),[166] was revived from obscurity in the 1980s.[167] Since that time it has been described as acting as a 'lynchpin of international human rights activism' in the context of extraterritoriality.[168] The basis for its invocation is a clause which states that: 'district courts shall have original jurisdiction of any civil action by an alien for a tort only, committed in violation of the law of nations or a treaty of the United States'.[169]

This clause, the usage of which is strongly resisted by the United States Chamber of Commerce,[170] has been invoked on a number of occasions in the context of extraterritorial responsibility of extractive companies operating in indigenous peoples' territories in relation to allegations of complicity in genocide and war crimes.[171]

---

160 Westra 2008: 139.
161 Skinner *et al.* 2013.
162 House of Lords and House of Commons, Joint Committee on Human Rights, *Any of Our Business? Human Rights and the UK Private Sector*, First Report of Session 2009–10, Volume I (24 November 2009), paras 203–205.
163 Ibid.; see also Couillard *et al.* 2009: 6.
164 UN Doc. CERD/C/USA/CO/6 (8 May 2008), para 30.
165 For a history of the Act, see Bradley 2002: 587–589.
166 *Alien Tort Claims Act* (ATCA), 28 U.S.C. §1350 (2001).
167 Bradley 2002: 587.
168 Developments in the Law of Extraterritoriality (2011), 124 *Harvard Law Review*, 1233.
169 28 U.S.C. § 1350: US Code - Section 1350: Alien's action for tort.
170 Howard 2002.
171 See, for example, *Kiobel v Shell* and *Alexis Holyweek Sarei v. Rio Tinto PLC*; see also Westra (2008): 161, 103–124.

Chapter 1 has posited that, from the inception of the law of nations, one of its core principles, which is inseparable from claims to title to territory, has been the requirement for voluntary and informed consent of indigenous peoples to assertions of State power over lands and resources under indigenous dominium. The US Supreme Court has itself recognised that in the absence of conquest, consent is the only basis for claims over indigenous territories.[172] It also recognises the inherent sovereignty and territorial rights of indigenous peoples.[173] Chapters 2–5 suggest that the requirement for indigenous peoples' consent continued, albeit in an increasingly emaciated form, throughout the colonial era and is manifested in the robust contemporary requirement for FPIC as a derivation of indigenous peoples' rights to self-determination and sovereignty. The requirement for indigenous peoples' consent has consequently never ceased to be a principle of the law of nations, albeit more frequently honoured in the breach than in the observance, and has applied to, and been applied by, States and corporations acting on their behalf since the commencement of the colonial encounter.[174]

If this hypothesis that obtaining the consent of indigenous peoples has always been a principle of the law of nations is accepted, then the Alien Claims Act would appear to extend to contexts in which corporations are complicit with host States in failing to obtain it where indigenous peoples' territorial and sovereignty rights are threatened. However, given the on-going challenges to the Act's applicability where acts which give rise to the claim occur abroad,[175] the prospect that such an argument will be considered, let alone entertained, may be remote.

At a more general level, it has been suggested that long-term possibilities for universal or extraterritorial jurisdiction over corporate actors revolve around the negotiation of an international instrument[176] or the emergence of custom.[177] The universal applicability of the self-determination-based consent requirement is an issue of practical as well as moral importance. The absence of a global governance framework for the mineral sector leads to competition for foreign direct investment which frequently results in a 'beggar-thy-neighbour' approach and a 'race to the bottom' in terms of regulatory protections in host States.[178] In such a context, equitable trade relations and obligations arising out of international cooperation necessitate that the requirement for indigenous peoples' consent be adhered to by all States. If this is not the case, scenarios may arise whereby certain States gain unjust

---

172 *Worcester v Georgia* U.S. (6 Pet.) 515 (1832), 541–563.
173 Ibid.: 559; *Cherokee Nation v. Georgia* 30 U.S. (5 Pet) 1 (1831), 17; *US v Wheeler*, 435 US 313, 322–3 (1978). Imai 2009: 293–294.
174 See Lugard F L Lady 1997 (first published in 1906); Galbraith 1974; Andrews 1978; Page and Sonnenburg 2003; Marshall 1968.
175 *Kiobel v. Royal Dutch Petroleum*, 261 F.3d 111 (2nd Cir. 2010); see also Developments in the Law of Extraterritoriality 2011: 1240–1242 and Fiechter 2011–2012; Skinner *et al.*; McCorquodale and De Schutter 2013.
176 De Schutter 2006: 51.
177 Bernaz 2013.
178 Report of the Special Rapporteur on the Right to Food, De Schutter, *Crisis into Opportunity: Reinforcing Multilateralism* A/HRC/12/31 (21 July 2009), para 22; Doyle and Whitmore 2014: 134–7; Doyle and Carino 2013: 79.

competitive advantage by effectively subsidising resource extraction through the denial of the potential for indigenous peoples to enter into mutually acceptable consent-based benefit-sharing arrangements in relation to resource exploitation in their territories.[179] In doing so, they may fall foul not only of human rights obligations but also of World Trade Organization rules prohibiting trade subsidies.[180]

Having considered host State practice and home State responsibility in relation to FPIC and the evolving role of international organisations, in particular, international financial institutions, in strengthening its normative status, the final section will consider the potential role of the UN's principal judicial organ, the ICJ, in strengthening the requirement's status under international law.

7.5 A window of opportunity for the ICJ to address FPIC?

The lack of standing of indigenous peoples before the International Court of Justice has meant that their rights and interests are generally deemed incidental, or mere facts to be considered, in cases addressing State claims to territorial sovereignty which have come before the court.[181]

Racial discriminatory doctrines justifying differential treatment of peoples based on external assessments of their 'backwardness' or their uncivilised nature continued to be reflected in national and international law well into the twentieth century. Indeed, it is frequently argued that these outdated modes of legal thinking premised on racist constructs and doctrines continue to have enduring effects on the manner in which contemporary legal reasoning affects indigenous peoples.[182] To a certain degree, this legacy is evident in the jurisprudence of the ICJ. The operation of international law's inter-temporal rule combined with the application of *uti possidetis juris* has meant that situations where title over indigenous peoples' territories had been obtained by conquest, under conditions of duress, or without even seeking their consent, would not be revisited.[183] Border disputes continue to be resolved by the ICJ without consideration of the implications of indigenous claims, as evidenced in the 1992 frontier dispute between El Salvador and Honduras where it held that: 'It was from the outset accepted that the new international boundaries should, in accordance with the principle generally applied in Spanish America of the *uti possidetis juris*, follow the colonial administrative boundaries.'[184]

179 See Barsh 2005: 4–7.
180 Ibid.: 9–11.
181 See, for example, *Western Sahara* Advisory Opinion, ICJ Reports 1975; *Land, Island and Maritime Frontier Dispute (Salvador/Honduras: Nicaragua intervening)*, ICJ No. 92/22 11 September 1992; *Territorial Dispute (Libyan Arab Jamahiriyai Chad)*, ICJ judgment of 3 February 1994; Case Concerning the *Frontier Dispute (Burkina Faso/Republic of Mali)* judgment of 22 December 1986.
182 Bell and Asch 1997; see also Williams 2005.
183 Castellino 2008.
184 ICJ No. 92/22, 11 September 1992, *Land, Island and Maritime Frontier Dispute (Salvador/Honduras: Nicaragua intervening)*. See Castellino 2008: 552; also Reisman 1995: 356–357.

Similarly, in 1994, the ICJ deemed irrelevant the *de facto* exclusive effective occupation by indigenous inhabitants of disputed uranium-rich territories which were claimed by Libya and Chad. Libya acknowledged 'that title to the territory was at all relevant times, vested in the peoples inhabiting the territory, who were tribes, confederations of tribes or other peoples' and argued that its own title was effectively a derivative of that title.[185] The court deemed the case to rest exclusively on the borders specified in a 1955 Treaty entered into by Libya and Chad. As a result, it judged it 'unnecessary to consider the history of the "Borderlands" claimed by Libya on the basis of title inherited from the indigenous people' or to address the role of the principle of *uti possidetis juris*.[186] In doing so, the ruling not only dismissed as irrelevant the exclusive effective occupation of the area by the indigenous peoples, but also facilitated an agreement between Libya and Chad which afforded no recognition of those indigenous peoples' contemporary rights and interests.[187] This approach to the application of the principle of *uti possidetis juris*, which ignored the prior territorial claims of indigenous peoples, served to deny potential challenges to their non-consensual inclusion within newly created States irrespective of the manner in which title over their territories had been acquired by the colonial powers.[188]

At the same time, international law can also be regarded as gradually evolving to explicitly reject some of its discriminatory doctrinal underpinnings, with the ICJ playing a constructive role in this regard. In its 1975 advisory opinion on the *Western Sahara* case, the court concluded that:

> [P]ractice of the relevant period indicates that territories inhabited by tribes or peoples having a social and political organisation were not regarded as *terra nullius*. It shows that in the case of such territories the acquisition of sovereignty was not generally considered as effected unilaterally through 'occupation' of terra nullius by original title but through agreements concluded with local rulers . . . such agreements with local rulers, whether or not considered as an actual 'cession' of the territory, were regarded as *derivative roots of title*, and not original titles obtained by occupation of terra nullius.[189]

Crawford suggests that the *Western Sahara* case 'provides a decisive refutation of the criterion of civilization as a test for *terra nullius*' and that it follows 'that a necessary condition for valid acquisition of nearly all inhabited territory was the consent of the native chiefs or peoples involved'.[190] The ICJ ruling nevertheless implies that in the period in question the principle of *terra nullius* applied in territories where

---

185 *Territorial Dispute (Libyan Arab Jamahiriya v. Chad)*, ICJ judgment of 3 February 1994 at 13.
186 Ibid.: 36–38.
187 Reisman 1995: 356–357.
188 Castellino 2008: 533; for a discussion on the principle of *uti possidetis juris*, see Castellino and Allen 2003.
189 Emphasis added. *ICJ Western Sahara Advisory Opinion* of 16 October 1975; see also UN Doc E/CN.4/Sub.2/1999/20, para 188.
190 Crawford 2007: 181–182.

there was a lack of 'social and political organisation'.[191] While past conceptions of some indigenous peoples as lacking in social and political organisation constituted the basis for deeming their territories *terra nullius*, contemporary sociological and anthropological understandings, that all peoples by definition correspond to socially organised groups, rejects the notion that any people's lands can be considered *terra nullius* on the basis of a lack of such organisation.[192] The ruling affirms that this was the criterion in the past, but indicates that it had relatively little purchase in practice.

The ICJ advisory opinion does not, however, legitimise cases where the criterion of political and social organisation was used as a basis for *terra nullius,* nor does it suggest that the on-going negative effects of such practices should be tolerated. This interpretation is supported by the invocation of the *Western Sahara* opinion by the Australian Supreme Court. In 1992, the court, in *Mabo v Queensland*, rejected the *terra nullius* doctrine which had been invoked to assert title to territory in a context where the native peoples were deemed to lack sufficient social and political organisation to exercise dominion.[193] *Mabo* clarified that the doctrine of *terra nullius* is discriminatory in all contexts where lands are inhabited by a people, regardless of the perceived level of political organisation. However, trapped within the legal constructs of the common law and rigid notions of national sovereignty, the Australian High Court was unable, or unwilling, to engage with the implications of this rejection of *terra nullius* for contemporary indigenous sovereignty and consent, and instead focused exclusively on its property rights implications.[194] Nevertheless, despite these shortcomings, this interpretation of the ICJ's *Western Sahara* advisory opinion as rejecting all contexts in which *terra nullius* was applied suggests that under modern international law the only acceptable case of *terra nullius* is territories that are devoid of population.[195]

The ICJ Vice President, in his separate opinion, described the Western Sahara opinion as 'a considerable step along the path marked out by Vitoria' due to its condemnation of the use of the notion of *terra nullius* as a basis for justifying conquest and colonisation, as had effectively been permitted in the Berlin Conference.[196]

The *Aerial Herbicides* case instigated by Ecuador against Colombia in 2008, and removed from its list of contentious cases in 2013 at Ecuador's request, would have afforded the court an opportunity to travel further down that path by engaging with a rights-compliant version of the legal principle of consent affirmed by

191 Castellino and Allen 2003: 1, 3.
192 A similar controversial statement was made in the Canadian Supreme Court case, *Calder v Attorney-General of British Columbia* [1973] SCR 313. For a critique, see Bell and Asch 1997: 61–74.
193 *Mabo v Queensland* [No. 2] (1992) 175 CLR 1. For a discussion on pre and post Mabo and the Native Title Act, see Mcrae *et al.* 2009: 278–319. See also Castellino and Keane 2009: 260, 57–70.
194 Thornberry 2002: 85.
195 Crawford 2007: 266 fn 55.
196 *Western Sahara* (Request for Advisory Opinion) Separate Opinion of Vice-President Ammoun ICJ Rep. 1975, 6, 86–87. For a discussion on the ICJ's engagement with the concept of *terra nullius*, see Castellino 1999: 523–559, see also Castellino 2000.

Vitoria and proposed by Kasson at the Berlin Conference. Ecuador has not ruled out the possibility of re-invoking the case, and similar cross-border issues affecting indigenous peoples may come before the court in the future. The hypothetical scenario of how the court could have engaged with the case therefore merits consideration.

The case addressed the aerial spraying by Colombia of toxic herbicides over Ecuadorian territory, including the territories of indigenous peoples which span the border between the countries.[197] In its arguments against Colombia's actions, Ecuador cites the observations of the Special Rapporteur on the rights of indigenous peoples that the spraying is threatening the subsistence rights of indigenous communities and their very survival.[198] It notes that the region affected by the spraying 'is home to communities of indigenous peoples, including the Awá, who continue to live according to their ancient traditions and are deeply dependent on their natural environment [maintaining a deep connection with their lands]'.[199]

Ecuador also claims that these peoples are equally affected on the Colombian side of the border.[200] In 2005, the Special Rapporteur addressed the issue of spraying in Colombia and concluded that '[e]xcept where expressly requested by an indigenous community which has been fully apprised of the implications, no aerial spraying of illicit crops should take place near indigenous settlements or sources of provisions'.[201]

In 2003, the Constitutional Court of Colombia affirmed that prior consultations seeking consent were necessary to protect the way of life of indigenous peoples threatened by such spraying.[202] It clarified that respect for the rights to property, cultural integrity and autonomy implied that consultations could not be used to impose a decision.[203] The requirement to obtain FPIC in such contexts has been substantially strengthened in subsequent developments under international human rights law and the jurisprudence of the Colombian Court.[204] The extant body of Colombian jurisprudence contextualises the contemporary international human rights law as it pertains to the specific issues raised by Ecuador in its application.

---

197 Letter from the Ambassador of Ecuador (Appointed) to the Kingdom of the Netherlands to the Registrar of the International Court of Justice Embajada del Ecuador en los Países Bajos No. 4-4-3/08. The Hague, 31 March 2008. 2008 General List No. 138.
198 Ibid.: paras 4, 24.
199 Ibid.: para 24.
200 Ibid.: para 18.
201 Report of the Special Rapporteur on the Situation of Human Rights and Fundamental Freedoms of Indigenous People, Mr. Rodolfo Stavenhagen (10 November 2004), Mission to Colombia, UN Doc E/CN.4/2005/88/Add.2.
202 Constitutional Court of Colombia judgment SU-383/03, May 13, 2003 (Rapporteur: Álvaro Tafur Galvis), Section 7.2, p. 179.
203 Ibid.: Section 7.2, p. 179.
204 Constitutional Court of Colombia, Sentencia T-769/09 (2009); and Colombia Constitutional Court, Sentencia T-129/11 (2011).

Ecuador's original application to the ICJ included a claim for 'any loss of or damage to the property or livelihood or human rights' of persons affected by the use of the herbicides.[205] It alleged violations of 'rights under customary and conventional international law' and noted that the ICJ had jurisdiction to address a broad range of issues under the 1948 Pact of Bogotá, including 'any question of international law' and 'the existence of any fact which, if established, would constitute the breach of an international obligation'.[206] In light of these 'broad claims' and the facts presented, it has been suggested that the case affords the ICJ the opportunity to evaluate competing essential interests and the hierarchy of laws pertaining to drug eradication and environmental protection.[207] It is likely that such an opportunity will arise again, and the ICJ would be afforded another opportunity to address recent developments in the recognition of the rights and the essential interests of indigenous peoples under international human rights law. If this particular case were addressed, this should provide guidance as to how these rights and interests could be balanced with those of the Colombian and Ecuadorian States.

Colombia's international obligation to respect the right of indigenous peoples to self-determination, including its subsistence dimension, would provide the ICJ with an opportunity to directly engage with the issue. In doing so, the court would have the opportunity to address a number of related issues raised in the progressive separate opinions and writings of its current and former judges. Among these are the following:

i. Judge Cançado Trindade's argument that the court needs to move beyond the intra-State dimension of international law and also address its 'human dimension'. His observations regarding the relevance of the general principles of law, such as the inter-temporal aspect of sustainable development and the precautionary principle, to indigenous peoples' issues would also be relevant.[208]

ii. Judge Weeramantry's recommendation to expand the content and relevance of international law through an engagement with the traditional wisdom of indigenous peoples and by addressing the relevance of their traditional system of environmental management and associated intergeneration considerations.[209] Also his important suggestion that the court ought to

---

205 *Aerial Herbicide Spraying Case* Application, op. cit. 197, para 38.
206 Ibid., para 37; Ecuador argued that the court has jurisdiction to hear the case under Article XXXI of the *American Treaty on Pacific Settlement of Disputes*, Bogotá, 30 April 1948, United Nations, 30 Treaty Series, 55 and Article 32 of the *United Nations Convention against Illicit Traffic in Narcotic Drugs and Psychotropic Substances*, UN Doc. E/CONF.82/15 (1988), reprinted in 28 *International Legal Materials* (ILM) 493 (1989).
207 Vinuales 2008–2009: 234–235.
208 Separate opinion of Judge Cançado Trindade in *Pulp Mills on the River Uruguay (Argentina V. Uruguay) Judgment I.C.J Reports, 2010,* 14, paras 125–131.
209 Separate Opinion of Judge C. G. Weeramantry in *Gabčíkovo-Nagymaros Project case (Hungary v. Slovakia), I.C.J. Reports 1997, 7,* at 97–111, in particular at 107, addressing intergenerational considerations and traditional systems of environmental management practices of indigenous peoples.

address the 'seminal issue' of the duties flowing to States from the right to self-determination of peoples could be engaged with.[210]

iii. Judge Vereshchetin's proposal that peoples' right to self-determination and the consent of peoples should be accorded similar weight to that of States, and that 'the people whose right to self-determination lies at the core of the whole case' should be able to participate in ICJ cases.[211]

iv. Judge Vinuesa's critique that the court, in the case concerning pulp mills on the River Uruguay, failed to give adequate consideration to the due diligence requirements associated with environmental impact assessments, in particular, the requirement for effective participation and meaningful consultations with affected populations.[212]

Addressing these and other issues pertaining to the rights of indigenous peoples would provide the ICJ with an opportunity to reconcile its jurisprudence,[213] and the broader field of international law, with the rapid development that has taken place in the arena of international human rights law, in particular, the recognition of indigenous peoples' right to self-determination and its intimate relationship with the consent requirement in the context of State-authorised activities impacting on their way of life and survival. It would also provide the court with the possibility of revisiting the broader implications of its acknowledgement in its *Western Sahara* advisory opinion that: 'the acquisition of sovereignty was not generally considered as effected unilaterally through "occupation" of terra nullius by original title but through agreements concluded with local rulers'.[214]

In light of the above, the court, in addressing a case such as that raised by Ecuador, could consider the implications of the historical recognition of the role of indigenous peoples' consent in the legitimisation of the title to territory for the status of the contemporary requirement for their FPIC for activities impacting on their rights and interests. The heightened interest around such issues makes another case of this nature inevitable and the opportunity would need to be grasped. As noted in Chapter 3, similar issues in relation to FPIC could come before the court if the ILO supervisory bodies were to affirm that a substantive consent requirement is implied in Convention 169.[215] It is worth recalling that the ICJ's charter empowers it to invoke 'general principles of law recognized by civilized nations' in making its decisions. The qualifier 'civilized' is no longer used to exclude principles of law recognised by non-European States that once were classified as 'uncivilized'. The aforementioned individual opinions suggest

---

210 Separate Opinion of Judge C. G. Weeramantry in *East Timor (Portugal v. Australia) Judgment I.C.J. Reports 1995, 90*, at 142.

211 Separate Opinion of Judge Vereshchetin in ibid., at 135–137.

212 Dissenting opinion of (ad hoc) Judge Vinuesa, *Pulp Mills on the River Uruguay (Argentina V. Uruguay) Judgment I.C.J Reports, 2010, 14*, paras 59–66.

213 Knop points to the trend in ICJ rulings of focusing on participation and identity as elements of self-determination, Knop 2002:110.

214 *Western Sahara*, Advisory Opinion, *I.C.J. Reports 1975, 12*, para 80.

215 See Chapter 3.8 in this volume.

that ICJ judges interpret these general principles of law to include those recognised by indigenous nations. Therefore, in addressing the principle of indigenous consent, it would be appropriate if due consideration were given to the relevant principles of law which indigenous nations recognise as governing self-determined FPIC processes.

Despite its withdrawal of the case, Ecuador has brought the issue of indigenous peoples' subsistence rights in the context of State-imposed activities in their territories to the court's attention. This is indicative of the growing, if at times begrudging and self-serving, awareness among States of the obligations flowing from the principles of international law in relation to indigenous peoples' right to permanently exist as culturally distinct peoples. The human rights discourse coupled with the political activism of indigenous peoples has also borne fruit in the adoption by the IFC of the FPIC standard. This in itself represents a game-changing development for the extractive industry's engagement with indigenous peoples. Its domino effect is already evident in the policies of the major global financial corporations that fund a significant percentage of projects in indigenous territories. It is also contributing to what has the potential to be a transformative step for some of the largest mining industry players in their move towards recognition of FPIC. Chapter 8 will address the normative and practical context which is propelling them on that trajectory.

8 FPIC and the corporate obligation to respect indigenous peoples' rights

8.1 Introduction

During much of the colonial era, corporate entities frequently obtained the native 'consent' necessary to legitimise colonial claims over territories which were not yet under European domination. In the contemporary era, delegation of State consent-seeking duties to extractive corporations continues to be a common practice, frequently due to the lack of State capacity or State will to engage in good faith consent-seeking dialogue with indigenous peoples. While the State maintains overall accountability for ensuring that rights are protected, the existence of an independent corporate responsibility to respect human rights is now accepted by most multinational extractive companies. Within the context of a growing corporate engagement with the human rights discourse, an increasing number of extractive industry firms are making public commitments to respect indigenous peoples' rights. Commitments to respect the requirement for free, prior and informed consent (FPIC) have been slower to emerge. This appears to be changing in light of the incorporation of FPIC into the policies and safeguards of influential actors such as the International Finance Corporation (IFC) and a number of indicators suggest that the industry stance on FPIC is changing.[1] The momentum behind these developments indicates that greater industry engagement with FPIC is inevitable, and that the future arena of contestation will revolve around the manner in which it is interpreted and operationalised. This chapter outlines the current landscape with regard to mining companies' engagement with FPIC. Section 8.2 provides an overview of the developments within the broader business and indigenous peoples' rights arena as they pertain to FPIC. Section 8.3 examines the position of the International Council Mining and Metals (ICMM) in relation to FPIC. Section 8.4 contextualises the requirement for FPIC in light of the risk of community hostility and the potential for corporate complicity in infringements on the rights of indigenous peoples, and Section 8.5 addresses some of the progressive approaches to FPIC which are emerging from corporate actors in extractive sector.

---

1 See, for example, Sabatini 2014: 3, noting that it may 'seem like heresy coming from a policy journal ... published by organisations with ties to business and investors: consulta previa [free, prior and informed consent] has to succeed'.

8.2 Consent requirement and UN processes addressing corporate human rights obligations

Developments in the normative framework of indigenous peoples' rights under the UN human rights regime have contributed significantly to the emergence of FPIC as a principle which is directly applicable to the extractive corporations and financial institutions funding them. The contemporary requirement for corporations to obtain FPIC was addressed in the 1994 report of the UN Centre for Transnational Corporations and affirmed in the 2003 commentary on the draft UN Norms on Transnational corporations.[2] Nevertheless, in 2007, some months prior to the adoption of the UN Declaration on the Rights of Indigenous Peoples (UNDRIP), the UN Special Representative to the Secretary General on the issue of human rights and transnational corporations and other business enterprises, John Ruggie, suggested that the affirmation of a corporate obligation to obtain indigenous peoples' FPIC was, at that time, inappropriate, as the principle was still being debated at the global level.[3] In light of the Special Representative's position on FPIC, the relatively low levels of indigenous participation in his consultative processes with civil society and business representatives were unsurprising. Nevertheless, calls were made for the Special Representative to incorporate FPIC into his framework in light of the adoption of the UNDRIP and the emergence of a substantial body of jurisprudence requiring FPIC.[4] While the position of the Special Representative in relation to FPIC clearly changed over the course of his mandate,[5] the requirement was not explicitly included in the UN framework on business and human rights or in its associated guiding principles and commentary, leading to some criticism of them.[6] The guiding principles did, however, state:

> [E]nterprises should respect the human rights of individuals belonging to specific groups or populations that require particular attention, where they may have adverse human rights impacts on them. In this connection, United Nations instruments have elaborated further on the rights of indigenous peoples.[7]

In doing so, they imply that the rights affirmed under ILO Convention 169 (C169) and the UNDRIP, including the requirement for FPIC, fall within the scope of

---

2 *Commentary on the Norms on the Responsibilities of Transnational Corporations and Other Business Enterprises with Regard to Human Rights*, UN Doc. E/CN.4/Sub.2/2003/38/Rev.2 (2003) at 10(c).

3 Ruggie also excluded the precautionary principle on similar grounds, see Ruggie 2007: 825.

4 Special Representative of the United Nations, Secretary-General for Business and Human Rights, *Online Forum* (New York, Business and Human Rights Resource Center, 2012), responses from C. Doyle (Middlesex University) and M. de Cordova (NEI Investments) at 66, 67, 99 available at http://en.hrsu.org/wp-content/uploads/2011/08/online-forum-re-guiding-principles-nov-2010-to-jan-2011.pdf; UNPFII (2009) UN Doc, E/C.19/2009/CRP. 8 Annex II: *Manila Declaration of the International Conference on Extractive Industries and Indigenous Peoples*, 23–25 March 2009, Legend Villas, Metro Manila, the Philippines (henceforth Manila Declaration 2009). See also *Indigenous Peoples' Declaration on Mining*, London, 16 May 1996.

5 Ruggie 2013.

6 Clavero 2012: 14.

7 *Guiding Principles on Business and Human Rights: Implementing the United Nations 'Protect, Respect and Remedy' Framework*. 21 March 2011, N Doc. A/HRC/17/31, para 12.

corporate human rights obligations. This fact is evidenced by the Special Representative's reference to the requirement for FPIC under international standards in his report addressing the negotiation of investment agreements. The report held that community consultation should take place prior to the finalising of investment agreements or contracts between States and corporations and that at the earliest stage possible in the project: 'Community engagement plans should be aligned at a minimum to the requirements of domestic and international standards. For example, free prior informed consent or consultation with those potentially impacted may be required.'[8]

The articulation of the requirement for FPIC under the human rights framework also played an influential role in its inclusion in the IFC's performance standards. This was perceived as necessary on the basis that, while the rights affirmed in the UNDRIP and C169: 'address the responsibilities of states, it is increasingly expected that private sector companies conduct their affairs in a way that would uphold these rights and not interfere with states' obligations under these instruments'.[9]

The Special Rapporteur on the rights of indigenous peoples has addressed the obligations of extractive companies to obtain consent, noting that they should have policies and practices consistent with the international framework of indigenous peoples' rights that comply with the requirements for consultation and consent.[10] Similar recommendations regarding corporate responsibility in relation to FPIC have been made by the Experts Mechanism on the Rights of Indigenous Peoples and UN treaty bodies which traditionally address the human rights obligations of States.[11] Perhaps the most encouraging signs of recognition of the requirement emerge from two UN initiatives aimed specifically at addressing Business and Human Rights and with which the industry has engaged extensively to date, namely, the UN Working Group on Business and Human Rights and the UN Global Compact.

8.2.1 The UN Working Group on Business and Human Rights

In its 2011 resolution 17/4, endorsing the Guiding Principles on Business and Human Rights, the Human Rights Council established a five-member Working Group on the issue of human rights and transnational corporations and other business enterprises. Under the resolution, the Working Group is tasked with the promotion and 'effective and comprehensive dissemination and implementation

---

8 *Principles for Responsible Contracts: Integrating the Management of Human Rights Risks into State-Investor Contract Negotiations: Guidance for Negotiators,* UN Doc A/HRC/17/31/, Add. 3.

9 IFC Guidance Note 7, Indigenous Peoples, 1 January 2012, para GN 1.

10 UN Doc A/HRC/24/41 (2013), para 89.

11 UN Doc. A/HRC/EMRIP/2012/2, Annex 1, Advice No. 4 (2012), para 27 d; UN Doc. CERD/C/KHM/CO/8–13 (2010) para 16; CESCR UN Doc. E/C.12/ARG/CO/3 (2011), para 9, citing Statement on the obligations of States Parties regarding the corporate sector and economic, social and cultural rights, UN Doc.E/C.12/2011/1, 20 May 2011.

of the Guiding Principles'. To achieve this, it is mandated to do the following: facilitate the exchange and promotion of good practices and lessons learned; make recommendations to all concerned actors; promote capacity building, and, where requested, provide 'advice and recommendations regarding the development of domestic legislation and policies relating to business and human rights'.[12] Its mandate also extends to the conduct of country visits, where invited to do so by States, and it is requested to give special attention to 'persons living in vulnerable situations'.[13] The Working Group is not expected to operate autonomously from the Human Rights regime, but is instead required to 'work in close cooperation and coordination' with UN and regional Human Rights bodies and organisations. Finally, it is required to 'report annually to the Human Rights Council and the General Assembly' and to guide the work of the UN Forum on Business and Human Rights established pursuant to the resolution.[14]

The Working Group's first annual report,[15] produced in 2013 and presented to the 68th session of the General Assembly, 'explores the challenges faced in addressing adverse impacts of business-related activities on the rights of indigenous peoples through the lens of the UN Guiding Principles on Business and Human Rights'.[16] The report addresses a number of core issues in the context of indigenous peoples' rights. It offers important clarifications on the scope of the obligations which are inherent in the Guiding Principles in relation to the State protection of and corporate respect for indigenous peoples' collective and individual rights, and the mechanisms which are necessary to guarantee effective remedies in cases where those rights are violated. The report therefore constitutes a valuable and necessary contribution to the pressing issue of ensuring respect for indigenous peoples' rights in the context of corporate activities. However, it also suffers from some limitations which merit future attention. Many of these limitations are reflective of the time and resource constraints which have restricted the full and effective participation of indigenous peoples in the report's elaboration. Others may reflect the fact that the Working Group is still in the process of developing a full understanding of the extant normative framework of indigenous peoples' rights and the implications of this framework for how the Guiding Principles should be interpreted and implemented in the context of indigenous peoples.

Three aspects of the report are particularly noteworthy and represent important contributions of the Working Group to the realisation of indigenous peoples' rights in the context of corporate activities. First is the report's affirmation of the fact that the duties and obligations outlined in the Guiding Principles have to be interpreted by States, businesses and other actors in a manner which is consistent

---

12 HRC Resolution 17/4 Human rights and transnational corporations and other business enterprises, UN Doc A/HRC/RES/17/4, para 6.
13 Ibid.: para 6f.
14 Ibid.: paras 6i and j.
15 UN Doc A/68/279, 6 August 2013.
16 Ibid.

with the UNDRIP and C169. Second is the report's acknowledgement that indigenous peoples' own customary judicial systems are on a par with other grievance mechanisms, and the requirement that these traditional systems be accorded due consideration by State and corporate actors. Third is the emphasis placed in the report on indigenous peoples' FPIC as a 'fundamental element of indigenous peoples' rights, on which the ability to exercise and enjoy a number of other rights rest'.[17] In relation to this latter point, the report recognises that the requirement for FPIC is derived from indigenous peoples' collective rights and is a component of the State duty to protect, as well as the corporate obligation to respect human rights. It also recognises that indigenous peoples' right to self-determination implies that, to the extent possible, FPIC processes must be determined and controlled by indigenous peoples themselves.[18] While the report recognises these important dimensions of FPIC, one of its more significant shortcomings is the relatively limited focus on the relationship between FPIC and the fundamental rights of indigenous peoples. This gives rise to an overly restrictive interpretation of the circumstances under which FPIC is required. It also leads to inadequate attention being directed to the necessary preconditions for the effective realisation of FPIC processes.

A second shortcoming is the rather cursory consideration giving to the issue of home State responsibility in relation to violations of indigenous peoples' rights by corporations registered in their jurisdictions. The report tends to underplay the potential role of extraterritorial obligations in the context of ensuring access to remedies and justice, and the increasing attention being placed on home State obligations in this regard by a range of actors. In doing so, it missed the opportunity to address the need, identified by the UN Human Rights treaty and charter bodies and recognised in the third pillar of the UN Guiding Principles, to move beyond the 'inadequacy of the status quo' in the context of extraterritorial obligations, in particular in relation to protecting indigenous peoples' rights.[19]

8.2.2 The UN Global Compact

The UN Global Compact, which was established in 2000, is the world largest corporate social responsibility (CSR) initiative. Its global network includes over 10,000 participants, of which some 7,500 are business participants, all of whom acknowledge the corporate responsibility to respect human rights. The Compact consists of 10 principles in the areas of human rights, labour, the environment, and anti-corruption, to which business sectors commit to align their operations and strategies.[20] In 2013, following an 18-month, primarily on-line consultation process, with which indigenous peoples, civil society and industry engaged, the

---

17 Ibid.: para 9.
18 Ibid., citing Doyle and Cariño 2013.
19 Ruggie 2013: 45.
20 Available at: www.unglobalcompact.org/AboutTheGC/index.html

UN Global Compact produced a Business Reference Guide to the UN Declaration on the Rights of Indigenous Peoples.[21]

The document offers useful advice for mining companies considering engaging in indigenous territories by offering them an overview of indigenous peoples' rights and represents an important and welcome contribution to the area of business and indigenous peoples' rights. A number of features of the guide are worthy of mention, given the reach which the document has within the business community. First, the manner in which the UNDRIP is framed in the guide is a welcome departure from the tendency of other industry guides to take a legalistic approach towards its importance and the associated responsibilities of business actors impacting on indigenous peoples' rights. Instead, the guide contextualises the UNDRIP within the broader framework of indigenous peoples' rights and places emphasis on its normative value, clarifying that it falls under the responsibility of businesses to understand and respect the rights it affirms. In doing so, it frames FPIC as a core element of the indigenous rights framework.

Consistent with the Working Group's report, it notes that as an expression of the rights to self-determination and lands and resources, FPIC 'should be as far as possible determined and controlled by the particular indigenous community' and explains that the requisites for obtaining consent are a function of indigenous peoples' cultures, practices, customary laws and institutions. The guide also serves a useful function in making the relationship between consultation and consent explicit. It highlights that the former has to serve to obtain the latter, and that consultation is not an end in and of itself. Particularly important is the guide's acknowledgement that indigenous peoples have 'a right' to give or withhold consent, and its recommendation that where consent has not been obtained, businesses should not proceed with the proposed projects.

In addition to addressing the substantive aspects of the right, the guide focuses on some of the procedural issues which typically arise when consent is being sought. Addressing the 'free' aspect, it highlights the importance for companies to ensure that their CSR projects are rights-compliant and do not serve to distort or undermine the legitimacy of consent-seeking processes. In relation to FPIC's 'prior' dimension, it clarifies that under international law 'prior' implies in advance of project authorisation, in addition to prior to commencement of project activities. It explains the rights basis of this, including the fact that it is necessary to guarantee the exercise of the right to self-determination. This clarification is also important as it is a common misconception among businesses that consent need only be obtained later in the project lifecycle, when actual physical impacts arise or when detailed impact assessment information is available.

Another important issue which the guide addresses is the corporate responsibility to respect indigenous peoples' rights in contexts where States fail in their duty to obtain their FPIC. In this regard, it notes the potential legal risks, which include

21 Available at: www.unglobalcompact.org/resources/541

those arising from the possibility of complicity in rights abuses, if projects are pursued against the wishes of the affected indigenous peoples.

Finally, its reference to concrete cases in which the requirement for FPIC has been recognised by companies is welcome as it demonstrates the challenges that both communities and companies face, given the frequently disastrous legacy of mining in indigenous territory and the potential role which respect for FPIC can play in overcoming these challenges.

A companion 'Good Practice Note' on FPIC was endorsed by the UN Global Compact in 2014, addressing the business case for FPIC, the challenges associated with its operationalisation, and existing good practice in the area. It offers further useful advice to companies complementing that in the business reference guide. The Note recommends that companies conduct adequate due diligence in relation to indigenous peoples' rights and 'adjust their policies and procedures to address the right to FPIC found in the UNDRIP'.[22] It also emphasises the need for FPIC processes to be developed in collaboration with the affected indigenous peoples and to respect their traditional decision-making methods.[23]

8.3 Analysis of the mining industry's position in relation to FPIC

The International Council for Minerals and Metals (ICMM) is a mining industry body consisting of 22 of the world's biggest mining companies, responsible for 30–50 per cent of global production, together with association members which provide it with access to an additional 1,500 companies. Changes in the position of the ICMM and its members in relation to FPIC over the last decade therefore provide one of the best barometers of the overall outlook of the industry.

In 2005, the ICMM engaged in discussions with representatives of indigenous peoples, leading to an expectation among some of those indigenous representatives present that it would adopt FPIC as the standard with which its members would abide.[24] The ICMM failed to do so, and in March 2007, while the UNDRIP was pending consideration by the General Assembly, the ICMM expressed its view that: [25] 'Practical implementation of FPIC presents significant challenges for government authorities as well as affected companies as the concept is not well defined and with very few exceptions, is not enshrined in local legislation.'[26]

---

22 Lehr, 'Indigenous Peoples' Rights and the Role of Free, Prior and Informed Consent. A Good Practice Note' (endorsed by the United Nations Global Compact Human Rights and Labour Working, 2014), 20.

23 Ibid.

24 Personal communication with Joji Cariño. See also ICMM 2005: 52. The International Council on Mining and Metals (ICMM) acknowledged that the feedback on its initial draft indicated that there was '[i]nadequate recognition of Indigenous Peoples' rights, particularly to [FPIC]'. See ICMM 2007.

25 ICMM 2008a; See also Moody, 2007: 10–11.

26 Forest Peoples Programme and Association of Saramaka Authorities, *Free, Prior and Informed Consent: Two Cases from Suriname* (Moreton-in-Marsh: FPIC Working Papers, Forest Peoples Programme, March 2007) 16. See also ICMM 2008b: 7.

Subsequent to the adoption of the UNDRIP, and following a series of roundtables with indigenous representatives, the Council maintained this position on the grounds that 'FPIC is not something companies can unilaterally grant.'[27] It reaffirmed its position in 2010 in its Good Practice Guide on Indigenous Peoples and Mining which, while acknowledging the reasons why FPIC is 'of particular concern to Indigenous Peoples involved with mining', nevertheless rearticulated the Council members' view that: 'a blanket endorsement of the right to FPIC is not currently possible, particularly given the difficulties entailed in applying the concept in practice'.[28] Instead the Council held its members to the lower standard of consulting with indigenous peoples in order to seek 'broad community support for new projects or activities', stating that: 'following consultation with local people and relevant authorities, a decision may sometimes be made not to proceed with developments or exploration even if this is legally permitted'.[29] The Council did, however, repeatedly commit ICMM members to participating: 'in national and international forums on Indigenous Peoples issues, including those dealing with the concept of free, prior and informed consent'.[30]

In May 2013, the ICMM adopted its current Position Statement on Indigenous Peoples and Mining, replacing the 2008 Position Statement, which its members are expected to implement by May 2015. The Statement, which draws on the IFC's Guidance Note to Performance Standard 7, includes a commitment to 'work to obtain the consent of Indigenous Peoples'[31] and clarifies that:

> FPIC comprises a process, and an outcome. Through this process Indigenous Peoples are: (i) able to freely make decisions without coercion, intimidation or manipulation; (ii) given sufficient time to be involved in project decision making before key decisions are made and impacts occur; and (iii) fully informed about the project and its potential impacts and benefits. The outcome is that Indigenous Peoples can give or withhold their consent to a project, through a process that strives to be consistent with their traditional decision-making processes while respecting internationally recognized human rights and is based on good faith negotiation.

The commitment to 'work to obtain consent' applies to 'new projects and changes to existing projects that are likely to have significant impacts on indigenous communities' and does not apply retrospectively.

The Position Statement is commendable in a number of regards. First, it acknowledges indigenous peoples' capacity to give or withhold consent to mining projects. It also recognises that FPIC should cater to the diversity of indigenous peoples' decision-making processes and consequently is defined by them. In doing

27 ICMM 2008b.
28 ICMM 2010: 23, 24.
29 Ibid.: 24.
30 Ibid.: 24; see also ICMM 2008a: 53.
31 ICMM 2013.

so, it appears to move beyond the position that obtaining indigenous peoples' consent could be unethical, or not pragmatic because of definitional or procedural issues, concerns which the ICMM had raised in its previous position paper and its associated good practice guidance. This represents important progress towards engagements based on principles of equality of peoples and respect for their decision-making capabilities and practices. Second, it acknowledges that FPIC should always be sought from indigenous peoples or those who share their characteristics, while holding that member companies may extend the commitment to non-indigenous people if they are also affected. In doing so, it addresses cases where governments may refuse to recognise the status of a particular group as indigenous and acknowledges that the rights of those groups must be respected, irrespective of this. The position statement is therefore a welcome development in so far as it constitutes an acknowledgement of mining companies' responsibilities to respect indigenous peoples' rights, independent of the actions of States. In this regard, it represents a tentative move from behind the shield of the State sovereignty argument, which in the past was a common reason provided for the refusal to recognise the requirement to obtain FPIC.

However, a caveat to the commitment to work to obtain consent raises some important questions as to the nature of the commitment being made and suggests that it falls short of the guidance of UN bodies that companies should ensure that their operations respect the rights of indigenous peoples by complying with the requirements of consultation and consent in conformity with international standards.[32] The caveat holds that:

> [Where] consent is not forthcoming despite the best efforts of all parties, in balancing the rights and interests of Indigenous Peoples with the wider population, government might determine that a project should proceed and specify the conditions that should apply. In such circumstances, ICMM members will determine whether they ought to remain involved with a project.

It is clear that the ICMM members are not making a commitment to respect the outcome of FPIC processes. What they appear to be committing to is: (a) to engage in FPIC processes; (b) to respect the outcome of the process in cases where the State respects that outcome; and (c) in cases where the State does not respect the outcome, each company will exercise its own decision-making agency and decide how to proceed. This may or may not be in accordance with the decision of the State.

The position statement is based on the premise which underpins the UN guiding principles, namely that the 'corporate responsibility to respect', exists independently of a State's ability or willingness to fulfil its human rights obligations. Therefore, this logically implies that in scenario (c) the corporation must assess if, by complying with the decision of the State, it would be infringing on the rights of the indigenous

---

32 UN Doc. A/HRC/27/52/Add.3 (2014), para 72.

people who have withheld their consent. The simple answer to this question is clearly, yes it would, as the right to give or withhold FPIC and by extension the right to self-determination is being denied. However, given that FPIC is also derived from a range of other rights which are affected by extractive industry projects, inevitably these other rights are also being infringed upon. As discussed earlier, the requirement for FPIC in the context of extractive projects exists precisely because these projects' inevitability have a significant impact on a broad spectrum of indigenous rights.

A question therefore arises as to the logical coherence of the ICMM Position Statement. It asks how its non-committal position with regard to the outcomes of FPIC processes accords with its commitment that ICMM members will 'respect the rights, interests, special connections to lands and waters, and perspectives of Indigenous Peoples'. FPIC is the mechanism through which indigenous peoples provide their perspectives on the acceptability, or not, of impacts to their rights and interests. The notion that FPIC outcomes related to extractive projects can be ignored, while indigenous rights and perspectives are respected, therefore appears to be inherently contradictory. It suggests that the ICMM position statement could imply that its members commit to respecting indigenous rights provided the State also does, but otherwise they will decide whether or not to respect those rights and perspectives on a case-by-case basis.

Another question to which the Position Statement gives rise is whether or not it is possible to hold a good faith process to obtain FPIC in a context where the party seeking FPIC does not commit to respecting the outcome of that process. In other words, can one commit to FPIC and at the same time reject its basic premise of respecting self-determined decisions? If one were to assume that the commitment 'to work to obtain FPIC' is consistent with rejecting the outcome of FPIC processes, then the question arises as to whether it is reasonable to expect indigenous peoples to engage in such FPIC processes when their decisions and rights may be ignored whenever the State decides to do so. This question is particularly important given that the primary reason why indigenous peoples have lobbied the ICMM and other private sector actors in relation to FPIC is precisely because States are failing to uphold their human rights obligations when taking decisions in relation to projects in their territories.

If the State genuinely balances the rights and interests of others against those of indigenous peoples in the context of proposed mining in their territories, the outcome would, in almost all cases, require the State to respect the decision of indigenous peoples. In general, however, where consent is withheld, genuine rights-balancing exercises are not performed on the basis of strict necessity and proportionality within a framework which guarantees respect for indigenous peoples' rights. This leads to the general presumption that the outcome of FPIC processes must be respected by corporate actors if they are to comply with the corporate responsibility to respect human rights.

Where the State does not comply with its human rights duties to consult and seek indigenous peoples' consent within a framework that guarantees respect for their rights, the subsidiarity principle implies that there is an independent responsibility on corporations to seek and obtain FPIC in a manner that is acceptable to, and agreed with, the communities concerned, thereby ensuring respect for their rights. A caveat to this general requirement exists where the conditions are such that the State obstructs or prevents the corporation from seeking consent in accordance with international standards – or in cases where there is repression or conflict under which 'free' consent is extremely difficult or impossible to obtain. In such contexts, proceeding with project operations would generally be inappropriate, as consent is unobtainable and respect for indigenous rights cannot be guaranteed.

The Special Rapporteur has suggested that:

> [I]n keeping with their independent responsibility to respect human rights, companies should conduct their own independent assessment of whether or not the operations, in the absence of indigenous consent, would be in compliance with international standards, and under what conditions. If they would not be in compliance, the extractive operations should not be implemented, regardless of any authorization by the State to do so.[33]

The only context in which overriding indigenous consent is permissible under international standards is stipulated in Article 46(2) of the UNDRIP, as discussed above.[34] This establishes an extremely high threshold which will rarely, if ever, be met by a mining project in indigenous peoples' territory. In cases where a project is outside their territories but nevertheless has an impact on their enjoyment of their rights, the threshold remains very high and would be a function of the extent of those impacts as perceived by the people themselves. The ICMM members' commitment to engage in good faith FPIC processes and to respect indigenous peoples' rights, interests and perspectives should therefore result in adherence to the outcome of FPIC processes becoming the norm, irrespective of State positions. An explanation in the Position Statement guidance outlining this would constitute an important step towards establishing constructive relations with indigenous peoples and ensuring compliance with the responsibility to respect their rights.

A number of other important issues arise in relation to the implementation of the ICMM Position Statement. The first relates to the empowerment of indigenous peoples to engage in good faith FPIC processes. The IFC guidance suggests that clients consider 'investment in building relevant institutions, decision-making processes and the capacity' of affected communities.[35] This is necessary in order to address power imbalances inherent in the negotiations between large corporations and indigenous peoples. The sector has a responsibility to contribute financially towards capacity building activities if it wishes to seek access to resources in

33 UN Doc. A/HRC/24/41, para 40.
34 See Chapter 5.
35 Ibid.: para GN 18.

indigenous peoples' territories. In the absence of sufficient community empower-ment and access to independent legal and technical expertise, good faith FPIC processes are not possible. However, the development of a transparent mechanism decoupling the source of such funds from their administration is essential for the integrity of FPIC processes which guarantees the autonomy of indigenous decision-making.[36]

The second issue which will be important for the ICMM members to appreciate is the bases for FPIC. While the ICMM has moved beyond the language of 'grant-ing' FPIC, its Position Statement nevertheless addresses FPIC and indigenous rights and perspectives as if the two were independent of each other and can be addressed in isolation. A proper understanding of this interdependency and the self-determination basis of FPIC will be necessary for its members to act appropriately in cases where consent is withheld. This understanding has impor-tant implications for consent-seeking processes and questions such as: if and when consent should be sought?: who defines its contents and controls the process?; how are divergent opinions between communities to be addressed?; and how consent once granted is to be maintained or, once refused, may or may not be sought again?

A third set of related issues which the ICMM will have to readdress in light of its move towards realising FPIC is the questions around benefit sharing, impact assessments and oversight. Within an FPIC and self-governance framework, indigenous peoples are empowered to negotiate the terms of benefit-sharing agreements and to regulate activities in their territories. This may imply partner-ship arrangements, ownership shares, and the adoption of management roles.[37] The requirement for informed consent places greater emphasis on the importance of impact assessments and the role of indigenous peoples in their conduct. These impact assessments will have to cater to cultural, spiritual, gender, economic and human rights considerations along with the more traditional social and environ-mental variables.[38] Indigenous peoples may be satisfied with participation in assessments, provided they have a determining say in who will conduct and review them, or they may decide to request the necessary financial resources to conduct some aspects themselves, free from outside interference. Finally, oversight of FPIC processes will be crucial to ensuring process and outcome integrity. The role which indigenous legal systems and institutions play in this will be of fundamental impor-tance for the operationalisation of FPIC in a manner consistent with indigenous perspectives and rights.

---

36 IFC Guidance Note 7, Indigenous Peoples, 1 January 2012, para GN 20; see also Baker 2013: 34; OECD Norwegian NCP 2011: 34.
37 UN Doc. A/HRC/24/41 (2013), paras 75–77.
38 Akwé: Kon, Voluntary guidelines for the conduct of cultural, environmental and social impact assessments regarding developments proposed to take place on, or which are likely to impact on, sacred sites and on lands and waters traditionally occupied or used by indigenous and local communities (Secretariat of the Convention on Biological Diversity, Geneva, 2004), Decision VII/16 F COP-7 UN Doc. UNEP/CBD/COP/7/21, 13 April 2004; see also Doyle and Cariño 2013.

Addressing these various issues will require open and inclusive dialogue with indigenous representatives. This necessitates trust and good faith on both sides. The challenge for the ICMM is that many indigenous representatives remain sceptical of engaging in discussions on FPIC with an organisation whose members maintain the right to ignore their FPIC decisions. Viewed from the perspective of the industry's legacy in indigenous territories, this stance is hardly surprising. A better starting point for such discussions would have been around the negotiation of the content of Position Statement itself, something which the ICMM may ultimately have to revisit in one way or another unless its members demonstrate their commitment to respect in practice what is currently obscured on paper.

8.4 Community resistance, corporate complicity and risk

One of the primary reasons why companies resist making public commitments to FPIC is 'the risk that they might not gain consent with regard to a highly valuable concession that they would be unwilling to forego, regardless of community opposition'.[39] Such concerns tend not to be raised in the position statements or policies. On the contrary, it is suggested that respecting indigenous peoples' rights may provide companies with a competitive advantage, an argument which is also made by NGOs promoting FPIC.[40] Fears of competitive disadvantage are, however, among the central justifications offered by company representatives in discussions or interviews probing reticence towards FPIC.[41] The notion that host governments may punish them for requiring consent by awarding contracts to their competitors is presented as placing responsible companies 'between a rock and a hard place'.[42] This serves to justify the invocation of the level playing field of State decisions or national legislation and practice as the appropriate baseline standard despite the fact that corporations do not satisfy their human rights obligations merely by complying with national legislation.[43] The ethical, and potentially legal, issues arising from ignoring principles of international human rights law which are not guaranteed by the State or enshrined in national legislation are compounded by the fact that it is precisely in contexts where legislation and State practices around natural resource governance are weakest that industry recognition of FPIC is most critical.[44] Reliance on State practice as the determining factor for whether FPIC should be obtained also downplays corporate agency in determining which projects to pursue, and

---

39 Lehr and Smith 2010: 18.
40 IPIECA 2012: 3. This view is also endorsed by one of its members, see ExxonMobil *Annual Report* (2010) at 24; see also Herz, La Vina and Sohn 2007.
41 Doyle and Cariño 2013: 46; Workshop of the OECD National Contact Points and the Extractive Sector, The British Academy, 10–11 Carlton House Terrace, London 23 March 2012 (notes on file with author); Balch 2012: 16.
42 Ibid.
43 UN Doc A/HRC/17/31 (2011), Principle 11; UN Doc. A/HRC/21/47 (2012), para 60.
44 Colchester 2010.

corporate influence over structural issues associated with the regulation of extractive projects.[45] Corporations promote themselves as proactive actors in the areas of emerging health and safety and environmental practices, begging the question as to why indigenous peoples' rights, including their FPIC, should be treated differently.[46]

A tension also exists between these commercial considerations for resisting FPIC and the growing financial risks associated with community opposition. Refusal to seek and obtain consent is resulting in conflicts which are delaying projects, sometimes by decades, tarnishing the reputation of companies and the sector as a whole and resulting in lost investment opportunities. In light of the restraints community resistance places on governments' capacity to guarantee the conditions necessary for mining operations, investor risk management strategies which focus exclusively on political risk have become antiquated. 'Community hostility risk' is gradually being recognised as constituting tangible material risk requiring serious attention, with corporate actors encouraged to adhere to the OECD guidelines on multinational enterprises to mitigate it.[47] Indeed, community risk and the challenge of obtaining and maintaining a social licence to operate were identified by industry analysts in 2014 as number four on the list of the top ten risks that mining and metal companies face in the coming decade.[48] These findings are corroborated by empirical research illustrating that 'the absence of opportunities for community stakeholders to provide consent at the outset of projects' was the second most prominent issue in a growing number of protracted and escalating conflicts and disputes pertaining to mining projects, and only preceded by concerns in relation to environmental impacts.[49]

On the other hand, the potential competitive advantage obtained through mitigating risk by respecting indigenous peoples' rights is a strong economic argument in favour of corporate engagement with FPIC.[50] The rationale behind this is that absent acknowledgement of the option to withhold consent to projects, project proposals will automatically tend to be opposed from the outset and will prove increasingly infeasible to implement. In social psychology this is referred to as a 'boomerang effect', which arises as result of 'psychological reactance' or 'the motivational state that is hypothesised to occur when a freedom is eliminated or threatened with elimination'.[51] In other words, attempts to force a 'choice', or 'persuade', in contexts where restrictions are placed on autonomy and self-determination, have a boomerang effect in that they arouse in the entity whose freedom is being constrained a tendency to automatically reject what is on offer. If the potential to exercise choice is clear and realistic from the outset, then rejection

45 Bebbington 2010.
46 See, for example, BHP performance indicators in *BHP Billiton Sustainability Report* 2011: 4.
47 Akpan 2005: 311–331.
48 Business risks facing mining and metals 2013–2014 (EY, 2013), available at: www.ey.com
49 Franks *et al.* 2014: 2; see also Schydlowsky and Thompson 2014: 84, noting that the number of conflicts in Peru 'reported in 2013 shot up to 216, from 63 in 2004'.
50 Laplante and Spears 2008.
51 Brehm 1966; Brehm and Brehm 1981: 37.

of what is being proposed is less likely. Experience in Australia's Northern Territories appears to support this argument, as resistance to extractive projects reportedly decreased following recognition of the right to withhold consent and the establishment of conditions for its good faith implementation.[52] In other jurisdictions, where the possibility of withholding consent does not exist, or where it exists under law but is denied in practice, the imposition of projects has generated a context of conflict in which rejection of projects is the *de facto* starting point for indigenous communities.[53] In these situations indigenous peoples are radicalised, leading to a phenomenon of criminalisation and exclusion,[54] with social conflicts surging,[55] some to the point of potentially destabilising the State.[56]

One response in Peru, a country in which social conflict over mining has escalated in the last decade, has been by the Superintendency of Banks, Insurance Companies and Pension Fund Administrators which will require all banks 'that lend to large mining developments and other large projects (defined as having an overall investment greater than $10 million) with the potential for socioeconomic conflict to engage in a targeted due diligence process'.[57] As part of this due diligence, which is aimed at reducing financial risk arising from conflict, banks will have to obtain information in relation to consultations that were conducted and the extent of community opposition to a borrower's proposed project.[58]

Increased focus on corporate responsibility in the human rights arena along with a growing tendency towards litigation[59] also suggests that companies may in the future face increasing legal risks if they knowingly contribute to measures leading to human rights violations. Among the scenarios identified by the International Commission of Jurists where allegations of corporate complicity are most common are those where a business makes use of security providers or partners with entities involved in gross human rights abuses.[60] The frequent use of force which accompanies non-consensual projects and the fact that the industry is associated with the 'worst abuses, up to and including complicity in crimes against humanity'[61] expose extractive companies to this risk. Currently corporate complicity is primarily addressed through civil suits, which are not necessarily framed in terms of human rights violations,[62] and corporate legal responsibility in

---

52 McIntosh 1997.
53 Anaya, 'Extractive industries operating within or near indigenous territories', UN Doc A/ HRC/18/35 (2011), para 65; see also Anaya, 'Observations on the situation of the indigenous peoples of Guatemala in relation to extractive and other types of industries affecting traditional indigenous territories - with an appendix on the Marlin mine case', UN Doc A/HRC/18/35/ Add.3. (2011).
54 Caoi 2008; Fulmer *et al.* 2008; see also García 2007.
55 Bebbington *et al.* 2008: 2889; Social Conflict and ILO 169 *American Quarterly Spring* 2014: 68–69.
56 UN Doc A/HRC/18/35/Add.3 (2011), para 73.
57 Schydlowsky and Thompson 2014: 86.
58 Ibid.
59 Skinner *et al.* 2013.
60 International Commission of Jurists (2008) Volume I: 27.
61 UN Doc. E/CN.4/2006/97 (2006), para 25.
62 UN Doc. A/HRC/17/31 (2011), Principle 11.

the criminal arena is generally limited to crimes such as 'genocide, slavery, human trafficking, forced labour, torture and some crimes against humanity'.[63] Corporate involvement in non-consensual projects threatening indigenous peoples' non-derogable subsistence and existence rights, or necessitating their forcible transfer leading to permanent and irreversible harm, have certain overlaps with these areas. The evolving international legal interpretation of the issue of corporate complicity may see greater attention focused on these areas in the future.[64]

Free, prior and informed consent is recognised as the safeguard for protecting indigenous peoples' fundamental rights in the context of resource extraction under the human rights regime. The universal acceptance that corporations have obligations to respect these rights implies that the industry can no longer hide behind definitional, procedural and ethical arguments or a thinly veiled self-interest in order to defend any obstruction to indigenous peoples' efforts to exercise their right to self-determination by operationalising FPIC in practice.

Given the market dominance and global reach of ICMM members, the development of a body of practice by these companies of engaging in FPIC processes whose outcomes are respected would have a transformative effect on overall industry practice and would be conducive to the incorporation of FPIC requirements into regulatory frameworks. It would also empower indigenous communities to insist that States only engage with companies that respect their decision-making rights. Companies should be proactive in this regard and negotiate clauses, requiring FPIC for projects to proceed, into contractual agreements with States. Consideration of any obstacles which States establish in relation to seeking and obtaining FPIC should consequently form part of corporate human rights' due diligence. As indigenous peoples gain greater power over decision-making in their territories, corporate reputation will become increasingly important. The endorsement of the ICMM members of the requirement for FPIC, if followed by actual respect for FPIC outcomes in practice, could therefore conceivably lead to respect for FPIC outcomes being associated with competitive advantage rather than disadvantage.

The fact that the ICMM's position does not commit its members to respect the outcome of FPIC processes implies that in the immediate future any such commitment will have to be made at the individual company level. The emerging references to FPIC in the policy statements of a small but growing number of companies,[65] and statements by those advising them that they can no longer

---

63 Ibid.: para 61.
64 Clapman 2011: 222–242; International Commission of Jurists 2008: Volume II, 56.
65 Rio Tinto, *Indigenous Communities, the UN Declaration on the Rights of Indigenous Peoples (UNDRIP) and Free Prior and Informed Consent (FPIC)* (Rio Tinto Communities/EA, January 2012), see also Section 8.5.2. Four other companies have made some form of conditional commitment to FPIC, namely: De Beers Canada; Inmet Mining Corporation (Inmet Mining Sustainability Report 2010 at 25); Newmont (Newmont Community Relationships Review Global Summary Report 2009 at 193); and Talisman Energy Inc, see Section 8.5.1 and Xstrata, see http://www.xstratacopper.com/EN/SustainableDevelopment/community/Pages/default.aspx. For extracts from these and other extractive companies' reports and policies addressing community engagement, see Voss and Greenspan (2012).

pre-empt the result of engagement with communities,[66] are signs of a tentative and important evolution in the industry position.

8.5 Emerging industry engagement with FPIC?

This view that the mining industry can no longer avoid engagement with FPIC is echoed in a review of the outcomes of industry's own 2002 Mining, Minerals, and Sustainable Development (MMSD) multi-stakeholder initiative which had led to the establishment of the ICMM. The 2002 report of this multi-stakeholder initiative included a recommendation which went some way towards recognising the requirement for consent.[67] A 2012 review of that report's implementation conducted by the organisation which had facilitated the initial MMSD process reflects shifting ground in relation to perceptions of FPIC. It describes FPIC as a challenge which would 'shape the agenda for the next 10 years',[68] and posited that the IFC's recognition of the requirement signalled that the industry may now be forced to engage with its implementation.[69] This, and other indicators of the pressure which the mining industry is facing to endorse FPIC, suggest that we may be rapidly approaching the tipping point at which FPIC crystallises into the incontestable standard to be met by governments and the private sector, in particular, the extractive industry.[70]

An interesting aspect of this development is that the exposure of the private sector to investor expectations and their vulnerability to reputational and financial risk may imply that the normative force of FPIC, as a principle applicable to all actors, is in practical terms of equal significance to its purely legal dimension. Moving towards FPIC as the operating standard for the industry would not only be ethically and legally sound practice, but may also potentially be in the industry's long-term economic interest.[71] However, this risk management-driven engagement with FPIC begs the question as to what it portends for indigenous peoples.

An analysis of the policy position of two extractive industry companies – Talisman Energy Inc. in relation to oil and gas, and Rio Tinto in the context of mining – which have been most forthright in their official position in relation to FPIC and have promoted the concept in the oil and gas and mining sectors may shed some light on this.

---

66 Balch 2012: 16.
67 *Breaking New Ground*, The Report of the Mining, Minerals and Sustainable Development Project (London: Earthscan Publications Ltd, 2002), MMSD, xviii, xxix, 25.
68 Buxton 2012: 3.
69 Ibid.: 3, 16 and 28.
70 For other indicators coming from the industry, investors and analysts, see Sosa 2011; Balch 2012: 15–17; Lehr 2010: 68; Indigenous Peoples Get Last Word on Mines, *The Wall Street Journal* (US edition), 27 March 2012. See also IMRA (2014); ASI (2014).
71 Herz *et al.* 2007.

8.5.1 Talisman Energy Inc. engagement with FPIC

In 2010 Talisman Energy Inc. issued its Global Community Relations Policy committing it to incorporating 'the broad principles of Free, Prior and Informed Consent'. Under the policy, consent is interpreted as meaning that Talisman will 'endeavor to obtain and maintain the support and agreement of Communities for its activities, in ways that are respectful and sensitive to local cultural and consultative processes and to the interests of the Community and Talisman'.[72]

The commitment was further qualified by Talisman's position 'that the authority for Free, Prior and Informed Consent is primarily derived from state domestic law'. In the context of its activities in the Maranon basin of northern Peru, the company interpreted this as requiring a vote with two-thirds majority support.[73] However, despite objections by representatives of the impacted Achuar people at its Annual General Meeting in 2010 and subsequent communications in 2011, Talisman continued with exploration activities. In 2012, it signalled its intention to wind down its Peruvian operations as it was 'unable to build a material resource position'.[74] NGOs working with the Achuar claimed that its withdrawal was triggered by indigenous resistance to its activities.[75]

The case is interesting as it raises the issue of what corporate commitments to FPIC mean in such a context, what the triggers for these commitments are and the problem with the wording of policies and public commitments in relation to FPIC which are framed towards maximising the ambiguity as to the circumstance in which they apply, while minimising any potentially binding implications which might flow from them. At the request of two responsible investors, Talisman Energy Inc. had commissioned an extensive study on FPIC which was completed in 2010.[76] The study is significant as it provides guidance in relation to FPIC to the extractive industry in general and formed the basis of Talisman's FPIC policy. It acknowledges the significant momentum behind FPIC,[77] addressing its component parts and development under human rights law, existing corporate policy and practices in relation to it, as well as implementation considerations from a corporate perspective.[78] In light of global trends, including the evolving legal, social and reputational risks that corporations face when operating in indigenous territories, the report recommends that 'it would be both timely and wise for Talisman to consider incorporating FPIC principles into its indigenous peoples or community policy'.[79]

---

72 Talisman Energy Inc. 2010b: 2.
73 Talisman Energy Inc. 2010a: 2.
74 R Dube, 'Talisman Energy to Withdraw from Peru', *Wall Street Journal*, 14 September 2012.
75 Ibid.
76 Lehr and Smith 2010: 6.
77 Ibid.
78 Ibid.
79 Ibid.: 8.

While the report was ground-breaking for the industry and offers very constructive advice in relation to FPIC, a number of contentious issues do emerge from its recommendations.[80] First, it acknowledges that communities should have the opportunity to refuse consent,[81] but does not explicitly address what the company should do if consent is not obtained. A second major concern is its conservative position as to when the consent requirement is triggered. The report holds that because States grant concessions, obtaining consent prior to their issuance, as envisaged under human rights law, is not under corporate control. In light of this, it suggests using the language 'gaining "community agreement based on FPIC principles" to clarify the fact that some of the terms in FPIC, especially "prior," may have different meanings for companies than for States'.[82]

As suggested above, given the power wielded by the industry, this idea that seeking consent prior to concession issuance and contract finalisation is outside industry control is contestable, in particular, if major industry players act collectively to implement FPIC as a matter of policy and practice or companies address this issue during their human rights due diligence and in contract negotiations. Individual corporations also have the potential to seek consent prior to each phase of the project and the commencement of any activities in indigenous territories. The report suggests that the trigger for consent only arises for large-scale extractive activities which are deemed to have substantial impacts.[83] This reasoning leads to the conclusion that FPIC is not required for exploration, and is only potentially required for exploitation.[84] This position is at odds with international human rights standards and jurisprudence and a self-determination rights-based FPIC framework. It also ignores the reality that the denial of a requirement for FPIC at the concession issuance and exploration stages renders communities relatively powerless to withhold consent and prevent projects proceeding to the exploitation stage.[85] Another potentially problematic aspect of the report is its suggestion that the company policy should define what constitutes 'substantial impacts'.[86] In the absence of a requirement that this be done in conjunction with the affected peoples, it can serve to further disempower them by denying them their central role in determining what constitutes a substantial impact on their territories and well-being, something which in many cases only they can determine. A third concern is the possibility of interpreting the recommendations as suggesting that, where corporations are impeded from seeking consent by governments, safeguards for indigenous peoples' rights can be subordinated to the exigencies of national governments. The report acknowledges

80 Ibid.: 94–99, Annex, *World Resources Institute's Commentary.*
81 Ibid.: 77.
82 Ibid.: 70.
83 Ibid.: 76–77.
84 Ibid.: 54.
85 Franks *et al.* 2014.
86 Ibid.: 78.

that it is unclear how significant the barriers to implementing FPIC are in States where governments are opposed to the principle.[87] It does not, however, suggest that operations should not proceed where these barriers prevent companies from seeking FPIC and thereby guaranteeing respect for indigenous rights. In light of the above, as well as developments in the international arena in relation to FPIC since its issuance, the report should be read in conjunction with the UN Global Compact Business Reference Guidance on the UNDRIP and its accompanying Good Practice Note on FPIC. These two more recent publications, the latter by one of the same authors of the Talisman report, provide important guidance to companies, which is aligned with the indigenous rights framework, and addresses the afore-mentioned concerns in the original report.

8.5.2 Rio Tinto

The second company which is noteworthy in terms of its official position on FPIC is Rio Tinto. Its 2012 policy guidance states that:

> The UN Declaration on the Rights of Indigenous Peoples (UNDRIP) primarily concerns the relationship between Indigenous peoples and sovereign governments. Rio Tinto seeks to operate in a manner that is consistent with the UNDRIP. In particular, we strive to achieve the Free, Prior, and Informed Consent (FPIC) of affected Indigenous communities as defined in the 2012 International Finance Corporation (IFC) Performance Standard 7 and supporting guidance. We are obliged to respect the law of the countries in which we operate, hence we will also seek consent as defined in relevant jurisdictions and ensure agreement-making processes are consistent with such definitions.[88]

This document also states: 'Neither Rio Tinto policy nor IFC PS7 intends that the implementation of FPIC contradicts the right of sovereign governments to make decisions on resource exploitation.'[89]

Rio Tinto's policy is currently the most advanced within the mining sector in relation to indigenous peoples' rights and FPIC. The driver for this may in part lie in the extent of Rio Tinto's portfolio which has extensive overlaps with indigenous territories, together with lessons learned from prior engagements.[90] The first paragraph above suggests a strong position supporting FPIC as framed in the UNDRIP, provided any ambiguities in the IFC's performance standards are interpreted consistently with indigenous peoples' rights. It clearly indicates that where a State does not seek FPIC, or there are deficiencies in State consent-seeking

87 Ibid.: 70.
88 Rio Tinto Community agreements guidance 2012: 14–15, referencing IFC guidance note 7, para GN 27.
89 Ibid.
90 Doyle and Cariño 2013.

processes, the company will attempt to compensate for this by attempting to obtaining FPIC in accordance with the requirements of the UNDRIP and the IFC's Performance Standard 7. A rights-based interpretation of the second sentence would lead to the conclusion that, in a context where a State refuses to accept the outcome of the consent process, Rio Tinto will acknowledge its own agency and independent obligations to respect indigenous rights and comply with the community decisions. An alternative reading of the second statement could lead to the interpretation that it weakens the commitment in the first paragraph by suggesting that there may be scenarios where the company will ultimately decide to act in accordance with the wishes of States which override FPIC outcomes.

It is too early to make any assessment of Rio Tinto's interpretation of its commitment or its implementation.[91] However, the language in the Rio Tinto policy represents a significant improvement on that of Talisman, and the company has been actively promoting the concept in public fora and within the ICMM, as reflected in the progress on its Position Statement. In 2005, Rio Tinto entered into a contractual agreement committing to obtain the consent of the Mirarr people in Australia's Northern Territory prior to the commencement of any mining activities in the Jabiluka lease area. The contractual agreement followed a decade-long struggle of the Mirarr to have their right to FPIC respected by ERA, the company which Rio Tinto acquired in 2000, and the struggle was entered into in the absence of a legislative requirement to obtain consent. This sets an important precedent for the company, and other extractive industry companies, in light of its policy commitment to FPIC.

This nascent engagement by the industry with FPIC may be reflective of a good faith intention to move towards a new engagement paradigm, and as such is to be welcomed. This shift in policy could indicate a genuine willingness on the part of industry, or at least some of its major actors, to transition to a more rights-compliant mode of operation and may offer an opportunity to build a body of practice around FPIC operationalisation. Building such a body of practice is essential not only to protect indigenous peoples' rights but is increasingly recognised by industry analysts as necessary for a functioning extractive industry. Nevertheless, in the absence of clear and unambiguous commitments not to proceed where consent is withheld, and apparent limitations on when consent will be sought, it may also be that hand in hand with the industry's acknowledgement of the FPIC requirement are the portents of an intent to minimise its implications. This suggests that Karr's pessimistic epigram *plus ça change, plus c'est la même chose* is one which may be relevant in gauging how far the industry has come and is willing to move towards guaranteeing respect for indigenous peoples' rights. As the terrain

---

91 Rio Tinto's current operations in Mongolia have, however, led to controversy with regard to the criteria for application of IFC Performance Standard 7. See First Peoples Worldwide Corporate Monitor, January 2013. Goodland was particularly critical of the IFC's position, conversation with R Goodland, February 2013.

of contestation shifts from the question of whether or not FPIC is required, to how it should be operationalised, constant vigilance for nuances in corporate positions and practices which seek to weaken the core rights-safeguarding nature, and self-determination basis, of requirement will remain essential. At the same time, there are concrete grounds for optimism that a new consent-based model of engagement between indigenous peoples and the extractive sector may be on the horizon. These models are being driven by indigenous peoples themselves and are briefly discussed in Chapter 9. Before addressing that fundamental issue, some of the challenges and limitations of the concept of FPIC will first be considered.

9 Operationalisation of consent, challenges, limitations and opportunities

9.1 Introduction

The operationalisation of free, prior and informed consent (FPIC) is a major but necessary undertaking. Successfully and fully operationalised, it implies a transformation of the *modus operandi* of the extractive sector and the sharing of decision-making power with predominantly vulnerable groups which State authorities have traditionally regarded as incidental to their decision-making processes. Realising this transformative potential is, however, a function of the prevailing political and economic circumstances. Political will, the availability of adequate technical and financial resources and the establishment of a relationship of trust between all parties are essential pre-conditions for its realisation. The book has argued that the arena of contestation in relation to FPIC in the extractive sector is shifting from the question of whether FPIC is required to how it will be operationalised. The realisation of this potential will be contingent on ensuring that a series of pre-conditions are met addressing limitations which are inherent to the concept of consent in contexts where major power asymmetries exist. It also necessitates that limitations are not placed on FPIC which are inconsistent with the right to self-determination. Ultimately, this means that indigenous peoples themselves must be in a position to define what the culturally appropriate contours of FPIC are, and how it should be operationalised. Only if this is the case, can FPIC deliver on its promise of transforming the existing self-determination-denying development paradigm into a self-determined development one which offers a genuine break with colonial-style models of the past.

The chapter is divided into four sections. Section 9.2 first looks at the evolution of the contemporary norm of FPIC through a social constructivist lens. Section 9.3 then proceeds to examine the challenges which the broader social, political and economic environments pose to the realisation of FPIC as well as the limitations that are inherent to the concept itself. These limitations raise questions as to the requirement's potential to act as a panacea for the complex challenges confronting indigenous peoples in whose territories much of the world's remaining mineral resources are located, giving rise to the conclusion that it is a necessary but not sufficient requirement for the pursuit of self-determined development. This leads to a discussion on the operationalisation of FPIC. The role which FPIC might play in transforming the extant extractive industry model with its colonial underpinnings is then touched on in Section 9.4 as are the pre-conditions that are necessary for meaningful widespread and systematic culturally appropriate FPIC processes. Finally the chapter closes with Section 9.5, addressing the issue which is at the heart of the indigenous rights project, namely the empowerment of indigenous peoples to pursue their own self-determined development paths and take control over their own futures. It suggests that indigenous control over the responses to the 'what, when, where, why, if, how and who' questions that inevitably arise in the context of operationalisation of FPIC are central to the realisation of this objective.

9.2 The development of FPIC as an international norm

Two distinct approaches to encouraging greater State and industry respect for indigenous peoples' rights have been evident in the context of international standard setting or 'norm building' processes since the 1980s. One, reflected in the aggressive timeframe for the drafting of ILO Convention 169 and more recently in the development of the UN guidelines on business and human rights, downplayed the significance of indigenous consent in the realisation of indigenous peoples' rights.[1] Illustrative of this was the decision of the Special Representative of the Secretary-General on human rights and transnational corporations and other business enterprises in 2005 to exclude FPIC from the scope of his work on the grounds that it was still under discussion by States. Such reasoning was aligned with his pragmatic approach as it avoided entering into the contentious terrain with industry and States in relation to FPIC. By the time the UN Protect, Respect, Remedy framework had been adopted, it nevertheless included the requirement for FPIC through its reference to the existence of UN standards applicable to vulnerable groups, including indigenous peoples, which by 2007 extended to the UN Declaration on the Rights of Indigenous Peoples (UNDRIP).

The second approach, reflected in the harder-edged discussions on UNDRIP and on the UN Norms on transnational corporations, was predicated on the more ambitious longer-term goal of reforming the extant social and institutional order where it is considered structurally incompatible with the recognition of indigenous peoples' right to self-determination.[2] This approach holds that the principle of self-determination implies that consent is the *sine qua non* of engagement between indigenous peoples, the extractive industry and State actors. From a pragmatic perspective, this approach also has validity, as if the lack of FPIC is a primary root cause of conflict in relation to extractive projects,[3] then obtaining it must be part of a pragmatic solution to their avoidance and resolution. The evolution in thinking in relation to the central role of FPIC in the context of business and indigenous peoples rights from the commencement of the Special Representative's

---

1 UN Doc. A/HRC/17/31 (2011).
2 See Clavero 2012: 483–580.
3 Franks *et al.* 2014, 2; Resolution of Philippine Commission on Human Rights in relation to the Case of the Subanon of Mt Canatuan (2002) (on file with author).

mandate, to the beginning of the second year of the UN Working Group on Business and Human Rights, is evident in the emphasis on FPIC in the latter's first annual report to the General Assembly in 2013 discussed in Chapter 8. As has been noted by the Special Rapporteur on the rights of indigenous peoples, the notion of 'principled pragmatism' now necessitates respect for the standards affirmed in the UNDRIP together with the 'Protect, Respect, Remedy' framework.[4]

In light of these and other developments over the last decade, we appear to be witnessing the crystallisation of the norm of FPIC at the international level, through its affirmation by a range of authoritative sources addressing both State and corporate responsibility and its adoption by some key actors, including multilateral institutions, States (albeit in a somewhat piecemeal manner), indigenous peoples, civil society organisations and more recently key industry players and actors. The process through which this evolution has occurred can be considered in light of the norm lifecycle stages involving norm emergence, norm cascade and internalisation outlined by Finnemore and Sikkink, and also invoked by Ruggie to explain a similar pattern in the adoption of the UN Guiding Principles.[5]

The 'norm entrepreneurs' involved in the emergence of FPIC are indigenous peoples themselves, through their promotion of the concept in the Working Group on Indigenous Populations and those experts advocating the concept, including those who participated in the C169 and UNDRIP drafting processes. Early adopters of the concept which facilitated its emergence include Australia's Northern Territories, the Philippines, CERD, the Inter-American Commission on Human Rights and the Working Group on Indigenous Populations itself. The process of socialisation that contributed to the norm's emergence also involved other human rights mechanisms which could be classified as somewhere along the spectrum of 'entrepreneurs' and 'norm consumers', engaged with the concept in a more gradual manner, at first, somewhat cautiously by focusing on its procedural aspect and later, as it gained more traction, focusing on its substantive aspect. Norm entrepreneurs also existed within a number of international processes which promoted respect for FPIC, such as the World Commission on Dams and the Extractive Industry Review. The adoption of UNDRIP in 2007 marked a step in the transition towards the norm cascade phase. UN organisations rapidly adopted the norm followed by international financial institutions. As Finnemore and Sikkink suggest, 'Agreement among a critical mass of actors on some emergent norm can create a tipping point after which agreement becomes widespread in many empirical cases.'[6] Viewed from this perspective, FPIC can probably be considered to have reached this tipping point in the international institutional practices and discourse towards the end of 2011 following its incorporation into the performance standards of the IFC. The subsequent uptake by the Equator Banks, and key

---

4   UN Doc. A/HRC/12/34 (2009), para 53.
5   Ruggie 2013.
6   Finnemore and Sikkink 1998: 892–893.

corporate actors, spanning a number of industry initiatives and resource-intensive industries, including Rio Tinto, Coca-Cola and Nestlé and the commitment of ICMM members to 'work to obtain consent' indicate that the norm has entered into the next stage of 'norm cascade' where it is being taken up, internalised and promoted by key actors. The evidence of initial engagement with the norm by some States is perhaps reflective of the changes in the 'mechanisms of influence' inherent in the norms evolution.[7] As private sector actors, international institutions, indigenous peoples and civil society converge on the principle, as an expected standard of behaviour, pressure on State actors to comply with it will increase. As Risse and Sikkink point out: 'The process of human rights change almost always begins with some instrumentally or strategically motivated adaptation by national governments to growing domestic and transnational pressures.'[8]

Viet Nam's pilot UN Reducing Emissions from Deforestation and forest Degradation (REDD) project is an example of this in the context of FPIC, as consistent with the "boomerang effect" described by Risse and Sikkink,[9] as the pressure being exerted on Viet Nam by international organisations to implement FPIC in this context is used by indigenous networks to promote broader recognition of their rights, including FPIC. These same indigenous networks were responsible for international organisations' uptake of the concept of FPIC. The extent to which States will respond to pressure from the indigenous peoples, civil society, international organisations and developments in the corporate sphere in the medium to long term remains to be seen. This will necessitate 'transnational advocacy networks'[10] of indigenous peoples together with their allies linking domestic organisations and local struggles to continue generating pressure on government structures from above and from below.[11] This will have to be coupled with pressure from within these structures. If, in response to external pressure, States adopt the principle, a process of 'indigenisation' of relevant State actors will be necessary for it to be internalised and given effect in a rights-consistent manner.[12] Viewed through a constructivist lens, which gives due consideration to the pervasive influence of social norms and shared ideas on law and policy-making processes in both the national and international spheres, the very fact that some States have constructed elaborate arguments in an attempt to justify non-compliance with the FPIC norm is itself a reflection of its emergence and growing recognition in the international and national spheres.[13] Decisions by authoritative international organisations, including the human rights bodies of the UN, can have 'ripple

---

7 Ibid.: 895.
8 Risse and Sikkink 1999: 10.
9 Ibid.: 18–19. The boomerang effect in international relations arises when domestic groups engage with international mechanisms to put external pressure on their States.
10 Finnemore and Sikkink 1998.
11 Brysk 1993.
12 Bennegan 2007.
13 Finnemore and Sikkink 1998: 892, referring to the US justifying the use of landmines in North Korea as an example of the emerging norm against the use of landmines.

effects in international relations'.[14] A clear trend exists among these institutions towards greater emphasis on State and corporate compliance with FPIC. This, combined with private sector influence and national and transnational advocacy of indigenous peoples, has the potential to create a context which is facilitative of norm cascade.[15] The pace of this cascade across States and among industry actors and international organisations will be uneven. Recent developments clearly suggest that multilateral institutions and the private sector, including banks, the extractive and other industry sectors, will continue to leapfrog States in FPIC adoption. The extensive and growing body of policies and standards incorporating the norm reflects its resonance with broader societal understandings of measures that are necessary to safeguard indigenous societies in contexts where they are vulnerable to potentially irreversible and profound impacts. This should eventually lead to the final stage of 'norm internalisation', where FPIC will be mainstreamed and acquires a 'taken-for-granted quality' with debates in relation to its legitimacy put aside.[16] The result should be a transformation of the political landscape pertaining to resource governance from one where FPIC is widely regarded as something which 'ought' to be obtained, to one where it is understood as something which must be obtained.

9.3 Limits placed on and limits inherent to consent

Respect for the requirement for FPIC has emerged as one of the central rallying cries of indigenous peoples and their support organisations in the context of protecting rights potentially affected by extractive projects. However, experience in contexts where consent is mandated by law, or commitments have been made to obtain it under voluntary standards, points to the limitations of the concept in practice and the challenges associated with operationalising it.[17]

These limitations have been noted by the Special Rapporteur on the rights of indigenous peoples who acknowledged the critical importance of understanding the contours of the principle of consent in the context of resource extraction, but has cautioned against a reductionist approach to the framework of indigenous peoples' rights which views it exclusively through the lens of consent. According to the Special Rapporteur, such an approach blurs 'understanding about the relevant human rights framework by which to discern the conditions under which extractive industries may legitimately operate within or near indigenous territories'.[18]

---

14 Anaya 2004: 248.
15 Finnemore and Sikkink 1998: 895.
16 Ruggie 2013: 129.
17 The author was involved in conducting consultations with communities throughout the Philippines in relation to their experience with FPIC. Philippines Indigenous Peoples, ICERD Shadow Report, Submission to the Committee on the Elimination of Racial Discrimination, 75th Session, 3–28 August 2009 (Manila: 2009), 42–65, available at: www2.ohchr.org/english/bodies/cerd/cerds75. htm. For commentaries on the effectiveness of voluntary standards, see Colchester and Farhan Ferrari 2007: 14–19; see also *UN-REDD Guidelines on Free, Prior and Informed Consent* (FPIC) (Geneva: UNREDD Programme, UNDP, FAO, UNEP, February 2012), 12.
18 UN Doc A/HRC/21/47 (2012), para 48.

The Special Rapporteur's proposal that FPIC might be best conceived as a 'safeguard' for indigenous peoples' rights is reflective of the need to minimise any potential disconnect between the concept of FPIC and the rights it seeks to protect. A number of important issues arise from a consideration of the limitations of FPIC as a mechanism for safeguarding these rights. These limitations can be grouped under two broad categories. The first category relates those limitations which are placed on the consent requirement by non-indigenous actors and are inconsistent with the rights framework underpinning it. The second addresses the limitations which are implicit in the concept of consent itself, and the importance of bearing these in mind within the larger struggle for the realisation of indigenous peoples' rights. Both point to the absolute necessity for the continued emphasis on a conception of consent based on indigenous rights.

9.3.1 Limitations imposed on consent

History is replete with examples of occasions when 'consent' has been given by indigenous peoples in contexts where they had no choice but to accept infringements on, or complete denial of, their rights. Nowhere is this more evident than in historical treaties imposed upon indigenous peoples, often through military presence or might,[19] which reflected positivist conceptions of consent. The effect of such 'consent' was to enable domination by contract.[20] It therefore begs the question whether contemporary conceptions of consent are capable of safeguarding rights and what other safeguards are necessary to guarantee procedural fairness and just outcomes. Indeed, it has been suggested that even under contemporary conditions, indigenous peoples may potentially achieve better protection for their rights by insisting on the State's fiduciary duties flowing from trust-based relationships, rather than pursuing consent-based treaty rights or contractual agreements.[21] However, it is widely accepted that this fiduciary model has failed to deliver on its rights-protecting promise and that the pursuit of an approach based on self-determination which guarantees indigenous control over decisions impacting on their future is in keeping with indigenous peoples' aspirations and rights.

The qualifiers 'free', 'prior' and 'informed' appended to the contemporary notion of indigenous peoples' consent aim to address the huge power asymmetries between companies, States and indigenous peoples and guarantee the voluntary nature and integrity of consent. However, the effectiveness of these protections is highly dependent on the interpretation accorded to them and how they are implemented in practice. Experience illustrates that legislative protection for the requirement for consent, in and of itself, is no guarantee that it will be operationalised in a rights-consistent manner, even if those rights have been

---

19 *Choctaw Nation v Oklahoma* 397 U.S. 620, 630–631 (1970); See also Clinebell and Thomson, 1978: 693.
20 Goodin 2000: 309.
21 Ibid.: 443.

afforded constitutional protection.[22] It also shows that once consent is mandated through law, or as a result of the convergence of opinion of key actors in a particular sector that it constitutes the appropriate standard of behaviour, contestation shifts to control over the rules governing its operationalisation.[23] This new struggle is between the efforts of indigenous peoples to keep FPIC rooted in its self-determination and human rights foundation and attempts to abstract it from this foundation by those who wish to control its content and minimise its impact. Framed as a stand-alone principle, it can be shaped by those whose vested interests conflict with indigenous peoples' control over resources. In a worst case scenario, a paradoxical situation arises where FPIC becomes widely accepted as the standard for corporate and State engagement with indigenous peoples but rather than constituting a mechanism for safeguarding rights, a process of 'bureaucratic terrorism'[24] transforms it into a technocratic tool designed to meet corporate exigencies.[25]

The only effective response to the inevitable tendency towards non-indigenous bureaucratisation of the concept is consistent insistence in anchoring consent to the self-governance and self-determination-based rights framework from which it has emerged. This necessitates emphasising that the determination of the scope and nature of FPIC is itself an exercise of indigenous peoples' right to self-determination without which the integrity of the consent requirement is compromised. One proactive manifestation of this is the development, promotion and implementation by indigenous peoples of their own conceptions of FPIC consistent with their customary laws and practices. Diverse manifestations already exist of this, ranging from community-initiated and community-controlled consultations and referenda to the use of manifestos, protocols, and policies aimed at promoting external actors' compliance with indigenous decision-making processes.[26]

Another potential limitation on the requirement for FPIC may unintentionally come from those who advocate for it from within the environmental movement. The particular emphasis placed on intergenerational considerations and relationships with the earth in many indigenous cultures is regarded as inherently compa-

---

22 CERD Early Warning Urgent Action letters to the Philippines, 7 March 2007; 28 August 2007, 7 March 2008, 15 August 2008 and 27 August 2010; CERD/C/PHL/CO/20, 28 AUGUST 2009, paras 24, 25.

23 Philippines National Indigenous Peoples Network (2009), 47–49; see also Muhi 2007; Gorre 2005; Uy Manuel Gorre and Trinidad 2004; Norwegian NCP 2011. For a perspective on other methods deployed by certain members of the industry in addressing the emerging FPIC requirement, see Cuffe 2012; see also AIDESEP, CONACAMI, and ONAMIAP 2012.

24 Moses 2002: 65.

25 For a discussion of a manifestation of this in the Philippines, see Manuel 2004: 3–14.

26 See, for example, *The Subanen Manifesto: Voice of the Subanen of the Zambaonga Peninsula*, Subanen Conference on Free Prior and Informed Consent Casa Emsa, Pagadian City, Zamboanga del Sur, 22 November 2009 (Zambaonga 2009); see also *Kitchenuhmaykoosib Inninuwug Protocols: A Set of Protocols for the Kitchenuhmaykoosib Inninuwug*, 5 July 2011 (Kitchenuhmaykoosib 2011).

tible with the sustainable development agenda.[27] This perspective is strengthened by the common-sense assumption that those most impacted by decisions are most likely to give due consideration to their long-term negative impacts and benefits. As a safeguard for their land and cultural rights which embody these relationships, FPIC acts as a fundamental enabler for sustainable development and is essential in ensuring environmental justice.[28] Attempts to obtain recognition of the require- ment for FPIC in the context of extractive projects have as a result led to synergies between indigenous peoples and the environmental movement.[29] In the process there has been a tendency towards the romanticisation or essentialisation of indig- enous identity as environmental activists or victims and as ecological guardians.[30] This has in turn led to the view that the requirement for their FPIC has emerged from the environmental arena,[31] and the associated classification of it as a form of 'Green radicalism' – an ecologically orientated position opposed to industrialisa- tion.[32] In addition to detaching FPIC from a rights and indigenous sovereignty- based framework, this conception of FPIC presumes the outcomes of indigenous peoples' decision-making processes. While FPIC processes should ensure that indigenous peoples are fully informed of environmental impacts, it would be unreasonable to place the burden of addressing broader environmental problems that are not of their making on indigenous peoples' shoulders. It could also lead to a context in which industry and government actors equate FPIC with a pre- ordained outcome, increasing their hostility to the concept. States should have adequate environmental safeguards in place and guarantee environmental justice for indigenous peoples, however, the burden of ensuring environmental sustain- ability should not fall on individual indigenous communities when faced with choices as to their social, economic and cultural futures. Instead prior indigenous participation at the strategic planning level and in the development of strategic environmental assessments which relate to their territories should be guaranteed before any projects are even considered. As a diverse collection of peoples, intent on ensuring their own survival and development, it is inevitable that the exercise of indigenous self-determination will on occasions come into conflict with the aims of environmentalists and those classified as green radicals.[33] Failure to acknowl- edge this and accept it as a necessary outcome of a rights-based process would constitute little more than a form of environmental despotism.

---

27 United Nations, World Commission on Environment and Development, Report to the General Assembly, General Assembly Resolution 42/187, 11 December 1987 (also referred to as the Brundtland Report); for a discussion on sustainable development, see Rogers *et al.* 2007. See also *Indigenous Peoples and Sustainable Development Roundtable Discussion Paper for the Twenty-Fifth Anniversary Session of IFAD's Governing Council* (Rome: IFAD, 2003). See also Doyle and Whitmore 2014: 121–133.
28 Westra 2008.
29 Perrett 1998: 377.
30 Richardson 2009b.
31 See, for example, Perrault 2004; Dutfield 2009: 58–59.
32 Buxton 2010: 11; see also Dryzek, 1997.
33 Richardson 2009b: 351.

9.3.2 Inherent limitations to the concept of consent

The primary purpose of consent is to safeguard the right to choice. Choice is, by definition, circumscribed by circumstance, being premised on the available options within a particular social, economic and cultural context. Consent therefore has to be 'assessed in the context of the surrounding circumstances',[34] and cannot be divorced from broader social, economic and political realities impacting on indigenous peoples' choices.[35] Considered in this light, it may be possible that consent is not always the appropriate mechanism for establishing boundaries for extractive operations in or near indigenous territories. Three scenarios where such considerations arise are briefly considered below.

The first is the context of indigenous peoples living in voluntary isolation. In this case, the choice to live in isolation is an exercise of the right to self-determination and should, in and of itself, be interpreted as an absolute prohibition on efforts to seek consent for extractive projects in or near the territories of these peoples.[36] This is consistent with the views of the Inter-American Commission on Human Rights and the Special Rapporteur on the rights of indigenous peoples. In 2006, the Inter-American Commission granted precautionary measures in favour of the Tagaeri and Taromenami peoples living in voluntary isolation in the Ecuadorian Amazon jungle. In doing so, it requested that 'the Ecuadorian State adopt the measures necessary to protect the territory inhabited by the beneficiaries from third parties'.[37] In 2008, a clause was introduced to the Constitution of Ecuador holding that the violation of the right to stay in voluntary isolation constitutes ethnocide. The government of Ecuador delimited the '*Zona Intangible Tagaeri-Taromenane*' within the *Yasuní* Biosphere Reserve and commenced efforts to secure funding from third parties, including governments, in order to offset revenues lost from not extracting oil.[38] While problems with the government's implementation of these measure have since arisen, the principle underpinning them and view expressed by the Special Rapporteur in his 2010 report which addressed the situation, is that no resource extraction activities should take place in or near the territories of these peoples. The Inter-American Development Bank policy on indigenous peoples also acknowledges that consultations and negotiations with indigenous peoples in voluntary isolation are not possible, and commits not to fund any project which jeopardises their rights.[39] In such contexts it is clear that there is

---

34 Appeals Chamber, *Prosecutor v. Dragoljub Kunarac Radomir Kovac and Zoran Vukovic*, Case no: IT-96-23-T and IT-96-23/1-T, Judgment of: 22 February 2001, para 460.
35 Leonen 1998.
36 Parellada (ed.) 2007; see also Annual Report of the UNCHR, *The Rights of Indigenous Peoples*, UN Doc. A/HRC/9/11 (3 September 2008), para 6.
37 Inter-American Commission on Human Rights 'Precautionary Measures granted by the IACHR during 2006', para 25, available at: www.cidh.oas.org/medidas/2006.eng.htm
38 An agreement was signed between the Government of Ecuador and the UNDP in August 2010 in relation to the Yasuni reserve, see http://www.cooperaccion.org.pe/index.php?option=com_cont entandview=articleandid=207:la-iniciativa-del-yasuni-en-ecuadorandcatid=54:comentario-institucionalandItemid=103
39 da Cunha 2007: 336.

an absolute prohibition on activities which in other contexts would trigger the mandatory consent requirement.

The second contextual issue relates to the economic reality within which indigenous peoples are expected to give or withhold consent. The recognition of legal title to land and the self-governing authority of indigenous structures is not sufficient to alter the economic marginalisation of most indigenous communities. Consent which is free from economic coercion can only exist in contexts where States uphold their responsibility to guarantee equality for all groups in society. As noted by Leonon: 'Liberal concepts such as free and informed consent will not work under conditions where the government is . . . abdicating its role in actively and immediately equalising economic opportunities.'[40] Viewed from this perspective, meaningful recognition of rights to ancestral territories must be coupled with the financial and technical means necessary to ensure alternatives exist to the 'sale or over-extraction of resources'.[41] In the absence of these alternatives, choice is denied and genuine consent is impossible. This issue is closely related to the broader requirement for indigenous peoples' participation in the formulation of the national and regional development plans, priorities and strategies. As a result of a global commodity boom, these strategies are frequently premised on increasingly pervasive extraction of resources located in indigenous territories. In the absence of an overarching and effective participatory framework, project-level FPIC processes become meaningless as the entire State apparatus is geared towards the pursuit of an extractive-orientated model of development.

Another determinant of the effectiveness of the consent-seeking processes is the institutional, technical and financial capacity of indigenous peoples to engage in them. Indigenous peoples confronted with decisions pertaining to complex development projects with intergenerational impacts, often on multiple communities and peoples, will face organisational, political and technical capacity-related challenges.[42] Lessons from the operationalisation of prior informed consent (PIC) procedures at the inter-State level indicate that in the absence of an adequate financial mechanism, and funding obligations on those States and entities seeking consent, a consent-based system can achieve little by way of practical outcomes.[43] Independent funding mechanisms, accessible to indigenous peoples sufficiently in advance of processes which seek their consent, covering a range of community empowerment and capacity-building needs, as well as the provision of independent technical assistance and guarantees of access to information on alternative development options are all necessary. The model for funding of the land councils in Australia indicates that financially sustainable approaches are possible in the long term.

---

40 Leonen 1998: 44.
41 Lynch 2005: 412.
42 Masaki 2009: 81; see also Macintyre 2007: 49–65; Ove Varsi 2010; see also Lasimbang and Heroepoetri 2010.
43 Barrios 2004: 738.

Adequate financial and technical assistance is also critical to address inherent power imbalances in relationships between indigenous peoples and extractive companies. The fundamental role which power plays in the vitiating individual consent has been acknowledged by the Appeal Chamber of the ICTY which quoted US jurisprudence addressing a similar issue in the context of sexual relations between prison guards and inmates and held that 'unequal positions of power and the inherent coerciveness of the situation with could not be overcome by evidence of apparent consent'.[44]

The power imbalance between indigenous peoples and external entities cannot be tackled merely by building the capacity of indigenous peoples' organisations and empowering communities. Education and capacity-building in relation to indigenous peoples' rights and perspectives within governmental and corporate institutions is an essential pre-requisite for the meaningful intercultural dialogue which should form the basis of FPIC. Ensuring that indigenous peoples maintain control over how, when and where all key aspects of FPIC processes function is also essential in efforts to avoid the consent-vitiating effect of power imbalances.

A third philosophical question is whether there are contexts in which seeking consent for certain types of projects or activities, including large-scale extractive activities, is inconsistent with human dignity and respect for fundamental rights.[45] In discussing the 'constitutional duty to defend deep core values which are part of emerging world jurisprudence', Justice Sachs of the South African Supreme Court suggests that: 'Respect for human dignity is the unifying constitutional principle for a society that is not only particularly diverse, but extremely unequal.'[46]

Consent is a necessary condition for otherwise unjustifiable infringements on indigenous rights. From a philosophical perspective it can serve as a 'defence against allegations of (wrongful) harm'.[47] It is not, however, a sufficient condition to protect the inherent dignity of indigenous peoples and guarantee protection and realisation of those rights. The jurisprudence of the human rights treaty bodies is somewhat ambiguous with regard to the role of consent in relation to measures which could lead to a violation of indigenous peoples' rights. The CESCR and HRC have emphasised that *in addition to* seeking and obtaining consent for resource exploitation, State parties must 'guarantee that in no case will such exploitation violate the rights recognised in the Covenant[s]'.[48] The wording 'in no case' could be interpreted as implying that consent cannot pre-legitimise certain limitations on, extinguishment, or the potential violations of rights. This would appear to

---

44 *Prosecutor v. Dragoljub Kunarac Radomir Kovac and Zoran Vukovic op.cit* 34, para 131, citing: *New Jersey v Martin*, 235 N.J. Super. 47, 56, 561 A.2d, 631, 636 (1989). The Chamber also noted that Chapter 13 of the German Criminal Code contained similar provisions.
45 For a discussion on the issue of limitations to individual informed consent that are particular to medical procedures and sexual activities, see O'Neill 2003: 4–7; See also European Court of Human Rights *Laskey, Jaggard and Brown v. The United Kingdom*, Application No. 21627/93, 21826/93, 21974/93, Judgment of 19 February 1997.
46 Sachs 2009: 213.
47 Goodin 2000: 314.
48 See, for example, CESCR Concluding Observations to Argentina UN Doc. E/C.12/ARG/CO/3 (14 December 2011), para 9; HRC Concluding Observations to Panama, UN Doc. CCPR/C/PAN/CO/3, 17 April 2008, para 21.

equate to a prohibition on pursuing extractive activities which could threaten a people's physical or cultural survival.[49] Similar issues arise in relation to destruction of sacred sites or disruptions of traditional economic or cultural activities. The case of an absolute prohibition on the disposal of toxic waste in indigenous territories is a good example of a prohibition supported by many indigenous peoples but modified during the negotiations on the UNDRIP, at the suggestion of Canada, to be permitted where indigenous consent is forthcoming. It has been argued that this was a case where the concept of consent, justified on the basis of market opportunities, operates outside of a framework of genuine choice and legitimates unacceptable risks to the enjoyment of rights.[50] In such a context, commentators conclude that a FPIC safeguard which leaves open the possibility of fundamental freedoms and rights being denied now or in the future is incompatible with the pursuit of justice and the long-term realisation of indigenous peoples' rights. Therefore, it would appear that there may a strong case to be made that there are things people and peoples should not be asked to consent to, either because they deny their dignity, freedoms and capabilities by causing severe negative impacts on their rights, or would constitute consenting to a form of domination which is morally reprehensible. Taking the analogy of perpetual slavery to which individual consent is no longer permissible, it could be argued that asking a people to consent to the abrogation of their 'inalienable' self-determination decision-making rights is similarly morally unacceptable.[51] However, it has also been argued that in many contexts adopting a protectionist approach whereby indigenous peoples are denied the option to consent to certain activities has the potential to lead to a situation in which their rights are frozen, condemning them to eternally perpetuating outsiders' poetic conception of their past.[52] This precise issue arose in the context of large-scale mining activities in Canada which the court deemed impermissible as they were incompatible with the First Nation's traditional way of life.[53]

The alternative approach holds that all rights are dynamic, including the right to exist, with boundaries determining legitimate infringements on, or extinguishment of, rights flowing from the exercise by a people of their right to self-determination. The jurisprudence of the Inter-American Court of Human Rights is consistent with such an interpretation. Under it, consent must be obtained for measures which could threaten the very physical and cultural survival of a people, leaving open the possibility that consent could be provided to measures with impacts which would otherwise be regarded as gross violations of fundamental rights and freedoms. This reasoning is consistent with the notion that the right to self-determination empowers a people to end its way of life and even collective

---

49 Canadian Supreme Court, *Delgamuukw v British Columbia* (1997) 3 SCR 1010, para 128; see also McNeil 2001: 116–122.
50 Engle 2011; Goodin 2000.
51 Goodin 2000.
52 Borrows 1997/1998: 37–64.
53 See also Canadian Supreme Court, *R. v. Van der Peet* [1996] 2 S.C.R. 507; for a controversial and provocative critique of the concept of 'indigenous' as contributing to this freezing of the past, see Kuper 2003: 389.

existence, should it voluntarily choose to do so. In light of the implications for current and future generations, the answer as to whether a people can legitimately take these decisions is a philosophical, legal and spiritual question which each people will have to answer within the framework of their own cultural, legal and spiritual worldviews and in accordance with their own conceptions of justice and rights. The requirement for consent should provide indigenous peoples with the possibility to calibrate risks and rewards in a manner they consider consistent with the realisation of their rights. The granting of consent is only to those impacts and mitigating measures which are fully disclosed. It does not absolve third parties from requirements to respect indigenous peoples' rights and for redress where violations occur.[54] Furthermore, over and above standard principles of contract negotiation, States or companies entering into an agreement with indigenous peoples should be duty bound, due to their dominant status, to act in good faith and ensure that the terms of any agreement are fair and guarantee indigenous peoples' rights and interests.[55] The failure to do so should constitute grounds to vitiate any consent provided.

A final observation is that a certain anomaly appears to exist in the position that consent is only required when cultural and physical survival is in jeopardy. This reduces consent to something akin to its manifestation under the positivist model – a once-off recognition of a people's self-determination or sovereign decision-making power which is necessary to justify a State action, after which that decision-making power is effectively extinguished. The right to self-determination in these contexts is reduced to a right to reject cultural and physical extinguishment, as opposed to an on-going right to determine future social, cultural and economic development and enjoy a relationship with external actors on the basis of equality. Under this restricted conception of consent, protectionist measures which would prevent extinguishment of rights are removed, but the liberal notion of freedom to make meaningful choices, which should come in their place, is denied. It is questionable if this restricted conception consent fulfils the role of a safeguard for the realisation of rights. Instead, it is suggested that consent has to be viewed as a component of self-determination which facilitates a people's possibility to preserve, gradually change or radically transform their way of life, as they so decide. For this to be possible, consent is necessary for *any* activity or project directly impacting on their control over their chosen way of life.

9.4 Realising the transformative potential of FPIC

9.4.1 Transformation of the extractive model

The extractive industry, States and global institutions have frequently relied on the argument that indigenous peoples, for their own 'narrow, pretended, cultural

---

54 UNDRIP Article 32(3).
55 Goodin 2000: 332.

integrity', threaten the development opportunities of the world's poor.[56] Moody suggests that this perspective, far from being based on facts and an objective analysis of the benefits to humankind of the mining industry, is instead premised on an 'industrio-centric view' of the world, which holds that the solution to poverty and environmental issues is to be found in international institutions and multinational corporations.[57] Within this worldview, indigenous peoples are regarded as having neither the knowledge nor sensitivity required to contribute to the resolution of these issues. The emergence of the sustainable development discourse, which presented indigenous peoples as partners from whom important lessons could be learned, promised a shift in this thinking. However, resistance from the industry and the on-going tendency among certain States to regard indigenous peoples as obstacles to the pursuit of sustainable development have denied the discourse's empowering potential. This was evident in the request of the United States, Canada, New Zealand and Australia that an explicit reference to the principle of indigenous peoples' FPIC be removed from the proposed text of the Conference on Sustainable Development, which would have constituted input to the 2012 Rio +20 *The Future We Want* Report.[58]

Despite its limitations, the self-determination-based right to freely give or withhold informed consent which has emerged from human rights law is central to the demands of indigenous peoples, many of whom view the current model of mineral exploitation as a systematic attack on their cultures and survival.[59] The 2011 report of the Special Rapporteur on the rights of indigenous peoples points to the structural nature of this problem which underpins the pervasive impacts of extractive projects on indigenous peoples, concluding that the prevailing extractive model 'appears to run counter to the self-determination of indigenous peoples in the political, social and economic spheres'.[60]

Many, if not most, indigenous peoples are hostile to the pervasive non-consensual expansion of the industry into their territories which this model implies. This hostility arises from the profound impact which it, and the practices of its colonial predecessor, have had on their well-being and capacity to determine their own models of development.[61] Even those peoples who have purportedly benefited from it describe the model as leading to little more than a shift from government welfare to 'mining welfare',[62] and a trading of rights for basic services.[63] As noted

56 Moody 1992: 13; see also ILO 1988c: 36/19, Statement of Mr Watchorn, Employers' adviser Australia; and *La Bugal-B'laan Tribal Association, Inc v. Director, Mines and Geosciences Bureau (MGB-DENR) and WMC (PHILIPPINES), Inc*, G.R. No. 127882,. 1 December 2004, para 4.
57 Moody 1992: 12–14.
58 *Earth Negotiations Bulletin Conference on Sustainable Development CSD-19*, Vol. 5, No. 304, International Institute for Sustainable Development, 16 May 2011 (IISD, 2011) at 6.
59 Tebtebba Foundation 2005.
60 UN Doc A/HRC/18/35 (2011), para 82.
61 *Manila Declaration* 2009, reproduced in UN Doc, E/C.19/2009/CRP. 8 Annex II; see also declarations in Tebtebba Foundation 2005.
62 Langton and Mazel 2008: 31.
63 Asian Indigenous Peoples Caucus Statement, Item no 6: Special Session on Asia, UNPFII 6th Session, May 2007, available at: www.docip.org

by O'Faircheallaigh, one of the world's experts on contractual agreements between indigenous peoples and mining companies, a tendency exists for governments to reduce service provision budgets where agreements are negotiated. This in turn leads communities to keep benefit arrangements confidential – something which is detrimental to the operationalisation of FPIC for other communities and peoples.[64] Indigenous leaders argue that this welfare-based, as opposed to rights-based, approach will be perpetuated as long as the extractive model is premised on the denial of their 'sovereignty over their land and the autonomy over their communities and destinies'.[65]

This rights-denying nature of the extant extractive-based development model is self-perpetuating. Economic imperatives facing developing countries dictate the legislative protection they afford to indigenous peoples vis-à-vis the interests of extractive corporations.[66] In keeping with this prescription for development, some international bodies, States, investors and mining companies have argued that the realisation of the Millennium Development Goals and poverty alleviation is dependent on increased foreign direct investment in the extractive sector.[67] This linking of the extractive industry to the realisation of the Development Goals, and potentially to their Post 2015 Sustainable Development successors, should place an even greater onus on all involved to ensure adherence to the highest human rights standards, including the standards articulated in the UNDRIP. Free, prior and informed consent constitutes the primary safeguard for indigenous peoples' rights in the context of extractive operations, and is indispensable when they are justified on the basis of developmental goals. As noted by the Eminent Person responsible for the World Bank Extractive Industry Review, the failure to respect the requirement for FPIC delegitimises any claims to be 'in the pursuit of sustainable development for poverty alleviation in the extractive industry sector'.[68] Such a failure could result in an untenable position whereby the realisation of the Goals, which should benefit indigenous peoples, becomes contingent on violations of their rights and potentially their existence as peoples.[69]

Recognition of the right to give or withhold FPIC would have a transformative effect on this extractive-based development model. As a facilitator of indigenous peoples' right to development, it would enable them to choose between maintaining their existing development models, pursuing genuine consent-based partnerships in extractive operations potentially with ownership stakes in companies and control

64 O'Faircheallaigh 2010: 77.
65 Statement of M. Woodley, CEO of Yindjibarndi Aboriginal Corporation Australia, *Yindjibarndi Aboriginal people take on WA FMG mining magnate* (3 August 2011) *Guardian Worker's Weekly*, available at: www.cpa.org.au/guardian/2011/1512/07-yindjibarndi.html
66 See Caruso and Colchester 2005; Tujan and Bella Guzman 2002. On agreements between host countries and companies, see UN Doc. A/HRC/8/5 (2008), para 35.
67 For an example of premising the ability to reach the goals on the widespread expansion of the mining industry, see *Philippines Medium-Term Philippine Development Plan 2004–2010*, Chapter 3, 58; See also United Nations Conference on Trade and Development (UNCTAD), World Investment Report 2007, *Transnational Corporations, Extractive Industries and Development*; and Salim 2005: 340–350.
68 Ibid.: 349.
69 Doyle 2009: 44.

over operations, or seeking out non-extractive-based alternative developmental models. This consent paradigm has yet, however, to prove its effectiveness, and major challenges will have to be overcome if it is to deliver on these aspirations. Among these challenges are the potential for power imbalances to lead to manipulation of specific consent-seeking processes and the risk that externally defined parameters governing their conduct are imposed on indigenous peoples. Accessible, independent and credible participatory oversight mechanisms, funding for empowerment and capacity-building and the opportunity for communities to consider alternative development options are all essential pre-requisites for the meaningful operationalisation of FPIC, as is the capacity-building of corporate and State actors in relation to indigenous peoples' rights leading to the internalisation of norms such as FPIC and the indigenisation of these institutions.[70]

Proactive measures by indigenous peoples will be necessary to address these external and internal challenges. A core element of this will involve an insistence on the maintenance of a clear link between self-determination, dignity and consent. Without a basis in dignity and self-determination, the notion of consent has the potential to become a disempowering distraction from the underlying rights it aims to protect. Grounded in dignity and the right to self-determination it is perhaps the most powerful and pragmatic tool available to indigenous peoples regardless of whether they seek to pursue their own development models or envisage potential future engagement in externally proposed extractive operations, but this time on their own terms through consensual partnerships premised on dignity.

9.4.2 Operationalisation of FPIC

Flowing, as it does, from the principles of indigenous self-determination and sovereignty, the content and implementation of FPIC should be primarily determined and controlled by indigenous peoples. However, given that FPIC seeks to regulate the engagement of State and non-State actors with indigenous peoples, its implementation will necessitate some degree of harmonisation of indigenous perspectives with the constitutional and legislative framework and the institutions of the States within which particular peoples reside and with the processes, practices and organisational structures of corporate entities with which they engage. This concept of harmonisation of indigenous and non-indigenous perspectives is embodied in the *sui generis* nature of indigenous peoples' rights.[71] As a derivate of these rights, indigenous peoples' FPIC is by extension a *sui generis* standard, infused with indigenous legal perspectives but orientated towards the just harmonisation of indigenous and non-indigenous laws and practices in a manner consistent with the principle of equality of peoples.

---

70 Risse and Sikkink 1999; Bennegan 2007.
71 Borrows and Rotman 1997: 451.

While the realisation of FPIC-based contractual agreements between indigenous peoples and companies is possible without State involvement, and, in the short to medium term, in some jurisdictions may present a pragmatic avenue towards FPIC implementation, the widespread and systematic operationalisation of FPIC will remain contingent on States fulfilling their human rights obligations. This necessity for the State to facilitate the realisation of a series of preconditions, which establish the enabling environment within which good faith consultations aimed at obtaining consent can take place and the integrity of the outcomes is guaranteed, is reflected in repeated demands and recommendations of indigenous peoples and international, regional and national supervisory bodies addressing their rights. These recommendations are echoed by international organisations, civil society and to a certain degree reflected in the concerns of corporate actors.

The transformative power of FPIC lies in its potential to restructure the relationship between indigenous peoples, States and industry from one based on power and dominance, to one premised on equality and consent. Given the small size of most indigenous groups, and their histories of oppression at the hands of the State and those seeking control over their resources, this is an ambitious project which implies a radical transformation of the *modus operandi* of the extractive sector. As such, it necessitates actions at a range of governance levels and across all economic, development, environment and technical spheres within which decisions are taken which have a bearing on both industry operations and indigenous peoples' rights. Cariño has argued that indigenous peoples need to invoke every argument available to them in these spheres to support the realisation of FPIC.[72] In keeping with this, indigenous peoples have been active participants in the negotiations on FPIC in a number of international contexts, including in relation to the role of a traditional knowledge intellectual property rights regime at the World Intellectual Property Organization (WIPO), the implementation guidelines and processes of the UN initiative on Reducing Emissions from Deforestation and Forest Degradation in Developing Countries (UN REDD) and the development of an access and benefit-sharing regime for the utilisation of genetic resources under the Convention on Biological Diversity (CBD). In the absence of similar fora for the extractive industry in the international sphere, which engages concerned parties in relation to the governance and regulation of the industry, the UN Human Rights mechanisms, with the involvement of the United Nations Permanent Forum on Indigenous Issues (UNPFII), may have a role in facilitating broad-based dialogue in relation to FPIC implementation in the sector premised on the principles affirmed in the UNDRIP. In doing so, they could build on the initial work conducted by the UNPFII and the Working Group on Indigenous Populations in the area. Indigenous peoples have also been involved in a range of multi-stakeholder roundtables and certification initiatives in sectors including forestry, palm oil, soya, biofuels and mining in which the requirement for FPIC is

72 Cariño 2005: 39.

recognised.[73] As will be discussed in Section 9.5, they are also proactively asserting their own conceptions of FPIC at the community, people and community of peoples levels.

At the national level identifying the high level components of a culturally appropriate framework may provide a useful lens through which consideration can be given to the measures which a State or a group of States, in cooperation with indigenous peoples and, where appropriate, the extractive industry and international organisations, could pursue in order create an enabling environment facilitative of the widespread operationalisation of FPIC. A generic framework for the realisation of FPIC, which would have to be made specific to each particular context, could consist of the following dimensions: (a) relationship building and strategic planning; (b) legal and policy architecture; (c) consultation and consent-seeking processes design; (d) organisational empowerment and capacity building; and (e) financing and continuous oversight and review. A brief consideration of these five interrelated dimensions can help to identify and classify some of the key components of a participatory 'FPIC operationalisation' programme.

The relationship-building and strategic planning dimension consists of two primary components, namely, trust-building and participatory determination of development models and strategic resource use planning. A basic starting point in a process seeking to guarantee good faith consultations in the context of proposed extractive industry projects is a genuine effort on the part of the State to realign its relationships with indigenous peoples to one based on respect for indigenous self-determination. Such engagement would be both remedial and forward-looking in nature, involving dialogue around legacy issues associated with extractive projects, an acknowledgement of the harm inflicted and consideration of their on-going implications for indigenous peoples. The need to address this legacy, in particular where there are on-going effects of projects implemented without consent, has long been a central call of indigenous peoples.[74] The outcome should be the entrenchment of indigenous peoples' rights into national regulatory frameworks either through constructive agreement with indigenous peoples or constitutional recognition of their rights. A component of this would involve culturally appropriate compensation for harm and a commitment to participation in policy decision-making as well as good faith consultations to obtain FPIC in relation to any future project proposals. The recognition of the principle of self-identification, the ratification of C169 and a reaffirmation of commitments to implement the UNDRIP would all be significant and tangible steps towards such reconciliation and trust-building.

Indigenous involvement in development policy formulation and strategic resource use planning acts as a necessary foundation for any subsequent project-specific FPIC proposals. Indigenous peoples' organisations should be involved in

---

73 Colchester 2010; see also Roundtable on Sustainable Biofuels (RSB) 2010: 5–6; Roundtable on Responsible Soy (RTRS) 2010: 5, Principle 3.2.2; Roundtable on Sustainable Palm Oil (RSPO) 2007: 8, Principle 2, Criterion 2.3. See also The Initative for Responsible Mining (IRMA) www.responsiblemining.net
74 Manila Declaration 2009; 'Indigenous Peoples' Declaration on Mining', London, 16 May 1996.

the evaluation of State-proposed development models, including those that are extractive industry-driven, which impact on their development agendas. The inter-societal nature of the engagement implies that alternative development models proposed by indigenous peoples, in accordance with their priorities and perspectives, should be evaluated alongside State proposals. Such models could potentially include indigenous-controlled extractive projects, conducted on the scale and at the pace they deem compatible with their development plans and aspirations. Alternatively they may involve development models that are incompatible with extractive industry activities within their territories. This implies that indigenous peoples must be afforded the space and means necessary to formulate their own self-determined development plans and priorities before any decisions are taken constraining the development options available to them. It also necessitates a process through which indigenous peoples can select, and hold accountable, those who will represent them in development planning-related dialogues with the State. Indigenous participation in strategic resource use planning is a precondition for project-level FPIC processes, as in its absence, their conduct can be rendered futile. Participation in such planning also increases the potential for meaningful and constructive engagement in the context of specific project proposals. Indigenous participation at this initial stage of resource use planning would provide an important perspective on community empowerment needs and aspirations and assist in identifying if contexts exist where moratoria on project proposals in indigenous territories are necessary. Along with addressing legacy issues, the need for moratoria on concession issuance in indigenous territories, until adequate State and indigenous structures, processes, and capacities are in place which enable consent to be sought and granted in a manner that is genuinely free prior and informed, has been a core demand of indigenous peoples, and has in recent years been echoed by UN treaty and charter bodies.[75]

While many States have taken steps to introduce some degree of regulatory and policy protection for indigenous rights,[76] and a growing corpus of commitments to respect indigenous peoples' rights have been made by States as part of the Universal Periodic Review process,[77] in the main, national frameworks continue to be inadequate in terms of the legal recognition afforded to indigenous rights and the associated requirements for consultation and consent. Where legislation does exist, it is frequently subordinated to conflicting laws and policies addressing resource exploitation. In such contexts, regulatory frameworks, including those

---

75 CERD Early Warning Urgent Action letter to Peru, 13 March 2010, CESCR Concluding Observations to Democratic Republic of Congo, UN Doc. E/C.12/COD/CO/4, 20 November 2009; Anaya, *Preliminary Note on the Application of the Principle of Consultation with Indigenous Peoples in Guatemala and the Case of the Marlin Mine.* UN Doc. A/HRC/15/37/Add.8, 8 July 2010, para 23.
76 Wiessner1999; Cuskelly 2011.
77 As of May 2014, 264 recommendations had been made by States to other States in relation to indigenous peoples' rights. Of these, 52 were rejected, 4 received no response, 13 were addressed in a general response and 195 were accepted. Of this total, 5 recommendations were in relation to FPIC of which 2 were accepted, 2 rejected and one received no response. See www.upr-info.org/database/

components related to indigenous rights, environmental protection and natural resource usage and exploitation would have to be jointly reviewed and harmonised in line with international standards addressing indigenous peoples' rights. A similar review of investment and trade agreements impacting on indigenous peoples' rights would be necessary, as would the development of procedures to ensure that investment and contractual agreements are consistent with indigenous peoples' rights and the requirements for indigenous consultation and FPIC.[78] In jurisdictions where indigenous ownership and control rights over sub-soil resources are not recognised, priority rights to use and exploit these resources should be vested in indigenous peoples.[79] Corporate compliance with their independent responsibility to respect human rights is an essential component of systematising FPIC implementation. This requires the conduct of indigenous rights' due diligence and avoidance of complicity in violations of indigenous rights, including the State duty to consult and obtain consent. Both home States and host States have a duty to ensure that adequate regulatory and policy frameworks are in place to promote and facilitate this corporate responsibility, and to sanction corporate-related human rights violations. Conversely, public commitments by corporations to obtaining FPIC and promotion of the concept as necessary corporate practice could contribute significantly to addressing host State concerns that FPIC represents a disincentive to foreign investment in the sector, thereby increasing their willingness to enact the necessary legislation.

Consultation and consent-seeking processes which are established under State regulatory regimes have to be capable of accommodating the diversity of indigenous-defined and autonomously controlled *sui generis* decision-making processes which may arise from self-determination-based assertions of FPIC. This implies consultation processes which are flexible enough to respect indigenous timeframes, decision-making institutions and procedures, customary laws and practices, and ensure indigenous participation in, or control over, key aspects of impact assessments, in particular those related to social, cultural and spiritual rights and interests. They should also be flexible enough to cater to the diversity of indigenous conceptions of FPIC whether formally documented in advance in manifestos, policies or protocols developed by indigenous peoples themselves or agreed with them during discussions prior to consultation processes commencing. Those communities who wish to formulate their own procedures should have the time and space to develop, agree and implement their contents. Consultation frameworks should ensure that indigenous peoples have access to the necessary independent legal and technical advice to engage in such negotiations, and include oversight mechanisms which ensure that they obtain reasonable benefits and compensation as a result of any negotiated agreement. This may involve imposing minimum thresholds for the royalties and establishing conditions which

78 Ruggie, *Principles For Responsible Contracts: Integrating the Management of Human Rights Risks into State-Investor Contract Negotiations: Guidance For Negotiators*, UN Doc A/HRC/17/31/Add.3.
79 See, for example, Philippines Indigenous Rights Act (1997), Section 57.

have to be met for agreements to be considered fair, just and compliant with indigenous peoples' rights.

Given the limited understanding of most State actors of indigenous rights, and the lack of technical expertise in relation to extractive projects or awareness of international standards protecting their rights which indigenous peoples may have, significant organisational capacity-building and community empowerment are required to ensure that all parties are in a position to engage in the participatory resource planning and consent-seeking processes. In the context of project-specific consent-seeking processes, empowerment of indigenous peoples in areas such as negotiation skills, as well as the provision of relevant legal and technical knowledge, would have to be facilitated in a manner which does not, and is not perceived to, compromise the outcomes of FPIC processes. Engagement at the national or regional levels in the development and resource planning will also demand financial and technical assistance to enable indigenous peoples to develop or strengthen pan-indigenous national or regional level networks or structures. Similarly indigenous peoples may also wish to strengthen their governance institutions or develop processes to address inter-community or inter-peoples-related considerations.

Financing of such an ambitious effort is an important consideration. The requirement under the UN Declaration on the Rights of Indigenous Peoples that indigenous peoples be provided with technical and financial assistance, and that this may come from States other than those in which they reside or from UN Agencies, is worth noting in this context. Initiatives of indigenous peoples to develop their own conceptions of FPIC are particularly worthy of support, as the sharing of lessons learned from these experiences offers the potential for considerable empowerment of indigenous peoples within and beyond national borders. Corporate actors are equipped both financially and logistically to assist in certain non-controlling aspects of an FPIC operationalisation, in particular, funding indigenous empowerment and capacity-building activities, provided structures are established which ensure that their involvement does not lead to undue influence over future FPIC outcomes. UN agencies and bodies, including the UNPFII, may also have a role to play in assisting with the establishment of independent participatory monitoring procedures. Civil society organisations engaged in dialogue with indigenous peoples can also contribute towards addressing resource constraints, providing independent technical expertise, and documenting indigenous peoples' experiences in relation to FPIC. These would have to be made accessible to other indigenous peoples and could contribute towards the building of a body of practice and knowledge around FPIC. A component of this would have to be great transparency around benefit-sharing models and outcomes. The financial sector, which benefits from investments in indigenous territories, could consider funding independent FPIC monitoring and oversight mechanisms to address its investments and client activities in indigenous territories. The sector has the potential to contribute greatly towards FPIC realisation provided it engages in dialogue with indigenous peoples and gains an understanding of their rights, perspectives and needs and addresses these in its human rights due diligence.

The principle of FPIC formalises the inter-societal relationships between indigenous peoples and external actors, including the State. These relationships are dynamic and evolve over time. Frameworks aimed at operationalising FPIC must therefore embody a degree of flexibility and a feedback mechanism which facilitates continuous learning and adaption. The creation and maintenance of a climate of good faith necessitates independent participatory oversight mechanisms, with powers to enforce sanctions and guarantee remedies. In the establishment of such mechanisms, appropriate consideration is required for the role which indigenous peoples' customary grievance mechanisms and legal systems will play in addressing violations of their rights.[80] In many contexts, at least until confidence is restored in national mechanisms and barriers to holding parent companies to account are overcome, regulatory measures with extraterritorial reach in home States of companies will have to be part of the mix. In addition, as with any ambitious undertaking, practical problems with FPIC implementation are inevitable. A regular participatory review of community experiences and legislative, policy and administrative frameworks, as well as institutional capacities and accountability would be necessary to guarantee procedural effectiveness and rights compliance.

For indigenous peoples to be free to exercise their right to self-determination a 'philosophical space' within which they can continue to construct their own perspectives and worldviews is essential.[81] The requirement for FPIC can facilitate the preservation or creation of these philosophical spaces by protecting indigenous peoples' 'physical spaces' and halting the historical trend which has forced them to retreat into ever more confined areas. This is fundamental for the emergence of a rights-based engagement paradigm which draws on both positive and negative experiences of the past. If this is realised, indigenous peoples will have the freedom to imagine their own futures, secure in the knowledge that they will have the physical spaces and the control over them necessary to translate these visions into reality. The struggle for respect of FPIC is therefore a struggle against widely held discriminatory perspectives in relation to indigenous peoples' capacity for adaptation and engagement with the other groups in society in a mutually beneficial imaginative, constructive and creative manner. The irony is that today's indigenous peoples exist precisely because they have demonstrated, and continue to demonstrate, a combination of imagination, creativity and pragmatism in their resilience to cultural and physical assimilation. This resilience is currently manifested in their struggles to assert their decision-making rights and insist on respect for their own conceptions of FPIC. A fundamental determinant of the success of any effort to operationalise FPIC, be it at the local, national or regional level, will therefore remain the extent to which control over it rests with the impacted indigenous peoples and communities.

---

80 Report of the Working Group on the issue of human rights and transnational corporations and other business enterprises, 'Human rights and transnational corporations and other business enterprises', UN Doc A/68/279, 6 August 2013, paras 45–47.
81 Borrowing from Arundhati Roy's conception that the philosophical space necessary for alternative imagination requires the preservation of their physical space. Roy 2011: 214.

9.5 Self-determined and indigenous-controlled models of FPIC

One of the central messages of this book is that the source of FPIC, as a derivate of indigenous peoples' *sui generis* self-determination rights, implies that indigenous peoples must be the pivotal actors in defining what FPIC means and how it will be operationalized in their particular contexts. Any discussion on the content and implementation of FPIC would therefore be seriously remiss if it did not attempt to project indigenous perspectives on the issue. The last chapter in the book will therefore close by offering some perspectives which emerge from indigenous advocacy and practice around FPIC. It is suggested that, given FPIC's central role as a vehicle for operationalising self-determination, primacy must be accorded to such perspectives and practices in any examination of its content. In many regards, these perspectives are reflected in the provisions of the UNDRIP, which, despite wording compromises accepted by indigenous peoples, nevertheless frames FPIC as a derivate of the indigenous self-determination which is necessary for the realisation of the rights to development, land, territories and resources and a host of other interrelated cultural and self-governance rights. The UNDRIP through its repeated affirmation of the requirement in a range of contexts also implicitly acknowledges the central and indispensable role which indigenous peoples attribute to FPIC in ensuring their continued survival and development in accordance with their own aspirations. This central role of FPIC in the normative framework of indigenous rights, and the nature and bases of the obligations which indigenous peoples regard it as imposing on all actors seeking to engage with them, were succulently captured in the statement on behalf of the Global Indigenous Caucus immediately following the adoption of the UN Declaration:

> Indigenous Peoples' right to self-determination is about our right to freely determine our political status and freely pursue our economic, social and cultural development. It also includes our right to freely manage our natural wealth and resources for mutual benefit, and our right to maintain and protect our own means of subsistence. 'Free, prior and informed consent' is what we demand as part of self-determination and non-discrimination from governments, multinationals and private sector.[82]

A review of the extensive body of indigenous peoples' declarations and statements over the last three decades confirms this status of FPIC as one of their most repeated demands in a host of national and international fora.[83] The 2009

---

82 Statement by the Chairman, Global Indigenous Caucus, Les Malezer, 13 September 2007 on the adoption of the UN Declaration on the Rights of Indigenous Peoples, available at: www.iwgia.org/images/stories/int-processes-eng/decl-rights-ind-peop/docs/07-09-13IP CaucusStatementAdoptionDeclaration%20.pdf

83 Tebtebba Foundation 2005; Statements made by indigenous leaders, organisations and community representatives from throughout the world demanding respect for free, prior and informed consent at various international fora are available at: www.docip.com

Manila Declaration was the product of a global indigenous peoples conference on the Extractive Industry. It demands that investors, companies, the UN, and States recognise and enforce the right of indigenous peoples to FPIC. The conference led to the establishment of a Global Indigenous Peoples Extractive Industry Network, which has the implementation of the Manila Declaration as one of its core objectives.[84] As both participants in international standard-setting processes and expert actors in the production of research and advocacy papers in relation to FPIC, indigenous peoples have contributed greatly to the understanding of the concept under international law and practice.[85] In a growing number of local struggles, indigenous communities are also invoking their own conceptions of FPIC as a tool to resist domination and to challenge discriminatory laws and practices. These peoples' formulations of FPIC are contributing to the international understanding of the concept. Given the momentum behind the principle of FPIC and its grounding in the right to self-determination, it is timely and appropriate that increased attention be accorded to these proactive stances with regard to the determination of its content.

A growing body of indigenous practice exists around the assertion of their own rights-based conceptions of FPIC in the context of attempts to impose extractive projects in their territories. One manifestation of this is an emerging practice among indigenous peoples in various geographies of formulating their own peoples' manifestos, policies, or protocols in relation to FPIC definition and implementation.[86] A common feature of these diverse articulations of FPIC is that the requirement's substantive and procedural aspects are grounded in indigenous self-determination and territorial rights and embodied in the notion of a prior and permanent indigenous sovereignty. These articulations of FPIC are shared with external actors and establish expectations of behaviour. Their potential to result in the codification of aspects of oral traditions, and hence potentially endanger those traditions, or to place constraints on a community's capacity for adaption of their customary processes in light of evolving circumstances, are factors which need to be considered during their formulation.[87] If these are borne in mind at the outset and the appropriate authorities within the communities are aware of them, conditionality and flexibility can generally be built into their design and their degree of specificity catered to the particular need and context.[88] An overview of some indigenous experiences in relation to asserting their right to give or withhold FPIC are addressed below. The first three cases involve the formulation by

84 Manila Declaration 2009. The author was responsible for producing the conference documentation.
85 Mining and Indigenous Peoples Conference, London, 6–16 May 1996; International Conference on Extractive Industries and Indigenous Peoples, 23–25 March 2009, Manila. See, for example, reports and papers of Asian Indigenous Peoples Pact (AIPP) and the International Indian Treaty Council (IITC) on Free, Prior and Informed Consent; see also Carling 2010; Cariño 2005; Carmen 2011.
86 For a discussion on their use for the protection of cultural heritage, see Bannister 2008.
87 Discussion at side event of the EMRIP 2010 with indigenous representatives.
88 Raja Devasish Roy, EMRIP side event 2010.

communities of FPIC guidance for external actors while the other cases present alternative strategies used.[89]

In the Philippines, as noted in Section 7.2, FPIC is required under the Indigenous Peoples Rights Act 1997, but its implementing rules no longer reflected the spirit and the letter of the law and have rendered FPIC ineffective as a safeguard for indigenous decision-making rights. Faced with this situation, and an increasing number of mining projects being authorised in their territories without genuine consent, the leaders of the Subanen communities from across the Zamboanga Peninsula in Mindanao, who number some 300,000 people, came together between 2007 and 2009 to hold their own consultation process with the objective of developing a Subanen peoples' set of culturally appropriate FPIC guidelines. The outcome of the process, itself an exercise of the right to self-determination, was a manifesto which the Subanen refer to as 'Voice of the Subanen across the Zamboanga Peninsula' which they submitted to the National Commission on Indigenous Peoples in November 2009.[90] Its purpose is to ensure that FPIC processes are culturally appropriate and consistent with their customary laws, worldview, practices and institutions. One of the interesting features of the manifesto is that it is a hybrid of customary law and western legal concepts, as it incorporates elements of the national guidelines on FPIC, adapting them into a culturally appropriate model of FPIC. It therefore constitutes a unique modular approach to the operationalisation of FPIC, which, on the one hand, guarantees cultural specificity and self-determined procedures and, on the other, is fully compatible and harmonised with an overarching but sufficiently flexible national framework for consent. By clarifying where the national guidelines were inconsistent with customary laws, the Manifesto removed any ambiguity with regard to what should happen in cases of incompatibility, and provided a clear set of customary law consistent FPIC rules and regulations. The Subanen had in effect presented the National Commission on Indigenous Peoples with a fully operable solution to addressing what had become an increasingly intractable problem, namely, how to operationalise FPIC in a self-determination consistent manner while at the same time providing a clear set of rules which were accessible to outsiders interested in proposing projects in indigenous territories. Unfortunately, the Commission, which is responsible for facilitating FPIC processes and for the development of the national guidelines, has refused to officially endorse the manifesto. Another important aspect of the Subanen experience is the role which indigenous peoples' traditional judicial bodies can play in the adjudication of the validity of consultation and consent-seeking processes where problems are encountered in its operationalisation. The Subanon community of Mt Canatuan is emblematic in this regard. Under their customary justice system the Subanon found the government agency and the company to have breached their customary

---

89 For further details on these cases see Doyle and Cariño 2013; IBIS 2013: 31–3.
90 Text of Subanon Manifesto, available at: www.piplinks.org/National+Commission+on+Indigeno us+Peoples+(NCIP)+

laws in relation to the flawed manner in which they obtained 'consent'. Following extensive national and international attention to the case as a result of the Subanon engagement with a Canadian Parliamentary hearing and CERD's Early Warning Urgent Action procedure, the Canadian company eventually accepted the legitimacy of the Subanon Court's decision and the authority of their traditional leader. A final aspect of FPIC that emerges from the Subanen experience is the intimate relationship they regard it as having with their right to formulate and implement their own development plans before any external proposals will be considered. In this way, FPIC and the right to self-determined development are regarded as two sides of the same coin.[91]

A second case, which has some parallels with the Subanen experience, relates to the Resguardo of Canamono Lomapretia, Riosucio y Supia Caldas in Colombia which comprises 22,000 Chami and Embera in 32 communities. As noted earlier the Colombian Constitutional Court has affirmed a requirement for FPIC in the context of mining projects in indigenous peoples' territories. However, despite this and its obligations under C169, the government issued a series of mining concessions covering the territories of 89 indigenous peoples, in the absence of any consultation. The Resguardo communities only became aware of the 48 concessions granted over their territories after flyovers were conducted and mining company representatives entered their territories to take samples. Drawing on the international standards and the jurisprudence of the Constitutional Court and the Inter-American Court, and in particular their own histories, traditional laws and practices the Resguardo communities developed their own regulatory framework consisting of a series of resolutions addressing the types of mining operations that are permissible within their territories and the protocols which must be followed in consulting with the communities. The development of the framework was a multi-year process involving extensive and inclusive community consultations which framed the communities' perspective in light of 500 years of history. It elaborates on how the community regulates mining activities in light of their traditional practice of artisanal mining and prohibits large-scale mining on the basis of its impact to their traditional livelihoods and their food security in light of the communities' small land base. Under the resolution addressing consultations, any company seeking to access the territory must commit to respecting the Resguardo's normative framework prior to the commencement of consultations. This provides the communities with leverage when attempting to assert their right to withhold consent and pursue their own development model, a right which is recognised by the Colombian Constitutional Court but is not recognised under Colombia's consultation law. It also lessens power imbalances in the consultation process as the terms and conditions are established by the community in accordance with their customary laws. The experience of communities in Colombia mirrors that of many communities in regions of the Philippines, where armed conflict continues, and highlights the incompatibility of the notion of 'free' consent

91 Doyle and Gilbert 2009.

with conflict areas where community leaders who assert their rights are threatened with violence.

A third case which demonstrates the growing effectiveness of indigenous assertions of FPIC both as a means of resistance and as a basis for establishing the conditions under which mining can proceed in indigenous territories is that of the Kitchenuhmaykoosib Inninuwug (KI) First Nation in Northwestern Ontario, Canada. Over a period of five years, KI leaders and community members successfully resisted the entry of two mining companies, developing a consultation and consent protocol with which they insisted any company seeking access to their territory would have to comply. In the process six KI community members were jailed for refusing to recognise a Court order to allow a mining company access to their lands. Both cases terminated in the government compensating mining companies in the region of eight million dollars for the withdrawal of their claims. The KI were successful in invoking their *de facto* right to withhold FPIC despite the fact that the State of Ontario and the Canadian Federal State do not recognise the right of the KI to determine if mining operations can proceed in their territories. They insist on exercising this right until issues pertaining to treaty rights and KI jurisdiction over their lands and resources are addressed in nation-to-nation negotiations with Canada. In both the KI and the Resguardo cases, the communities have managed to assert their right to decide what happens in their territories and in both cases, as a result, companies which had claims or concessions in their territories have committed to respecting the community's consultation and FPIC processes.

One of the lessons which emerges from the experience of all three cases is that FPIC must include the right to establish moratoria on consultations in relation to proposed projects.[92] If this is not guaranteed, communities run the risk of facing consultation fatigue, a phenomenon whereby they are expected to repeatedly engage in consultation processes with different companies every time a concession is sought in their territories. This drains a community's resources and places them under constant strain and also denies them the possibility of implementing their own development plans as they have no certainty over the future of their territories. The cases also point to the fact that there is a range of issues underpinning community assertions of FPIC, varying from the need to protect community-determined development models and plans; to efforts to establish basic preconditions for a consultation processes, such as the recognition of territorial rights; to attempts to rectify rights-denying deficiencies inherent in homogeneous State FPIC guidelines which cater more to the interests of corporate actors than to protecting indigenous rights.

Indigenous peoples, such as the Kaska Dena First Nation in Yukon, Northwest Territories and British Colombia, Canada, have also had experience in leveraging laws which do not require consent in order to negotiate exploration contracts with companies which include a clause requiring consent, should projects proceed

---

92 In 2013, Guatamala issued a two-year moratorium on mining licences aimed at minimising social conflict, see Elías and Sánchez 2014: 74.

beyond the exploration stage. Rather than develop protocols or policies outlining how FPIC should be obtained, they have developed legal templates which they adapt and use for entering into benefit-sharing agreement with companies. The Kaska Dena First Nation, which has extensive experience of engaging with extractive industry companies both in adversarial and non-adversarial contexts, made use of the negotiations around its exploration agreement to include the contractually binding clause for exploitation. The fact that the company felt relatively confident that the First Nation would come to an agreement based on negotiated terms in part explains the willingness to voluntarily submit to including a contractually binding consent requirement. In most cases what are negotiated are Impact Benefit Agreements (IBAs) which, if communities are in a reasonable position from which to negotiate, can deliver benefits but lack a consent requirement and consequently do not start from the same rights bases as FPIC.

Similar formal binding commitments to obtaining consent for any mining activities have been voluntarily entered into by Rio Tinto in 2005 with the Mirarr People in Australia's Northern Territory, in the context of the Jabiluka mining concession. In that case the commitment followed two decades of Mirarr struggles to stop the project proceeding, mostly prior to Rio Tinto's acquisition of the concession in 2000. The Mirarr insistence that the original 'consent' obtained in 1982 under the *Aboriginal Land Rights (Northern Territories) Act* 1976 was granted under 'confusion and unconscionable pressure', and their eventual success in preventing mining operations from proceeding, point to the necessity for FPIC to be genuine if it is to serve corporate interests as well as those of indigenous peoples. Together with the Kaska Dena case it is highly significant as it constitutes tangible evidence of the possibility for contractually binding consent requirements to be negotiated outside of a regulatory requirement for FPIC. As with the Subanen case, it demonstrates the need for strong independent agencies tasked with facilitating FPIC processes which are not subject to pressure from governments acting on behalf of mining company interests.

Communities throughout Latin America have also taken proactive and creative steps to assert their right to give or withhold consent, despite the absence of legislative recognition of the requirement. In Guatemala, Colombia, Ecuador and Peru, indigenous communities have initiated their own community *'consultas'* (or self-consultations), effectively community referenda whereby the community consult among themselves in accordance with their own customary practices and reach a decision in relation to a project that has been proposed in their territories. The communities assert that this is both an exercise of their right to consultation which is affirmed under C169 and their right to self-determination and that the outcomes of their *consultas* should therefore be respected. Guatemalan indigenous communities have been the most prominent in the use of such referenda holding 74 in 2012 above.[93] The failure of the Guatemalan State to recognise the positions expressed in these referenda has given rise to a polarised situation and increased

---

93 Vittor 2014: 50; Informe anual de la Alta Comisionada de las Naciones Unidas para los Derechos Humanos sobre las actividades de su oficina en Guatemala (A/HRC/22/17/Add.1) (2013).

levels of conflict.[94] In Peru, a somewhat similar picture emerges.[95] Indigenous communities have also engaged in a series of community referenda and have stalled various mining projects, with widespread protest and conflict caused by the failure to seek consent and protect rights to water and the environment.[96] In Africa, similar approaches to asserting community conceptions of FPIC to those addressed above are emerging.[97] Examples can also be found in South Africa where indigenous peoples hold rights over sub-soil resources and have significant ownership stakes in extractive industry projects in their territories.[98] In Australia's Northern Territory traditional owners' rights over sub-soil resources are not recognised, however, a thriving mining industry coexists with a functioning FPIC requirement.[99]

The overarching message which emerges from this body of indigenous practice is threefold. First, FPIC is seen by indigenous peoples as fundamental to the protection of their rights, at both the conceptual and implementation levels, and cannot be divorced from those rights. It is therefore necessary that indigenous peoples' rights be recognised before seeking FPIC and until such time indigenous communities should be entitled to refuse to even consider activities in their territories. Second, indigenous peoples themselves will decide how, when, where and why their FPIC should be sought and will determine the manner, process and conditions through which it is granted or withheld. This implies that they can decide not to enter into consultation processes, or to consult purely among themselves in relation to any proposed activity and to demand that the outcome of these consultations be recognised as legitimate. Third, while indigenous communities are either managing to engage in consent-based contractual agreements with companies, or forcing them to abandon their operations, the burden imposed on communities from doing so can be enormous. The failure to involve indigenous peoples at the strategic planning phases; the absence of consultations prior to issuing concessions; the limiting of participatory rights to mere consultations, while ignoring the outcome of those consultations; the ignoring of community-held self-consultations and community-defined FPIC processes; and the failure to comply with the spirit and intent of the law in contexts where consent is recognised are common practices by States which serve to create a environment in which the only realistic option available to many indigenous peoples is to say 'no' from the outset and adopt FPIC as a strategy of resistance rather than as a means for engagement. By refusing to engage on the basis of FPIC States are themselves rejecting the potential for indigenous peoples to say yes. On the other hand, where rights to resources are recognised and effective structures

---

94 For a corporate perspective holding that these are 'false consultations', see Cemento Progreso 2014: 93–96; for a contrasting indigenous perspective that 75 consultations representing the peoples' voice have been carried out in good faith, see Mash-Mash and Gómez 2014: 90–92.
95 IBIS 2013: 33.
96 Vittor 2014: 50; Franks *et al.* 2014: 2.
97 Guri Yangmaadome *et al.* 2012.
98 Comaroff and Comaroff 2009: 107–110.
99 Doyle and Cariño 2013: 60–63.

are in place to guarantee the integrity of FPIC processes and outcomes, consent-based projects can and do proceed in indigenous territories. Ultimately, indigenous peoples are advocating for models of FPIC which imply new consensual and equality-based relationships with all actors engaging with them and mandate a diversity of processes which are facilitative of 'meaningful choices by indigenous peoples about their development path'.[100]

---

100 Commission on Human Rights, Sub-Commission on the Promotion and Protection of Human Rights, Working Group on Indigenous Populations, Twenty-second session, 19–13 July 2004, 5.

Conclusion

International human rights law recognises that obtaining indigenous peoples' free, prior and informed consent in relation to extractive projects impacting on their territories and well-being is a *condicio sine qua non* for the exercise of their right to self-determination. The operationalisation of this self-determination right to give or withhold free, prior and informed consent (FPIC) is increasingly urgent in light of threats to the survival of indigenous peoples arising from the unabated encroachment of extractive operations into their territories and the level of social conflict which this is generating. Within the human rights regime, while there is clear acknowledgement of the necessity for FPIC, there has been some divergence of opinion as to when it should be mandatory. The book has argued that these divergent opinions and practices are not inconsistencies within the human rights regime but are instead reflective of an evolution along the spectrum of participative rights.[1] The clear trend within international human rights law and across a range of policies of international organisations is towards recognition of FPIC as the necessary safeguard for protecting the rights and well-being of indigenous communities, in a manner consistent with their right to self-determination and is particularly evident in the context of large-scale extractive projects.

At the level of policy and discourse among international institutional and corporate actors, the momentum behind the FPIC norm since the adoption of the UNDRIP has been unprecedented. International organisations, in particular, UN agencies and bodies, have responded to the developments within the human rights regime by adopting indigenous rights policies which incorporate a consent requirement. Effective lobbying of the financial sector by the transnational indigenous advocacy network has led to almost all of the major international development banks doing likewise, with the exception of the World Bank, which has included FPIC as a core theme in its on-going policy review. The major private sector banks, investing in developing countries, have also made similar policy commitments to ensure that FPIC is obtained for their investment projects. The need for State and corporate actors to address FPIC has emerged as a central theme in

1 Clavero 2005b: 41.

the context of the implementation of the UN Guiding Principles on Business and Human Rights and has also gained centre stage in the guidance developed by the UN Global Compact. Consequently, it is now incontestable that the right of indigenous peoples to give or withhold FPIC falls within the universe of rights which corporations are expected to respect independent of State actions. Roundtables, certification processes and multi-stakeholder initiatives, spanning a broad range of resource-intensive industries, are also engaging with the requirement. At the individual company level, some of the world's biggest consumer brand companies, which are major users and consumers of land and natural resources, have publicly committed to FPIC. Individual extractive industry companies are also making significant steps towards FPIC recognition. The 2013 International Mining and Metals position statement, which commits its members to work to obtain FPIC, represented a welcome shift in the organisation's position on the subject, and depending on how its members interpret the commitment, and how effective indigenous peoples are at ensuring they abide by it, this could have profound implications for the industry's *modus operandi*.

State practice currently evidences varying degrees of recognition of FPIC. This ranges from States which deny any requirement for FPIC, to States which have enshrined it in legislation or have considered affording it constitutional protection. The number of States which have afforded some recognition to the requirement in the context of extractive projects, either through legislative, judicial or administrative processes, remains relatively low but is on the increase. As indigenous rights become entrenched within national legislative frameworks, the requirement for consent will logically follow. In addition, States are recognising the requirement in the context of climate change mitigation and access to traditional knowledge associated with genetic resources. In the medium to longer term, these disparate initiatives addressing FPIC should have mutually reinforcing outcomes. A number of States, which do not necessarily have indigenous populations themselves, have also committed to respecting indigenous peoples' FPIC in their development cooperation strategies. Human rights bodies are placing increased emphasis on the responsibility of home States of corporations to hold them to account for human rights and have linked this responsibility with the requirement for FPIC in the context of extractive corporations.

This move towards respect for the FPIC norm involves a shift in the established balance of power and will, as a result, occur at different rates in differing contexts. Commitments by international organisations, financial institutions, industry bodies, and individual companies are all relatively recent, and consequently have yet to be transformed into practice. In States where the requirement is recognised for significant periods of time there have been mixed experiences with its implementation, some rights-empowering and some rights-denying. This body of experience points to the significant issues around power imbalances and lack of accountability of State structures to indigenous peoples. It also highlights the importance of addressing a series of pre-conditions which range from relationship building to indigenous involvement in strategic resource use planning, and from the need for flexible legislative and policy frameworks that are capable of accommodating the diversity of indigenous decision-making processes, to the mechanics of ensuring structures are established to provide funding for indigenous empowerment in a manner that does not influence FPIC process outcomes. One of the primary lessons is that indigenous control over the processes definition and its execution is fundamental to ensuring the integrity of FPIC decisions. This is reflective of FPIC's status as a central tenet of an on-going dynamic right to self-determination.

This book has sought to demonstrate that the contemporary substantive consent requirement affirmed under international human rights law is rooted in the inherent sovereignty and self-determination of peoples. Its emergence under human rights law can be traced from the initial incorporation into ILO Convention 107 of a highly compromised consent requirement which only applied in the context of removals – a requirement reflecting a palliative approach to indigenous existence. The assumed temporary nature of this existence automatically implied that the consent requirement could be overridden in the interest of national development. It nevertheless provided the platform for a more procedurally sound, yet still, on the surface, substantively wanting, consent requirement under ILO Convention 169. The book has argued that the substantive aspect of this consent requirement logically emerges from a right to permanently exist and to maintain a chosen way of life, and could be affirmed by the ILO Supervisory bodies. Considered outside of the framework of self-determination, it is, however, a somewhat restricted right, as external actors continue to dictate the conditions governing indigenous existence. Subsequent evolutions in the normative framework of human rights were reflected in CERD's General Recommendation XXIII of 1997, which affirmed a non-discrimination rights-based requirement for State parties to obtain indigenous peoples' informed consent in relation to all 'decisions that directly impact on their rights and interests'. This was reinforced by the self-determination-based FPIC obligations articulated in the UNDRIP and the recognition of the right to under common Article 1 of the Human Rights Covenants, by the bodies responsible for their oversight, as vested in indigenous peoples. A growing body of UN treaty and charter body jurisprudence, along with decisions under regional systems and national courts, all attest to the fact that the requirement for FPIC constitutes a minimal standard for resource extraction in indigenous territories. These affirmations of the requirement for consent are framed in light of the recognition of indigenous peoples' right to self-determination. Consent, under this contemporary normative framework, therefore not only safeguards the right to exist but also the right to determine the terms of that existence.

The book also posited that when considering the potential future impact of the requirement to obtain FPIC it is fundamental not to lose sight of its historical as well as contemporary manifestations. Recognition of the requirement for consent played a fundamental role in legitimising the acquisition of title to territory under the law of nations. In many regards, indigenous consent, albeit in practice frequently uninformed or coerced, forms the cornerstone upon which the territorial State was founded. Under Vitoria's framework justifying title to territory, consent was to be voluntarily given, with those providing it aware of what they were consenting to. However, a series of far-reaching limitations legitimising 'just war', where consent was withheld, rendered the requirement ineffective as a means of asserting sovereignty. Las Casas espoused a more rights-consistent version of consent, rejecting Vitoria's limitations. However, his model was not accepted by the colonists as it challenged existing claims over territory and has been criticised for failing to reflect indigenous perspectives – instead being framed in a manner consistent with the colonial Christianising objective. During the seventeenth and eighteenth centuries treaties and agreements were entered into with indigenous peoples, some of which embodied indigenous notions of consent and provide important insights for the contemporary consent-based engagements. Over these centuries the law of nations gradually shifted from its natural law roots towards a positivist model and by the nineteenth century native peoples were excluded from the community of civilised nations whose consent determined its rules and to whom those rules applied. As outsiders, they were only empowered with a once-off capacity to provide consent for the benefit of the colonial power's acquisition of title to territory, but with no positive implications for their own current or future legal status. Driven by pragmatism, the colonial project expanded across Africa on the basis of consent-based agreements with native peoples. As with early colonial consent seeking the extent to which this consent was voluntarily given, on the basis of full understanding, is highly questionable. Despite its rights-denying doctrines and the use of duress to obtain consent, recognition of native peoples as sovereign entities with the capacity to legitimise third party claims to title to territorial sovereignty was integral to the formation of international law itself. Throughout this colonial history indigenous peoples exercised their *de facto* sovereignty, either by entering into agreements or by refusing to provide consent through resistance to, or retreat from, colonial encroachment. Consistent with this, indigenous peoples have always presented their claims in international legal and political arenas as those of sovereign peoples. This was true of their attempts to engage with colonial powers and post-colonial States.[2] Their initial attempts to seek recognition in the League of Nations in the 1920s were premised on assertions of equality with sovereign nation-states.[3] Subsequent efforts to engage with the UN were again in the context of seeking recognition as self-determining sovereign nations, following their exclusion from the decolonisation agenda and their continued subordination within post-colonial States.[4]

The ideological return to some form of recognition of indigenous sovereignty under international law, as represented by the affirmation of an inherent right to self-determination and to lands, territories and resources, embodies natural law-based elements underpinning prior theoretical positions acknowledging indigenous

2 Sanders 1983: 13.
3 Sanders 1998: 73–74; see also Garrow 2008: 341; and Simpson 2008: 205–206.
4 Treaty Council News 1977: 25–26; see also Vinding and Hitchcock 2009; and Rostkowski 1998; Van Langenhove 1954; Statement of Mr Ryckmans, in GAOR, 9th session, 4th Committee, 419th meeting, 2 November 1954, 150; and Belgian Government Information Center 1953.

sovereignty, as framed by the fathers of the discipline during the early years of the initial colonial encounter. However, while both positions affirm that a consent requirement derives from indigenous peoples' existence as peoples, the FPIC paradigm under the contemporary normative framework differs in a fundamental manner from that of centuries past, in so far as it is premised on indigenous definition and control over its content and operationalisation, and is no longer framed in the light of 'legitimate' exceptions to its realisation or overarching proselytising objectives.

The human rights regime has provided the crack through which indigenous peoples were eventually able to reassert their status as peoples vested with the right to self-determination, and by extension, vested with the power to give or withhold consent to States. Their success in doing so extends their struggle for recognition beyond the ambit of human rights law. They have traced a line along the broader canvas of international law bridging the disconnection between their status under contemporary international law, and their prior status under earlier manifestations of international law as sovereign entities with the right to give or withhold their consent to States and other actors infringing on their territorial dominion.

The contextualisation of the consent requirement in light of its historical grounding in indigenous peoples' sovereignty also brings to the fore the unresolved issue of indigenous peoples' claims over resources. Viewed in light of this unaddressed issue, the requirement for FPIC, rather than being a radical position, constitutes a moderate demand and indeed compromise on behalf of indigenous peoples. In addition to limiting any potential for extinguishment of indigenous land and resources rights, it assists in establishing a context which is facilitative of reconciliation between competing claims to territorial dominium and is consistent with the realisation of the right to self-determination of all peoples within legally pluralistic and democratic States.

Historical pacts between indigenous peoples themselves, and subsequently between indigenous peoples and States, show that consent has long been a basic operational principle in agreements and treaties involving indigenous peoples. They also offer insights into long-standing indigenous conceptions of consent. Revisiting and drawing from these conceptions of consent can help inform the contemporary requirement for the FPIC in light of its *sui generis* nature which is grounded in indigenous law, tradition and perspectives. Unfortunately, history also shows that increasing power imbalances gave rise to inherently unjust agreements and States' failure to abide by earlier treaties. This suggests that in the absence of adequate independent oversight and accountability mechanisms, caution is necessary in engagement with the consent paradigm. In light of this, the book has argued that the operationalisation of the principle of FPIC must be under the direction and control of indigenous peoples themselves, with decision-making within the FPIC framework understood and respected by all as an exercise of the right to self-determination.

It has been suggested that despite the contemporary recognition of indigenous peoples' rights, these peoples may eventually become no more than a footnote in history, with the homogenising and pervasive forces of globalisation eventually leading to their disappearance. Ultimately there can be no definitive response to this hypothesis as the future is indeterminate. In a worst case scenario, the recognition of the right to self-determination and FPIC provides these peoples with the opportunity to write that footnote themselves, and should they so choose to transition from their current way of life with dignity, at a pace and in a manner of their own choosing. A more optimistic perspective, held by those advocating for indigenous self-determination, regards all cultures as dynamic and existing in overlapping interdependent spheres. It holds that according a more prominent position to indigenous cultures, which is premised on the recognition of the right to self-determination and FPIC, would not only provide the context in which they can survive and flourish, but would also serve to infuse mainstream contemporary cultures with enriching perspectives and worldviews that may ultimately be essential for their own survival and transformation.

This prospect raises a number of further questions in relation to FPIC, the answers to which will determine how the principle evolves and what its significance will be for the future of indigenous peoples. A first question asks what protections and pre-conditions are necessary to ensure that FPIC operationalisation proceeds in a manner which is consistent with the exercise of the right to self-determination. Issues which arise are the role that oversight mechanisms should play, how these mechanisms should be constructed, the extent to which they should be accountable to indigenous peoples and how they relate to indigenous judicial processes. Other considerations include how national rules and regulations and corporate policies pertaining to consultation and FPIC can guarantee respect for local decision-making processes and indigenous assertions of FPIC as reflected in emerging indigenous practices outlined in Chapter 9; and the existence of a potential facilitative role, premised on human rights principles including indigenous consent and participation, for UN actors, in particular UN human rights mechanism in conjunction with national human rights institutions, in the context of FPIC operationalisation, oversight and dispute resolution.

An overarching question would query the extent to which FPIC can potentially constitute the basis for a more meaningful consideration of indigenous peoples' resource rights and ultimately their sovereignty and self-determination rights. The book has posited that FPIC has this potential. It challenges the compartmentalisation of rights, bridging their proprietorial and governance dimensions and forces a reconsideration of non-indigenous delineations between land rights, territorial rights, resource rights and self-governmental rights. However, further research is necessary to examine its capacity to realise this in practice. This involves greater consideration of the role which recognising the right to give or withhold consent can play in altering the rights-constraining power dynamics between indigenous peoples and external actors, as well as the potential impact on internal power relations within and between communities and peoples. A related question asks what conditions are necessary for a good faith intercultural dialogue between the industry, States and indigenous peoples to occur.

The requirement for FPIC also has a potentially significant role to play in the adoption of legislative and administrative measures and broader national and regional strategic developmental and resource use planning and in international investment and trade agreements. The nature of participation in consent processes in relation to such measures would be different from more localised project-specific consent processes. The question therefore arises as to how consent can be operationalised in relation to measures which may directly affect all indigenous peoples in a State or potentially across multiple States.

Finally, the requirement for indigenous peoples' consent strikes at the core of the State-centric international legal project, raising the unresolved issue of the status of these peoples as subjects under international law. The resolution of this issue has long been obstructed by the notion that it is a question which falls under the exclusive prevue of sovereign States. The re-emergence of the requirement for indigenous peoples' consent, which since the formation of international law constituted a legitimising basis for claims to title to territory, challenges this assumption. It raises the question as to whether or not the self-determination-based requirement to obtain consent from these peoples, in relation to measures impacting their territorial dominion, constitutes a general principle of law which all States are bound to respect. It also highlights the need for authoritative international organs such as the International Court of Justice to engage in determination of indigenous peoples' claims and interests when these come into conflict with States' claims, and address the role of the legal principle of indigenous peoples' free prior and informed consent in such contexts.

The book has argued that FPIC has reached a tipping point at which the arena of contestation is shifting from the question of whether FPIC is required to how it will be operationalised. Genuine implementation of FPIC implies a significant transformation of the *modus operandi* of the extractive sector. The realisation of this transformative potential of FPIC in the context of major power asymmetries will be contingent on ensuring that limitations which are inconsistent with the right to self-determination are not placed on FPIC, and that those limitations which are inherent in the concept of consent are given due consideration in efforts to operationalise it. As noted in Chapter 5, FPIC is referred to as a principle and a safeguard for indigenous rights, but is often appropriately conceived of as a self-determination right. Many, if not most, indigenous peoples hold this view. They regard the empowered decision-making between development choices based on consent, which FPIC encapsulates, as an inherent right, without which the rights to self-determination, lands, territories, resources, culture and develop-ment can be rendered effectively meaningless. Denial of the requirement for FPIC implies that control over decisions pertaining to their lands and resources, and by extension over their futures, is taken from them. Consultation with indigenous peoples is essential. However, consultations, negotiations, parti-cipation and partnership without a requirement for consent freeze existing power relations and leave indigenous peoples with little leverage to influence the outcome of decision-making processes. States, international organisations, global financial institutions and transnational extractive corporations currently hold this decision-making power and many of them are clearly reluctant to share it with indigenous peoples. In this sense, indigenous peoples' struggle for what they regard as their self-determination right to give or withhold FPIC is perhaps best conceived in terms of Shivji's conceptualisation of human rights when he argues that:

> seen as a means of struggle, 'right' is therefore not a standard granted as charity from above but a standard-bearer around which people rally for struggle from below. By the same token the correlate of 'right' is . . . power/ privilege where those who enjoy such power/privilege are the subject of being exposed and struggled against.[5]

Seen in this light, the assertion of a right to FPIC is a powerful tool in indigenous peoples' struggle to alter long-standing discriminatory power equations, irrespective of State or industry acknowledgement of the requirement, and is consistent with the notion of self-determination as on-going resistance to cultural and territorial encroachment.[6]

To ensure the effective implementation of their right to FPIC, indigenous peoples will have to continue to assert it at the community, people and community of peoples levels, while rallying and demanding respect for it in all national, regional and international fora available to them. Ultimately, it is indigenous peoples themselves who must define what the culturally appropriate contours of FPIC are, and how it should be operationalised. Only if this is the case, can it deliver on its promise of facilitating a future premised on self-determined development which does not repeat the false promises of the past. The adoption of the UNDRIP, and the affirmation of a self-determination based right to FPIC by the human rights regime, were a reflection of the adeptness of indigenous peoples in terms of getting their rights recognised. The extent to which, and the manner in which, FPIC is implemented, will be a measure of how successful they are in ensuring that they are upheld in practice.

---

5 Shivji 1989: 71.
6 Imai 2009: 290; for a discussion on the maintenance of cultural differences in the context of inter-ethnic interaction, see Barth 1998: 10–38.

Appendix I
Regional documents and jurisprudence

Regional documents

African [Banjul] Charter on Human and Peoples' Rights, OAU Doc. CAB/LEG/67/3 rev. 5, 21 ILM 58 (1982), adopted 27 June 1981, entered into force 21 October 1986.

African Union Assembly, *Decision on the United Declaration on the Rights of Indigenous Peoples*, African Union Assembly/AU/Dec. 141 (VIII), 30 January 2007.

American Convention on Human Rights, OAS Treaty Series No. 36, 1144 UNTS 123, entered into force 18 July 1978, reprinted in Basic Documents Pertaining to Human Rights in the Inter-American System, OEA/Ser.L.V/II.82 doc.6 rev.1 at 25 (1992).

American Treaty on Pacific Settlement of Disputes, Bogotá, 30 April 1948 30 UNTS 55 *Proposed American Declaration on the Rights of Indigenous Peoples* (Approved by the Inter-American Commission on Human Rights on 26 February 1997, at its 1333rd session, 95th Regular Session), OEA/Ser/L/V/.II.95 Doc.6 (1997).

Protocol to the [European] Convention for the Protection of Human Rights and Fundamental Freedoms, 213 UNTS 262, entered into force 18 May 1954.

Inter-American Court of Human Rights Jurisprudence

Inter-American Court of Human Rights Advisory Opinion Oc-18/03 of 17 September 2003, [Requested by the United Mexican States Juridical Condition and Rights of Undocumented Migrants].

Kichwa People of Sarayaku and its members v. Ecuador Inter-Am. Com. H.R. Case 12.465, 26 April 2010.

Mayagna (Sumo) Awas Tingni Community v. Nicaragua, Inter-Am. Ct. H.R., (ser. C) No. 79 (31 August 2001).

Pueblo Indígena Kichwa De Sarayaku v. Ecuador [De 27 De Junio De 2012 (Fondo y Reparaciones)].

Saramaka People v. Suriname, Interpretation of Judgment of Preliminary Objections, Merits, Reparations and Costs. Judgment of 12 August 2008. Series C No. 185.

Saramaka People v. Suriname, Judgment of 28 November 2007 (Preliminary Objections, Merits, Reparations, and Costs) Inter-Am. Ct. H.R., (Ser. C) No. 172 (2007).

Sarayaku People v. Ecuador, 17 July 2005, Separate Opinion of Judge Cançado Trindade (Spanish version only).

Sawhoyamaxa Indigenous Community v. Paraguay Inter-Am. Ct. H.R., Merits, Reparations and Costs (ser. C) No. 146 (29 March 2006).

Yatama v. Nicaragua (Preliminary Objections, Merits, Reparations and Costs) Judgment of 23 June 2005.

Inter-American Commission of Human Rights Jurisprudence

Mary and Carrie Dann v. United States Inter-American Comm. H.R, Case No. 11.140 Report 75/02 para 131 (2001).

Maya Indigenous Communities of the Toledo District (Belize), Inter-American Comm. H.R., Report No. 40/04, Case 12.053, 12 October 2004.

Precautionary Measure PM 382/10 - Indigenous Communities of the Xingu River Basin, Pará, Brazil, 1 April 2011.

African Commission on Human and Peoples Rights Jurisprudence

Centre for Minority Rights Development (Kenya) and Minority Rights Group International on behalf of Endorois Welfare Council v Kenya African Commission on Human and Peoples' Rights, Communication No. 276/2003, 4 February 2010.

Human Rights-Based Approach to Natural Resources Governance, African Comm. H.P.R Res. 224 (51st Ordinary Session), 18 April-2 May 2012, Banjul, The Gambia, available at: www.achpr.org/sessions/51st/resolutions/224/

The Social and Economic Rights Action Center for Economic and Social Rights v Nigeria (Ogoni v Nigeria) African Commission on Human and Peoples Rights Communication No. 155/96 (2001).

European Court of Human Rights Jurisprudence

Freedom and Democracy Party (OZDEP) v Turkey No. 23885/94, Judgment of 8 December 1999.

Handolsdalen Sami village and others v Sweden, Application No. 39013/04.

Laskey, Jaggard & Brown v. The United Kingdom, Application No. 21627/93, 21826/93, 21974/93, Judgment of 19 February 1997.

Appendix II
Domestic documents
and jurisprudence

Constitutions

Bolivia: *Political Constitution of the State of Bolivia 2009*.
Brazil: *Constitution of the Federal Republic of Brazil 1998*.
Ecuador: *Constitution of the Republic of Ecuador 2008*.
Mexico: *Political Constitution of the United Mexican States (1917, last updated 2013)*.
Namibia: *The Constitution of the Republic of Namibia* (1988, amended 2010).
The Philippines: *The Constitution of the Philippines*, 1987.

Legislation and administrative guidelines

Australia: *Australia Aboriginal Land Rights (Northern Territories) Act* 1976.
Australia: *Native Title Act* 1993 (Cth).
Bolivia: *Ley de Consulta a los Pueblos Indígenas del Territorio Indígena y Parque Nacional Isiboro Sécure* TIPNIS Ley 222 (10-Febrero-2012).
Bolivia: *Ley de Hidrocarburos* (Bolivia, Ley No 3058) del 17 Mayo 2005.
Bolivia: *Ley Nº 3760* de 7 de noviembre de 2007, modificada por *Ley Nº 3897* de 26 de junio de 2008.
Canada: *Corporate Accountability of Mining, Oil and Gas Corporations in Developing Countries Act*, Canadian Bill C-300 (Historical) 2010.
Canada: *Oil and Gas Act*, 2002, Revised Statutes of the Yukon (R.S.Y).
Colombia: *Codigo de Minas* (Colombia, Ley 685, 15 Augusto 2001).
Fiji: *Native Land Trust Act* [Fiji, Cap 134 of 2000].
Greenland: *Act on Greenland Self-Government*, adopted 19 May 2009.
Greenland: *Greenland Home Rule Act*, (1978) Act No. 577.
Guyana: *Amerindian Act* (Guyana, 20 October 2005).
India: Forest Rights Act (2006).
Mexico: *Ley Agraria* Nueva Ley publicada en el *Diario Oficial de la Federación*, el 26 de febrero de 1992, Texto Vigente Última reforma publicada Mexico, DOF 09–04–2012.
Mexico: *Ley de Derechos de los Pueblos Indígenas del Estado de Chihuahua* P.O.E. 2013.06.29/ No. 52.
Mexico: *Ley Forestal Diario Oficial de la Federación* (Mexico, 22 de diciembre de 1992).
New Zealand: *Ngai Tahu Land Report Waitangi Tribunal Claim* 27 (Waitangi Tribunal, 1991).
Papua New Guinea: *Land Act* (PNG, No.45 of 1996).
Peru: *Ley del Derecho a la Consulta Previa a los Pueblos Indígenas u Originarios Reconocido en el Convenio No 169 de la Organización International del Trabajo Ley No. 29785*, 23 augusto 2011.

Peru: *Reglamento de la Ley No 29785, Ley del Derecho a la Consulta Previa a los Pueblos Indígenas u Originarios Reconocido en el Convenio No 169 de la Organización International del Trabajo Decreto Supremo* No 001–2012 MC, 3 abril 2012.

The Philippines: *Indigenous Peoples Rights Act* 1997, Republic Act No. 8371 (the Philippines).

The Philippines: *The Revised Guidelines on Free and Prior Informed Consent (FPIC) and Related Processes of 2012* NCIP Administrative Order No. 3 Series of 2012.

Spain: *Spanish Judiciary Act Ley Orgánica 6/1985*, de 1 de julio, del Poder Judicial.

United States of America: *Alien Tort Claims Act*, 28 USC §1350 (2001) *Act of 3 March 1911*, Ch 231 § 24, 36 Stat. 1087, 1093 (1911) *Judiciary Act*, Ch. 20 § 9, 1 Stat. 73, 77 (1789); Revised Statutes tit. 13, ch 3, § 563, para 16 (1873).

Statements

Australia: *Declaration on the Rights of Indigenous Peoples General Assembly 13 September 2007 Explanation of vote by the Hon. Robert Hill Ambassador and Permanent Representative of Australia to the United Nations* (As delivered) 2007, available at: http://www.unny.mission.gov.au/unny/GA_070913.html

Australia: *Note verbale dated 2 August 2006 from the Permanent Mission of Australia to the United Nations Office at Geneva addressed to the Office of the United Nations High Commissioner for Human Rights*, see UN Doc A/HRC/2/G/1 (24 August 2006).

Australia: *Statement of Peter Vaughn to the Permanent Forum on Indigenous Issues, Representative of Australia, on behalf of Australia, New Zealand and the United States of America, on Free, Prior and Informed Consent*, 22 May 2006, New Zealand Ministry of Foreign Affairs and Trade, available at: http://www.australiaun.org/unny/soc_220506.html

Australia: *Statement on the United Nations Declaration on the Rights of Indigenous Peoples Parliament House Canberra* (3 April 2009), available at: http://www.un.org/esa/socdev/unpfii/documents/Australia_official_statement_endorsement_UNDRIP.pdf

Australia: *The Declaration on the Rights of Indigenous Peoples Statement by H.E. Ambassador Rosemary Banks on behalf of Australia, New Zealand and the United States*, Statements and Speeches by Ministry Representatives 2006 United Nations General Assembly 61st session Third Committee: Item 64(a) (16 October 2006), available at: www.mfat.govt.nz/Media-and-publications/Media/MFAT-speeches/2006/0–16-October-2006b.php

Canada: *'Canada's Statement of Support on the United Nations Declaration on the Rights of Indigenous Peoples'* Indian and Northern Affairs Canada, (12 November 2010), available at: www.ainc-inac.gc.ca/ap/ia/dcl/stmt-eng.asp

Canada: *Canada's Position: United Nations Draft Declaration on the Rights of Indigenous Peoples* (2006) available at: www.ainc-inac.gc.ca/ap/ia/pubs/ddr/ddr-eng.asp

Canada: *Statement of Support on the United Nations Declaration on the Rights of Indigenous Peoples* (12 November 2010), available at: www.aadnc-aandc.gc.ca/eng/1309374239861

New Zealand: *Ministry of Foreign Affairs and Trade (MFAT), Explanation of Vote HE Rosemary Banks, New Zealand Permanent Representative to the United Nations*, 13 September 2007, available at: www.mfat.govt.nz/Media-and-publications/Media/MFAT-speeches/2007/0–13-September-2007.php

New Zealand: *Parliament Ministerial Statements—UN Declaration on the Rights of Indigenous Peoples—Government Support* [Volume: 662; Page: 10229] (20 April 2010), available at http://www.parliament.nz/en-NZ/PB/Debates/Debates/6/5/a/49HansD_20100420_00000071-Ministerial-Statements-UN-Declaration-on.htm

United States of America: *Announcement of U.S. Support for the United Nations Declaration on the Rights of Indigenous Peoples* (16 December 2010), available at: www.state.gov/documents/organization/153223.pdf

United States of America: *Department of State Announcement of U.S. Support for the United Nations Declaration on the Rights of Indigenous Peoples* (16 December 2010), available at: www.state.gov/documents/organization/153223.pdf

United States of America: *Observations of the United States with Respect to the Declaration on the Rights of Indigenous Peoples*, USUN press release #204(07) 13 September 2007, reproduced in Cummins, S.J. (ed.) (2007) *Digest of United States Practice in International Law*. Washington, DC: International Law Institute, Oxford University Press.

Development strategies

Denmark: *Strategy for Danish Support to Indigenous Peoples* (Danish Ministry of Foreign Affairs, Danida, May 2004.

The Philippines: Philippines Medium-Term Philippine Development Plan 2004–2010.

Spain: *Estrategia Sectorial Española de Cooperación Española con los Pueblos Indígenas* (2006).

National cases

Argentina: *Antiman, Víctor Antonio y Linares, José Cristóbal Linares s/usurpación*, of 30 October 2007, [Argentina Magistrate's Court of the Fourth District of the Province of Neuquén].

Argentina: *Etcheverry Ruben A. y Otros C/ Provincia del Neuquen* Tribunal Superior de Justicia de Argentina S/ Accion De Inconstitucionalidad, Nro de Fallo 1532/08.

Australia: *Mabo v. Queensland* [No 2] (1992) 175 CLR 1.

Australia: *Wik Peoples v. Queensland* (1996) 134 ALR 637.

Australia: *Western Australia v. Ward* [2002] HCA 28; 213 CLR 1; 191 ALR 1; 76 ALJR 1098 (8 August 2002).

Australia: *Western Desert Lands Aboriginal Corporation (Jamukurnu - Yapalikunu)/Western Australia/Holocene Pty Ltd* [2009] NNTTA 49 (27 May 2009).

Belize: *Aurelio Cal and the Maya Village of Santa Cruz v. Attorney General of Belize & Manuel Coy and Maya Village of Conejo v. Attorney General of Belize* (Consolidated) Claim Nos 171 & 172, 2007, Supreme Court of Belize (18 October 2007).

Belize: *The Maya Leaders Alliance and the Toledo Alcaldes Association on Behalf of the Maya Villages of Toledo District v. the Attorney General of Belize and the Minister of Natural Resources and Environment*, Claim No. 366 of 2008 Supreme Court of Belize, A.D. 2010.

Belize: Supreme Court of Belize CLAIM NO. 394 OF 2013 3 April 2014.

Bolivia: *Corte Suprema de Justicia de Bolivia Sentencia Constitucional 0045/2006*, Expediente 2005–12440–25-RDL, sentencia de 2 de junio de 2006, II.5.1.

Canada: *Calder v. Attorney-General of British Columbia*, [1973] SCR 313.

Canada: *R. v. Sparrow* [1990] 1 SCR 1075.

Canada: *Blueberry River Indian Band v. Canada* (Department of Indian Affairs and Northern Development), [1995] 4 SCR 344.

Canada: *R. v. Gladstone* [1996] 2 SCR 723.

Canada: *Delgamuukw v. British Columbia* [1997] 3 SCR.

Canada: *Reference re Secession of Quebec*, [1998] 2 SCR 217.

Canada: *Haida Nation v. British Columbia (Minister of Forests)* 2004 SCC 73.

Canada: *Platinex Inc. v. Kitchenuhmaykoosib Inninuwug First Nation* 2006 CanLII 26171.

Canada: *Taseko Mines Limited v. Phillips*, 2011 BCSC 1675 Date: 20111202 Dockets: S117685, 114556.

Canada: *Wahgoshig First Nation (WFN) v. Her Majesty the Queen in Right of Ontario et al* 2011 ONSC 7708 2012 01.

Colombia: *Constitutional Court of Colombia Judgment SU -383/03*, 13 May 2003.

Colombia: *Constitutional Court of Colombia Judgment T-704/06* of 22 August 2006 (Rapporteur: Humberto Antonio Sierra Porto).

Colombia: *Constitutional Court of Colombia Judgment T-769* (2009) Expediente T-2315944.

Colombia: *Constitutional Court of Colombia Judgment T-129/*11 (2011) Expediente T-2451120.

Costa Rica: *Constitutional Court of Costa Rica Vote 1992–3003*, Case 3003 07/10/1992 L, Judgment of 7 October 1992.

Guatamala: *Apelación De Sentencia De Amparo Expediente*, Guatamala Constitutional Court 3878–2007, 21 December 2009.

India: *Orissa Mining Corporation. Vs. MoEF & Ors* Indian Supreme Court judgement dated 18/04/2013 in W.P.(C) No.180/2011.

Malaysia: *Kerajaan Negeri Selangor & 3 Ors v Sagong Bin Tasi & 6 Ors* 2005 [CA].

Papua New Guinea: *Musa Valley Management Company Ltd et al v/s the Department of Lands and Physical Planning et al*, PNG National Court of Justice OS (JR) No 10 of 2009 N3827 16, 17 June 2009, 22 January 2010.

Peru: *Lima Asociación Interétnica De Desarrollo De La Selva (Aidesep)*, Peru Consitutional Court EXP. N.° 05427–2009-PC/TC.

The Philippines: *Isagani Cruz et al v. Secretary of Environment and Natural Resources et al* G.R. No. 135385 6 December 2000.

The Philippines: *La Bugal-B'lann Tribal Ass'n v. Ramos*, G.R. No 127882 421 S.C.R.A. 148 (1 December 2004).

The Philippines: *Didipio Earth-Savers' Multi-Purpose Association, [DESAMA] Inc. et al. v. Elisea Gozun, et al* G.R. No. 157882 (30 March 2006).

South Africa: *Alexkor Ltd and Another v. Richtersveld Community and Others* (CCT19/03) [2003] ZACC 18; 2004 (5) SA 460 (CC).

South Africa: *Richtersveld Community v. Alexkor Ltd & Another* [2004] 3 All SA 244 (LCC).

United States of America: *Vanhorne's Lessee v. Dorrance*, 2 U.S. 304 (1795) 2 U.S. 304 (F.Cas.) 2 Dall.

United States of America: *Cherokee Nation v. Georgia*, 30 U.S. (5 Pet.) 1, 16 (1831).

United States of America: *Worchester v Georgia* 31 U.S. (6 Pet.) 515 (1832).

United States of America: *Fletcher v Peck* (1810)10 US 87.

United States of America: *Johnson v. M'Intosh*, 21 U.S. 543, 5 L.Ed. 681, 8 Wheat. 543 (1823).

United States of America: *US v. Shoshone Tribe* 304 US 111, 115–18 (1938).

United States of America: *Choctaw Nation v. Oklahoma*, 397 U.S. 620, 630–31 (1970).

United States of America: *US v. Wheeler*, 435 US 313, 322–3 (1978).

United States of America: *New Jersey v. Martin*, 235 NJ Super 47, 56, 561 A.2d, 631, 636 (1989).

United States of America: *Te-Moak Tribe of Western Nevada v. US Department of the Interior*, No. 07–16336, (9th Cir. 18 June 2010).

United States of America: *US Kiobel v. Royal Dutch Petroleum*, 261 F.3d 111 (2nd Cir. 2010).

Appendix III
International documents
and jurisprudence

United Nations Human Rights Treaties and Protocols

International Convention on the Elimination of All Forms of Racial Discrimination, GAOR 2106 (XX), Annex, 20 UN GAOR Supp. (No. 14) 47, UN Doc. A/6014 (1966), 660 UNTS 195, entered into force 4 January 1969.

International Covenant on Civil and Political Rights, GAOR 2200A (XXI), 21 UN GAOR Supp. (No. 16) 52, UN Doc. A/6316 (1966), 999 UNTS 171, entered into force 23 March 1976.

International Covenant on Economic, Social and Cultural Rights GAOR 2200A (XXI), 21 UN GAOR Supp. (No. 16) 49, UN Doc. A/6316 (1966), 993 UNTS 3, entered into force 3 January 1976.

Optional Protocol to the International Covenant on Economic, Social and Cultural Rights, UN GAOR A/RES/63/117 (10 December 2008).

UN Human Rights Committee (HRC) Jurisprudence

Concluding Observations

Canada, UN Doc. CCPR/C/79/Add.105 (7 April 1999); Panama UN Doc. CCPR/C/PAN/CO/3, (17 April 2008); Nicaragua, UN Doc. CCPR/C/NIC/CO/3, (12 December 2008); Colombia, UN Doc. CCPR/C/COL/CO/6, (4 August 2010); Togo, UN Doc. CCPR/C/TGO/CO/4 (2011).

Communications

Communication No. 167/1984 *Lubicon Lake Band v. Canada*, UN Doc. Supp. No. 40 (UN Doc. A/45/40) at 1 (1990).

Communication No. 511/1992 *Lansman v. Finland*, UN Doc. CCPR/C/52/D/511/1992 (1994).

Communication No. 1457/2006 *Angela Poma Poma v Peru* CCPR/C/95/D/1457/2009 (2009).

Communication No. 1023/2001 *Lansman v. Finland*, UN Doc. CCPR/C/83/D/1023/2001 (2005).

Communication No. 167/1984 *Lubicon Lake Band v. Canada*, (26 March 1990), UN Doc. Supp. No. 40 (A/45/40) at 1 (1990).

General comments

General Comment 12, Article 1 (1984), Compilation of General Comments and General Recommendations Adopted by Human Rights Treaty Bodies, UN Doc. HRI/GEN/1/Rev.1 at 12 (1984).

UN Committee on the Elimination of Racial Discrimination (CERD) Jurisprudence

CERD Concluding Observations

Suriname UN Doc. CERD/C/64/CO/9/Rev.2, (2004); Lao UN Doc. CERD/C/LAO/CO/15, 18 April 2005; United States of America UN Doc. CERD/C/USA/DEC/1 (b) 11 April 2006; Guyana UN Doc. CERD/C/GUY/CO/14, 4 April 2006; India UN Doc. CERD/C/IND/CO/19, 5 May 2007; Ethiopia UN Doc. CERD/C/ETH/CO/15, 20 June 2007; Russia UN Doc. CERD/C/RUS/CO/19 20 (2008); Ecuador UN Doc. CERD/C/ECU/CO/19, 15 August 2008; United States of America UN Doc. CERD/C/USA/CO/6 (7 March 2008); Colombia CERD/C/COL/CO/14, (28 August 2009); The Philippines UN Doc. CERD/C/PHL/CO/20, 28 August 2009; Cambodia UN Doc. CERD/C/KHM/CO/8–13 (2010); Norway UN Doc. CERD/C/NOR/CO/19–20 (8 April 2011).

CERD Early Warning Urgent Action communications and decisions

Letters to: Guyana (24th August 2007); Philippines (24th August 2007); Canada (15th August 2008); The Philippines (7th March 2008); Peru (13th March 2009), (13th March 2010), (2nd September 2011); Papua New Guinea (11th March 2011), France (28th September 2009).

Decisions issued to: United States (2006) UN Doc. CERD/C/USA/DEC/1; Suriname (2005) UN Doc. CERD/C/DEC/SUR/2.

CERD Early Warning Urgent Action procedure guidelines (2007).

CERD Summary Records

1215th meeting, UN Doc. CERD/C/SR.1215 (7 August 1997).

1235th meeting, UN Doc. CERD/C/SR.1235 (5 August 1997); 1183rd meeting, UN Doc. CERD/C/SR.1183 (3 January 1997).

1171st meeting, UN Doc. CERD/C/SR.1171 (14 November 1996).

Briefing on the United Nations Declaration on the Rights of Indigenous Peoples UN Doc. CERD/C/SR.1848/Add.1 (22 February 2008).

CERD General Recommendations

General Recommendation XX, *Non-discriminatory implementation of rights and freedoms* (Art. 5) 03/15/1996 contained in UN Doc. A/51/18.

General Recommendation XXIII, *Rights of indigenous peoples* (Fifty-first session, 1997), U.N. Doc. A/52/18, annex V at 122 (1997), reprinted in Compilation of General Comments and General Recommendations Adopted by Human Rights Treaty Bodies, U.N. Doc. HRI\GEN\1\Rev.6 at 212 (2003).

UN Committee on Economic Social and Cultural Rights (CESCR) Jurisprudence

CESCR Concluding Observations

Canada UN Doc. E/C.12/CAN/CO/5, 19 May 2006; Mexico, UN Doc. E/C.12/MEX/CO/4 9 June 2006; Democratic Republic of Congo, UN Doc. E/C.12/COD/CO/4 (20 November 2009); Cambodia UN Doc. E/C.12/KHM/CO/1 (22 May 2009); Sri Lanka UN Doc. E/C.12/LKA/CO/2–4 (9 December 2010); Colombia, UN Doc. E/C.12/COL/CO/5 (21 May 2010); Russia UN Doc. E/C.12/RUS/CO/5 (11 May 2011); Argentina UN Doc. E/C.12/ARG/CO/3 (14 December 2011); China UN Doc. E/C.12/CHN/CO/2 (2014).

CESCR General Comments and Statements

General Comment 14, (Twenty-second session, 2000): *Article 12: The Right to the Highest Attainable Standard of Health*, UN Doc. E/2001/22 (2000).

General Comment 15, *The right to water* (29th session, 2003), UN Doc. E/C.12/2002/11 (2002).

General Comment 18, *Article 6: the equal right of men and women to the enjoyment of all economic, social and cultural rights* (35th session, 2006), UN Doc. E/C.12/GC/18 (2006).

General Comment 19, *The right to social security (art. 9)* (39th session, 2007), UN Doc. E/C.12/GC/19 (2008).

General Comment 21, *The right of everyone to take part in cultural life*, UN Doc. E/C.12/GC/21 (21 December 2009).

Statement on the obligations of States Parties regarding the corporate sector and economic, social and cultural rights, UN Doc. E/C.12/2011/1 (20 May 2011).

UN Committee on the Rights of the Child (CRC) Jurisprudence

CRC General Comment No. 16 (2013) *on State obligations regarding the impact of business on children's rights*, UN Doc. CRC/C/GC/16.

UN Human Rights Council Resolutions

Adoption of the text of the United Nations Declaration on the Rights of Indigenous Peoples, Resolution 2/2006 29 June 2006 UN Doc. A/HRC/Res/2006/2.

Institution-building of the United Nations Human Rights Council, Resolution 5/1 18 June 2007 UN Doc. A/HRC/Res/2007/5/1.

Human rights and transnational corporations and other business enterprises, Human Rights Council Resolution A/HRC/RES/17/4 (6 July 2011).

UN Special Rapporteurs

Country Reports of the Special Rapporteur on the Situation of Human Rights and Fundamental Freedoms of Indigenous People, Rodolfo Stavenhagen

Mission to Philippines, UN Doc. E/CN.4/2003/90/Add.3 (2003); Mission to Colombia, UN Doc. E/CN.4/2005/88/Add.2 (2004).

Annual Reports of the Special Rapporteur on the Rights of Indigenous Peoples, James Anaya

UN Doc. A/HRC/9/9 (2008); UN Doc. A/HRC/12/34 (2009); UN Doc. A/HRC/15/37 (2010); UN Doc. A/HRC/18/35 (2011); UN Doc. A/HRC/21/47 (2012); UN Doc. A/HRC/24/41 (2013).

Country Reports and Statements of the Special Rapporteur on the Rights of Indigenous Peoples, James Anaya

Declaración pública del Relator Especial sobre los derechos humanos y libertades fundamentales de los indígenas, James Anaya, sobre la "Ley del derecho a la consulta previa a los pueblos indígenas u originarios reconocido en el Convenio No. 169 de la Organización Internacional de Trabajo", aprobada por el Congreso de la República del Perú, 7 de julio de 2010. UN Doc. A/HRC/9/9/ Add.1, 15 August 2008, Annex 1.

Statement on the right to participation, EMRIP 3rd Session, 12 July 2010.

Statement on the situation of the human rights and fundamental freedoms of indigenous people, Ninth Session of the UN Permanent Forum on Indigenous Issues, 22 April 2010.

Preliminary note on the application of the principle of consultation with indigenous peoples in Guatemala and the case of the Marlin mine. UN Doc. A/HRC/15/37/Add.8 (8 July 2010).

La situación de los pueblos indígenas afectados por el proyecto hidroeléctrico El Diquís en Costa Rica, UN Doc. A/HRC/18/35/Add.8 (2011).

Observations on the situation of the indigenous peoples of Guatemala in relation to extractive and other types of industries affecting traditional indigenous territories – with an appendix on the Marlin mine case, UN Doc. A/HRC/18/35/Add.3. (2011).

The situation of indigenous peoples in Canada, UN Doc. A/HRC/27/52/Add.2 (2014).

La situación de los derechos de los pueblos indígenas en Perú, en relación con las industrias extractivas, UN Doc. A/HRC/27/52/Add.3 (2014).

Reports of other UN Special Rapporteurs

Report of the Special Rapporteur on the Right to Food, Jean Ziegler 24 January 2005 UN Doc E/ CN.4/2005/47.

Report of the Independent Expert on Minority Issues, Gay McDougall Addendum Mission to Colombia, 25 January 2011, UN Doc. A/HRC/16/45/Add.1.

Report of the Special Rapporteur on Adequate Housing as a component of the right to an adequate standard of living, UN Doc. A/HRC/4/18 (11 June 2007), *Annex 1 Basic Principles and Guidelines on Development based Evictions and Displacement.*

UN Experts Mechanism on the Rights of Indigenous Peoples (EMRIP)

Follow-up report on indigenous peoples and the right to participate in decision-making, with a focus on extractive industries, UN Doc. A/HRC/EMRIP/2012/2 (2012) and Annex 1: Advice 4.

Final report of the study on indigenous peoples and the right to participate in decision-making, UN Doc. A/HRC/18/42 (2011) and Annex: Advice no. 2.

Progress report on the study on indigenous peoples and the right to participate in decision-making, UN Doc. A/HRC/EMRIP/2010/2 (17 May 2010).

UN Universal Periodic Review (UPR) Reports

UPR 12th Session October 2011 (8 December 2011), UN Doc. A/HRC/19/4; UPR 8th Session (May 2010) (17 June 2010), UN Doc. A/HRC/15/8; UPR 5th Session May 2009 (4 June 2009), UN Doc. A/HRC/12/8; UPR 4th Session February 2009 (3 March 2009), UN Doc. A/HRC/11/17.

UN General Assembly Reports and Resolutions

The future we want, General Assembly resolution 66/288 (11 September 2012).

Declaration on the Rights of Indigenous Peoples, G.A. Res. 61/295, UN Doc. A/RES/47/1 (13 September 2007), 46 ILM 1013 (2007).

Sixty-first General Assembly Plenary 107th & 108th Meetings *General Assembly Adopts Declaration on Rights of Indigenous Peoples* UN Doc. GA/10612.

General Assembly 61st Session 2007 UN Doc. A/61/PV.107.

Note verbale dated 2 August 2006 from the Permanent Mission of Australia to the United Nations Office at Geneva addressed to the Office of the United Nations High Commissioner for Human Rights, UN Doc. A/HRC/2/G/1 (24 August 2006).

Second International Decade of the World's Indigenous People (2005–2014), GAOR 59/174 (20 December 2004).

Draft Programme of Action for the Second International Decade of the World's Indigenous People, UN Doc. A/60/270 (18 August 2005).

Declaration on Principles of International Law concerning Friendly Relations and Cooperation among States in accordance with the Charter of the United Nations, GA Res 2625 Annex, 25 UN GAOR, Supp. (No. 28), UN Doc. A/5217 at 121 (1970).

Annotations on the text of the draft International Covenants on Human Rights, UN Doc. A/2929 (1955).

Text of Replies to the Ad Hoc Committee on Factors (8 May 1952) UN Doc. A./AC.67/2.

UN Commission and Sub-Commission on Human Rights Reports and Resolutions

Cristescu, A., *The Right to Self-Determination Historical and Current Development on the Basis of United Nations Instruments,* E/CN.4/sub.2/404/Rev.1 (1981).

Espiel, H. G., *Implementation of United Nations Resolutions Relating the Right of People Under Colonial and Alien Domination to Self-Determination,* UN Doc. E/CN.4/Sub.405 (20 June 1978) and UN Doc E/CN.4/Sub.2/405/Rev.1 (1980).

Study of the Problem of Discrimination Against Indigenous Populations, Final report submitted by the Special Rapporteur, Mr. José Martínez Cobo, UN Doc. E/CN.4/Sub.2/476 & Add. 1–6 (1981); UN Doc. E/CN.4/Sub.2/1982/2 & Add. 1–7 (1982); UN Doc. E/CN.4/Sub.2/1983/21 & Add. 1–7 (1983).

Study of the problem of discrimination against indigenous populations. Economic and Social Council Resolution, 1982/34 (7 May 1982).

Commission on Human Rights resolution 1982/19, 10 March 1982.

United Nations Study on Treaties, Agreements and Other Constructive Arrangements between States and Indigenous Populations – Second Progress Report, E/CN.4/Sub.2/1995/27.

Study on Treaties, Agreements and Other Constructive Arrangements Between States and Indigenous Populations, Final report by Miguel Alfonso Martínez, Special Rapporteur, UN Doc. E/CN.4/Sub.2/1999/20.

Indigenous peoples and their relationship to land, Final working paper prepared by the Special Rapporteur, Mrs. Erica-Irene A. Daes E/CN.4/Sub.2/2001/21 (11 June 2001).

Indigenous peoples' permanent sovereignty over natural resources, Final report of the Special Rapporteur, Erica-Irene A. Daes E/CN.4/Sub.2/2004/30 and E/CN.4/Sub.2/2004/30/Add.1 (13 July 2004).

Report of the seminar on Treaties, Agreements and other Constructive Arrangements between States and Indigenous Peoples, UN Doc. E/CN.4/Sub.2/AC.4/2004/7.

Conclusions and Recommendations of the Seminar on Treaties, Agreements and Other Constructive Arrangements between States and Indigenous Peoples, UN Doc. E/CN.4/2004/111.

UN Initiatives on Business and Human Rights

Commentary on the Norms on the Responsibilities of Transnational Corporations and Other Business Enterprises with Regard to Human Rights, UN Doc. E/CN.4/Sub.2/2003/38/Rev.2 (2003).

Outcome of the second session of the Working Group on the issue of human rights and transnational corporations and other business enterprises, UN Doc. A/HRC/WG.12/2/1 (2012).

Report of the Working Group on the issue of human rights and transnational corporations and other business enterprises 'Human rights and transnational corporations and other business enterprises', UN Doc. A/68/279 (6 August 2013).

Reports of the Special Representative of the Secretary-General on the Issue of Human Rights and Transnational Corporations and Other Business Enterprises, John Ruggie

Interim Report UN Doc. E/CN.4/2006/97 (22 February 2006).

Protect, Respect and Remedy: A Framework for Business and Human Rights, A/HRC/8/5 (7 April 2008).

Guiding Principles on Business and Human Rights: Implementing the United Nations "Protect, Respect and Remedy" Framework, UN Doc. A/HRC/17/31 (21 March 2011).

Principles for responsible contracts: integrating the management of human rights risks into State-investor contract negotiations: guidance for negotiators, UN Doc. A/HRC/17/31/Add.3 (2011).

UN Permanent Forum on Indigenous Issues (UN PFII)

Special Theme: Millennium Development Goals Information Received from the United Nations System, UNPFII 4th session, New York, UN Doc. E/C.19/2005/4/Add.13 (28 March 2005).

International Workshop on FPIC and Indigenous Peoples, *Contribution of the ILO* (Geneva: ILO, 2005) UN Doc. PFII/2005/WS.2/4.

Report of the International Workshop on Methodologies regarding Free, Prior and Informed Consent and Indigenous Peoples (New York, 17–19 January 2005), UN Doc. E/C.19/2005/3.

Information received from non-governmental organizations with ECOSOC consultative status International Work Group for Indigenous Affairs (IWGIA) and Tebtebba Foundation, UN Doc. E/C.19/2007/7 (13 March 2007).

Report of the Government of Spain to the PFII 6th session, 21 February 2007, UN Doc. E/C.19/2007/4.

Report of the international expert group meeting on extractive industries, Indigenous Peoples' rights and corporate social responsibility (4 May 2009), UN Doc. E/C.19/2009/CRP. 8 and *Annex II: Manila Declaration of the International Conference on Extractive Industries and Indigenous Peoples*, 23–25 March 2009 Legend Villas, Metro Manila, the Philippines.

Report on the UNPFII 8th session, UN Doc. E/C/19/2009/14, Annex, *General Comment on Article 42 of the UN Declaration*.

Report on the UNPFII ninth session (19–30 April 2010) *Special theme: "Indigenous peoples: development with culture and identity: articles 3 and 32 of the United Nations Declaration on the Rights of Indigenous Peoples"*, UN Doc. E/2010/43-E/C.19/2010/15.

Indicators of Well-being, Poverty and Sustainability Relevant to Indigenous Peoples, February 2008, UN Doc. E/C.19/2008/9.

Consolidated report on extractive industries and their impact on indigenous peoples, Permanent Forum on Indigenous Issues Twelth session (20 February 2013) UN Doc. E/C.19/2013/16.

UN Working Group on Indigenous Populations and UN Working Group on the Draft Declaration on the rights of indigenous peoples

Report of the Working Group on Indigenous Populations on its first session, (E/CN.4/Sub.2/1982/33) 25 August 1982.

Standard-Setting Legal Commentary on the Concept of Free, Prior and Informed Consent, Expanded Working Paper, submitted by A. I. Motoc, UN Doc. E/CN.4/Sub.2/AC.4/2005/WP.1, 14 July 2005.

A Preliminary Working Paper on the Principle of Free, Prior and Informed Consent of Indigenous Peoples in Relation to Development Affecting Their Lands and Natural Resources That Would Serve as a Framework for the Drafting of a Legal Commentary by the Working Group on This Concept, submitted by A. I. Motoc, UN Doc. E/CN.4/Sub.2/AC.4/2004/4 (2004).

International Workshop on the Draft United Nations Declaration on the Rights of Indigenous Peoples, Patzcuaro, Michoacán, Mexico, 26–30 September 2005, Information provided by the Government of Mexico E/CN.4/2005/WG.15/CRP.1 (29 November 2005).

Establishment of a Working Group of the Commission on Human Rights to Elaborate a Draft Declaration in Accordance with Paragraph 5 of General Assembly Resolution 49/21, Resolution of the Commission on Human Rights 1995/32, 3 March 1995.

Universal Declaration on Indigenous Rights: A Set of Preambular Paragraphs and Principles, UN Doc. E/CN.4/Sub.2/1988/25.
Analytical Commentary on the Draft Principles Contained in the First Revised Text of the Draft Declaration on the Rights of Indigenous Peoples, UN Doc. E/CN.4/Sub.2/AC.4/1990/1/Add.1.
Draft Universal Declaration on the Rights of Indigenous Peoples, August 1993, UN Doc. E/CN.4/Sub.2/1993/29/Annex I.
Draft Declaration on the Rights of Indigenous Peoples, UN Doc. E/CN.4/Sub.2/1994/2/Add.1 (1994).

Reports of the Working Group on the Draft Declaration on the Rights of Indigenous Peoples group established in accordance with Commission on Human Rights resolution 1995/32 of 3 March 1995

UN Doc. E/CN.4/2006/79; UN Doc. E/CN.4/2005/89; UN Doc. E/CN.4/2003/92; UN Doc. E/CN.4/2002/98; UN Doc. E/CN.4/2001/85; UN Doc. E/CN.4/2000/84; UN Doc. E/CN.4/1999/82; UN Doc. E/CN.4/1998/106; UN Doc. E/CN.4/1997/102; UN Doc. E/CN.4/1996/84; UN Doc. E/CN.4/1996/WG.15/CRP.2.

Reports of the Working Group on Indigenous Populations (WGIP)

Report of the 1st session UN Doc. E/CN.4/Sub.2/1982/33, (1982); Report of 4th Session UN Doc. E/CN.4/Sub.2/1985/22, (27 August 1985) Annex III *Declaration of Principles;* Report of the 5th Session UN Doc. E/CN.4/Sub.2/1987/22 and Annex.5 *Declaration of Principles Adopted by the Indigenous Peoples;* Report of the 6th session UN Doc. E/CN.4/Sub.2/1988/24 and Annex II; Report of 7th session UN Doc. E/CN.4/Sub.2/1989/36; Report of 8th Session UN Doc. E/CN.4/Sub.2/1990/42; Report of 10th session UN Doc. E/CN.4/Sub.2/1992/33.

Other United Nations and International Documents

Declaration on Principles of International Law concerning Friendly Relations and Cooperation among States in accordance with the Charter of the United Nations, GAOR 2625 (XXV) Annex, 25 UN GAOR, Supp. (No. 28), UN Doc. A/5217 (1970).
Vienna Convention on the Law of Treaties, 1155 UNTS 331, 8 ILM 679, entered into force 27 January 1980.
Declaration of San Jose, 1982, adopted UNESCO Meeting of Experts on Ethno-Development and Ethnocide in Latin America UNESCO Doc. FS 82/WF.32 (1982).
Draft articles on the law of treaties between States and international organizations or between international organizations with commentaries, 1982 YB ILC, Vol. II, Part II 1982, UN Doc. A/CN.4/SER.A/1982/Add.1.
Declaration on the Right to Development, G.A. res. 41/128, annex, 41 U.N. GAOR Supp. (No. 53), 186, UN Doc. A/41/53 (1986).
United Nations Convention against Illicit Traffic in Narcotic Drugs and Psychotropic Substances, UN Doc. E/CONF.82/15 (1988), reprinted in 28 International Legal Materials (ILM) 493 (1989).
Vienna Declaration and Programme of Action, adopted by the World Conference on Human Rights on 25 June 1993, UN Doc. A/CONF.157/23, 12 July 1993.

Rotterdam Convention on the Prior Informed Consent Procedure for Certain Hazardous Chemicals and Pesticides in International Trade, 1998, 224 UNTS 337; C.N.846.2002.
Annual Report of the UNCHR, *The Rights of Indigenous Peoples.* UN Doc. A/HRC/9/11 (3 September 2008).
Draft Declaration on the rights of peasants and other people working in rural areas, UN Doc. A/HRC/15/1/2 (2013).

International Court of Justice (ICJ) Jurisprudence

Corfu Channel Case (UK v. Albania) ICJ Reports [1949] 4.
Legal Consequences for States of the continued presence of South Africa in Namibia (South West Africa) Notwithstanding Security Council Resolution 276 (1970) Advisory Opinion of 21 June 1971, ICJ Reports [1971] 78.
Western Sahara, Advisory Opinion, ICJ Reports [1975] 12.
Frontier Dispute (Burkina Faso/Republic of Mali) ICJ Reports [1986].
Land, Island and Maritime Frontier Dispute (El Salvador v. Honduras. Nicaragua intervening) ICJ Reports [1992] 22.
Territorial Dispute (Libyan Arab Jamahiriyai v. Chad) ICJ Reports [1994].
East Timor (Portugal v. Australia) Judgment ICJ Reports [1995] 90.
Gabčíkovo-Nagymaros Project case (Hungary v. Slovakia), ICJ Reports [1997] 7.
Legal Consequences of the Construction of a Wall in the Occupied Palestinian Territory, Advisory Opinion, ICJ Reports [2004] 136 [Advisory Opinion on the Legal Consequences on the Construction of a Wall in the Occupied Palestinian Territory (2004) 43 ILM 1009].
Application of the Convention on the Prevention and Punishment of the Crime of Genocide (Croatia v. Serbia), Preliminary Objections, Judgment, ICJ Reports [2008] 412.
Letter from the Ambassador of Ecuador (Appointed) to the Kingdom of the Netherlands to the Registrar of the International Court of Justice Embajada del Ecuador en los Países Bajos No. 4–4-3/08. The Hague, 31 March 2008. 2008 General List No. 138.
Pulp Mills on the River Uruguay (Argentina V. Uruguay) Judgment ICJ Reports [2010] 14.

International Arbitration

Award on the claims of Great Britain and Portugal to certain territories formerly belonging to the Kings of Tembe and Mapoota, on the eastern coast of Africa, including the islands of Inyack and Elephant (Delagoa Bay or Lorenzo Marques), 24 July 1875 XXVIII.
Cayuga Indians (Great Britain) v. United States, 6 UNRIAA 173 (1926).
Island of Palmas (United States v. Netherlands) 2 UNRIAA 831 (1928).
Trail Smelter Case (US v. Canada) 3 Rep International Law Arbitration 1905, 1965–66 (1949) U.N. Sales No. 1949 v.2.

Permanent Court of International Justice (PCIJ)

Legal Status of Eastern Greenland (Denmark v. Norway), 1933 PCIJ (ser. A/B) No. 53 (Apr. 5).

International Criminal Tribunal for the former Yugoslavia (ICTY)

Prosecutor v. Dragoljub Kunarac Radomir Kovac and Zoran Vukovic Case no: IT-96–23-T& IT-96–23/1-T Judgement of 22 February 2001.

International Labour Organization (ILO)

ILO Conventions and Declarations

Convention concerning Indigenous and Tribal Peoples in Independent Countries (ILO No. 169) 72 ILO Official Bull. 59; 28 ILM 1382 (1989), entered into force 5 September 1991.

Convention concerning the Protection and Integration of Indigenous and Other Tribal and Semi-Tribal Populations in Independent Countries C107 – Indigenous and Tribal Populations Convention, 1957 (No. 107) (Entry into force: 2 June 1959) Adoption: Geneva, 40th ILC session (26 June 1957) – Status: Outdated instrument (Technical Convention).

ILO Convention No. 50 on the Recruiting of Indigenous Workers 1936.

ILO Convention No. 64 on Contracts of Employment 1939.

ILO Convention No. 111 Discrimination (Employment and Occupation) Convention 25 June 1958 362 UNTS 31.

ILO Recommendation No. 104, 40th Session, 5 June 1957.

ILO Reports and Observations

El Salvador Observation, Discrimination (Employment and Occupation) Convention, 1958 (No. 111) CEACR 2008/79th Session reproduced in *Monitoring indigenous and tribal peoples' rights through ILO Conventions A compilation of ILO supervisory bodies' comments 2009–2010* (Geneva: ILO, 2010).

General observation Indigenous and Tribal Peoples Convention, 1989 (No. 169), Governing Body, 282nd Session, Colombia, GB.282/14/3 (2001). Reproduced in International Labour Conference, 100th Session, 2011 *Report of the Committee of Experts on the Application of Conventions and Recommendations* Report III (Part 1A).ILC.100/III/1A.

Observation CEACR 2009/80th Session, Argentina Indigenous and Tribal Peoples Convention, 1989 (No. 169).

Report of the Committee Set Up to Examine the Representation Alleging Non-Observance by Brazil of the Indigenous and Tribal Peoples Convention, 1989 (No. 169), Union of Engineers of the Federal District (SENGE/DF). (GB.295/17);(GB.304/14/7) [2009].

Report of the Committee Set Up to Examine the Representation Alleging Non-Observance by Guatemala of the Indigenous and Tribal Peoples Convention, 1989 (No. 169), made under Article 24 of the ILO Constitution by the Federation of Country and City Workers (FTCC) GB.294/17/1; GB.299/6/1 (2007).

Report of the Committee Set up to Examine the Representation Alleging Non-Observance by Colombia of the Indigenous and Tribal Peoples Convention, 1989 (No. 169), Central Unitary Workers' Union (CUT) and the Colombian Medical Trade Union Association (GB.277/18/1); (GB.282/14/4) (1999).

Direct Request (CEACR) Discrimination (Employment and Occupation) Convention, 1958 (No. 111), adopted 2010, published 100th ILC session (2011).

Organisation for Economic Cooperation and Development (OECD) Documents

OECD Guidelines for Multinational Enterprises [2011 Edition]. Paris: OECD, 2011.

Final Statement by the UK National Contact Point for the OECD Guidelines for Multinational Enterprises Complaint from Survival International against Vedanta Resources plc. London: OECD, 2009.

Final Statement Complaint from the Future in Our Hands (FIOH) against Intex Resources ASA and the Mindoro Nickel Project, The Norwegian National Contact Point for the OECD Guidelines for Multinational Enterprises. Oslo: OECD, 2011.

OECD Recommendation of the Council on Common Approaches for Officially Supported Export Credits and Environmental and Social Due Diligence TAD/ECG(2012)5 (28 June 2012).

Convention on Biological Diversity (CBD)

Convention on Biological Diversity (1992–06–05) (entry into force 1993–12–29) 1760 UNTS 79; 31 ILM 818 (1992).

Akwé: Kon Voluntary guidelines for the conduct of cultural, environmental and social impact assessments regarding developments proposed to take place on, or which are likely to impact on, sacred sites and on lands and waters traditionally occupied or used by indigenous and local communities (Secretariat of the Convention on Biological Diversity, Geneva, 2004) Decision VII/16 F COP-7, UN Doc. UNEP/CBD/COP/7/21 (13 April 2004).

Nagoya Protocol on Access to Genetic Resources and the Fair and Equitable Sharing of Benefits Arising from their Utilization to the Convention on Biological Diversity. Nagoya, 29 October 2010 C.N.782.2010.TREATIES-1 (Depositary Notification).

Report of the Second Part of the Ninth Meeting of the ad hoc Open-Ended Working Group on Access and Benefit-Sharing, UN Doc. UNEP/CBD/COP/10/5/Add.4 (28 July 2010).

Financial Sector Standards

Asian Development Bank Safeguard Policy Statement (July 2009).

European Bank for Reconstruction and Development (EBRD) Environmental and Social Policy (May 2008).

Equator Principles III (June 2013) available at: www.equator-principles.com

IFC Environmental and Social Review Procedures Manual Version 5. Washington, DC: IFC, 2012.

IFC Guidance Note 7 Indigenous Peoples. Washington, DC: IFC (January 2012).

IFC Performance Standard 1 Assessment and Management of Environmental and Social Risks and Impacts. Washington, DC: IFC (January 2012).

IFC Performance Standard 7 Indigenous Peoples. Washington DC: IFC (January 2012).

IFC-CESI *Environmental and Social Review Procedures Manual Financial Intermediary Investments: Early Review and Appraisal, Disclosure and Commitment, & Supervision*, Version 4. Washington, DC: IFC (2009).

Inter-American Development Bank 'Operational Policy on Indigenous Peoples' (February 2006).

World Bank Operational Policy on Indigenous Peoples no 4.10 (2005).

Historical International Documents

Pope Adrian's Bull "Laudabiliter" And note upon it' (1155), reprinted in Appendix 1 of Hull E., (1931) *A History of Ireland and Her People.* London: G. G. Harrap & Company Ltd.

Pope Innocent IV, Commentary on *Quod super his* (ca. 1245).

Papal Bull of Pope Nicolas V, 1453.

Treaty between Spain and Portugal concluded at Tordesillas June 7, 1494 Ratification by Spain, July 2, 1494, ratification by Portugal, 5 September 1494 (Original manuscript National Archives at Lisbon, gav. 17, maco 2, no. 24).

Laws of Burgos (Leyes de Burgos), Promulgated on 27 December 1512.

Treaty of Saragossa, 22 April of 1529.

Papal Bull Sublimis Deus, promulgated, May 1537.

Ordenanzas de Descubrimientos Nueva Población y Pacificación de la Indias 1573, Felipe II, 13 Julio, 1573.

Recopilación de Leyes de los Reinos de las Indias' (Madrid: first published 1681).

The Pacific Islanders Protection Act 1875, 38 & 39 Vict. C. 51.

General Act of the Berlin Conference on West Africa, 26 February 1885.

Privy Council Re Southern Rhodesia (1919) A.C. 211.

Treaty of Peace between the Allied and Associated Powers and Austria; Protocol, Declaration and Special Declaration (St. Germain-en-Laye, 10 September 1919) 16 July 1920 Austrian Treaty Series (1920) No. 3.

Montevideo Convention on the Rights and Duties of States (1933), 49 Stat 3097, TS 881.

Bibliography

Books

Abbot, W.W. (1975) *The Colonial Origins of the United States, 1607–1763*. New York: Wiley.

Aikio, P. and Scheinin, M. (eds) (2000) *Operationalizing the Right of Indigenous Peoples to Self-Determination*. Åbo, Finland: Institute for Human Rights, Åbo Akademi University.

Alexandrowicz, C.H. (1967) *An Introduction to the History of the Law of Nations in the East Indies*. Oxford: Oxford University Press.

Alexandrowicz, C.H. (1973) *The European-African Confrontation: A Study in Treaty Making*. Leiden: A.W. Sijthoff.

Alston, P. (ed.) (2005) *Non-State Actors and Human Rights*. Oxford: Oxford University Press.

Anaya, S.J. (2004) *Indigenous Peoples in International Law*. Oxford: Oxford University Press.

Andrews, K.R. (1978) *The Westward Enterprise: English Activities in Ireland, the Atlantic, and America, 1480–1650*. Liverpool: Liverpool University Press.

Anghie, A. (2007) *Imperialism, Sovereignty and the Making of International Law*. Cambridge: Cambridge University Press.

Austin, J. and Austin, S. (1869) *Lectures on Jurisprudence, or, the Philosophy of Positive Law*, ed. R Campbell. London: John Murray.

Auty, R.M. (1998) *Resource Abundance and Economic Development*. New York: Oxford University Press.

Baer, G.W. (1976) *Test Case: Italy, Ethiopia, and the League of Nations*. Stanford, CA: Hoover Press.

Bannister, S. (1838) *British Colonization and Coloured Tribes*. London: W. Ball Paternoster Row.

Belgian Government Information Center (1953) *The Sacred Mission of Civilization: To Which Peoples Should the Benefits Be Extended? The Belgian Thesis*. New York: Belgian Government Information Center.

Bellich, J. (1988) *The New Zealand Wars and the Victorian Interpretation of Racial Conflict*. Auckland: Auckland University Press.

Bennett, G. (1978a) *Aboriginal Rights in International Law*. London: Anthropological Institute [for] Survival International.

Bennett, J.M. and Castles, A.C. (eds) (1979) *A Sourcebook of Australian Legal History: Source Materials from the Eighteenth to the Twentieth Centuries*. Sydney: Law Book Co.

Beyleveld, D. and Brownsword, R. (2007) *Consent in the Law*. Oxford: Hart Publishing.

Blackstone, Sir W. (1765) *Commentaries on the Laws of England in Four Books*. Clark, NJ: The Law Book Exchange.

Blaser, M., Feit, H.A. and Mcrae, G. (2004) *In the Way of Development: Indigenous Peoples, Life Projects and Globalization*. London: Zed Books.

Boas, F. (1921) *The Mind of Primitive Man*. New York: Macmillan Company.

Bolt, C. (1971) *Victorian Attitudes to Race*. London: Routledge and Kegan Paul

Brehm, J.W. (1966) *A Theory of Psychological Reactance*. New York: Academic Press.

Brehm, S. and Brehm, J.W. (1981) *Psychological Reactance: A Theory of Freedom and Control*. New York: Academic Press.

Brennan, F. (1998) *The Wik Debate: Its Impact on Aborigines, Pastoralists and Miners*. Sydney, UNSW Press.

Brierly, J.L. (1963) *The Law of Nations: An Introduction to the International Law of Peace*, 6th edn. Oxford: Clarendon Press.

Brownlie, I. (1963) *International Law and the Use of Force by States*. Oxford: Clarendon Press.

Brownlie, I. (1990) *Principles of Public International Law*, 4th edn. Oxford: Oxford University Press.

Brownlie, I. (1992) *Treaties and Indigenous Peoples: The Robb Lectures*. Oxford: Clarendon Press.

Brownswood, R. (ed.) (1993), *Law and the Public Interest*. Stuttgart: Franz Steiner.

Calhoun, J.C. (1947) *A Disquisition on Government*. New York: Political Science Classics.

Cambrensis, G. and Dimock, J.F. (1867) *Giraldi Cambrensis Opera*. Vol. 5, *Topographia Hibernica, et Expugnatio Hibernica*. London: Longman and Co.

Cariño, J. and Nettleton, G. (1983) *The Philippines: Indigenous Peoples and Development Series: 1 Authoritarian Government, Multinationals and Ancestral Lands*. London: Anti-Slavery Society.

Caruso, E. and Colchester, M. (eds) (2005) *Extracting Promises: Indigenous Peoples, Extractive Industries and the World Bank*, 2nd edn. Manila: Tebtebba Foundation.

Casas, B., De Las, ([1552] 1974) *The Devastation of the Indies: A Brief Account*, trans. H. Briffault. Baltimore, MD: Johns Hopkins University Press.

Casas, B. De Las (1559) *Apologética Historia Sumaria De Las Gentes Destas Indias* 3 Obras Escogidas, 165–6.

Casas, B., De Las (1992) *Obras Completas* [Complete Works]. 14 Vols. Madrid: Alianza Editorial.

Casas, B., De Las, and Abril Castello, V. (eds) (1992a) *Apologética Historia Sumaria de Las Gentes Destas Indias* in *Obras Completas* Volumes 6–8. Madrid: Alianza Editorial (First Published 1559).

Casas, B., de Las, Hernández, R. and Galmés, L. (eds) (1992e) *Tratado Comprobatorio dDel Imperio Soberano y Principado Universal que los Reyes de Castilla y Leon Tienen sobre las Indias*. In *Obras Completas*, Vol. 10. Madrid: Alianza Editorial (First published 1553).

Casas, B., de Las, Losada, A. and Lassègue, M. (eds) ([1958] 1992e) *De Thesauris*, in *Obras Completas* Vol. II.1. Madrid: Alianza Editorial.

Casas, B., de Las and Poole, S. (ed.) (1992b) *In Defense of the Indians: The Defense of the Most Reverend Lord, Don Fray Bartolome De Las Casas, of the Order of Preachers, Late Bishop of Chiapa, Against the Persecutors and Slanderers of the Peoples of the New World Discovered Across the Seas*. Dekalb, IL: Northern Illinois University Press.

Casas, B., De Las and Sanderlin, G.W. (eds) (1992d) *Witness: Writings of Bartolomé De Las Casas*. New York: Orbis Books.

Cassese, A. (1995) *Self Determination of Peoples: A Legal Reappraisal*. Cambridge: Cambridge University Press.

Castellino, J. (2000) *International Law and Self-Determination: The Interplay of the Politics of Territorial Possession with Formulations of Post-Colonial 'National' Identity*. The Hague: Martinus Nijhoff Publishers.

Castellino, J. and Allen, S. (2003) *Title to Territory in International Law: A Temporal Analysis*. Aldershot: Ashgate Publishing Limited.

Castellino, J. and Keane, D. (2009) *Minority Rights in the Pacific Region: A Comparative Legal Analysis*. Oxford: Oxford University Press.

Castellino, J. and Walsh, N. (eds) (2005) *International Law and Indigenous Peoples*. Boston: Martinus Nijhoff.

Castro, D. (2007) *Another Face of Empire: Bartolomé De Las Casas, Indigenous Rights, and Ecclesiastical Imperialism*. Durham, NC: Duke University Press.

Charters, C. and Stavenhagen, R. (eds) (2009) *Making the Declaration Work: The United Nations Declaration on the Rights of Indigenous Peoples*. Copenhagen: IWGIA.

Clapham, A. (2006) *Human Rights Obligations of Non-State Actors*. Oxford: Oxford University Press.

Clavero, B. (2002) *Genocidio y Justicia: La Destrucción de las Indias, Ayer y Hoy*. Madrid: Marcial Pons Historia.

Clavero, B. (2005a) *Tratados con Otros Pueblos y Derechos de Otras Gentes en la Constitución de Estados por América*. Madrid: Centro de Estudio Políticos y Constitucionales.

Comaroff, J.L. and Comaroff, J. (2009) *Ethnicity Inc*. Chicago: University of Chicago Press.

Coomans, F. and Kunnemann, R. (eds) (2012) *Cases and Concepts on Extraterritorial Obligations in the Area of Economic, Social and Cultural Rights*. Cambridge: Intersentia.

Coret, A. (1960) *Le Condominium*. Paris: Librairie Générale de Droit et de Jurisprudence.

Cornell, S. (1988) *The Return of the Native: American Indian Political Resurgence*. New York: Oxford University Press.

Crawford, J. (2007) *The Creation of States in International Law*, 2nd edn. Oxford: Oxford University Press.

Crozier, M.J., Huntington, S.P. and Watanuki, J. (1975) *The Crisis of Democracy*. New York: New York University Press.

Curtin, P. (1964) *The Image of Africa: British Ideas and Action, 1780–1850*. Madison, WI: University of Wisconsin Press.

Cuskelly, K. (2011) *Customs and Constitutions: State Recognition of Customary Law Around the World*. Bangkok: IUCN.

Damerow, H. (1978) *A Critical Analysis of the Foundations of International Law*, Doctoral dissertation. Rutgers University, New Brunswick, NJ.

Davenport, F.G. and Paullin, C.O. (1917) *European Treaties Bearing on the History of the United States and its Dependencies to 1648*. Washington, DC: Carnegie Institution of Washington.

Davidson, B. (1992) *The Black Man's Burden: Africa and the Curse of the Nation-State*. London: James Currey.

De Sadeleer, N. (2002) *Environmental Principles: From Political Slogans to Legal Rules*. Oxford: Oxford University Press.

Donnelly, J. (2003) *Universal Human Rights in Theory and Practice*. Ithaca, NY: Cornell University Press.

Downing, T. (2002) *Indigenous Peoples and Mining Encounters: Strategies and Tactics, Minerals Mining and Sustainable Development Project*. London: International Institute for Environment and Development and World Business Council.

Doyle, C. (forthcoming 2015) *Free Prior and Informed Consent: A Universal Self-Determination Norm and Framework for Consultation and Benefit Sharing*. Copenhagen: IWGIA.

Doyle, C. and Cariño, J. (2013) *Making Free Prior and Informed Consent a Reality: Indigenous Peoples and the Extractive Sector*. London: ECCR, Middlesex University, PIPLinks.

Doyle, C. and Whitmore, A. (2014) *Indigenous Peoples and the Extractive Sector: Towards a Rights Respecting Engagement*. Bagnio: Tebtebba, Piplinks and Middlesex University.

Driedger, E. (1983) *Construction of Statutes*. Toronto: Butterworths.

Dryzek, J.S. (1997) T*he Politics of the Earth: Environmental Discourses*. New York: Oxford University Press.

Dryzek, J.S. (2000) *Deliberative Democracy and Beyond: Liberals, Critics, Contestations*. Oxford: Oxford University Press.

Duncan Hall, H. (1948) *Mandates, Dependencies and Trusteeships*. Washington, DC: Carnegie Endowment for International Peace.

Eccles, W.J. (1972) *France in America*. New York: Harper and Row.

Egerton, H.E. (1897) *A Short History of British Colonial Policy*. London: Methuen and Co.

Egerton, H.E. (1903) *The Origin and Growth of the English Colonies and of Their System of Government*. Oxford: Clarendon Press.

Ehler, S. and Morrall, J. (trans. and ed.) (1967) *Church and State Through the Centuries*. New York: Biblo and Tannen Publishers.

Evans, G., Goodman, J. and Lansbury, N. (eds) (2002) *Moving Mountains: Communities Confront Mining and Globalization*. London: Zed Books.

Falkowski, J.E. (1992) *Indian Law / Race Law: A Five Hundred Year History*. New York: Praeger.

Ferguson, J. (1990) *The Anti-Politics Machines: 'Development,' Depoliticization, and Bureaucratic Power in Lesotho*. New York: Cambridge University Press.

Fernández, I.P. (2001) *El Derecho Hispano-Indiano: Dinamica Social de Su Proceso Histórico Constituyente*. Salamanca: Editorial San Esteban.

Field, D.D. (1876) *Outlines of an International Code*. New York: Baker, Voorhis and Company.

Follesdal, A. and Maliks, R. (eds) (2014) *Kantian Theory and Human Rights*. New York: Routledge.

Francis, J.M. (2006) *Iberia and the Americas: Culture, Politics, and History: A Multidisciplinary Encyclopedia*, Vol. 1. Santa Barbara: ABC-CLIO.

Fukuyama, F. (2011) *The Origins of Political Order*. Croyden: Profile Books.

Galbraith, J.S. (1974) *Crown and Charter: The Early Years of the British South Africa Company*. Berkeley, CA: University of California Press.

Gilbert, J. (2006) *Indigenous Peoples' Land Rights Under International Law: From Victims to Actors*. New York: Transnational Publishers.

Gong, G.W. (1984) *The Standard of Civilization in International Society*. Oxford: Clarendon Press.

Green, L.C. and Dickason, O.P. (1989) *The Law of Nations and the New World*. Alberta: University of Alberta Press.

Grinde, D.A., and Johansen, J.R. (1991) *Exemplar of Liberty: Native America and the Evolution of Democracy*. Berkeley, CA: University of California Press and UCLA American Indian Studies.

Grotius, H. De ([1625] 2004) *On the Law of War and Peace*. Whitefish: Kessinger Publishing.

Grotius, H. De ([1633] 1916) *Mare Liberum* (trans. R. van D. Magoffin). New York: Oxford University Press.

Hakluyt, R. ([1584] 1877) *A Discourse Concerning Western Planting*. Cambridge, MA: Press of J. Wilson.

Hall, W.E. (1890) *A Treatise on International Law*. Oxford: Clarendon Press.

Hall, W.E. (1894) *A Treatise on the Foreign Powers and Jurisdiction of the British Crown*. Oxford: Clarendon Press.

Halleck, H.W. (1878) *Halleck's International Law or Rules Regulating the Intercourse of States in Peace and War*. London: C. Kegan Paul and Co.

Hanke, L. (1949) *The Spanish Struggle for Justice in the Conquest of America*. Philadelphia, PA: University of Pennsylvania Press.

Hanke, L. (1959) *Aristotle and the American Indians: A Study in Race Prejudice in the Modern World*. Chicago: Henry Regneree Company.

Hanke, L. (ed.) (1967) *History of Latin American Civilization: Sources and Interpretations*. Boston: Little, Brown, and Company.

Hannum, H. (1996) *Autonomy, Sovereignty, and Self-Determination: The Accommodation of Conflicting Rights*. Philadelphia, PA: University of Pennsylvania Press.

Himmericky Valernisa, R. (1996) *The Encomierderos of New Spain, 1521–1555*. Austin, TX: University of Texas Press.

Hull, E. (1926) *A History of Ireland and Her People*. Dublin: The Phoenix Publishing Company, Ltd.

Humphreys, M., Sachs, J. and Stiglitz, J.E. (eds) (2007) *Escaping the Resource Curse*. New York: Columbia University Press.

Hyde, C.C. (1922) *International Law Chiefly as Interpreted and Applied by the United States*. Boston: Little Brown & Co,

Icaza Dufour, F. de (ed.) ([1681] 1987) *Recopilación de Leyes de los Reynos de las Indias*, 5 vols. Mexico: Miguel A. Porrúa.

Jennings, F. (1975) *The Invasion of America: Indians, Colonialism, and the Cant of Conquest*. Chapel Hill, NC: University of North Carolina Press.

Jennings, F. (1984) *The Ambiguous Iroquois Empires: The Covenant Chain Confederation of Indian Tribes with English Colonies*. New York: W.W. Norton.

Jennings, F. (ed.) (1985a) *The History and Culture of Iroquois Diplomacy: An Interdisciplinary Guide to the Treaties of the Six Nations and Their League*. Syracuse, NY: Syracuse University Press.

Jennings, R.Y. (1963) *The Acquisition of Territory in International Law*. New York: Oceana Publications.

Kawharu, I.H. (1977) *Maori Land Tenure: Studies of a Changing Institution*. New York: Oxford University Press.

Keal, P. (2003) *European Conquest and the Rights of Indigenous Peoples: The Moral Backwardness of International Society*. Cambridge: Cambridge University Press.

Kingsbury, B. and Straumann, B. (2010) *The Roman Foundations of the Law of Nations: Alberico Gentili and the Justice of Empire*. Oxford: Oxford University Press.

Kirsch, S. (2006) *Reverse Anthropology: Indigenous Analysis of Social and Environmental Relations in New Guinea*. Stanford, CA: Stanford University Press.

Knop, K. (2002) *Diversity and Self-Determination in International Law*. Cambridge: Cambridge University Press.

Koskenniemi, M. (1989) *From Apology to Utopia*. Helsinki: Finnish Lawyers' Publishing Company.

Koskenniemi, M. (2001) *The Gentle Civilizer of Nations: The Rise and Fall of International Law, 1870–1960*. Cambridge: Cambridge University Press.

Kymlicka, W. (1995) *Multicultural Citizenship*. Oxford: Clarendon Press.

Lâm, M.C. (2000) *At the Edge of the State: Indigenous Peoples and Self-Determination*. New York: Transnational Publishers.

Langford, M., Vandenhole, W., Scheinin, M. and Van Genugten, W. (2013) *Global Justice, State Duties: The Extraterritorial Scope of Economic, Social, and Cultural Rights in International Law*. Cambridge: Cambridge University Press.

Lauterpacht, E. (1988) *International Law Reports*. Cambridge: Cambridge University Press.

Lawrance, T.J. (1895) *The Principles of International Law*. Boston: D.C. Heath and Co.

Lenzerini, F. (ed.) (2008) *Reparations for Indigenous Peoples: International and Comparative Perspectives*. Oxford: Oxford University Press.

Levaggi, A. (2002) *Diplomacia Hispano-Indígena en Las Fronteras de América: Historia de Los Tratados entre la Monarquía Española y las Comunidades Aborígenes*. Madrid: Centro de Estudios Políticos y Constitucionales.

Libby, R.T. (1989) *Hawke's Law: The Politics of Mining and Aboriginal Land Rights in Australia.* Nedlands, WA: University of Western Australia Press.

Lindley, M.F. (1926) *The Acquisition and Government of Backward Territory in International Law: A Treatise on the Law and Practice Relating to Colonial Expansion.* London: Longmans, Green and Co.

Lorimer, J. (1883–1884) *The Institutes of the Law of Nation: A Treatise of the Jural Relations of Separate Political Communities.* Edinburgh: William Blackwood and Sons.

Lüdert, J. (2008) *Deliberating Justice: Indigenous Peoples, the World Bank and the Principle of Free Prior Informed Consent.* Munich: Grün Verlag.

Lugard, F.D. (1922) *The Dual Mandate in British Tropical Africa.* Edinburgh and London: William Blackwood and Sons.

Lugard, Lady F.L. (1997) *A Tropical Dependency: An Outline of the Ancient History of the Western Sudan with an Account of the Modern Settlement of Northern Nigeria.* Baltimore, MD: Black Classic Press.

Lukes, S. (1974) *Power: A Radical View.* Old Tappan, NJ: Macmillan.

Lupher, D.A. (2006) *Romans in a New World: Classical Models in Sixteenth-Century Spanish America.* Ann Arbor, MI: University of Michigan Press.

Mackay, A. (1873) *A Compendium of Official Documents Relative to Native Affairs in the South Island* (Vol. One). Wellington: Government Printer. (Republished in microfiche by Wellington: The Alexander Turnbull Library Wellington, 1990).

Mackay, F. (1999) *Los Derechos de los Pueblos Indígenas en el Sistema Internacional.* Lima: FIDH.

Macnutt, F.A. (1909) *Bartholomew de Las Casas: His Life, Apostolate, and Writings.* Cleveland, OH: The Arthur H. Clark Company.

Mander, G. and Tauli-Corpuz, V. (2006) *Paradigm Wars: Indigenous Peoples' Resistance to Globalization.* San Francisco: Sierra Club Books.

Marshall, P.J. (1968) *Problems of Empire: Britain and India, 1757–1813.* London: Allen and Unwin.

Masferré, E. (1999) *A Tribute to the Philippine Cordillera.* Manila: Asiatype, Inc.

Mcnair, A.D. (1961) *The Law of Treaties.* New York: Clarendon Press (1986 edition).

Mcneil, K. (2001) *Emerging Justice? Essays on Indigenous Rights in Canada and Australia.* Saskatoon: Native Law Centre of Canada.

Mcrae, H., Nettheim, G., Anthony, T., Beacroft, L., Brennan, S., Davis, M. and Janke, T. (2009) *Indigenous Legal Issues: Commentary and Materials.* Pyrmont, NSW: Thomson Reuters.

Meisels, T. (2009) *Territorial Rights.* New York: Springer.

Mellor, G.R. (1951) *British Imperial Trusteeship, 1783–1850.* London: Faber and Faber.

Meredith, M. (2006) *The State of Africa: A History of Fifty Years of Independence.* London: Free Press.

Miller, R.J. (2006) *Native America, Discovered and Conquered: Thomas Jefferson, Lewis and Clark, and Manifest Destiny.* Westport, CT: Greenwood Publishing Group.

Miller, R.J., Behrendt, L., Ruru, J. and Lindberg, T. (2010) *Discovering Indigenous Lands: The Doctrine of Discovery in the English Colonies.* Oxford: Oxford University Press.

Montgomery, J. (2001) *Tikal: An Illustrated History of the Ancient Maya Capital.* New York: Hippocrene Books, Inc.

Moody, R. (1992) *The Gulliver File Mines: People and Land, a Global Battleground.* London: Minewatch.

Moody, R. (2007) *Rocks and Hard Places: The Globalization of Mining.* London: Zed Books.

Morales, F. (1979) *Padrón, Teoría y Leyes de la Conquista.* Madrid: Ediciones Cultura Hispánica del Centro Iberoamericano de Cooperación.

Muldoon, J. (1977) *The Expansion of Europe.* Philadelphia, PA: University of Pennsylvania Press.

Muldoon, J. (1979) *Popes, Lawyers and Infidels: The Church and the Non-Christian World, 1250–1550.* Liverpool: Liverpool University Press.

Naito, K., Remy, F. and Williams, J.P. (2001) *Review of Legal and Fiscal Frameworks for Exploration and Mining.* London: Mining Journal Books Limited.

Niezen, R. (2003) *The Origins of Indigenism: Human Rights and the Politics of Identity.* Berkeley, CA: University of California Press.

Nussbaum, A. (1954) *A Concise History of the Law of Nations.* New York: Macmillan Company.

Olcott, C. (1916) *Life of William McKinley.* Boston: Houghton Mifflin Co.

Oppenheim, L. (ed.) (1914) *The Collected Papers of John Westlake on Public International Law.* Cambridge: Cambridge University Press.

Oppenheim, L. (1920) *International Law: A Treatise,* Vol. 1, ed. R. Roxburgh. Clark, NJ: The Lawbook Exchange, Ltd.

Orange, C. (2011) *The Treaty of Waitangi.* Wellington: Bridget Williams Books.

Orique, D.T. (2011) The Unheard Voice of Law in Bartolomé de Las Casas's *Brevisima Relación de la Destrucción de las Indias.* Doctoral dissertation.: University of Oregon.

O'Sullivan, M. and Ó Síocháin, S. (2003) *The Eyes of Another Race: Roger Casement's Congo Report and 1903 Diary.* Dublin: University College Dublin Press.

Özden, M. and Golay, C. (2010) *The Right of Peoples to Self-Determination and to Permanent Sovereignty Over Their Natural Resources Seen from a Human Rights Perspective.* Geneva: CETIM.

Padel, F. and Das, S. (2010) *Out of this Earth: East India, Adivasis and the Aluminium Cartel.* Hyderabad: Orient Black Swan.

Pagayatan, A.T. and Victoria, F.J. (eds) (2001) *A Divided Court, a Conquered People? Case Materials from the Constitutional Challenge to the Indigenous Peoples' Rights Act of 1997.* Quezon City: Legal Rights and Natural Resources Centre Inc, Kasama sa Kalikasan LRC-KSK, Friends of the Earth-Philippines.

Pagden, A.R. (1995) *Lords of All the World: Ideologies of Empire in Spain, Britain and France, C. 1500–C. 1800, and: Theories of Empire, 1450–1800.* New Haven, CT: Yale University Press.

Page, M.E. and Sonnenburg, P.M. (2003) *Colonialism: An International, Social, Cultural, and Political Encyclopedia.* Santa Barbara, CA: ABC-CLIO.

Parellada, A. (ed.) (2007) *Pueblos Indígenas en Aislamiento Voluntario y Contacto Inicial en la Amazonia e el Gran Chaco.* Copenhagen: IWGIA.

Parry, J.H. (1940) *The Spanish Theory of Empire in the Sixteenth Century.* Cambridge: Cambridge University Press.

Phillimore, R. (1871) *Commentaries upon International Law,* 2nd edn. London: Butterworth.

Prescott, W.H. (1847) *History of the Conquest of Peru,* vol. II, ed.. W.H. Munro. Philadelphia, PA: J. B. Lippincott Company (Republished New York: Cosimo Classics, 2007).

Pufendorf, S. (1672) *De Jure Naturae et Gentium Libri Octo.* Oxford: Clarendon Press (1934 edition).

Rens, J. (1961) *The Andean Programme* Geneva: ILO.

Richardson, B.J., Imai, S. and Mcneil, K. (eds) (2009) *Indigenous Peoples and the Law: Comparative and Critical Perspectives.* Oxford: Hart Publishing.

Ritter, D. (2009) *Contesting Native Title.* Sydney: Allen and Unwin.

Robertson, L.G. (2005) *Conquest by Law: How the Discovery of America Dispossessed Indigenous Peoples of Their Lands.* Oxford: Oxford University Press.

Rodríguez-Piñero, L. (2005) *Indigenous Peoples, Postcolonialism, and International Law: The ILO Regime (1919–1989).* Oxford: Oxford University Press.

Rogers, P., Jalal, K. and Boyd, J. (2007) *An Introduction to Sustainable Development.* London: Earthscan.

Rowbottom, J. (2010) *Democracy Distorted: Wealth, Influence and Democratic Politics*. Cambridge: Cambridge University Press.

Roy, A. (2011) *Broken Republic*. London: Penguin Books.

Rufus Davis, S. (1978) *The Federal Principle: A Journey Thought Time in Quest of Meaning*. Berkeley, CA: University of California Press,

Ruggie, J. (2013) *Just Business*. New York: W. W. Norton and Company

Sachs, A. (2009) *The Strange Alchemy of Life and Law*. Oxford: Oxford University Press.

Sanderlin, G. (ed. and trans.) (1971) *Bartolomé de Las Casas: A Selection of His Writings*. New York: Knopf.

Scheppele, K.L. (1988) *Legal Secrets: Equality and Efficiency in the Common Law*. Chicago: University of Chicago Press.

Scott, J.B. (1934) *The Spanish Origin of International Law: Francisco de Vitoria and His Law of Nations*. Oxford: Clarendon Press.

Secret Instructions to Lieutenant Cook (1768) *Letterbook Containing Secret Instructions For Lieutenant James Cook Appointed to Command His Majesty's Bark The Endeavour (30 July 1768)*. Canberra: National Library of Australia. Scanned copy available at: http://www.migrationheritage.nsw.gov.au/exhibition/objectsthroughtime/secret

Sepúlveda, G. De and Losada, A., (eds) (1951) *Democratas Segundo, o de las Justas Causas de la Guerra contra los Indios*. Madrid: CSCI.

Sereni, A.P. (1943) *The Italian Conception of International Law*. New York: Columbia University Press.

Sharma, S.P. (1997) *Territorial Acquisition, Disputes, and International Law*. The Hague: Martinus Nijhoff Publishers.

Shaw, M. (1986) *Title to Territory in Africa: International Legal Issues*. Oxford: Clarendon Press.

Shivji, I.G. (1989) *The Concept of Human Rights in Africa*. London: Council for the Development of Economic and Social Research in Africa.

Simpson, L.B. (ed. and trans.) (1960) *The Laws of Burgos of 1512–1513: Royal Ordinances for the Good Government and Treatment of the Indians*. San Francisco: J. Howell.

Smith, J.H. (1950) *Appeals to the Privy Council from the American Plantations*. New York: Colombia University Press.

Smith, S. (1877) *The History of the Colony of Nova-Caesaria, Or New Jersey*. Burlington, VA: James Parker, William S. Sharp. First published 1765.

Snow, A.H. (1919) *The Question of Aborigines in the Law and Practice of Nations*. Washington, DC: Government Printing Office.

Stanlis, P.J. (1993) *Edmund Burke*. New Brunswick, NJ: Transaction Publishers.

Stavenhagen, R. (1997) Los organizaciones indígenas: actors emergentes en América Latina. in *Comisión Nacional de Derechos Humanos Guía para Pueblos Indígenas*. Mexico: OHCHR.

Stogre, M.J. (1992) *That the World May Believe: The Development of Papal Teaching on Aboriginal Rights*. Sherbrooke, QC: Editions Paulines.

Szablowski, D. (2007) *Transnational Law and Local Struggles Mining, Communities and the World Bank*. Oxford: Hart Publishing.

Tebtebba Foundation (2005) *We Indigenous Peoples: A Compilation of Indigenous Peoples' Declarations*. Baguio City: Tebtebba.

Thomas, H. (2004) *Rivers of Gold: The Rise of the Spanish Empire, from Columbus to Magellan*. New York: Random House.

Thornberry, P. (1992) *International Law and the Rights of Minorities*. Oxford: Clarendon Press.

Thornberry, P. (2002) *Indigenous Peoples and Human Rights*. Manchester: Manchester University Press.

Tierney, B. (1988) *The Crisis of Church and State, 1050–1300: With Selected Documents*. Toronto: University of Toronto Press, the Medieval Academy of America.

Tierney, B. (1997) *The Idea of Natural Rights: Studies on Natural Rights, Natural Law, and Church Law, 1150–1625*. Grand Rapids, MI: Eerdmans Publishing.

Tomuschat, C. (ed.) (1993) *Modern Law of Self-Determination*. The Hague: Martinus Nijhoff Publishers.

Trelease, A.W. ([1960] 1997) *Indian Affairs in Colonial New York: The Seventeenth Century*. Lincoln: University of Nebraska Press.

Tuck, R. (1999) *The Rights of War and Peace: Political Thought and the International Legal Order from Grotius to Kant*. Oxford: Oxford University Press.

Tujan, A. and Bella Guzman, R. (2002) *Globalizing Philippine Mining*. Manila: IBON.

Tully, J. (1980) *A Discourse on Property: John Locke and His Adversaries*. Cambridge: Cambridge University Press.

Tully, J. (1993) *An Approach to Political Philosophy: Locke in Contexts*. Cambridge: Cambridge University Press.

Twiss, T. (1846) *The Oregon Territory: Its History and Discovery*. New York: D. Appleton and Co. (Republished by forgotten books 2013).

Umozurike, U.O. (1997) *The African Charter on Human and Peoples' Rights*. The Hague: Martinus Nijhoff Publishers.

Van Dyke, V. (1985) *Human Rights, Ethnicity and Discrimination*. London: Greenwood Press.

Vanhanen, T. (1990) *The Process of Democratization: A Comparative Study of 147 States, 1980–1988*. New York: Crane Russak.

Van Langenhove, F. (1954) *The Question of the Aborigines Before the United Nations: The Belgian Thesis*. Brussels: Royal Colonial Institute of Belgium, Section of Social and Political Sciences.

Vattel, E.D. ([1758] 2008) *The Law of Nations, or the Principles of Natural Law*, ed. K. Haakonssen. Indianapolis: Liberty Fund.

Vitoria, F. de, Scott, J.B. and Nys, E. (eds) ([1532] 1917) *The Classics of International Law: De Indis et de Ivre Belli Relectiones* [Reflections on the Indians and the Law of War], trans. J. P. Bate. Washington, DC: Carnegie Institute of Washington.

Vladimiri, P. (1414) Opinio Hostiensis. In Hermannus von der Hardt, *Magnum Oecumenicum Constantiense Concilium* (1700) Frankfurt and Leipzig. Reprinted in J. Muldoon (ed.) (1977) *Expansion of Europe: The First Phase*. Philadelphia, PA: University of Pennsylvania Press.

Wallace-Bruce, N.L., (1994) *Claims to Statehood in International Law*. New York: Carlton Press.

Wallerstein, I. (2011) *The Modern World-System* I: *Capitalist Agriculture and the Origins of the European World-Economy in the Sixteenth Century*. Berkeley, CA: University of California Press.

Walters, F.L. (1952) *A History of the League of Nations*, Vol. II. New York: Oxford University Press.

Weckman, L. (1949) *Las Bulas Alejandrinas de 1493 y la Teoría Política del Papado Medieval: Estudio de la Supremacía Papal Sobre Islas, 1091–1493*. Mexico: Universidad Nacional Autonoma de Mexico, Instituto de Historia.

Weddle, R.S. (1985) *Spanish Sea: The Gulf of Mexico in North American Discovery, 1500–1685*. College Station, TX: Texas A and M University Press.

Westlake, J. (1894) *Chapters on the Principles of International Law*. Cambridge: Cambridge University Press.

Westra, L. (2008) *Environmental Justice and the Rights of Indigenous Peoples: International and Domestic Legal Perspectives*. London: Earthscan.

Weyl, M. and Weyl, R. (2008) *Sortir le Droit International du Placard*. Geneva: Cetim.

Wheaton, H. (1866) *Elements of International Law*. London: Sampson Low Son and Co.

White, R. (1991) *The Middle Ground: Indians, Empires, and Republics in the Great Lakes Region, 1650–1815*. Cambridge: Cambridge University Press.

Whitmore, A., Nettleton, G. and Abayao, L. (eds) (2012) *Pitfalls and Pipelines: Indigenous Peoples and Extractive Industries*. Manila: Tebtebba.

Williams, R.A. Jr (1990) *The American Indian in Western Legal Thought: The Discourses of Conquest*. Oxford: Oxford University Press.

Williams, R.A. Jr (1999) *Linking Arms Together: American Indian Treaty Visions of Law and Peace, 1600–1800*. New York: Routledge.

Williams, R.A. Jr. (2005) *Like a Loaded Weapon: The Rehnquist Court, Indian Rights, and the Legal History of Racism in America*. Minneapolis, MN: University of Minnesota Press.

World Commission on Dams (2000) *Dams and Development, A New Framework for Decision Making: The Report of the World Commission on Dams*. London: Earthscan.

Wright, Q. (1930) *Mandates Under the League of Nations*. Chicago: University of Chicago Press.

Wright Mills, C. ([1956] 2000) *The Power Elite*. Oxford: Oxford University Press.

Xanthaki, A. (2007) *Indigenous Rights and United Nations Standards Self-Determination, Culture and Land*. Cambridge: Cambridge University Press.

Young, I.M. (2000) *Inclusion and Democracy*. Oxford: Oxford University Press.

Zavala, S. (1963) *La Defensa de los Derechos del Hombre en América Latina (Siglos XVI–XVIII)*. Paris: UNESCO.

Zibechi, R. (2012) *Territories in Resistance: A Cartography of Latin American Social Movements* trans. R. Ramor. Oakland, CA: AK Press.

Book chapters

Ahren, M. (2007) The UN Declaration on the Rights of Indigenous Peoples: How Was it Adopted and Why Is It Significant? in *The UN Declaration on the Rights of Indigenous Peoples, What Made it Possible? The Work and Process Beyond the Final Adoption 4*. Gáldu Čála, Tromso: Gáldu Resource Centre for the Rights of Indigenous Peoples, 84–129.

Åhrén, M. (2009) The Provisions on Lands, Territories and Natural Resources in the UN Declaration on the Rights of Indigenous Peoples: An Introduction, in C Charters and R Stavenhagen (eds) *Making the Declaration Work: The United Nations Declaration on the Rights of Indigenous Peoples*. Copenhagen: IWGIA, 200–215.

Akpan, G.S. (2005) Host Community Hostility to Mining Projects: A New Generation of Risk? in E Bastida, T W. Waelde, and J. Warden-Fernández (eds) *International and Comparative Mineral Law and Policy: Trends and Prospects*. Dordrecht: Kluwer Law International, 311–331.

Alfredsson, G. (1998) Indigenous Peoples and Autonomy, in M. Suksi (ed.) *Autonomy: Applications and Implications*. The Hague: Martinus Nijhoff Publishers, 125–138.

Allen, S. (2011) The UN Declaration on the Rights of Indigenous Peoples and the Limits of the International Legal Project, in S. Allen and A. Xanthaki (eds) *Reflections on the UN Declaration on the Rights of Indigenous Peoples*. Oxford: Hart Publishing, 255–258.

Alston, P. (2005) The "Not-a-Cat" Syndrome: Can the International Human Rights Regime Accommodate Non-State Actors? In P. Alston (ed.) *Non-State Actors and Human Rights*. Oxford: Oxford University Press, 3–36.

Altman, J. (2009) Benefit Sharing is No Solution to Development: Experiences from Mining on Aboriginal Land in Australia, in R. Wynberg, D. Schroeder and R. Chennells (eds) *Indigenous Peoples, Consent and Benefit Sharing: Lessons from the San-Hoodia Case*. London: Springer, 285–301.

Anaya, S.J. (2009) The Right of Indigenous Peoples to Self-Determination in the Post-Declaration Era, in C. Charters and R. Stavenhagen (eds) *Making the Declaration Work: The United Nations Declaration on the Rights of Indigenous Peoples*. Copenhagen: IWGIA, 184–199.

Bank, A. (1999) Losing Faith in the Civilizing Mission: The Premature Decline of Humanitarian Liberalism at the Cape, 1840–60, in M. Daunton and R. Halpern (eds) *Empire and Others: British Encounters with Indigenous Peoples, 1600–1850*. London: UCL Press.

Bannister, K. (2008) Non-Legal Instruments for the Protection of Intangible Cultural Heritage: Key Roles for Ethical Codes and Community Protocols, in C. Bell and R. K. Paterson (eds) *Protection of First Nations Cultural Heritage Laws, Policy, and Reform*. Vancouver: UBC Press, 278–310.

Barsh, R.L. (2005) Trade and Intellectual Property Rights: How Do They Affect Indigenous Knowledge, Local Plant Varieties, and the Other "Ecological and Intellectual Resources" of Indigenous Peoples? in *Globalization, Cultural Resources and Indigenous Peoples, Forum for Development Cooperation with Indigenous Peoples Conference Report*. Tromso: University of Tromso Centre for Sami Studies, 4–7.

Barth, F. (1998) Introduction, in F. Barth (ed.) *Ethnic Groups and Boundaries: The Social Organization of Culture Difference*. Long Grove, CA: Waveland Press, 10–38.

Barume, A. (2009) Responding to the Concerns of the African States, in C. Charters and R. Stavenhagen (eds) *Making the Declaration Work: The United Nations Declaration on the Rights of Indigenous Peoples*. Copenhagen: IWGIA, 170–182.

Bebbington, A. (2010) Extractive Industries and Stunted States: Conflict, Responsibility and Institutional Change in the Andes, in R. Raman (ed.) *Corporate Social Responsibility: Discourses, Practices and Perspectives*. London: Palgrave Macmillan, 97–115.

Bell, C. and Asch, M. (1997) Challenging Assumptions: The Impact of Precedent in Aboriginal Rights Litigation, in M. Asch (ed.), *Aboriginal and Treaty Rights in Canada: Essays on Law, Equality and Respect for Difference*. Vancouver: UBC Press, 38–74.

Bennagen, P.L. (2007) "Amending" IPRA Negotiating Autonomy, Upholding the Right to Self-Determination, in A.B. Gatmaytan (ed.) *Negotiating Autonomy: Case Study on Philippine Indigenous Peoples Land Rights*. Quezon City/Copenhagen: LRC/IWGIA, 179–198.

Bradlow, D.D. (2012) The Reform of the Governance of the IFIs: A Critical Assessment, in H. Cisse, D.D. Bradlow and B. Kingsbury (eds) *The World Bank Legal Review*. Washington, DC: The World Bank, 37–58.

Breen, L.A. (1999) Praying with the Enemy: Daniel Gooking, King Philip's War, and the Dangers of Intercultural Mediatorship, in M. Daunton and R. Halpern (eds) *Empire and Others: British Encounters with Indigenous Peoples, 1600–1850*. London, UCL Press, 101–122.

Bull, H. (1984) European States and African Political Communities, in H. Bull and A. Watson (eds) *The Expansion of International Society*. Oxford: Clarendon Press, 99–114.

Burroughs, P. (1999) Imperial Institutions and the Government of Empire, in A. Porter (ed.) *The Oxford History of the British Empire*, Vol. III. Oxford: Oxford University Press, 170–197.

Campbell, B. (2005) The Challenges of Development. Mining Codes in Africa, in E. Bastida, T.W. Waelde and J. Warden-Fernández (eds) *International and Comparative Mineral Law and Policy: Trends and Prospects*. The Hague: Kluwer Law International, 800–816.

Carling, J. (2010) Indigenous Peoples' Right to Free, Prior and Informed Consent (FPIC) in Policy Making and Development, in Forum Conference 2010, *Indigenous Participation in Policy-Making: Ideals, Realities and Possibilities, Forum for Development Cooperation with Indigenous Peoples Conference Report*. Tromso: University of Tromso Centre for Sami Studies, 28–37.

Carmen, A. (2011) The Right to Free Prior and Informed Consent: A Framework for Harmonious Relations and New Processes for Redress, in J. Hartley, P. Joffe and J. Preston (eds) *Realizing the UN Declaration on the Rights of Indigenous Peoples: Triumph, Hope, and Action*. Saskatoon: Purich Publishing Ltd, 120–134.

Carro, V.D. (1971) The Spanish Theological-Juridical Renaissance and the Ideology of Bartolomé de Las Casas, in J. Friede and B. Keen (eds) *Bartolomé de Las Casas in History*. DeKalb, IL: Northern Illinois University Press, 237–349.

Cassese, A. (1998) *Self-Determination of Peoples: A Legal Reappraisal*. Cambridge: Cambridge University Press.

Castellino, J. (2011) Indigenous Rights and the Right to Development: Emerging Synergies or Collusion? in S. Allen and A. Xanthaki (eds) *Reflections on the UN Declaration on the Rights of Indigenous Peoples*. Oxford: Hart Publishing, 367–386.

Castellino, J. and Doyle, C. (forthcoming, 2015) Who Are 'Indigenous Peoples'? An Examination of Concepts Concerning Group Membership in the United Nations Declaration on the Rights of Indigenous Peoples, in M. Weller and J. Hohmann (eds) *The UN Declaration on the Rights of Indigenous Peoples: A Commentary*.

Chan, T.M. (2004) The Richtersveld Challenge: South Africa Finally Adopts Aboriginal Title, in R.K. Hitchcock and D. Vinding (eds) *Indigenous Peoples' Rights in Southern Africa*. Copenhagen: IWGIA, 114–133.

Charters, C. (2009) Indigenous Peoples and International Law and Policy, in B.J. Richardson, S. Imai and K. Mcneil (eds) *Indigenous Peoples and the Law*. Oxford: Hart Publishing, 161–194.

Chávez, L.E. (2010) The Declaration on the Rights of Indigenous Peoples: Breaking the Impasse: the Middle Ground, in C. Charters and R. Stavenhagen (eds) *Making the Declaration Work: The United Nations Declaration on the Rights of Indigenous Peoples*. Copenhagen: IWGIA, 96–107.

Clapman, A. (2011) Corporations and Criminal Complicity, in G. Nystuen, A. Follesdal, and O. Mestad (eds) *Human Rights, Corporate Complicity and Disinvestment*. Cambridge: Cambridge University Press, 222–242.

Clarke, J. (2009) Australia: The White House with Lovely Dot Paintings Whose Inhabitants Have 'Moved On' from History? In B.J. Richardson, S. Imai and K. Mcneil (eds) *Indigenous Peoples and the Law: Comparative and Critical Perspectives*. Oxford: Hart Publishing, 81–110.

Colley, P. (2002) Political Economy of Mining, in G. Evans, J. Goodman and N. Lansbury (eds) *Moving Mountains: Communities Confront Mining and Globalization*. London: Zed Books, 19–36.

Comas, J. (1971) Historical Reality and the Detractors of Father Las Casas, in J. Friede and B. Keen (eds) *Bartolomé de Las Casas in History: Toward an Understanding of the Man and His Work*. Dekalb, IL: Northern Illinois University Press, 487–539.

Crawford, J. (1992) The Rights of Peoples: Peoples or Governments? in J. Crawford (ed.) *The Rights of Peoples*. Oxford: Clarendon Press, 55–67.

Cunha, M. da. (2007) El BID y los Pueblos Aislados Política Institucional y Cooperación Regional, in *Pueblos Indígenas en Aislamiento Voluntario y Contacto Inicial en la Amazonia y el Gran Chaco*. Copenhagen: IWGIA, 328–332.

Daes, E.I. (2000) The Spirit and Letter of the Right to Self-Determination of Indigenous Peoples: Reflections on Making of the United Nations Draft Declaration, in P. Aikio and M. Scheinin (eds) *Operationalizing the Right of Indigenous Peoples to Self-Determination*. Åbo, Finland: Institute for Human Rights, Åbo Akademi University, 67–83.

Daes, E.I. (2010) The Contribution of the Working Group on Indigenous Populations to the Genesis and Evolution of the UN Declaration on the Rights of Indigenous Peoples, in C. Charters and R. Stavenhagen (eds) *Making the Declaration Work: The United Nations Declaration on the Rights of Indigenous Peoples*. Copenhagen: IWGIA, 48–76.

Daes, E.I. (2011) The UN Declaration on the Rights of Indigenous Peoples: Background and Appraisal, in S. Allen and A. Xanthaki (eds) *Reflections on the UN Declaration on the Rights of Indigenous Peoples*. Oxford: Hart Publishing, 11–40.

De Schutter, O. (2012) Foreword, in F. Coomans and R. Künnemann (eds) *Cases and Concepts on Extraterritorial Obligations in the Area of Economic, Social and Cultural Rights*. Cambridge: Intersentia, v–x.

Diffie, B.W. (1967) Population Statistics and Social History, in L. Hanke (ed.) *History of Latin American Civilization: Sources and Interpretations*, vol. 1: *The Colonial Experience*. Boston: Little, Brown and Company, 193–200.

Donelan, M. (1984) Spain and the Indies, in H. Bull and A. Watson (eds) *The Expansion of International Society*. Oxford: Clarendon Press, 75–85.

Doyle, C. (2010a) The Effectiveness of Legal and Non-Legal Remedies for Addressing the Rights of Indigenous Peoples at Mindoro Island and Elsewhere, in *Indigenous Participation in Policy-Making: Ideals, Realities and Possibilities, Forum for Development Cooperation with Indigenous Peoples Conference Report*. Tromso: University of Tromso Centre for Sami Studies, 85–94.

Doyle, C. and Gilbert, J. (2009) Indigenous Peoples and Globalization: From "Development Aggression" to "Self-Determined Development", in *European Yearbook of Minority Issues* Vol. 8. Leiden: Martinus Nijhoff Publishers, 219–262.

Dutfield, G. (2009) Protecting the Rights of Indigenous Peoples: Can Prior Informed Consent Help? in R. Wynberg, D. Schroeder, and R. Chennells (eds) *Indigenous Peoples, Consent and Benefit: Sharing Lessons from the San-Hoodia Case*. London: Springer, 53–68.

Eide, A. (2007) Rights of Indigenous Peoples: Achievements in International Law During the Last Quarter of a Century, in *The UN Declaration on the Rights of Indigenous Peoples: What Made it Possible? The Work and Process Beyond the Final Adoption 4*. Gáldu Čála, Tromso: Gáldu Resource Centre for the Rights of Indigenous Peoples, 40–82.

Eide, A. (2009) The Indigenous Peoples, the Working Group on Indigenous Populations and the Adoption of the UN Declaration on the Rights of Indigenous Peoples, in C. Charters and R. Stavenhagen (eds) *Making the Declaration Work: The United Nations Declaration on the Rights of Indigenous Peoples*. Copenhagen: IWGIA, 32–47.

Errico, S. (2011) The Controversial Issue of Natural Resources, in S. Allen and A. Xanthaki (eds) *Reflections on the UN Declaration on the Rights of Indigenous Peoples*. Oxford: Hart Publishing, 329–366.

Erueti, A. (2011) The International Labour Organization and the Internationalisation of the Concept of Indigenous Peoples, in S. Allen and A. Xanthaki (eds) *Reflections on the UN Declaration on the Rights of Indigenous Peoples*. Oxford: Hart Publishing, 93–120.

Fenton, W.M. (1985) Structure, Continuity, and Change in the Process of Iroquois Treaty Making, in F. Jennings (ed.) *The History and Culture of Iroquois Diplomacy: An Interdisciplinary Guide to the Treaties of the Six Nations and Their League*. Syracuse, NY: Syracuse University Press, 3–36.

Fisch, J. (1988) Africa as *terra nullius*: The Berlin Conference and International Law, in S. Förster, W.J. Mommsen and R. Robinson (eds) *Bismarck, Europe and Africa: The Berlin Africa Conference 1884–1885 and the Onset of Partition*. Oxford: Oxford University Press, 347–375.

Foster, M.K. (1985) Another Look at the Function of *Wampum* in Iroquois-White Councils, in F. Jennings (ed.) *The History and Culture of Iroquois Diplomacy: An Interdisciplinary Guide to the Treaties of the Six Nations and Their League*. Syracuse, NY: Syracuse University Press, 99–114.

Friede, J. (1971) Las Casas and Indigenism in the Sixteenth Century, in J. Friede and B. Keen (eds) *Bartolomé de Las Casas in History*. DeKalb, IL: Northern Illinois University Press, 127–234.

Gilbert, J. and Doyle, C. (2011) A New Dawn over the Land: Shedding Light on Collective Ownership and Consent, in S. Allen and A. Xanthaki (eds) *Reflections on the UN Declaration on the Rights of Indigenous Peoples*. Oxford: Hart Publishing.

Goodall, H. (1999) Authority under Challenge: Pikampul Land and Queen Victoria's Law during the British Invasion of Australia, in M. Daunton and R. Halpern (eds) *Empire and Others: British Encounters with Indigenous Peoples, 1600–1850*. London: UCL Press, 260–279.

Goodland, R. (1985) Tribal Peoples and Economic Development: The Human Ecological Dimension, in J.A. McNeely and D.C. Pitt (eds) *Culture and Conservation: The Human Dimension in Environmental Planning*. Copenhagen: IUCN, 13–32.

Goodland, R. (2008) The Institutionalized Use of Force in Economic Development: With Special Reference to the World Bank, in C.L. Soskolne (ed.) *Sustaining Life on Earth*. Lanham, MD: Lexington Books, 339–354.

Goodland, R. and Wicks, C. (2009) *Philippines: Mining or Food?* Doyle C., E. Teague, S. Sexton and F. Nally (eds) London: Society of St Colombans.

Guri Yangmaadome, B., Banuoko Faabelangne, D., Kanchebe Derbile, E., Hiemstra, W. and Verschuuren, B. (2012) Sacred Groves Versus Gold Mines: Biocultural Community Protocols, in *Ghana Biodiversity and Culture: Exploring Community Protocols, Rights and Consent*. London: IIED, 121–130.

Henriksen, J.B. (2009) The UN Declaration on the Rights of Indigenous Peoples: Some Key Issues and Events in the Process, in C. Charters and R. Stavenhagen (eds) *Making the Declaration Work: The United Nations Declaration on the Rights of Indigenous Peoples*. Copenhagen: IWGIA, 78–85.

Hunt, M. (2005) Indigenous Land Rights and their Impact on the Minerals Industry, in E. Bastida, T.W. Waelde, and J. Warden-Fernández (eds) *International and Comparative Mineral Law and Policy: Trends and Prospects*. The Hague: Kluwer Law International, 661–680.

Imai, S. (2009) Indigenous Self-Determination and the State, in B.J. Richardson, S. Imai and K. Mcneil (eds) *Indigenous Peoples and the Law*. Oxford: Hart Publishing, 285–314.

Jennings, F. (1985b) Introduction, in F. Jennings (ed.) *The History and Culture of Iroquois Diplomacy: An Interdisciplinary Guide to the Treaties of the Six Nations and Their League*. Syracuse, NY: Syracuse University Press, xiii–xviii.

Jorgensen, D. (2007) Clan-Finding, Clan-Making and the Politics of Identity in a Papua New Guinea Mining Project, in J. Weiner and K. Glaskin (eds) *Customary Land Tenure and Registration in Australia and Papua New Guinea*. Canberra: Australian National University E Press, 57–69.

Keen, B. (1971) Introduction: Approaches to Las Casas, 1535–1970, in J. Friede and B. Keen (eds) *Bartolomé de Las Casas in History*. DeKalb, IL: Northern Illinois University Press, 3–63.

Kingsbury, B. (1999) Operational Policies of International Institutions as Part of the Law-Making Process: The World Bank and Indigenous Peoples, in G.S. Goodwin-Gill and S. Talmon (eds) *The Reality of International Law: Essays in Honour of Ian Brownlie*. Oxford: Clarendon Press, 323–342.

Kingsbury, B. (2000) Reconstructing Self-determination: A Relational Approach, in P. Aikio and M. Scheinin (eds) *Operationalizing the Right of Indigenous Peoples to Self-Determination*. Åbo, Finland: Institute for Human Rights, Åbo Akademi University, 19–37.

Kymlicka, W. (2011) Beyond the Indigenous/Minority Dichotomy, in S. Allen and A. Xanthaki (eds) *Reflections on the UN Declaration on the Rights of Indigenous Peoples*. Oxford: Hart Publishing, 183–208.

Littlechild, Chief W. (2011) Consistent Advocacy, Treaty Rights and the UN Declaration, in J. Hartley, P. Joffe and J. Preston (eds) *Realizing the UN Declaration on the Rights of Indigenous Peoples: Triumph, Hope, and Action*. Saskatoon: Purich Publishing Ltd, 112–119.

Lynch, O. (2005) Concepts and Strategies for Promoting Legal Recognition of Community-Based Property Rights: Insights from the Philippines and Other Nations, in J.P. Brosius, A. Lowenhaupt Tsing and C. Zerner (eds) *Communities and Conservation: Histories and Politics of Community-Based Natural Resource Management*. Walnut Creek, CA: Alta Mira Press, 391–426.

Masaki, K. (2009) Recognition or Misrecognition? Pitfalls of Indigenous Peoples' Free, Prior, and Informed Consent (FPIC), in S. Hickey and D. Mitlin (eds) *Rights-Based Approaches to Development: Exploring the Potential Pitfalls*. Greenwich, CT: Kumarian Press, 69–86.

M'baye, K. (1978) Les Droits de l'Homme en Afrique, in K. Vasak (ed.) *Les Dimensions Internationales des Droits de l'Homme*. Paris: UNESCO, 645–663.

Minde, H. (1996) The Making of an International Movement of Indigenous Peoples, in F. Horn (ed.) *Minorities and Their Right of Political Participation*. Rovaniemi: Lapland University Press, 90–128.

Moore, R.J. (1999) Imperial India, 1858–1914, in A. Porter (ed.) *The Oxford History of the British Empire*, vol. III. Oxford: Oxford University Press, 422–446.

Morgan, P.D. (1999) Encounters between British and "Indigenous" Peoples, c.1500–c.1800, in M. Daunton and R. Halpern (eds) *Empire and Others: British Encounters with Indigenous Peoples 1600–1850*. London: UCL Press, 42–78.

Moses, T. (2002) Renewal of the Nation, in E-I. A. Daes, G. Alfredsson and M. Stavropoulou (eds) *Justice Pending: Indigenous Peoples and Other Good Causes: Essays in Honour of Erica-Irene A. Daes*. The Hague: Martinus Nijhoff Publishers, 57–68.

Myntti, K. (2000) The Right of Indigenous Peoples to Self-Determination and Effective Participation, in P. Aikio and M. Scheinin (eds) *Operationalizing the Right of Indigenous Peoples to Self-Determination*. Åbo, Finland: Institute for Human Rights, Åbo Akademi University, 85–130.

Ove Varsi, M. (2010) The Sami Parliament: Its Relevance as a Model in Democratic and Undemocratic States, in *Forum Conference 2010, Indigenous Participation in Policy-making: Ideals, Realities and Possibilities*. Tromso: University of Tromso, 38–46.

Porter, A. (1999a) North American Experience and British Missionary Encounters in Africa and the Pacific, c. 1800–50, in M. Daunton and R. Halpern (eds) *Empire and Others: British Encounters with Indigenous Peoples, 1600–1850*. London: UCL Press, 345–363.

Porter, A. (1999b) Introduction, in A. Porter (ed.) *The Oxford History of the British Empire*, Vol. III. Oxford: Oxford University Press, 1–30.

Pritchard, S. (1998) Working Group on Indigenous Populations: Mandate, Standard-Setting and Future Perspectives, in S. Pritchard (ed.) *Indigenous Peoples, the United Nations and Human Rights*. Annandale, Australia: Federation Press, 40–62.

Quane, H. (2011) The UN Declaration on the Rights of Indigenous Peoples: New Directions for Self-Determination and Participatory Rights? In S. Allen and A. Xanthaki (eds) *Reflections on the UN Declaration on the Rights of Indigenous Peoples*. Oxford: Hart Publishing, 259–288.

Regino Montes, A. and Torres Cisneros, G. (2009) The United Nations Declaration on the Rights of Indigenous Peoples: The Foundation of a New Relationship between

Indigenous Peoples, States and Societies, in C. Charters and R. Stavenhagen (eds) *Making the Declaration Work: The United Nations Declaration on the Rights of Indigenous Peoples*. Copenhagen: IWGIA, 138–169.

Richardson, B.J. (2009a) The Dydic Character of US Indian Law, in B.J. Richardson, S. Imai and K. Mcneil (eds) *Indigenous Peoples and the Law: Comparative and Critical Perspectives*. Oxford: Hart Publishing, 51–80.

Richardson, B.J. (2009b) The Ties That Bind: Indigenous Peoples and Environmental Governance, in B.J. Richardson, S. Imai and K. Mcneil (eds) *Indigenous Peoples and the Law*. Oxford: Hart Publishing, 337–370.

Risse, T. and Sikkink, K. (1999) The Socialization of International Human Rights Norms into Domestic Practices: Introduction, in T. Risse, S. Ropp and K. Sikkink (eds) *The Power of Human Rights: International Norms and Domestic Change*. Cambridge: Cambridge University Press, 1–38.

Rodríguez-Piñero, L. (2011) The Inter-American System and the UN Declaration on the Rights of Indigenous Peoples: Mutual Reinforcement, in S. Allen and A. Xanthaki (eds) *Reflections on the UN Declaration on the Rights of Indigenous Peoples*. Oxford: Hart Publishing, 457–484.

Ruru, J. (2009)The Maori Encounter with Aotearoa: New Zealand's Legal System, in B.J. Richardson, S. Imai and K. Mcneil (eds) *Indigenous Peoples and the Law: Comparative and Critical Perspectives*. Oxford: Hart Publishing, 111–134.

Salim, E. (2005) Business as Usual with Marginal Change: EIR Final Comment on the World Bank Group Management Response to the Extractive Industry Review (Jakarta, 2004), reproduced in E. Caruso and M. Colchester (eds) *Extracting Promises: Indigenous Peoples, Extractive Industries and the World Bank*. Manila: Tebtebba Foundation, 340–350.

Sanders, D. (1985) Aboriginal Rights: The Search for Recognition in International Law, in M. Boldt, J. Long and L. Little Bear (eds) *The Quest for Justice: Aboriginal Peoples and Aboriginal Rights*. Toronto: University of Toronto Press, 292–303.

Sanders, D. (1998) The Legacy of Deskaheh: Indigenous Peoples as International Actors, in C. Cohen (ed.) *Human Rights of Indigenous Peoples*. Ardsley: Transnational Publishers, 73–88.

Schabas, W.A. (2005) Cultural Genocide and the Protection of the Right of Existence of Aboriginal and Indigenous Groups, in J. Castellino and N. Walsh (eds) *International Law and Indigenous Peoples*. Boston: Martinus Nijhoff Publishers, 117–132.

Schabas, W.A. (2011) On the Binding Nature of the Findings of the Treaty Bodies, in M. Cherif Bassiouni and W.A. Schabas (eds) *New Challenges for the UN Human Rights Machinery*. Cambridge: Intersentia, 97–108.

Scheinin, M. (2000) The Right to Self-Determination Under the Covenant on Civil and Political Rights, in P. Aikio and M. Scheinin (eds) *Operationalizing the Right of Indigenous Peoples to Self-Determination*. Åbo, Finland: Institute for Human Rights, Åbo Akademi University, 179–199.

Scheinin, M. (2005) What Are Indigenous Peoples? In N. Ghanea-Hercock and A. Xanthaki (eds) *Minorities, Peoples, and Self-Determination: Essays in Honour of Patrick Thornberry*. Boston: Martinus Nijhoff Publishers, 3–13.

Schroeder, D. (2009) Justice and Benefit Sharing, in R. Wynberg, D. Schroeder, and R. Chennells (eds) *Indigenous Peoples, Consent and Benefit Sharing: Lessons from the San-Hoodia Case*. London: Springer, 11–26.

Ssenyonjo, M. (2011) Economic, Social and Cultural Rights in the African Charter, in M. Ssenyonjo (ed.) *The African Regional Human Rights System: 30 Years After the African Charter on Human and Peoples' Rights*. Boston: Martinus Nijhoff Publishers, 55–100.

Stavenhagen, R. (2011) The Rights of Indigenous Peoples to Work: The Challenge Ahead, in S. Allen and A. Xanthaki (eds) *Reflections on the UN Declaration on the Rights of Indigenous Peoples*. Oxford: Hart Publishing, 147–170.

Strelein, L. (1996) The Price of Compromise: Should Australia Ratify ILO Convention 169? In C. Bird, G. Martin and J. Nielsen (eds) *Majah: Indigenous Peoples and the Law*. Leichhardt, NSW: Federation Press, 63–86.

Sturtevant, W.C. (1974) Woodsmen and Villagers of the East, in J.B. Billard (ed.) *The World of the American Indian*. Washington, DC: National Geographic Society, 101–149.

Suarez-Franco, A.M. (2013) Land Grabbing South America (Inter-American Human Rights Commission), in M. Gibney and W. Vandenhole (eds) *Litigating Transnational Human Rights Obligations: Alternative Judgments*. New York: Routledge, 283–300.

Swepston, L. (1998) The ILO Indigenous and Tribal Peoples Convention (No. 169): Eight Years After Adoption, in C.P. Cohen (ed.) *Human Rights of Indigenous Peoples*. New York: Transnational Publishers, 17–36.

Swepston, L. (2005) Indigenous Peoples in International Law and Organizations, in J. Castellino and N. Walsh (eds) *International Law and Indigenous Peoples*. Boston: Martinus Nijhoff Publishers, 53–66.

Thornberry, P. (1993) The Democratic or Internal Aspect of Self-Determination with Some Remarks on Federalism, in C. Tomuschat (ed.) *Modern Law of Self-Determination*. Boston: Martinus Nijhoff Publishers, 128–131.

Thornberry, P. (2000) Self-Determination and Indigenous Peoples: Objections and Responses, in P. Aikio and M. Scheinin (eds) *Operationalizing the Right of Indigenous Peoples to Self-Determination*. Åbo, Finland: Institute for Human Rights, Åbo Akademi University, 39–64.

Thornberry, P. (2011) Rights of Indigenous Peoples into CERD Practice, in S. Allen and A. Xanthaki (eds) *Reflections on the UN Declaration on the Rights of Indigenous Peoples*. Oxford: Hart Publishing, 61–92.

Tobin, B. (2014) *Indigenous Peoples, Customary Law and Human Rights – Why Living Law Matters*. London: Routledge.

Urteaga Crovetto, P. (2009) Fundamentación Jurídica del Derecho a la Consulta y al Consentimiento Libre, Previo e Informado en el Marco del Convenio 169 de la OIT; el Caso de Perú, in *El Derecho a la Consulta Previa en América Latina*. Bogotá: Instituto Latinoamericano de Servicios Legales Alternativos, 123–162.

Valbuena Wouriyu, A. (2005) Colombia: License to Plunder, in E. Caruso and M. Colchester (eds) *Extracting Promises: Indigenous Peoples, Extractive Industries and the World Bank*. Manila: Tebtebba Foundation, 157–163.

Van Dyke, V. (1995) The Individual, the State, and Ethnic Communities in Political Theory, in W. Kymlicka (ed.) *The Rights of Minority Cultures*. Oxford: Oxford University Press, 31–56.

Van Genugten, W. (2003) Tilburg Guiding Principles on World Bank, IMF and Human Rights, Tilburg University, The Netherlands, April 2002, reproduced in P. Hunt and S. Mathews (eds) *World Bank, IMF and Human Rights*. Nijmegen: Wolf Legal Publishers, 247–255.

Vermeylen, S. (2009) Trading Traditional Knowledge: San Perspectives from South Africa, Namibia and Botswana, in R. Wynberg, D. Schroeder and R. Chennells (eds) *Indigenous Peoples, Consent and Benefit Sharing Lessons from the San-Hoodia Case*. London: Springer, 193–210.

Voyiakis, E. (2011) Voting in the General Assembly: Evidence of Customary International Law? In S. Allen and A. Xanthaki (eds) *Reflections on the UN Declaration on the Rights of Indigenous Peoples*. Oxford: Hart Publishing, 209–224.

Walters, M.D. (2009) The Emergence of Indigenous Rights Law in Canada, in B.J. Richardson, S. Imai and K. Mcneil (eds) *Indigenous Peoples and the Law*. Oxford: Hart Publishing, 21–50.

Willemsen Díaz, A. (2009) How Indigenous Peoples' Rights Reached the UN, in C. Charters and R. Stavenhagen (eds) *Making the Declaration Work: The United Nations Declaration on the Rights of Indigenous Peoples*. Copenhagen: IWGIA, 16–31.

Woods, N. (2003) The United States and the International Financial Institutions: Power and Influence with the World Bank and the IMF, in R. Foot, N. Macfarlane and M. Mastanduno (eds) *US Hegemony and International Organizations*. Oxford: Oxford University Press, 92–114.

Wynberg, R., Schroeder, D. and Chennells, R. (2009) Introduction, in R. Wynberg, D. Schroeder and R. Chennells (eds) *Indigenous Peoples, Consent and Benefit Sharing Lessons from the San-Hoodia Case*. London: Springer, 3–10.

Yanez, A. ([1942] 2014) *Fray Bartolome de las Casas El Conquistador Conquistado*. Mexico: Joaquin Mortiz.

Young, I.M. (1995) Together in Difference: Transforming the Logic of Group Political Conflict, in W. Kymlicka (ed.) *The Rights of Minority Cultures*. Oxford: Oxford University Press, 155–176.

Youngblood Henderson, J. (1985) The Doctrine of Aboriginal Rights in Western Legal Tradition, in M. Boldt, J.A Long and L. Little Bear (eds) *The Quest for Justice*. Toronto: University of Toronto Press, 185–220.

Journal articles

Aguilar, G., Lafosse, S., Rojas, H. and Steward, R. (2010) The Constitutional Recognition of Indigenous Peoples in Latin America, 2(2) *Pace International Law Review Online Companion* 44.

Albro, R. (2006) The Culture of Democracy and Bolivia's Indigenous Movements, 26(4) *Critique of Anthropology* 387.

Alvarez, A. (1909) Latin America and International Law, 3 *American Journal of International Law* 269.

Anaya, S.J. (2005a) Divergent Discourses about International Law, Indigenous Peoples, and Rights over Lands and Natural Resources: Toward a Realist Trend, 16 *Colorado Journal of International Environmental Law and Policy* 237.

Anaya, S.J. (2005b) Indigenous Peoples' Participatory Rights in Relation to Decisions about Natural Resource Extraction: The More Fundamental Issues of What Rights Indigenous Peoples Have in Lands and Resources, 22 *Arizona Journal of International and Comparative Law* 7.

Anaya, S.J. and Wiessner, S. (2007) The UN Declaration on the Rights of Indigenous Peoples: Towards Re-Empowerment. 3 *Jurist*. Available at: http://jurist.law.pitt.edu/forumy/2007/10/un-declaration-on-rights-of-indigenous.php

Anaya, S.J. and Williams, R.A. (2001) The Protection of Indigenous Peoples' Rights over Lands and Natural Resources Under the Inter-American Human Rights System, 14 *Harvard Human Rights Journal* 33.

Anon (1965–1966) Purely Economic Justifications Sufficient to Permit Exercise of Federal Eminent Domain Power: United States v. Certain Parcels of Land, 64 *Michigan Law Review* 347.

Anon (2011) Developments in the Law: Extraterritoriality, 124 *Harvard Law Review* 1226.

Andrews, J.A. (1978) The Concept of Statehood and the Acquisition of Territory in the Nineteenth Century, 94 *Law Quarterly Review* 408.

Anghie, A. (1999) Finding the Peripheries: Sovereignty and Colonialism in Nineteenth-Century International Law, 40 *Harvard International Law Journal* 3.

Bachrach, P. and Baratz, M.S. (1962) Two Faces of Power, 56(4) *The American Political Science Review* 947.

Baker, S.H. (2013) Why the IFC's Free, Prior, and Informed Consent Policy Doesn't Matter (Yet) to Indigenous Communities Affected by Development Projects, 30(3) *Wisconsin International Law Journal* 668.

Barcia, C. (1927) Francisco de Vitoria et l'Ecole du Droit International, 17(2) *Recueil des Cours de l'Académie de Droit International de La Haye* 109.

Barrios, P. (2004) Rotterdam Convention on Hazardous Chemicals: A Meaningful Step Towards Environmental Protection?, 16 *Georgetown International Environmental Law Review* 679.

Barsh, R.L. (1983) Indigenous North America and Contemporary International Law, 62 *Oregon Law Review* 73.

Barsh, R.L. (1987) Revision of ILO Convention No. 107, 81 *American Journal of International Law* 756.

Barsh, R.L. (1990) An Advocate's Guide to the Convention on Indigenous and Tribal Peoples, 15 *Oklahoma City University Law Review* 209.

Barsh, R.L. (1992) Democratization and Development, 14 *Human Rights Quarterly* 120.

Barsh, R.L. (1994) Indigenous Peoples in the 1990s: From Object to Subject of International Law, 7 *Harvard Human Rights Journal* 33.

Barsh, R.L. (1998) Indigenous Peoples and the UN Commission on Human Rights A Case of the Immovable Object and the Irresistible Force, 18(4) *Human Rights Quarterly* 782.

Beaglehole, E. (1953) A Technical Assistance Mission in the Andes, 67 *International Labour Review* 520.

Bebbington, A.H., Bebbington, D., Bury, J., Lingan, J., Mun Oz, P. and Scurrah, M. (2008) Mining and Social Movements: Struggles over Livelihood and Rural Territorial Development in the Andes, 12(36) *World Development* 2888.

Bennett, G. (1978b) Aboriginal Title in the Common Law: A Stony Path through Feudal Doctrine, 27 *Buffalo Law Review* 617.

Bennett, G. (1979) The Developing Law of Aboriginal Rights, 22 *International Commission of Jurists: The Review* 42.

Berman, H.R. (1978) The Concept of Aboriginal Rights in the Early Legal History of the United States, 27 *Buffalo Law Review* 637.

Berman, H.R. (1985) Are Indigenous Populations Entitled to International Juridical Personality?, 79 *American Society of International Law* 190.

Berman, H. (1988) The International Labour Organization and Indigenous Peoples: Revision of ILO Convention No. 107 at the 75th Session of the International Labour Conference, 41 *International Commission of Jurists* 48.

Bernaz, N. (2013) Enhancing Corporate Accountability for Human Rights Violations: Is Extraterritoriality the Magic Potion? 117(3) *Journal of Business Ethics* 493.

Beuchot, M. (1994) Bartolomé de Las Casas, el Hhumanismo Indígeno y los Derechos Humanos, 6 *Anuario Mexicano de Historia del Derecho* 37.

Borrows, J. (1997/1998) Frozen Rights in Canada: Constitutional Interpretation and the Trickster, 22(1) *American Indian Law Review* 37.

Borrows J. and Rotman, L.I. (1997) The *Sui Generis* Nature of Aboriginal Rights: Does It Make a Difference? 36 *Alberta Law Review* 9.

Boruchoff, D.A. (2008) Another Face of Empire: *Bartolomé de las Casas, Indigenous Rights, and Ecclesiastical Imperialism* (review), 43(2) *Early American Literature*, 497.

Bradley, C.A. (2002) The Alien Tort Statue and Article III, 42 *Virginia Journal of International Law*, 587.

Bridge, G. (2004) Mapping the Bonanza: Geographies of Mining Investment in an Era of Neoliberal Reform, 56 *The Professional Geographer* 406.

Brilmayer, L. (1989–1990) Consent, Contract, and Territory, 74 *Minnesota Law Review* 1.

Brito Vieira, M. (2003) Mare Liberum vs. Mare Clausum: Grotius, Freitas, and Selden's Debate on Dominion over the Seas, 64(3) *Journal of the History of Ideas* 361.

Brysk, A. (1993) From Above and Below: Social Movements, the International System, and Human Rights in Argentina, 26(3) *Comparative Political Studies* 259.

Burger, J. (1996) The United Nations Draft Declaration on the Rights of Indigenous Peoples, 6 *St. Thomas Law Review* 209.

Buxton, A. (2010) Democratic Pragmatism or Green Radicalism? A Critical Review of the Relationship between Free, Prior and Informed Consent and Policymaking for Mining, Development Destiny Studies Institute Working Paper Series No. 10–102. London: LSE.

Calma, T. (2003) Self-Determination and Effective Participation 'Within the Life of the Nation'? An Australian Perspective on Self-Determination. Sydney: Australian Human Rights Commission. Available at: http://www.hreoc.gov.au/social_justice/international_docs/self_determination.htm

Campbell, M.S. and Anaya, S.J. (2008) The Case of the Maya Villages of Belize: Reversing the Trend of Government Neglect to Secure Indigenous Land Rights, 8(2) *Human Rights Law Review* 377.

Cariño, J. (2005) Indigenous Peoples and the Right to Free Prior and Informed Consent: Reflections on Concepts and Practice, 22(1) *Arizona Journal of International and Comparative Law* 19.

Cariño, J. and Colchester, M. (2010) From Dams to Development Justice: Progress with 'Free, Prior and Informed Consent' since the World Commission on Dams, 3(2) *Water Alternatives* 423.

Carozza, P.G. (2003) From Conquest to Constitutions: Retrieving a Latin American Tradition of the Idea of Human Rights, 25 *Human Rights Quarterly* 286.

Caso, A. (1948) Definición del Indio y de lo Indio, 8(5) *America Indigena* 239.

Castellino, J. (1999) A Territorial Interpretation of Identity in International Law: The Case of the Western Sahara, 29(3) *Millennium Journal of International Studies* 523.

Castellino, J. (2006) A Re-Examination of the International Convention for the Elimination of All Forms of Racial Discrimination, 2 *Revista iberoamericana de derechos humanos* 1.

Castellino, J. (2008) Territorial Integrity and the "Right" to Self-Determination: An Examination of the Conceptual Tools, 33(2) *Brooklyn Journal of International Law* 503.

Castellino, J. and Gilbert, J. (2003) Self-Determination, Indigenous Peoples and Minorities, 8 *Macquarie Law Journal* 455.

Cemento Progreso (2014) A View from the Private Sector, Spring Issue, *American Quarterly* 93.

Clavero, B. (2005b) The Indigenous Rights of Participation and International Development Policies, 22 *Arizona Journal of International and Comparative Law* 41.

Clavero, B. (2008) Perú: Convenio Necesario y Ley Innecesaria, Available at: http://servindi.org/actualidad/5211.

Clavero, B. (2009) Why Are Only Indigenous Peoples Internationally Entitled to a Specific Right to Their Own Culture? Available at: http://hrcolumbia.org/indigenous/lecture-columbia-1–21–09.pdf

Clavero, B. (2011) Principios Contra Garantías: Empresas Transnacionales y Pueblos Indígenas en el Orden Internacional de los Derechos Humanos Tras 2011, (Sevilla). Available at: http://www.elcorreo.eu.org/IMG/pdf/Empresas_transnacionales_y_pueblos_indigenas.pdf

Clavero, B. (2012a) ¿Globalización del Constitucionalismo? Transnacionalidad de Empresas entre Poderes y Derechos por Tiempos Postcoloniales, 1947–2011. 41 *Quaderni Fiorentini per la Soria del Pensiero Giuridico Moderno* 483.

Clavero, B. (2012b) Principios Contra Garantías: Empresas Transnacionales y Pueblos Indígenas en el Orden Internacional de los Derechos Humanos Tras 2, *Revista Latinoamericana de Derecho y Políticas Ambientales* 63.

Clinebell, J.H. and Thomson, J. (1977–1978) Sovereignty and Self-Determination: The Rights of Native Americans Under International Law, 27 *Buffalo Law Review* 699.

Coelho, V. S.P. and Favareto, P. (2008) Questioning the Relationship between Participation and Development: A Case Study of the Vale do Ribeira, Brazil, 36(12) *World Development* 29–37.

Cohen, F.S. (1942) The Spanish Origin of Indian Rights in the Law of the United States, 31 *The Georgetown Law Journal* 1.

Colopy, J.H. (1994/1995) Poisoning the Developing World: The Exportation of Unregistered and Severely Restricted Pesticides from the United States, 13 *UCLA Journal of Environmental Law and Policy* 167.

Corntassel, J., (2003) Who Is Indigenous? 'Peoplehood' and Ethnonationalist Approaches to Rearticulating Indigenous Identity, 9(1) *Nationalism and Ethnic Politics* 75.

Coumans, C. (2010) Alternative Accountability Mechanisms and Mining, in M. Beck, E. Canel, U. Idemudia, L.L. North, D. Szablowski and A. Zalik (eds) Rethinking the Extractive Industry: Regulation, Dispossession and Emerging Claims, 30(1–2) *Canadian Journal of Development Studies* 27.

Cuffe, S. (2012) Marketing Consent: A Journey into the Public Relations Underside of Canada's Mining Sector in Latin America, 84 *The Dominion* 9.

Daes, E.I. (1993) Some Considerations on the Rights of Indigenous Peoples to Self-Determination, 3 *Transnational Law and Contemporary Problems*, 1.

Davis, M. (2008) Indigenous Struggles in Standard-Setting: The United Nations Declaration on the Rights of Indigenous Peoples, 9 *Melbourne Journal of International Law* 439.

Dobyns, H.F. (1966) Estimating Aboriginal American Populations: An Appraisal of Techniques with a New Hemispheric Estimate, 7 *Current Anthropology* 395.

Domínguez-Redondo, E. (2011) Rethinking the Legal Foundations of Control in International Human Rights Law: The Case of Public Special Procedures, 29(3) *Netherlands Quarterly of Human Rights* 261.

Domínguez Redondo, E. (2012) The Universal Periodic Review: Is There Life Beyond Naming and Shaming in Human Rights Implementation? 4 *New Zealand Law Review* 673.

Doyle, C. (2009) Indigenous Peoples and the Millennium Development Goals: 'Sacrificial Lambs' or Equal Beneficiaries? 13 *International Journal of Human Rights*, Special Edition 44.

Duruigbo, E. (2006) Permanent Sovereignty and Peoples' Ownership of Natural Resources in International Law, 38 *George Washington International Law Review* 33.

Elías S. and Sánchez, G. (2014) Case Study Guatemala, Spring Issue, *American Quarterly* 71.

Ely, J.W., Jr (2003) Can the "Despotic Power" Be Tamed? Reconsidering the Public Use Limitation on Eminent Domain, November/December *American Bar Association Probate and Property* 30.

Engle, K. (2011) Legislative Comment on Fragile Architecture: The UN Declaration on the

Rights of Indigenous Peoples in the Context of Human Rights, 22(1) *European Journal of International Law* 141.

Dannenmaier, E. (2008) Beyond Indigenous Property Rights: Exploring the Emergence of a Distinctive Connection Doctrine, 86 *Washington University Law Review* 53.

De Schutter, O., Eide, A., Khalfan, A., Orellana, M., Salomon, M. and Seiderman, I. (2012) Commentary to the Maastricht Principles on Extraterritorial Obligations of States in the Area of Economic, Social and Cultural Rights, 34 *Human Rights Quarterly* 1084.

Ferch, M.L. (1992) Indian Land Rights: An International Approach to Just Compensation, 2 *Transnational Law and Contemporary Problem* 301.

Fiechter, M.K. (2011–2012) Extraterritorial Application of the Alien Tort Statute: The Effect of Morrison v. National Australia Bank, Ltd. on Future Litigation, 97 *Iowa Law Review* 959.

Finnemore, M. and Sikkink, K. (1998) International Norm Dynamics and Political Change, 52(4) *International Organization* 887.

Franck, T.M. (1992) The Emerging Right to Democratic Governance, 86 *American Journal of International Law* 46.

Franks, D., Davis, M.R., Bebbington, A.J., Ali, S.H. Kemp, D. and Scurrah, M. (2014) Conflict Translates Environmental and Social Risk into Business Costs, *PNAS* (published ahead of print May 12, 2014, doi:10.1073/pnas.1405135111). Available at: http://www.pnas.org/content/111/21/7576.full

Freeman, M. (1995) Are There Collective Human Rights? 43(1) *Political Studies* 25.

Fulmer, A.M., Snodgrass, A. and Neff, P. (2008) Indigenous Rights, Resistance and the Law: Lessons from a Guatemalan Mine, 50(4) *Latin American Politics and Society* 91.

Garrow, C. E. (2008) Following Deskaheh's Legacy: Reclaiming the Cayuga Indian Nation's Land Rights at the Inter-American Commission on Human Rights, 35 *Syracuse Journal of International Law and Commerce* 341.

Gilbert, G. (2002) Autonomy and Minority Groups: A Right in International Law? 35 *Cornell International Law Journal* 324.

Goodin R.E. (2000) Waitangi Tales, 20 *Australasian Journal of Philosophy* 309.

Goodland R. (2004) Free, Prior and Informed Consent and the World Bank Group, 4(2) *Sustainable Development Law and Policy* 66–74.

Goodland, R. (2012) Responsible Mining: The Key to Profitable Resource Development, Defining "Best Practice Responsible Mining" Research Series: A1–2012–4. Vermont: IEDS.

Greig, D.W. (1988) Sovereignty, Territory and the International Lawyer's Dilemma, 26 *Osgoode Hall Law Journal* 127.

Grote, R. (1999) The Status and Rights of the Indigenous Peoples of America, 59 *Heidelberg Journal of International Law* 427.

Hales, R.J., Rynne, J., Howlett, C., Devine, J. and Hauser, V. (2013) Indigenous Free Prior Informed Consent: A Case for Self-Determination in World Heritage Nomination Processes, 19(3) *International Journal of Heritage Studies* 270.

Henriksen, J.B. (1999) Implementation of the Right of Self-Determination of Indigenous Peoples within the Framework of Human Security, paper presented at International Conference on Indigenous Peoples' Self-Determination and the Nation State in Asia, Baguio, the Philippines.

Holder, C. and Corntassel, J. (2002) Indigenous Peoples and Multicultural Citizenship: Bridging Collective and Individual Rights, 24 *Human Rights Quarterly* 126.

Houghton, J. (2011) Debates Indígenas ante la Reconquista Minera del Cauca, 1 *Señas, Revista de la Casa del Pensamiento de la Cxhab Wala Kiwe*, 89.

Hutchinson, A. C. (1989) The Three 'R's': Reading / Rorty / Radically, 103 *Harvard Law Review* 555.

IISD (2011) Earth Negotiations Bulletin Conference on Sustainable Development CSD-19 5(304) International Institute for Sustainable Development 1.

Iorns, C. J. (1992) Indigenous Peoples and Self Determination: Challenging State Sovereignty, 24 *Case Western Reserve Journal of International Law* 199.

Katz, J. (1994) Informed Consent – Must It Remain a Fairy Tale?, 10 *Journal of Contemporary Health Law and Policy* 69.

Keith, R G. (1971) *Encomienda, Hacienda* and *Corregimiento* in Spanish America: A Structural Analysis, 51(3) *Hispanic American Historical Review* 43.

Khee-Jin Tan, A. (2005–2006) All that Glitters: Foreign Investment in Mining Trumps the Environment in the Philippines, 23 *Pace Environment Law Review* 183.

Kingsbury, B. (1998) "Indigenous Peoples" in International Law: A Constructivist Approach to the Asian Controversy, 92(3) *The American Journal of International Law* 414.

Kingsbury, B. (2001–2002) Reconciling Five Competing Conceptual Structures of Indigenous Peoples' Claims in International and Comparative Law, 34 *New York University Journal of International Law and Politics* 189.

Koivurova, T. (2011) Jurisprudence of the European Court of Human Rights Regarding Indigenous Peoples: Retrospect and Prospects, 18 *International Journal on Minority and Group Rights* 1.

Kunz, J.L. (1954) Chapter XI of the United Nations Charter in Action, 48 *American Journal of International Law* 98.

Kuper, A. (2003) The Return of the Native, 44(3) *Current Anthropology* 389.

Kymlicka, W. (1999) Theorizing Indigenous Rights, 49 *University of Toronto Law Journal* 281.

Langton, M. and Mazel, O. (2008) Poverty in the Midst of Plenty: Aboriginal People, the Resource Curse and Australia's Mining Boom, 26 *Journal of Energy and Natural Resources Law* 31.

Laplante, L.J. and Spears, S.A. (2008) Out of the Conflict Zone: The Case for Community Consent Processes in the Extractive Sector, 11 *Yale Human Rights and Development Law Journal* 69.

Leonen, M.M.V.F. (1998) The Indigenous Peoples Rights Act of 1997: Will This Legal Reality Bring Us to a More Progressive Level of Political Discourse? 9(1) *Philippine Natural Resources Law Journal* 7.

Leonen, M.M.V.F. (2000) Weaving Worldviews: Implications of Constitutional Challenges to the Indigenous Peoples' Rights Act of 1997, 10 *Philippines Natural Resources Law Journal* 3.

Lipschutz, A. (1952) La Noción o Definición del Indio en la Reciente Legislación Protectora en los Américas, 41(1) *Journal de la Société des Américanistes* 63.

Loarca, C (2009) El Deber de Consultar a los Pueblos, Guatemala. Available at: www.politicaspublicas.net/panel/biblioteca/cat_view/146-consulta-previa.html

Lugard, F. (1893) Treaty Making in Africa, 1 *Geographical Journal* 53.

Lynch, O. (1988) The Philippines Colonial Dichotomy: Attraction and Disenfranchisement, 63(1) *Philippine Law Journal* 112.

MacDonell J., Sir (1911) International Law and Subject Races, 12 *Journal of the Society of Comparative Legislation* 280.

Macintyre, M. (2007) Informed Consent and Mining Projects: A View from Papua New Guinea, 80(1) *Pacific Affairs: An International Review of Asia and the Pacific* 49.

MacKay, F. (2004a) Indigenous Peoples' Right to Free, Prior and Informed Consent and the World Bank's Extractive Industries Review, 4(2) *Sustainable Development Law and Policy* 42.

MacKay, F. (2004b) Indigenous Peoples' Rights and Resource Exploitation, 12(1) *Philippines Natural Resources Law Journal* 43.

MacKay, F. (2005) The Draft World Bank Operational Policy 4.10 on Indigenous Peoples Progress or More of the Same? 22 *Arizona Journal of International and Comparative Law* 81.

MacKay, F (2009) Internacional: ¿Por qué es Importante la Nueva Sentencia Interpretativa de la CIDH en el Caso Saramaka-Surinam? Available at: http://servindi.org/actualidad/4601

MacKlem, P. (1993) Distributing Sovereignty: Indian Nations and Equality of Peoples, 45 *Stanford Law Review* 1311.

MacKlem, P. (2007) What is International Human Rights Law? Three Applications of a Distributive Account, 52 *McGill Law Journal* 575.

Manuel, E.L. (2004) The Free Prior Informed Consent Paradox: Recreating an Existing Tool for Empowerment, 12(1) *Philippines Natural Resources Law Journal* 3.

Marks, C.G. (1990–1991) Indigenous Peoples in International Law: The Significance of Francisco De Vitoria and Bartolomé De Las Casas, 13 *Australian Year Book of International Law* 1.

Martínez de Bringas, A. (2009) La Aplicación Extraterritorial del Convenio 169 de la OIT ante la Actuación de las Empresas Trasnacionales Españolas que Afecten a los Derechos Indígenas, 85 *Revista Vasca de Administración Pública*. Herri-Arduralaritzako Euskal Aldizkaria, 83–105.

Mash-Mash and Gómez G. (2014) A View from Indigenous Peoples, (Spring Issue) *American Quarterly* 90.

Matz, N. (2005) Civilization and the Mandate System under the League of Nations as Origin of Trusteeship, 9 *Max Planck Yearbook of United Nations Law* 47.

McCorquodale, R., and Simons, P. (2007) Responsibility Beyond Borders: State Responsibility for Extraterritorial Violations by Corporations of International Human Rights Law, 70(4) *Modern Law Review* 598.

McGee, B. (2009) The Community Referendum: Participatory Democracy and the Right to Free, Prior and Informed Consent to Development, 27(2) *Berkeley Journal of International Law* 570.

McIntosh, I. (1997) Australian Aboriginal Property Rights Under Threat, 21(2) *Cultural Survival Quarterly*. Available at: www.culturalsurvival.org/ourpublications/csq/article/australian-aboriginal-property-rights-under-threat

McNeil, K. (1998) Aboriginal Rights in Canada: From Title to Land to Territorial Sovereignty, 5 *Tulsa Journal of Comparative and International Law* 253.

Merlan, F. (2009) Indigeneity Global and Local, 50(3) *Current Anthropology* 303.

Meron, T. (1986) On a Hierarchy of International Human Rights, 80 *American Journal of International Law* 16.

Miller, J. (2008) Inter-Tribal and International Treaties for American Indian Economic Development, 12(4) *Lewis and Clark Law Review* 1103.

Muldoon, J. (1980) John Wyclif and the Rights of the Infidels: The *Requerimiento* Re-Examined, 36(3) *The Americas* 301.

Nakagawa, M. (2004) Overview of Prior Informed Consent from an International Perspective, IV(2) *Sustainable Development Law and Policy* 27.

Nikolakis, W., Cohen, D.H., and Nelson, H.W. (2012) What Matters for Socially Responsible Investment (SRI) in the Natural Resources Sectors? SRI Mutual Funds and Forestry in North America, 2(2) *Journal of Sustainable Finance and Investment* 136.

Obinna Okere, B. (1984) The Protection of Human Rights in Africa and the African

Charter on Human and Peoples' Rights: A Comparative Analysis with the European and American Systems, 6 *Human Rights Quarterly* 141.

O'Faircheallaigh, C. (2010) Aboriginal-Mining Company Contractual Agreements in Australia and Canada: Implications for Political Autonomy and Community Development, 30(1–2) *Canadian Journal of Development Studies* 69.

O'Neill, O. (2003) Some Limits of Informed Consent, 29 *Journal of Medical Ethics* 4.

Pennington K.J. (1970) Bartolomé de Las Casas and the Tradition of Medieval Law, 39 *Church History* 149.

Perrault, A. (2004) Facilitating Prior Informed Consent Context of Genetic Resources and Traditional Knowledge, 4(2) *Sustainable Development Law and Policy* 21.

Perrault, A., Herbertson, K. and Lynch, O.J. (2007) Partnerships for Success in Protected Areas: The Public Interest and Local Community and Rights to Prior Informed Consent (PIC), 19 *The Georgetown International Environmental Law Review* 501.

Perrett, R.W. (1998) Indigenous Rights and Environmental Justice, 20 *Environmental Ethics* 377.

Phelan, J. (1957) Some Ideological Aspects of the Conquest of the Philippines, 13 *The Americas: A Quarterly Review of Inter-American Cultural History* 221.

Quane H. (2005) The Rights of Indigenous Peoples and the Development Process, 27 *Human Rights Quarterly* 652.

Quane, H. (2012) A Further Dimension to the Interdependence and Indivisibility of Human Rights?: Recent Developments Concerning the Rights of Indigenous Peoples, 25 *Harvard Human Rights Journal* 49.

Reisman, M. (1995) Protecting Indigenous Rights in International Adjudication, 89 *American Journal of International Law* 350.

Rosenthal, J.P. (2006) Politics, Culture, and Governance in the Development of Prior Informed Consent in Indigenous Communities, 47(1) *Current Anthropology* 119.

Ross, J. (1999) Legally Binding Prior Informed Consent, 10 *Colorado Journal of International Environmental Law and Policy* 499.

Rostkowski, J. (1998) Les Indiens des États-Unis: Hérauts de l'Autochtonie sur la Scène International, 84(1) *Journal de la Société des Américanistes* 264.

Rubies, J.P. (2007) Book review: Daniel Castro, "Another Face of Empire. Bartolomé de Las Casas, Indigenous Rights and Ecclesiastical Imperialism", 58(4) *Journal of Ecclesiastical History* 767.

Ruggie, J.G. (2007) Business and Human Rights: The Evolving International Agenda. Corporate Social Responsibility Initiative, 101 *American Journal of International Law* 819.

Sabatini, C. (2014) Editorial, (Spring Issue) *American Quarterly* 3.

Sachs, J.D. and Warner, A.M. (1997) Natural Resource Abundance and Economic Growth Papers 517a, *Harvard Institute for International Development*.

Sachs, J.D., and Warner, A.M. (2001) The Curse of Natural Resources, 45 *European Economic Review* 827.

Samson, K. (1989) Response to Review 41 Article on ILO Convention 107 Extract from a Letter by Klaus Samson to the ICJ, 42 *International Commission Jurists Review* 43.

Sanders, D. (1983) The Re-Emergence of Indigenous Questions in International Law, *Canadian Human Rights Yearbook* 3.

Sanders, D. (1991) Collective Rights, 13 *Human Rights Quarterly* 368.

Sarfaty, G.A. (2005) The World Bank and the Internationalization of Indigenous Rights Norms, 114 *Yale Law Journal* 1791.

Sarfaty, G.A. (2009) Why Culture Matters in International Institutions: The Marginality of Human Rights at the World Bank, 103 *American Journal of International Law* 647.

Schachter, O. (1998) Decline of the Nation-State and its Implications for International Law, 36 *Columbia Journal of Transnational Law* 7.

Schilling-Vacaflor, A. (2012) Democratizing Resource Governance through Prior Consultations? Lessons from Bolivia's Hydrocarbon Sector, GIGA Working Paper No. 184, Hamburg: German Institute of Global and Area Studies (GIGA).

Schwebel, S.M. (1979) The Effect of Resolutions of the U.N. General Assembly on Customary International Law Proceedings of the Annual Meeting, 73 *American Society of International Law* 301.

Schydlowsky, D.M. and Thompson, R.C. (2014) Reducing the Financial Risk of Social Conflict, (Spring Issue) *American Quarterly* 83.

Shelton, D. (2011) Self-Determination in Regional Human Rights Law: From Kosovo to Cameroon, 105 *American Journal of International Law* 60.

Simpson, A. (1987) The Role of Indigenous Nongovernment Organizations in Developing Human Rights Standards Applicable to Indigenous Peoples, 81 *American Society of International Law Proceedings*, 282.

Simpson, A. (2008) Subjects of Sovereignty: Indigeneity, the Revenue Rule, and Juridics of Failed Consent, 71 *Law and Contemporary Problems* 191.

Stennett, B (1985) Constitutional Law – Eminent Domain – Fifth Amendment Public Use Test Is Satisfied If a Public Purpose Is Served, 5 *Mississippi Law Journal* 213.

Swepston, L. (1987) Indigenous and Tribal Populations: A Return to Centre Stage, 126 *International Labour Review* 447.

Swepston, L. (1989) Response to Review 41 Article on ILO Convention 107: Reply to Howard Berman by Lee Swepston, 42 *International Commission of Jurists* 44.

Swepston, L. (1990) A New Step in the International Law on Indigenous and Tribal Peoples: ILO Convention No 169 of 1989, 15(3) *Oklahoma City University Law Review* 677.

Szablowski, D. (2010) Operationalizing Free, Prior, and Informed Consent in the Extractive Industry Sector? Examining the Challenges of a Negotiated Model of Justice, 30 (1–2) *Canadian Journal of Development Studies* 111.

Tammes, A.J.P. (1958) Decisions of International Organs as a Source of International Law, 94 *Recueil des Cours* 261.

Tennant, C. (1994) Indigenous Peoples, International Institutions, and the International Legal Literature from 1945–1993, 16 *Human Rights Quarterly* 1.

Thornberry, P. (1989) Self-Determination, Minorities, Human Rights: A Review of International Instruments, 38(4) *The International and Comparative Law Quarterly* 867.

Tierney, B. (1987) Hierarchy, Consent, and the "Western Tradition", 15 *Political Theory* November 646.

Tierney, B. (2004) The Idea of Natural Rights-Origins and Persistence, 2 *Northwestern University Journal of International Human Rights* 2.

Touval, S. (1966) Treaties, Borders and the Partition of Africa, 7(2) *Journal of African History* 279.

Uram, C. (1990) International Regulation of the Sale and Use of Pesticides, 10 *Northwestern Journal of International Law and Business* 460.

Van Dyke, V. (1982) Collective Entities and Moral Rights: Problems in Liberal-Democratic Thought, 44(1) *The Journal of Politics* 21.

Van Langenhove, F. (1956) Le Problème de la Protection des Populations Aborigènes aux Nations Unies, 89 *Recueil des cours de l'Académie de droit international de La Haye* 321.

Venne, S. (1990) The New Language of Assimilation: A Brief Analysis of ILO Convention 169, 2(2) Without Prejudice, *The EAFORD International Review of Racial Discrimination* 53.

Vinding, D., and Hitchcock, R.K. (2009) A Chronology of Important Events in the Genocides and Rights of Indigenous Peoples, 4(1) *Genocide Studies and Prevention* 111.

Vinuales, J.E. (2008–2009) The Contribution of the International Court of Justice to the Development of International Environmental Law: A Contemporary Assessment, 32 *Fordham International Law Journal* 232.

Vittor, L. (2014) Indigenous Peoples and Resistance to Mining Projects, (Winter 2014) *ReVista: Harvard Review of Latin America* 50.

Walls, M.P. (1988) Chemical Exports and the Age of Consent: The High Cost of International Export Control Proposals, 20 *New York University Journal of International Law and Politics* 753.

Walters, M. (1995) *Mohegan Indians v Connecticut* (1705–1773) and the Legal Status of Customary Laws and Government in British North America, 33 *Osgoode Hall Law Journal* 785.

Weissbrodt, D. and Mahling, W. (1994) Highlights of the 46th Session of the Sub-Commission. Available at: http://www1.umn.edu/humanrts//demo/subrept.htm

Whitmore, A. (2006) The Emperor's New Clothes: Sustainable Mining? 14 *Journal of Cleaner Production* 309.

Wiessner, S. (1999) Rights and Status of Indigenous Peoples: A Global Comparative and International Legal Analysis, 12 *Harvard Human Rights Journal* 57.

Wiessner, S. (2008) Indigenous Sovereignty: A Reassessment in Light of the UN Declaration on the Rights of Indigenous Peoples, 41 *Vanderbilt Journal of Transnational Law* 1141.

Wiessner, S. (2011) The Cultural Rights of Indigenous Peoples: Achievements and Continuing Challenges, 22 *European Journal of International Law* 121.

Wilkinson C.F. and Volkman, J.M. (1975) Judicial Review of Indian Treaty Abrogation: 'As Long as Water Flows, or Grass Grows Upon the Earth' – How Long a Time Is That? 63 *California Law Review* 601.

Williams, R.A. (1983) The Medieval and Renaissance Origins of the Status of the American Indian in Western Legal Thought, 57 *Southern California Law Review* 1.

Williams, R.A. (1991) Columbus's Legacy: Law as an Instrument of Racial Discrimination against Indigenous Peoples' Rights of Self-Determination, 8(2) *Arizona Journal of International and Comparative Law* 51.

Wolfrum, R. (1999a) The Committee on the Elimination of Racial Discrimination, 3 *Max Planck Yearbook of United Nations Law* 489.

Wolfrum, R. (1999b) The Protection of Indigenous Peoples in International Law, 59 *Zeitschrift für ausländisches öffentliches Recht und Völkerrecht* 369.

Zavala, S. (1944) Las Casas ¿esclavista? III (2) *Cuadernos Americanos* 149.

Zion, J.W. and Yazzie, R. (1997) Indigenous Law in North America in the Wake of Conquest, 20 *Boston College International and Comparative Law Review* 55.

Business reports and statements

ASI (2014) *Aluminium Stewardship Imitative (ASI) Performance Standard Draft 1 version 2* (July 2014). Available at: http://aluminium-stewardship.org/

Balch, O. (2012) *Engaging Stakeholders: Legitimate Concerns Prompt Complex Negotiations,* in Ethical Corporations, Indigenous Peoples and the Extractive Sector.

BHP (2011) *BHP Billiton Sustainability Report.* Available at: www.bhp.com

BHP Billiton Sustainability Reports (2009) (2010) and (2011). Available at: www.bhpbilliton. com/home/aboutus/sustainability/reports/Pages/default.aspx

Buxton, A. (2012) *MMSD+10: Reflecting on a Decade.* IIED Discussion Paper. London: International Institute for Environment and Development.

De Cordova (NEI Investments) (2012) *Response to Special Representative of the United Nations Secretary-General for Business and Human Rights, Online Forum.* New York: Business and Human Rights Resource Centre, 99. Available at: http://en.hrsu.org/wp-content/uploads/2011/08/online-forum-re-guiding-principles-nov-2010-to-jan-2011.pdf

EIRIS (2010) *Improving Vedanta Resources' Governance of Responsible Business Practices.* London: Experts in Responsible Investment Solutions (EIRIS). Available at: www.eiris.org/

EITI (2011) *Second National Reconciliation Study of the Extractive Industries Transparency Initiative (EITI) in Peru (2008–2010): Final Version Consultancy for the EITI Peru Multi-Sector Working Committee 13 December 2011.* Lima: Ernst and Young.

EITI (2012) *Mongolia Extractive Industries Transparency Initiative (ÐEITI) Fifth EITI Reconciliation Report 2010,* Ulaanbaatar: EITI.

Ethical Funds Company (2008) *Sustainability Perspectives Winning the Social License to Operate Resource Extraction with Free, Prior, and Informed Community Consent.* Toronto: Ethical Funds. Available at: http://www.neiinvestments.com/neifiles/PDFs/5.4%20Research/FPIC.pdf

ExxonMobil *Annual Report* (2010).

Howard, J.E. (2002) The Alien Tort Claims Act: Is Our Litigation. (International Policy and Programs at the U.S. Chamber of Commerce). Available at: http://www.uschamber. com/press/opeds/2002/alien-tort-claims-act-our-litigation

ICMM (2005) *Mining and Indigenous Peoples Issues Review,* ed. J.M. Render. London: ICMM. Available at: www.icmm.com

ICMM (2007a) *Releases: Findings of Survey on Indigenous Peoples Issues* (17 April 2007). Available at: www.icmm.com

ICMM (2008a) *Position Statement, Mining and Indigenous Peoples Issues,* released May 2008. Available at: http://www.icmm.com

ICMM (2008b) *Mining and Indigenous Peoples Issues: Roundtable: Continuing a Dialogue between Indigenous Peoples and Mining Companies.* IUCN-ICMM Dialogue on Mining and Biodiversity. Sydney: ICMM, IUCN. Available at: www.icmm.com

ICMM (2010) *Good Practice Guide Indigenous Peoples and Mining' Guidance 2010–3.* London: ICMM. Available at: www.icmm.com

ICMM (2013) *Position Statement on Indigenous Peoples and Mining Effective from May 2015.* London: ICMM. Available at: www.icmm.com

IFC (2007a) *Convention 169 and the Private Sector: Questions and Answers for IFC Clients.* Washington DC: IFC. Available at: www.ifc.org

IFC (2007b) *Policy and Performance Standards on Social and Environmental Sustainability and Disclosure Policy: Commentary on IFC's Progress Report on the First 18 Months of Application,* Office of the Compliance Advisor/Ombudsman (CAO) IFC and MIGA. World Bank Group, Advisory Note. Washington, DC: IFC.

IFC (2010a) *Compliance Advisor Ombudsman, The CAO at 10: Annual Report FY2010 and Review FY2000–10.* Washington DC: IFC. Available at: www.cao-ombudsman.org

IFC (2010b) *Progress Report on IFC's Policy and Performance Standards on Social and Environmental Sustainability, and Policy on Disclosure of Information Review and Update Process.* Washington, DC: IFC.

IFC (2012a) *IFC Performance Standards on Environmental and Social Sustainability - Performance Standard No. 7 on Indigenous Peoples.* Washington, DC: IFC. Available at: www.ifc.org

IFC (2012b) *Guidance Note 7.* Indigenous Peoples (January 1, 2012).

IFC (2012c) *IFC Updated Sustainability Framework Fact Sheet.* Washington, DC: IFC. Available at: www.ifc.org

Institute for Business and Human Rights (2012) *OECD National Contact Points and the Extractive Sector Workshop Report* (23 March 2012). London: Institute for Business and Human Rights, OECD NCP Norway.

IPIECA (2012) *Indigenous Peoples and the Oil and Gas Industry Context, Issues and Emerging Good Practice.* London: IPIECA. Available at: http://www.ipieca.org/

IMRA (2014) *Draft Standard for Responsible Mining v1.0* (July 2014). Initiative for Responsible Mining Assurance (IRMA). Available at: www.responsiblemining.net/

Knoepfel, I. (2011) *Responsible Investment in Commodities: The Issues at Stake and a Potential Role for Institutional Investors.* Zurich: On Values, Investment Strategies and Research.

Kropp, R. (2010) Investors Urge US to Support Rights of Indigenous Peoples. *Sustainability Investment News,* July 30. Available at: www.socialfunds.com/news/article.cgi?sfArticleId=3003

Lehr, A.K. and Smith, G.A. (2010) *Foley Hoag LLP: Implementing a Corporate Free, Prior, and Informed Consent Policy: Benefits and Challenges.* Boston: Foley Hoag LLP.

Rio Tinto (2009) *Annual Report.*

Rio Tinto (2011) *Communities Standard.*

Rio Tinto (2012) *Indigenous Communities, the UN Declaration on the Rights of Indigenous Peoples (UNDRIP) and Free Prior and Informed Consent (FPIC).* Rio Tinto, January.

Roundtable on Responsible Soy (RTRS) (2010) *Principles and Criteria for Responsible Soy Version 1.0.* ITG1-OUT-01-ENG (22 April 2010).

Roundtable on Sustainable Biofuels (RSB) (2010) *Guidance for RSB Principles and Criteria.* RSB-GUI-01–000 (Version 2.0). Available at: http://rsb.org/pdfs/standards/11–03–08%20RSB%20Guidance%20for%20PCs%20Version%202.pdf

Roundtable on Sustainable Palm Oil (RSPO) (2007) *Principles and Criteria for Sustainable Palm Oil Production Roundtable on Sustainable Palm Oil.* Available at: http://www.rspo.org/sites/default/files/RSPO%20Principles%20and%20Criteria.pdf

Talisman Energy Inc (2010a) *Corporate Responsibility Report: Safe Profitable Growth.* Available at: http://www.talisman-energy.com/upload/report_link/19/02/tal_cr_final.pdf

Talisman Energy Inc (2010b) *Global Community Relations Policy* (9 December 2010). Available at: http://www.talisman-energy.com/responsibility/policies_management_systems/cr_policy.html

NGO and indigenous peoples' reports and documents

Amnesty International (2010) Open Letter to the Authorities of the Plurinational State of Bolivia in the Context of the Dispute Concerning the Isiboro Sécure Indigenous Territory and National Park (Territorio Indígena y Parque Nacional Isiboro Sécure - TIPNIS) 3 May 2010. Available at: http://www.amnesty.org/en/library/info/AMR18/002/2012

Anaya S.J. (2011) *Memorandum Re: Draft Performance Standard 7 on Indigenous Peoples to: Reider Kvam IFC Environment and Social Development Department Policy and Quality Assurance.*

Bascopé, I. (2010) *Case Study: Bolivian Government Consultation with the Guaraní Indigenous Peoples of Charagua Norte and Isoso.* La Paz: OXFAM and CEJIS.

CAOI (2008) *Being Sued, Defending the Mother Country? Criminalization of the Exercise of Indigenous Peoples' Rights, Political and Legal Analysis, Colombia – Chile – Peru.* Lima: Coordination of Andean Indigenous Organizations.

Clean Trade Project (2012) *Guide to Transnational Tort Litigation in the United Kingdom and the*

United States Regarding the Spoliation of Natural Resources Clean Trade Project: The Resource Curse and Consumer Demand for Oil, Gas, and Minerals. Clean Trade Project.

Colchester, M. (2010) *Free, Prior and Informed Consent: Making FPIC Work for Forests and Peoples.* New Haven, CT: Yale University, The Forests Dialogue.

Colchester, M. and Farhan Ferrari, M. (2007) *Making FPIC Work: Challenges and Prospects for Indigenous People.* Moreton-in-Marsh: Forest Peoples Programme.

Colchester, M. and MacKay, F. (2004) *In Search of Middle Ground: Indigenous Peoples, Collective Representation and the Right to Free, Prior and Informed Consent.* Morten on Marsh: Forest Peoples Programme.

Colchester, M., Sirait, M. and Wijardjo, B. (2003) *The Application of FSC Principles 2 and 3 in Indonesia: Obstacles and Possibilities.* Walhi and Aman.

Doyle, C. (2010b) *Statement on behalf of Indigenous Peoples Links (PIPLinks); the Forest Peoples Programme (FPP); the Asian Indigenous Peoples Pact (AIPP); the Foundation for Aboriginal and Islander Research Action (FAIRA); Russian Association of Indigenous Peoples of the North (RAIPON); Organizacions de Naciones y Pueblos Indigenas en Argentina (ONPIA) and Middlesex University Department of Law to the Third Session of the UN Expert Mechanism on the Rights of Indigenous Peoples Presentation under Agenda Item 4.* Geneva: EMRIP. Available at: http://www.forestpeoples.org/sites/fpp/files/publication/2010/08/ifcunemripstatementjul10eng.pdf

Doyle, C. (2010c) *Statement on Behalf of University of Middlesex Department of Law and Philippines Indigenous Peoples Links (PIPLinKs)* (Geneva, 2010) *to the Third Session of the UN Expert Mechanism on the Rights of Indigenous Peoples Presentation under Agenda Item 3.* Available at: www.docip.org

Doyle, C. (2011) *Input to IFC Sustainability Policy and Performance Standards Review. Phase 3 Suggestions Aimed at Clarifying Language in IFC Performance Standard 7, Sustainability and Access to Information Policies and Guidance Note 7 to Facilitate the Effective Implementation of the Requirement to Obtain Indigenous Peoples' Free, Prior and Informed Consent.* 25 February.

Doyle C. (forthcoming 2015) *Free Prior and Informed Consent: A Self-Determination Norm and Framework for Consultation and Benefit Sharing.*

Doyle, C., Wicks, C. and Nally, F. (2007) *Mining in the Philippines: Concerns and Conflicts.* Solihull: Society of St. Columban.

First Peoples Worldwide (2012) *Indigenous Peoples Guidebook on Free Prior Informed Consent and Corporate Standards.* Fredericksburg, VA: First Peoples Worldwide, IITC and Trillium Asset Management.

Forest Peoples Programme (2008) *Free Prior and Informed Consent and the Roundtable on Sustainable Palm Oil: A Guide for Companies.* Moreton-in-Marsh: FPP.

Forest Peoples Programme and Association of Saramaka Authorities, *Free, Prior and Informed Consent: Two Cases from Suriname* (FPIC Working Papers, Forest Peoples Programme, Moreton-in-Marsh, March 2007) 16. Available at: www.forestpeoples.org/documents/law_hr/fpic_suriname_mar07_eng.pdf

Gibson G. (2012) *Free, Prior, and Informed Consent in Canada A Summary of Key Issues, Lessons, and Case Studies Towards Practical Guidance for Developers and Aboriginal Communities.* Boreal Leadership Council.

Gorre, I. (2005) *Initial Comments on National Commission on Indigenous Peoples Draft Guidelines on Free and Prior Informed Consent Issue Paper 2005–02.* Quezon City, LRC.

Greenspan E. (2014) *Free, Prior, and Informed Consent in Africa: An Emerging Standard for Extractive Industry Projects* Washington, DC: Oxfam America.

Griffiths, T. (2005) *Indigenous Peoples and the World Bank: Experiences with Participation.* Moreton-in-Marsh: Forest Peoples Programme.

Harvard Project on American Indian Economic Development (2014) *On Improving Tribal-Corporate Relations in the Mining Sector: A White Paper on Strategies for Both Sides of the Table.*

Harvard Project on American Indian Economic Development, John F. Kennedy School of Government. Cambridge. MA: Harvard University Press.

Herz, S., La Vina, A., and Sohn, J. (2007) *Development without Conflict: The Business Case for Community Consent*. Washington, DC: World Resource Institute.

IBIS (2013) *Guidelines on Free Prior and Informed Consent*. Copenhagen: IBIS.

International Commission of Jurists (2008) *Corporate Complicity and Legal Accountability: Report of the International Commission of Jurists, Expert Legal Panel on Corporate Complicity in International Crimes*, Volumes I, II, III. Geneva: International Commission of Jurists.

Jimeno Santoyo, G. (2002) *Possibilities and Perspectives of Indigenous Peoples with Regard to Consultations and Agreements within the Mining Sector in Latin America and the Caribbean: Thematic Exploration*. Ottawa: North South Institute.

Lasimbang, J. and Heroepoetri, A. (2010) *Evaluation Report on Free, Prior and Informed Consent Project, "Support for Organizational Development and for Training and Technical Assistance to Help Indigenous Communities to Negotiate Agreements based on Free, Prior and Informed Consent (FPIC) in the Forestry Sector"*. Oslo: Rainforest Foundation.

Ligue Internationale des Femmes pour la Paix et la Liberté (1981) *International NGO Conference on Indigenous Peoples and the Land*. Geneva: WILPF.

Maastricht Principles on Extraterritorial Obligations of States in the Area of Economic, Social and Cultural Rights (Maastricht University, 28 September 2011).

Mackay, F. (2008) *Compilations of UN Treaty Body Jurisprudence Volumes I, II and III Covering the Years 1993–2008*. Moreton-in-Marsh: Forest Peoples Programme.

MacKay, F. (2011) *Amicus Curiae Brief in the Case of the Pueblo Indígena Kichwa de Sarayaku v. Ecuador*. Amsterdam: Forest People Programme.

MacKay, F. (2013) *The Rights of Non-Indigenous Forest Peoples*. Moreton-in-Marsh: FPP.

Martin, S. (2007) *Free Prior Informed Consent: The Role of Mining Companies*. Melbourne: Oxfam Australia.

Moncloa, A.A. (2007) *No Pero Si Communidades y Mineria Consulta y Consentimiento Previo, Libre e Informado en el Peru*. Lima: CooperAcción and Oxfam America.

Moore, E. (2011) *The Administration of Special Purpose Agricultural and Business Leases Customary Land and the Lease-Lease-Back System, The National Research Institute of Papua New Guinea, Discussion Paper No. 118*. Boroko: The National Research Institute.

Muhi, A.R.T. (2007) *A Critique on the Philippines Free and Prior Informed Consent Guidelines of 2006*, LRC-KsK Issue Paper 2007–01. Quezon City, LRC.

Nijar, G. (2011) *The Nagoya Protocol on Access and Benefit-Sharing of Genetic Resources: An Analysis*. CEBLAW Brief, Kuala Lumpur: Universitii Malaya.

Oxfam America (2009) *Review of Major Mining, Oil, and Gas Company Policies on Free Prior and Informed Consent and Social License: A Discussion Paper*. Washington, DC: Oxfam America.

Philippines National Indigenous Peoples Network (2009) *Philippines Indigenous Peoples ICERD Shadow Report*. Manila: Philippines National Indigenous Peoples Network.

Picq, M. (2012) *Is the Inter-American Commission of Human Rights Too Progressive?* 9 June. Available at: http://www.aljazeera.com/indepth/opinion/2012/06/2012658344220937.html

Power, T. M. (2002) *Digging to Development: A Historical Look at Mining and Economic Development*. Washington, DC: Oxfam America.

Rumler, M. (2011) *Free, Prior and Informed Consent: A Review of Free, Prior and Informed Consent in Australia: An Independent Research Report*. Victoria: Oxfam Australia.

Sibaud, P. (2012) *Opening Pandora's Box: The New Wave of Land Grabbing by Extractive Industries and the Devastating Impact on Earth*. London: Gaia Foundation.

Skinner, G., McCorquodale, R. and De Schutter, O. (2013) The Third Pillar Access to

Judicial Remedies for Human Rights Violations by Transnational Business. CORE, ICAR, ECCJ.

Smith, H., Nindi, S. and Beckhaus, G. (2011) *Complex Commons Under Threat of Mining: The Process for and Content of Community Consent*. Cape Town: Legal Resources Centre.

Sosa, I. (2011) *Indigenous Relations and Free Prior and Informed Consent in the Mining Industry*. Amsterdam: Sustainalytics.

Tobin, B., Burton, G., and Fernandez-Ugalde, J.C. (2008) *Certificates of Clarity or Confusion: The Search for a Practical, Feasible and Cost Effective System for Certifying Compliance with PIC and MAT*. UNU-IAS Report.

Treaty Council News (1977) *Report of the International NGO Conference on Discrimination Against Indigenous Populations in the Americas, September 20–23 1977, Palais des Nations, Geneva, Switzerland*. 1(7) Treaty Council News.

Uy, D.M.F., Manuel, E.L., Gorre, I., and Trinidad, J. (2004) *Notes on NCIP Administrative Issuance 2002–2003* Issue Paper 2004–02. Quezon City: LRC.

Voss, M. and Greenspan, E. (2012) *Community Consent Index: Oil, Gas and Mining Company Public Positions on Free, Prior, and Informed Consent (FPIC)*, Oxfam America Research Backgrounder series. Washington, DC: Oxfam America.

Wicomb, W. and H. Smith (2011) *Customary Communities as 'Peoples' and Their Customary Tenure as 'Culture': What Can We Do with the Endorois Decision?* Legal Resources Centre 429.

Declarations, statements, submissions and interventions

Ahren, M. (2010) *Statement on Behalf of the Arctic Council under Agenda Item 3, Study on Indigenous People's Right to Participate in Decision-Making*. Geneva: Experts Mechanism on the Rights of Indigenous Peoples, 3rd session. Available at: www.docip.org

AIDESEP, CAN, CONACAMI, CPP, ONAMIAP (2011) *Pacto de Unidad Principios Mínimos no Negociables para la Aplicación de los Derechos de Participación, Consulta Previa y Consentimiento Previo, Libre e Informado*. Lima: CAN, CPP, CONACAMI, AIDESEP, ONAMIAP, December 2011.

AIDESEP, CONACAMI, ONAMIAP (2012) *Pronunciamiento Estado Peruano Consuma Violación de Derechos de los Pueblos Indígenas, Mediante la Reglamentación de una Inconstitucional Ley de Consulta Pacto de Unidad Confederación Nacional Agraria Perú*. 4 de marzo de 2012, Lima.

Carmen, A. (2012) *Strengthening Partnership between States and Indigenous Peoples: Treaties, Agreements and Other Constructive Arrangements: A Framework for Conflict Resolution, Reparations, Restitution and Redress of Treaty Violations based on the United Nations Declaration on the Rights of Indigenous Peoples and Free Prior and Informed Consent* (International Indian Treaty Council) UN Doc. HR/GENEVA/ /SEM/NGOs/2012/BP.5.

Couillard, V., Doyle, C., Gilbert, J. and Tugendhat, H. (2009) *Business, Human Rights and Indigenous Peoples: The Right to Free, Prior and Informed Consent, Submission to the House of Lords, House of Commons, Joint Committee on Human Rights*. Moreton-in-Marsh/Hendon: Forest Peoples Programme and Middlesex University.

Coulter, R. (2005) *Indigenous Peoples' Right of Free Prior Informed Consent with Respect to Indigenous Lands, Territories and Resources*. New York: UNPFII Workshop on Free, Prior and Informed Consent, Contribution of the Indian Law Resource Center.

García Hierro P. (2014) *Gobernanza Territorial y Pueblos Indígenas*. New York: UNPFII, statement at the 14th session.

Indigenous Peoples' Declaration on Mining (16 May 1996) London.

Indigenous Peoples' Plan of Implementation on Sustainable Development (2 September 2002) Johannesburg, South Africa.

KI First Nation (2011) *Kitchenuhmaykoosib Inninuwug Protocols: A Set of Protocols for the Kitchenuhmaykoosib Inninuwug*, Ottawa, Kitchenuhmaykoosib Inninuwug: KI First Nation.

Malezer, L. (2007) *Statement on the Adoption of the UN Declaration on the Rights of Indigenous Peoples on Behalf of the Global Indigenous Caucus*. New York: Global Indigenous Caucus.

Manila Declaration (2009) *Manila Declaration of the International Conference on Extractive Industries and Indigenous Peoples*, 23–25 March 2009. Legend Villas, Metro Manila, Philippines. "Indigenous Peoples' Declaration on Mining", London, 16 May 1996, reproduced in UN Doc. E/C.19/2009/CRP Annex II.

Maya Leaders Alliance (Belize) (2012) Update to the Committee on the Elimination of Racial Discrimination 81st Session in Anticipation of the Committee's Review of Belize in the Absence of a State Report. Available at: http://www2.ohchr.org/english/bodies/cerd/docs/ngos/TheMayaleadersAlliance.pdf

Moses, T. (1996) Statement on Behalf of the Grand Council of the Crees, 53rd Session of the Working Group on the Draft Declaration on the Rights of Indigenous Peoples (WGDDIP), 21 October--1 November, Geneva: WGDDIP.

Roy R.D. (2011) Intervention on Follow-up to the Recommendations of the Permanent Forum on "Free, Prior and Informed Consent" to the 10th Session of the United Nations Permanent Forum on Indigenous Issues, May 16–27, New York Agenda Item 3(c). Available at: http://www.docip.org

Subanen People (2009) *Subanen Manifesto: Voice of the Subanen of the Zambaonga Peninsula*. Subanen Conference on Free Prior and Informed Consent Casa Emsa, Pagadian City, Zamboanga del Sur, 22 November 2009, Pagadian: Subanen People of Zambaonga.

University of Arizona Indigenous Peoples Law and Policy (2008) *Program Submission to the Universal Period Review*: Belize. Available at: http://lib.ohchr.org/HRBodies/UPR/Documents/Session5/BZ/UA_BLZ_UPR_S5_2009_TheUniversityofArizona-IndigenousPeoplesLawandPolicyProgram.pdf

Williams, R.A. Jr. (2010) The University of Arizona Rogers College of Law (July 28) Statement to United States Federal Committee on Natural Resources Hearing on H.R. 5023 *Requirements, Expectations, and Standard Procedures for Executive Consultation with Tribes Act ("RESPECT Act") in Legislative Hearing Before the Committee on Natural Resources U.S. House of Representatives One Hundred Eleventh Congress Second Session* Wednesday, July 28, 2010 Serial No. 111–63, 28–34. Available at: http://www.gpo.gov/fdsys/pkg/CHRG-111hhrg57666/pdf/CHRG-111hhrg57666.pdf

Reports by international organisations

Alexander, M., Kayeh, D., Hardison, P. and Ahren, M. (2009) *Study on Compliance in Relation to the Customary Law of Indigenous and Local Communities, National Law, across Jurisdictions and International Law*. UN Doc. UNEP/CBD/ABS/GTLE/2/INF/3, 21 January 2009.

Allen & Overy (2013) Equator Principles EP-III released. Available at: http://www.thelawyer.com/briefings/equator-principles-financial-ep-iii-released/3005362.article

Canada, Report of the Royal Commission on Aboriginal Peoples (1996) Volume 2 *Restructuring the Relationship*.

Cristescu, A. (1981) *The Right to Self-Determination Historical and Current Development on the Basis of United Nations Instruments*. UN Doc. E/CN.4/sub.2/404/Rev.1.

Daes, E.-I. (2001) Final working paper prepared by the Special Rapporteur, Mrs. Erica-

Irene A. Daes *Indigenous Peoples and their Relationship to Land* UN Doc. E/CN.4/Sub.2/2001/21.

Daes, E.-I. (2004) Final Report of the Special Rapporteur, Erica-Irene A. Daes, 12 July 2004, *Indigenous Peoples' Permanent Sovereignty over Natural Resources*. UN Doc. E/CN.4/Sub.2/2004/30/Add.1.

De Schutter, O. (2006) *Extraterritorial Jurisdiction as a Tool for Improving the Human Rights Accountability of Transnational Corporations*, Submission to the UN Special Representative. Available at: http://www.reports-and-materials.org/Olivier-de-Schutter-report-for-SRSG-re-extraterritorial-jurisdiction-Dec-2006.pdf

Doyle, C. (2008) Free Prior Informed Consent (FPIC) – A Universal Norm and Framework for Consultation and Benefit Sharing in Relation to Indigenous Peoples and the Extractive Sector, paper prepared for OHCHR Workshop on Natural Resource Companies, Indigenous Peoples and Human Rights, Moscow, 3–4 December 2008 (Middlesex University). Available at: http://www2.ohchr.org/english/issues/indigenous/resource_companies.htm

Doyle, C. (2012) Response to Special Representative of the United Nations Secretary-General for Business and Human Rights *Online Forum*. New York: Business and Human Rights Resource Centre, 66–67. Available at: http://en.hrsu.org/wp-content/uploads/2011/08/online-forum-re-guiding-principles-nov-2010-to-jan-2011.pdf

Espiel, H.G. (1978) *Implementation of United Nations Resolutions Relating the Right of People Under Colonial and Alien Domination to Self-Determination* UN Doc. E/CN.4/Sub.405.

ILO (1953) *Indigenous Peoples, Living and Working Conditions of Aboriginal Populations in Independent Countries*. International Labour Office Studies and Reports, new ser., no. 35 Geneva: ILO.

ILO (1955) *International Labour Conference*, 39th Session 1956. *Eighth Item on the Agenda: Living and Working Conditions of Indigenous Populations in Independent Countries*, Report VIII (1). Geneva: ILO.

ILO (1956a) *International Labour Conference*, 39th Session 1956, *Eighth Item on the Agenda: Living and Working Conditions of Indigenous Populations in Independent Countries*, Report VIII (2). Geneva: ILO.

ILO (1956b) *International Labour Conference*, 40th Session 1957 *Eighth Item on the Agenda: Living and Working Conditions of Indigenous Populations in Independent Countries*, Report VI (1). Geneva: ILO in ILO II/40/4–8.

ILO (1956c) International Labour Conference, 39th Session, *Record of Proceedings*. Geneva: ILO.

ILO (1957a) *International Labour Conference*, 40th Session 1957, *Eighth Item on the Agenda: Living and Working Conditions of Indigenous Populations in Independent Countries*, Report VI (2). Geneva: ILO in ILO II/40/4–8.

ILO (1957b) International Labour Conference, 40th Session, *Record of Proceedings*. Geneva: ILO.

ILO (1987) International Labour Conference, 75th Session., 1988 *ILO Partial Revision of the Indigenous and Tribal Populations Convention, 1957 (no. 107): Sixth Item on the Agenda* Report VI(1). Geneva: ILO.

ILO (1988a) International Labour Conference, 75th Session. 1988 *ILO Partial Revision of the Indigenous and Tribal Populations Convention, 1957 (no. 107): Sixth Item on the Agenda* Reports VI(2). Geneva: ILO.

ILO (1988b) International Labour Conference, 76th Session 1989, *ILO Partial Revision of the*

Indigenous and Tribal Populations Convention, 1957 (No. 107), Report IV(1). Geneva: ILO.

ILO (1988c) *Record of Proceedings*, International Labour Conference. 75th Session.

ILO (1989a) International Labour Conference, 76th Session 1989, *ILO Partial Revision of the Indigenous and Tribal Populations Convention, 1957 (No. 107)*, Reports IV(2A) and IV(2B). Geneva: ILO.

ILO (1989b) *Record of Proceedings* International Labour Conference 76th Session. Geneva: ILO.

ILO (2001) Representation (Article 24) Colombia C169 2001 Report of the Committee set up to Examine the Representation Alleging Non-Observance by Colombia of the Indigenous and Tribal Peoples Convention, 1989 (No. 169), made under Article 24 of the ILO Constitution by the Central Unitary Workers' Union (CUT) and the Colombian Medical Trade Union Association. Submitted: 1999 Document: (GB.277/18/1): (GB.282/14/4). Geneva: ILO.

ILO (2002) *Convenio núm. 169, sobre Pueblos Indígenas y Tribales en Países Independientes*. San José, Costa Rica, 1st Edition 1996, 5th edition 2002, Doc. No. RLA/98/O1M/UNF. San Jose: ILO.

ILO (2003) *ILO Convention on Indigenous and Tribal Peoples 1989 (No. 169)*: Manual. Geneva: ILO.

ILO (2007a) *Guía para la aplicación del Convenio núm.* 169 de la OIT Documentación para taller pro Ratificación Convenio 169 OIT - CHILE 2007. Geneva: ILO.

ILO (2007b) *Eliminating Discrimination against Indigenous and Tribal Peoples in Employment and Occupation A Guide to ILO Convention No. 111*. Geneva: ILO.

ILO (2009) *Application of Convention No. 169 by Domestic and International Courts in Latin America: A Casebook*. Geneva: ILO.

ILO (2010) *Monitoring Indigenous and Tribal Peoples' Rights Through ILO Conventions A Compilation of ILO Supervisory Bodies' Comments 2009–2010*. Geneva: ILO.

Khara, H. (2010) *The Emerging Middle Class in Developing Countries*. Paris: OECD.

Norwegian NCP (2011) *Final Statement Complaint from the Future In Our Hands (FIOH) against Intex Resources ASA and the Mindoro Nickel Project*. The Norwegian National Contact Point for the OECD Guidelines for Multinational Enterprises. Oslo: OECD.

OECD (2011): *Update of OECD Guidelines for Multinational Enterprises: Informal Expert Meeting on Human Rights Issues Summary of Remarks of Invited Experts (25 January 2011)*. Paris, OECD.

OECD (2012) OECD National Contact Points and the Extractive Sector. The British Academy, 10–11 Carlton House Terrace, London, 23 March 2012 (notes on file with author).

OECD Norwegian NCP (2011) *The Norwegian National Contact Point for the OECD Guidelines for Multinational Enterprises, Final Statement Complaint from the Future In Our Hands (FIOH) against Intex Resources ASA and the Mindoro Nickel Project*. Oslo: OECD.

OECD UK NCP (2009) *Final Statement by the UK National Contact Point for the OECD Guidelines for Multinational Enterprises Complaint from Survival International against Vedanta Resources plc*. London: OECD.

Report of the Experts Mechanism on the Rights of Indigenous Peoples (2011) UN Doc. A/HCR//18/42 Advice no 2.

Tauli-Corpuz, V. (2008) *The Concept of Indigenous Peoples' Self-Determined Development or Development with Identity and Culture: Challenges and Trajectories*. Baguio City: Tebtebba Foundation, UN Doc. CLT/CPD/CPO/2008/IPS/02.

World Bank (2003) *The World Bank Group and Extractive Industries: The Final Report of*

World Bank Extractive Industry Review: Striking a Better Balance. Volume 1. Washington, DC: World Bank.

World Bank (2004) *The World Bank Group and Extractive Industries, Legal Note on Free Prior and Informed Consultation.* Sec M2004–0369/IDA/SecM2004–0559 3 August 2004.

World Investment Report (2010) Geneva, United Nations Conference on Trade and Development.

Newspaper articles

García, A. (2007) El Perro del Hortelano, *El Comercio,* 28 October 2007, Lima, Peru. Available at: http://www.aidesep.org.pe/editor/documentos/58.pdM

Guardian Worker's Weekly (2011) Yindjibarndi Aboriginal People Take on WA FMG Mining Magnate (3 August 2011). Available at: www.cpa.org.au/guardian/2011/1512/07-yindjibarndi.html

Miller, J. and MacDonald, A. (2012) Indigenous Peoples Get Last Word on Mines. *The Wall Street Journal* (U.S. edition), 27 March 2012. Available at: http://online.wsj.com/news/articles/SB10001424052702303863404577283321113646182

Monet, J. (2012) James Anaya: A Sit-Down with the UN's Man in Indian Country May 9, 2012. Available at: http://indiancountrytodaymedianetwork.com/2012/05/09/james-anaya-a-sit-down-with-the-un%E2%80%99s-man-in-indian-country-111990

The Western Australian, (1898) Delagoa Bay: The Railway Arbitration Case. *The Western Australian,* 18 July 1898. Available at: http://trove.nla.gov.au/ndp/del/article/3213374

Index

Lightning Source UK Ltd.
Milton Keynes UK
UKOW04f0322241217
314957UK00008B/101/P